T0264916

Measurements and Instrumentation for Machine Vision

Editors

Oleg Sergiyenko
Universidad Autónoma de Baja California
México

Wendy Flores-Fuentes
Universidad Autónoma de Baja California
México

Julio C. Rodríguez-Quiñonez
Universidad Autónoma de Baja California
México

Jesús E. Miranda-Vega
Tecnológico Nacional de México/IT de Mexicali
México

CRC Press
Taylor & Francis Group
Boca Raton London New York

CRC Press is an imprint of the
Taylor & Francis Group, an **informa** business

A SCIENCE PUBLISHERS BOOK

First edition published 2024
by CRC Press
2385 NW Executive Center Drive, Suite 320, Boca Raton FL 33431

and by CRC Press
4 Park Square, Milton Park, Abingdon, Oxon, OX14 4RN

Library of Congress Cataloging-in-Publication Data (applied for)

ISBN: 978-1-032-38161-9 (hbk)
ISBN: 978-1-032-38163-3 (pbk)
ISBN: 978-1-003-34378-3 (ebk)

DOI: 10.1201/9781003343783

Typeset in Times New Roman
by Radiant Productions

Preface

Measurements and Instrumentation for Machine Vision is the first book in a series from the Taylor & Francis Engineering/Measurement and Instrumentation field at CRC Press. This book is a reference for the scholars' audience, it includes advanced students, early career and established researchers. Readers are provided with selected topics in the state of the art and relevant novelty content in the frontier of knowledge for the engineering implementation, scientific knowledge and technological innovation development related to machine vision. Each chapter is the result of an expert's research and a collaborative work evaluated by a peer review process and consulted by a book editorial board. The importance of this book's topic relies on the fact that machine vision is the basis of cyber-physical systems to be capable of interrelating with humans.

Machine vision is considered the eyes of cybernetics systems and plays a fundamental role in Industry 4.0 and Society 5.0 for the joining of the virtual and real world to coexist in a new era in human lives that integrates the technologies into their daily lives with creativity, and globalization through interconnectivity.

Industry 4.0 implies the development of cyber-physical systems capable of seeing, making decisions and acting; while society 5.0 searches for solutions for real problems to better human life conditions, based on the application of all the benefits and advantages that offers Industry 4.0, this is the last and is also known as the fourth industrial revolution. Although it is not an easy task, it requires the application of measurement fundamentals and methods and the development of instrumentation strategies and technologies for the achievement of machine vision systems for every specific application.

It is a revolution that seeks to replace some of the functions that humans perform with optimal, efficient, automated and interconnected processes; called the Industrial Internet of Things (IIoT). A multidisciplinary integration of mainly electronic and mechatronic devices for signal emitters, sensors and cameras, artificial intelligence algorithms, embedded systems, instrumentation and control, actuators, robotics, interconnectivity, data science and cloud computing, that is the application and development of multiple interconnected disciplines.

In the beginning, one of the dreams of humans has been for machines to do our work, while we enjoy rest and other activities that give us pleasure. This gave rise to the industrial revolution, which brought as a benefit an increase in the world population, an increase in the average rate of living, as well as new lifestyles, with tasks that involve less physical effort and that provide us with better quality of life. But now the dreams of humans are a green, healthy and intelligent life, interconnected, under continuous monitoring and with accurate control for sustainability, not only for living on the Earth but also to be able to search and live in other places in the universe.

The integration of optoelectronics devices for emitters, sensors and cameras, artificial intelligence algorithms, embedded systems, robust control, robotics, interconnectivity, big data, and cloud computing is the core of machine vision developments for cyber-physical systems to collaborate with humans and their real and virtual environments and activities. It is required to focus on the theory, methods, tools and techniques for the design, instrumentation and measurement methods applied in machine vision systems.

Measurements are values assigned to refer to a physical quantity or phenomenon; they play an important role in science development. One of the most crucial points in the measurement of machine vision is the proper estimation of information transform quality: such parameters as sensitive part calibration, scene size traceability, accuracy/uncertainty, receiver operating characteristic, repeatability, reproducibility, etc.

The use of current technology requires measuring essential attributes from objects, health data, dimensions of a surface and weather, to mention some. These are necessary to do breakthrough innovations in a wide range of fields. The artificial intelligence (AI) field is one of them. This field is aimed at the research for imitating human abilities, above all, how they learn. AI can be divided into two main branches such as machine learning and deep learning. These components are methods and algorithms that are used for prediction and analysis in the case of machine perception. Although deep learning is also used for forecasting as well as machine learning, the way how the model is created is different. This sub-branch is inspired by how the human brain can learn. In other words, this is based on behavior's neurons to make connections among others to solve a particular problem. In other contexts, measurements are known as data or instances and depending on the quality of them a problem can be solved. Convolutional neural networks (CNN) have catalyzed several vision recognition systems.

Accuracy measurement for medical data is valuable information for a doctor because it can prevent a patient's illness. Health monitoring is required for people who need to constantly check for signs of illness. Data generated by applications can be used by specialists or a smart health system to send an alert in real-time. For example, as well as blood pressure and pulse monitoring are common requirements of a doctor, also medical images obtained by machine vision systems are fundamental. These medical diagnostics can be assisted by machine learning algorithms with the purpose to offer better outcomes.

With the advancements in technology, community researchers have access to better computers in comparison to decades ago. Smart applications aided by computer technology are designed to solve many problems. This progress has increased the interest in the development of cognitive machines, especially in industry. Measurements provided by machine vision systems dotted by AI technology help factories become more efficient and productive. The interaction of humans and machines is possible thanks to accurate smart sensors. Robots safely interact with humans by taking care of the distance between them, they are called cobots. Optical sensors and cameras are the main elements that regularly can be used for this purpose.

SPAD (Single Photon Avalanche Diode) sensors open new possibilities for the development of an accurate vision system by counting individual photon particles instead of the volume of the light by pixel (CMOS technology). Cameras RGB-D depict an important advancement that has recently gained attention in the design of vision systems. Depth information can be estimated with this type of camera to solve the most promising vision tasks.

The application of measurements and instrumentation are infinitive, while the submissions of the present book are addressed to machine vision applications, where the challenge to provide the ability to see, measure, track, create models, interconnect, take decisions and self-adaptation of cyber-physical systems involves multidisciplinary and interdisciplinary requirements with always in mind the sustainability and human-centred resolution of local, regional, and global needs and problems.

Each chapter's contribution demonstrates a deep review of the state of the art, as well as reports the most recent theoretical novelty backgrounded with research results of novel proposals that contribute to current knowledge and development challenges toward futurist trends.

Chapter 1 Machine Learning Approaches for Single Photon Direct Time of Flight Imaging: Reviews the state-of-art deep learning techniques based on processing approaches in the context of SPAD (Single-photon avalanche diodes) sensors. These sensors can offer advantages for operation in outdoor environments with satisfactory results and maintaining a high frame rate. Furthermore, a general description of machine vision tasks such as surface and object detection and super-resolution depth mapping are discussed in detail. Spiking Neural Networks (SNN) are analyzed for Direct time-of-flight (dToF) sensors, which can better exploit SPAD's discrete event-based nature.

Chapter 2 Experimental Evaluation of Depth Measurements Accuracy in Indoor and Outdoor Environments: One of the main goals of this chapter is to integrate a TVS with a stereovision system. For the purpose of the work, a red laser is used to be reflected on a surface, and then a camera RGB-D can capture the scene under observation. Color and depth frames were collected from the depth camera. The main idea is to find the laser point in the color frame to get the corresponding depth information. Four different image processing techniques were applied for smoothing the color frames of the beam laser. An overview of the methods for depth measurements and the key concepts of machine vision is presented.

Chapter 3 Design and Evaluation Support System for Convolutional Neural Network, Support Vector Machine and Convolutional Autoencoder proposes a design, training, and application evaluation based on convolutional neural network (CNN), support vector machine (SVM), convolutional autoencoder (CAE). These authors designed a front-end tool implemented on Matlab based on deep learning structures. The application shown in this work can be addressed to industry for material surface defects detection, such as burrs, cracks, protrusions, chippings, spots and fractures.

Chapter 4 Classification of Objects in IR Images using Wavelet Filters based on Lifting Scheme describes an emerging model using a small CNN and wavelet filters based on a lifting scheme (multi-resolution analysis (MRA) to improve the feature extraction process. A brief overview of infrared image processing is presented. Experiments are conducted with four benchmark datasets for training and testing the models.

Chapter 5 Image Dataset Augmentation: A Survey and Taxonomy Highlight that the lack of training data can affect the performance of a machine learning model. This work is focused on image dataset augmentation approaches to enhance a computer vision system. The key concepts of deep learning and data collection for data augmentation are discussed. The main data image augmentation techniques such as color and geometric transformation, as well as a practical application of this technique, are discussed.

Chapter 6 A Filter-based Feature Selection Methodology for Vehicle/Non-Vehicle Classification presents a machine learning-based model to detect vehicles from a dataset having classes: vehicles and non-vehicles. The main focus of the chapter is to implement a Histogram of Oriented Gradients (HOG) as feature extraction. The method proposed is validated with two benchmark datasets, such as GTI and Kaggle.

Chapter 7 Augmented Visual Inertial Wheel Odometry Through Slip Compensation: This chapter proposes a strategy for compensating wheel slip, based on a differential drive robot kinematics model. The mobile robot presented in this work is equipped with wheel encoders which measure the left and right wheel linear velocities. The key components of a visual-inertial wheel odometry (VIWO) scheme are described. Experimental results obtained through the KAIST dataset to verify the method proposed are presented.

Chapter 8 Methodology for Developing Models of Image Color of Terrain with Landmarks for their Detection and Recognition by Autonomous Mobile Robots: This chapter suggests the creation of a virtual dynamic system based on an image that is scanned by an imaginary fan-shaped beam. A general overview of the construction of automobile mobile robots is presented. The authors describe a methodology for creating models of the color of landmarks against the background of arbitrary terrain. These models are addressed to use in robot navigation.

Chapter 9 Machine Vision – A Measurement Tool for Agricultural Automation: Describes how machine vision applications can improve the agriculture sector. Activities such as fruit counting, fruit robotic harvesting and fruit yield estimation can be automated for attending to an important issue for food security. A modeling of the visual feedback control system was proposed for the navigation task of a mobile robot. The vision system for the agriculture approach is based on the Orchard robot (OrBot) that includes an RGB-D camera. A practical fruit harvesting is carried out in which processing time is measured.

Chapter 10 Occlusion-Aware Disparity-based Direct Visual Servoing of Mobile Robots: Refers to position control of a mobile robot taking into account the camera's velocity and a disparity map computed from the stereo images. This visual servoing system is integrated by a stereo camera. The proposed visual servoing framework is verified by simulations and experiments. Physical experiments with a mobile robot were carried out for positioning tasks, in which occlusion information in the controller design was integrated.

Chapter 11 Development of a Software and Hardware Complex for the Visualization of Sedimentation Inside a Vortex Chamber develops an application system for visualizing sedimentation inside a vortex chamber. This system works under difficult operating conditions and temperatures over 1000°C. A complete software and hardware package for the operation of the system mentioned is developed for the monitoring process. Image enhancement algorithms such as distortion correction and background subtraction are detailed and validated with a practical application.

Chapter 12 Machine Vision for Astronomical Images Using the Modern Image Processing Algorithms Implemented in the CoLiTec Software: Big data in astronomy requires high-dimensional information. As a consequence, scientific analysis and data mining represent a challenge for astronomers and scientists around the world. This chapter describes a general overview of the different modern image processing algorithms and their implementation of them in the Collection Light Technology (CoLiTec) software. CoLitec was designed to perform MV tasks for astronomical objects.

Chapter 13 Gallium Oxide UV Sensing in Contemporary Applications explores advanced applications of UV-C photodetectors in contemporary computer machine vision systems. Sensing UV light has become challenging for researchers and arrays of a component such as Gallium oxide can be useful in imaging and machine vision applications. This chapter also gives an overview of photosensors based on vacuum and solid-state devices.

Chapter 14 Technical Vision System for Alive Human Detection in an Optically Opaque Environment focuses on the technical problems of creating a highly sensitive vision system for detecting and identifying living people behind optically opaque obstacles by estimation of Doppler phase shifts in reflected signals caused by the process of breathing and heartbeat of the living human. This work also discusses the advantages and disadvantages of hardware implementations for this task.

Chapter 15 The Best Linear Solution for a Camera and an Inertial Measurement Unit Calibration is addressed for applications where one or more sources of noise are present in a system. In this work, a set of experiments were carried out to find a rotational offset between the two sensors as well as to verify the robustness of the solution proposed based on basic least squares. The effect of noise concerning multiple positioning of the camera's rotational matrix versus IMU's rotational matrix was analyzed, to measure the offset between the two sensors for geometrical calibration between them to enhance visual perception and pattern recognition capabilities.

Chapter 16 Methods of Forming and Selecting a Reference Image to Provide High-Speed Navigation for Maneuvering Aircraft provides a given speed and accuracy of navigation of high-speed manoeuvring aircraft by reducing the computational complexity of processing superimposed images in combined extremal-correlation flyers navigation systems. This work is focused on eliminating emerging uncertainties when using multispectral sensors as part of combined navigation systems of flyers.

Chapter 17 Application of Fibre Bragg Grating Arrays for Medical Diagnosis and Rehabilitation Purposes: gives an overview of a human health application based on a semiconductor material such as Ga2o3 used on sensors for physiological parameters measurements. This study is based on Fibre Bragg Grating Arrays (FBGA) for physiological pulse detection. The work highlights the advantages of using FBGAs due to it being provided multiple data from a region of interest simultaneously. These applications minimize the effects of sensor location and facilitate locational referencing capabilities.

Acknowledgement

The editors would like to offer our acknowledgement to all the contributors for their time and effort. We are delighted to have this academic product with a global vision. It was a pleasure to work with researchers in the areas of Machine Vision, Navigation, Robotics, Control, and Artificial Intelligence. Seventy-five researchers from around the world have collaborated on this project, representing the participation of fourteen countries: Canada, China, Egypt, France, India, Japan, Malaysia, Mexico, Russia, Spain, Thailand, Ukraine, the United Kingdom and the United States. A whole list of authors with affiliations is available in the "List of Authors" section of this book.

We are grateful for the indispensable role of the following reviewers who have done a wonderful job reading and suggesting improvements for each chapter. Oleksandr Tsymbal, Thomas Tawiah, Andrey Somov, Abdulkader Joukhadar, Swagato Das, Moises Jesus Castro Toscano, Oscar Real Moreno, Javier Sanchez Galan, Giovanni Fabbrocino, Hang Yuan, Huei-Yung Lin, Miti Ruchanurucks, Junzhi Yu, Piotr M. Szczypiński, Tadeusz Uhl, Shahnewaz Ali, Subhajit Maur, Oleksandr Tymochko, Guilherme B. Pintarelli, Sergey V. Dvoynishnikov, Oleksander Poliarus, Dah-Jye Lee, Pr. Azzeddine Dliou, Alberto Aloisio, Dayi Zhang, Junfan Wang, Oleg Starostenko, Jonathan Jesús Sanchez Castro, Ruben Alaniz-Plata, Jacek Izydorczyk, Muaz Khalifa Alradi, Radhakrishna Prabhu, Tanaka Kanji and Sergii Khlamov.

Special thanks also go to the editorial board and the officials at CRC Press/Taylor & Francis Group for their invaluable efforts, great support and valuable advice for this project towards the successful publication of this book. We are also grateful to our institutions Universidad Autónoma de Baja California, and Tecnológico Nacional de México/IT de Mexicali to provide us with a location and time where to develop this project.

Oleg Sergiyenko
Universidad Autónoma de Baja California, México

Wendy Flores-Fuentes
Universidad Autónoma de Baja California, México

Julio C. Rodríguez-Quiñonez
Universidad Autónoma de Baja California, México

Jesús E. Miranda-Vega
Tecnológico Nacional de México/IT de Mexicali, México

Contents

List of Contributors

Afanasiev Volodymyr
Kharkiv National Air Force University named after Ivan Kozhedub, Kharkiv, Ukraine

Andrey Somov Skoltech
Skolkovo Institute of Science and Technology Russia

Arnoldo Díaz-Ramirez
Department of Computer Systems, Tecnológico Nacional de México, IT de Mexicali, Mexicali, BC 21376, México

Arup Roy
School of Computing and Information Technology, Reva University, Bengaluru, Karnataka- 560064, India

Atikul Islam
Department of Computer Science & Engineering, Annex College of Management Studies, BD-91, Salt Lake Bypass, Sector 1, Bidhannagar, Kolkata, West Bengal 700064, India

Azman Jalar
Department of Applied Physics, Faculty of Science and Technology, Universiti Kebangsaan Malaysia, 43600 Bangi, Selangor, Malaysia

Baris Fidan
Department of Mechanical and Mechatronics Engineering University of Waterloo

Brian Stewart
STMicroelectronics

Brice Allen
Department of Engineering and Physics, Northwest Nazarene University

Chaker Tlili
Chongqing Key Laboratory of Multi-scale Manufacturing Technology, Institute of Green and Intelligent Technology, Chinese Academy of Sciences, Chongqing, People's Republic of China.

Daniel Trevino-Sanchez
Department of Computing, Electronics and Mechatronics Universidad de las Américas Puebla, Sta. Catarina Martir, San Andres Cholula, Puebla 72810, México

Dmitriev Oleg
Flight Academy of National Aviation University, Kropyvnytzkyy, Ukraine

DO Semenov
Kutateladze Institute of thermophysics SB RAS Lavrentyeva avenue 1 , Novosibirsk, Russia

Duke M Bulanon
Department of Engineering and Physics, Northwest Nazarene University

Ehsan Hashemi
Department of Mechanical Engineering University of Alberta

Fusaomi Nagata
Sanyo-Onoda City University, 1-1-1 Daigaku-Dori, Sanyo-Onoda, 756-0884, Japan

Fustii Vadim
Kharkiv National Air Force University named after Ivan Kozhedub, Kharkiv, Ukraine

Garrisen Cizmich
Department of Engineering and Physics, Northwest Nazarene University

GV Bakakin
Kutateladze Institute of thermophysics SB RAS Lavrentyeva avenue 1 , Novosibirsk, Russia

IK Kabardin
Kutateladze Institute of thermophysics SB RAS Lavrentyeva avenue 1 , Novosibirsk, Russia **Iryna Tabakova**
Kharkiv National University of Radio Electronics, 14 Nauki Avenue, 61166 Kharkiv, Ukraine

Isaac Compher
Department of Engineering and Physics, Northwest Nazarene University

Istvan Gyongy
School of Engineering, Institute for Integrated Micro and Nano Systems, The University of Edinburgh

Jack Iain MacLean
School of Engineering, Institute for Integrated Micro and Nano Systems, The University of Edinburgh, STMicroelectronics

Jesús E Miranda-Vega
Department of Computer Systems, Tecnológico Nacional de México, IT de Mexicali, Mexicali, BC 21376, México

Joseph Ichiro Bulanon
Department of Engineering and Physics, Northwest Nazarene University

Julio C Rodríguez-Quiñonez
Universidad Autónoma de Baja California, México

Keigo Watanabe
Okayama University, Okayama, Japan

Kento Nakashima
Sanyo-Onoda City University, 1-1-1 Daigaku-Dori, Sanyo-Onoda, 756-0884, Japan

Kohei Miki
Sanyo-Onoda City University, 1-1-1 Daigaku-Dori, Sanyo-Onoda, 756-0884, Japan

Koki Arima
Sanyo-Onoda City University, 1-1-1 Daigaku-Dori, Sanyo-Onoda, 756-0884, Japan

Maki K Habib
Mechanical Engineering Department, School of Sciences and Engineering, American University in Cairo, AUC Avenue, P.O. Box 74, New Cairo 11835, Egypt

Manish Mishra
School of Electrical Sciences, Indian Institute of Technology, Bhubaneswar, Argul - Jatni Road, Kansapada, Odisha – 752050, India

Marina Kolendovska
Kharkiv National University of Radio Electronics, 14 Nauki Avenue, 61166 Kharkiv, Ukraine

Maroi Agrebi
LAMIH UMR CNRS 8201, Department of Computer Science, Université Polytechnique Hauts-de-France, 59313 Valenciennes, France

Miti Ruchanurucks
Electrical Engineering Department, Kasetsart University, Thailand

Mohd Firdaus Raih
Department of Applied Physics, Faculty of Science and Technology, Universiti Kebangsaan Malaysia, 43600 Bangi, Selangor, Malaysia/ Institute of Systems Biology, Universiti Kebangsaan Malaysia, 43600 UKM Bangi, Selangor, Malaysia

Muhammad Azmi Abdul Hamid
Department of Applied Physics, Faculty of Science and Technology, Universiti Kebangsaan Malaysia, 43600 Bangi, Selangor, Malaysia

Naif H Al-Hardan
Department of Applied Physics, Faculty of Science and Technology, Universiti Kebangsaan Malaysia, 43600 Bangi, Selangor, Malaysia

Naser M Ahmed
School of Physics, Universiti Sains Malaysia, 11800 USM, Penang, Malaysia

Niraj Reginald
Department of Mechanical and Mechatronics Engineering University of Waterloo

Oleg Sergiyenko
Universidad Autónoma de Baja California, México

Oleg Sytnik
O.Ya. Usikov Institute for Radio Physics and Electronics, National Academy of Sciences of Ukraine, 12 Academician Proskura St., Kharkov 61085, Ukraine

Olizarenko Serhij
Flight Academy of National Aviation University, Kropyvnytzkyy, Ukraine

Oleksandr Poliarus
Kharkiv National Automobile and Highway University, Ukraine

Omar Al-Buraiki
Department of Mechanical and Mechatronics Engineering University of Waterloo

Pawan Kumar Singh
Department of Information Technology, Jadavpur University, Jadavpur University Second Campus, Plot No. 8, Salt Lake Bypass, LB Block, Sector III, Salt Lake City, Kolkata-700106, West Bengal, India

Prasant Kumar Sahu
School of Electrical Sciences, Indian Institute of Technology, Bhubaneswar Argul - Jatni Road, Kansapada, Odisha – 752050, India

Ratchakorn Srihera
Ryowa Co., Ltd., 10-5 Torigoe-Cho, Kanda-Machi, Miyako-Gun, Fukuoka, Japan

Saurav Mallik
Center for Precision Health, School of Biomedical Informatics, The University of Texas Health Science Center at Houston, Houston, TX, 77030, USA

Sergey Nesteruk
Skolkovo Institute of Science and Technology Russia

Sergii Khlamov
Kharkiv National University of Radio Electronics, 14 Nauki Avenue, 61166 Kharkiv, Ukraine

Soo Jeon
Department of Mechanical and Mechatronics Engineering University of Waterloo

Sotnikov Oleksandr
Kharkiv National Air Force University named after Ivan Kozhedub, Kharkiv, Ukraine

Stepanenko Dmitryy
Flight Academy of National Aviation University, Kropyvnytzkyy, Ukraine

Surangrak Sutiworwan
Office of Information and Communications Technology, United Nations, Thailand

SV Dvoinishnikov
Kutateladze Institute of thermophysics SB RAS Lavrentyeva avenue 1 , Novosibirsk, Russia

Svetlana Illarionova
Skolkovo Institute of Science and Technology Russia

Tatsuki Shimizu
Sanyo-Onoda City University, 1-1-1 Daigaku-Dori, Sanyo-Onoda, 756-0884, Japan

Tetiana Trunova
Kharkiv National University of Radio Electronics, 14 Nauki Avenue, 61166 Kharkiv, Ukraine

Tiurina Valeriia
Kharkiv National Air Force University named after Ivan Kozhedub, Kharkiv, Ukraine

Trystan Andriy
State Scientific Research Institute of Armament and Military Equipment Testing and Certification, Cherkasy, Ukraine

Tymochko Oleksandr
Flight Academy of National Aviation University, Kropyvnytzkyy, Ukraine

VA Pavlov
Kutateladze Institute of thermophysics SB RAS Lavrentyeva avenue 1 , Novosibirsk, Russia

Vadym Savanevych
Kharkiv National University of Radio Electronics, 14 Nauki Avenue, 61166 Kharkiv, Ukraine

VG Meledin
Kutateladze Institute of thermophysics SB RAS Lavrentyeva avenue 1 , Novosibirsk, Russia

Vicente Alarcon-Aquino
Department of Computing, Electronics and Mechatronics Universidad de las Américas Puebla, Sta. Catarina Martir, San Andres Cholula, Puebla 72810, México

Vladimir Kartashov
Kharkov National University of Radio Electronics,14 Nauky Ave., Kharkov 61085, Ukraine

Vladimir Kartashov
Kharkiv National University of Radio Electronics, 14 Nauki Avenue, 61166 Kharkiv, Ukraine

VV Rakhmanov
Kutateladze Institute of thermophysics SB RAS Lavrentyeva avenue 1 , Novosibirsk, Russia

Wendy Flores-Fuentes
Universidad Autónoma de Baja California, México

Wendy García-Gonzalez
Universidad Autónoma de Baja California, México

Xiule Fan
Department of Mechanical and Mechatronics Engineering University of Waterloo

Yevhen Poliakov
Kharkiv National Automobile and Highway University, Ukraine

1

Machine Learning Approaches for Single Photon Direct Time of Flight Imaging

Jack Iain MacLean,[1,*] *Brian Stewart*[2] *and Istvan Gyongy*[1]

1.1 Introduction

1.1.1 LiDAR

LiDAR sensors are becoming increasingly widespread in applications requiring 3D imaging or proximity sensing, such as autonomous navigation or machine vision. These optical sensors typically use one of two types of time-of-flight (ToF) approach, indirect time-of-flight (iToF) and direct time-of-flight (dToF), which emit a wave or light pulse to illuminate a scene of interest and time the returning, back-scattered photons to estimate distance, as in Figure 1.1. As the speed of light in the air is constant, the duration for incident photons to return is directly proportional to the distance of the object from the sensor. A sensor is made up of many pixels which are able to independently measure the ToF of objects within the field-of-view (FoV). The difference between iToF and dToF lies in the methodology of time measurement. iToF-based sensors do not directly measure the time between emitted and received pulses, instead, it measures the delay between signals by integrating the received signal during specific windows of time synchronized with the emitted signal.

[1] School of Engineering, Institute for Integrated Micro and Nano Systems, The University of Edinburgh.
[2] STMicroelecronics (R&D) Ltd.
* Corresponding author: s2110140@ed.ac.uk

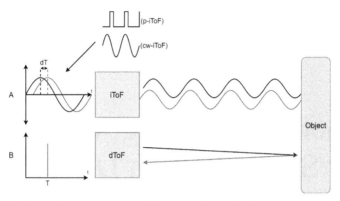

Figure 1.1: The figure illustrates the two different methods of ToF measurement (black: emitted, red: reflected). (A) iToF. The two types of iToF shown are the square waved pulsed-light (p-iToF) and the sinusoidal continuous wave (cw-iToF). (B) dToF.

Sensors based on the dToF principle directly measure the time taken between the laser emission towards the scene and the detection of back-scattered photons. Timing is often performed using an electronic stopwatch called a time-to-digital converter (TDC). The distance (d) can be extracted from the time between the sensor and object using equation 1.1 [Shahnewaz and Pandey, 2020].

$$d = \frac{ct_m}{2} \qquad (1.1)$$

where t_m is the time measured by the sensor with a precision of Δt, and c is the speed of light.

Single-photon avalanche diodes (SPADs) are photodetectors that are seeing increased use in 3D depth imaging sensors as they provide a high sensitivity to photons, low timing jitter, and a fast response time to detected photons. SPADs operate in an unstable state called Geiger-mode, where the SPADs are reverse-biased above their breakdown voltage. While operating in Geiger mode, a single photon hitting the SPAD could trigger an avalanche of self-sustaining current flow which can be detected. The resultant current flow caused by photon events activates a Schmitt trigger, as seen in Figure 1.2. The Schmitt trigger outputs a square wave digital pulse which can then be processed by accompanying electronics. The chance of a SPAD detecting a photon event is measured by its photon detection probability (PDP) which, depending on the wavelength of light, can range from a few percent up to fifty percent [Piron et al., 2021]. After the photon is detected and the SPAD avalanches, the bias voltage of the SPAD must be reduced to reset its state. The time taken to reset the SPAD is typically only a few nanoseconds long and is called dead time due to the inability to detect new photons. Two quenching and recharge circuits exist in order to reset the SPAD back to its Geiger-mode operating point. Passive quenching can be seen in Figure 1.2(a) and active quenching in Figure 1.2(b). The difference between these two methods is that active quenching utilizes a MOSFET to connect the SPAD circuit to a voltage source below the SPADs breakdown voltage, which decreases the time to quench the avalanche current. When the MOSFET is closed the avalanche current is quickly quenched as the circuit is biased to the low voltage source. The addition of active recharge can be seen in Figure 1.2(c) and is achieved by adding a low-capacitance MOSFET in parallel with the quenching resistor. When the switch is closed, due to a photon event being detected, the SPAD circuit voltage quickly returns to its operating voltage thus further reducing the dead time [Vilà et al., 2012].

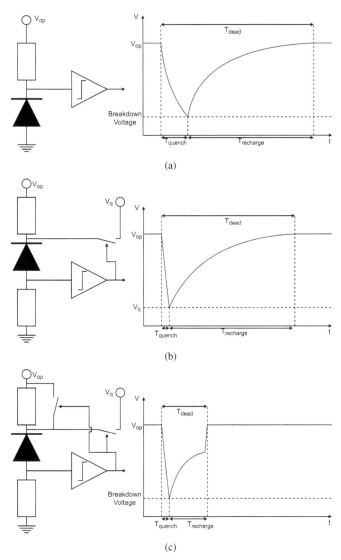

Figure 1.2: (a) SPAD Circuit utilizing passive quenching and recharging, (b) SPAD Circuit utilizing active quenching and passive recharging, (c) Active quenching and active recharge.

The SPAD is also affected by two main types of noise, afterpulsing and the dark count rate (DCR). Afterpulsing is caused by carriers being trapped during an avalanche which are then released after the reset process, causing the SPAD to be triggered again. The DCR is the rate at which SPADs avalanches can be triggered by thermally generated carriers rather than photon events. The main drawbacks of using SPAD-based sensors is that the SPAD pixel requires excess circuitry to operate quenching, counting, timing, and buffering all of which reduce the sensor's fill factor (FF). Typically, this means that SPAD-based sensors have a lower FF when compared to sensors based on other photodetectors. To increase the FF, and reduce the effects of dead time, multiple SPADs are combined via a combination tree, typically OR or XOR, into macro pixels which act as one pixel.

As SPAD-based sensors can generate large quantities of data, the bottleneck inherent in the data readout for off-chip processing is only exacerbated, see Figure 1.3. The most common method for data compression is on-chip per-pixel histogramming, Figure 1.4, which takes advantage of new 3D stacking technology to integrate SPAD and CMOS circuitry onto the same silicon die. The histograms are built up over multiple laser cycles using a TDC which is triggered on each SPAD event to create a timestamp. This timestamp is used to measure increments in the photon count in the corresponding histogram bin in memory. Photon event timestamps are allocated to the appropriate histogram bin in memory, with the histogram being built up over multiple laser cycles until the desired SNR is achieved. The histogram memory is then read out from the sensor and a peak estimation algorithm is applied to extract detected surface depths.

Under high photon fluxes, photon pile-up can occur which prevents the detection of additional photons after the first due to the SPAD quenching circuit being paralyzed by additional detections preventing a recharge. Even at lower photon rates, TDC pile up may occur which distorts the histograms and prevents the detection of back-scattered photons at longer ranges [Gyongy et al., 2022]. One method to prevent this is the use of multi-event TDCs, such as the one implemented in [Al Abbas et al., 2018], which uses a one-hot encoding scheme to encode the photon events combined with a processing pipeline that allows for the recording of time stamps at a much higher rate.

The completed histogram is then read off-chip where a peak detection algorithm is used to extract the depths of the surfaces detected in the pixels FoV. While histogramming does achieve a high degree of data compression, it introduces higher power consumption and requires a significant area of silicon to implement. The general process flow for SPAD-based LiDAR, as seen in Figure 1.5, is that when the reflected incident and ambient photons arrive at the SPAD pixels of the sensor, only a fraction are detected based on the SPAD sensors Photon Detection Efficiency (PDE). The detected photon events cause an avalanche current which activates the Schmitt triggers to output a digital pulse, these pulses are then buffered and optionally shortened. A combination tree, usually consisting of OR or XOR gates, are used to combine multiple SPAD pixel signals into one macro-pixel. A TDC synchronized with a clock then generates timestamps based on the photon events represented in the macro pixel signal and increments the count in the corresponding histogram bin stored in

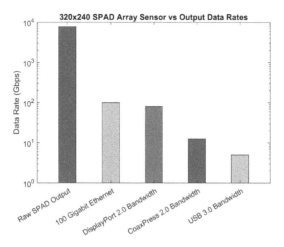

Figure 1.3: Maximum output data rate of a 320x240 SPAD array, assuming each SPAD is firing at 100 Mega counts per second (Mcps), compared to current data transfer solutions.

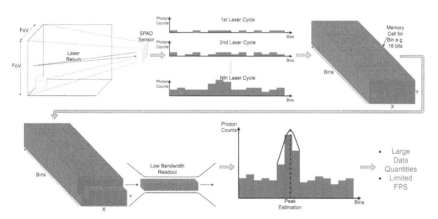

Figure 1.4: On-chip histogram buildup process.

memory. The histogram is then read off the chip and processed into a depth map or 3D point cloud for further processing.

However, in recent years some of these steps have begun to be replaced with neural network implementations. As will be demonstrated in this chapter, the depth estimation algorithms and point cloud generation steps which were integral to machine vision can be replaced with deep neural network implementations, improving latency and reducing power consumption. Even histogramming could be replaced with an appropriate neural network architecture. Such implementations which bypass point cloud generation and output a form of metadata using neural networks can be seen in sensors such as the Sony IMX500 [imx,].

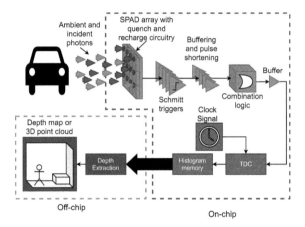

Figure 1.5: Typical SPAD-based dToF processing pipeline.

1.1.2 Deep neural and neuromorphic networks

Artificial Neural Networks (ANNs) are seeing increased use in 3D LiDAR applications to perform tasks such as object detection, autonomous navigation, and upsampling. Recently it can be seen that deep learning approaches are outperforming classical machine learning methods. A prime example is in object detection where Convolutional Neural Networks (CNNs) exceed the accuracy of methods such as k-nearest neighbors or gradient boosting trees. The concept of deep learning networks has been around for decades but has only recently become the predominant machine learning method. The main causes for the growing use of deep neural networks are the increase in cheap and powerful computational resources, larger datasets, and more refined training methods for the models [Goodfellow et al., 2016]. Previous issues which plagued deep networks such as vanishing and exploding gradients have effectively been solved with the improvement of the gradient descent optimization algorithm.

As the improvement of training techniques and resources for deep neural networks have grown, and so too has the use of Spiking Neural Networks (SNNs). These neuromorphic networks are predisposed to take advantage of event-based nature of the SPAD. SNNs operate asynchronously and encode information as spikes allowing for better integration of time, frequency, and phase information. Other appealing qualities offered are the greater data sparsity and relatively lower power consumption when compared to traditional synchronous networks. The difference in SNNs architecture when compared to analogue networks can be seen in Figure 1.6, where a Leaky Integrate-and-Fire (LIF) neuron [Koch and Segev, 1998] is compared with traditional artificial neurons. Traditional artificial neurons operate with fixed update periods with constant activation levels. These inputs are then summed with each other and a bias term, with the result being passed through an activation function (typically a ReLU). Spiking neurons operate asynchronously, with each neuron maintaining its own membrane potential. The membrane potential is increased by the arrival of an

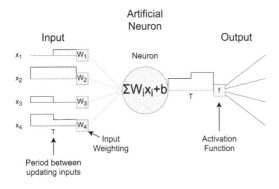

(a)

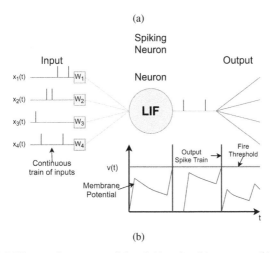

(b)

Figure 1.6: Difference between traditional (a) and spiking neuron (b) architecture.

input spike and, in the case of an LIF neuron, decreases over time in the absence of input spikes. When the membrane potential reaches a set threshold an output spike is produced and the membrane potential is reset.

While the advantages of spiking architecture are clear, the main problem preventing their widespread use is the lack of a developed training method [Taherkhani et al., 2020] which also limits their size to a few layers. One method to circumvent this is to convert a traditionally trained ANN network into a spiking equivalent [Rueckauer et al., 2016]. However, the process for conversion does put limitations on the layer and activation types that can be used in the architecture design. As the activations of the original network are approximated using spiking equivalents, the overall accuracy deteriorates for every layer in the network. Despite these drawbacks, SNNs have still seen some tentative use in dToF based object detection.

1.2 Surface detection

Surface detection is the process of extracting the depth of objects encoded in the timing information output by the dToF SPAD sensors, typically in histogram format. Peak Detection (PD), as in Figure 1.7, locates the detected surfaces based on the reflected photon rates, which is the superposition of the background photons and incident photons. Various algorithms have been developed to perform PD such as Gaussian curve fitting and Continuous wavelet transform [Nguyen et al., 2013]. Digital filters have also been previously applied to perform PD, such as a Center-of-Mass filter [Tsai et al., 2018], but demand a higher computational cost to process the entire histogram using small sliding steps to maintain high precision. Neural network approaches have seen increased use in this field over the last few years, with some approaches outlined below.

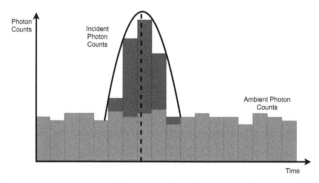

Figure 1.7: Peak detection using a histogram with a Gaussian pulse shape. Light blue represents the ambient photon bed, and dark blue is the incident back-scattered photons detected by a SPAD sensor. The solid black line represents the beam shape, in this case, a Gaussian, and the dashed black line is the estimated peak.

1.2.1 Artificial Neural Networks

The work of [Chen et al., 2022] explores a method to perform feature extraction on SPAD histogram data using a neural network-based multi-peak analysis (NNMPA) to improve the robustness of the distance measurement under harsh environmental conditions with the goal to predict the target distance's coarse position in a noisy histogram. The datasets used to train the system can be seen in Table 1.1, the first being a synthetic dataset based on the Montecarlo principle and the second being real data captured using the "OWL" flash LiDAR sensor by Fraunhofer IMS [owl,]. The first stage of the system is to extract features from the histogram, this is done by first convolving over the raw histogram and then splitting it into multiple regions with a feature extracted from each, 12 being shown as the optimum number. The local maximum M_n and the corresponding bin number b_n from each region are extracted and the background is estimated and subtracted from this value. The features are then normalized, f_n, and combined into a feature group $F_n = \{f_n, b_n\}$. These features are then processed by the NN which uses the softmax function to assign soft decisions to each feature where the highest scoring feature is chosen as the final prediction. As the resolution of the classification is lower than the histogram resolution, a distance recovery process is used to reduce loss from the low precision in the final distance estimation. The paper provides a detailed comparison between the proposed NNMPA network and the chosen classical method, showing that the former outperforms the latter on both datasets. However, under certain conditions, i.e., short distance and low ambient, in the synthetic dataset the classical method outperforms the NNMPA network. The classical comparison method is an average filter with background estimation and subtraction with a final global maximum detection applied. For instance, in the synthetic dataset at a distance of 50–60 m and ambient rates of 4Mcps, the NNMPA has an accuracy of 57.17% compared with 18.33% for the classical. However, at a distance of 0–10m at the same ambient, the NNMPA method has an accuracy of 83.17% compared with 89.00% for the classical. The overall performance of the NNMPA exceeds that of the classical method in most situations where either the ambient is >3Mcps and the distance is <30m. No detailed analysis was provided as to why the CDP outperforms NNMPA at shorter distances and lower ambient levels, so it remains an open question. When tested on the real dataset the NNMPA reaches accuracies approaching 100%, exceeding the CDP across all measured distances. The NNMPA method also outperforms the classical in computation time, 0.26ms vs 0.32ms when simulated using LabView [ni,] on a PC (not specified whether CPU or GPU utilized), with the largest contribution of 0.23s from the initial convolution over the histogram.

An FPGA implementation of this system is also outlined by [Chen et al., 2021] which is compared to the performance of the PC implementation. To increase the efficiency of the networks FPGA implementation, fixed point arithmetic replaces floating point to reduce the computational demands. Approximated values in a Look-Up-Table (LUT) replaces the background light estimation for increased computational efficiency, however, this caused a large quantization error in low ambient levels with the maximum error for ambient estimation being 39.28% at 1–1.5 Mcps ambient photon rate. The conversion to an FPGA implementation caused a maximum accuracy loss of 2.76% with a negligible accuracy reduction at low ambient levels despite the high quantization error, as can be seen in Figure 1.8. The FPGA used, an Enclustra Mas ZX3, cannot stably use the full 384 pixels of the SPAD sensor due to timing violations, instead only 96 pixels are used resulting in the resource occupation in Table 1.2. The end result for the FPGA implementation was a marked reduction in computation time by 0.17 ms per histogram in each pixel while having an overall accuracy drop of 1.21% (maximum of 2.76%).

The work outlined in [Aßmann et al., 2021] first presents an approach to perform super-resolution on LiDAR waveforms using a CNN. It is trained using 25,000 synthetic histograms where one reflector is separated from another with random separation distance, amplitude, and noise within experiment parameters. This dataset is designed to replicate the experiment first presented in [Hernández-Marín et al., 2008] which proposes the statistical Reverse Jump Markov Chain Monte Carlo (RJMCMC) method. The proposed CNN details can be seen in Table 1.3. The goal of the network is to process the synthetic histograms to extract the principal peak location compo-

Table 1.1: Details of datasets used in [Chen et al., 2022].

	Synthetic dataset	Real dataset
Dataset size	96,000	7,000
Histogram size	1310 bins	1310 bins
TDC resolution	312.5ps	312.5ps
Max ranges	60m	25m
Incident rate	10 Mcps	
Background Rate	1-8 Mcps	7-9 Mcps
Sensor array size		2x192
Pulse width	5ns	18.75ns
Peak power		75W

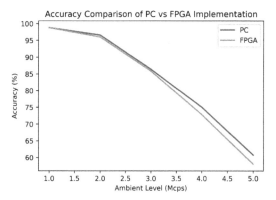

Figure 1.8: Accuracy comparison of PC and FPGA implementation on 2360 bin histograms where the PC configuration is a simulation run using the software LabView [Chen et al., 2021].

Table 1.2: NNMPA FPGA resource occupation [Chen et al., 2021].

Resources	384 Pixels	96 Pixels
LUT as Logic	6594 (12.39%)	6373 (11.98%)
LUT as memory	496 (2.85%)	496 (2.85%)
Slice registers as flip-flop	9549 (8.97%)	9416 (8.85%)
Slice registers as latch	0 (0%)	0 (0%)
BRAM	101.5 (72.50%)	29.50 (21.07%)
DSP blocks	15 (6.82%)	15 (6.82%)

nents present and attach a confidence value to each peak detected. The histograms consist of 4096 bins representing a max distance of 65m. The trained network is tested on the same real data used in [Hernández-Marín et al., 2008] and compared to its proposed method RJMCMC, with the results presented in Table 1.4. While Li-DARNet has an overall worse performance than the classical method, LiDARNet is better able to detect multiple surfaces in the input waveform while RJMCMC either mislocates or fails to identify the secondary surfaces.

[Aßmann et al., 2021] also presented an automotive LiDAR model which uses a similar CNN as the super-resolution, with the same application to extract the depths

Table 1.3: Super resolution and automotive LiDAR networks parameters EB stands for Encode Block which consists of a 1D convolutional layer, a dropout layer, and a max-pooling layer [Aßmann et al., 2021].

	Super Resolution		Automotive		Activation
	L, W	#Params	L, W	#Params	
EB1	64, 64	4,160	96, 48	4704	ReLU
EB2	64, 32	131,136	96, 48	442,464	ReLU
EB3	-	-	64, 24	147,520	ReLU
Conv1D	32, 32	65,568	32, 24	49,184	ReLU
Conv1D	16, 32	16,400	16, 24	12,304	ReLU
	C	#Params	C	#Params	
Dense	128	2,097,280	256	3,842,304	ReLU
Dense	4096	528,384	7500	1,927,500	SoftMax
Total		2,842,928		6,425,980	

Table 1.4: Evaluation of a real Super-Resolution Benchmark using the synthetically trained LiDARNet [Aßmann et al., 2021] [Hernández-Marín et al., 2008].

	RJMCMC		LiDARNet	
Ground Truth (cm)	Mean (cm)	Error (cm)	Mean (cm)	Error (cm)
1.7	1.462	0.238	1.281	0.419
3.2	3.281	0.081	3.843	0.643
5.2	5.086	0.114	5.489	0.289
7.2	7.053	0.147	7.136	0.064
9.2	9.108	0.092	9.332	0.132
11.2	11.092	0.108	11.345	0.145
13.2	13.155	0.045	13.357	0.157

of all surfaces present in the histogram data. This model is also trained using synthetic data, which was proven to be viable in the super-resolution model. The automotive synthetic datasets utilize existing labeled scenes in [Ros et al., 2016] and [Gaidon et al., 2016] to provide detailed ground truth data that acts as a base scene for a SPAD sensors FoV to be projected. Beam expansion is simulated by employing a spatial down-sampling routine to emulate each SPAD pixel detecting multiple returns, while this results in the loss of objects spatial location their depth is retained. The paper sets the maximum number of separate surfaces present in each pixel as 9 with the surface reflectivity determined using generic values for each label type scaled by their brightness in the RGB image. 14,000 Synthetic waveforms of distances up to 300m are represented with 7500 bin histograms. The parameters of the trained network can also be seen in Table 1.3. The final network is then compared to RJMCMC on 1000 test waveforms, with the results being presented in Table 1.5. The main advantage that can be seen is the total time required to process a single waveform, with LiDARNet having total run times order lower than that of RJMCMC while also providing a slightly better Peak Signal-to-Noise Ratio (PSNR).

The work presented by [Sun et al., 2020] presents a network that fuses SPAD histogram data and monocular (RGB) data for robust depth estimation to overcome noisy or corrupted data. The final depth is estimated by using a CNN to combine

Table 1.5: Evaluation of LiDARNet in automotive configuration for 1,000 simulated waveforms compared to ideal waveforms [Aßmann et al., 2021] [Hernández-Marín et al., 2008].

	Signal	JMCMC	LiDARNet
PSNR (dB)	8.25	40.43	43.50
MSE	0.2935	0.0008	0.0006
time (ms)		>5000	3.4

the noisy output of the SPAD sensor with the depth information extracted from an RGB image using a pre-trained monocular depth estimation neural network. The network is trained on synthetic data generated using the NYUv2 [Silberman et al., 2012] with depths of under 10m where the SPAD histograms consist of 1,024 bins with a temporal resolution of 80ps, and a total input resolution of 512x512x1,024 (processed in smaller patches and recombined at the output due to memory constraints). Pre-processing is used to convert the histogram bins from a linear to a logarithmic scale, reducing the bin count from 1,024 to 128 in order to reduce the runtime and memory consumption by a factor of 7. In total, there are 7,600 training scenes and 766 testing scenes. Real-depth data is captured using the LinoSPAD [Burri et al., 2017] sensor with an array size of 256x256 SPADs and 1,536 bin histograms with a temporal resolution of 26ps. Monocular data is captured at 5Hz using a PointGrey camera. The network structure can be seen in Figure 1.9. The monocular depth estimator used in SPADnet is pre-trained (DORN [Fu et al., 2018] and DenseDepth [Alhashim and Wonka, 2018]) with the resultant depth estimation being converted into the z axis index for each x,y spatial coordinate where the corresponding indice is set to 1 and all other locations set to 0. The process is referred to as "2D to 3D up-projection". The results of the trained SPADnet network compared to other solutions can be seen in Table 1.6. It can be seen that the SPADnet model using the log-scaled bins produces the best results, with under half the RMSE of the linear implementation. It also produces the highest accuracy within 1.25% of the ground truth, with 99.6% of results falling within the accuracy metric. When tested on the captured data with cases where areas of the scene has low reflectivity, optical misalignment, and multipath interference, the proposed log SPADnet has a greater ability to reconstruct the depth maps than the other approaches. In examples with extremely weak returns, SPADnet produces an RMSE of 7.15cm versus the 24.01cm and 11.68cm of [Rapp and Goyal, 2017] and [Lindell et al., 2018] (log) respectively. The main issue with the log scale re-binned histogram architecture is that the resolution decreases with distance, so further depths will be combined into the larger time bins increasing the quantization error. The monocular depth estimator also has a tendency to fail when used on previously unseen datasets or when objects are too close, causing SPADnet to not benefit from the monocular depth in these cases. The benefits of utilising ToF data with the monocular depth data is demonstrated when the DORN network [Fu et al., 2018] is swapped for the DenseDepth [Alhashim and Wonka, 2018] monocular network. When trained on the NYUv2 dataset DORN and DenseDepth have a RMSE (cm) error of 53.7 and 71.2 respectively, however, when combined into SPADnet this RMSE reduces to 14.4 and

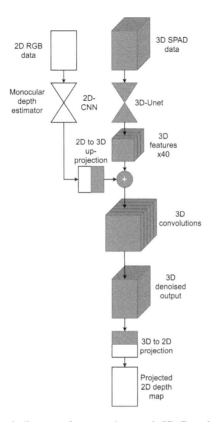

Figure 1.9: Network diagram of proposed network SPADnet [Sun et al., 2020].

13.3 respectively. The addition of SPAD ToF data is able to compensate for monocular depths shortcomings in prediction when objects are too close or there is low texture data available [Ali and Pandey, 2022]. While the monocular data provides accurate of relative depth which can be used to de-noise SPAD LIDAR's high accuracy but low resolution depth data. These results demonstrate that the combination of monocular RGB data and SPAD histograms provide a more robust solution than either in isolation.

The work presented by [Zang et al., 2021] proposes a 3D CNN to process ToF data utilizing multi-dimensional spatial and temporal features into depth maps under low photon flux and SNR conditions. The architecture is also compressed using low-bit parametric quantization to allow for implementation on FPGA while maintaining high reconstruction quality. The network is trained on synthetic data generated using the NYUv2 [Silberman et al., 2012] and Middlebury [Scharstein and Pal, 2007] datasets. The synthetic dataset consists of 13,000 and 1,300 ToF tensors for training and validation respectively, with input data being 64x64x1,024 bins. Real data for testing is collected using the LinoSPAD [Burri et al., 2017] which provides SPAD data at a resolution of 256x256x1,536 with a bin width of 26ps. The network uses a 3D version of U-net++ [Zhou et al., 2019] as the core, with the main network being

Table 1.6: Results of proposed and existing methods on synthetic data. Note that the different image sizes depended on whether the bins were in linear or log scale due to memory constraints during training. $*^1$ [Fu et al., 2018] (Pre-trained Monocular depth estimator), $*^2$ [Rapp and Goyal, 2017], $*^3$[Lindell et al., 2018]. [Sun et al., 2020].

| | | Signal photons = 2, background photons = 50, SBR = 0.04 | | | |
	Patch size	$\delta < 1.25$	$\delta < 1.25^2$	RMSE (cm)	Abs rel
$*^1$		0.881	0.976	53.7	0.117
$*^2$		0.965	0.986	43.9	0.032
$*^3$ (linear)	64x64	0.935	0.952	72.1	0.058
$*^3$ (log)	128x128	0.993	0.998	18.2	0.011
SPADnet (linear)	64x64	0.970	0.993	34.7	0.031
SPADnet (log)	128x128	**0.996**	**0.999**	**14.4**	**0.010**

split into a feature extraction module and a refinement module. The network learns to filter the noise during the training to output a 2D depth map without using any guiding images such as monocular or intensity data. As the main obstacle to embedding the network on FPGA is the large quantity of memory used for data transfer and the low on-chip memory available for parameters, a 2D low-bit quantization method outlined in [Zhou et al., 2016] was utilized to quantize the 3D data parameters to compress the model, with the floating point parameters converted into a fixed point format. In order to reduce the loss from quantization, the weight parameters of the first and last layers were not changed. The bit widths for the weights of other hidden layers are reduced to 2 bits while the bit widths of outputs from activation functions are reduced to 4 bits. The result is an impressive reduction in network size compared to the original floating point model, allowing for implementation on FPGA. The compressed version of the network is referred to as W2A4, and relative compression to other existing networks can be seen in Table 1.7. The proposed and existing networks were tested on 7 indoor scenes of the Middlebury dataset using three different SNRs, with the results shown in Table 1.8. These results demonstrate that despite the small size of the network, it produces high accuracy with a low error rate. The Absolute relative difference (ABS rel) shows a difference of 2.94×10^{-5} between the proposed method and [Sun et al., 2020] and 16.2×10^{-3} with [Peng et al., 2020].

Table 1.7: Comparison of different existing and proposed networks in terms of No. of parameters, training time, and the relative compression compared to W2A4. $*^1$ without utilizing intensity data. $*^2$ utilizing intensity data [Zang et al., 2021].

	No. parameters	Training time	Compression rate
[Lindell et al., 2018] $*^1$	3.95M	24h	21.99x
[Lindell et al., 2018] $*^2$	3.93M	24h	21.83x
[Sun et al., 2020]	3.95M	24h	21.99x
[Peng et al., 2020]	1.01M	36h	5.61x
32-bit floating point	2.19M	17h	12.17x
W2A4	0.18M	16h	-

Table 1.8: Results of proposed and existing algorithms over three different SNR levels [Zang et al., 2021].

	Accuracy		Error	
Signal photons = 2, background photons = 10, SBR = 0.2				
	$\delta < 1.25$	$\delta < 1.25^2$	RMSE (m)	ABS rel
[Lindell et al., 2018]	0.9962	0.9982	0.066	0.0110
[Sun et al., 2020]	0.9966	0.9981	0.062	0.0070
[Peng et al., 2020]	0.9966	**0.9987**	0.064	0.0087
32-bit floating point	**0.9968**	0.9983	**0.059**	0.0069
W2A4	0.9967	0.9980	0.061	**0.0056**
Signal photons = 2, background photons = 50, SBR = 0.04				
[Lindell et al., 2018]	0.9827	0.9951	0.149	0.0260
[Sun et al., 2020]	0.9948	0.9971	0.073	0.0082
[Peng et al., 2020]	0.9961	**0.9980**	0.064	0.0087
32-bit floating point	0.9961	**0.9980**	**0.063**	0.0067
W2A4	**0.9962**	**0.9980**	0.064	**0.0060**
Signal photons = 2, background photons = 100, SBR = 0.02				
[Lindell et al., 2018]	0.9357	0.9729	0.321	0.0580
[Sun et al., 2020]	0.9952	0.9978	0.069	0.0081
[Peng et al., 2020]	0.9961	**0.9981**	0.065	0.0087
32-bit floating point	**0.9963**	0.9980	**0.064**	**0.0060**
W2A4	**0.9963**	**0.9981**	0.065	**0.0060**

1.2.2 Comparison

[Chen et al., 2022] demonstrated a system that can operate well in adverse conditions, though its accuracy deteriorates in ideal conditions when compared to classical methods. It has the lowest computation time at only 0.26ms per histogram vs LiDAR-NET's 3.4ms. Its FPGA implementation only has a minor drop in depth prediction despite the high quantization error in the ambient estimation. Sadly it doesn't have any detailed information on the exact number of parameters used in the NNMPA fully connected structure, but as the FPGA BRAM utilization is high so to will be the network size. [Aßmann et al., 2021] demonstrates a very low error when detecting multiple close surfaces at distances of up to 300m using a convolutional structure without any feature extraction being performed on the histograms. While the network has relatively few parameters due to its convolutional architecture, making it easier to implement on a chip, it is still a larger network than [Zang et al., 2021] which uses 180,000 parameters. [Zang et al., 2021] presented a small network that is able to outperform multiple state-of-the-art schemes under various conditions, as seen in Table 1.8. One of the key results is the minimal effect quantization had on the performance of the network compared to its 32-bit floating-point equivalent. While [Sun et al., 2020] presented good results utilizing both depth and RGB, it was outperformed by [Zang et al., 2021] in accuracy prediction on similar datasets. A key takeaway from this is that while additional guiding information, such as monocular, is useful in detecting the surfaces present in a scene, it is not a necessary step as proven by the presented systems. Quantisation has also been shown to reduce the size of a network dramatically, Table 1.7, to allow for easier implementation on hardware with minimal increase in error. The main advantage that [Chen et al., 2022] and

Table 1.9: Comparison table of surface detection schemes. $*^1$ also uses RGB data 1: [Chen et al., 2022], 2: [Aßmann et al., 2021], 3: [Sun et al., 2020], and 4: [Zang et al., 2021].

	1	2	3	4
Implementation level	FPGA	Simulation	Simulation	Simulation
Accuracy metric	Accuracy	MSE	$\delta < 1.25$	$\delta < 1.25$
Reported result	83.54%	0.0006	0.9960	0.9962
No. parameters		6,425,980		180,000
Input data type	Histograms	Histograms	Histograms$*^1$	Histograms
Data resolution	1x1,310	1x7,500	1x128	1x1,024
SPAD array size	2x192		256x256	64x64
Max range	61.26m	300m	10m	
Peak laser power	75W			
Pulse width	18.75ns			
Repetition rate	10KHz			
Temporal resolution	312.5ps			
Frame rate	20			
Computation time	0.26ms	3.4ms		
Power Consumption				

[Aßmann et al., 2021] have over the other schemes presented is the ability to output multiple detected surfaces from the same pixel. The more detailed output of these networks make them ideal for use in combination with spatial super-resolution schemes and algorithms such as that presented in [Gyongy et al., 2020].

1.3 Super-resolution depth mapping

Super-resolution imaging is a series of techniques used to increase the resolution of an imaging system, such as in 1.10. Traditional approaches such as linear and bicubic interpolation [Keys, 1981] can be fast but yield results that have been overly smoothed. Recently deep learning approaches, such as SR-GAN [Ledig et al., 2016], are achieving state-of-the-art performances driving them into becoming more common in super-resolution tasks [Yang et al., 2019]. These techniques have also seen increased use in the upsampling of low spatial resolution depth maps captured using SPAD LiDAR for use in applications such as automotive vehicles.

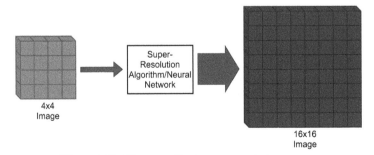

Figure 1.10: Diagram of basic super-resolution output.

1.3.1 Artificial Neural Networks

The work presented by [Ruget et al., 2021a] proposes a deep neural network that de-noises and up-samples a depth map from 64x32 to 256x128 using multi-scale photon count histogram information and exploiting high-resolution intensity images for guided up-sampling. The network is modeled on use with the Quantic 4x4 [Hutchings et al., 2019] sensor which provides both the intensity and depth information at resolutions of 256x128 and 64x32 respectively. The training and testing of the neural network uses synthetic histogram and intensity data generated using the MPI Sintel Depth dataset [Butler et al., 2012], [Wulff et al., 2012] (training) and Middlebury dataset [Scharstein and Pal, 2007], [Hirschmuller and Scharstein, 2007] (test) as the ground truth. The designed network utilizes U-net architecture [Ronneberger et al., 2015] and incorporates guidance information as in [Guo et al., 2019]. The network uses as an input the concatenation of two depth maps (up-sampled from 64x32 to 256x128 using the nearest neighbor algorithm), with the first depth map being comprised of the surfaces with the highest photon counts. The second depth map consists of any pixels which contain secondary surfaces where the photon counts exceed a certain threshold, if not then that pixel entry remains 0. Multi-scale information is also utilized to de-noise the data and is included in both the decoder and encoder using guiding branches, with depth features being incorporated in the encoder and intensity in the decoder. The four multiscale depth features connected to the encoder consist of D1, D2, D3, and D4. D1 is the first depth map down sampled using nearest-neighbor interpolation from 256x128 to 128x64. D2 is computes the depths using center of mass on the source 64x32x16 histograms. D3 and D4 are the source histograms down-sampled by a factor of 2 and 4 respectively by summing adjacent pixels. The intensity image used to guide the upsampling process has a resolution of 256x128. The size of each component of the network can be seen in Table 1.10. The results of the trained network are compared to four other methods, first the nearest-neighbor interpolation, Guided Image Filtering [He et al., 2013], DepthSR-Net (retrained on the same dataset) [Guo et al., 2019], and an algorithm presented in [Gyongy et al., 2020]. Each system was tested under three different conditions, High SNR of 2 and signal photon counts per pixel (ppp) of 1200 with secondary surfaces present, medium SNR of 0.02 and ppp of 4 with no secondary surfaces, and low SNR of 0.006 and ppp of 4 with no secondary surfaces. The results can be seen in Table 1.11 where Absolute Depth Error (ADE) is calculated as $ADE = |R + d - d^{ref}|$, with R being the residual map predicted by Histnet, d being an up-scaled low-resolution depth map, d^{ref} being ground truth. Additional results can also be found in [Ruget et al., 2021b]. The results show that guided upsampling using intensity images and multi-scale depth features significantly improves the accuracy of the final HR image. The main drawback, however, is that even when implemented on a NVidia RTX 6000 GPU the processing time for one frame is significant. With the total processing time reaching 7 seconds, Histnet would be unlikely to be usable in any live scenarios.

Another super-resolution and denoising scheme by [Martín et al., 2022] devises a method to upscale and denoise dToF video sequences using past, present, and future

Table 1.10: No. of parameters per network component of Histnet [Ruget et al., 2021a].

Network section	No. of parameters
Encoder	25,108,992
Decoder	31,058,368
Depth guidance	9,600
Intensity guidance	1,549,824
Total	57,726,784

Table 1.11: Quantitive comparison of the different methods of reconstruction for the 4x upsampling of the MPI Sintel dataset [Ruget et al., 2021a]. ADE stands for Absolute Depth Error. $*^1$ is Nearest neighbour interpolation, $*^2$ is [He et al., 2013], $*^3$ is [Guo et al., 2019], $*^4$ is [Gyongy et al., 2020], and $*^5$ is Histnet.

	$*^1$	$*^2$	$*^3$	$*^4$	$*^5$
Time per frame	1ms	0.4s	7s (on GPU)	4s	7s (on GPU)
	Training on high SNR with secondary surface				
Scene	ADE	ADE	ADE	ADE	ADE
Art	0.038	0.039	0.008	0.0076	0.0027
Reindeer	0.035	0.035	0.0051	0.004	0.0018
	Training on medium SNR without secondary surface				
Art	0.22	0.17	0.023	0.05	0.019
Reindeer	0.21	0.16	0.024	0.06	0.019
	Training on low SNR without secondary surface				
Art	0.276	0.22	0.064	0.187	0.055
Reindeer	0.272	0.206	0.053	0.168	0.05

depth frames based on the network presented in [Li et al., 2022]. It is trained using 15,500 images using synthetic depth data generated from high-resolution depth maps (256x128) and RGB data (256x128 converted to grayscale) recorded in Airsim [Shah et al., 2017]. As these depth maps don't contain the Poisson noise inherent in photonics, histograms are created from the Airsim data using a Poisson distribution to generate incident and background photon counts which form a 16-bin histogram. The FoV of the scenes is 30°with different frame rates simulated to vary the object movement per frame, the SNR is also varied between video sequences, and finally, the depth is varied between 0 and 35m. From these generated histograms, new depth maps are created using center of mass peak extraction [Gyongy et al., 2020]. The depth maps are normalized and consecutive frames with a set temporal radius T_R are concatenated, i.e., in groups of $2T_R + 1$ frames such that the input to the network is of the shape 64x32x($2T_R$+1). When the temporal radius is 0, only a single depth frame is used as input as opposed to if the radius is set to one, where it uses one frame from the past and one from the future. If the frame is at the start or end of the video sequence, then the system replicates the current frame to fulfill the required input size. The network output is a super-solved depth frame of the size 256x128 and is compared with the normalised ground truth depth map from Airsim and evaluated using the metrics Peak Signal-to-Noise Ratio (PSNR) [Fardo et al., 2016] and Structure Similarity Index (SSIM) [Nilsson and Akenine-Möller, 2020]. The network architecture

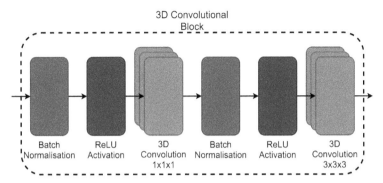

Figure 1.11: Diagram of 3D convolutional blocks used in super-resolution scheme [Martín et al., 2022].

itself is based on blocks of 3D convolutions and dynamic upsampling filters. The structure of the 3D blocks can be seen in Figure 1.11, with the full network shown in Figure 1.12. The number of convolutional blocks varies with the size of the temporal resolution such that there are $3 + T_R$ blocks per network. Initial testing to investigate the impact of different temporal resolutions was completed using a dataset of 1500 frames (3 recordings of 500 frames). The results show that while a higher T_R improves PSNR and SSIM, the trade-off is a large decrease in FPS from 43.4 FPS at $T_R = 1$ to 30.8 FPS at $T_R = 4$. An investigation was also made into an object's speed and the network's ability to exploit the temporal information, and was found that as long as an object didn't move more than 2-3 pixels in between frames then there would be no degradation in accuracy. The proposed system is also compared to other contemporary methods such as Bicubic [Keys, 1981], Histnet [Ruget et al., 2021a], and iSeeBetter [Chadha et al., 2020] using the same 1,500 frame dataset. It can be seen in Table 1.12 that the proposed approach has a greater accuracy at upsampling the depth maps with only a slightly lower frame rate than other approaches presented. The images produced from this scheme are better able to replicate the flat surfaces of an object, but have a tendency to blur the edges of an object with the background.

Table 1.12: Comparison of work presented in [Martín et al., 2022] at different temporal resolutions with other contemporary methods. Scenes 1 and 2 have an SNR of 1.3 and scene 3 has a SNR of 3, with different SNR values used to demonstrate the robustness of the network.

Method	Scene 1 PSNR	Scene 1 SSIM	Scene 2 PSNR	Scene 2 SSIM	Scene 3 PSNR	Scene 3 SSIM	FPS
Bicubic	15.82	0.538	17.60	0.607	26.80	0.841	**185**
iSeeBetter	20.47	0.784	21.96	0.837	28.74	0.843	33
Histnet	19.14	0.812	20.14	0.858	27.18	0.881	0.25
$T_R = 1$	21.20	0.890	22.72	0.910	31.17	0.901	43.4
$T_R = 4$	**22.05**	**0.909**	**23.00**	**0.916**	**31.31**	**0.906**	30.8

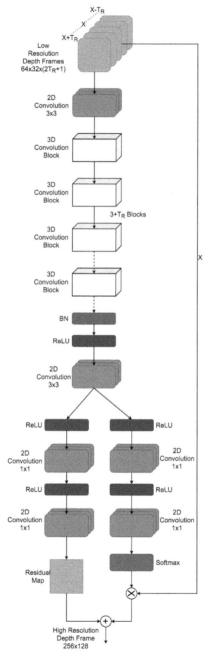

Figure 1.12: Diagram of the full network used in the super-resolution scheme [Martín et al., 2022].

1.3.2   Spiking Neural Networks

The work presented by [Kirkland et al., 2020] presents a single pixel SPAD sensor that utilizes a spiking neural network to upscale the output 1x8,000 bin ToF histogram into a 64x64 resolution depth map. A fully spiking convolutional architecture is used where the depth histogram is encoded using 1D convolutions, then decoded into a 2D depth map using 2D convolutional layers. The network is trained on synthetic data created by simulating a flood illuminated single point SPAD sensor with depths ranging from 2 to 4m. 4 different experiments comprised the 11,600 sample dataset, with the variance of photon count and IRF from 1,000 to 9,500 photon counts and 20 to 100 ps time windows and histogram bin widths of 2.3ps. The synthetic scenes are generated using object silhouettes, with the background objects being static throughout all images and the foreground object moving between 200 locations which only vary along the x and z axis. In total, 29 different object silhouettes are used.

The structure of the devised Spiking Convolutional Neural Network (SCNN) and the network it is compared to can be seen in Table 1.13. The SCNN is trained as a synchronous CNN but is converted into its spiking equivalent using Nengo [Bekolay et al., 2014]. The results of the conversion versus the traditional ANN approach can be seen in Table 1.14. It can be seen that Spike-SPI performs better on all reported metrics except SNR and RMSE. Spike-SPI spatial reconstruction of the scene is superior to the ANN as seen in the Intersection over Union (IoU) and accuracy metrics. While 87% of all depth estimates made by Spike-SPI are accurate, the predictions for the background are considerably noisy which is the root of the low SNR and RMSE. Spike-SPI also benefits from lower processing power over the ANN implementation. While the average firing rate of the neurons is around 1Hz, with a max of 150Hz, only around 11% of the neurons are active as low connection weights inherited from the CNN version don't significantly increase the spiking neurons' membrane potentials to their threshold essentially filtering them out. This reduction in information propagation can reduce the accuracy of the reconstruction, but also reduces the power consumption. The paper reports however that there was no tangible difference between the results of the CNN and SCNN implementations. There is also a marked reduction in processing time for each frame due to the asynchronous nature of the network. By varying the firing rates of the neurons, the time taken to converge on a result reduces with the trade-off of more neural activity. The main flaw of this reconstruction scheme is its reliance on a the background remaining static, with only the foreground changing.

1.3.3   Comparison

The largest difference between the presented schemes is the input data that they use, shown in Table 1.15. Histnet utilizes the most data inputs but does not achieve greater SSIM over the method of [Martín et al., 2022], as seen in Table 1.12, which uses multiple depth frames. Histnet also presents a far slower computation time than the scheme presented in [Martín et al., 2022] of 7s vs 32ms respectively. This shows that there does not appear to be an added advantage in utilizing Depth, intensity,

Table 1.13: Details of Spike-SPI and its comparison network [Kirkland et al., 2020].

			Spike-SPI					
Layer	Ce1	Ce2-3	Ce4-10	Cd8-5	Cd4-3	Cd2	Cd1	Up
Kernel size	7	7	7	5	5	5	5	2
Feature no.	64	128	256	256	128	64	1	
			ANN					
Layer	FC1		FC2		FC3			
Kernel size								
Feature no.	1024		512		256			

Table 1.14: Results of the Spike-SPI vs the ANN solution [Kirkland et al., 2020] where δ relates to the accuracy of the predictions within 1.25% of the ground truth. IoU results performed on a mask of the Spike-SPI depth map outputs where the data is converted into a binary value to represent the presence of an object in the scene.

	Photon count	IRF	IoU	SNR	RMSE	$\delta < 1.25$
ANN		100ps	0.650	**14.844dB**	**0.189**	0.853
Spike-SPI	1,000		**0.783**	14.284dB	0.201	**0.871**
ANN		20ps	0.650	**14.708dB**	**0.192**	0.853
Spike-SPI			**0.760**	14.155dB	0.202	**0.868**
ANN		100ps	0.637	**15.076dB**	**0.187**	0.856
Spike-SPI	9,500		**0.780**	14.391dB	0.198	**0.871**
ANN		20ps	0.631	**15.070dB**	**0.188**	0.856
Spike-SPI			**0.778**	14.424dB	0.198	**0.870**

and histogram data over just depth. Histograms however are shown in the Spike-SPI to provide a wealth of information, providing the most impressive performance in super-resolution. [Kirkland et al., 2020] up-scales the input histogram into a 64x64 depth map. The catch is that it relies on a known static background, so has limited applications in the real world. Its spiking nature compounded with the low neural activity does imply it would have the lowest power consumption out of the presented methods. A comparison in computation time was not investigated in Spike-SPI, but it would be interesting to see the time taken to process the histogram using the ANN vs the SNN. An interesting network would seem to be a structure similar to [Martín et al., 2022] using the raw histograms instead of the depth maps, which could then be converted into a spiking equivalent for the reduction in power consumption and potential computation time.

1.4 Object detection

Object detection is the image processing task that detects and extracts semantic objects of a predefined class (such as boat, airplane, human, etc.) in digital images or videos, such as in Figure 1.13. Every object class defined has its own set of features that is used to identify it, for instance, a square class would be identified b perpendicular corners. However, while in algorithms such as Scale-invariant feature transform (SIFT) [Lowe, 2004] where each class is predefined using reference images, in neural network approaches based on convolutional layers the features of a class are learned

Table 1.15: Comparison table of reviewed super resolution depth mapping solutions $*$[1]also utilises intensity (256x128) and histogram (64x32x16) data. $*$[2] approximated from paper. 1: [Ruget et al., 2021a], 2: [Martín et al., 2022], and 3: [Kirkland et al., 2020].

	1	2	3
Implementation level	Simulation	Simulation	Simulation
Accuracy metric	ADE	SSIM	RMSE
Reported result	0.00225	0.91	≈ 0.20
No. parameters	57,726,784		n/a
Input data type	Depth maps$*$[1]	Depth maps	Histograms
Input resolution	64x32x2	64x32	1x8000
Output data type	Depth maps	Depth maps	Depth maps
Output resolution	256x128	256x128	64x64
SPAD array size	256x128/64x32	64x32	1x1
Computation time	7s	32ms$*$[2]	54ms$*$[2]

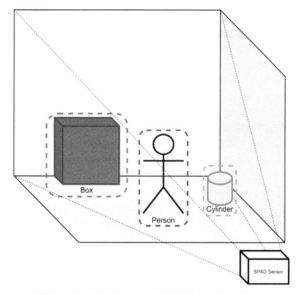

Figure 1.13: Diagram of basic object detection.

and not defined. Object detection applications include face recognition, object tracking, and image annotation. Over time CNN implementations of object detection have seen increased use and has now become state of the art.

1.4.1 Artificial Neural Networks

The first system [Ruvalcaba-Cardenas et al., 2018] is a flash LiDAR which compares a modified version of the VGG-16 [Simonyan and Zisserman, 2014] 2D CNN and compares it to a 3D CNN at identifying three classes (airplane, chair, and drone). These two systems are trained using a limited dataset of only 1,983 and 1,900 images

Table 1.16: Details of datasets used in [Ruvalcaba-Cardenas et al., 2018].

	Indoor	Outdoor
Range	25m	400m, 600m, and 700m
Ambient	<1 lux	
SPAD array		64x64
Pulse width		7ns
Pulse energy		18mj
Repetition rate		100Hz
Depth resolution		0.5m

captured on a SPAD LiDAR setup for the 2D and 3D network respectively, with an example shown in Table 1.16. For the indoor images, a 16mm to 160mm zoom lens was used with different zooms for each object. The outdoor data also used a meade telescope with the SPAD sensor while the laser was mounted using a telescopic sight and a beam expander which was set to give a 3m diameter beam at each of the 3 ranges. The sensor outputs histograms which are processed into depth maps, with distance thresholding, and then median and spatial filters are applied to remove any background data or noise until finally, the image is binarised. A nearest-neighbor interpolation algorithm is used to upsample the binarised images to 320x320, with the data for the 2D network being resized again down to 224x224 while the 3D network converts the images into a 16x16x16 voxel grid where the binary image is projected along the z-axis. The 2D modified VGG-16 network is retrained using transfer learning [Yosinski et al., 2014], where the first 14 layers of VGG-16 are frozen while the last 4 are replaced with 4 unfrozen layers for a total of 18 layers where the final two are a dense and a classification layer. The new network is then trained on 1,923 images (641 per class) and 60 images for testing. The 3D network structure can be seen in Figure 1.14 (using ReLU activation functions) and was trained on a dataset of 1,900 voxel grids with 1,615 training, 285 validation, and 60 testing voxel grids. The results of these networks are given in F1 score over the 60 test images, not accuracy or any other metric. The results show that the modified VGG-16 network provides an average F1 score of 0.95 while the 3D network provides an F1 score of 0.97, indicating that there are clear advantages utilizing the 3D information even when using a smaller network. While the results are impressive, the source dToF data applies significant pre-processing and the depth information is lost before being used with the NN.

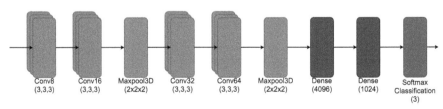

Figure 1.14: Proposed 3D Convolutional Network Architecture [Ruvalcaba-Cardenas et al., 2018].

The work performed by [Nash and Devrelis, 2020] presents a flash LiDAR system that is used to classify 6 different vehicles as if mounted to a drone using a CNN which is contrasted with other traditional methods such as Gaussian naive Bayes Classifier and a nearest neighbor classifier [Goldberger et al., 2004]. The training data consists of 116 vehicle datasets varying from a few to several thousand frames captured using the a 32x32 SPAD array outdoors during twilight. The sensor itself is mounted on a tower 16m above the ground to simulate a drone's elevation with a DJI gimbal used to provide movement and stability, while the target vehicles are placed 30m from the base. The SPAD array is illuminated by a 35mj, 5ns laser with a repetition rate of 20Hz and a beam divergence of 115°providing a depth resolution of 0.75m. The SPAD array uses a first photon TDC, so to reduce the effect of noise histogram averaging of 15-50 frames is used to filter out ambient photon detections. The depth images are pre-processed to remove the ground plane, convert the depth into meters, and reorient the vehicle. The structure of the CNN used to process the final depth images can be seen in Figure 1.15, unfortunately, no detailed information on the parameters was given. The CNN is compared to two traditional approaches, principle component analysis (PCA) with a Gaussian Classifier and PCA with a Nearest Neighbour classifier. The results of the work can be seen in Table 1.17. The CNN-based approach is shown to outperform the traditional methods but only by a small margin. The performance of the system overall is impressive given the low spatial and depth resolution. The low resolution reduces the data throughput making it more applicable for embedding on a drone, however, the network has only been tested using the CPU of an NVIDIA Jetson TX2 board and took multiple seconds to process and single frame. The work did express its desire to implement the system on a GPU which would improve the computation time.

The work presented by [Ito et al., 2017] is a small SPAD LiDAR system that utilizes depth, monocular, and intensity data to perform localization in an environment using a Deep Convolutional Neural Network (DCNN). The LiDAR system, named SPAD LiDAR, is targeted as a low-cost and compact sensor and is used with two CNN schemes: SPAD DCNN and Fast SPAD DCNN. The SPAD LiDAR sensor has a range of up to 80m using two SPAD arrays on the same chip, with one used to detect backscattered photons and the other to measure the ambient light. The main specifications can be seen in Table 1.18. The SPAD DCNN network uses all three data inputs to determine if there is a target and then resolve its 3D coordinates. The network is small, consisting of only three convolutional layers, three pooling layers, and two fully connected layers. Fast SPAD DCNN is a version with improved runtime performance over the original and integrates peak intensity data with the depth data so that results with low certainty are filtered out. This is done pixel-wise by binarising the peak intensity data and multiplying the result with the depth data. The data and ground truth data were collected indoors with trajectories being captured using a vicon motion capture system [vic, 2022] and later resized from the native 202x96 into 112x112. The networks are compared to the same network structure, but as if only depth data was used instead of all 3 inputs. The datasets used to train consist of three recordings of the sensor slowly moving towards a wooden pallet, with two used for training and one for testing. Three experiments were carried out to

Table 1.17: Classification accuracy of Algorithms [Nash and Devrelis, 2020].

Classification Algorithm	Accuracy (%)
PCA with Gaussian	63.0
PCA with Nearest Neighbour	85.2
CNN	86.3

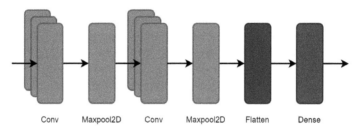

Conv   Maxpool2D   Conv   Maxpool2D   Flatten   Dense

Figure 1.15: Proposed 3D Convolutional Network Architecture [Nash and Devrelis, 2020].

test SPAD DCNN and Fast SPAD DCNN. The first experiment compared the ability of the conventional method vs the SPAD DCNN at localising the target in the scene, with the conventional achieving an error of 6.7cm and SPAD DCNN achieving an error of 4.4cm. As the depth resolution of the SPAD LiDAR is 3.5cm, the result is not only an improvement over the conventional method but close to the resolution limitation. The 2nd experiment compares the runtime of SPAD DCNN and Fast SPAD DCNN. It reuses the dataset from the first experiment and measures the computational demands and runtime to process one frame when the networks are implemented on a CPU (core i7) and a GPU (GTX Titan X), with the results shown in Table 1.19. The third test examines the increase in localization error as the guided vehicle moves off course from the training data. Five trajectories with 5 variations are used to test the system's ability to cope with variance in sensor movement. The results are that for a deviation of 50cm off the path of the training set, the average localization error increases to 0.15m. Overall, it can be seen that by providing the neural network multiple sources of data to leverage, it was able to reduce the error by 2.3cm when compared to depth data alone.

Table 1.18: SPAD LiDAR sensor specifications [Ito et al., 2017].

Pixel resolution	202×96 pixels
Field of view	55°×9°
Frame rate	10fps
Size	W 0.067 × H 0.073 × D 0.177 m
Range	80m (reflectivity 9%)
Laser	Class 1 laser
Distance resolution	0.035m

The work of [Scholes et al., 2022] presents a SPAD LiDAR system called Drone-sense which is capable of determining the type, orientation, and segmentation

Table 1.19: Runtime Results of Fast SPAD DCNN and SPAD DCNN [Ito et al., 2017].

	SPAD DCNN	Fast SPAD DCNN
CPU runtime	36.03ms	25.5ms
GPU runtime	4.1ms	2.9ms

(body, engines, camera) of drones in flight using a CNN that utilizes a decision tree and an ensemble structure. The system utilizes the SPAD sensor Quantic 4x4 [Hutchings et al., 2019] which is 256x256 SPAD pixel array able to provide both intensity data and depth histograms (64x64 resolution). The sensor outputs 16 bin histograms with 500ps temporal resolution. In this work, the sensor resolution was set differently from the default at 80x240 pixels for intensity and depth at 20x60 pixels. The network is trained on a synthetic dataset of 72,000 images generated by placing two drones in an Unreal Engine environment at random positions, orientations, and distances within the camera FoV. The simulated intensity images are created using a Poisson filter and are resized to 80x240, while the depth maps are downsampled to 20x60 and converted into 15 bin histograms. The proposed large network structure can be found in the original paper. The core of the network is referred to as the Drone Feature Encoder (DFE), and it extracts features from depth and intensity data into a space of 1x3x32 filters. The remainder consists of either the segmentation or the decision trees for orientation and identification predictions. The testing uses two angular regimes, "full angle" and "reduced angle" as seen in Table 1.20, with the reduced angle having the drone constrained to the specifications of the manufacturer. The trained network was then tested using real data captured by the Quantic 4x4 camera of a drone in flight, with an example of the results shown in Table 1.21. The network was able to correctly distinguish between the two drone types with average accuracies of over 90%. The training and testing data seem to not contain any background noise, so either some pre-processing is performed or the synthetic data does not take into account any ambient light and background objects. The work also experiments with the network's ability to perform using only the depth histograms or only the intensity data. When using only the histograms, the average reduction in accuracy for orientation prediction was less than 0.5% while the reduction when using only intensity data was just under 2%. The small loss when only using histograms suggests the benefit is minimal with the intensity included. The impact of a reduction in resolution was also investigated, with the resolution being halved and quartered. The main result was an overall reduction in the segmentation accuracy, with the largest reduction being the segmentation of engines resulting in a loss of accuracy of 7% and 23% for the half and quarter resolution respectively. The ability to detect the camera was not greatly impacted, however, with only a reduction of 2% and 3% for half and quarter resolution respectively. The resolution also impacted the orientation prediction with the yaw predictions accuracy reducing by 1.7% and 7.6% for the half and quarter resolution respectively.

The work by [Mora-Martín et al., 2021] presents a short-range 3D depth imager that uses CNNs to investigate the accuracy of gesture recognition using 3D depth data with low lateral resolution at high speeds. It uses the Quantic 4x4

Table 1.20: Full angle and reduced angle regimes for drone orientation [Scholes et al., 2022].

	Full angle	Reduced angle
Yaw range	0°, 360°	0°, 360°
Roll range	0°, 360°	140°, 220°
Pitch range	0°, 180°	140°, 220°

Table 1.21: Dronesense predictions on real data example [Scholes et al., 2022].

Metric	Ground truth	Prediction, accuracy %
Classification	Mavic2	Mavic2, 100
Orientation		
Yaw	31	19, 93
Roll	180	177, 96
Pitch	90	92, 96

[Hutchings et al., 2019] sensor to capture both depth and intensity data at resolutions of 64x32 and 256x128 respectively. The laser is a 2W max power flood illumination source with a FoV of 20°. It has a pulse length of 10ns and a repetition rate of 6MHz. The sensor itself is set with a temporal resolution of 4ns per bin and captured data at approximately 200FPS. 4 different combinations of input data was tested, specifically depth (64x32), intensity (256x128), histogram (64x32x16), and intensity and depth (I+D) (256x128x2). I+D stacks depth data up-scaled to 256x128 using nearest neighbor interpolation onto the third axis of the intensity data for a final resolution of 256x128x2. The system comprises two networks, the first is a U-net [Ronneberger et al., 2015] network version that was modified to handle the 4 different data schemes, which outputs a binary mask with 0 being the background and 1 being an object of interest in the pixel. The second is a simpler classification network that predicts the gesture. The network was trained using a RTX2070 GPU using three datasets, the first dataset being a hand in front of a plain background without ambient light, the second introducing objects into the background, and the third introducing objects and ambient light. 1,000 frames for each of the 3 gestures are captured for each dataset, resulting in a 9,000 frame dataset. The network training results can be seen in Table 1.22. The Histogram and I+D network proved to get the best results, though the histogram-based network has the added advantage of faster processing time. The faster processing time can be attributed to only needing one data frame from the sensor which halves the data acquisition time and requires no additional pre-processing to upscale and combine the data. It also shows that while the histogram data has a lower spatial resolution, it benefits from information such as object reflectivity, ambient level, object edges, and the depth that the histogram contains resulting in similar or better performance than that of higher resolution data.

1.4.2 Spiking Neural Networks

The work [Ara Shawkat et al., 2020] presents a SPAD-based vision system that utilizes on-chip memristive spiking neural networks for object detection. It is currently

Table 1.22: Average processing speed, classification accuracy, and standard deviation over all three datasets [Mora-Martín et al., 2021].

	Processing Speed	Average accuracy (%)	St. dev
Intensity (256x128)	41 FPS	98.78	0.31
Depth (64x32)	**45 FPS**	98.59	0.17
Histogram (64x32x16)	41 FPS	99.26	**0.16**
I+D (256x128x2)	32 FPS	**99.31**	0.28

a prototype design that uses a 5x5 SPAD array to recognize shapes but not differentiate them, i.e., square, diamond, plus, and triangle. The main difference in its architecture is that it utilizes an asynchronous Address Event Representation (AER) readout scheme presented in [Shawkat and Mcfarlane, 2020] instead of traditional histogramming. The AER generates a pixel event when enough photons were detected which is then encoded using a 7-bit pixel address (3 bits for row, 3 for column, and 1 for data validation). The SNN which processes the address events consists of analog CMOS Integrate-and-Fire (IF) neurons and memristive synapses, and only 3 input neurons and one output neuron as seen in Figure 1.16. The design is implemented in two portions, with the CMOS section implemented in 65nm CMOS whereas the memristors are modeled in Verilog-A. The address events of each row of the SPAD array are not fed directly into the SNN as the input order is not based on their arrival, but on their position in the array. This suggests that the AER is simply used to show which pixels had an event over the laser cycle and does not represent any specific timing information. The pixels in the row which had an event are then represented in an input signal by a binary 1 so that if only the middle pixel in the bottom row had an event, the signal to the SNN would be 00100. The results presented in [Ara Shawkat et al., 2020] show some advantages over similar systems, particularly the dynamic range and power consumption, 152dB and 2.1mW respectively, but do not provide any accuracy metrics for the predictions. The power consumption achieved is very impressive, as it presents energy consumption of just 0.48pj per synaptic spike and per neuron spike of 12.5pj which is far better than the power consumption achieved in the SNN Loihi [Davies et al., 2018] which has an energy consumption of 23.6pj per synaptic spike and 81pj per neuron spike.

The work outlined by [Afshar et al., 2020] presents a neuromorphic object detection scheme that uses spatio-temporal patterns generated by SPAD pixels in an event-based manner to increase frame rates and reduce noise and redundant data. It uses a flash LiDAR with data captured by a 32x32 SPAD array which is then up-sampled to 128x128 for training before being implemented on a 128x128 flash SPAD sensor. Instead of recording the photon time of flight information, the proposed approach utilizes photon events directly with asynchronous neuromorphic processing operating on the inter-spike arrival times within the local regions of the SPAD array such that it only records the inter-pixel photon arrival order. The event generation system is called First-AND and requires no TDC or associated memory to be implemented.

he sensor consists of 128x128 SPAD pixels which are grouped together into 125x125 overlapping 4x4 receptive fields. These receptive fields contain the circuitry

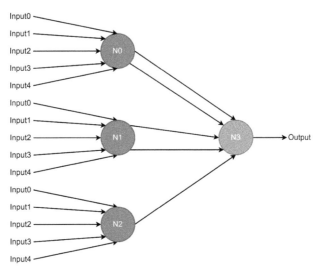

Figure 1.16: SNN topology outlined in [Ara Shawkat et al., 2020] for pattern recognition In-put0 to Input4 represents the 5 rows of the SPAD array.

to perform real-time feature extraction and event generation. Each receptive field can produce 4 types of features, North, East, South, and West as seen in Figure 1.17. These features are created by using 4 overlapping AND gates patterned to connect 8 SPADs together, triggering a feature event only if all 8 SPADs were triggered by photons at the same time. Only one feature per receptive field can be triggered and output during each laser cycle, with the first feature detected being stored in memory as a 2-bit address. Digital AND gates are used instead of analog summing and comparator circuits which simplifies the design and ensures that the output at each AND gate is deterministic. To minimize the impact of noise, a receptive field must report the same feature over multiple laser cycles before it is transmitted. When a receptive field's feature reaches the threshold, an event is generated using an AER scheme to output the location of the feature. The full First-AND block diagram is shown in Figure 1.18. The events generated by First-AND are processed by a 16-neuron network which creates a binary feature map from the event stream, trained using the Feature Extraction using Adaptive Selection Thresholds (FEAST) algorithm [Afshar et al., 2019]. The binarised features are then used as inference on the input event stream to create a first-layer feature map that can be processed by an event-based classifier after a 1D or 2D pooling operation.

The First-AND event generation method is compared with two other event schemes: On-Off events, and On-Off Bi-polar and Uni-polar (OOBU) events. The On-Off events are generated by using a thresholding operation to convert the differences between consecutive SPAD frames into a sparse event stream. While this provides single-pixel resolution, it requires the measurement and storage of timing information for each SPAD pixel. OOBU is an augmented version of On-Off events, where uni-polar and bi-polar events are generated by counting recent event types in adjacent pixels to the current event, i.e., 3x3 pixel region. If all recent detected events are all on or all off events and exceed the selected threshold, then it generates a Uni-polar event. If both on and off events are detected, however, then a Bi-polar event is generated if the total event number exceeds the threshold. This method only considers local event counts and not the shape of the feature, causing different-shaped features to cause the same event type.

The dataset used to train the network consists of 24,000 images with 15 classes of plane. Each plane is dropped in front of the camera with 200 images of each plane. To increase the dataset's size, each image is rotated 4 times and flipped for a total of 1,600 images per plane. The results of the network trained on this data is outlined in Table 1.23. The per-recording results demonstrate the accuracy of the system when predicting a class with the greatest number frames won over the whole recording, effectively performing a pooling and max operation on the recording. While the 2D pooling method provides consistently higher results, it is significantly faster to compute and simpler to implement the 1D pooling in hardware. The total data reduction of the proposed event schemes over the original recordings was an 81, 57, and 25-fold reduction in data rates for First-AND, On-Off, and OOBU respectively. As the OOBU method provides consistently better results, it was used in the hardware implementation. The hardware implementation utilized approximately 30% of Cyclone IVE FPGAs resources and takes $29.24\mu s$ to process a single AER event and update the output. The main bottleneck of the FPGA implementation is loading the 3x3 ROI around the current event, which only becomes more exacerbated as the number of event polarities and ROI increases.

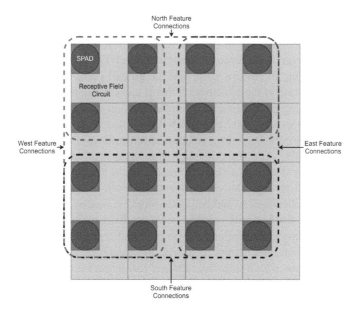

Figure 1.17: Layout of the receptive fields and the 4 feature areas [Afshar et al., 2020].

Figure 1.18: Functional block diagram of ASIC implemented First-AND network receptive field [Afshar et al., 2020].

Table 1.23: Classification accuracy of proposed event generation schemes OOBU+FEAST combines the OOBU event generation scheme with the feature extraction network used with First-AND [Afshar et al., 2020].

	Accuracy			
	Per frame		Per recording	
	1D pooling	2D pooling	1D pooling	2D pooling
First-AND	63%	70%	71%	80%
On-Off	55%	65%	62%	76%
OOBU	63%	72%	78%	85%
OOBU+FEAST	75%	87%	79%	90%

1.4.3 Comparison

[Ruvalcaba-Cardenas et al., 2018] proved the benefit of 3D over 2D input data, increasing the F1 score to 0.97 from 0.95 respectively, but the input data relied on a noise removal scheme to pre-process the data. The 3D voxel grids are also just versions of the 2D image projected over the z-axis. [Nash and Devrelis, 2020] are able to perform impressive classification accuracy on different models of cars given the low spatial resolution of the sensor, as seen in Table 1.17. However, the system also uses frame averaging to remove noise and the ground plane from the image. This impacts the frame rate of the system such that it takes multiple seconds to process a single image, making the likelihood of implementation on a drone in real-time low. [Ito et al., 2017] presented Fast SPAD DCNN for object localization utilizing depth, range, and intensity data. It achieves an impressive run-time of 2.9ms per frame when implemented on GPU. The key difference from other methods is the integration of depth and intensity data into a single frame. It has a low error of only 0.15m for tracking the object through the environment, however, the dataset is limited so it isn't clear how applicable it would be in real-world scenarios. [Scholes et al., 2022] utilizes both depth and intensity to improve its results, with its key difference being the output of not only classification but also pose and segmentation. However, when only using histogram data, it reports a drop in orientation prediction accuracy of 0.5%, so it is curious why it does not only use histogram information to streamline the process. As it doesn't state the effect on classification or segmentation operations, it could be assumed that only using histograms has a significant impact on these metrics. [Mora-Martín et al., 2021] produce a system with excellent classification accuracy that can be used in real time. While the main implementation uses both depth and intensity, just as in [Scholes et al., 2022] it also tests performance when

Table 1.24: Comparison table of reviewed object detection solutions *[1] Depth D, Intensity I, and Monocular M, *[2] 80x240 being the resolution of source data, *[3] Neurons implemented in CMOS and Synapses in Verilog A 1: [Ruvalcaba-Cardenas et al., 2018], 2: [Nash and Devrelis, 2020], 3: [Ito et al., 2017], 4: [Scholes et al., 2022], 5: [Mora-Martín et al., 2021], 6: [Ara Shawkat et al., 2020], and 7: [Afshar et al., 2020].

	1	2	3	4
Implementation level	Simulation	Simulation	Simulation	Simulation
Accuracy metric	F1 score	Accuracy	MAE*	Accuracy
Reported result	0.97	86.3%	0.044	> 90%
No. parameters				
Input data type	Voxel grid	Depth maps	D+I+M*[1]	D+I*[1]
Data resolution	16x16x16	32x32	112x112	20x60*[2]
SPAD array size	64x64	32x32	202x96	256x256
Max range	700m	≈30m	80m	
Pulse energy	18mj	35mj		
Pulse width	7ns	5ns		
Repetition rate	100Hz	20Hz		
Temporal resolution	333ns	5ns	2.33ns	500ps
Frame rate			10	
Computation time		2+s	2.9ms (GPU)	t
Power Consumption				

	5	6	7
Implementation level	Simulation	*[3]	FPGA
Accuracy metric	Accuracy		Accuracy
Reported result	99.31		87%
No. parameters			
Input data type	D+I*[2]	Binary signal	SPAD events
Data resolution	64x32/256x128	5x1	125x125
SPAD array size	256x256	3x5	128x128
Max range			
Pulse energy			
Pulse width	10ns		
Repetition rate			
Temporal resolution	4ns	N/A	N/A
Frame rate	32		
Computation time			29.24µs per event
Power Consumption		2.1mW	

using the raw histograms. This only resulted in a reduction of average accuracy by 0.05%, while reducing the standard deviation by 0.12 and increasing FPS by 9. The gains in FPS and STD are a good trade-off considering the negligible accuracy loss. The main takeaway from [Ara Shawkat et al., 2020] is the low power consumption of just 0.48pj per synaptic spike and per neuron per spike of 12.5pj using SNNs, though what the average activity and power consumption of the entire network and sensor were not expressed. [Afshar et al., 2020] show the benefit of using photon events with spiking neural networks, achieving a data compression rate of x81 and x21 for First-AND and OOBU respectively. OOBU allowed for fast output updates due to the presence of new photon events in only 29.24µs. The main drawback of the First-AND scheme would be its vulnerability to dead pixels, as it will essentially disable entire receptive fields from generating certain event types.

The key takeaway from these is that there will likely be an increase in the number of systems that begin to use the raw histogram output from the SPAD sensors as the input data due to the amount of information that is encoded within. The processing of histograms into depth maps or voxel grids results in the loss of key information, hindering the network which always benefits from more data instead of less. With the decreased run time and power consumption that comes with SNNs, I also expect to see an increase in their use as they mature and current issues, such as a lack of developed learning algorithms, are resolved. As opposed to SNNs, traditional ANNs require large numbers of parameters to be stored as floats in memory making it difficult to implement on-chip, however, as techniques for network quantization develops, I expect to see more compressed ANN networks implemented on-chip or on FPGA.

1.5 Conclusion

In conclusion, the presented papers show that the performance of neural network schemes is improved by the utilization of multiple data sources at the input, however, the results are not significantly better than networks that utilize raw histograms and have the added drawback of increased computation time. This can be seen in the object detection scheme by [Mora-Martín et al., 2021] where depth and intensity combined only provides a 0.05% average accuracy increase over histograms alone with the trade-off being a reduction of 9fps. Due to this, we should expect to see input data to shift closer to raw sensor output, i.e., histograms or ideally the SPAD events themselves, as it inherently contains more information that could be exploited by neural networks than using only depth maps or point clouds. This benefit is shown by [Afshar et al., 2020] work where the proposed OOBU+FEAST event based implementation achieves a 90% classification accuracy while also reducing the data rate by a factor of 25.

The structure of the neural networks discussed has shown that convolutional architecture utilizing ReLU activation remains the favored design, however, spiking implementations of these may see increased use in the future as the development of learning algorithms used to train or convert them mature. While ANN to SNN conversion process introduces minor degradation in reconstruction accuracy and imposes limits on the network architecture, we expect it to also see increased use, especially for systems integrated on-chip. It's use by [Kirkland et al., 2020] demonstrates that SNNs converted from ANNs are still able to achieve state of the art performance, and with only 11% of the networks neurons being active implying a significant power saving when implemented on chip. The use of network quantization and its limited effect on network accuracy is also making on-chip implementation of neural networks increasingly viable, with the work by [Zang et al., 2021] achieving a 12.7x compression rate compared to its 32-bit floating point implementation and a 21.99x compression rate compared to [Lindell et al., 2018]. As more sophisticated compression schemes develop, we should expect to see an increase in neural networks implemented on-chip, FPGA, etc.

References

Afshar, S., Hamilton, T. J., Davis, L., Van Schaik, A., and Delic, D. 2020. Event-based processing of single photon avalanche diode sensors. IEEE Sensors Journal, 20(14): 7677–7691.

Afshar, S., Xu, Y., Tapson, J., van Schaik, A., and Cohen, G. 2019. Event-based feature extraction using adaptive selection thresholds. CoRR, abs/1907.07853.

Al Abbas, T., Dutton, N. A., Almer, O., Finlayson, N., Rocca, F. M. D., and Henderson, R. 2018. A CMOS spad sensor with a multievent folded flash time-to-digital converter for ultra-fast optical transient capture. IEEE Sensors Journal, 18(8): 3163–3173.

Alhashim, I., and Wonka, P. 2018. High quality monocular depth estimation via transfer learning. CoRR, abs/1812.11941.

Ali, S., and Pandey, A. K. 2022. Arthronet: A monocular depth estimation technique with 3d segmented maps for knee arthroscopy. Intelligent Medicine.

Ara Shawkat, M. S., Sayyarparaju, S., McFarlane, N., and Rose, G. S. 2020. Single photon avalanche diode based vision sensor with on-chip memristive spiking neuromorphic processing. In 2020 IEEE 63rd International Midwest Symposium on Circuits and Systems (MWSCAS), pp. 377–380.

Aßmann, A., Stewart, B., and Wallace, A. M. 2021. Deep learning for lidar waveforms with multiple returns. In 2020 28th European Signal Processing Conference (EUSIPCO), pp. 1571–1575.

Bekolay, T., Bergstra, J., Hunsberger, E., DeWolf, T., Stewart, T., Rasmussen, D. et al. 2014. Nengo: A python tool for building large-scale functional brain models. Frontiers in Neuroinformatics, 7.

Burri, S., Bruschini, C., and Charbon, E. 2017. Linospad: A compact linear spad camera system with 64 fpga-based tdc modules for versatile 50 ps resolution time-resolved imaging. Instruments, 1(1).

Butler, D. J., Wulff, J., Stanley, G. B., and Black, M. J. 2012. A naturalistic open source movie for optical flow evaluation. pp. 611–625. *In*: Fitzgibbon, A., Lazebnik, S., Perona, P., Sato, Y., and Schmid, C. (eds.). Computer Vision – ECCV 2012, Berlin, Heidelberg. Springer Berlin Heidelberg.

Chadha, A., Britto, J., and Roja, M. M. 2020. Iseebetter: Spatio-temporal video super-resolution using recurrent generative backprojection networks. CoRR, abs/2006.11161.

Chen, G., Kirtiz, G. A., Wiede, C. and Kokozinski, R. 2021. Implementation and evaluation of a neural network-based lidar histogram processing method on fpga. In 2021 IEEE 34th International Systemon-Chip Conference (SOCC), pp. 1–6.

Chen, G., Landmeyer, F., Wiede, C., and Kokozinski, R. 2022. Feature extraction and neural network-based multi-peak analysis on time-correlated lidar histograms. Journal of Optics, 24(3): 034008.

Davies, M., Srinivasa, N., Lin, T.-H., Chinya, G., Cao, Y., Choday, S. H. et al. 2018. Loihi: A neuromorphic manycore processor with on-chip learning. IEEE Micro, 38(1): 82–99.

Engineer ambitiously.

Fardo, F. A., Conforto, V. H., de Oliveira, F. C., and Rodrigues, P. S. 2016. A formal evaluation of PSNR as quality measurement parameter for image segmentation algorithms. CoRR, abs/1605.07116.

Fu, H., Gong, M., Wang, C., Batmanghelich, K., and Tao, D. 2018. Deep ordinal regression network for monocular depth estimation. CoRR, abs/1806.02446.

Gaidon, A., Wang, Q., Cabon, Y., and Vig, E. 2016. Virtualworlds as proxy for multi-object tracking analysis. In 2016 IEEE Conference on Computer Vision and Pattern Recognition (CVPR), pp. 4340–4349.

Goldberger, J., Hinton, G. E., Roweis, S., and Salakhutdinov, R. R. 2004. Neighbourhood components analysis. *In*: Saul, L., Weiss, Y., and Bottou, L. (eds.). Advances in Neural Information Processing Systems, volume 17. MIT Press.

Goodfellow, I., Bengio, Y., and Courville, A. 2016. Deep Learning. MIT Press.

Guo, C., Li, C., Guo, J., Cong, R., Fu, H., and Han, P. 2019. Hierarchical features driven residual learning for depth map super-resolution. IEEE Transactions on Image Processing, 28(5): 2545–2557.

Gyongy, I., Dutton, N. A. W. and Henderson, R. K. 2022. Direct time-of-flight single-photon imaging. IEEE Transactions on Electron Devices, 69(6): 2794–2805.

Gyongy, I., Hutchings, S. W., Halimi, A., Tyler, M., Chan, S., Zhu, F. et al. 2020. Highspeed 3d sensing via hybrid-mode imaging and guided upsampling. Optica, 7(10): 1253–1260.

He, K., Sun, J., and Tang, X. 2013. Guided image filtering. IEEE Transactions on Pattern Analysis and Machine Intelligence, 35(6): 1397–1409.

Hernández-Marín, S., Wallace, A., and Gibson, G. 2008. Bayesian analysis of lidar signals with multiple returns. IEEE Transactions on Pattern Analysis and Machine Intelligence, 29: 2170–80.

Hirschmuller, H., and Scharstein, D. 2007. Evaluation of cost functions for stereo matching. In 2007 IEEE Conference on Computer Vision and Pattern Recognition, pp. 1–8.

https://developer.sony.com/develop/imx500/.

https://www.ims.fraunhofer.de/content/dam/ims/de/newsroom/kernkompetenzen/smartsensor-systems/qvga-photo-detector-for-indirect-tof-imaging.pdf.

https://www.vicon.com/hardware/cameras/.

Hutchings, S. W., Johnston, N., Gyongy, I., Al Abbas, T., Dutton, N. A. W., Tyler, M. et al. 2019. A reconfigurable 3-d-stacked spad imager with in-pixel histogramming for flash lidar or high-speed time-of-flight imaging. IEEE Journal of Solid-State Circuits, 54(11): 2947–2956.

Ito, S., Hiratsuka, S., Ohta, M., Matsubara, H., and Ogawa, M. 2017. Spad DCNN: Localization with small imaging lidar and dcnn. In 2017 IEEE/RSJ International Conference on Intelligent Robots and Systems (IROS), pp. 3312–3317.

Keys, R. 1981. Cubic convolution interpolation for digital image processing. IEEE Transactions on Acoustics, Speech, and Signal Processing, 29(6): 1153–1160.

Kirkland, P., Kapitany, V., Lyons, A., Soraghan, J., Turpin, A., Faccio, D. et al. 2020. Imaging from temporal data via spiking convolutional neural networks. In: Buller, G. S., Hollins, R. C., Lamb, R. A., Laurenzis, M., Camposeo, A., Farsari, M., Persano, L., and Busse, L. E. (eds.). Emerging Imaging and Sensing Technologies for Security and Defence V; and Advanced Manufacturing Technologies for Microand Nanosystems in Security and Defence III, volume 11540, pp. 115400J. International Society for Optics and Photonics, SPIE.

Koch, C., and Segev, I. 1998. Methods in Neuronal Modeling: From Ions to Networks. MIT Press.

Ledig, C., Theis, L., Huszar, F., Caballero, J., Aitken, A. P., Tejani, A. et al. 2016. Photo-realistic single image super-resolution using a generative adversarial network. CoRR, abs/1609.04802.

Li, Y., Zhu, H., Hou, Q., Wang, J., and Wu, W. 2022. Video super-resolution using multi-scale and non-local feature fusion. Electronics, 11(9).

Lindell, D. B., O'Toole, M., and Wetzstein, G. 2018. Single-photon 3d imaging with deep sensor fusion. ACM Trans. Graph., 37(4).

Lowe, D. 2004. Distinctive image features from scale-invariant keypoints. International Journal of Computer Vision, 60: 91–110.

Martín, G. M., Scholes, S., Ruget, A., Henderson, R. K., Leach, J., and Gyongy, I. 2022. Video super-resolution for single-photon lidar.

Mora-Martín, G., Turpin, A., Ruget, A., Halimi, A., Henderson, R., Leach, J. et al. 2021. High-speed object detection using SPAD sensors. In: Soskind, Y. and Busse, L. E. (eds.). Photonic Instrumentation Engineering VIII, volume 11693, page 116930L. International Society for Optics and Photonics, SPIE.

Nash, G., and Devrelis, V. 2020. Flash lidar imaging and classification of vehicles. In 2020 IEEE Sensors, pp. 1–4.

Nguyen, K., Fisher, E. M.,Walton, A., and Underwood, I. 2013. An experimentally verified model for estimating the distance resolution capability of direct time of flight 3d optical imaging systems. Measurement Science and Technology, 24: 12.

Nilsson, J., and Akenine-Möller, T. 2020. Understanding SSIM.

Peng, J., Xiong, Z., Huang, X., Li, Z. -P., Liu, D., and Xu, F. 2020. Photon-efficient 3d imaging with a non-local neural network. pp. 225–241. In: Vedaldi, A., Bischof, H., Brox, T., and Frahm, J. -M. (eds.). Computer Vision – ECCV 2020, Cham. Springer International Publishing.

Piron, F., Morrison, D., Yuce, M. R., and Redouté, J. -M. 2021. A review of single-photon avalanche diode time-of-flight imaging sensor arrays. IEEE Sensors Journal, 21(11): 12654–12666.

Rapp, J. and Goyal, V. K. 2017. A few photons among many: Unmixing signal and noise for photon-efficient active imaging. IEEE Transactions on Computational Imaging, 3(3): 445–459.

Ronneberger, O., Fischer, P., and Brox, T. 2015. Unet: Convolutional networks for biomedical image segmentation. pp. 234–341. *In*: Navab, N., Hornegger, J., Wells, W. M., and Frangi, A. F. (eds.). Medical Image Computing and Computer-Assisted Intervention – MICCAI 2015, Cham. Springer International Publishing.

Ros, G., Sellart, L., Materzynska, J., Vazquez, D., and Lopez, A. M. 2016. The synthia dataset: A large collection of synthetic images for semantic segmentation of urban scenes. In 2016 IEEE Conference on Computer Vision and Pattern Recognition (CVPR), pp. 3234–3243.

Rueckauer, B., Lungu, I. -A., Hu, Y., and Pfeiffer, M. 2016. Theory and tools for the conversion of analog to spiking convolutional neural networks.

Ruget, A., McLaughlin, S., Henderson, R. K., Gyongy, I., Halimi, A., and Leach, J. 2021a. Robust and guided super-resolution for single-photon depth imaging via a deep network. In 2021 29th European Signal Processing Conference (EUSIPCO), pp. 716–720.

Ruget, A., McLaughlin, S., Henderson, R. K., Gyongy, I., Halimi, A., and Leach, J. 2021b. Robust super-resolution depth imaging via a multi-feature fusion deep network. Opt. Express, 29(8): 11917–11937.

Ruvalcaba-Cardenas, A. D., Scoleri, T., and Day, G. 2018. Object classification using deep learning on extremely low resolution time-of-flight data. In 2018 Digital Image Computing: Techniques and Applications (DICTA), pp. 1–7.

Scharstein, D., and Pal, C. 2007. Learning conditional random fields for stereo. In 2007 IEEE Conference on Computer Vision and Pattern Recognition, pp. 1–8.

Scholes, S., Ruget, A., Mora-Martín, G., Zhu, F., Gyongy, I., and Leach, J. 2022. Dronesense: The identification, segmentation, and orientation detection of drones via neural networks. IEEE Access, 10: 38154–38164.

Shah, S., Dey, D., Lovett, C., and Kapoor, A. 2017. Airsim: High-fidelity visual and physical simulation for autonomous vehicles. CoRR, abs/1705.05065.

Shahnewaz, A., and Pandey, A. K. 2020. Color and depth sensing sensor technologies for robotics and machine vision. Springer International Publishing, Cham, pp. 59–86.

Shawkat, M. S. A., and Mcfarlane, N. 2020. A digital CMOS silicon photomultiplier using perimeter gated single photon avalanche diodes with asynchronous aer readout. IEEE Transactions on Circuits and Systems I: Regular Papers, 67(12): 4818–4828.

Silberman, N., Hoiem, D., Kohli, P., and Fergus, R. 2012. Indoor segmentation and support inference from rgbd images. pp. 746–760. *In*: Fitzgibbon, A., Lazebnik, S., Perona, P., Sato, Y., and Schmid, C. (eds.). Computer Vision – ECCV 2012, Berlin, Heidelberg. Springer Berlin Heidelberg.

Simonyan, K., and Zisserman, A. (2014). Very deep convolutional networks for large-scale image recognition. arXiv preprint arXiv:1409.1556.

Sun, Z., Lindell, D. B., Solgaard, O., and Wetzstein, G. 2020. Spadnet: Deep rgb-spad sensor fusion assisted by monocular depth estimation. Opt. Express, 28(10): 14948–14962.

Taherkhani, A., Belatreche, A., Li, Y., Cosma, G., Maguire, L. P., and McGinnity, T. 2020. A review of learning in biologically plausible spiking neural networks. Neural Networks, 122: 253–272.

Tsai, S. -Y., Chang, Y. -C., and Sang, T. -H. 2018. Spad lidars: Modeling and algorithms. In 2018 14th IEEE International Conference on Solid-State and Integrated Circuit Technology (ICSICT), pp. 1–4.

Vilà, A., Arbat, A., Vilella, E., and Dieguez, A. 2012. Geiger-Mode Avalanche Photodiodes in Standard CMOS Technologies.

Wulff, J., Butler, D. J., Stanley, G. B., and Black, M. J. 2012. Lessons and insights from creating a synthetic optical flow benchmark. pp. 168–177. *In*: Fusiello, A., Murino, V., and Cucchiara, R. (eds.). Computer Vision – ECCV 2012. Workshops and Demonstrations, Berlin, Heidelberg. Springer Berlin Heidelberg.

Yang, W., Zhang, X., Tian, Y., Wang, W., Xue, J. -H., and Liao, Q. 2019. Deep learning for single image super-resolution: A brief review. IEEE Transactions on Multimedia, 21(12): 3106–3121.

Yosinski, J., Clune, J., Bengio, Y., and Lipson, H. 2014. How transferable are features in deep neural networks? CoRR, abs/1411.1792.

Zang, Z., Xiao, D., and Li, D. 2021. Non-fusion timeresolved depth image reconstruction using a highly efficient neural network architecture. Optics Express, 29.

Zhou, S., Wu, Y., Ni, Z., Zhou, X., Wen, H., and Zou, Y. 2016. Dorefa-net: Training low bitwidth convolutional neural networks with low bitwidth gradients.

Zhou, Z., Siddiquee, M. M. R., Tajbakhsh, N., and Liang, J. 2019. Unet++: Redesigning skip connections to exploit multiscale features in image segmentation.

2

Experimental Evaluation of Depth Measurements Accuracy in Indoor Environments

Wendy García-Gonzalez,[1] *Wendy Flores-Fuentes,*[1] *Oleg Sergiyenko,*[1]
Julio C Rodríguez-Quiñonez,[1] *Jesús E Miranda-Vega,*[2,*]
Arnoldo Díaz-Ramirez[2] and *Marina Kolendovska*[3]

2.1 Introduction

Recent advancements in computer vision (CV) technology increases the quality of life of the whole society. The constant enhancements of computer systems allow the developing vision of powerful applications. Research fields are interested in applying computer vision to solve their main problems. For example, healthcare applications are enhanced by using computer-aided diagnosis (CAD). Medical images play an important role in developing diagnostics. Using different diagnostic imaging techniques with CAD, an early disease prediction is possible.

On the other hand, health monitoring uses cameras 2D and 3D for collection as a general framework for CV. This can be used to analyze or extract useful information for safety and health monitoring based on object detection, object tracking, and action recognition CV techniques [Seo et al. 2015].

Nowadays, cameras RGB-D are the main part of any CV due to their commercial availability at low cost. These cameras are devices widely used in industry to solve complex challenges in machine vision (MV) that humans cannot do. Color (RGB) and depth (D) can be obtained with this technology. Mobile robots interact with operators in warehousing, where depth measurement can be critical for safety.

---

[1] Universidad Autónoma de Baja California, México.
[2] Department of Computer Systems, Tecnológico Nacional de México, IT de Mexicali, Mexicali, BC 21376, México.
[3] Kharkiv National University of Radio Electronics, 14 Nauki Avenue, 61166 Kharkiv, Ukraine.
* Corresponding author: elias.miranda@itmexicali.edu.mx

The development of MV applications requires flexible and robust devices like cameras RGB-D to execute activities without human intervention. The concept of Industry 4.0 is performed during an industrial inspection process when computer science (CS) is implemented to become a process smarter.

Furthermore, areas of research in CS fields such as artificial intelligence (AI), machine learning (ML), robotics, and CV require RGB-D (Red-Green-Blue-Depth) cameras to develop algorithms to enhance depth calculations. These results increase the accuracy and reduce the cost of visual inspections in the industry. Their cost-effective cameras and the development of more sophisticated industrial robot applications are demanded.

A camera can be exposed to external factors that reduce its performance in a real scenario. Sunlight, temperature, and humidity are a few examples of factors that cause interference with the cameras or any camera technology. The performance of an RGB-D can be affected by these factors in harsh environments.

A technical vision system (TVS) is a device that can scan an object or a surface to obtain 3D coordinates by using a laser and an aperture to capture the returned light. In a real scenario, the performance of a TVS can be affected by a lack of illumination. Depending on the distance this system cannot reach to capture the laser beam.

The object of study of the present work is to apply the main techniques of machine vision to enhance the performance of a TVS to detect a laser beam under a controlled environment. A practical implementation of the integration of a TVS and a stereo system can be a mobile robot that receives the depth from a TVS and an RGB-D camera. When an RGB-D camera cannot estimate the depth a TVS can still receive the measurements by dynamical triangulation. Several experiments were carried out to characterize an RGB-D camera. The results will be used to analyze the suitability of integration of both camera and TVS systems. An overview of the technology from camera D415 and TVS is discussed in this work as depth measurement depth devices. The key concepts of CV are also discussed. Additionally, recommendations from the literature for enhancing depth measures implemented based on image processing are detailed.

2.2 State of ART of depth measurement technologies for indoors and outdoors

This section reviews the state-of-the-art technologies used in a controlled environment for depth measurements. Also, a brief review of relevant technology and methods applied for CV applications will be analyzed and commented on.

2.2.1 Lidar system

Technology such as Light Detection and Ranging (LiDAR) and cameras caught researchers' attention in the last five years. This allows working in real operations and can reduce environmental interferences. This feature is of utmost importance for designers of autonomous navigation. A laser-pulsed signal is an example of the first technique used to avoid ambient light interferences. The following authors

[Zhang et al. 2018], carried out experiments using laser pulsed to eliminate sunlight interference.

LiDAR and cameras are indispensable for the depth perception of autonomous vehicles, these are the heart of CV technologies.

A general description of a LiDAR device can be detailed as follows:

- This device uses an active optical imaging approach that uses lasers pulsed to determine the 3D environment around an object.
- Allows remote sensing technology.
- The main industries using these technologies are civil engineering, roadwork, meteorology, terrestrial mapping, and mining.
- The operation of this system can be in moving or stationary.

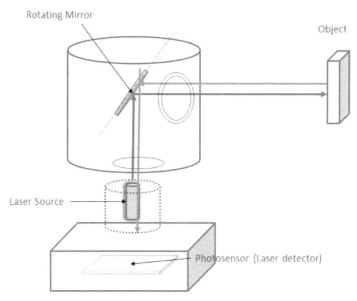

Figure 2.1: Components of a Lidar.

The main components of a LiDAR system are illustrated in Figure 2.1. It is important to note that Global Positioning System (GPS) and Inertia Measurement Unit (IMU) are also part of this system; however, this chapter is focused on optical devices.

On the other hand, laser wavelengths of 905, 1300, or 1550 nm are commonly preferred for lidar systems [Behroozpour et al. 2017]. In this portion of the wavelength range, the solar radiation responsivity of the sun is weak due to the atmospheric absorption phenomenon. Although the wavelength in the 905 nm band is broadly used for LiDAR, this represents a disadvantage due to its harmful to the human eye and requires a high cost for digital signal processing [Kim and Jung 2020]. Three different configurations or principles of operation are commonly used such as pulsed time-of-flight (TOF), Amplitude modulated continuous wave (AMCW), and frequency-modulated continuous wave (FMCW) [Li et al 2022].

The first principle called pulsed ToF is a well-known operation principle that measures the time delay between emitted and received pulsed signal. Then the distance *d* can be denoted as follows:

$$d = c\frac{\Delta_t}{2} \tag{1.1}$$

where Δ_t and *c*, corresponds to the time delay and speed of light, respectively.

The following equation 1.1 is also used for ToF; however, this considers the index of refraction *n* of the medium, $d = c\dfrac{\Delta_t}{2n}$.

The second operational principle, based on the Doppler effect, corresponds to the FMCW Lidar method. A frequency-modulated is used to study an object or surface where the depth and velocity can be obtained. The advantage of this method is that distance and velocity can be obtained at the same time. FMCW technology can mitigate the interferences from similar radiation sources and strong sunlight [Rogers et al. 2020].

Li and Ibanez-Guzman [2020] detail how to calculate velocity information by applying the FMCW method.

$$f_{if} = \frac{4rB}{ct} = \frac{f_{if}^+ + f_{if}^-}{2}, f_d = \frac{f_{if}^+ + f_{if}^-}{2}\left(when\ f_d < f_{if}\right) \tag{1.2}$$

where *B* and *T* are parameters of modulation bandwidth. f_d is the Doppler frequency shift, f_i corresponds to the intermediate frequency.

By knowing f_d and λ as a laser wavelength, the velocity can be calculated as follows.

$$v = \frac{f_d\lambda}{2} \tag{1.3}$$

The operational principle AMCW is based on the intensity modulation of a continuous light wave as [Royo and Ballesta-Garcia 2019] give a brief explanation for the measurement of a depth distance by using the intensity modulation of a continuous light wave based on (1.4).

$$\Delta\Phi = \kappa_M d = \frac{2\pi f_M}{c}R \Rightarrow R = \frac{c}{2}\frac{\Delta\Phi}{2\pi f_M} \tag{1.4}$$

where *R* is the distance to the object studied, *c* is the speed of light; κ_M is the wavenumber associated to the modulation frequency, *d* is the total distance travelled and f_M is the modulation frequency of the amplitude of the signal.

According to [Qiu et al. 2016] accurate depth measurements for the outdoor environment plays an important role where LiDAR represents a reliable solution.

The following work [Sun et al. 2016] developed a technique to separate lidar signal and sunlight noise. They implemented a laser with orbital angular momentum for the space-borne lidar with the photon sieve filter.

Zhu et al. [2021] proposed a simultaneous localization and mapping (SLAM) system that can operate in an outdoor strong-sunlight environment using Livox lidar for depth measurements. The accuracy of a Livox Mid-40 sensor can reach an accuracy of 2 cm at 20 m.

Asvadi et al. [2016] use a Velodyne LiDAR and they highlight that these devices are less sensitive to weather conditions. According to [Velodyne Lidar 2022] HDL-32E model can reach a typical accuracy of ±2 cm at 100 m.

Although, this is more expensive due to being integrated by optical elements that can perform tasks in harsh environments.

2.2.2 Cameras

With the irruption of Industry 4.0, the inspection and evaluation of objects play an important role in the manufacturing process. Although a human has accomplished these tasks, nowadays, machine vision cameras can do them automatically at high accuracy. A camera is responsible for capturing the scene by an algorithm of computer vision (CV). This can enhance productivity in any industry that requires a smart process and being interconnected in the cloud. Industrial cameras require to execute high performance in uncertain environments. For example, the operators can be aware by improving their safety and reducing risk.

Cameras are important devices that can be implemented in complex environments. These devices give vision to a computer that is superior to the human eye in the context of wavelength sensitivity. For example, the human eye can see about 400 nm–700 nm, and UV (ultraviolet), CCD, and near IR (infrared radiation) cameras can reach more qualities of light. Many industrial processes require cameras to manufacture products of high quality.

The main industry developers of machine vision cameras are well-known, such as Cognex Corp., Basler AG, Omron Corp., Keyence, National Instruments, and Sony Corporation. Cognex developed the In-Sight D900 that is used in industrial image analysis based on DL in which processing is taken on-device. This represents an advantage over other cameras; however, the price is quite high.

Basler introduced an embedded vision system with cloud connectivity to develop IoT applications and access to cloud services. The model of the camera is daA4200-30 mci (S-Mount). This camera can reach 30 frames per second at 13 MP resolution. This camera has been used for robotic fertilization [Ulloa et al. 2022].

Low-cost RGB-D cameras caught the attention of machine vision research. Microsoft Kinect is a pioneer developer of a machine vision camera to get depth. Intel is another player in the camera market that can offer the designer of MV the third dimension (depth). The price of these cameras can vary from 200 $ to 900 $. The price can increase according to their features or the high performance required. The following authors [Kuan et al. 2016] conducted practical evaluations with Intel R200, Kinect v2, and Prime sense RGB-D Sensors where strong sunlight NIR interference was present. They concluded that the Kinect v2 is better than the R200 for the task of capturing 3D surface data of objects outdoors.

Liu et al. [2022] mentioned that to increment the performance in terms of sensitivity of a vision system, the use of high-power lasers can be implemented. They developed a novel stereo vision measurement system comprising a line scan camera (Dalsa, LA-GM-2K08A), a frame camera (Sick, Ranger E50414), and a line laser system (CNI, OEM-FM-660&PL-880) as well as the calibration method.

Azure Kinect DK is a camera that can be used to develop artificial vision applications. This camera can exploit the Azure Cognitive Services for AI applications. The following work [Antico et al. 2021] evaluates the accuracy in terms of assessments of postural control.

D415 and D435 (2018) are based on active stereo vision which utilizes a NIR texture projector paired with 2 NIR cameras for depth sensing. Servi et al. [2021] evaluated these cameras at close range in a controlled environment. D415 has a good metrological performance for short range compared to D435 and LiDAR Camera L515.

The authors [Andriyanov et al. 2022] used a D415 with YOLOv3 neural network for detection and recognition applications in a controlled environment. The purpose of that work was to detect and recognize the spatial position of apples with this camera and AI algorithms.

Curto and Araujo [2022] evaluated a depth estimation performance with a particularly transparent and translucent object. The RGB-D cameras used for these experiments were D415, L515, and SR305 (structured light principle). According to the experimental setup described by the authors, these were carried out indoor environment. The best performance for depth estimation with a transparent/translucent object was reached with D415.

The following work [Carfagni et al. 2022] also evaluates the performance of D415 and SR300 for short range (150 mm to 500 mm) in a controlled environment. D415 showed better results in terms of systematic depth error.

Infrared techniques for image acquisition

Infrared thermography (IRT) is a technology that allows non-contacting with the object understudy, meaning that features of the element are conserved without altering them. This technique is mostly used for remote diagnosis that allows no contact with the object or area under study. The next three studies describe fault detection by applying infrared cameras. The following work deal with rotating machinery in a harsh environment [Yongbo et al. 2020]. These authors used the thermal camera Hawk-1384. The thermal camera T660 model was used for fault detection of a power system. DL was integrated to create an intelligent system to enhance the diagnosis [Kim et al. 2021]. The following authors also use the thermal camera Hawk-1384. They proposed to avoid vibration methods to diagnose a failure in a gearbox. CNN technique was applied for IRT images to identify common gear faults [Li et al. 2019].

2.3 Computer vision

It is well known that CV was born in the 1960s as an academic discipline. This is part of computer science. One of the first works in this field was developed by Larry Roberts. That work was focused on extracting 3D geometrical information from a 2D perspective view of blocks. Hanson [1978] defined CV as scene analysis or image understanding. In its early beginnings, CV focused on studying visual data.

The following work Lamport [1966] was focused on the first CV tasks about image classification. In the late 1970's, David Marr defined the vision as constructing efficient symbolism from images from the world Marr [1977].

Current computers can see and learn about images with a high level of understanding of their environment with minimum effort. The key point to this advancement is the increasing development of artificial intelligence (AI) and optical devices such as cameras and lasers.

CV applications are growing exponentially due to the contribution of an immense community interested in designing vision systems. AI is integrated into two layers such as machine learning (ML) and deep learning (DL) to imitate a human's behavior. Arthur Samuel who was recognized as a distinguished computer programmer, defined ML as a field of study that allows computers to learn. This interdisciplinary field is integrated into many areas of science and engineering, such as optics, robotics, image processing, machine learning, and neuroscience.

2.3.1 Machine learning

The main objective of this branch of AI is to create mathematical models to solve human tasks. It is well-known that the power of ML comes from mathematical tools, in which linear algebra, vector calculus, probability, and statistics are the most identified by ML developers. The quality of this layer depends mainly on past experiences to build a robust model.

Depending on the scenarios ML can be categorized as supervised, unsupervised learning, and reinforcement learning. The categorization selected by an ML developer depends on how the model is being trained. For example, supervised learning needs to be trained with labeled data, and an unsupervised model can work with unlabeled data.

2.3.2 Supervised learning

One of the main tasks of supervised learning is classification. Figure 2.2 details a supervised learning workflow, a workflow which is separated sequentially. The process starts given raw data that a developer of ML knows. Some developers prefer to apply data preprocessing before to feature extraction step. Schmidt et al. [2019] also describe a supervised learning workflow.

The preprocessing of raw data deals with transforming data to express them in a convenient way. Data filtering and cleaning are important processes at this stage. Sometimes developers receive multiple data from different sensors, and many problems could appear. The first problem is the scale of the data, due to transductors can manage different output voltages for the. In this case, the processing of data is focused to standardize them. Another important issue is when the signal is mixed with noise. The use of digital filters can reduce it. A digital filter is a mathematical tool that manipulates the input signal or a vector to remove redundant information.

Feature engineering is an interesting process to convert raw data into relevant information for improving the models created. The new data transformed contains the main characteristics of a phenomenon studied. In many cases, the raw data size is

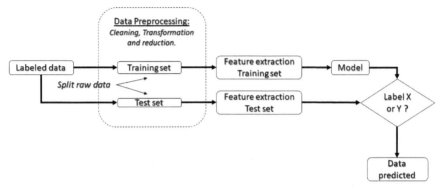

Figure 2.2: Classical supervised learning workflow.

reduced by extracting their features. The essence of this stage relies on the algorithm selected. For example, Mel-frequency cepstral coefficients (MFCC) [Ghaffar et al. 2021], these authors indicate that the novel of using MFCC was to carry out experiments and analyze functional near-infrared spectroscopy in brain-computer interface. Regularly, this technique has been used for audio. They also implemented ML classifiers such LDA, SVM, and KNN to distinguish brain activities during four different mental tasks.

The following research is about applying MFCC, and principal component analysis (PCA) used as feature extraction for Structural Health Monitoring (SHM) applications [Mei et al. 2019]. SHM deals with opportune maintenance of infrastructure by damage detection. This can be identified by installing sensors on the infrastructure to study its dynamic properties.

Another feature extractor is linear predictive coefficients (LPC). This technique can enhance the performance of any ML method. LPC is also widely used for digital audio signal processing. The mathematical expression to obtain the LPC coefficients of order is the following.

$$P_t = \sum_{k=1}^{M} a_k s_{t-k} \tag{1.5}$$

where s_t is the signal at time t.

In the case of image processing edge detection, local binary pattern features (LBP) are the technique used for extracting features. As per your definition, the LBP value can be calculated by transforming decimal numbers from array 3×3 into a binary number. The center pixel is used as a threshold intensity to encode neighbor pixels according to the following equation (1.6).

$$LBP_{P,R} = \sum_{i=0}^{P-1} s\left(n_i - G_c\right)2^i \tag{1.6}$$

$$s_x = \{1, \quad if \ x > 0 \ 0, \quad otherwise$$

Two relevant properties of LBP are its tolerance regarding monotonic illumination changes and its computational simplicity [Huang et al. 2011]. Figure 2.3 shows a graphical representation of how LBP values are calculated. A matrix input

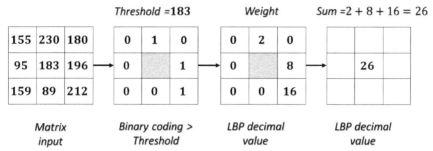

Figure 2.3: Graphical representation of the calculation of LBP values.

3×3 is selected from an image where the threshold corresponds to 183. The LBP decimal value resulted is only where appears 1's binary representation.

Another feature extractor is the Gabor filter (GF). This two-dimensional filter can be defined as a Gaussian kernel modulated by an oriented complex sinusoidal wave, this is detailed in [Sun et al. 2006] as follows:

$$g(xy) = \frac{1}{2\pi\sigma_x\sigma_y}\left(-\frac{x^2+y^2}{2\sigma^2}\right)e^{2\pi j\omega\tilde{x}} \tag{1.7}$$

$$\tilde{x} = x\cos\theta + y\sin\theta \text{ and } \tilde{y} = x\sin\theta + y\cos\theta \tag{1.8}$$

where σ_x and σ_y represent scaling parameters, and the center frequency is denoted by ω, θ is the orientation of the GF. One disadvantage of the GF's is their "ring" effect near the edges because of their high-frequency response [Moraru et al. 2006].

2.3.3 Unsupervised learning

The unsupervised approach is commonly used for clustering tasks. ML designers study the relationship between groups of clusters with the purpose of making better decisions. They try to find hidden patterns in the data given.

Workflow unsupervised learning is illustrated in Figure 2.4, in which the process starts with raw data unlabeled. In the case of feature extraction with unsupervised

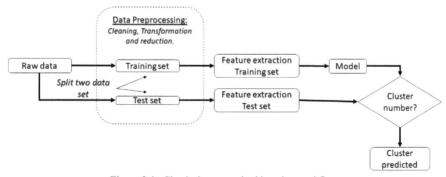

Figure 2.4: Classical unsupervised learning workflow.

learning, the Locally Linear Embedding (LLE) algorithm is a method used for dimensionality reduction. Clustering is another main task of the unsupervised method, the k-means algorithm is a well-known example. The following work [Ghareeb 2022], describes an unsupervised learning workflow.

2.3.4 Semi-supervised learning

According to the literature, semi-supervised learning is a category in the middle of the supervised and unsupervised learning model. This category is a form of classification that involves labeled and unlabeled data to enhance the ML model's performance. The following work is a detailed revision of surveys on this topic [Van Engelen 2020]. They give an up-to-date overview of semi-supervised learning methods.

2.3.5 Reinforcement learning

The third category of ML corresponds to reinforcement learning (RL). The authors [Moerland 2023] define model-based RL as: 'any MDP approach that (i) uses a model (known or learned) and (ii) uses learning to approximate a global value or policy function'. This method allows the system to minimize the gaps in the scenarios, with neither known data nor data collected. Temporal-Difference (TD) learning and Q-learning are common algorithms used for RL models.

The main components of RL are agents, environment and policies [Tzorakoleftherakis 2019].

Figure 2.5 shows a general representation of reinforcement learning interacting with the components previously mentioned.

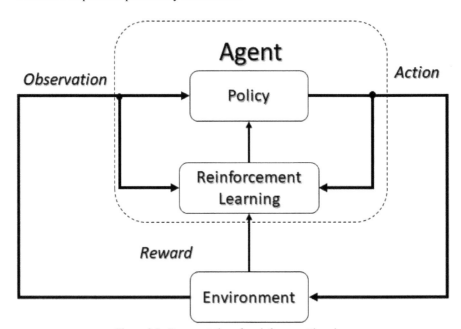

Figure 2.5: Representation of a reinforcement learning.

The techniques most used in ML for classification tasks correspond to support vector machines (SVM), decision trees, linear regression, linear discriminant analysis (LDA), random forests, naive Bayes, and K-nearest neighbors (KNN). These techniques are commonly known as classical algorithms. Advances in ML focused on time series forecasting can be consulted in [Masini et al. 2021].

Quantum computation is based on of laws of quantum mechanics. ML and quantum computers could be the next industrial revolution. This combination can enhance traditional techniques such as SVM, KNN, K-means clustering, and others. The ML algorithms will be called quantum support vector machine (QSVM), Q-KNN. The main algorithms are Grover's algorithm, Swap-test, Phase Estimation, and HHL Algorithm [Zhang and Ni 2021].

2.3.6 Deep learning

AI accelerates using of real-time applications for depth perception, object detection, and mapping surfaces. In other contexts, AI algorithms can help to predict the vertical deflection of structures. DL is another subset of AI, specifically convolutional neural networks (CNN or ConvNet). The advantage of CNN's is that they can automatically detect particular features of any class.

Figure 2.6 shows an architecture of a deep neural network (DNN), in which fully connected layers are strength joined. The main difference between DNN with ANN is that this includes many hidden layers. That means DNN is capable of extracting relevant information by itself. This gives an advantage for feature extraction without any developer ML intervention.

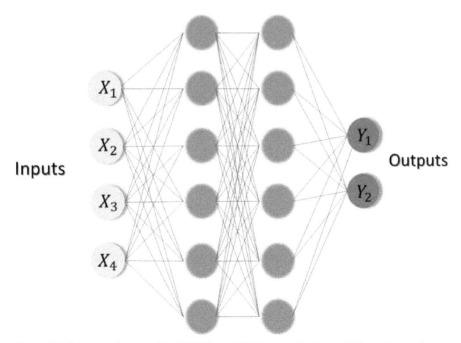

Figure 2.6: Schematic diagram of the DNN: The model is integrated by inputs, hidden, and output layers.

2.4 Signal and image processing

This section gives an overview of essential steps to adequate the signal and images extracted from sensors and devices. The purpose is to convert them into a convenient form because several issues can appear in a real environment. For example, the case of optical devices that work with optoelectrical signals should be taken into account the electrical noise. This undesired signal can affect the performance of the optical system by confusing the signal of interest.

In the literature, two types of filters can be found, analog and digital filters. An analog filter requires physically using a resistor, inductor, and capacitor to design a filter. Computers conduct digital filters to manipulate the data through the convolution of particular coefficients. Depending on the techniques these coefficients should be calculated. Digital filters are classified as Finite Impulse Response (FIR) and Infinite Impulse Response (IIR).

The impulse response of an FIR filter is finite in duration. In the case of IIR, it is infinite. Equation (1.9) describes an FIR filter.

$$y[n] = \sum_{k=0}^{M-1} b_k x[n-k] \tag{1.9}$$

where

$y[n]$ represents the output of the filter. b_k are the filter coefficients and $x[n-k]$ is the filter input delayed by k samples.

Equation (1.10) describes an IIR filter in the form of a linear difference equation.

$$y[n] + \sum_{k=1}^{N} b_k y[n-k] = \sum_{k=0}^{M} a_k x[n-k] \tag{1.10}$$

One advantage of using FIR filters is that they are stable and simple to design in comparison with IIR. However, IIR filters require fewer coefficients to reach the same frequency response compared to FIR filters.

A **moving average filter** is a wide tool for smoothing a signal. This filter operates by averaging several points named a window M from the input signal $x[]$ to produce each point in the output signal $y[]$, see equation (1.11).

$$y[n] = \frac{1}{M} \sum_{j=0}^{N-1} x[i+j] \tag{1.11}$$

Digital images can be acquired with different conditions found in their environment that can affect their quality to show relevant information. These also need to be pre-processed to remove information that does not correspond with the rest of the image. In other words, digital signals and images can be treated the same way as a sequence of numbers that can be manipulated numerically to reduce the undesired outliers.

Image processing

Before going forward, first, we should define what an image is. An image can be defined as a representation of a matrix of pixels intensity composed mainly of 2D or 3D arrays of numbers. An image is everywhere in thousands of applications thanks to the advancements in cameras and computers. It is important to note that the purpose of an image is to represent a phenomenon or a scene under study.

The main applications of image processing are the following:

- **Image restoration** brings back the appropriate sharpness from out-of-focus images. This process tries to recover the main characteristics of a degraded image. The next authors give a brief overview of state-of-the-art underwater image restoration and enhancement of underwater by analyzing an in-depth survey [Zhang et al. 2019, Yang et al. 2019].

- **Super-Resolution (SR):** This technique combines different low-resolution images into high-resolution images to show relevant information. Wang et al. [2020] proposed an in-depth review of the advances and trends of deep learning techniques focused on SR.

- **Compression:** This application focuses on reducing images' space in the storage device. To improve the data transmission, the volume data size should be reduced. The compression methods for image processing can be divided into two types, lossless and lossy compression [Geetha et al. 2021]. The format Joint Photographic Expert Group (JPEG) is a widely known image compression format. In the case of video MPEG, AVS (Audio and Video Coding Standard in China) and H.264 or MPEG-4 AVC (Advanced Video Coding).

  Vector quantization (VQ) and discrete cosine transform (DCT) are techniques used for the lossy compression of an image. Deep generative models are applied for lossless compression [Kang et al. 2022].

- **Edges detection** applications are used to detect when brightness changes sharply or discontinuities are present in an image. In the literature, it is well known that edge detection techniques can be divided into two domains: Spatial Domain and Frequency Domain. The classical edge detectors are:

  1. Gradient edge Detectors (*first derivative or classical, Sobel, Prewitt, Kirsch*)
  2. Zero crossing (*second derivative, Laplacian operator and second directional derivative*)
  3. Laplacian of Gaussian (LoG), *Marr-Hildreth*
  4. Gaussian edge detectors (*Canny and ISEF (Shen-Castan)*)
  5. Colored edge detectors.

  Sharifi et al. [2002] realized an analysis with these algorithms in which they conclude that under noisy conditions ISEF, Canny, Marr-Hildreth, Kirsch, Sobel, Lapla2, Lapla1 show better performance, respectively.

- **Object segmentation:** takes an image of a group of pixels into meaningful areas to be extracted from its background. Researchers of the MV community associate the object segmentation problem with the object tracking problem. Solving one problem can solve another implicitly or explicitly [Yao et al. 2020].

- **Face detection:** Another problem of computer vision and widely studied. Viola-Jones, Gabor feature, ANN, PCA, and SVM are algorithms that can solve the face detection problem. Current research focuses on face detection, and recognition is the detection of faces in occlusion and non-uniform illumination [Kumar et al. 2019].

Blurring Images: Sometimes developers are interested in smoothing an image before another process, like thresholding. A Gaussian filter is an algorithm that can be used for this purpose. The mathematical expression is as follows:

$$G(x,y) = \frac{1}{2\pi} e^{-\frac{x^2+y^2}{2\sigma^2}} \tag{1.12}$$

One disadvantage of the Gaussian filter is that it cannot remove salt-and-pepper noise. This type of noise appears on digital images and is known as impulse noise. The following authors propose to remove the salt-and-pepper noise by applying an adaptive frequency median filter (AFMF) [Erkan et al. 2020].

Median filter: is another technique used in image processing for blurring images. This function can conserve edges while noise is removed from the image. However, the high computational cost is the price of using this filter. Figure 2.7 details the process of smoothing an image.

A study of the median filter was carried out for noise removal and quality preservation of images can be consulted in [Shah et al. 2022].

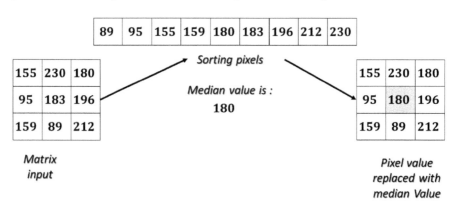

Figure 2.7: Calculation of a median value.

2.5 Depth measurement systems principles and applications

Depth measurements play a vital role in many applications to make decisions that impact the quality of people's lives. One example of this can be found in the automotive industry with smarter cars to warn about possible collisions. Also, object detection is an important task desirable. According to the literature, several methods and devices are implemented to calculate the depth.

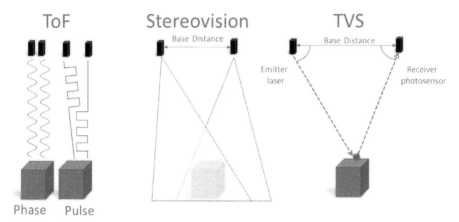

Figure 2.8: Main technologies for measuring the depth.

Figure 2.8 shows three different technologies for depth measurements: Time-of-Flight Systems (ToF), stereovision and a TVS.

2.5.1 ToF

ToF based on phase-shift technique and signal pulsed, dynamic triangulation, and stereoscopic vision, and structure light is commonly used in several areas. Laser scanners also use this technique in which a signal pulsed can be emitted to strike near objects. Then the traveling time of a signal returned is measured. The Microsoft Kinect Sensor V2 provides this technology for depth measurements. According to the specifications, the maximum depth distance is 4.5 m.

Stereovision

This method is a first approximation for depth measurement by trying to find corresponding points in different images captured by two cameras. This technology is commonly used in autonomous driving. Here, two cameras capture the same scene; then, the depth can be inferred by finding the corresponding points in the two RGB images acquired (by comparing the parallax difference between them). One example of an RGB-D camera corresponds to the Intel RealSense D455, which utilizes two passive infrared cameras to make the measurements.

Li et al. [2021] describes how to determine the depth by applying SV by (1.13) and (1.14).

$$\frac{P_l P_r}{O_c} = \frac{PP_m}{PP_n} \tag{1.13}$$

$$\frac{L_B - x_l - \left(-x_r \right)}{L_B} = \frac{z_c - f}{z_c} \tag{1.14}$$

where

O_l and *correspond* to the optical center from camera left and right, respectively.

L_B is the baseline.

The depth z_c with respect to the point P can be expressed as follows:

$$z_c = \frac{L_B f}{x_l - x_r} \qquad (1.15)$$

H_l and H_r represents the main points of the imaging plane of the left and right images respectively. f is the focal length (vertical distance from the optical center O_c to the imaging plane).

Condotta et al. [2020] carried out experimentations with five different cameras that can be illustrated in Table 2.1. The main purpose was to test their suitability to be used in agriculture applications. The importance of this study relies on the suitability of the camera in a harsh environment.

Structured Light

Structured Light: this is another technique that provides depth information by emitting coding light patterns on an object or a surface to be analyzed. Distortion of projection of structured-light pattern is indispensable to calculate the 3D coordinates of an object or a surface. Recent signs of progress in creating and controlling structured light can be consulted in [Forbes 2019].

Figure 2.9 shows a graphical representation of structured light. Pixels from the camera and projector are key points to determining depth information by calculating their correspondences from the pixels observed. According to [Geng 2011], the expression to calculate the geometric relationship between a camera and a structured light projector, and an object under study is as follows:

$$R = B \frac{sin(\theta)}{sin(\alpha + \theta)} \qquad (1.16)$$

where,

B corresponds to the distance between the camera and the projector. α and θ are angles by triangulation formed of the camera, projector and object (point P).

Table 2.1: Main cameras for measuring the depth and their specifications.

Camera	Principle	Measuring Range (m)	Depth resolution (HxV)	Frame Rate (FPS)
Real Sense D415	Structured Light/Steroscopy	0.16 – 10	63° x 40°	90
Real Sense D435	Structured Light/Steroscopy	0.11 – 10	82.5° x 58°	90
Kinect v.1	Structured Light	0.4 – 3.5	57° x 43°	15/30
Kinect v.2	Time of Flight	0.5 – 4.5	70° x 60°	15/30
Xtion PRO Live	Structured Light	0.8 – 3.5	58° x 45°	30/60
Xtion 2	Structured Light	0.8 – 3.5	74° x 52°	30

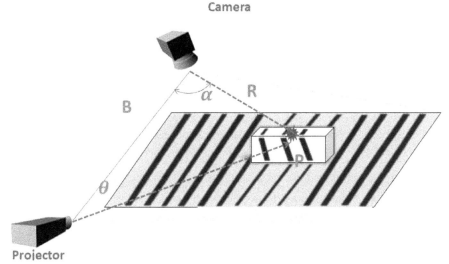

Figure 2.9: Schematic diagram of a typical structured light system.

2.5.2 *Optoelectronic scanning*

The systems or devices that allow remote sensing are based on electromagnetic waves. A few examples are GPS, LiDAR, ultrasonic sensors, and technical vision systems (TVS). The main difference between these devices is related to their wavelength used. This section focuses on the visible light portion, especially with optoelectronic devices commonly used for noncontact applications, such as lasers, photodiodes, and phototransistors.

When we talk about optical scanning, people often think of LiDAR. However, other devices can perform the same task as a TVS cheaply. For example, the Leica BLK360 Imaging Laser Scanner has an accuracy of 6 mm at 10 m. This device is enabled to collect 360,000 points per second. A full scan of the environment can take about 3 minutes.

TVS system is a novel optical system that can also be used for depth measurement. This system can capture a scene a laser scanner. The operational functioning of this system is based on a dynamical triangulation method (DTM). One of the applications of TVS is structural health monitoring (SHM). TVS can be used for SHM applications for displacement and scanning measurements. The advantage of this system is that it can be developed with minimal economic and computational cost compared with LiDAR technology. Autonomous navigation is another application of a TVS. For example, this system can be mounted on a mobile robot (MR) for obstacle detection [Básaca-Preciado et al. 2014]. This work can reach a 98% confidence level on its coordinate measurements. Levenberg–Marquardt's method helped them significantly increase the metrological accuracy of the 3D coordinates.

The basic components of the TVS system can be divided into three groups: Optical, optoelectrical, and mechanical. Optical elements such as lenses and mirrors. Optoelectrical devices are photosensors (photodiodes or phototransistors), and radiation sources such as laser (active method) or LED or incandescent lamps (passive methods). Positioner laser (PL) and scanning aperture (SA) are indispensable optoelectronic elements. PL emits a radiation laser and SA is the receiver system to capture the radiation of a laser. The third element is the mechanical part. This element gives support to Optical and optoelectrical components. A motor DC for the scanning process is the main part of a structural mechanical. With these elements mentioned before is possible to scan objects and surfaces under study.

The operational principle of a TVS for optoelectronic scanning

TVS emits a laser point under a desired object on the surface. Then, the light radiation stroked on a surface under analysis is detected at some angle by an aperture. Due to the PL angle and distance between the SA and PL being known (distance a), it is possible to apply DTM.

Figure 2.10, shows the elements detailed before. Note that the signal received by SA has a Gaussian shape. This is due to the rotational mirror, and the power radiation reflected by the photosensor. The global maximum of the Gaussian shape is taken for depth measurements. Oscilloscope shows the rising edge (aqua) of the start of the motorcycle, and the Gaussian signal is distinguished in yellow.

The square signal illustrated in an oscilloscope is generated by an encoder (opto-interrupter) every complete revolution of a motor DC.

In the case of this study, the global maximum was used to measure the angular position of a light source about pulses shown in an oscilloscope. These pulses are used to measure the period of a complete rotation. By knowing that the full rotation is 360 degrees, we can estimate the angular position of the light source used.

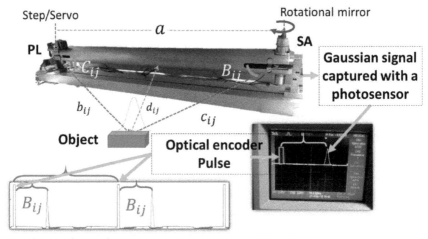

Figure 2.10: Main elements of a TVS.

By knowing SA and PL angles the coordinates X_{ij}, Y_{ij} and Z_{ij} can be calculated with the next equations (1.17), (1.18), (1.19) and (1.20).

$$X_{ij} = a \frac{sin(B_{ij})sin(C_{ij})cos \Sigma_{j=1}^{j} B_j}{sin(180° - B_{ij} + C_{ij})} \tag{1.17}$$

$$Y_{ij} = a \left(\frac{1}{2} - \frac{sin(B_{ij})cos(C_{ij})}{sin(180° - B_{ij} + C_{ij})} \right) \text{at } B_{ij} \leq 90° \tag{1.18}$$

$$Y_{ij} = -a \left(\frac{1}{2} + \frac{sin(B_{ij})cos(C_{ij})}{sin(180° - B_{ij} + C_{ij})} \right) \text{at } B_{ij} > 90° \tag{1.19}$$

$$Z_{ij} = a \left(\frac{1}{2} + \frac{sin(B_{ij})sin(C_{ij})tan \Sigma_{j=1}^{j} B_j}{sin(180° - B_{ij} + C_{ij})} \right) \text{at } B_{ij} > 90° \tag{1.20}$$

In optoelectronic scanning, it is well known that to find the angular position of a light source, the signal desired looks like a Gaussian signal shape. To minimize errors in angular position measurements, the best solution is to take measurements in the energy center of the signal generated by the scanner; see [Rivas et al. 2013]. Peak detection is a common task in time-series analysis and signal processing. Standard approaches to peak detection include smoothing and then fitting a known function (e.g., a polynomial) to the time series and matching a known peak shape to the time series [Palshikar 2009]. Peak detection and localization in a noisy signal with an unknown baseline are fundamental tasks in signal processing applications such as spectroscopy [Schmidt et al. 2019].

One of the most important problems to solve is that signals need to be smoothed before the measurements of each peak. Due to the acquisition process of the optical signal requiring different conditioning processes, such as analog-to-digital conversion and amplification, a number of issues can appear, especially distortion and noise. These issues alter the position of the local maximum; as a consequence, the accuracy of the angular position measurements decreases. Another typical problem observed in TVS systems is when digital filters are applied due to shifting the input signal.

Photosensors used for TVS

TVS can use photosensors such as photodiodes and phototransistors to extract environmental information on a structure under study. The integrated photodiode OPT301 includes an internally trans-impedance amplifier. The better response of this device is on 750 nm. The phototransistor BPW77NA is another device used as a transductor of a TVS. This device can reach better sensitivity at 850 nm. The advantage of this in comparison with OPT301 is the low cost and availability. Using a LED as a photosensor can be considered due to the narrow spectral selectivity, low cost, and commercial availability. One of the disadvantages of a LED is that it requires an additional circuit to amplify the photo-current generates by the photoelectric effect.

2.6 Implementation of MV for depth measurements

Depth measurements are based on a white wall placed at different distances. The results of the experiments are compared with a technical vision system TVS and laser distance-measuring instrument.

2.6.1 Practical evaluation of laser beam detection for depth measurements

After getting depth frames, it is important to filter the noise. A gaussian filter (GF) was used for this purpose. The mathematical expression of a GF is:

$$G(x,y) = \frac{1}{2\pi} e^{-\frac{x^2+y^2}{2\sigma^2}} \tag{1.21}$$

This algorithm can be implemented by applying the method *cv2.GaussianBlur(image,kernel size,sigmaX,sigmaY)*. The parameters taken for our experiments were *cv2.GaussianBlur(color_image,(5,5),0)*. Note that the kernel size was 5 (width and height), it should be odd. To standardize the experimentations a matrix 5 × 5 was selected for the rest of the filters.

The function used for blur, median and a box filters are as follows: *cv2. blur(color_image,(5,5)), cv2.medianBlur(color_image, 5) and cv2.boxFilter(color_ image,-1,(5,5))*.

After obtaining the image blurred with GF, it is important to apply a background subtractor method like *cv2.createBackgroundSubtractorMOG2*. However, in this case, object *detector.apply* cv2 library was applied directly to the frame denoised. We get a blurred mask frame.

The current frame is converted into hsv color space with *cv2.cvtColor(blurred_ frame, cv2.COLOR_BGR2HSV)*.

cv2.inRange function is used to check if the array elements of the red color of the image are between the elements of the other two arrays, the lower and upper ranges. The array selected for the experimentations are:

lower_red = np.array([155,155,200]) and *upper_red = np.array([180,255,255])*

Frame differencing is used to identify the laser light with the function *cv2.bitwise_and*. This method ensures the difference between the current frame and the next frame. Then *cv2.minMaxLoc* function is applied to find the brightest spot in the current frame.

cv2.circle functions it is used to highlight the laser point stroked on the surface studied. For showing distance for a specific point, is used *depth_image* variable. This get frame data by the instruction *np.asanyarray(depth_frame.get_data())*. *cv2. putText* function displays the result of depth measurement on the screen.

The source code used for the experiments is the following

```
import cv2
import numpy as np
import argparse
cap = cv2.VideoCapture(1)
# construct the argument parse and parse the arguments
ap = argparse.ArgumentParser()
ap.add_argument("-i", "--image", help = "path to the image file")
ap.add_argument("-r", "--radius", type = int,
        help = "radius of Gaussian blur; must be odd")
args = vars(ap.parse_args())
# Create a context object. This object owns the handles to all connected realsense
devices
pipeline = rs.pipeline()

# Configure streams
config = rs.config()
config.enable_stream(rs.stream.depth, 640, 480, rs.format.z16, 30)
config.enable_stream(rs.stream.color, 640, 480, rs.format.bgr8, 30)

# Start streaming
pipeline.start(config)

object_detector = cv2.createBackgroundSubtractorMOG2()
list = []
while True:
  # This call waits until a new coherent set of frames is available on a device
  # Calls to get_frame_data(...) and get_frame_timestamp(...) on a device will
return stable values until wait_for_frames(...) is called
  frames = pipeline.wait_for_frames()
  depth_frame = frames.get_depth_frame()
  color_frame = frames.get_color_frame()
  depth_image = np.asanyarray(depth_frame.get_data())
  color_image = np.asanyarray(color_frame.get_data())

  if not depth_frame or not color_frame: continue   # cv2.blur(color_image,(5,5))
# cv2.boxFilter(color_image,-1,(5,5))

  blurred_frame = cv2.GaussianBlur(color_image,(5,5),0) # cv2.GaussianBlur(-
color_image,(5,5),0) # cv2.medianBlur(color_image, 5)
  mask_blurred_frame = object_detector.apply(blurred_frame)
img_hsv = cv2.cvtColor(blurred_frame, cv2.COLOR_BGR2HSV) #image_RGB
= cv2.cvtColor(blurred_frame, cv2.COLOR_BGR2RGB  ) # cv.COLORMAP_
HOT  COLOR_BGR2LAB COLOR_BGR2RGB
```

```
  lower_red = np.array([155,155,200])
 upper_red = np.array([180,255,255])
 mask = cv2.inRange(img_hsv,lower_red,upper_red) # mask
 res = cv2.bitwise_and(color_image,color_image,mask =mask)
 (minVal, maxVal, minLoc, maxLoc) = cv2.minMaxLoc(mask)
 cv2.circle(color_image, maxLoc, args["radius"], (255, 0, 255), 10)
 distance = depth_image[maxLoc[1], maxLoc[0]] # Show distance for a specific
point
 cv2.putText(color_image, "{}mm".format(distance), (maxLoc[0], maxLoc[1] -
20), cv2.FONT_HERSHEY_PLAIN, 2, (0, 0, 0), 2)
 cv2.imshow('color_frame', color_image)
 cv2.imshow('mask_blurred_frame', mask_blurred_frame)
# average calculated
 for i in range(100):
   if distance <= 0:
     print("There is no data")
   list.append(distance)
 avg =( float(sum(list)/len(list) ))
 print(avg)
 list=[]

 if cv2.waitKey(1) & 0xFF == ord('q'):
   break

cap.release()
cv2.destroyAllWindows()
```

2.7 Discussion

The experimental results were obtained by applying four different image-smoothing techniques such as blur, gaussian, median, and a box filter. The experimental set-up was carried out under a controlled environment to avoid light conditions affecting the performance of the measurements. The scene observed corresponds to the red laser beam (Leica D810) striking the wall. The camera used for these experiments was the depth camera D415 with a depth and color frame resolution of 640 × 480. The depth measurements from the target were calibrated with a Leica D810. According to the specification of this laser distance meter, the wavelength of the laser is 650 nm < 1 mW with an accuracy of 1mm. The samples used in this experiment were 100 samples per target with a frame rate of 30 frames per second (fps). The average of these samples was taken to compare with the distance meter measurement.

Figure 2.11 details the dimension of the laboratory in which they carried out the experimentations. It is important to mention that the experiments were taken in a dark environment.

Although the minimum depth distance provided for the camera D415 is 0.3 meters, the dimension of the laboratory allowed for having different targets such as (3, 4, 5, and 6 meters). At short distances (1 and 2 meters), the laser power affects

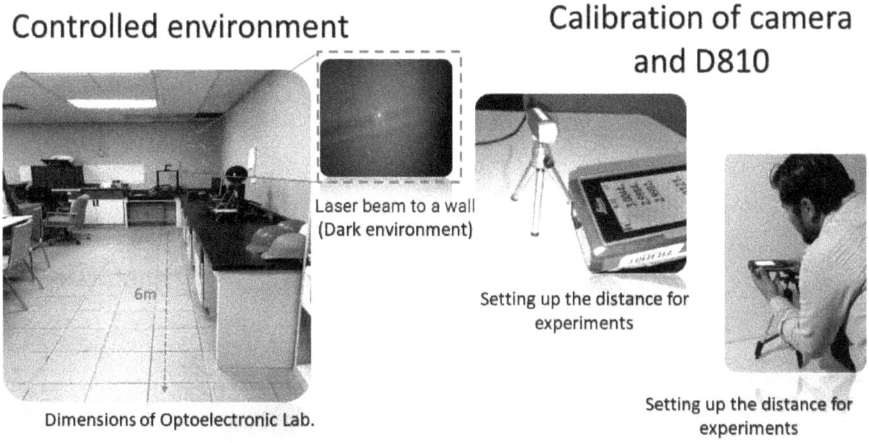

Controlled environment

Laser beam to a wall
(Dark environment)

6m

Dimensions of Optoelectronic Lab.

Calibration of camera and D810

Setting up the distance for experiments

Setting up the distance for experiments

Figure 2.11: Experimental set up.

the performance of the experiments. This added noise to the color frames captured by RGB sensors.

It is important to note that targets greater than 6 meters were not possible to consider for these experiments due to RGB camera did not detect the beam of a laser. The only way to detect the laser beam for greater distances is to change the parameters of its color space. To maintain the standardization of the experiments (input stream and image processing parameters), it was decided to work with the same parameters. The following instructions lower_red = np.array([155,155,200]) and upper_red = np.array([180,255,255]) were taken into account for the color space conversion.

Tables 2.2, 2.3, 2.4 and 2.5 show statistical results from the experimentations carried out in an indoor environment. According to the difference from the depth measurements of a Leica and RGB-D camera, all smooth functions had the same performance for 3 and 4 meters. One important difference is when the depth is taken directly by creating a mouse event to select the target position from the color frame the accuracy will improve. This is due to the light conditions of the laser Leica causing interference with the projection of the IR spectrum of camera D415. It is clear that the standard deviation of the measures increases while the RGB-D camera is moving away from the target.

The best performance for 5 and 6 meters is reached by applying the blur function compared with the rest of the algorithms. This algorithm provided a difference of 0.016 and 0.017 meters according to Leica measurements. Gauss function can reach a difference of 0.025 m and 0.026 m for a depth distance of 5 and 6 meters respectively. This represents the second-best performance of the experiments. The behavior of the median filter for the depth of 5 meters is satisfactory, however, the depth distance estimated (0.12 m) for the target at 6 meters is poor in comparison with the rest of the image filters. Finally, the box filter is the worst image filter for these experiments by considering the parameters mentioned before.

Table 2.2: Statistical data for the performance of the median filter for smoothing the color frames.

Distance (m)	Absolutes difference (m)	Standard deviation (m)
3	0.1191	11.010
4	0.12450	28.323
5	0.02981	43.54
6	0.12515	104.73

Table 2.3: Statistical data for the performance of the Gaussian filter for smoothing the color frames.

Distance (m)	Absolutes difference (m)	Standard deviation (m)
3	0.1309	12.318
4	0.1178	26.787
5	0.0257	58.935
6	0.0268	78.520

Table 2.4: Statistical data for the performance of the blur filter for smoothing the color frames.

Distance (m)	Absolutes difference (m)	Standard deviation (m)
3	0.1233	12.100
4	0.0992	26.545
5	0.0162	52.495
6	0.0174	111.289

Table 2.5: Statistical data for the performance of the box filter for smoothing the color frames.

Distance (m)	Absolutes difference (m)	Standard deviation (m)
3	0.1136	17.364
4	0.1084	23.662
5	0.0901	66.080
6	0.0432	108.759

2.8 Conclusions

This chapter has provided a brief review of the vision technology used for depth measurements. The key concepts of machine vision are also shown. Furthermore, the purpose of analyzing the use of laser light with a camera RGB was achieved. The main idea was to investigate the suitability of the integration of a TVS with an RGB-D camera for enhancing depth measurements. According to the indoor experiments, we can conclude that the blur and Gauss filter can offer satisfactory results for depth measurements.

References

Andriyanov, N., Khasanshin, I., Utkin, D., Gataullin, T., Ignar, S., Shumaev, V. et al. 2022. Intelligent system for estimation of the spatial position of apples based on YOLOv3 and real sense depth camera D415. Symmetry, 14(1): 148.

Antico, M., Balletti, N., Laudato, G., Lazich, A., Notarantonio, M., Oliveto, R. et al. 2021. Postural control assessment via Microsoft Azure Kinect DK: An evaluation study. Computer Methods and Programs in Biomedicine, 209: 106324.

Asvadi, A., Premebida, C., Peixoto, P., and Nunes, U. 2016. 3D Lidar-based static and moving obstacle detection in driving environments: An approach based on voxels and multi-region ground planes. Robotics and Autonomous Systems, 83: 299–311.

Básaca-Preciado, L. C., Sergiyenko, O. Y., Rodríguez-Quinonez, J. C., García, X., Tyrsa, V. V., Rivas-Lopez, M. et al. 2014. Optical 3D laser measurement system for navigation of autonomous mobile robot. Optics and Lasers in Engineering, 54: 159–169.

Behroozpour, B., Sandborn, P. A., Wu, M. C., and Boser, B. E. 2017. Lidar system architectures and circuits. IEEE Communications Magazine, 55(10): 135–142.

Carfagni, M., Furferi, R., Governi, L., Santarelli, C., Servi, M., Uccheddu, F. et al. 2019. Metrological and critical characterization of the Intel D415 stereo depth camera. Sensors, 19(3): 489.

Condotta, I. C., Brown-Brandl, T. M., Pitla, S. K., Stinn, J. P., and Silva-Miranda, K. O. 2020. Evaluation of low-cost depth cameras for agricultural applications. Computers and Electronics in Agriculture, 173: 105394.

Curto, E., and Araujo, H. 2022. An experimental assessment of depth estimation in transparent and translucent scenes for Intel RealSense D415, SR305 and L515. Sensors, 22(19): 7378.

Erkan, U., Enginoğlu, S., Thanh, D. N., and Hieu, L. M. 2020. Adaptive frequency median filter for the salt and pepper denoising problem. IET Image Processing, 14(7): 1291–1302.

Forbes, A. 2019. Structured light from lasers. Laser & Photonics Reviews, 13(11): 1900140.

Geetha, K., Anitha, V., Elhoseny, M., Kathiresan, S., Shamsolmoali, P., and Selim, M. M. 2021. An evolutionary lion optimization algorithm-based image compression technique for biomedical applications. Expert Systems, 38(1): e12508.

Geng, J. 2011. Structured-light 3D surface imaging: a tutorial. Advances in Optics and Photonics, 3(2): 128–160.

Ghaffar, M. S. B. A., Khan, U. S., Iqbal, J., Rashid, N., Hamza, A., Qureshi, W. S. et al. 2021. Improving classification performance of four class FNIRS-BCI using Mel Frequency Cepstral Coefficients (MFCC). Infrared Physics & Technology, 112: 103589.

Ghareeb, S., Hussain, A. J., Al-Jumeily, D., Khan, W., Al-Jumeily, R., Baker, T. et al. 2022. Evaluating student levelling based on machine learning model's performance. Discover Internet of Things, 2(1): 1–25.

Hanson, A. (Ed.). 1978. Computer vision systems. Elsevier.

Huang, D., Shan, C., Ardabilian, M., Wang, Y., and Chen, L. 2011. Local binary patterns and its application to facial image analysis: A survey. IEEE Transactions on Systems, Man, and Cybernetics, Part C (Applications and Reviews), 41(6): 765–781.

Kang, N., Qiu, S., Zhang, S., Li, Z., and Xia, S. T. 2022. PILC: Practical image lossless compression with an End-to-End GPU Oriented Neural Framework. In Proceedings of the IEEE/CVF Conference on Computer Vision and Pattern Recognition (pp. 3739–3748).

Kim, C., Jung, Y., and Lee, S. 2020. FMCW LiDAR system to reduce hardware complexity and post-processing techniques to improve distance resolution. Sensors, 20(22): 6676.

Kim, J. S., Choi, K. N., and Kang, S. W. 2021. Infrared thermal image-based sustainable fault detection for electrical facilities. Sustainability, 13(2): 557.

Kuan, Y. W., Ee, N. O., and Wei, L. S. 2019. Comparative study of intel R200, Kinect v2, and primesense RGB-D sensors performance outdoors. IEEE Sensors Journal, 19(19): 8741–8750.

Kumar, A., Kaur, A., and Kumar, M. 2019. Face detection techniques: A review. Artificial Intelligence Review, 52(2): 927–948.

Lamport, L. 1966. Summer Vision Programs.

Li, L., Wang, J., Yang, S., and Gong, H. 2021. Binocular stereo vision based illuminance measurement used for intelligent lighting with LED. Optik, 237: 166651.

Li, N., Ho, C. P., Xue, J., Lim, L. W., Chen, G., Fu, Y. H. et al. 2022. A progress review on solid-state LiDAR and nanophotonics-based LiDAR sensors. Laser & Photonics Reviews, 16(11): 2100511.

Li, Y., and Ibanez-Guzman, J. 2020. Lidar for autonomous driving: The principles, challenges, and trends for automotive lidar and perception systems. IEEE Signal Processing Magazine, 37(4): 50–61.

Li, Y., Gu, J. X., Zhen, D., Xu, M., and Ball, A. 2019. An evaluation of gearbox condition monitoring using infrared thermal images applied with convolutional neural networks. Sensors, 19(9): 2205.

Liu, Z., Wu, S., Wu, Q., Quan, C., and Ren, Y. 2018. A novel stereo vision measurement system using both line scan camera and frame camera. IEEE Transactions on Instrumentation and Measurement, 68(10): 3563–3575.

Marr, D. 1977. Representing visual information.

Masini, R. P., Medeiros, M. C., and Mendes, E. F. 2021. Machine learning advances for time series forecasting. Journal of Economic Surveys.

Mei, Q., Gül, M., and Boay, M. 2019. Indirect health monitoring of bridges using Mel-frequency cepstral coefficients and principal component analysis. Mechanical Systems and Signal Processing, 119: 523–546.

Moerland, T. M., Broekens, J., Plaat, A., and Jonker, C. M. 2023. Model-based reinforcement learning: A survey. Foundations and Trends® in Machine Learning, 16(1): 1–118.

Moraru, L., Obreja, C. D., Dey, N., and Ashour, A. S. 2018. Dempster-shafer fusion for effective retinal vessels' diameter measurement. In Soft Computing Based Medical Image Analysis (pp. 149–160). Academic Press.

Nebiker, S., Meyer, J., Blaser, S., Ammann, M., and Rhyner, S. 2021. Outdoor mobile mapping and AI-based 3D object detection with low-cost RGB-D cameras: The use case of on-street parking statistics. Remote Sensing, 13(16): 3099.

Palshikar, G. 2009, June. Simple algorithms for peak detection in time-series. In Proc. 1st Int. Conf. Advanced Data Analysis, Business Analytics and Intelligence (Vol. 122).

Qiu, J., Cui, Z., Zhang, Y., Zhang, X., Liu, S., Zeng, B. et al. 2019. Deeplidar: Deep surface normal guided depth prediction for an outdoor scene from sparse lidar data and single color image. In Proceedings of the IEEE/CVF Conference on Computer Vision and Pattern Recognition (pp. 3313–3322).

Reinforcement Learning: A Brief Guide. (s. f.). MATLAB & Simulink. https://la.mathworks.com/company/newsletters/articles/reinforcement-learning-a-brief-guide.html.

Rivas, M., Flores, W., Rivera, J., Sergiyenko, O., Hernández-Balbuena, D., and Sánchez-Bueno, A. 2013. A method and electronic device to detect the optoelectronic scanning signal energy centre. Optoelectronics-Advanced Materials and Devices, Mexico.

Rogers, C., Piggott, A. Y., Thomson, D. J., Wiser, R. F., Opris, I. E., Fortune, S. A. et al. 2021. A universal 3D imaging sensor on a silicon photonics platform. Nature, 590(7845): 256–261.

Royo, S., and Ballesta-Garcia, M. 2019. An overview of lidar imaging systems for autonomous vehicles. Applied Sciences, 9(19): 4093.

Schmidt, J., Marques, M. R., Botti, S., and Marques, M. A. 2019. Recent advances and applications of machine learning in solid-state materials science. npj Computational Materials, 5(1): 1–36.

Schmidt, M. N., Alstrøm, T. S., Svendstorp, M., and Larsen, J. 2019, May. Peak detection and baseline correction using a convolutional neural network. In ICASSP 2019-2019 IEEE International Conference on Acoustics, Speech and Signal Processing (ICASSP) (pp. 2757–2761). IEEE.

Seo, J., Han, S., Lee, S., and Kim, H. 2015. Computer vision techniques for construction safety and health monitoring. Advanced Engineering Informatics, 29(2): 239–251.

Servi, M., Mussi, E., Profili, A., Furferi, R., Volpe, Y., Governi, L. et al. 2021. Metrological characterization and comparison of D415, D455, L515 RealSense devices in the close range. Sensors, 21(22): 7770.

Shah, A., Bangash, J. I., Khan, A. W., Ahmed, I., Khan, A., Khan, A. et al. 2022. Comparative analysis of median filter and its variants for removal of impulse noise from gray scale images. Journal of King Saud University-Computer and Information Sciences, 34(3): 505–519.

Sharifi, M., Fathy, M., and Mahmoudi, M. T. 2002, April. A classified and comparative study of edge detection algorithms. In Proceedings. International conference on information technology: Coding and computing (pp. 117–120). IEEE.

Sun, W., Hu, Y., MacDonnell, D. G., Weimer, C., and Baize, R. R. 2016. Technique to separate lidar signal and sunlight. Optics express, 24(12): 12949–12954.

Sun, Z., Bebis, G., and Miller, R. 2006. Monocular precrash vehicle detection: features and classifiers. IEEE Transactions on Image Processing, 15(7): 2019–2034

Ulloa, C. C., Krus, A., Barrientos, A., Del Cerro, J., and Valero, C. 2022. Trend technologies for robotic fertilization process in row crops. Frontiers in Robotics and AI, 9.

Van Engelen, J. E., and Hoos, H. H. 2020. A survey on semi-supervised learning. Machine Learning, 109(2): 373–440.

Velodyne Lidar. 2022, 7 octubre. Velodyne's HDL-32E Surround Lidar Sensor. https://velodynelidar.com/products/hdl-32e/.

Wang, Z., Chen, J., and Hoi, S. C. 2020. Deep learning for image super-resolution: A survey. IEEE Transactions on Pattern analysis and Machine Intelligence, 43(10): 3365–3387.

Yang, M., Hu, J., Li, C., Rohde, G., Du, Y., and Hu, K. 2019. An in-depth survey of underwater image enhancement and restoration. IEEE Access, 7: 123638–123657.

Yao, R., Lin, G., Xia, S., Zhao, J., and Zhou, Y. 2020. Video object segmentation and tracking: A survey. ACM Transactions on Intelligent Systems and Technology (TIST), 11(4): 1–47.

Yongbo, L. I., Xiaoqiang, D. U., Fangyi, W. A. N., Xianzhi, W. A. N. G., and Huangchao, Y. U. 2020. Rotating machinery fault diagnosis based on convolutional neural network and infrared thermal imaging. Chinese Journal of Aeronautics, 33(2): 427–438.

Zhang, W., Dong, L., Pan, X., Zou, P., Qin, L., and Xu, W. 2019. A survey of restoration and enhancement for underwater images. IEEE Access, 7: 182259–182279.

Zhang, X., Wu, R., Shen, C., and Dai, W. 2018, February. Anti-sunlight jamming technology of laser fuze. In 2018 International Conference on Computer Science, Electronics and Communication Engineering (CSECE 2018) (pp. 59–63). Atlantis Press.

Zhang, Y., and Ni, Q. 2020. Recent advances in quantum machine learning. Quantum Engineering, 2(1): e34.

Zhu, Y., Zheng, C., Yuan, C., Huang, X., and Hong, X. 2021, May. Camvox: A low-cost and accurate lidar-assisted visual slam system. In 2021 IEEE International Conference on Robotics and Automation (ICRA) (pp. 5049–5055). IEEE.

3

Design and Evaluation Support System for Convolutional Neural Network, Support Vector Machine and Convolutional Autoencoder

Fusaomi Nagata,[1,*] *Kento Nakashima,*[1] *Kohei Miki,*[1] *Koki Arima,*[1] *Tatsuki Shimizu,*[1] *Keigo Watanabe*[2] and *Maki K Habib*[3]

3.1 Introduction

Recently, deep learning approaches such as Convolutional Neural Network (CNN), Support Vector Machine (SVM), convolutional autoencoders (CAE) are widely applied to solve various kinds of industrial defect detection problems. Since 2017, the authors have developed a design, training, and evaluation support software available on MATLAB® for CNN, SVM, CAE, etc. Figure 3.1 shows the main dialogue of the developed application. Original models designed through the application can be applied to various classification and anomaly detection problems. As for CNN, not only initial learning-based CNN (ILCNN) with an original series-type structure but also the transfer learning-based CNN (TLCNN) using the convolutional blocks of already trained large-scaled CNNs such as AlexNet, GoogLeNet, VGG16, VGG19 and so on can be designed. As for SVM, two types of models can be constructed. They are called one class learning-based SVM (OCSVM) and two class learning-

---

[1] Sanyo-Onoda City University, 1-1-1 Daigaku-Dori, Sanyo-Onoda, 756-0884, Japan.
[2] Okayama University, Okayama, Japan.
[3] Mechanical Engineering Department, School of Sciences and Engineering, American University in Cairo, AUC Avenue, P.O. Box 74, New Cairo 11835, Egypt.
* Corresponding author: nagata@rs.socu.ac.jp

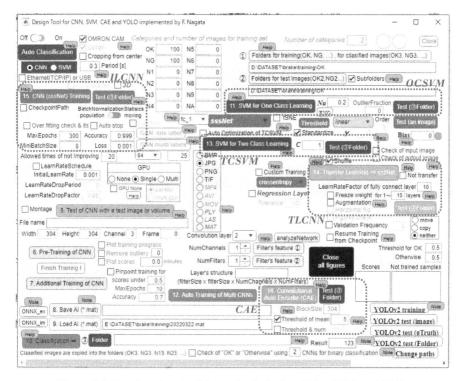

Figure 3.1: Developed main dialogue for designing CNN, SVM, and CAE.

based SVM (TCSVM). Training of OCSVM does not require images including defects, i.e., OCSVM can be trained only using images of non-defective products [Zhang et al., 2006].

Also, as with OCSVM, CAE for anomaly detection can be constructed only using images of non-defective products. Essentially, CAE is trained through one-class learning using images of non-defective products until visually similar images can be generated from the final output layer when training images are given to the input layer. The trained CAE can produce a visual image like an input image without a defect. However, when an image with a defect is introduced to the CAE, the region around the defect will not be successfully produced in the corresponding output image. By utilizing this property, the region around a defect can be visualized as shown in Figure 3.2 by subtracting the output image from the input one.

In this chapter, some models designed and based on the deep network structures such as CNN, SVM and CAE are applied to actual problems concerning defect detection of industrial products. Design, training, and evaluation processes are presented.

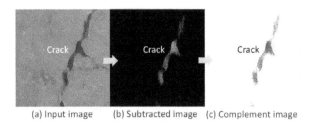

(a) Input image   (b) Subtracted image   (c) Complement image

Figure 3.2: Example of output in applying a test image to a trained CAE.

3.2 Support Vector Machine

In this section, SVMs designed for binary classification are introduced. For example, Zhang et al. reported the effectiveness of one-class learning-based SVM for anomaly detection [Zhang et al., 2006]. Then, SVM-based defect detection method for industrial applications was presented by Chittilappilly and Subramaniam [A.J. Chittilappilly and Subramaniam, 2017]. As shown in Figure 3.1, the authors have also developed a user-friendly design software for convolutional neural networks (CNNs) and support vector machines (SVMs) [Nagata et al., 2018a, Nagata et al., 2018b]. CNNs generally include several layered blocks composed of convolutional layer, rectified linear unit layer called ReLU, and pooling layer to process image data given from the former layers, after which fully-connected layers and a softmax function layer are located for final output. Even if students and novice engineers are unfamiliar with software development using Matlab, C#, C++, or Python, the application shown in Figure 3.1 is able to support them to effectively construct desired CNN and SVM models for defect detection.

After this, binary classification systems using CNNs, SVMs, and template matching techniques are described for visual defect inspection of industrial products and materials. Two kinds of one-class learning-based SVMs are first designed and trained using the proposed application. The two SVM models are trained using typical OK images without any defects to be able to distinguish images including defects from all images. It is assumed in this section that the defects are fracture, cracks, burrs, protrusions, chipping, and spot, that frequently appear in the manufacturing process of resin-molded articles. Some examples of typical defects are shown in Figure 3.3. Two kinds of pre-trained CNN models are selected as feature extractors for OCSVMS, which are placed at the fore parts of the two OCSVMs. Compressed feature vectors are extracted by the CNNs and are used as input vectors for the OCSVMs. The performance of the OCSVMs incorporated with the two kinds of CNNs is compared and evaluated through training and classification experiments. Then, TCSVM incorporated with the AlexNet is constructed through a two-class learning, and then the binary classification performance is evaluated.

In addition, a template matching method to extract important target regions from original training and test images is implemented in the application and applied to the OCSVM with the AlexNet. It is expected that this preprocess is able to improve the accuracy and its reliability in binary classification using SVMs.

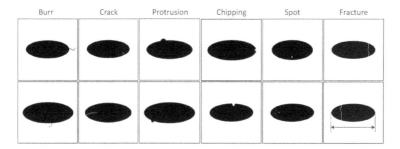

Figure 3.3: Examples of six kinds of defects that are seen in the resin molded articles production line. The horizontal lengths are about 30 mm.

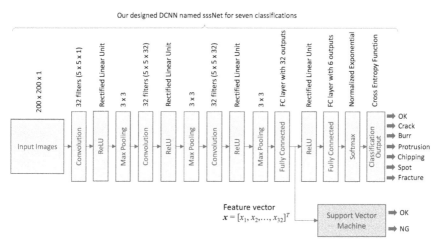

Figure 3.4: The proposed OCSVM whose input is the feature vector generated from our designed DCNN named sssNet.

3.2.1 OCSVMs collaborated with two kinds of CNNs

In the following subsections, two kinds of OCSVMs for binary classification are designed and trained using our developed CNN&SVM design application, in which CNN models are deployed at the front of SVMs to extract feature vectors in images. Actually, It is the most important function required for a defect inspection system that defective products are removed from all products. Any defective product is not allowed to be mixed with many non-defective products. Two kinds of OCSVMs are designed and trained to cope with this need using the DCNN&SVM design application. It is expected that the optimized OCSVMs will be able to classify product images into OK or NG categories, including several defects such as fracture, spot, chipping, cracks, burrs, and protrusions.

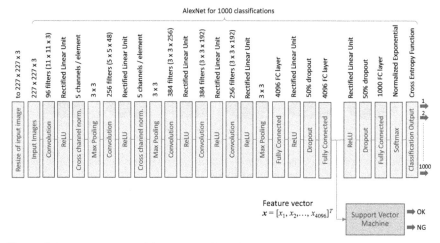

Figure 3.5: The proposed OCSVM to which feature vectors generated from the fully-connected layer of AlexNet are given.

3.2.1.1 OCSVM incorporated with originally designed CNN model named sssNet

As for the first designed OCSVM, our original CNN model named sssNet is applied to the extraction of multidimensional feature vector $x = [x_1, x_2, \cdots, x_{32}]^T$ from input images. The designed OCSVM for binary classification, whose input requires the feature vector x generated from the 1st fully connected layer (11th layer) in the sssNet, is shown in Figure 3.4. Gaussian kernel function given by Equation (3.2) is used for one-class training of the OCSVM. In the training, only the feature vectors $x_1, x_2, \cdots, x_{5100} \in \Re^{32 \times 1}$ extracted from 5,100 OK images are used for unsupervised learning of the OCSVM with the sssNet. No NG images with defects are not needed for the unsupervised learning. The quadratic programming (QP) of the OCSVM is solved by the sequential minimal optimization (SMO) algorithm [Platt, 1998].

Here, anomaly detection process is explained. If a feature vector $x \in \Re^{32 \times 1}$ extracted from a test image using the sssNet is given to the trained OCSVM, an output $f(x)$ called the score is calculated by

$$f(x) = \sum_{i=1}^{N} \alpha_i y_i G(x_i^*, x) + b \tag{3.1}$$

where $x_i^* \in \Re^{1 \times 32}$ $(i = 1, 2, \cdots, N)$ is the determined support vectors; N is the number of support vectors determined in the training process using the training data set of OK category; α_i $(i = 1, 2, \cdots, N)$ and b are the Lagrange multipliers and the bias respectively, which are important SVM parameters optimized through the training. y_i is the label set to 1 in the case of one-class learning. $f(x)$ is the signed distance to the optimized hyperplane. $G(x_i^*, x)$ is the kernel function used, which is

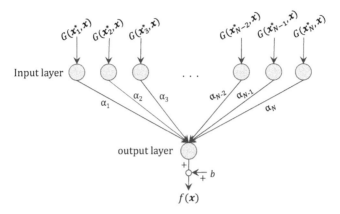

Figure 3.6: OCSVM is given by Equation (3.1) after training through one-class learning.

represented by

$$G(x_i^*,x) = \exp\left(-\left\|\frac{x_i^* - x_s}{k}\right\|^2\right) \qquad (3.2)$$

where k is the kernel scale, and x_s is the standardized input vector calculated by

$$x_s = (x - x_\mu) \oslash x_\sigma \qquad (3.3)$$

with

$$x_\mu = \frac{\sum_{j=1}^{5100} x_j}{5100} \qquad (3.4)$$

$$x_\sigma = \left[\frac{1}{5100}\sum_{j=1}^{5100}(x_j - x_\mu)^{\circ 2}\right]^{\circ\frac{1}{2}} \qquad (3.5)$$

where $\oslash$, $\circ 2$, $\circ\frac{1}{2}$ are the Hadamard operators for element-wise division, power and root, respectively.

In this test trial, after it took about several minutes to complete the training, k, N, and b were optimized as 1.1875, $2{,}621$, and -1.0639, respectively. Figure 3.6 illustrates the optimized OCSVM after trained through one-class learning. Consequently, a feature vector extracted from a test image can be classified by evaluating the sign of $f(x)$ such that $f(x) > 0$ and $f(x) < 0$ mean OK category and NG one, respectively.

Incidentally, for example, the nth-order polynomial equation can also be used as another kernel function, which is given by

$$G(x_i^*,x) = \left[1 + \frac{(x_i^*)^T}{k}\frac{x_s}{k}\right]^n \qquad (3.6)$$

3.2.1.2 OCSVM incorporated with widely-known AlexNet

As for the second OCSVM, a widely-known CNN called AlexNet is used to extract the feature vector $x = [x_1, x_2, \cdots, x_{4096}]^T$ from input images. Note that the feature vector has 4096 elements to originally deal with one thousand classification task. Figure 3.5 illustrates the OCSVM for binary classification whose input is the feature vector generated from the 2nd fully connected layer (20th layer) in the AlexNet. Equally, 5100 feature vectors obtained from OK images $x_1, x_2, \cdots, x_{5100} \in \mathfrak{R}^{4096 \times 1}$ were used for unsupervised learning of the OCSVM with the AlexNet. It also took several minutes for completing the optimization. The same conditions in the case of the OCSVM with the sssNet were used to this training. As a result, k, N, and b were optimized as 26.7690, 2,667, and -1.0635, respectively, after the training.

3.2.1.3 Classification experiments using two kinds of trained OCSVMs

After training the two kinds of OCSVMs, classification experiments were conducted to evaluate the generalization ability to OK and NG test images. Needless to say, the test images were not used in the training process. The classification results using the SVM shown in Figure 3.4 is given by histograms as Figure 3.7. The horizontal and vertical axes denote the output values from the OCSVM trained with our designed sssNet and the number of image samples, respectively. It is confirmed from the histogram given in Figure 3.7 that the OCSVM can satisfactorily discriminate NG images from OK ones.

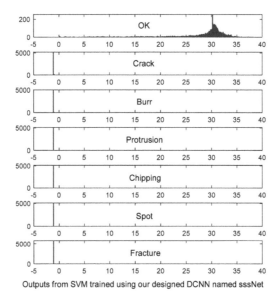

Figure 3.7: Classification results using the OCSVM shown in Figure 3.4. The horizontal and vertical axes denote the output from the SVM trained with the sssNet and the number of test images, respectively.

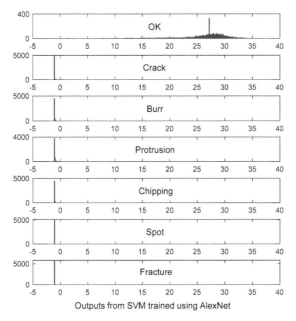

Outputs from SVM trained using AlexNet

Figure 3.8: Classification results using the OCSVM shown in Figure 3.5. The horizontal and vertical axes also denote the AlexNet-based SVM's output and the number of image samples, respectively.

On the other hand, Figure 3.8 shows the classification results using the OCSVM shown in Figure 3.5. It is confirmed from Figure 3.8 that the OCSVM with AlexNet can also discriminate NG images from OK ones with the almost same performance as the OCSVM with sssNet. The lengths of feature vectors generated from sssNet and AlexNet are pretty different as 32 and 4096; however, almost the same discrimination ability can be observed. In the case of the target images given by $200 \times 200 \times 1$ resolution, as shown in Figure 3.3, the feature vectors with 4096 components given to OCSVM seem to be redundant. The detailed comparison result of the number of misclassified images with defects is shown in Table 3.1. These images were unfortunately classified as non-defective articles. It is observed from Table 3.1 that the OCSVM with the sssNet is superior to that with AlexNet.

Table 3.1: Comparison result of the number of misclassified images.

SVM	Burr	Crack	Chipping	Knob	Spot	Fracture
sssNet	13	4	1	0	0	0
AlexNet	167	20	298	127	0	0

In the next subsection, supervised learning of the TCSVM, i.e., two-class learning, is introduced as an alternative approach.

3.2.2 TCSVM obtained by two-class learning

The two kinds of OCSVMs described in the previous subsections were obtained by one-class learning process, i.e., only images of non-defective articles were used for optimization. In this subsection, TCSVM trained by two-class learning is explained, and the generalization ability is compared to the OCSVMs. The TCSVM is trained using two classes of images of non-defective and defective articles. In this test trial, AlexNet is used for the feature extractor. After the optimization process, the classification function $f(x)$ of TCSVM can also calculate the score given by Equation (3.1). Note that the label y_i is set to 1 or -1 in the case of two-class learning. $f(x)$ is the signed distance from x to the decision boundary called a hyper plane. If the linear kernel is selected as given by

$$G(x_i^*, x) = \frac{(x_i^*)^T}{k} \frac{x_s}{k} \tag{3.7}$$

then the function given by Equation (3.1) can be simplified to

$$f(x) = \frac{x_s^T}{k}\beta + b \tag{3.8}$$

where k is called the kernel scale, $\beta \in \Re^{4096 \times 1}$ is the fitted linear coefficient vector, b is the bias. k, β and b are the important TCSVM parameters to be optimized. The structure of the designed TCSVM is shown in Figure 3.9. It is regarded as one of the linear classifiers. The feature vector $x \in \Re^{4096 \times 1}$ is extracted from the second flatten fully-connected layer in AlexNet.

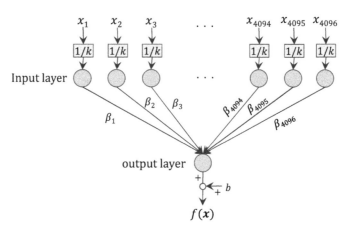

Figure 3.9: Network structure of TCSVM given by Equation (3.8) after trained through two-class learning.

5,100 normal images and 30,600 (5,100 × 6 categories) anomaly ones are prepared for optimizing the TCSVM shown in Figure 3.9. The images of anomalies

Table 3.2: Confusion matrix to check the trained situation of the two-class learning-based SVM (TCSVM), in which training images are evaluated.

Actual/Predicted	Normal	Anomaly
Normal	5092	8
Anomaly	27	30573

Table 3.3: Confusion matrix to check the generalization ability of the two-class learning-based SVM (TCSVM), in which test images are evaluated.

Actual/Predicted	Normal	Anomaly
Normal	997	3
Anomaly	13	5987

include one of the six kinds of defects as shown in Figure 3.3. k, N and b were optimized as 63.8168, 698 and 4.9334, respectively. After the training, the trained situation was checked using the training data, so that the comparison result was given by the confusion matrix shown in Table 3.2. Note that since not hard margin concept but soft margin one is adopted in this chapter, the misclassification of this degree should be allowed even though the training images are evaluated. After the optimization, the generalization ability is also checked using test images of 1,000 normals and 6,000 (1,000 × 6 categories) anomalies. Table 3.3 shows the comparison result by the confusion matrix. As can be seen, desirable generalization ability can be confirmed; however, complete classification with the misclassification rate of 0 could not be achieved. Although the decision boundary called hyper plane is determined by the soft margin concept, in which a certain degree of misclassification is allowable unless falling in the situation of extreme overfitting, the desirable classification result can be seen from Table 3.2. It should be noted that the misclassification as this degree can not be helped, i.e., unavoidable because actual anomaly detection applications have to deal with images regarded as outliers.

3.3 Template matching method to narrow down the target area

3.3.1 *Image cropping based on normalized cross-correlation*

In this subsection, a template matching operation implemented in the MATLAB application is introduced. If a template image made in advance, whose size is (M,N), is applied as shown in Figure 3.10, then a padding operation makes the original target image larger to be able to check even the edge area. The original target image and the padded area are together called an expanded target image. The similarity rate between the template image and an area with the same size in the target image expanded with the padding operation can be quantitatively evaluated by the correlation

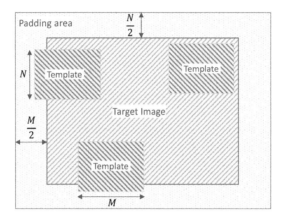

Figure 3.10: Configuration among a target image, padding area, and template image whose size is (M, N).

coefficient $\alpha(u, v)$ calculated by [Lewis, 1995]

$$\alpha(u, v) = \frac{s_{it}(u, v)}{s_i(u, v)s_t(u, v)} \tag{3.9}$$

$$s_{it}(u, v) = \sum_{y=v}^{v+N-1} \sum_{x=u}^{u+M-1} \{f(x, y) - \bar{f}_{u,v}\}\{t(x-u, y-v) - \bar{t}\} \tag{3.10}$$

$$s_i(u, v) = \sqrt{\sum_{y=v}^{v+N-1} \sum_{x=u}^{u+M-1} \{f(x, y) - \bar{f}_{u,v}\}^2} \tag{3.11}$$

$$s_t(u, v) = \sqrt{\sum_{y=v}^{v+N-1} \sum_{x=u}^{u+M-1} \{t(x-u, y-v) - \bar{t}\}^2} \tag{3.12}$$

where (u, v) is the left upper position of the template image in the expanded target image coordinate; $s_{it}(u, v)$ is the covariance, $s_i(u, v)$ and $s_t(u, v)$ are the standard deviations; $f(x, y)$ is the normalized value of grayscale at the position (x, y) in the expanded target image coordinate; $t(x-u, y-v)$ is the normalized value of grayscale at the position $(x-u, y-v)$ in the template image coordinate; M and N are the width and height of the template image, respectively; $\bar{t}$ is the mean value of grayscale in the template; $\bar{f}(u, v)$ is the mean value of grayscale in an area just below the template.

The correlation coefficient $\alpha(u, v)$ written by Equation (3.9) is sequentially calculated by conducting raster scanning in the template image from the top left to the bottom right in the expanded target image. After completing the raster scanning operation, an area best matched to the template image can be extracted by finding the maximum value of $\alpha(u, v)$. Figure 3.11 shows a template image and examples of cropped images using the template matching method.

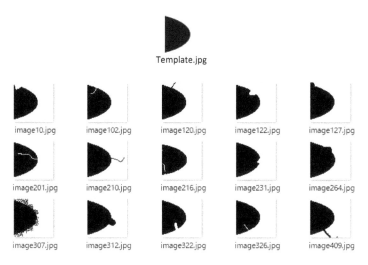

Figure 3.11: Examples of cropped images using the template matching method.

3.3.2 Classification experiment

Here, the effectiveness of the template matching is appraised. 3,000 OK images as shown in Figure 3.12 are cropped from the original OK ones. Then, an OCSVM is constructed based on the block diagram shown in Figure 3.5 and trained using the 3,000 cropped OK images. After the training is completed, the OCSVM is appraised using 120 test images as shown in Figure 3.13. The test images contain OK ones without a defect and NG ones with one of the defects shown in Figure 3.3. Figure 3.14 shows the binary classification result of the 120 test images shown in Figure 3.13, in which images with minus and plus scores are predicted as NG and OK, respectively. It is observed from the classification result that all the test images are successfully classified into the OK or NG category.

3.4 Convolutional autoencoder

In this section, two types of Convolutional Autoencoder (CAE) models are designed, trained and deployed in our developed Matlab application. They are applied to visualizing defective areas included in images of brake rotors as an industrial product. The visualization ability of defective regions in images is appraised [Arima et al., 2022].

3.4.1 Design of two types of CAEs

The first introduced CAE is a SegNet-based model named CAE1, and the second one is our original model named CAE2. Original SegNet has a deep convolutional encoder-decoder structure for image segmentation. SegNet can output labels for each pixel in the input image to which object class the pixel be-

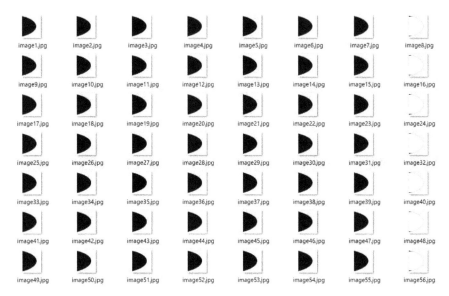

Figure 3.12: Some of 3000 OK cropped images for training the OCSVM incorporated with AlexNet.

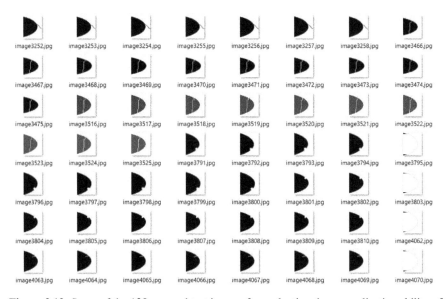

Figure 3.13: Some of the 120 cropped test images for evaluating the generalization ability of the OCSVM trained using images shown in Figure 3.12.

longs [Badrinarayanan et al., 2022]. On the other hand, CAE2 has a shallower network structure and fewer weight parameters than CAE1. The CAEs are applied to

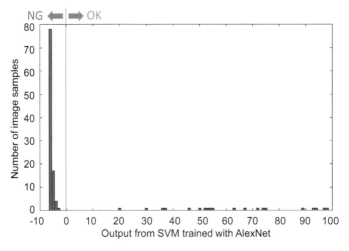

Figure 3.14: Binary classification result of 120 test images shown in Figure 3.13.

the visualization of defective parts in images of brake rotors, and to the identifying of their positions in these images. Their performances are qualitatively compared through visualization experiments of faulty areas.

In the case of conventional AE (Auto Encoder) with three layers, the input and output layers have the same number of neurons; the hidden layer has fewer neurons than those. In the case of training such an AE, weights are adjusted so that the input patterns are equally generated from the output layer as they are. If the training is completed, then it is expected that essential features of input data are successfully squashed into the middle hidden layer. CAE was proposed as an extended model that applied the concept of AE to CNN models [Hinton and Salakhutdinov, 2006]. The authors have constructed and deployed two types of CAEs as shown in Figures 3.15 and 3.16. Note that CAE1 is designed based on VGG16, and also CAE2 is constructed based on our originally designed CNN model named sssNet. They are trained only using the same 2,875 non-defective images of brake rotors.

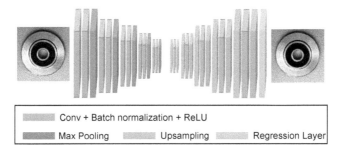

Figure 3.15: CAE structure designed using VGG16 for the encoder part called CAE1.

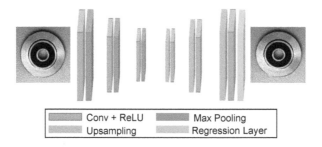

▨ Conv + ReLU	▨ Max Pooling
▨ Upsampling	▨ Regression Layer

Figure 3.16: CAE structure designed using sssNet for the encoder part called CAE2.

3.4.2 Evaluation of visualization performance of defective areas by two CAEs

Only non-defective images are generally used to train CAE models. After training a CAE model using a dataset of non-defective images, if a non-defective test image A is given to the CAE, then it will be able to output an almost similar image A'. Therefore, an image identical to only black color can be obtained by displaying the absolute pixel values of the subtraction $|A - A'|$ since all the pixel elements became almost zero.

On the other hand, when test image B, including defective areas, is given to the CAE, the features of the defective areas can not be reconstructed by the CAE. This means that the output image B' could not accurately have the features of defective areas. Consequently, when the subtracted image $|B - B'|$ is displayed, the defective areas can be successfully mapped as brighter white (see subfigures (b) in Figure 3.17). Moreover, their complement and emphasis lead to clear maps, in which the defective

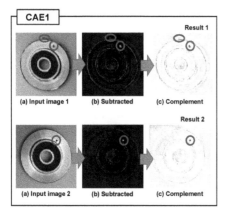
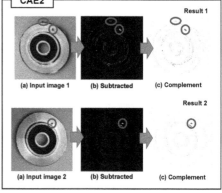

Figure 3.17: Examples of visualization results using two types of CAEs, in which two test images, i.e., input images 1 and 2, are given to the CAEs for evaluation.

areas are finally visualized with black color (see subfigures (c) in Figure 3.17). As proposed in this subsection, CAE1 and CAE2 are designed based on VGG16 and sssNet, respectively. In the case of using CAE1, it is observed that defects located around the edge and on the rotor can be successfully visualized as the output images from CAE1. On the other hand, also in the case of CAE2, defective areas can be visualized; however, it seemed that the clearness of the defective areas was slightly weaker than in CAE1.

3.5 Conclusions

This chapter proposes a design, training, and application evaluation for CNN, SVM, and CAE. In trail tests, two types of one-class learning-based SVMs (OCSVMs) for binary classification are designed and trained using the developed CNN&SVM design tool, and evaluated to discriminate NG sample images including typical defects from OK ones appearing in the manufacturing line of resin molded articles. Consequently, it is confirmed in spite of the shorter feature vector that the OCSVM with our designed sssNet can perform almost the same discrimination ability as well as that with AlexNet . Then, another type of TCSVM constructed by two-class learning is designed and evaluated, which makes it possible to develop a cascade-type SVM consisting of multiple different types of SVMs for binary classification in the future. In addition, a template matching technique is successfully applied together with OCSVM using AlexNet to extract the important featured areas in training and test images, so that the overall calculation load until the SVM is able to have a desired binary classification ability can be reduced.

Moreover, two types of CAEs are built and deployed on the Matlab system. One is SegNet-based CAE, the other is our originally designed CAE with a shallower network structure and fewer weight parameters. After training these two CAEs using images without defects, visualization performances of defective areas are evaluated and compared. Consequently, it is confirmed that the SegNet-based CAE including VGG16 in the encoder part can more clearly visualize defective areas than the latter CAE including sssNet.

Generally speaking, the shallower the network structure is better if the classification abilities are almost the same. To cope with the need, the proposed Matlab application introduced in this chapter efficiently supports the design, training and evaluation processes of CNNs, SVMs and CAEs.

Acknowledgment

This work was supported by JSPS KAKENHI Grant Number 16K06203 and MITSUBISHIPENCIL CO., LTD.

References

Arima, K., Nagata, F., Shimizu, T., Miki, K., Kato, H., Otsuka, A. et al. 2022. Visualization and location estimation of defective parts of industrial products using convolutional autoencoder. Artificial Life and Robotics, 27: 804–811.

Badrinarayanan, V., Kendall, A., and Cipolla, R. 2022. A deep convolutional encoder-decoder architecture for image segmentation. In Proceedings of IEEE Transactions on Pattern Analysis and Machine Intelligence, pp. 2481–2495.

Chittilappilly, A. and Subramaniam, K. 2017. SVM based defect detection for industrial applications. In Proceedings of 2017 4th International Conference on Advanced Computing and Communication Systems (ICACCS2017), pp. 782–786.

Hinton, G. and Salakhutdinov, R. 2006. Reducing the dimensionality of data with neural networks. Journal of Science, 313(5786): 504–507.

Lewis, J. 1995. Fast Normalized Cross-correlation. Technical Report, Industrial Light & Magic.

Nagata, F., Tokuno, K., Ochi, H., Otsuka, A., Ikeda, T., Watanabe, K. et al. 2018a. A design and training application for deep convolutional neural networks and support vector machines developed on matlab. In Proceedings of the 6th International Conference on Robot Intelligence Technology and Applications, pp. 27–33.

Nagata, F., Tokuno, K., Watanabe, K., and Habib, M. 2018b. Design application of deep convolutional neural network for vision-based defect inspection. In Proceeding of 2018 IEEE International Conference on Systems, Man, and Cybernetics, pp. 1701–1706.

Platt, J. 1998. Sequential minimal optimization: A fast algorithm for training support vector machines. Technical Report MSR–TR–98–14, pp. 1–24.

Zhang, X., Gu, C., and Lin, J. 2006. Support vector machines for anomaly detection. In Proceedings of 2006 6th World Congress on Intelligent Control and Automation, pp. 2594–2598.

4

Classification of Objects in IR Images using Wavelet Filters based on Lifting Scheme

Daniel Trevino-Sanchez and *Vicente Alarcon-Aquino**

4.1 Introduction

Detecting, locating, and classifying objects correctly is a hard task. It is essential to have reliable models with high-accuracy levels, especially when handling challenging images, such as Infrared (IR) scenarios. A convolutional neural network (CNN) is a highly accurate classifier that may detect and identify objects within an image as stated in [Voulodimos et al., 2018], including IR images. CNN presents more image recognition and object detection advantages than standard fully connected neural networks. Many models perform all the object detection, location, and recognition tasks with a single CNN, but as a result, they become larger, more complex, and consume more computational resources [Nielsen, 2015]. Some examples are [Malik et al., 2020], [Ölmez and Dokur, 2003], and [Akula et al., 2017] which present a CNN-based deep learning framework for the recognition of targets in IR images. Another good example of object identification and recognition for IR imaging using complex CNN is addressed in [d'Acremont et al., 2019], which is performed in the wild for defense applications where no large-scale datasets are available. In the case of IR images, the number of features is limited, and a grayscale single-channel is the only available information source. This makes them much more challenging to work with than the common color images (RGB), which have three information

Department of Computing, Electronics and Mechatronics, Universidad de las Americas Puebla, Sta. Catarina Martir, San Andres Cholula, Puebla, Mexico.
Email: daniel.trevinosz@udlap.mx
* Corresponding author: vicente.alarcon@udlap.mx

channels available, among other things. The chapter aims to provide relevant theoretical frameworks and some of the latest empirical research findings. It is written for professionals who want to improve their understanding of the strategic techniques to detect and locate objects in challenging images, and the measurements employed to assess them. Finally, an emerging model using a small CNN and wavelet filters based on a lifting scheme (multi-resolution analysis (MRA)) to improve the feature extraction process is presented. The performance of the proposed hybrid model is assessed using an IR benchmark dataset, comparing its performance with the standard pooling methods: maximum, average, and mixed pooling.

4.2 Theoretical background

To better understand the classification techniques of the previous section and the proposed model, it is essential to clarify some key concepts before focusing on the importance of this contribution and the advantages and disadvantages of some other approaches. For that purpose, this section gives a brief explanation of infrared (IR) images and the techniques used in the model to classify their objects, such as convolutional neural networks, Fourier transforms, wavelet transforms, multi-resolution analysis, and, more concretely, the lifting scheme transform, and the pooling layers specifically involved in the feature extraction process.

4.2.1 *Infrared spectrum and imaging*

Infrared radiation is waves that belong to the electromagnetic spectrum, and its name originates from the Latin word *infra*, which means below. This means the IR band is located below the visual red light band since it has a longer wavelength [Larkin, 2011]. IR is split into four bands: Near IR (NIR), short-wave IR (SWIR), mid-wave IR (MWIR), and long-wave IR (LWIR). SWIR imaging occurs at $1.5\mu m$, an eye-safe wavelength preferred by the military. All bands are classified by the length of the waves in meters, as shown in Figure 4.1. The wavelength for visible light is only around 1% and goes from 380 *nm* to 780 *nm*, while the IR rays have a wider range from 780 *nm* to 1 *mm*, as shown in Figure 4.2. Although humans cannot see IR rays, they can perceive them as heat.

An IR camera converts thermal energy into a visual image showing variations across an object or scene. Furthermore, thermography displays the temperature val-

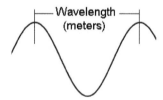

Figure 4.1: Wavelength of an electromagnetic wave.

Figure 4.2: Visible light within the electromagnetic spectrum [Larkin, 2011].

ues of an object without any physical contact. This is because IR radiation is emitted by all objects at temperatures above absolute zero, and the amount of radiation increases with temperature [Larkin, 2011]. In this sense, IR rays also consist of discrete bundles of energy called photons emitted from all the objects. The image sensor in a camera holds millions of photo-sensitive spots, pixels that detect the number of incoming photons. A camera sensor's ability to detect photons depends on their energy or wavelength. Visible light photons (400 *nm* to 700 *nm*) are generally detected. Still, in the near-infrared part of the electromagnetic spectrum, the sensor may also detect photons with slightly longer wavelengths (700 *nm* to 1000 *nm*). Artificial light sources are utilized to help some cameras better perceive an IR scene. Like, Near-infrared illumination is commonly used in surveillance scenes that could be too dark for commercial cameras. Standalone IR luminaries used for day-and-night cameras generally provide a longer reach than camera-integrated IR illumination. This IR illumination consists of a larger number of Light Emitting Diodes (LEDs) to provide more light. A camera for day and night operation uses visible and near-infrared light. It produces color videos during the day and gray-scale videos at night. When it uses night mode, the camera makes a one-channel video, a gray-scale one. This video has the advantage of using a low bit rate, and therefore, a reduced bandwidth, which minimizes storage needs [Axis-Communications, 2018].

It is important to clarify that IR imaging is not night vision. Night vision collects what little amount of light is available and amplifies it so that the naked eye can discern it. Differently, IR devices perceive IR waves emitted by any object dissipating heat. Tracking objects is not an easy task especially at night not even using night vision, as shown in Figure 4.3a. However, using IR allows that the differences in temperature between objects and background provides the necessary contrast to detect them, as shown in Figure 4.3b. If in some scenarios, there is no light available, night vision is blind. At the same time, IR cameras still collect thermal energy emit-

Figure 4.3: Tracking a walking person is difficult [Kristan et al., 2016], at night is harder even with night vision technology (left side), however using IR imaging (right side) objects are not easy to hide.

ted by the objects, whose amounts vary according to how much heat each body has. Therefore IR technology can be used in total darkness. However, an object can be at the same temperature as the background. Even more, some camouflage technology is able to control the object's surface temperature to appear invisible to IR vision. To counter cases like that, the newest military vision combines Night Vision, Infrared Vision, and Artificial Intelligence algorithms to get the best from all worlds.

4.2.2 *Convolutional Neural Networks*

Neural networks and many other pattern-detection methods have existed for over 50 years. However, relevant developments in the area of CNN have taken place in recent years. CNN, also known as ConvNets, is one of the most important tools for image recognition, object classification, or object localization. Faces and fingerprints are just some examples of CNN applications widely used. CNN's invariance to shifting features is due to its configuration that keeps the same weight across the space. This can also be achieved by using fully connected layers, which are the simplest neural networks but are also extremely dense. The CNN is made of neurons, which are nodes where inputs come from the previous layer and the output connects to the next layer. Inside the neuron, all the inputs are multiplied by some weight, added all together, and passed through an activation function before reaching the output of the neuron [Williams and Li, 2018a]. The activation function keeps the output values from 0 to 1, this function can be linear or exponential, as shown in Figure 4.4. The general equation for a single cell is also presented in Equation 4.1

$$Y_{i,j} = \sigma\left(b + \sum_{l=0}^{n-1}\sum_{m=0}^{n-1} W_{l,m}a_{i+l,j+m}\right) \qquad (4.1)$$

where $Y_{i,j}$ is the output at a certain layer position (i, j), σ is the activation function of that position, b represents the bias, $W_{l,m}$ are the weights of the filter component, and $a_{j+l,k+m}$ is the input activation at a combined position of the filter and the layer, and n is the window size of the convolution filter.

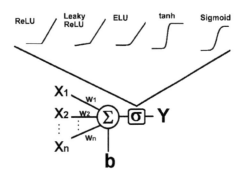

Figure 4.4: The general description of a single cell, selecting from five possible activation functions.

The training process would also require massive instances to cover all possible variations. To design a CNN is important to consider the number of parameters and mathematical operations required in every layer, as well as know their operation in detail. There are already many popular architectures of CNNs, such as AlexNet [Krizhevsky et al., 2012], VGGNet [Simonyan and Zisserman, 2014], ResNet [He et al., 2016], and GoogLeNet [Szegedy et al., 2015]. CNN image classification process receives an image as input, then labels it under a predefined category (car, person, dog, tiger, etc.). The input image is a matrix of values representing all pixels. Depending on the image dimensions, it would be Height (h) x Width (w) x Channels (c). For instance, a 7x7x3 image array would be a color image in RGB format (Red-Green-Blue color combination), and a 7x7x1 image array would be a grayscale image.

4.2.2.1 Stride and padding

Stride is the shifting factor used over convolution or pooling layers input. The layer processes pixels one by one using a stride equal to 1. If the stride is equal to 2, the filter processes one-pixel position jumps the next, and so on. When the filter does not match the input image, it can either add rows and columns of zeros, known as zero padding, or it can only use the part of the image that fits. This is named valid padding because it only keeps the valid region of the image. Another method is mirror padding which fills any needed row or column by reflecting the internal values into them [Liao et al., 2019].

4.2.2.2 Convolution layer

The convolution layer extracts features from the input. It keeps pixels relationship by using trainable square matrices of different sizes, known as kernels or filters. These filters and all the portions of the input data perform many mathematical operations that give the name to the layer, as shown in Figure 4.5. The result of such operations is known as a "Feature Map". Using different filters allows operations like detecting edges, colors, or corners. It may find patterns, or even blur or sharpen different features.

4.2.2.3 Pooling layer

The pooling layer is mainly used for downsampling, reducing the input's dimensions. The most widely known pooling methods are max-pooling and average pooling [Lee et al., 2018]. This technique summarizes a region into one single value calculating some statistical value. Max-pooling takes the highest value of a region R_{ij}, while the region slides at a stride of $S \times S$ (in this case $S = 2$) through the entire image to reduce its feature map. The padding of one or more values (pixels) is sometimes added to the image's perimeter (up, down, left, and right) to compensate for the size and fit into the next layer. In this case, no padding is added. Therefore $P = 0$. The

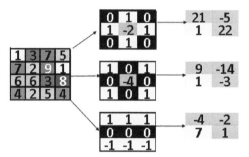

Figure 4.5: In this example, the convolution uses three different kernels. Each filter multiplies a 3 x 3 section of the input, then the results are added to obtain the new value in that position. The output is one channel for every filter. However, since there is no padding and the stride is one, the results also reduce their size to 2x2.

equation for max-pooling is described in Equation (4.2).

$$F_{max}(l,m) = max(R(i,j)_{a,b});$$
$$\{F_{max}(l,m)|\forall(l,m)\exists!(a,b), \forall R(i,j)_{a,b} \in I(x,y)\};$$

(4.2)

where R is the pooling region, (i,j) are its dimensions. F_{max} is the obtained output, (l,m) are its dimensions. I is the input image, (x,y) its dimensions. The indexes (a,b) points out a unique R in the image. Finally, to obtain the dimensions (l,m), the stride S, the padding P, and the image dimensions (x,y) must be considered, as shown in Equations (4.3) and (4.4).

$$l = \frac{x-i+2*P}{S} + 1;$$

(4.3)

$$m = \frac{y-j+2*P}{S} + 1;$$

(4.4)

Similarly to max pooling, average pooling reduces the feature map by calculating the average value of each region. The general equation for average pooling is shown in Equation (4.5).

$$F_{avg}(l,m) = \frac{1}{|R_{i,j}|}\sum_{}^{i}\sum_{}^{j}(R(i,j)_{a,b});$$
$$\{F_{avg}(l,m)|\forall(l,m)\exists!(a,b), \forall R(i,j)_{a,b} \in I(x,y)\}$$

(4.5)

where F_{avg} is the produced output, and $|R_{ij}|$ is the magnitude or number of elements in the pooling region.

There are two probabilistic pooling methods, mixed pooling [Yu et al., 2014], and stochastic pooling [Zeiler and Fergus, 2013]. Mixed pooling selects between max and average pooling randomly over training. The general equation for mixed pooling is presented in Equation (4.6).

$$F_{mix}(l,m) = \lambda F_{max} + (1-\lambda)F_{avg}$$

(4.6)

where F_{mix} is the obtained output, and λ value is 0 or 1 randomly.

On the other hand, stochastic pooling randomly selects values of the region depending on its probability, which is calculated based on its magnitude. The Equation (4.7) is the first step, it normalizes all the values in the pooling region $R(i,j)$ to obtain the probability of each element $p(i,j)$.

$$p(i,j) = \frac{R(i,j)}{\sum_{i}\sum_{j}(R(i,j))}; \quad (4.7)$$

The next step is done by applying Equation (4.8), which is the general form for stochastic pooling.

$$F_{stoch}(l,m) = P(p_{ij})_{a,b};$$
$$\{F_{stoch}(l,m)|\forall(l,m)\exists!(a,b),\forall R(i,j)_{a,b} \in I(x,y)\}; \quad (4.8)$$

where F_{stoch} is the generated output, the function $P()$ selects a sample from the multinomial distribution created with the probabilities obtained by the Equation (4.7).

As a summary, Figure 4.6 illustrates the four different pooling methods previously presented.

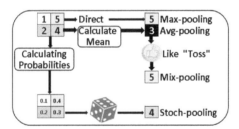

Figure 4.6: The pooling methods are presented as four paths obtaining different results from the same region.

4.2.3 *Fourier transform and short time Fourier transform*

Analyzing frequencies in one-dimension signals is very common using the Fourier Transform (FT). But it only has the frequency and no time resolution, which is a big disadvantage. This means that although we can determine all the frequencies in a signal, we do not know when they are present. FT is a useful method only for stationary signals. Stationary signals keep their statistical attributes constant all the time. To analyze signals, FT requires sines and cosines functions of different frequencies. The coefficients of these basis functions are calculated by taking the inner product in $L^2(\mathbb{R})$ (a set of square integrable real-valued functions) of the signal with sine wave basis functions of infinite duration, as shown in Equation (4.9).

$$FT(f) = \int_{-\infty}^{\infty} x(t)e^{-j2\pi ft} dt \quad (4.9)$$

where $FT(f)$ [Rioul and Vetterli, 1991a] is the Fourier Transform, and $x(t)$ is the analyzed signal. The component $e^{-j2\pi ft}$ is a periodic signal, and along with the integral, it produces a frequency sweep. The product of the signal with the periodic function generates peaks that identify all the stationary frequencies present in the signal $x(t)$. The FT is the appropriate tool when the signal $x(t)$ comprises only stationary frequencies. But unexpected changes in frequency or time will expand on the frequency axis. To address this problem, solutions like the Short Time Fourier Transform (STFT) or the Gabor Transform [Gabor, 1946] were developed to show signal behavior in time and frequency at one. The STFT uses a window that slides over the entire signal to construct spectra localized in time. The signal $x(t)$ multiplied with the fixed window function is confined to that small interval, this is how the the Fourier analysis of the product is done, as shown in Equation (4.10)

$$STFT(b,f) = \int_{-\infty}^{\infty} x(t)g^*(t-b)e^{-j2\pi ft}dt \qquad (4.10)$$

where $*$ denotes complex conjugate and $g(t)$ is the analysis window. The window $g(t-b)$ is a localized function that is shifted over time to calculate the transform throughout the signal in all positions b. The main disadvantage of the STFT is that the time-frequency window can't be adapted to the signal's shape at any time or frequency. The window width is constant regardless of the frequency producing a single resolution for the entire analysis.

4.2.4 Wavelet transform

The wavelet analysis calculates the correlation between the signal under consideration and a wavelet function $\psi(t)$. The similarity between the signal and the analyzing wavelet function is computed separately for different time intervals, resulting in a two-dimensional representation. The analyzing wavelet function $\psi(t)$ is called the mother wavelet. Compared to the FT, the analyzing function of the wavelet transform does not need to be sine-form. A wavelet function $\psi(t)$ is a small wave, which must oscillate somehow to discriminate between different frequencies. The wavelet contains the analyzing shape and the window. Several functions have been developed for the Continuous Wavelet Transform (CWT) with specific properties [Mallat, 1999, Daubechies, 1992], as shown in Figure 4.7.

To classify an analyzing function as a wavelet, the following mathematical criteria must be met [Mallat, 1989, Mallat, 1999]:

1. A wavelet must have finite energy, as shown in Equation (4.11)

$$E = \int_{-\infty}^{\infty} |\psi(t)|^2 dt < \infty \qquad (4.11)$$

the energy E equals the integrated squared magnitude of the analyzing function and must not be infinity.

2. If $\Psi(f)$ is the FT of the wavelet $\psi(t)$, the following condition must hold, as shown in Equation (4.12)

$$C_\psi = \int_0^{\infty} \frac{|\Psi(f)|^2}{f} df < \infty \qquad (4.12)$$

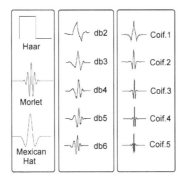

Figure 4.7: A few wavelet functions are presented as examples. However, there are plenty of wavelet functions for endless application. Some of them are the Mexican Hat (related to its shape), Haar, Daubechies or db (related to its designer's name), and Coiflet of Coif. (requested by Ronald Coiflet).

where C_ψ denotes the admissibility condition that depends only on ψ. This condition implies that the FT of $\psi(t)$ vanishes at the zero frequency, which entails that the average value of the wavelet in the time domain must be zero. The value of C_ψ is not the same for all wavelets.

3. For complex wavelets the FT $\Psi(f)$ must be both real and vanish for negative frequencies [Rioul and Vetterli, 1991b], [Lee and Schwartz, 1995].

The CWT is defined in Equation (4.13)

$$CWT(\tau, s) = \frac{1}{\sqrt{s}} \int_{-\infty}^{\infty} x(t) \psi^* \left(\frac{t - \tau}{s} \right) dt \qquad (4.13)$$

where $CWT(\tau, s)$ is transformed signal, τ is the translation parameter, and s is the scale parameter. ψ stands for the mother wavelet, and $*$ denotes the complex conjugate in the case of a complex wavelet. To guarantee that the wavelets keep the same energy at every scale, the signal energy must be normalized. To normalize it, the wavelet coefficients must be divided by $\frac{1}{\sqrt{|s|}}$ at every scale. Changing the scale parameter s stretches and expands the mother wavelet. This modifies the central frequency f_c of the wavelet and the window length. Therefore, the scale s replaces the frequency to represent the wavelet analysis results. The parameter τ modifies the wavelet's location in time. When τ is modified the wavelet is relocated over the signal. Fixing the scale s and changing translation τ, modifies the rows of the time-scale plane, but changing the scale s and fixing the translation τ alters the columns of the same plane. The wavelet coefficients are the elements in CWT (τ, s), all of them are associated with a scale or frequency, and a location in time ([Mallat, 1989, Daubechies, 1992]). To reverse the process the CWT has an inverse transformation. The Inverse Continuous Wavelet Transformation (ICWT) is defined in Equation (4.14)

$$x(t) = C_\psi^{-1} \int_0^{+\infty} \int_{-\infty}^{+\infty} CWT(\tau, s) \frac{1}{\sqrt{|s|}} \psi_{\tau,s}^* \left(\frac{t - \tau}{s} \right) \frac{d\tau ds}{s^2} \qquad (4.14)$$

the admissibility constant C_ψ must fulfill the second wavelet condition. The central frequency f_c of a wavelet function is inversely proportional to the specific scale s. Large scales mean low frequencies or general information about the signal, while small scales mean high frequencies or signal's detail. The CWT performs a multi-resolution analysis which analyzes a signal at different frequencies and times (time-frequency resolution). This multi-resolution analysis can also be achieved using filter banks.

4.2.5 Multi-resolution analysis

It is important to differentiate between Multi-Scale Analysis (MSA) and Multi-Resolution Analysis (MRA). Sometimes these terms are used as synonyms despite their differences. When referring to Scale, it has to do with sizes and proportions. For example, all images have dimensions, the total number of pixels along their width and height. Resolution is a degree of detail in a bitmap image, measured in pixels per inch (ppi). The maximum resolution of an image is reached when the pixels per inch match the size of the image in the lower dimension. Increasing the resolution beyond this point and having the image's size fixed would be like zooming in. Some well-known methods are the pyramid representation, an MSA, and the continuous wavelet transform (CWT), an MRA.

The definition of MRA are sequences of closed subspaces $\{V_j \subset L^2(\mathbb{R}) : j \in \mathbb{Z}\}$ that satisfy the following properties [Mallat, 1989]:

1. $...V_2 \subset V_1 \subset V_0 \subset V_{-1} \subset V_{-2} \subset ... \subset L^2(\mathbb{R})(i.e., V_j \subset V_{j-1})$;

2. $\cap_{j\in\mathbb{Z}}V_j = \{0\}, and, \overline{\cup_{j\in\mathbb{Z}}V_j} = L^2(\mathbb{R})$;

3. $\forall j \in \mathbb{Z}, x(t) \in V_j \Leftrightarrow x(2t) \in V_{j-1}$;

4. $\forall k \in \mathbb{Z}, x(t) \in V_0 \Rightarrow x(t-n) \in V_0$;

5. There exists a function $\phi(t) \in V_0$ such that $\phi_{j,n}(t) = 2^{-j/2}\phi(2^{-j}t - n) : j,n \in \mathbb{R}\}$ satisfies the stability condition $A \parallel x(t) \parallel^2 \leq \sum_{j\in\mathbb{Z}}\sum_{n\in\mathbb{Z}} | \langle x(t), \psi_{j,n}(t)\rangle |^2 \leq B \parallel x(t) \parallel^2$ and forms an orthonormal basis of V_0 where $A > 0$ and $B < \infty$ for all signals $x(t)$ in $L^2(\mathbb{R})$.

The following is an explanation of these properties. Property (1) describes the successive subspaces that represent the different scales or resolutions, property (2) ensures the completeness of these subspaces and that $lim_{j\to-\infty}x_j(t) = x(t)$. Property (3) describes that V_{j-i} comprises all rescaled versions of V_j, property (4) indicates that any translated version of a function shares the original's space. Finally, the property (5), denotes that the function $\phi(\bullet)$ is the scaling function in the MRA [Daubechies, 1992].

MRA approaches intend to have the best look at each level by varying frequency resolution, but this has some lateral effects. According to the Heisenberg uncertainty principle, frequency and time are both sides of the same coin, implying that increasing time resolution will decrease frequency resolution and vice versa. MRA is a series of successive approximations representing the signal at different levels of detail. Each level contains specific features' information of the signal. The signal is expressed at a particular resolution level by eliminating all higher-resolution information. While the resolution level increases, finer details are added to the signal until the same signal is recovered. In other words, local data is processed at high-resolution levels, where higher frequencies and short wavelengths are present. And global information is processed at low-resolution levels, using low frequencies and long wavelengths. And for complete processing of the signal, a cross-resolution technique can be used. Some advantages of multi-resolution representations are image compression and feature extraction, among other applications.

4.3 Related work

The number of cameras in major cities is exponentially growing and cannot be handled manually anymore. They need to be monitored permanently, 24 hours a day, every day. All images produced by those cameras need to be analyzed to find anything considered a potential risk or a condition that may require some action to report. Most of these situations happen at night or in places where the light is too low. To overcome such scenarios, the surveillance systems are equipped with IR technology. IR Technology is helpful to see during the day or in complete darkness and enables Toxic Gas Detection by Absorption Spectroscopy. It helps to avoid collisions or threats hidden in the fog or underneath the pathway. It is much better at spotting hidden objects. For example, a person hidden inside a cardboard box or behind some bushes cannot be seen with the naked eye, but it can be seen with IR technology. IR is better for camouflaged targets than night vision. A thermal can detect warm targets at a much greater distance. A high-end thermal can see warm-blooded animals in a field at or beyond 1,000 yards. Although, it is not possible to identify the animal kind.

However, IR images require filtering and more processing. Despite the ability to see in total darkness, it only produces one information channel at grayscale instead of the three color channels (Red-Green-Blue) of regular images. Additionally, all objects must be Detected, Recognized, and Identified (DRI) to find potentially dangerous things in an image, like vehicles, people, drones, or even wild animals.

These three concepts are references that have been established by The Night Vision Thermal Imaging Systems Performance Model, also referred to as the Johnson criteria [Chevalier, 2016]. They have become universally accepted standards. Initially, they were created by the US Army to provide a metric for the distance, whereby a thermal sensor can make a picture of a specific target [Bareła et al., 2013]. These criteria are defined as follows. Detection means that the objective is visible. It means that the target can be seen on at least two pixels, and there is a high probability that it is something of suspicion. Recognition is when the objective can be classify into a class (human, animal, vehicle, etc.). Identification of an object allows you to differentiate two objects of the same kind (type of vehicle, its maker, its model, and even some particular characteristics like bumps, stamps, or distinctive scratches) [Chevalier, 2016]. The terms detection, recognition, and identification can be mistaken, especially by the public who do not have a military background. They are based on 1950s standards used for lower resolution CRT displays. Newer high-resolution digital sensors have change the perception of the magnitude of these measurements, but the standards remain.

Every helpful technology like the IR gives strong advantages, but it only comes along with some challenges. Even though CNNs are excellent at classifying objects, they can be improved using MRA to help its weakest layers to retain more and better details. The pooling layers are used to downsample the information within the network. However, a lot of information needs to be recovered in the process. In studies like [Malik et al., 2020] and [Li et al., 2019], the MRA is used to extract features to create an input image to feed the network for training, and the MRA is not part of the CNN. CNN has been helped by being provided with the key data. However, it needs to improve its internal feature extraction process and, therefore, its performance. Although they have simpler networks, these models have two or more stages. Some other studies like [Fujieda et al., 2018], [Fujieda et al., 2017] and [Ferrà et al., 2019] are models embedding the MRA into CNN. On the other hand, objects in IR images are difficult to detect and especially to classify due to many changing variables for the same thing in the thermal image. However, the CNN observes good performance when the image is large enough, and the training set is abundant in samples and object variety. If one of these issues is limited CNN needs other techniques to achieve the task. That is one of the main reasons to implement the MRA in CNN applied to IR imagery.

In summary, CNNs are excellent tools for classifying objects, but IR images are challenging. The proposed hybrid model includes a pre-processing block that cleans the IR images and enhances relevant characteristics before using the CNN. This model also incorporates a technique called Lifting Scheme within the CNN. The Lifting Scheme is an MRA that can perfectly fit within the CNN. The presented model serves as a pooling layer; therefore, to improve CNN's overall performance, the hybrid model must replace all pooling layers. The research reported by [Akula et al., 2017] is one of the first studies using CNN for detecting and classifying IR objects. In this approach, the central idea is to differentiate between the background and in-front objects. They create four categories: background, ambassador (luxury car), auto (small cars), and pedestrians. They adapted the architecture from LeNet-5 [LeCun et al., 1998] and used ten layers in their CNN. One issue to be highlighted is that they fixed the input images to 200×200 to obtain all the features they needed to perform the detection with high accuracy. A smaller image may not present the same results.

Another important research is reported in [d'Acremont et al., 2019], their model uses only twelve layers and classifies eight classes of military vehicles. There are few datasets for IR images available, and military datasets, most of the time, are restricted. The main contribution of this study is that they create synthetic datasets based on a small amount of real military IR images. After training the CNN, they tested its performance, and it achieved high accuracy levels for both real and synthetic datasets. The input image is smaller in other studies (128×128). This study pointed directly to one of the most important problems in developing the research field for civil applications. [Malik et al., 2020] propose a method to classify heart sounds. These signals help detect heart abnormalities. The dataset consists of five subsets one normal and four abnormal conditions. As a first step, this method cuts the audio signal every three heart cycles to produce numerous segments. Then it uses the CWT to generate 2D Images based on the frequencies found on each audio signal segment, the time when they appear, and their amplitude or intensity represented by a color scale. The reason is that CNN is designed to handle images and is very accurate in classifying them. Before they feed them into the CNN, the scalograms are resized to fit the input dimensions requirements. The input, as a Scalogram, has a lot of organized information in such a way that the CNN can be small to perform with high accuracy and simultaneously have a low computational cost. The CNN comprises five convolutional layers and three fully connected layers. It also utilizes some normalization, pooling layers, and Relu activation functions. In summary, CWT is not part of CNN. On the contrary, the CWT is used to create the input images to train the CNN. The CNN, as a final step and based on the training images, classifies the input into the five available categories.

Another method is presented by [Ölmez and Dokur, 2003] for classifying of seven heart sounds. The CWT using the Daubechies 2 (Haar) function wave is applied to extract features, forming vectors using the detail coefficients at six decomposition levels. In this case, the signal is 1D, and they do not require a CNN; instead, they used a Grow-and-Learn (GAL) algorithm. The GAL is an incremental algorithm that makes a growing network for supervised learning. The GAL has advantages like fast training, implementation simplicity, better performance over other networks, and the number of nodes in the hidden layers is automatically determined during the training. When it learns, this network grows and changes its structure dynamically (categories, nodes, and weights). Also, [Gupta et al., 2005] conducted a similar study with two main differences. They used the wavelet transform to extract features from only two decomposition levels. The other difference is that only three classes of heart sounds were classified. In both studies, the features extracted using the wavelet transform were easily separable into the desired classes that no other technique like Mel-frequency Cepstrum was needed. Besides, this advantage also allowed the use of a smaller network for 1D to reduce computational costs and achieve a simpler and more practical model.

The investigation reported by [Fortuna-Cervantes et al., 2020] evaluates a learning model in the aerial navigation of a drone detecting one sort of object (obstacle) to be able to avoid it. They propose two models, one without image preprocessing and the other based on 2D discrete wavelet transform (2D-DWT). However, in this application, the main use of the wavelet transform is to reduce the image until it can go through the small CNN input. It only uses the approximation coefficients extracted with the wavelet function Haar. And to fit the input size of the CNN, it applies three decomposition levels.

Additionally, the wavelet transform is applied to each one of the three color channels (Red-Green-Blue) to keep color images as inputs. The CNN consists of four convolutions, four max pooling, and three fully connected layers ending with a binary classification class, images with or without texture cube. This cube is part of an image plane for navigation in simulated environments. The results show that the model using the 2D-DWT presents an improvement over the raw model. The author points out some of the advantages of the MRA and its ability to retain some details using the frequency domain.

The works reported by [Williams and Li, 2016] and [Williams and Li, 2018a] use Convolutional Neural Networks (CNN) to classify objects in four benchmark datasets. They propose two methods for decomposing the images on one level using the fast wavelet transform. The first model decomposes pictures into the four wavelet coefficients. These four coefficients are used independently, one by one, and are applied as input to the CNN. Every trained CNN is used to generate an output vector. Once all four vectors are obtained, an OR operator is applied to get the classification. The second model is similar but leaves the approximation coefficients alone while combining the three detail coefficients. Each detail coefficient is multiplied by a different scalar to normalize them, then all three are added as a single input image. Each scalar was obtained during the testing stage of the first model. Just like the first model, the results are used as inputs to generate a classification vector. In this case, two vectors are generated for the OR operator to obtain the final result. Although the first model shows relevant results, the computational cost is high, and each coefficient has to go through the CNN in a sequence, not in parallel. In this study, the preprocessing of the input data is different, and for example, they normalized IR images to help the CNN to recognize features and to increase the convergence speed, according to Equation 4.15

$$X_{new} = \frac{X_{old} - m}{SD} \tag{4.15}$$

where X_{new} is the normalized pixel value, X_{old} is the initial pixel value, m is the mean value of the pixel from the image, and SD is the standard deviation of pixels.

All the studies mentioned above use the wavelet transform to prepare the input signal for the CNN as a previous stage. They modify the inputs to make them easier to extract features using the MRA as a pre-processing tool. The MRA is not part of any CNN layer for the group of studies already mentioned. However, it is essential for each model. The study [Williams and Li, 2018b] introduces the use of wavelets directly as a pooling layer. Their model, named Wavelet Pooling for Convolutional Neural Networks, uses the fast wavelet transform (FWT) algorithm. Although it uses the second level of decomposition, it decomposes the coefficients to the first level again, and then the pooling method downsamples the data by half. This increases the computational cost of the model. Every time a pooling layer is used in the CNN, it affects the overall performance. On the other hand, this method increases the accuracy compared with the traditional techniques (maximum, average, mixed, and stochastic pooling methods) by testing four benchmark classification datasets. It reduces features more structurally, not just by neighborhood regions. Another breakthrough was made by [Bastidas-Rodriguez et al., 2020], this study not only incorporates the wavelet transform within the CNN but also uses an implementation of the lifting scheme, which has more advantages in fitting as another layer or layers set. This study also generates a wavelet design to learn the optimal wavelet coefficients and configuration. This is done automatically during the training stage of the CNN. This study served as the base and inspiration for the approach reported in this chapter.

The research models combining CNN with MRA keep creating combinations inspired by CNN breakthroughs. For instance, the solution proposed by [Fujieda et al., 2018] and [Fujieda et al., 2017] is similar to the residual net in the sense that it utilizes the wavelet to skip the pooling layer and then concatenate it again; however, in this case, more convolutional layers are required to match sized between the wavelet output with the mainstream of the CNN. This hybrid method eliminates the use of traditional pooling layers by applying both techniques, high-stride convolutional layers and wavelet transform as parallel layers. Combing these techniques allows for saving key features and details to improve the accuracy of the CNN. On the other hand, it significantly increases the computational cost, first for the wavelet decomposition process (even though only the approximations coefficient is used), then the parallel paths to process, and finally for additional convolutional layers needed to match both data branches.

4.4 Proposed approach

The related works previously presented have in common that their solutions are based on CNN, which is widely applied to extract features and classify classes. But either they have a previous stage using MRA, or they replace a layer or a function completely with an MRA implementation. The latter has a high computational cost. Nevertheless, feature extraction is known to be the trouble's core. As a result, some new approaches combine more than one technique to extract better features to improve CNN results. The most suitable MRA solution for the CNN is the lifting scheme. This method was already presented in some related studies and is the base for the proposed model. In this sense, reviewing this analysis before going deeper into the proposed model is essential.

4.4.1 The lifting scheme

Since the lifting scheme is an MRA, its applications goes from designing wavelets to applying the DWT. It uses the same scaling function to keep a simple relationship with the MRA. Then by fulfilling the biorthogonal relations and isolating the degrees of freedom left, it has total control over the degrees of freedom to satisfy and design a wavelet function for a specific function. It also can speed up the fast wavelet transform. For these reasons, it is considered the second-generation wavelet transform. The lifting scheme applies convolutions rather than filters, reducing importantly the arithmetic operations required, demonstrated in [Sweldens, 1998] and [Daubechies and Sweldens, 1998]. The DWT utilizes filters dividing the signal by its composed frequencies. Contrarily the lifting scheme separates the input sequentially to form to sample groups the odds and the evens. Finally each group pass through some arithmetic operations, as shown in Figure 4.8. The general form of the lifting scheme was presented by [Sole and Salembier, 2007]. The original lifting scheme

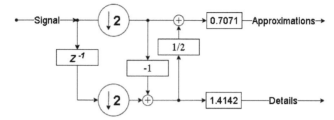

Figure 4.8: The lifting scheme decomposes a signal into two frequency subbands, low and high. Initially the signal is divided into odd and even sample groups Z^{-1}, where ($\downarrow$ 2) indicates that the number of elements of each sample group is reduced by half [Daubechies and Sweldens, 1998].

was transformed into a general form to solve some restrictions. It has the following four steps:

1. The signal is divided into two groups, odd and even. Therefore each group is downsampled by half ($\downarrow$ 2), as shown in Equations (4.16) and (4.17)

$$x_e[n] = x[2n] \tag{4.16}$$

$$x_o[n] = x[2n+1] \tag{4.17}$$

   where n is the discrete signal sample, x_e is the even sample group, x_o is the odd sample group.

2. The operator $P()$ is called prediction, it subtracts the odd from the even samples to obtain variations or details, as shown in Equation (4.18). The simplest case is the Haar wavelet function.

$$d[n] = x_o[n] + P(x_e[n]) \tag{4.18}$$

   where d are the obtained variations or detail coefficients. These coefficients contain high-frequency information.

3. The operator $U()$ is called update, it obtains average values between sample groups, as shown in Equation (4.19).

$$c[n] = x_e[n] + U(d[n]) \tag{4.19}$$

   where c are the average obtained between samples or approximation coefficients. These coefficients contain low-frequency information.

4. The last step normalizes both outputs multiplying them by $\sqrt{2}$ and $\frac{1}{\sqrt{2}}$, respectively.

To recover the original signal, the process need to reverse the order of the operations and change the signs.

The 2D version of the lifting scheme applies to images. The process used for the 1D version is repeated three times. The fist one as seen before separates the signal into low and high frequency subbands. The next two processes divide each output subband into low and high frequency subbands. At the end we obtain four groups (low-Low, Low-High, High-Low, and High-High). The first stage divides the image in one direction (horizontal), while the second divides it in the other direction (vertical). The following are the steps for the 2D version of the lifting scheme [Daubechies and Sweldens, 1998]:

1. Each subband of the first stage is divided into odd and even sample groups in the second stage, as shown in Equations (4.20) to (4.23).

$$d_{even}[n] = d[2n] \tag{4.20}$$

$$d_{odd}[n] = d[2n+1] \tag{4.21}$$

$$c_{even}[n] = c[2n] \tag{4.22}$$

$$c_{odd}[n] = c[2n+1] \tag{4.23}$$

where d_{even} are the even and d_{odd} are odd sample groups obtained from the detail coefficients, while c_{even} are the even and c_{odd} are odd sample groups obtained from the approximation coefficients.

2. The prediction operator is applied in Equations (4.24) and (4.25) for the vertical direction.

$$HH[n] = d_{odd}[n] + P(d_{even}[n]) \tag{4.24}$$

$$LH[n] = c_{odd}[n] + P(c_{even}[n]) \tag{4.25}$$

where HH is the high-high frequency and LH is the low-high frequency coefficients.

3. The update operator is applied in Equations (4.26) and (4.27) for the vertical direction.

$$HL[n] = d_{even}[n] + U(HH[n]) \tag{4.26}$$

$$LL[n] = c_{even}[n] + U(LH[n]) \tag{4.27}$$

where HL is the high-low frequency and LL is the low-low frequency coefficients.

4. The operator $N1$ and $N2$ are used to normalize the low and high-frequency subbands multiplying them by $\sqrt{2}$ and $\frac{1}{\sqrt{2}}$, accordingly.

The four sets of coefficients obtained at the end of the decomposition process are known as approximations (LL), verticals (HL), horizontals (LH), and diagonals (HH), as shown in Figure 4.9. As mentioned before, the previous example is for the Haar wavelet function only. There are several wavelet functions, and each one

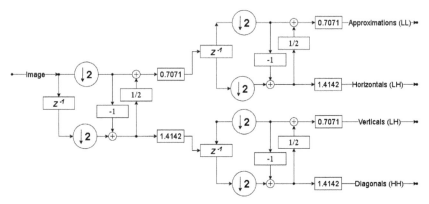

Figure 4.9: The 2D lifting scheme for the Haar function case decomposes an image into four subbands. The subband are known as approximations (LL), horizontals (LH), verticals (HL), and diagonals (HH).

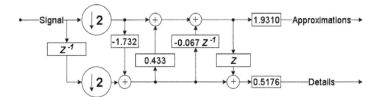

Figure 4.10: The lifting scheme for the Daubechies 4 (Db4) contrarily to the Haar case, is more complex and requires more operations [Daubechies and Sweldens, 1998].

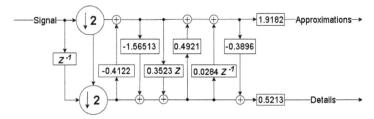

Figure 4.11: Lifting scheme for the Daubechies 6 (Db6) similar to the Db4 case, but the degree of complexity is even higher [Daubechies and Sweldens, 1998].

have different characteristics that can be useful for a specific application. Two more wavelet functions of the same family were implemented for this study.

Figure 4.10 shows the lifting scheme for the Daubechies 4 (Db4). Regardless of the wavelet function, the lifting scheme always initiates separating the samples in odd and even by the operator Z^{-1}. Due to this separation, each group of samples are half-sized. Therefore the symbol ($\downarrow 2$) is used to indicate it as downsampling the signal by 2. The addition operators are used. For software reasons the subtraction is made using the addition operator and its negative scalar. This case also takes previous samples, indicated by the operator Z, and future samples, indicated by operator Z^{-1}. The lifting scheme for the Daubechies 6 (Db6) is shown in Figure 4.11. The process is very similar to the DB4 case. However, this wavelet function is more complex and requires more operations. All the variables and parameters were calculated, established and confirmed in other studies like in [Daubechies and Sweldens, 1998].

4.4.1.1 Random wavelet pooling model

The proposed model was used as a first experiment, a random model.

This study [Treviño-Sanchez and Alarcon-Aquino, 2021] randomly selects one of the four sets of wavelet transform coefficients on every iteration. It also incorporates the Lifting Scheme, a second-generation of MRA in a formal model as a pooling layer inside the CNN. The general idea is to emulate the Max-pooling effect that prevents the CNN from overfitting. During this research, it was observed that the max-pooling has a changing behavior in the frequency spectrum.

The initial hypothesis was that max-pooling acts like a dynamic filter, changing from a low-pass filter to a high-pass filter, then to a band-pass filter and so on (in all cases, the filter was irregular). However, the amplitude is positive, like an amplifier. Finally, it was determined that max-pooling was creating an increasing effect with the signal's harmonics. In other words, the max-pooling effect depended on the signal. The shape and frequencies trigger the non-linear behavior that makes max-pooling popular for preventing overfitting. However, if the signal characteristics are little or not enough to stimulate this effect, then the result for the CNN may constantly be overfitting obtaining poor results. For this reason, to create a model that emulates the max-pooling nonlinear effect without depending on the signal. The MRA was chosen to reduce dimensions like a pooling layer, and at the same time all four coefficient sets obtained from the wavelet transform were ready to add up with their features. The approximations set (LL) was fixed in all cases since it keeps most of the input energy. One of the other three coefficient sets was selected randomly to produce a limited dynamic filter. The complete model is shown in Figure 4.12. Seven pooling methods, including the proposed model, are tested to validate this study using three different wavelet functions and one benchmark dataset. The results are compared

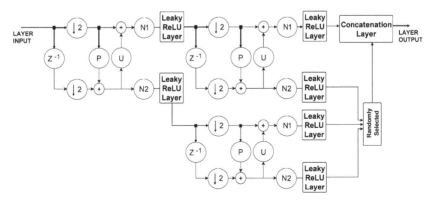

Figure 4.12: Random Model embedded in the CNN replaces pooling layers approaching to emulate the Max-pooling effect [Treviño-Sanchez and Alarcon-Aquino, 2021].

with five of the most used pooling methods, which are also considered state-of-the-art. Although it reaches similar numbers to traditional pooling techniques, it also has a high computational cost.

4.4.1.2   Hybrid wavelet pooling model

As a second experiment, a new study presenting a hybrid solution was performed by [Treviño-Sanchez and Alarcón-Aquino, 2022]. It proposes a pooling method that mixes a standard pooling method with the MRA within the CNN. The model is a new pooling layer to reduce the feature map size without losing details. It combines in parallel the max-pooling layer, which is the standard pooling method most commonly used, and the 2D Lifting Scheme, considered a second generation of MRA. Placing these two methods together does not add much computational cost compared to other studies. However, they achieve better quality characteristics that in consequence, improve CNN accuracy. The model is constructed based on blocks to forms a network layer that replaces each pooling layer inside the CNN. It is built of two lifting scheme architectures, as presented in Figure 4.13. The lifting scheme has the advantage of being very suitable as a CNN layer. Even when reducing dimensionality the space and frequency information is preserved. Its mathematical operations are few and simple to calculate.

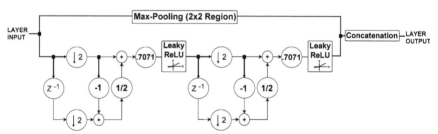

Figure 4.13: The proposed pooling method mixes the max-pooling technique and the 2D lifting scheme. They are connected in parallel forming a single pooling layer embedded in the CNN. This model uses the lifting scheme for the Haar function, although it only requires the LL coefficients [Treviño-Sanchez and Alarcón-Aquino, 2022].

As explained in the theoretical background, the lifting scheme includes a downsampling process. However, there is no information loss at this point, and it is only a notation to indicate that the signal is divided into odd and even sample groups. For the Haar wavelet function, the operator P obtains the differences between the two sample groups to form the details, while the operator U calculates the arithmetic mean to generate the approximations. This is done twice since the images going through the CNN are 2D signals. The parameter N1 is just for normalization. The model also uses the activation function layers called leakyReLU to connect the lifting output to the concatenation layer. This activation function also keeps negative values from vanishing without giving them much weight. At the same time, the max-pooling looks for the largest magnitude of the region to simply it. A 2 × 2 pooling region, and a 2 × 2 stride, with no padding are considered. It is well-known that max-pooling loses some information but retains some frequency details. Max-pooling behavior improves CNN's accuracy and prevents it from overfitting, which is the main reason it is included in the model.

The last experiment used an IR benchmark dataset known as FLIR for training and testing. This research uses the hybrid pooling method proposed in the study [Treviño-Sanchez and Alarcón-Aquino, 2022] to replace each pooling layer. The IR dataset images are used to extract the different-sized objects and resized to 28x28 pixels in order to fit the small CNN input. As mentioned, the MRA helps CNN keep essential features to improve its performance. Additionally, the accuracy of each case classifying IR objects are measured, as well as the performance of the CNN related to the original size of the IR objects. However, this has yet to be tested in IR images, mainly because of the previously mentioned challenges. This procedure allows increasing the number of samples to train the CNN and to handle all different objects in a unique format. By doing this, the CNN can be specialized on the object features rather than their size.

4.4.2 Experimental setup

Four benchmark datasets comprising RGB images were used for training and testing the models. This tests not only establish that the proposed wavelet model is improves the CNN performance and the effect of using different wavelet function. However, the model was validated and measured using three information channels datasets. To conclude the experiment a IR dataset with only one data channel and all related challenges is needed. This last part of the experiment is to determine the accuracy level the CNN can reach with all the limitations related to IR images, and to establish if there is a specific wavelet (among the three wavelet functions) that improves CNN performance. All experiments used MATLAB® R2020b& Deep Learning Toolbox, and the CNN utilized was the MatConvNet, which is also reported in [Williams and Li, 2018b]. All are trained using stochastic gradient descent, the initial learning rate of 0.001, minibatch of 64, and 20 max epochs. All tests are run on a 64-bit operating system (windows 10). The core was an AMD RYZEN 7 4800H series with Radeon Graphics @ 2.90 GHZ, with 16.0 GB RAM. And the GPU utilized was an NVIDIA GEFORCE GTX 1050.

The first one is the MNIST dataset [LeCun and Cortes, 2010], it contains color images of handwritten single digits divided into ten classes, and their size is 28x28 pixels. The training set comprises 60,000 images, and the testing set of 10,000 images. The network structure used for this dataset is made of four convolutions, three normalizations, one ReLU, one softmax, one classification, and two pooling.

The second dataset is KDEF [Goeleven et al., 2008]. It contains the emotional faces of 70 people between 20 and 30 years old, half females and half males. There are seven emotions (afraid, angry, disgusted, happy, neutral, sad, and surprised) and five poses (full left and right profiles, half left and right profiles, and straight). The color images were modified to fit 128x128 pixels and reduce computational cost. The CNN is configured for seven classes, and the CNN layers architecture is formed by five convolutions, four normalizations, four ReLU, two dropouts, one softmax, one classification, and four pooling. The dropout layers were used to prevent the network from overfitting.

The third dataset is CIFAR-10 [Krizhevsky, 2009], it has 10 classes of different objects: airplane, automobile, bird, cat, deer, dog, frog, horse, ship, and truck. The color images are 32x32 pixels. The training set has 50,000 images and testing set 10,000 images.

The fourth dataset is SVHN [Netzer et al., 2011], it also has ten classes, but it is made of street view house numbers (SVHN), one class for each digit. The training set comprises 73,257 digits, the testing test of 26,032, and the validation set of 30,000. The color image size is 32x32 pixels. Both CNN architectures for CIFAR-10 and SVHN are almost the same. They are formed by: five convolutions, three normalizations, four ReLU, two dropouts, one softmax, one classification, and three pooling. The difference is that CIFAR-10 uses 32 filters in the first 3 convolution blocks and 64 in the fourth convolution block, while SVHN uses 64 and 128.

The last dataset is the FLIR [Teledyn-FLIR, 2019] includes $8,861$ IR images containing $9,695$ IR objects. The four classification classes are people, bicycles, cars, and dogs. The original size of the IR images is 640x512 pixels. However, in this study, the image size used is 28x28 pixels. The CNN is a small CNN constituted by the following layers: four convolutional, two pooling, one ReLU, one softmax, and one classification.

4.5   Results and discussion

Ten pooling methods, including the proposed model, are tested using four benchmark datasets. The results are reduced to compare the best five evaluated methods. The pooling methods considered in Tables 4.1 to 4.4 are the five most relevant: Average (Avg), Maximum (Max.), the LL output of the lifting scheme (Lift.), lifting scheme LL coefficients concatenated with the Average pooling, and lifting scheme LL coefficients concatenated with the Max-pooling. Two standard methods are also considered state-of-the-art.

The first experiments' results are concentrated in Tables 4.1 to 4.4. The percentage in the first table shows the accuracy of the models classifying the MNIST dataset, the second refers to CIFAR-10 dataset, the third is about the SVHN dataset, and the last one reports the results for the KDEF dataset. They have organized one method per column and one wavelet function per row. Three wavelet functions with different vanishing moments were used: Haar, Daubechies 4, and Daubechies 6. In addition, the first row is for the model that does not use MRA. An asterisk indicates the proposed model.

The hybrid method reaches the highest accuracy value for the MNIST dataset using the Haar and the Daubechies 4 wavelet functions. For the CFAR-10 dataset, the result is the same, except that the method using only the approximations set coefficients (LL) with the Daubechies 4 also reaches the same highest value. If we observe wavelet methods without a max-pooling combination, the proposed method using random selection by 2×2 region is the most consistent and reaches the second-

Table 4.1: Accuracy results using the MNIST dataset.

Wavelet	Avg.	Max.	Lift.	Random	*Hybrid
None	98.7%	99.2%	-	-	-
Haar	-	-	99.2%	99.3%	99.4%
Daubechies 4	-	-	99.3%	99.3%	99.4%
Daubechies 6	-	-	99.3%	99.3%	99.2%
Proposed Model.					

Table 4.2: Accuracy results using the CIFAR-10 dataset.

Wavelet	Avg.	Max.	Lift.	Random	*Hybrid
None	74.7%	73.7%	-	-	-
Haar	-	-	74.7%	74.7%	74.8%
Daubechies 4	-	-	74.8%	74.7%	74.8%
Daubechies 6	-	-	74.7%	74.7%	74.7%
Proposed Model.					

Table 4.3: Accuracy results using the SVHN dataset.

Wavelet	Avg.	Max.	Lift.	Random	*Hybrid
None	88.2%	87.9%	-	-	-
Haar	-	-	88.0%	88.1%	88.2%
Daubechies 4	-	-	88.1%	88.1%	88.2%
Daubechies 6	-	-	88.1%	88.1%	88.0%
Proposed Model.					

Table 4.4: Accuracy results using the KDEF dataset.

Wavelet	Avg.	Max.	Lift.	Random	*Hybrid
None	76.3%	75.4%	-	-	-
Haar	-	-	74.1%	74.2%	76.3%
Daubechies 4	-	-	74.1%	74.2%	74.2%
Daubechies 6	-	-	74.2%	74.2%	74.1%
Proposed Model.					

highest accuracy. The hybrid model with max-pooling goes the highest accuracy (99.4%), but as explained before, this may change drastically using different datasets since max-pooling is signal dependable. On the contrary, the random model reaches the second-highest values but is consistently invariant to signal effects. The last test results are concentrated in Table 4.5. Three rows are used for the wavelet functions: Haar, Daubechies 4, and Daubechies 6. In addition, one row for the max-pooling model alone does not use MRA. All the models are tested for the FLIR dataset [Teledyn-FLIR, 2019].

The hybrid model is suitable for IR objects and reaches good accuracy levels. However, the FLIR dataset is composed of IR images that are one-gray channels; as mentioned before, details are difficult to obtain. In this case, the three wavelet

Table 4.5: Accuracy results using the FLIR dataset.

Wavelet	Hybrid
Max-Pool	96.1%
Haar	96.0%
Daubechies 4	95.6%
Daubechies 6	96.0%

function belongs to the same family. The results indicate little or no difference among the details extracted by the Haar and the Db6 wavelet functions. In contrast, the Db4 extracts fewer useful details than the others. Finally, the max-pooling has a marginal decimal over the closest wavelet, a statistical tie. Also, the CNN used is intended to be small to reduce computational costs and limited to small objects. CNN's small number of kernels retains fewer features and patterns than others. These small CNN work fine for color images (Red, Green, and Blue) but they are unsuitable for IR images.

4.6 Conclusions and future work

This chapter presented diverse approaches to applying MRA to strengthen CNNs. Some of them prepare the input data to be more detectable and classifiable, while others use different types of wavelet transforms looking to improve the CNN feature extraction process. Also, IR image challenges and how some studies focus on critical issues to solve them were mentioned. Finally, five experiments were presented; the first emulates the max-pooling method by randomly selecting the detail coefficient set and concatenating it with the approximations coefficients set. This approach was based on the idea that the max-pooling acted as a dynamic filter. The main advantage of this model was its independence of the signal shape or sample values, and it does not depend on the max-pooling in any part of the model. Although the max-pooling model resulted in an amplified harmonic stimulus, the model's behavior reached close values. The other model used a hybrid combination and has lower computational costs and high accuracy levels, although it incorporates max-pooling as part of it. It is important to mention that the only optimizer used in this study was the stochastic gradient descent. It was important to maintain all CNN variables constants as much as possible to prove that all differences were caused by the only variation, different pooling approaches. Once the best pooling method was established, other parameters like the CNN optimizer may be improved.

In future studies, bigger CNNs and larger images will be needed to take advantage of the hybrid model and to have clearer evidence about the differences in the model's performance. Furthermore, implementing three different wavelet functions allows one to complete more comparative tests to find better results. They also open the door to implementing even more wavelet functions to fit particularly into the required applications. Additionally, using heuristic methods may be more effective for some processes than a CNN with high computational costs. Just to mention one of them, the process to find regions of interest may be suitable for that purpose.

References

Akula, A., Singh, A., Ghosh, R., Kumar, S., and Sardana, H. 2017. Target Recognition in Infrared Imagery Using Convolutional Neural Network, volume 460, pp. 25–34. Springer Singapore.

Axis-Communications. 2018. IR in surveillance Day-and-night cameras and Optimized IR. White Paper, Sweden.

Bareła, J., Kastek, M., Firmanty, K., and Trzaskawka, P. 2013. Determining the range parameters of observation thermal cameras on the basis of laboratory measurements. Proceedings of SPIE - The International Society for Optical Engineering, 8541.

Bastidas-Rodriguez, M., Gruson, A., Polanía, L., Fujieda, S., Prieto-Ortiz, F., Takayama, K. et al. 2020. Deep adaptive wavelet network. IEEE Winter Conference on Applications of Computer Vision, pp. 3100–3108.

Chevalier, P. 2016. On the specification of the DRI requirements for a standard nato target. OIP Sensor Systems.

d'Acremont, A., Fablet, R., Baussard, A., and Quin, G. 2019. CNN-based target recognition and identification for infrared imaging in defense systems. Sensors, 19(9).

Daubechies, I. 1992. Ten lectures on wavelets. Society for Industrial and Applied Mathematics, pp. 350.

Daubechies, I., and Sweldens, W. 1998. Factoring wavelet transforms into lifting steps. The Journal of Fourier Analysis and Applications, 4(3): 247–269.

Ferrà, A., Aguilar, E., and Radeva, P. 2019. Multiple wavelet pooling for CNNS. European Conference on Computer Vision 2018 Workshops.

Fortuna-Cervantes, J., Ramírez-Torres, M., Martínez-Carranza, J., Murguía-Ibarra, J., and Mejía-Carlos, M. 2020. Object detection in aerial navigation using wavelet transform and convolutional neural networks: A first approach. Programming and Computer Software, 46(8): 536–547.

Fujieda, S., Takayama, K., and Hachisuka, T. 2017. Wavelet convolutional neural networks for texture classification. Computing Research Repository.

Fujieda, S., Takayama, K., and Hachisuka, T. 2018. Wavelet convolutional neural networks. Computing Research Repository.

Gabor, D. 1946. Theory of communication. Journal of the IEEE, 93(26): 429–457.

Goeleven, E., Raedt, R. D., Leyman, L., and Verschuere, B. 2008. The karolinska directed emotional faces: A validation study (kdef). Cognition and Emotion, 22: 1094–1118.

Gupta, C., Palaniappan, R., and Swaminathan, S. 2005. Classification of homomorphic segmented phonocardiogram signals using grow and learn network.

He, K., Zhang, X., Ren, S., and Sun, J. 2016. Deep residual learning for image recognition. IEEE Conference on Computer Vision and Pattern Recognition, pp. 770–778.

Kristan, M., Matas, J., Leonardis, A., Vojir, T., Pflugfelder, R., Fernandez, G. et al. 2016. A novel performance evaluation methodology for single-target trackers. IEEE Transactions on Pattern Analysis and Machine Intelligence, 38(11): 2137–2155.

Krizhevsky, A. 2009. Learning multiple layers of features from tiny images. Canadian Institute for Advanced Research (CIFAR).

Krizhevsky, A., Sutskever, I., and Hinton, G. E. 2012. Image net classification with deep convolutional neural networks. Advances in Neural Information Processing Systems, 25(2).

Larkin, P. J. 2011. IR and Raman Spectroscopy, Principles and Spectral Interpretation. Elsevier, Oxford.

LeCun, Y., and Cortes, C. 2010. Mnist handwritten digit database. National Institute of Standards and Technology.

LeCun, Y., Bottou, L., Bengio, Y., and Haffner, P. 1998. Gradient-based learning applied to document recognition. Proceedings of the IEEE, 86: 2278–2323.

Lee, C., Gallagher, P., and Tu, Z. 2018. Generalizing pooling functions in convolutional neural networks: Mixed, gated, and tree. IEEE Transactions on Pattern Analysis and Machine Intelligence, 40(4): 863–875.

Lee, N., and Schwartz, S. 1995. Linear time-frequency representations for transient signal detection and classification. Department of Electrical Engineering, Princeton University, Technical Report, 23.

Li, F., Liu, M., Zhao, Y., Kong, L. L., Dong, X. L., and Hui, M. 2019. Feature extraction and classification of heart sound using 1D convolutional neural networks. EURASIP Journal on Advances in Signal Processing, pp. 1–1.

Liao, L. -J., Lin, M. -H., Chen, C., and Chen, Y. -S. 2019. Thyroid nodule diagnosis system based on the densely connected convolutional network. Conference: Applications of Digital Image Processing XLII.

Malik, A. F., Barin, S., and Yuksel, M. 2020. Accurate classification of heart sound signals for cardiovascular disease diagnosis by wavelet analysis and convolutional neural network: Preliminary results. 28th Signal Processing and Communications Applications Conference, pp. 1–4.

Mallat, S. 1989. A theory for multiresolution signal decomposition: The wavelet representation. IEEE Transactions on Pattern Analysis and Machine Intelligence, 11(7): 674–693.

Mallat, S. 1999. A Wavelet Tour of Signal Processing. Academic Press, Cambridge, Massachusetts.

Netzer, Y., Wang, T., Coates, A., Bissacco, A., Wu, B., and Ng, A. 2011. Reading digits in natural images with unsupervised feature learning (svhn). NIPS Workshop on Deep Learning and Unsupervised Feature Learning.

Nielsen, M. 2015. Neural Networks and Deep Learning. Determination Press, San Francisco, CA, USA.

Ölmez, T., and Dokur, Z. 2003. Classification of heart sounds using an artificial neural network. Pattern Recognition Letters, 24(1-3): 617–629.

Rioul, O. and Vetterli, M. 1991a. Wavelets and signal processing. IEEE Signal Processing Magazine, pp. 14–38.

Rioul, O. and Vetterli, M. 1991b. Wavelets and signal processing. IEEE Signal Processing, pp. 14–38.

Simonyan, K. and Zisserman, A. 2014. Very deep convolutional networks for large-scale image recognition. Computing Research Repository Arxiv.

Sole, J. and Salembier, P. 2007. Generalized lifting prediction optimization applied to lossless image compression. IEEE Signal Processing Letters, 14(10): 695–698.

Sweldens, W. 1998. The lifting scheme: A construction of second generation wavelets. Siam Journal on Mathematical Analysis, 29(2): 511–546.

Szegedy, C., Liu, W., Jia, Y., Sermanet, P., Reed, S., Anguelov, D. et al. 2015. Going deeper with convolutions. IEEE Conference on Computer Vision and Pattern Recognition, pp. 1–9.

Teledyn-FLIR. 2019. Flir Thermal Starter Dataset Introduction Version 1.3. Teledyn FLIR, Oregon, USA.

Treviño-Sanchez, D. and Alarcon-Aquino, V. 2021. Random wavelet coefficients pooling for convolutional neural networks. 4to. Coloquio de Tecnología, Ciencia y Cultura: una visión global, Universidad de las Americas Puebla, Mexico.

Treviño-Sanchez, D. and Alarcón-Aquino, V. 2022. Hybrid pooling with wavelets for convolutional neural networks. Journal of Intelligent and Fuzzy Systems, 42(5): 4327–4336.

Voulodimos, A., Doulamis, N., Doulamis, A., and Protopapadakis, A. 2018. Deep learning for computer vision: A brief review. Computer Intelligence Neuroscience, pp. 1–13.

Williams, T., and Li, R. 2016. Advanced image classification using wavelets and convolutional neural networks. 15th IEEE International Conference on Machine Learning and Applications, pp. 233–239.

Williams, T., and Li, R. 2018a. An ensemble of convolutional neural networks using wavelets for image classification. Journal of Software Engineering and Applications, 11: 69–88.

Williams, T., and Li, R. 2018b. Wavelet pooling for convolutional neural networks.

Yu, D., Wang, H., Chen, P., and Wei, Z. 2014. Mixed pooling for convolutional neural networks. Rough Sets and Knowledge Technology, Lecture Notes in Computer Science, 8818: 364–375.

Zeiler, M., and Fergus, R. 2013. Stochastic pooling for regularization of deep convolutional neural networks. 1st International Conference on Learning Representations.

5

Image Dataset Augmentation
A Survey and Taxonomy

Sergey Nesteruk, Svetlana Illarionova and *Andrey Somov**

5.1 Introduction

Modern Computer Vision (CV) methods heavily rely on neural networks. Models based on convolutional and transformer blocks achieve state-of the-art performance on challenging tasks, including classification, semantic and instance segmentation, object and visual relationship detection, monocular depth estimation, and image reconstruction [He et al., 2016, Dosovitskiy et al., 2020]. One reason behind the rapid growth of neural-based solutions is in the advance of computational resources over last few decades. It allows for training larger models which are capable of recognising more complex patterns [Brown et al., 2020]. Another essential underlying condition is in the accessibility of training data from which the patterns can be retrieved [Birhane and Prabhu,]. Figure 5.1 shows the typical relation between accuracy and the amount of available training data.

From a practical standpoint, the development of neural model architectures has reached a point when a considerable amount of effort gives a small improvement for most of the common problems [Nesteruk et al., 2022]. The lack of training data, on the contrary, remains the crucial difficulty [Sun et al., 2017, Nesteruk et al., 2021b].

In this chapter, we comprehensively review image dataset augmentation approaches. More precisely, we describe a number of techniques helping extend the number of training samples.

We introduce the reader to the relevance of the deep learning approach for computer vision. First, we discuss the typical problems it helps to address, then switch

Skolkovo Institute of Science and Technology Russia.
* Corresponding author: a.somov@skoltech.ru

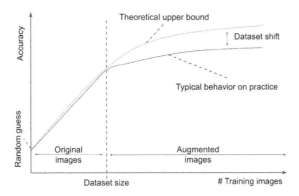

Figure 5.1: The typical dependence of accuracy from the dataset size.

to the specifics of the data and present the model architectures. After familiarizing the reader with the key definitions, we discuss image augmentation and image dataset augmentation topics. Afterwords, we dig deeper into detail of image dataset augmentation by providing the basics of augmentation, followed by the discussion of several augmentation techniques from different perspectives. To make the chapter practically feasible we cover a topic on implementation, i.e., which augmentation pipeline is best for a given issue. Each sample receives a single augmentation, which results in minimal variability and potential bias. Training data can become overly noisy when several augmentations are combined for each sample. A general strategy is to manually stack many augmentations with a defined range of magnitudes. We provide a reader with other options as well. Finally, we end with concluding remarks.

5.1.1 Deep Learning approach for Computer Vision

5.1.1.1 Computer Vision tasks

Deep learning is a rapidly growing technology. It involves advanced approaches for various tasks. Object recognition, scene understanding, and extraction of particular characteristics from images are one of the most frequently encountered application of deep learning for computer vision. Among the computer vision tasks, one can distinguish the most common problems including the object detection, image classification, object counting, as well as semantic and instance segmentation. Although neural network architectures can vary drastically for any specific problem, the fundamental point of difference among the problems is the way how a computer vision algorithm perceives input data. In supervised learning, the perception is determined by the target type. One can split target type by the strength of supervision into image-level, object-level, and pixel-level. In image classification problem, a single label is set for the entire image without any localization (Figure 5.2). Often, beyond image class estimation, one can consider a regression problem where an image is assigned with a single real number. For example, a problem of a fruit freshness estimation based on its photo or some product price estimation.

Figure 5.2: Original panda image.

Bounding boxes accompany the semantic label for each object in the object detection task. Another frequently occurring problem in computer vision is object counting, when instead of objects localization, the goal is to count individual instances within each image.

We can consider the semantic segmentation task by moving from an entire image to a single pixel. Semantic segmentation is a pixel-level task. In this regard, every pixel is set for a particular class, and the idea can consist of several target classes' masks. Another common example of pixel-level tasks is scene depth estimation. In this task, a continuous value is ascribed to each pixel. Pixel-level and object-level tasks can be combined. In instance segmentation task, one detects each distinct object and creates its mask simultaneously.

5.1.1.2 Computer Vision data

Computer vision techniques, and profound learning algorithms, help to reduce human labor, enhance performance, and speed up the processes in various domains. It poses challenges and encourages adjustment of approaches for particular tasks. However, only some fields are easily automated. Although there is almost the exact task definition in computer vision problems, each practical application has its specifics.

In this chapter, we use the terms *general-domain dataset*, *domain-specific dataset*, and *task-specific dataset* referring to the following definitions (Figure 5.3). General-domain datasets comprises common objects. Well-known examples of general-domain datasets include Imagenet [Deng et al., 2009], COCO [Lin et al., 2014], Pascal-VOC [Everingham et al., 2010], LAION [Schuhmann, 2022]. Imagenet consists of 1000 classes and includes more than 14 millions images. These datasets are often parsed from the Internet. For example, LAION dataset consists of 400 millions automatically annotated images using CLIP [Radford et al., 2021]. Imagenet is used for classification task, while PASCAL and COCO datasets are used for semantic segmentation, object detection. These datasets can be used for neural networks pre-training and further transferring for specific-domains datasets. It means that such data is usually large enough to train a model for extracting significant visual features and to improve prediction quality comparing with training from scratch. We usually do not use a distinct domain-specific datasets for ensuring a model pre-training and its consequent transfer to an-

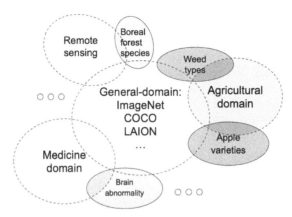

Figure 5.3: Example of general-domain datasets, domain-specific datasets, and task-specific datasets.

other specific- or general-domain datasets. However, if our target domain is close to some domain-specific dataset, this dataset can be more robust for transfer learning that a large general domain dataset [Mensink et al., 2021]. Often, domain-specific datasets require expert knowledge to markup data, for instance, when one works with medical images. That results in smaller labeled datasets comparing with case of general domain. Also, it usually requires special equipment for imaging, not only RGB cameras. General-domain and domain-specific datasets can intersect, although specific domains rarely overlap. In practice, when we solve an applied task, it has a very specific problem statement and unique context. Therefore, there is noticeable data shift between general-domain and task-specific datasets. Task-specific domain is partially nested in domain-specific datasets but with more unconventional problems. It results in necessity to collect a new dataset for an applied problem. Such datasets are usually smaller than both datasets from general domain and the entire specific domain to which it belongs. It can be formally expressed:

$$\Omega = \{I, T\}, \tag{5.1}$$

where I is the set of all possible images, T is the set of possible tasks.

$$\#(\Omega_T \cap \Omega_D) > \#(\Omega_T \cap \Omega_G), \tag{5.2}$$

where Ω_G is a general domain, Ω_D is a specific domain, Ω_T is a task-specific domain.

We can consider the following problem. We need to distinguish twenty apple varieties. Pre-training on such general-domain dataset as Imagenet will provide us with a better starting point than learning from scratch. It allows neural network model to extract basic features. However, Imagenet only includes a few examples of different fruits. A more specific agricultural dataset such as INaturalist [Van Horn et al., 2018], contains many fruit varieties, but it does not have sufficient number of target samples of specific classes. Therefore, INaturalist is helpful for model pre-training [Lemikhova et al., 2022], but additional dataset collection is vital.

In remote sensing domain, pretraining on a large dataset can be helpful, but adaptation and fine-tuning for a certain environmental conditions is necessary and it often requires additional data collection and labelling [Illarionova et al., 2021b].

Another difference between these domains is the data format and image characteristics. RGB image bands are usually considered in the general domain, although some specific domains involve a more comprehensive spectral range. Typically, in the remote sensing domain the multispectral satellite data with more than ten channels or hyperspectral imagery with hundreds channels [Illarionova et al., 2022b] is used. Medical image gathering includes different techniques, such as radiography, magnetic resonance imaging, etc., resulting in non-RGB data representation. 3D data frequently occurs in self-driving automobiles, health monitoring, and other applications [Georgiou et al., 2020]. Point cloud are also used to reconstruct surface in various task-specific applications, particularly, in remote sensing and environmental analysis [Tuominen et al., 2018].

Besides learning from multi-dimensional data, computer vision algorithms can gain knowledge from image-text representation. One can use images accompanied with text descriptions both for general and specific domains. LAION-400M is an example of general domain dataset collected from the Internet and filtered by CLIP. It can be used for various vision and language tasks. Example of more specific image-text dataset is Recipe1M+ [Marin et al., 2019] that includes cooking recipes and food images for computer vision models training.

5.1.1.3 Simplified scheme of Computer Vision model

Although, there are many various computer vision model architectures for different problems, in terms of data transformation within a model for the most of them we can rely on the following scheme. Typical model cutouts are:

- input image;

- intermediate representations;

- latent representation;

- output target.

Any of them can be considered for image dataset augmentation. Input image usually has three channels: red, green, blue. In some datasets it can be single grayscale channel. Sometimes in contains more that three channels for multi-spectral imagery. It is also possible to have auxiliary input data that can differ in resolution from the main RGB image. Regardless of the specific input combination and the way input data fuses inside a model, it is possible to augment this data before passing to a model. Most of the augmentations are applied at this stage. The main limitation at this point is to be aware of the spatial characteristics of data. If we change one channel's geometry, we should likely alter other media of all spatial modalities.

Inside a model, data passes through many layers of filters. Usually, deeper layers have more filters but lower spatial resolution. It may differ for the problems where

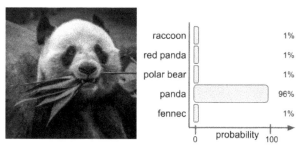

raccoon	1%
red panda	1%
polar bear	1%
panda	96%
fennec	1%

Figure 5.4: An example of label smoothing for the classification problem.

the target also has high resolution. We can apply image transformations to any intermediate layer that preserves spatial information [Chu et al., 2020]. This type of augmentation is relatively new and weakly studied [Kumar et al., 2020], and we recommend to be cautious with it. To add noise to a model moderately, it is better to lower the magnitude of geometrical transformations for the deeper layers. A very popular regularization technique that is applied to intermediate representations is called Dropout [Baldi and Sadowski, 2013]. One can consider it an augmentation because it randomly masks out different representation channels at every iteration and, thus, increases data diversity.

A special case of intermediate representation is an embedding vector. Here by an embedding, we mean a one-dimensional vector without spacial information usually obtained after the second last layer of a model [Ko and Gu, 2020]. It is easier to directly change the distribution of an embedding because it contains the most of semantic information and no spatial information [Abrishami et al., 2020]. It is the most natural to augment embeddings when using metric learning models. Interestingly, it is possible to apply augmentation to the latent space even if a problem requires spacial predictions [Du et al., 2021].

The last place to apply augmentation is the target itself. A simple example is label smoothing [Müller et al., 2019]. It overwrites the correct answer with the least confident version of it (Figure 5.4).

5.1.2 Image augmentation

It is a common practice to augment the training sets artificially for overcoming the limitation in the available training data. There are various ways to do it, and the main criteria of the successful augmentation is the increase of the model performance. A crucial part of a pipeline is model validation. A good practice is to assign the data into the following three parts: (i) training, (ii) validation, (iii) holdout. The first *training* subset is applied for a gradient calculation and weights update. The second *validation* subset is applied for checking the performance of model during the training process and for tuning the hyper-parameters. The holdout (aka. test) subset is used to declare model performance. In the few-shot learning pipelines one can apply cross-validation scheme [Browne, 2000].

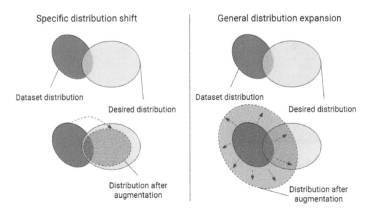

Figure 5.5: Influence of augmentation on data distribution.

Neural networks are supposed to work in real-life scenarios, on new data. But we need to test a model before deploying with the available training data. The critical assumption here, is that the distribution of data on inference should match the distribution of data in the holdout subset. If it is not valid, one should expect the model performance drop after the deployment [Moreno-Torres et al., 2012]. Therefore, it is important to remember that augmentation can be applied only to the training subset. If one augments the test data, the efficiency of a model can be overstated in the case it is trained using the identical type of augmentations.

By the influence on data distribution, we can distinguish two types of augmentation 5.5. The first aims for general distribution expansion, and the second adds a specific distribution shift. General distribution expansion is helpful in most of the applied cases. The concept behind it is that we do not know in advance how inference data distribution will differ from the test set. To compensate it, we try to cover all probable options. For example, if the training set consists only of good-quality images taken under the daylight conditions, but the inference light conditions can vary; it is a good idea to degrade image quality and randomly change brightness and contrast.

On the contrary, a specific distribution shift is applicable when a data scientist has domain-specific knowledge about model exploitation and can use it to fit the training set better. For example, we usually collect data for indoor agriculture datasets under daylight. However, a greenhouse will have phyto-light turned on most of the time. It changes the images significantly. Therefore, using image transformations that purple color photos can be sustainable.

Data augmentation is rather the art than the science. That is why it is not a trivial task to formally describe why does it work. We will show the intuition behind augmentation by referring to Figure 5.6. Suppose we have a function M (Equation 5.3) that maps an image to a latent vector so that the images with similar semantics have a smaller distance between the corresponding latent vectors than the images that are not similar. In that case, we can use this function to obtain the semantic distribution of our initial dataset. This function can be estimated by a model trained with metric

Figure 5.6: The idea behind image augmentation.

learning objective [Suárez et al., 2021]. However, we will assume that function M is an oracle that knows the semantics of any image regardless of the training data.

$$M : I \rightarrow E, \tag{5.3}$$

where I is the set of all possible images; E is the set of latent vectors (aka. embeddings).

Now we can introduce two distance functions. A function

$$D_v : I, I \rightarrow d_v, d_v \in \mathbb{R}, \tag{5.4}$$

measures visual distance between two images. It is also an oracle function that we assume to have. Function D_v must satisfy several conditions:

- $D_v(I_a, I_a) = 0$;

- $D_v(I_a, I_{\hat{a}}) < D_v(I_a, I_b)$,

where $I_a, I_{\hat{a}}$ are two different images of class A, and I_b is an image of class B.

Another distance function measures semantic difference between image embeddings:

$$D_s(e_1, e_2) = \frac{e_1 \cdot e_2}{\|e_1\| \|e_2\|} = d_s, e_1, e_2 \in E, d_s \in \mathbb{R}, \tag{5.5}$$

The semantic distance between latent vectors (and their corresponding images) is considered small if the ground truth labels for the current CV problem are the same for this data sample. Note that the semantics change depends on the problem. For instance, if our goal is to distinguish cats from dogs, a flipped copy of an image shares the same semantics with the original one. But if the goal is to determine the orientation, than any geometrical transformation changes the semantics.

Let us define an arbitrary image transformation function:

$$\tau : I, m \rightarrow \hat{I}, \tag{5.6}$$

where $m \in [0,1]$ is the transformation magnitude such that for every $m_1 < m_2, D_v(I_a, \tau(I_a, m_1)) < D_v(I_a, \tau(I_a, m_2))$.

To achieve better accuracy, one needs more training data. However, not all samples are equally useful. The same exact copy of an image contributes no extra information for a model.

Definition 5.1   Image augmentation is an image transformation that changes visual representation, but preserves original semantics.

A transformation must provide visually different results to obtain multiple informative copies of an image. Moreover, we want training samples not to be biased. For example, if a particular angle rotates all images or they have the same noise, a model will generalize poorly. Therefore, randomness is an important component of image augmentation.

5.1.3   Image dataset augmentation

One of the general definitions of image augmentation is the process of applying numerous alterations to original images in order to improve the diversity of training data. [Buslaev et al., 2020]. The critical observation is that it is assumed that the fresh samples are generated from the previously available data. However, there are efficient approaches beyond image augmentations via transformations that can improve a dataset. To overcome this terminology limitation, we introduce the term image dataset augmentation. Non-deterministic data manipulations performed to preprocess data before or during training are referred to as 'dataset augmentation'.

Definition 5.2   A group of methods known as 'dataset augmentation' are used to artificially enhance the quantity of data samples utilized in model inference or training.

It entails techniques like data collection, image augmentation, feature space manipulation, and others. Additionally, keep in mind that while augmentation is often employed for model training, some techniques may also be successfully utilized for test-time augmentation (TTA) [Shanmugam et al., 2021].

5.2   Image dataset augmentation primitives

In this section we describe the building block that are used to construct dataset augmentation pipelines. Figure 5.7 reflects the overall taxonomy of image dataset augmentation primitives.

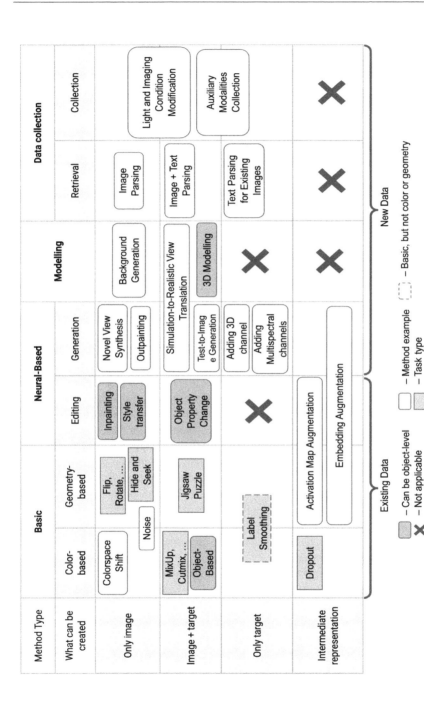

Figure 5.7: The taxonomy of image dataset augmentation primitives.

5.2.1 Basic augmentations

We use a very wide definition of basic augmentation. It is a single image augmentation that conduct transformations over existing samples and does not require sophisticated techniques. Example of original image and augmented image are shown in Figure 5.2 and Figure 5.8.

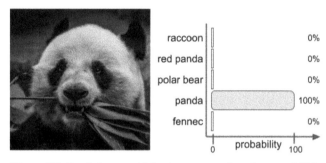

Figure 5.8: Panda image with basic augmentations (crop and flip).

5.2.1.1 Color transformations

Color transformations are frequently applied in various computer vision tasks. Different light conditions and variability of target object appearance make color transformations useful to extend training dataset. One can vary brightness, contrast, and saturation to get a modified image. RGB channels shifting or shuffling are another way how we can transform an original image. Such transformations usually do not corrupt the original labels of an image or its parts. Image plausibility with channel shifting augmentation depends on transformation magnitude, and slight changes while mixing can lead to a significant difference in actual image representation. A combination of color transformations produces a new previously unseen sample for a computer vision algorithm. Although such an approach enhances model generalization ability, it only provides less complex examples that usually occur in practice. Also, color transformations become less effective when a single band is considered or in case of multispectral data.

One can also implement random noise augmentation that distorts some pixels. Adding random noise to training data makes a neural network model less sensitive to particular features and more focused on the entire image semantics. It prevents memorizing training samples and reduces overfitting. Noise values can be generated from Gaussian (normal) distribution. Another noise example is Salt-and-pepper noise that is represented by black and white pixels. It was shown that neural network model trained with additive Gaussian and Speckle noise is capable of strong generalization to corrupted images [Rusak et al., 2020]. Speckle and Gaussian noise occur in various domain-specific datasets, such as medical ultrasound images [Sezer and Sezer, 2020] and remote sensing synthetic aperture radar data [Brisco et al., 2020]. Therefore, creating of robust models against this type of distortion is vital.

Besides RGB color space, one can consider the color model based on Hue, Saturation, Value (HSV). In the scope of this model *hue* refers to an actual pure color, *saturation* represents color intensity, *value* defines illumination level. Real-world objects are often affected by illumination conditions, shadows, etc. HSV color space provides an opportunity to work with a primary color. It can be helpful in some CV tasks to reduce illumination variations. In remote sensing domain, advantage of HSV model over conventional RGB color-space representation was declared in [Ganesan and Rajini, 2014] for satellite image segmentation. In medical domain, HSV image representation improved the brain magnetic resonance images segmentation [Singh, 2020]. In agricultural domain, an appropriate choice of a color space helps to solve some problems without neural networks [Nesteruk et al., 2020].

5.2.1.2 Geometric transformations

Another type of commonly used image augmentation is geometrical transformations. We can observe a target object or an entire scene from different view angles and different distances to them, and it usually does not change semantic (labels) of scene. Therefore, one can apply rotation, flipping, shifting, zooming, shearing, etc., to reconstruct more possible variants of real-life imaging conditions. It allows to train more spacial-invariant algorithms. Besides being considered from new viewpoints, objects or scenes can slightly modify their shapes. To change the shape of observed objects, elastic distortion is often utilized. Random cropping helps to create a new sample by choosing a smaller area from the entire scene. The range for crop size depends on a task and often does not affect image semantics. Although geometrical augmentations are a simple and efficient way to enrich dataset, there are also some limitations of their usage. For instance, in medicine, image flipping or rotation can lead to wrong data representation that is out the scope of practical interest. The same is for landscape classification tasks or facial recognition, where horizontal flipping is useless.

Hide-and-seek augmentation another useful approach that works well in CV tasks [Kumar Singh and Jae Lee, 2017]. It suggests splitting images into several patches according to some grid and discarding (masking) some of them with particular probability. Neural network model observes just randomly selected areas of input images.

5.2.2 Image mixing

5.2.2.1 Image-level mixing

Images mixing is another augmentation technique that works simultaneously with two (or multiple) images. Mixup augmentation leads mixing augmentations [Zhang et al., 2018]. This transformation combines two images using pixel-wise weighted average. The weighted mean of images' labels is used to create a new label for augmented samples. These transformations can be expressed using the

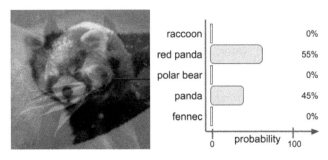

Figure 5.9: The example of the Mixup augmentation of panda image and red panda image.

following formulas:

$$\tau([I_a, I_b], \lambda) = \lambda I_a + (1 - \lambda)I_b, \tag{5.7}$$

$$\tau([L_a, L_b], \lambda) = \lambda L_a + (1 - \lambda)L_b, \tag{5.8}$$

where I_a, I_b are images from class A and B, L_a, L_b are one-hot label encodings, $\lambda \in [0, 1]$.

An example of Mixup augmentation is shown in Figure 5.9. Mixup addresses the problem of neural network overfitting, namely, its tendency to overestimate feature importance for a certain class. It has been shown, that mixing images of different classes leads to better neural network results. The Mixup image augmentation approach was extended in Puzzle Mixup [Kim et al., 2020]. The bottom line is to use the saliency information and the natural examples' underlying statistics.

Cutmix is another augmentation approach that accepts two images as an input and creates a new training sample [Yun et al., 2019]. In contrast to MixUp, Cutmix substitute some areas from one image with patches from another image. Pixel values are not mixed, but we combine labels proportionally to the pasted and original areas' sizes.

Mosaic augmentation was introduced as an adjustment for training the YOLO detection model [Bochkovskiy et al., 2020]. The augmentation mixes four images, instead of two images such as in Cutmix augmentation. For object detection task, new markup of generated sample includes bounding boxes from selected parts of original images.

In the case of multispectral imagery, mixing augmentation techniques can involve multiple input images such as in MixChannel augmentation [Illarionova et al., 2021a]. Usually, more than one satellite image can be obtained for a particular area during high vegetation period. Some spectral bands can be substitute by bands from another observation date but for the same study area. It supports multispectral data variability.

5.2.2.2 Object-level mixing

Besides mixing entire images, one can take only some target areas. Object-level mixing augmentation is a popular approach to enlarge training dataset providing diverse samples with target objects and new background. A neural network learns to recognize target objects in a previously unseen context based on generated examples. It improves model robustness and leads to better performance. CutPas augmentation takes object instances and pastes them on a new image [Dwibedi et al., 2017]. In [Ghiasi et al., 2021], semantic segmentation masks are also used to paste target objects to another image from general-domain dataset. The same transformation is applied to image mask. The mask of original image (background) is merged with pasted object's mask. In agricultural domain, object-based augmentation approach is described by [Nesteruk et al., 2022]. It is shown, that one can collect images with new backgrounds free of target objects. This data can be effectively used to generate new training samples without additional manual labelling. It is also useful in various remote sensing applications that are sensitive to new environmental conditions [Illarionova et al., 2021b]. For instance, moving from one geographical region to another results in land cover and land type changes. For more robust model transferring, new training samples are required [Illarionova et al., 2022a].

The major limitation of object-level mixing augmentations is that they require labeled masks for the objects. However, one can apply weakly-supervised learning techniques [Li et al., 2022a] to obtain pseudo-labels and to use coarse masks for object cutting and pasting.

The idea of object-level augmentation naturally expands for object parts. If we have the corresponding annotation, we can transform object parts independently. This approach can provide extremely high flexibility during dataset formation.

5.2.3 Neural augmentation

Beyond basic augmentations, one can use deep learning models for data augmentation. Two options are to edit existing images or to generate new samples.

Neural network approaches for image editing and new samples generation are more computationally expensive than basic augmentation but can lead to various unique samples [Gatys et al., 2015]. Depending on task, style transfer between datasets can be considered. It involves creating new samples with high similarity with target observations. For instance, lightning condition is crucial for vehicle detection task. Therefore, plausible image transfer from day to night is crucial to solve the task accurately. In [Lin et al., 2020], the GAN-based augmentation approach (AugGAN) is proposed to conduct image translation across domains. Image inpainting is another approach to image transformation. It can be realized through neural network models [Elharrouss et al., 2020]. For example, probabilistic diverse GAN (PD-GAN) for inpainting creates visually realistic content for a masked region [Liu et al., 2021]. It can be used for image restoration and dataset extension. Another option is to apply image outpainting [Xiao et al., 2020]. In aims at elongating beyond image borders. Also, a DNN can mix several images to produce a new sample that has something in common with both of the original samples [Hong et al., 2021].

To generate image, text description can be utilized as input [Qiao et al., 2019]. To use GANs to produce new training samples, we also need a target of a new samples to be known. One way to to it is to use conditioning on the class of generated image [Patel et al., 2020]. We can specify not only the class label of a new sample, but also a mask [Zhu et al., 2018]. In SCIT [Xu et al., 2021] they use a DNN to transfer specific object characteristics. More precisely, they make a healthy plant leaf look diseased. GANs are just one type of model architecture that is efficient for augmentation. Three most popular approaches are generative adversarial networks (GANs), variational autoencoders (VAEs), and diffusion models. There is a known trade-off between the performance of these approaches: GANs produce high-quality images but has relatively low variability; VAEs has high variability, but low quality; diffusion models has very high quality and high variability, but they are very time-consuming. Also, there are successful attempts to combine different generative techniques. In IDA-GAN [Yang and Zhou, 2021] they use the combination of conditional GAN with a VAE.

In many cases, generating new modalities for original samples is reasonable instead of developing unique examples. This type of dataset augmentation can also be named feature engineering. When multispectral data is considered, one can generate additional spectral bands using available bands from another range of wavelengths. For instance, we can create a near-infrared band from RGB to conduct environmental studies more effectively using limited datasets [Illarionova et al., 2021c]. It reduces requirements for sensors and lowers data cost. Another type of auxiliary channel is depth, which can be estimated over monocular image via MiDaS [Ranftl et al., 2022].

Another very promising approach is to reconstruct a 3D scene based on one or multiple images [Mildenhall et al., 2021], and sample new images from different viewpoints. It is also possible to obtain 3D scene or other image features from motion [Schonberger and Frahm, 2016].

When there are multiple modalities, it is reasonable to augment them simultaneously [Hao et al., 2023].

5.2.4   Synthetic data modeling

For many tasks the only efficient way to collect training data is to use graphical simulations [Gu et al., 2022]. A simulator is the first thing one needs for this type of synthetic data collection. There are many freely available simulators depending on the task. They can support indoor [Wu et al., 2018] and outdoor [Misra et al., 2018] scenes. Image quality can be either schematic [Kolve et al., 2017] or photo-realistic [Chang et al., 2017, Szot et al., 2021, Xia et al., 2018]. One can use generative models to make simulated images more realistic[Shrivastava et al., 2017]. It is also possible to use game engines such as Unity3D or Minecraft. Beyond simulators there exist application programming interfaces (APIs) for open-world street views such as Google Street View. The data scientist can use the above tools to generate a dataset or use off-the-shelf datasets generated with simulators for some other tasks [Shridhar et al., 2020, Thomason et al., 2020, Jayannavar et al., 2020].

5.2.5   *Data collection*

In real-world use cases it is almost always not enough to use available datasets. The bypass is to gather new images. The process of obtaining and analyzing data on certain variables in an established system is known as data collection. This procedure allows one to analyze outcomes and provide answers to pertinent queries. Nowadays, data collection is a significant barrier to machine learning and is a hotly debated topic in many communities. Data collection has recently become a crucial concern due to the following reasons. First, as machine learning is utilized more often, new applications are emerging that may not have enough labeled data. Second, unlike conventional machine learning, deep learning algorithms create features automatically, saving money on feature engineering but maybe requiring more labeled data. Third, as noticed earlier the emergence of new applications and severe requirements for the accuracy of inference may require the multimodal data collection, e.g., time-series from sensors and images [Kovalenko et al., 2022]. It requires the application of relevant data fusion methods with with further analysis of multimodal data [De Bernardis et al., 2016].

As more datasets are made available on the Web and in corporate data lakes, data discovery has become crucial for sharing and searching for new datasets [Halevy et al., 2016]. When no external dataset is readily available, data generation can be utilized.

5.2.5.1   *Image retrieval*

The volume of digital imaging data is increasing along with the quick advancement of computer technology. Information is often best communicated visually. Practical approaches that can aid in finding and obtaining the visual data a user is interested in are unavoidably needed. The image retrieval system retrieves images from a database upon the user request. Image retrieval refers to *data discovery* method in the scope of data collection.

To execute retrieval over the words annotated to the images, the majority of conventional and traditional techniques of image retrieval employ some method of adding information, i.e., image annotation, such as captioning, keywords, title, or descriptions to the images. This method refers to *image meta search* based on associated metadata. Since human picture annotation is time-consuming, expensive, and labor-intensive, substantial study [Wei et al., 2021b] has been done on automatic image annotation.

An alternative solution is *content-based image retrieval* [Long et al., 2003]. This method enables comparison of the image contents, e.g., textures, colors, forms, to a user-supplied query image or user-specified image attributes. It is based on the application of CV to the image retrieval [Scherer, 2020] [Janjua and Patankar, 2022].

The drawbacks of metadata-based systems and the wide range of applications for effective image retrieval have increased interest in content-based systems. Existing technology makes searching for textual descriptions of photographs simple, but it requires humans to annotate each image in the database manually; this may not be feasible for massive datasets or automatically generated photos. Additionally, it is easy to overlook pictures whose descriptions use several synonyms.

The pioneer content-based systems were designed in the way to search databases using images' color, texture, and shape characteristics. User-friendly interfaces were clearly needed after these technologies were created. Human-centered design initiatives have started to be put into practice in the field of content-based information retrieval in order to suit the demands of the user doing the search. This usually entails including query techniques that could support descriptive semantics, queries that could incorporate the user feedback, as well as the systems that could support ML, and systems that could comprehend the user satisfaction levels.

5.2.5.2   Image collection

When collecting image data, video/multi-spectral/hyper-spectral cameras, and laser scanners are frequently used to generate image data. RGB are the three fundamental hues that are frequently used to create colors in photographs. One is able to create new colors in the visible spectrum by mixing these three hues in various ratios. A typical Complementary Metal Oxide Semiconductor (CMOS) sensor is included in an RGB camera, which is how the colored images are captured. The number of pixels that make up a picture is typically represented in megapixels when describing the capture of static photos. The RGB camera determines the exact color of every pixel via a technique known as interpolation, according to [Weerasinghe et al., 2002]. Multi-spectral cameras can record picture data at specific frequencies in the electromagnetic spectrum. The main distinction between multi-spectral and conventional RGB cameras is that some objects have unique wavebands of reflection that may be outside of the visible spectrum. One disadvantage is that high-quality commercial multi-spectral cameras are more expensive than conventional RGB cameras. Spectral resolution and a wide range of spectrum measurements are characteristics of hyper-spectral cameras. For surface monitoring tasks, laser scanners are utilized as an alternative option to substitute cameras [Alexander et al., 2013]. The triangulation principle is the foundation of a laser scanner. The scanner consists of two components: (i) a positioning laser which performs projecting of a laser beam onto the surface, and (ii) a scanning aperture which rotates at the necessary speed to catch the laser energy's reflected beam. The triangle is fixed for a brief amount of time to allow the system to compute the laser point 3D coordinates relying on the law of sines [Lindner et al., 2014].

Contrary to camera vision, laser scanners are distinguished by their capacity to operate in total darkness and acquire the 3D coordinates of the points located on the surface. However, they can only perform the analyses of some scanned characters at a time and need a specific amount of time to complete 3D scanning of a critical area. Due to a technological constraint of a stepper motor operating the positioning laser, *dead zones* may simultaneously form between two neighboring scanning sites. It stops impediments between these places from being detected. Engaging the robotic swarm to accurately scan the necessary surface is one possibility, as reported in [Ivanov et al., 2020].

Data collection is an expensive and time-consuming process, so it is essential to organize it thoughtfully. The critical thing to remember is that training dataset must be as representative and rich as possible to achieve reasonable accuracy. It may seem not obvious, but dataset augmentation can be applied while data collection as well. It is also called hardware image augmentation [Nesteruk et al., 2022]. The idea behind it to vary lighting or imaging conditions during image collection [Silwal et al., 2021]. It is beneficial in two cases. The first case is expected variability of conditions during the inference. The second case occurs when there are strict limitations on data collection time or scale.

In practice, one needs to find a trade-off between data amount and variability while hardware image augmentation. For some applications, we can have extra profit from augmentation during data collection. In tasks requiring specific manual labeling, such as instance segmentation, having several images from the same viewpoint but with different imaging conditions provides us with free annotations for auxiliary images.

5.2.5.3 Image annotation

Collecting new images is not the only way to augment dataset. One can also increase the quality of annotations. Better annotation suits better for the specific problem.

The straightforward approach is to download an existing dataset and to manually label it for a new task. A special case is make classification more specific. For example, instead of binary cat vs. dog labels, one can determine their varieties. Other possibility is to increase the complexity of labels. A complex label provides a model with stronger signal. We can sort popular computer vision tasks by the time needed for their annotation: classification, object detection, semantic segmentation, instance segmentation. The exact annotation time can depend on image complexity, the number of classes, the required mask detalization, the proficiency of annotators, etc.

Also, there are several options to make labelling semi-automated. To accelerate annotation for segmentation, one can use interactive segmentation [Sofiiuk et al., 2022]. It approximate local mask region given a single point from an annotator. By adding more positive points, one can expand a mask. By adding negative points, one can reduce it. With this approach ten points if enough to approximate an average object accurately.

There are convenient tools that generate instance masks based on box-level annotations [Tian et al., 2021, Lan et al., 2021, Li et al., 2022b].

There are more general methods. If we already have a fraction of data that is labeled, we can use it to train a model. Then, we can use the predictions to obtain pre-computed labels. It can be easier for an annotator to correct prediction that to label from the scratch. This approach gives more value for complex tasks. A single mask can require several minutes of annotators' time, which is much longer than the time for border correction. Classification, on the contrary, requires comparable time for annotation and for correction. But, it depends on the case. For example, if there are thousands of classes in the dataset, a model that provides top ten most confident predictions, helps to search the correct class faster.

Even if there is no labeled data for a specific task, it is still possible to automate the process. Weakly supervised learning methods can generate more complex annotations (such as semantic masks), based on weaker signal (such as classification label) [Zhang et al., 2020]. The resulting masks will be not perfect, but they can be further corrected or filtered manually. Moreover, if the dataset is large enough, a model can be successfully trained with noisy data.

If there is no annotations for some dataset at all, a solution is to try zero-shot models. Fore general domain open-vocabulary approach can produce decent results [Minderer et al., 2022].

Another technique that helps to spend less time for manual annotation is active learning [Ren et al., 2021]. The idea behind it is to choose samples that are more informative for a model. It allows to annotate only the most useful fraction of images instead of the whole dataset.

Every dataset is unique, so there is no single universal tool. A data scientist have to study the data, and to find an appropriate solution. In some cases, it is possible to find a way to pseudo-label a dataset [Baek et al., 2019]. If the dataset is large enough, a model can be trained on noisy annotations.

5.3 Augmentation pipelines

In previous section we described augmentation primitives. The most challenging question is how to choose a proper augmentation pipeline for a specific problem. Applying a single augmentation for every sample gives a low variability and can include an unexpected bias. Combining many augmentations for every samples can make training data too noisy. A generic approach is to stack several augmentations with the specified range of magnitudes manually. In this section, we discuss other options.

5.3.1 Augmentation optimization

When there are many transformation options and a clear way to measure performance, the specific augmentation configuration can be determined via discrete optimization. The direct optimization of transformation types and their magnitudes is not suitable, because the desired behavior includes randomness. To overcome this issue, a common choice is to optimize augmentation policy instead.

Some of the popular augmentation optimization methods are based on reinforcement learning (RL): Autoaugment [Cubuk et al., 2019], Randaugment [Cubuk et al., 2020]. Fast Autoaugment performs density matching [Lim et al., 2019]. Faster Autoaugment uses a differentiable policy search through approximate gradients [Hataya et al., 2020]. In ADA [Fawzi et al., 2016], they try to find an augmentation pipeline that maximizes the loss. It is a way of producing hard training examples.

In [Takase et al., 2021], authors show an efficient way to choose samples for augmentation instead of applying it to every image. A similar idea is to produce many augmented samples offline, and to choose the most informative during the training. In [Paul et al., 2021] they compute loss on an ensemble of ten small models, and use the gradient to drop simplest samples. In [Toneva et al., 2018], the authors use sample forgetting score to decide which samples to prune. In [Mindermann et al., 2022], samples are prioritized and split on informative and less informative. One can expand training samples ranking to select better augmented ones.

5.3.2 Augmentation for the curriculum learning

When there are a lot of dataset augmentation options, it is natural to have several subsets with different quality. For example, we can have a small labeled subset that is the most relevant, and at the same time, a larger dataset that is less relevant. The relevance drop can be caused by domain shift, by the lack of annotations, or the quality of data. A data scientist can use this data either to pretrain a model or to mix the subsets within regular model training.

The augmentation strategy can be different during training. In curriculum learning training paradigm, the difficulty of samples usually increases from epoch to epoch. It allows a model to learn basic concepts before solving more complex problems. While it is challenging to find easy and hard samples in the original dataset, it is much more straightforward to change the difficulty via augmentation [Wei et al., 2021a]. For example, one can increase the overlapping of samples and add more noise [Nesteruk et al., 2021a].

5.3.3 Other applications of augmentation

The authors of negative augmentation [Sinha et al., 2021] show that another option is to go beyond hard example, and change the original image so that it does not represent original class anymore. To broaden this idea, we must recall that the augmentation parameters can become a new target for a model instead of originally collected label. It is a widely accepted solution for self-supervised learning [Chen et al., 2020] where a model can be trained in the way that an image and its augmented copy shares closer semantics with each other than with other image. Another option is to randomly permute the patches of the original image and to teach a model to reconstruct it [Wei et al., 2019].

Test-time augmentation is another way to adjust model performance applying image transformations. Test-time augmentation, in contrast to training dataset augmentation, uses both original test images and augmented images for model prediction. The final result is the average of these predictions. It allows one to reduce overconfidence of algorithms by bringing diversity to test data. This technique can be implemented for various computer vision tasks to achieve more accurate results. In the image classification task, the image label is defined by majority voting. The same is applicable for semantic or instance segmentation, adjusted for the fact that after geometrical augmentations the results are transformed back to fit the corresponding reference mask. Test-time augmentation can be used for detection problems. Usually, the bounding box on the test image is defined based on the original image, while object class is ascribed based on a set of augmented images and an original one. This approach boosts model performance in different tasks such as microscopy image analysis [Moshkov et al., 2020], brain tumor segmentation [Wang et al., 2019], satellite hyperspectral image segmentation [Nalepa et al., 2019].

One can verify model performance using not only transformations of original test images, but artificially generated samples. Small training dataset is a common issue for specific domains. Therefore, it can be beneficial for model performance to preserve additional images for training instead of using them for model validation. Test sample generation is a way to evaluate developed algorithms on diverse conditions and target object views. It is always assumed that images in training and test sets are sampled from the same distribution, so it should be taken into account while choosing an approach for test set generation. GAN models aim at approximating target distribution and can deliver strong results in synthetic test set creation. When generator yields images from the same distribution as for training set these images can be used for model evaluation. A GAN-based approach for predicting generalization was proposed in [Zhang et al., 2021] and showed a way to estimate model error using just synthetic data without the need for test set.

5.4 Conclusions

Deep learning enables myriads of applications involving computer vision. These applications include biomedicine, video gaming, precision agriculture, intelligent city/transport. However, the lack of training data limits their potential realization. In this chapter, we did a comprehensive survey and demonstrated the overall taxonomy of image dataset augmentation, an approach allowing for the increase of dataset. We begin by explaining the value of the deep learning approach for computer vision. Then we talk about common issues that it can help with, after which we move on to the specifics of the data and proceed with the discussion on the model architectures. After acquainting the reader with the fundamental terminology, we move on to talk about image augmentation and image dataset augmentation. After that, we go into greater detail on enhancing image datasets by outlining the fundamentals of augmentation and then talking about a variety of augmentation strategies from various angles. Finally, we discuss practical aspects in order to make the chapter practically feasible, namely which augmentation pipeline is suitable for a certain problem. The presented outlook is promising for enabling more applications based on computer vision and improving the performance of all existing tasks.

References

Abrishami, M. S., Eshratifar, A. E., Eigen, D., Wang, Y., Nazarian, S., and Pedram, M. 2020. Efficient training of deep convolutional neural networks by augmentation in embedding space. In 2020 21st International Symposium on Quality Electronic Design (ISQED), pp. 347–351. IEEE.

Alexander, C., Moeslund, J. E., Bøcher, P. K., Arge, L., and Svenning, J. -C. 2013. Airborne laser scanner (lidar) proxies for understory light conditions. Remote Sensing of Environment, 134: 152–161.

Baek, Y., Lee, B., Han, D., Yun, S., and Lee, H. 2019. Character region awareness for text detection. In Proceedings of the IEEE/CVF Conference on Computer Vision and Pattern Recognition, pp. 9365–9374.

Baldi, P., and Sadowski, P. J. 2013. Understanding dropout. Advances in Neural Information Processing Systems, 26.

Birhane, A., and Prabhu, V. U. 2021. Large image datasets: A pyrrhic win for computer vision? In Proceedings of the IEEE/CVF Winter Conference on Applications of Computer Vision, pp. 1537–1547.

Bochkovskiy, A., Wang, C. -Y., and Liao, H. -Y. M. 2020. Yolov4: Optimal speed and accuracy of object detection. arXiv preprint arXiv:2004.10934.

Brisco, B., Mahdianpari, M., and Mohammadimanesh, F. 2020. Hybrid compact polarimetric sar for environmental monitoring with the radarsat constellation mission. Remote Sensing, 12(20): 3283.

Brown, T., Mann, B., Ryder, N., Subbiah, M., Kaplan, J. D., Dhariwal, P. et al. 2020. Language models are few-shot learners. Advances in Neural Information Processing Systems, 33: 1877–1901.

Browne, M. W. 2000. Cross-validation methods. Journal of Mathematical Psychology, 44(1): 108–132.

Buslaev, A., Iglovikov, V. I., Khvedchenya, E., Parinov, A., Druzhinin, M., and Kalinin, A. A. 2020. Albumentations: Fast and flexible image augmentations. Information, 11(2): 125.

Chang, A., Dai, A., Funkhouser, T., Halber, M., Niebner, M., Savva, M. et al. 2017. Matterport3d: Learning from rgb-d data in indoor environments. In 2017 International Conference on 3D Vision (3DV), pp. 667–676. IEEE.

Chen, T., Kornblith, S., Norouzi, M., and Hinton, G. 2020. A simple framework for contrastive learning of visual representations. In Proceedings of the 37th International Conference on Machine Learning, pp. 1597–1607.

Chu, P., Bian, X., Liu, S., and Ling, H. 2020. Feature space augmentation for long-tailed data. In European Conference on Computer Vision, pp. 694–710. Springer.

Cubuk, E. D., Zoph, B., Mane, D., Vasudevan, V., and Le, Q. V. 2019. Autoaugment: Learning augmentation strategies from data. In Proceedings of the IEEE/CVF Conference on Computer Vision and Pattern Recognition, pp. 113–123.

Cubuk, E. D., Zoph, B., Shlens, J., and Le, Q. V. 2020. Randaugment: Practical automated data augmentation with a reduced search space. In Proceedings of the IEEE/CVF Conference on Computer Vision and Pattern Recognition Workshops, pp. 702–703.

De Bernardis, C., Vicente-Guijalba, F., Martinez-Marin, T., and Lopez-Sanchez, J. M. 2016. Contribution to real-time estimation of crop phenological states in a dynamical framework based on NDVI time series: Data fusion with sar and temperature. IEEE Journal of Selected Topics in Applied Earth Observations and Remote Sensing, 9(8): 3512–3523.

Deng, J., Dong, W., Socher, R., Li, L. -J., Li, K., and Fei-Fei, L. 2009. Imagenet: A large-scale hierarchical image database. In 2009 IEEE Conference on Computer Vision and Pattern Recognition, pp. 248–255. IEEE.

Dosovitskiy, A., Beyer, L., Kolesnikov, A., Weissenborn, D., Zhai, X., Unterthiner, T. et al. 2020. An image is worth 16x16 words: Transformers for image recognition at scale. In International Conference on Learning Representations.

Du, X., Wang, Z., Cai, M., and Li, Y. 2021. Vos: Learning what you don't know by virtual outlier synthesis. In International Conference on Learning Representations, pp. 1–12.

Dwibedi, D., Misra, I., and Hebert, M. 2017. Cut, paste and learn: Surprisingly easy synthesis for instance detection. In Proceedings of the IEEE International Conference on Computer Vision, pp. 1301–1310.

Elharrouss, O., Almaadeed, N., Al-Maadeed, S., and Akbari, Y. 2020. Image inpainting: A review. Neural Processing Letters, 51(2): 2007–2028.

Everingham, M., Van Gool, L., Williams, C. K., Winn, J., and Zisserman, A. 2010. The pascal visual object classes (VOC) challenge. International Journal of Computer Vision, 88(2): 303–338.

Fawzi, A., Samulowitz, H., Turaga, D., and Frossard, P. 2016. Adaptive data augmentation for image classification. In 2016 IEEE International Conference on Image Processing (ICIP), pp. 3688–3692. IEEE.

Ganesan, P., and Rajini, V. 2014. Assessment of satellite image segmentation in RGB and HSV color space using image quality measures. In 2014 International Conference on Advances in Electrical Engineering (ICAEE), pp. 1–5. IEEE.

Gatys, L. A., Ecker, A. S., and Bethge, M. 2015. A neural algorithm of artistic style. arXiv preprint arXiv:1508.06576.

Georgiou, T., Liu, Y., Chen, W., and Lew, M. 2020. A survey of traditional and deep learning-based feature descriptors for high dimensional data in computer vision. International Journal of Multimedia Information Retrieval, 9(3): 135–170.

Ghiasi, G., Cui, Y., Srinivas, A., Qian, R., Lin, T. -Y., Cubuk, E. D. et al. 2021. Simple copy-paste is a strong data augmentation method for instance segmentation. In Proceedings of the IEEE/CVF Conference on Computer Vision and Pattern Recognition, pp. 2918–2928.

Gu, J., Stefani, E., Wu, Q., Thomason, J., and Wang, X. 2022. Vision-and-language navigation: A survey of tasks, methods, and future directions. In Proceedings of the 60th Annual Meeting of the Association for Computational Linguistics (Volume 1: Long Papers), pp. 7606–7623, Dublin, Ireland. Association for Computational Linguistics.

Halevy, A., Korn, F., Noy, N. F., Olston, C., Polyzotis, N., Roy, S. et al. 2016. Goods: Organizing google's datasets. In Proceedings of the 2016 International Conference on Management of Data, SIGMOD '16, pp. 795–806, New York, NY, USA. Association for Computing Machinery.

Hao, X., Zhu, Y., Appalaraju, S., Zhang, A., Zhang, W., Li, B. et al. 2023. Mixgen: A new multi-modal data augmentation. In Proceedings of the IEEE/CVF Winter Conference on Applications of Computer Vision, pp. 379–389.

Hataya, R., Zdenek, J., Yoshizoe, K., and Nakayama, H. 2020. Faster autoaugment: Learning augmentation strategies using backpropagation. In European Conference on Computer Vision, pp. 1–16. Springer.

He, K., Zhang, X., Ren, S., and Sun, J. 2016. Deep residual learning for image recognition. In Proceedings of the IEEE Conference on Computer Vision and Pattern Recognition, pp. 770–778.

Hong, M., Choi, J., and Kim, G. 2021. Stylemix: Separating content and style for enhanced data augmentation. In Proceedings of the IEEE/CVF Conference on Computer Vision and Pattern Recognition, pp. 14862–14870.

Illarionova, S., Nesteruk, S., Shadrin, D., Ignatiev, V., Pukalchik, M., and Oseledets, I. 2021a. Mixchannel: Advanced augmentation for multispectral satellite images. Remote Sensing, 13(11): 2181.

Illarionova, S., Nesteruk, S., Shadrin, D., Ignatiev, V., Pukalchik, M., and Oseledets, I. 2021b. Object-based augmentation for building semantic segmentation: Ventura and santa rosa case study. In Proceedings of the IEEE/CVF International Conference on Computer Vision, pp. 1659–1668.

Illarionova, S., Shadrin, D., Ignatiev, V., Shayakhmetov, S., Trekin, A., and Oseledets, I. 2022a. Augmentation-based methodology for enhancement of trees map detalization on a large scale. Remote Sensing, 14(9): 2281.

Illarionova, S., Shadrin, D., Tregubova, P., Ignatiev, V., Efimov, A., Oseledets, I. et al. 2022b. A survey of computer vision techniques for forest characterization and carbon monitoring tasks. Remote Sensing, 14(22): 5861.

Illarionova, S., Shadrin, D., Trekin, A., Ignatiev, V., and Oseledets, I. 2021c. Generation of the nir spectral band for satellite images with convolutional neural networks. Sensors, 21(16).

Ivanov, M., Sergyienko, O., Tyrsa, V., Lindner, L., Flores-Fuentes, W., Rodríguez-Qui˜nonez, J. C. et al. 2020. Influence of data clouds fusion from 3D real-time vision system on robotic group dead reckoning in unknown terrain. IEEE/CAA Journal of Automatica Sinica, 7(2): 368–385.

Janjua, J., and Patankar, A. 2022. Comparative review of content based image retrieval using deep learning. pp. 63–74. *In*: Balas, V. E., Semwal, V. B., and Khandare, A. (eds.). Intelligent Computing and Networking, Singapore. Springer Nature Singapore.

Jayannavar, P., Narayan-Chen, A., and Hockenmaier, J. 2020. Learning to execute instructions in a minecraft dialogue. In Proceedings of the 58th Annual Meeting of the Association for Computational Linguistics, pp. 2589–2602.

Kim, J. -H., Choo, W., and Song, H. O. 2020. Puzzle mix: Exploiting saliency and local statistics for optimal mixup. In International Conference on Machine Learning, pp. 5275–5285. PMLR.

Ko, B., and Gu, G. 2020. Embedding expansion: Augmentation in embedding space for deep metric learning. In Proceedings of the IEEE/CVF Conference on Computer Vision and Pattern Recognition, pp. 7255–7264.

Kolve, E., Mottaghi, R., Han, W., VanderBilt, E., Weihs, L., Herrasti, A. et al. 2017. Ai2-thor: An interactive 3d environment for visual AI. arXiv preprint arXiv:1712.05474.

Kovalenko, E., Shcherbak, A., Somov, A., Bril, E., Zimniakova, O., Semenov, M. et al. 2022. Detecting the Parkinson's disease through the simultaneous analysis of data from wearable sensors and video. IEEE Sensors Journal, 22(16): 16430–16439.

Kumar Singh, K. and Jae Lee, Y. 2017. Hide-and-seek: Forcing a network to be meticulous for weakly-supervised object and action localization. In Proceedings of the IEEE International Conference on Computer Vision, pp. 3524–3533.

Kumar, D., Sharma, D., and Goecke, R. 2020. Feature map augmentation to improve rotation invariance in convolutional neural networks. In International Conference on Advanced Concepts for Intelligent Vision Systems, pp. 348–359. Springer.

Lan, S., Yu, Z., Choy, C., Radhakrishnan, S., Liu, G., Zhu, Y. et al. 2021. Discobox: Weakly supervised instance segmentation and semantic correspondence from box supervision. In Proceedings of the IEEE/CVF International Conference on Computer Vision, pp. 3406–3416.

Lemikhova, L., Nesteruk, S., and Somov, A. 2022. Transfer learning for few-shot plants recognition: Antarctic station greenhouse use-case. In 2022 IEEE 31st International Symposium on Industrial Electronics (ISIE), pp. 715–720.

Li, J., Jie, Z., Wang, X., Zhou, Y., Wei, X., and Ma, L. 2022a. Weakly supervised semantic segmentation via progressive patch learning. IEEE Transactions on Multimedia.

Li, W., Liu, W., Zhu, J., Cui, M., Hua, X. -S., and Zhang, L. 2022b. Box-supervised instance segmentation with level set evolution. In European Conference on Computer Vision, pp. 1–18. Springer.

Lim, S., Kim, I., Kim, T., Kim, C., and Kim, S. 2019. Fast autoaugment. Advances in Neural Information Processing Systems, 32.

Lin, C. -T., Huang, S. -W., Wu, Y. -Y., and Lai, S. -H. 2020. Gan-based day-to-night image style transfer for nighttime vehicle detection. IEEE Transactions on Intelligent Transportation Systems, 22(2): 951–963.

Lin, T. -Y., Maire, M., Belongie, S., Hays, J., Perona, P., Ramanan, D. et al. 2014. Microsoft coco: Common objects in context. In European Conference on Computer Vision, pp. 740–755. Springer.

Lindner, L., Sergiyenko, O., Tyrsa, V., and Mercorelli, P. 2014. An approach for dynamic triangulation using servomotors. In IEEE 23rd International Symposium on Industrial Electronics (ISIE), pp. 1926–1931.

Liu, H., Wan, Z., Huang, W., Song, Y., Han, X., and Liao, J. 2021. Pd-gan: Probabilistic diverse gan for image inpainting. In Proceedings of the IEEE/CVF Conference on Computer Vision and Pattern Recognition, pp. 9371–9381.

Long, F., Zhang, H., and Feng, D. D. 2003. Fundamentals of Content-Based Image Retrieval, pp. 1–26. Springer Berlin Heidelberg, Berlin, Heidelberg.

Marin, J., Biswas, A., Ofli, F., Hynes, N., Salvador, A., Aytar, Y. et al. 2019. Recipe1m+: A dataset for learning cross-modal embeddings for cooking recipes and food images. IEEE Transactions on Pattern Analysis and Machine Intelligence, 43(1): 187–203.

Mensink, T., Uijlings, J., Kuznetsova, A., Gygli, M., and Ferrari, V. 2021. Factors of influence for transfer learning across diverse appearance domains and task types. IEEE Transactions on Pattern Analysis & Machine Intelligence, (01): 1–1.

Mildenhall, B., Srinivasan, P. P., Tancik, M., Barron, J. T., Ramamoorthi, R., and Ng, R. 2021. Nerf: Representing scenes as neural radiance fields for view synthesis. Communications of the ACM, 65(1): 99–106.

Minderer, M., Gritsenko, A., Stone, A., Neumann, M., Weissenborn, D., Dosovitskiy, A. et al. 2022. Simple open vocabulary object detection with vision transformers.

Mindermann, S., Brauner, J. M., Razzak, M. T., Sharma, M., Kirsch, A., Xu, W. et al. 2022. Prioritized training on points that are learnable, worth learning, and not yet learnt. In International Conference on Machine Learning, pp. 15630–15649. PMLR.

Misra, D., Bennett, A., Blukis, V., Niklasson, E., Shatkhin, M., and Artzi, Y. 2018. Mapping instructions to actions in 3d environments with visual goal prediction. In Proceedings of the 2018 Conference on Empirical Methods in Natural Language Processing, pp. 2667–2678.

Moreno-Torres, J. G., Raeder, T., Alaiz-Rodríguez, R., Chawla, N. V., and Herrera, F. 2012. A unifying view on dataset shift in classification. Pattern Recognition, 45(1): 521–530.

Moshkov, N., Mathe, B., Kertesz-Farkas, A., Hollandi, R., and Horvath, P. 2020. Test-time augmentation for deep learning-based cell segmentation on microscopy images. Scientific Reports, 10(1): 1–7.

Müller, R., Kornblith, S., and Hinton, G. E. 2019. When does label smoothing help? Advances in Neural Information Processing Systems, 32.

Nalepa, J., Myller, M., and Kawulok, M. 2019. Training and test-time data augmentation for hyperspectral image segmentation. IEEE Geoscience and Remote Sensing Letters, 17(2): 292–296.

Nesteruk, S., Illarionova, S., Akhtyamov, T., Shadrin, D., Somov, A., Pukalchik, M. et al. 2022. Xtremeaugment: Getting more from your data through combination of image collection and image augmentation. IEEE Access, 10: 24010–24028.

Nesteruk, S., Shadrin, D., and Pukalchik, M. 2021a. Image augmentation for multitask few-shot learning: Agricultural domain use-case. arXiv preprint arXiv:2102.12295, pp. 1–12.

Nesteruk, S., Shadrin, D., Kovalenko, V., Rodríguez-Sánchez, A., and Somov, A. 2020. Plant growth prediction through intelligent embedded sensing. In 2020 IEEE 29th International Symposium on Industrial Electronics (ISIE), pp. 411–416. IEEE.

Nesteruk, S., Shadrin, D., Pukalchik, M., Somov, A., Zeidler, C., Zabel, P. et al. 2021b. Image compression and plants classification using machine learning in controlled-environment agriculture: Antarctic station use case. IEEE Sensors Journal.

Patel, M., Wang, X., and Mao, S. 2020. Data augmentation with conditional gan for automatic modulation classification. In Proceedings of the 2nd ACM Workshop on Wireless Security and Machine Learning, pp. 31–36.

Paul, M., Ganguli, S., and Dziugaite, G. K. 2021. Deep learning on a data diet: Finding important examples early in training. Advances in Neural Information Processing Systems, 34: 20596–20607.

Qiao, T., Zhang, J., Xu, D., and Tao, D. 2019. Mirrorgan: Learning text-to-image generation by redescription. In Proceedings of the IEEE/CVF Conference on Computer Vision and Pattern Recognition, pp. 1505–1514.

Radford, A., Kim, J. W., Hallacy, C., Ramesh, A., Goh, G., Agarwal, S. et al. 2021. Learning transferable visual models from natural language supervision.

Ranftl, R., Lasinger, K., Hafner, D., Schindler, K., and Koltun, V. 2022. Towards robust monocular depth estimation: Mixing datasets for zero-shot cross-dataset transfer. IEEE Transactions on Pattern Analysis and Machine Intelligence, 44(3).

Ren, P., Xiao, Y., Chang, X., Huang, P. -Y., Li, Z., Gupta, B. B. et al. 2021. A survey of deep active learning. ACM Computing Surveys (CSUR), 54(9): 1–40.

Rusak, E., Schott, L., Zimmermann, R. S., Bitterwolf, J., Bringmann, O., Bethge, M. et al. 2020. A simple way to make neural networks robust against diverse image corruptions. In European Conference on Computer Vision, pp. 53–69. Springer.

Scherer, R. 2020. pp. 1–137. Springer Cham, Switzerland.

Schonberger, J. L., and Frahm, J. -M. 2016. Structure-from-motion revisited. In Proceedings of the IEEE Conference on Computer Vision and Pattern Recognition, pp. 4104–4113.

Schuhmann, C. 2022. Laion-400-million open dataset. Accessed: 2022-06-06.

Sezer, A., and Sezer, H. B. 2020. Deep convolutional neural network-based automatic classification of neonatal hip ultrasound images: A novel data augmentation approach with speckle noise reduction. Ultrasound in Medicine & Biology, 46(3): 735–749.

Shanmugam, D., Blalock, D., Balakrishnan, G., and Guttag, J. 2021. Better aggregation in test-time augmentation. In Proceedings of the IEEE/CVF International Conference on Computer Vision (ICCV), pp. 1214–1223.

Shridhar, M., Thomason, J., Gordon, D., Bisk, Y., Han, W., Mottaghi, R. et al. 2020. Alfred: A benchmark for interpreting grounded instructions for everyday tasks. In Proceedings of the IEEE/ CVF Conference on Computer Vision and Pattern Recognition, pp. 10740–10749.

Shrivastava, A., Pfister, T., Tuzel, O., Susskind, J., Wang, W., and Webb, R. 2017. Learning from simulated and unsupervised images through adversarial training. In Proceedings of the IEEE Conference on Computer Vision and Pattern Recognition, pp. 2107–2116.

Silwal, A., Parhar, T., Yandun, F., Baweja, H., and Kantor, G. A. 2021. Robust illumination-invariant camera system for agricultural applications. In 2021 IEEE/RSJ International Conference on Intelligent Robots and Systems (IROS), pp. 3292–3298. IEEE.

Singh, P. 2020. A neutrosophic-entropy based clustering algorithm (NEBCA) with HSV color system: A special application in segmentation of parkinson's disease (PD) MR images. Computer Methods and Programs in Biomedicine, 189: 105317.

Sinha, A., Ayush, K., Song, J., Uzkent, B., Jin, H., and Ermon, S. 2021. Negative data augmentation. In International Conference on Learning Representations.

Sofiiuk, K., Petrov, I. A., and Konushin, A. 2022. Reviving iterative training with mask guidance for interactive segmentation. In 2022 IEEE International Conference on Image Processing (ICIP), pp. 3141–3145. IEEE.

Suárez, J. L., García, S., and Herrera, F. 2021. A tutorial on distance metric learning: Mathematical foundations, algorithms, experimental analysis, prospects and challenges. Neurocomputing, 425: 300–322.

Sun, C., Shrivastava, A., Singh, S., and Gupta, A. 2017. Revisiting unreasonable effectiveness of data in deep learning era. In Proceedings of the IEEE International Conference on Computer Vision (ICCV).

Szot, A., Clegg, A., Undersander, E., Wijmans, E., Zhao, Y., Turner, J. et al. 2021. Habitat 2.0: Training home assistants to rearrange their habitat. In Advances in Neural Information Processing Systems (NeurIPS).

Takase, T., Karakida, R., and Asoh, H. 2021. Self-paced data augmentation for training neural networks. Neurocomputing, 442: 296–306.

Thomason, J., Murray, M., Cakmak, M., and Zettlemoyer, L. 2020. Vision-and-dialog navigation. In Conference on Robot Learning, pp. 394–406. PMLR.

Tian, Z., Shen, C., Wang, X., and Chen, H. 2021. Boxinst: High-performance instance segmentation with box annotations. In Proceedings of the IEEE/CVF Conference on Computer Vision and Pattern Recognition, pp. 5443–5452.

Toneva, M., Sordoni, A., des Combes, R. T., Trischler, A., Bengio, Y., and Gordon, G. J. 2018. An empirical study of example forgetting during deep neural network learning. In International Conference on Learning Representations.

Tuominen, S., Näsi, R., Honkavaara, E., Balazs, A., Hakala, T., Viljanen, N. et al. 2018. Assessment of classifiers and remote sensing features of hyperspectral imagery and stereo-photogrammetric point clouds for recognition of tree species in a forest area of high species diversity. Remote Sensing, 10(5): 714.

Van Horn, G., Mac Aodha, O., Song, Y., Cui, Y., Sun, C., Shepard, A. et al. 2018. The inaturalist species classification and detection dataset. In Proceedings of the IEEE Conference on Computer Vision and Pattern Recognition, pp. 8769–8778.

Wang, G., Li, W., Ourselin, S., and Vercauteren, T. 2019. Automatic brain tumor segmentation using convolutional neural networks with test-time augmentation. In International MICCAI BrainlesionWorkshop, pp. 61–72. Springer.

Weerasinghe, C., Kharitonenko, I., and Ogunbona, P. 2002. Method of color interpolation in a single sensor color camera using green channel separation. In IEEE International Conference on Acoustics, Speech, and Signal Processing, 4: 3233–3236.

Wei, C., Xie, L., Ren, X., Xia, Y., Su, C., Liu, J. et al. 2019. Iterative reorganization with weak spatial constraints: Solving arbitrary jigsaw puzzles for unsupervised representation learning. In Proceedings of the IEEE/CVF Conference on Computer Vision and Pattern Recognition, pp. 1910–1919.

Wei, J., Huang, C., Vosoughi, S., Cheng, Y., and Xu, S. 2021a. Few-shot text classification with triplet networks, data augmentation, and curriculum learning. In Proceedings of the 2021 Conference of the North American Chapter of the Association for Computational Linguistics: Human Language Technologies, pp. 5493–5500.

Wei, W., Wu, Q., Chen, D., Zhang, Y., Liu, W., Duan, G. et al. 2021b. Automatic image annotation based on an improved nearest neighbor technique with tag semantic extension model. Procedia Computer Science, 183: 616–623. Proceedings of the 10th International Conference of Information and Communication Technology.

Wu, Y., Wu, Y., Gkioxari, G., and Tian, Y. 2018. Building generalizable agents with a realistic and rich 3d environment. arXiv preprint arXiv:1801.02209.

Xia, F., Zamir, A. R., He, Z., Sax, A., Malik, J., and Savarese, S. 2018. Gibson ENV: Real-world perception for embodied agents. In Proceedings of the IEEE Conference on Computer Vision and Pattern Recognition, pp. 9068–9079.

Xiao, Q., Li, G., and Chen, Q. 2020. Image outpainting: Hallucinating beyond the image. IEEE Access, 8: 173576–173583.

Xu, M., Yoon, S., Fuentes, A., Yang, J., and Park, D. S. 2021. Style-consistent image translation: A novel data augmentation paradigm to improve plant disease recognition. Frontiers in Plant Science, 12: 773142–773142.

Yang, H., and Zhou, Y. 2021. Ida-gan: A novel imbalanced data augmentation gan. In 2020 25th International Conference on Pattern Recognition (ICPR), pp. 8299–8305. IEEE.

Yun, S., Han, D., Oh, S. J., Chun, S., Choe, J., and Yoo, Y. 2019. Cutmix: Regularization strategy to train strong classifiers with localizable features. In Proceedings of the IEEE/CVF International Conference on Computer Vision, pp. 6023–6032.

Zhang, H., Cisse, M., Dauphin, Y. N., and Lopez-Paz, D. 2018. Mixup: Beyond empirical risk minimization. In International Conference on Learning Representations.

Zhang, M., Zhou, Y., Zhao, J., Man, Y., Liu, B., and Yao, R. 2020. A survey of semi-and weakly supervised semantic segmentation of images. Artificial Intelligence Review, 53(6): 4259–4288.

Zhang, Y., Gupta, A., Saunshi, N., and Arora, S. 2021. On predicting generalization using gans. arXiv preprint arXiv:2111.14212.

Zhu, Y., Aoun, M., Krijn, M., Vanschoren, J., and Campus, H. T. 2018. Data augmentation using conditional generative adversarial networks for leaf counting in arabidopsis plants. In BMVC, pp. 324.

6

A Filter-based Feature Selection Methodology for Vehicle/ Non-Vehicle Classification

Atikul Islam,[1] *Saurav Mallik,*[2] *Arup Roy,*[3] *Maroi Agrebi*[4] and
Pawan Kumar Singh[5],*

6.1 Introduction

Today the number of vehicles around is growing exponentially, which has been a cause for concern amongst the population living in major cities, metropolitan areas, and urban areas. As a result of the high traffic volume and limited space in dense urban areas, monitoring vehicles is particularly important [Batavia et al. 1997]. From real-time traffic management to supporting traffic planners, vehicle detection has many valuable applications. It is therefore difficult for law enforcement agencies to monitor every single vehicle. In addition to the rapid growth in the world's population, the number of vehicles on the road is also rising every day. People, their

---

[1] Department of Computer Science & Engineering, Annex College of Management Studies, BD-91, Salt Lake Bypass, Sector 1, Bidhannagar, Kolkata, West Bengal 700064, India.
Email: atikul060594@gmail.com
[2] Center for Precision Health, School of Biomedical Informatics, The University of Texas Health Science Center at Houston, Houston, TX, 77030, USA.
Email: saurav.mallik@uth.tmc.edu
[3] School of Computing and Information Technology, Reva University, Bengaluru, Karnataka-560064, India.
Email: aruproy.cse@gmail.com
[4] LAMIH UMR CNRS 8201, Department of Computer Science, Université Polytechnique Hauts-de-France, 59313 Valenciennes, France.
Email: maroi.agrebi@gmail.com
[5] Department of Information Technology, Jadavpur University, Jadavpur University Second Campus, Plot No. 8, Salt Lake Bypass, LB Block, Sector III, Salt Lake City, Kolkata-700106, West Bengal, India.
* Corresponding author: pawansingh.ju@gmail.com/pawankrsingh@ieee.org

families, and nations are adversely affected by road traffic accidents and injuries. In most countries, road traffic accidents result in a loss of 3% of the Gross Domestic Product (commonly known as GDP) caused by the death of approximately 1.3 million people each year [Sonka et al. 1993]. Despite the fact that there are several accident-avoidance methods available, deep learning-based accident prevention is gaining a lot of attention currently [Maity et al. 2022]. However, deep learning-based methods require more training images and also require more computational resources which may not be available in real-time. So, it is better to apply machine learning-based collision avoidance methods. The collision avoidance algorithm generally involves several steps, including detecting the vehicle and locating it using semantic segmentation, followed by recognizing the segmented objects [Nidhyananthan and Selva 2022]. Data from active sensors has been widely studied in the past few years for object detection. A more important consideration is the cost of these kinds of sensors. Our research focuses on passive sensors such as cameras to detect objects using vision-based methods. Images provide a more detailed picture of the environment than passive sensors. Object detection systems can be designed using the information conveyed by live images. Also, it is advantageous to have a higher resolution. Obtaining on-road information has never been easier, more affordable, and more accessible than with a camera. In addition to being able to use the data from these cameras to enhance intelligent security systems, these images can also be used to minimize traffic congestion through traffic management strategies [Bhattacharya et al. 2022]. Vehicle recognition (or classification) is very crucial for implementing intelligent transportation systems. The purpose of this technique is to identify moving vehicles and classify them accurately based on the flow rate [Arora and Kumar 2022].

With the help of technology, we can solve the above problem. It is possible to make vehicles capable of making intelligent decisions rather than humans. Driving autonomously is the result of this objective. Detection and classification of vehicles that are also part of autonomous driving are the objectives of our paper. For traffic management purposes, such as counting vehicles, measuring vehicle speed, and identifying traffic accidents, vehicle detection plays an important role [Kumar et al. 2022].

Detecting vehicles in different weather conditions, traffic jams, shadow effects, and many other challenges have been faced by researchers in this field. As a result of the different models, the following challenges are faced [Patil and Patil 2014]:

- Joint Random Fields (JRF) models fail to account for vehicle velocity.
- Traffic jams and shadow reductions are not addressed by the Color Transform Model.
- Vehicle classification is not accurate in cloudy or rainy weather conditions due to Background Estimation Algorithm.
- It is impossible to minimize the shadow effect during cloudy and rainy weather with a traffic monitoring system that relies on image analysis and rule-based reasoning.
- Due to its reliance on Illuminating Invariance, road detection doesn't handle overlapped vehicles but detects roads instead.

This chapter aims to classify road scene images from a dataset consisting of images into two categories, vehicle and non-vehicle, using the concepts of Histogram of Oriented Gradients (HOG) and Support Vector Machine (SVM). In this work, pre-processing is used which consists of changing the color format of the image from BGR to YUV and then resizing the image to 64 × 64. The process of pre-processing data involves transforming raw data into clean data. An initial pre-processing step detects missing values, noisy data, and other anomalies in the dataset before running the algorithm [Gupta et al. 2021]. When reducing processing resources is necessary without losing relevant or significant information, feature extraction is an effective process. An analysis can also be simplified by reducing redundant data through feature extraction. As a result, machine learning is also capable of learning and generalizing faster due to the reduction of data and the machine's effort in building variable combinations (features) [Bhagat et al. 2019]. A feature selection process is used to improve the accuracy of the process. Eliminating redundant and irrelevant variables, it increases the predictive power of the algorithms [Jain and Salau 2019]. The HOG feature descriptor is used here to extract features from the vehicle and non-vehicle images. By applying a correlation matrix to our filter-based feature selection procedure, some of the redundant features will be reduced. The input feature vector is reduced in order to select features in a predictive model. Reducing the number of original features will decrease the computation value of the modeling as well as improve the model's performance in some cases [Hira and Gillies 2015]. To detect vehicles and non-vehicles, we train our SVM classifier using the optimal number of features. It has been demonstrated that SVMs work well in multiple areas of biological analysis and image processing [Furey et al. 2000]. SVMs can be used for regression and classification. An SVM algorithm considers cross-parameter violations of the margin constraint when categorizing data using SVMs. The machine learning community has focused its research on SVMs because of their effective merchandising and higher accuracy [Zhang 2012].

6.2 Literature survey

Vehicle detection research has been conducted around the world by a variety of researchers. Model-based, optical-flow-based, feature-based, deep learning-based, and regression-based methods are typically used for vehicle detection [Hu 2021].

6.2.1 Vehicle detection based on optical flow

Batavia et al. [1997] detected vehicles approaching a car's blind spot using implicit optical flow. This method has the advantage of avoiding explicit optical flow calculations. Using this method for systems operating at speeds between 8 and 15 frames per second would be ineffective because it would not be able to identify the optical flow.

An improved method for calculating feature points in vehicle detection was developed using a pyramid model in Lucas-Kanade optical flow [Shi et al. 2017]. The Lucas-Kanade method is basically a two-frame differential method for estimating optical flow. In this case, the optical flow of an individual pixel around the central pixel at any given time is assumed to be constant at any given time. This method has the advantage of effectively removing the wrong optical flow. Several factors can affect this method, including changes in weather, harsh lighting, camera jitter, and noise.

6.2.2 Model-based vehicle detection

With a single Gaussian background model [Hu et al. 2021], proposed a method of detecting vehicles and determining background areas through threshold values. As a result of this technique, real-time vehicle detection is more accurate. When the background and vehicle are close to each other, the vehicle's profile cannot be extracted effectively from the Gaussian model.

The method has been further improved by [Yang and Qu 2018]. An image with a low rank and sparse decomposition was subtracted from the background. Due to the large amount of information stored and the long matching algorithm, the disadvantage of this method is that it does not perform fast matching.

6.2.3 Feature-based vehicle detection

The detection of vehicles based on features consists of two types: single and multi-feature detections. In single feature-based vehicle detection proposed by [Li et al. 2015], in order to extract vehicle features, dimensions were reduced in the color space, and a Bayes classifier was used for training and classification. For static vehicle targets, this method had an accuracy of 63.05%. Lighting, deflection, and real-time situations are the disadvantages of this method.

A number of feature extraction methods can be used to improve single feature-based vehicle detection, including scale-invariant feature transform (SIFT), Haar, and HOG. Han et al. [2009] used SIFT for vehicle detection using images with relatively obvious features. In addition to its high performance, this method is also flexible in terms of size and rotation. Using Haar-like features, local binary patterns (LBPs), and the Adaboost classifier sequentially, the Haar-like features, LBPs, and Adaboost classifier are used to detect vehicles ahead. In addition, a sample vehicle-detection video may be misjudged when complex structures appear when using this method, which can lead to poor vehicle detection at a distance.

As part of the multi-feature-based vehicle detection, focused on a multi-resolution directional HOG feature and an LBP fusion algorithm. Compared to single-feature extraction methods, this method has a higher detection rate and it is faster than single feature extraction methods.

Lin et al. [2021] proposed a vehicle detection algorithm combining the Haar and HOG features. Real-world scenarios guarantee that this algorithm is accurate and time-efficient. Lin et al. [2012] presented a method for detecting vehicles and estimating inter-vehicle distances. Urban/suburban roads perform well with this method.

6.2.4 Deep learning based vehicle detection

R-CNN [Girshick et al. 2015] is based on a candidate-box detection algorithm. An algorithm that generates 2000 boxes is used to implement the candidate box. An input image for a convolutional neural network (CNN) is a fixed-size image wrapped around each candidate box. In order to generate candidate boxes on the last layer of the feature map, fast R-CNN and Region of Interest (RoI) pooling is used instead of R-CNN because R-CNN has very low efficiency.

In the work done by Girshick, 2015, the RoI pooling layer is inserted before the full connection layer, removing the need to crop the image before it can be connected. It eliminates the need to scale and clip candidate block subgraphs.

A region proposal network (RPN) is added to fast R-CNN to improve it. Candidate boxes are generated by this layer, which uses the Softmax classifier to determine whether they are foreground or background. Succeeding this, a bounding-box regression is used to regulate the position of the bounding boxes and as a result, feature sub-maps are generated. This allows fast R-CNN to predict more correctly.

6.2.5 Regression-based vehicle detection

Regression-based detection algorithms named You Only Look Once (YOLO) [Redmon et al. 2016] and Single-Shot Multibox Detector (SSD) [Liu et al. 2016] have been applied for this type of detection method. In YOLO, the input images are resized to 448 × 448, a convolutional network is run on them and the results are thresholded by their confidence scores. It has a number of advantages over other real-time systems, such as the ability to process images straightforwardly, its speed, and its precision which is twice as high. However, YOLO is relatively inaccurate and detects fewer events than CNN.

This CNN uses a feed-forward approach in which bounding boxes and scores are generated for each object class instance, followed by a non-maximum suppression step. With SSD, you can get significantly better accuracy and speed than with YOLO.

6.3 Proposed methodology

The present section describes the proposed filter-based feature selection framework for vehicle/non-vehicle classification problems. Figure 6.1 illustrates the schematic diagram of the overall proposed methodology. Section 6.3.1 deals with the pre-processing steps whereas Section 6.3.2 explains the features that are extracted using the HOG feature descriptor. Implementation of datasets with feature selection and removing redundant features using a correlation matrix Section 6.3.3. Finally, a brief description of the machine learning model (which is an SVM classifier in our case) is provided in Section 6.3.4.

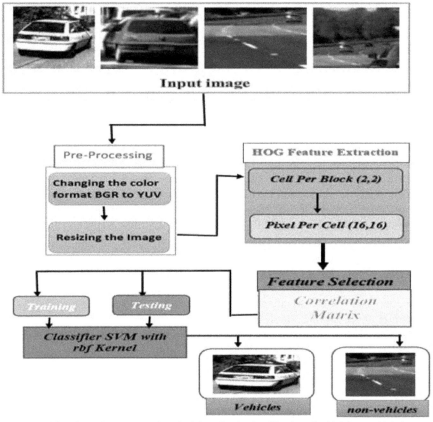

Figure 6.1: Flowchart of our proposed methodology for the classification of vehicle/non-vehicle images.

6.3.1 Pre-processing

6.3.1.1 Change color format

The RGB image is converted to YUV through a color conversion process. Because of the YUV color space, bandwidth is reduced more dramatically than with RGB colorspace. The majority of video cards render luminance/chrominance images directly via YUV or luminance/chrominance. The luminance component, or Y component, is always the most significant component in YUV capture. Raster graphics files with the YUV extension are often associated with Color Space Pixel Formats. The YUV format stores bitmap image data with color values across three Y, U, and V dimensions. Color (chrominance) is stored as U and V values, while brightness (luminance) is stored as Y values. Images can be formatted in YUV format to reduce processing time and memory requirements. Colors in the YUV range utilize the human eye's sensitivity to light and brightness. Figure 6.2 shows a YUV format image created by changing the color format of an original image.

a) Original RGB Image   b) YUV color format

Figure 6.2: Conversion of original image from RGB to YUV color format.

6.3.1.2 Resize the image

In this work, the input image is resized to 64 × 64 resolution. Computer vision relies heavily on resizing images before processing them. Smaller images are generally more conducive to deep-learning models. The learning time for an architecture increases when a neural network has to learn from four times as many pixels as an input image. By using the resize command, the file can be resized to a specified modulo and the apparent contiguous portion (or modulo) of that file can be increased or decreased without having to restore the original file. By adding or releasing overflow, a new modulo can be reached, and all items are rehashed for accuracy. When dealing with pictures of different sizes, downscaling them to the smallest available dimension is the most practical solution. Figure 6.3 shows the resizing of the input image. The size of the image should also be changed to reduce the file size. In addition, when an image is downsized, its quality is not affected.

a) YUV color format   b) Resizing the image

Figure 6.3: Resizing the image to 64 × 64 pixels.

6.3.2 Feature extraction

Different features like color and shape can be used to detect vehicles. There may be a lot of variation in colors between vehicles. Therefore, it would be appropriate to determine vehicles by their shape. HOG [Dalal and Triggs 2005] can therefore be used to determine the shape of an object present in an image. HOG finds its application in solving many typical pattern recognition problems such as Face recognition [Déniz et al. 2011], Human detection from video [Surasak et al. 2018], Handwritten script classification [Singh et al. 2015], Handwritten digit recognition [Ebrahimzadeh and Jampour 2014], etc. An image is divided into blocks containing cells where pixels are observed in order to extract the feature vector. Each gradient direction is computed for each sample, and each orientation bin is grouped and the gradient magnitude is summed. This gives us an indication of the shape of the image once we get a dominant orientation for each cell. In the domain of computer vision, the HOG descriptor describes features that are useful for detecting objects. An image is counted according to how many places in it have gradient orientation. For improved accuracy, this method uses the concept of overlapping local contrast normalization. However, this is calculated on a dense grid of uniformly spaced cells, similar to edge orientation histograms and SIFT descriptors. As a result, a dominant orientation of each cell is produced which when implemented for all cells gives us a representation of the shape of the input image.

In Figure 6.4, the objects are cropped to 16 × 16 pixels to show a tight crop. A computer vision algorithm is commonly trained on images like these. This proposed algorithm is also based on many studies in visual cognition that have focused on tight objects and cropped objects without a background.

A new block is formed by clubbing 4 blocks from the 9-point histogram matrix into one (2 × 2). Using a stride of 8 pixels, the clubbing overlaps. All 4 cells in a block are concatenated to form 36 feature vectors by concatenating all 9-point histograms. Here, each block of HOG consists of 4 cells in the image (as shown in Figure 6.5).

Figure 6.4: The original image of resolution 64 × 64 is divided into 16 cells of resolution 16 × 16.

Figure 6.5: One block of HOG consists of 4 cells in the image.

A YUV color space feature extraction was performed for all components. A total of 972 features can be found by multiplying 324 by 3 components.
An image is selected, and HOG features are extracted.

Total number of blocks = 9

Number of cells in each block = 4

Number of features per cell = 9

Number of features per block = 9 × 4 = 36

Total number of features = 36 × 9 = 324

6.3.3 Feature selection

A total of 972 features are extracted using the HOG feature descriptor. It may be possible to overfit our model by using many of these redundant features. For improving the classification accuracy as well as the speed of our proposed methodology, in this work, we have also removed some redundant features using a filter-based feature selection method. It is possible to reduce classification time as well as improve the final classification rate by excluding these ambiguous features using the feature selection method. In order to select attributes hidden from dominant patterns of the vehicle or non-vehicle images, discriminative feature vectors have been used [Laopracha et al. 2019]. This method computes local decisions at each image point using abstractions of image information. Image features of a specific type are present or not at that point. An image processing operation that detects features is known as feature detection. Feature selection techniques help reduce the number of features by selecting the most significant ones and discarding the rest.

Our data is split into test and train sets after HOG is used to extract images' features. The process is made more accurate by selecting features. The most critical variables are selected, and the redundant and irrelevant ones are eliminated, which increases the predictability of algorithms. A high correlation between features has been removed [Kumar et al. 2022, Taherzadeh et al. 2016]. As a result of applying a filter-based feature selection procedure, a set of 448 features are selected from the original feature set.

Figure 6.6 shows the illustration of the heatmap of the correlation matrix which is used after the implementation of the proposed filter-based feature selection methodology. It is already known that the value of the correlation coefficient ranges from −1 to +1. If there exists a positive relationship between the two variables (i.e., +1), it is known as a Positive correlation. On the other hand, if there is a negative relationship between the two variables (i.e., −1), we call it a Negative correlation. The correlation between the two variables is zero if the value is 0. Mathematically, for a pair of variables (a, b), the correlation coefficient r_{ab} can be defined as follows:

$$r_{ab} = \frac{\sum \left(a_i - \underline{a_i}\right)\left(b_i - \underline{b_i}\right)}{\sqrt{\sum \left(a_i - \underline{a_i}\right)^2 \times \sum \left(b_i - \underline{b_i}\right)^2}} \tag{1}$$

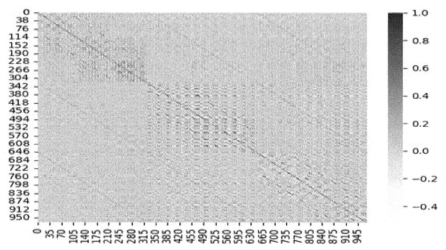

Figure 6.6: Illustration of a heatmap of correlation matrix used for the feature selection procedure in the present work. (Darker cells represent a higher correlation between variables and vice-versa).

In order to determine the correlation between the continuous feature and the class feature, the proposed work merely uses a sample correlation coefficient. The correlation coefficient, having a higher value for a sample, may not produce favorable results for the complete population due to the quick rise of the original feature set. Therefore, it is necessary to ascertain, across the entire population (or original feature vector), whether there is a significant correlation between the features [Blessie and Karthikeyan 2012]. The t-test is the most popular method for determining if two or more features are statistically correlated or not. In order to choose the most important features from the set of features, the proposed methodology in the suggested algorithm uses a t-test [Singh et al. 2016] which can be calculated as follows:

$$t = r_{ab} \sqrt{\frac{N-2}{1-r_{ab}^2}} \tag{2}$$

where N is the total number of features and r_{ab} is the correlation coefficient. If the calculated t-value is found to be greater than the critical value at 0.05 level of significance and $(N-2)$ degrees of freedom, then the feature is said to be significant and it is included in the final feature set. Else, the feature is discarded. The pseudocode for our filter-based feature selection algorithm used in the proposed methodology has been described below:

Proposed Filter-based Feature Selection

Input: Original feature set $F_{list} = \{F_1, F_2, \ldots \ldots F_k, F_c\}$ and the number of classes C.
Output: F_{best} with selected features

$$F_{best} = \varnothing$$
$$count = 1$$

while *count < k* do
 for *i = 1 to k*
  Calculate Pearson correlation coefficient r_{ab} using Eqn. (1)
 End for
 Assume $r_c = 0$ //intital assumption
 for *i = 1 to k*
  Calculate *t = significance (r_{ab}, r_c)* using Eqn. (2)
 End for
 If *t > Critical value // for (N – 2) degrees of freedom and 0.05 significance level*
 $F_{best} = F_{best} \ U \ F_{list}$
 count = count +1
end

6.3.4 Support Vector Machine (SVM)

In SVMs, sample data over time is analyzed. This technology locates a suitable segmentation hyperplane using Linear Separable SVM [Tanveer et al. 2016]. Calculating the interval in the sample space is significant since a maximum interval is sought in this study. Based on the following linear equation, the hyperplane in the sample space is divided as follows:

$$w^t x + b = 0 \tag{3}$$

This is a hyperplane whose direction is determined by W, and whose distance from the origin is determined by b. The following formula will apply to the training samples if the hyperplane correctly classifies them, i.e., the hyperplane classifies them correctly:

$$w^t x_i + b \geq 1 \quad y = 1 \tag{4}$$

$$w^t x_i + b \leq -1 \quad y = -1 \tag{5}$$

The maximal interval hypothesis is based on the above formula.

6.4 Experimental evaluation

6.4.1 Dataset used

6.4.1.1 Dataset 1

The present work primarily involves two classes of classification: vehicles and non-vehicles. GTI dataset provides the images [https://www.kaggle.com/datasets/iamprateek/vehicle-images-gti]. Among the 3425 images in the database are 3,900 images extracted from road sequences without vehicles and 3,425 images taken from different points of view of vehicle rears. This process maximizes the proportion of representative images in the class of vehicles, whose variability is naturally high. Considering the vehicle's position relative to the camera, we believe that it significantly affects the appearance of the rear [Arróspide et al. 2012]. In this dataset, images of size 64x64 are used. Some sample images of the images taken from the GTI dataset are shown in Figure 6.7.

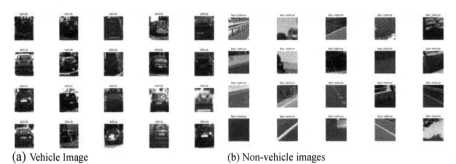

(a) Vehicle Image (b) Non-vehicle images

Figure 6.7: Sample images showing: (a) vehicle, and (b) non-vehicle images taken from GTI dataset.

6.4.1.2 Dataset 2

We downloaded this dataset from the Kaggle website which contains 8,792 vehicle images and 8,968 non-vehicle images [https://www.kaggle.com/datasets/brsdincer/vehicle-detection-image-set?resource=download]. Figure 6.8 shows some sample images of this dataset.

(a) Vehicle images (b) Non-vehicle images

Figure 6.8: Sample images showing vehicle and Non-vehicle images taken from Kaggle dataset.

6.4.2 *Evaluation metrics used*

The purpose of this section is to discuss evaluation metrics that can be used to measure the performance of machine learning classification algorithms. Optimization of a model is based on performance metrics. In this experiment, we will train a machine-learning model to find out whether or not an image contains a vehicle or not. It is imperative for this model to be accurate, but it is more significant to identify false predictions.

Whenever the output of a machine learning classification problem can be split into more than one class, the confusion matrix is used as a performance measure. The actual value is combined with the predicted values in the table. The following examples will help you understand the terminology of the confusion matrix:

- True Positive (TP): In fraud cases, the model detects the transaction as fraud.
- False Positive (FP): Fraud is detected when a transaction is not fraudulent. Type I errors are also known as these.
- True Negative (TN): Transactions that are detected as not fraudulent are not fraudulent.
- False Negative (FN): We predicted a negative outcome and it did not come true. Our prediction was that the image in the image was not a vehicle.

In classification models, confusion matrices are tables that describe how a classification model performs with a set of data. Please refer to Figure 6.9 for more details.

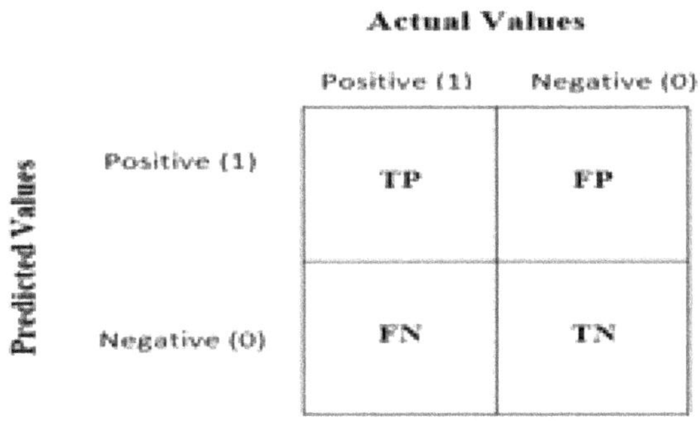

Actual Values

	Positive (1)	Negative (0)
Positive (1)	TP	FP
Negative (0)	FN	TN

Predicted Values

Figure 6.9: Schematic diagram representing a confusion matrix for a two-class classification problem.

6.4.2.1 *Accuracy*

We think it is a pretty significant metric, and it is also easy to comprehend. As a percentage of the total number of cases, the true results count represents the proportion of true results. An accurate prediction is one that is right the majority of the time.

$$Accuracy = \frac{(TP+TN)}{(TP+TN+FP+FN)} \tag{6}$$

Suppose a model can produce only two results for a binary classification problem. There are two types of models: those that give correct or incorrect predictions. In this example, we need to classify images to determine if they are vehicles or non-vehicles. Table 6.1 shows the classification accuracy attained before and after applying filter-based feature selection procedure on both the datasets by four different state-of-the-art machine learning models such as Naïve Bayes [Murphy 2006], Decision Tree [Safavian and Landgrebe 1991], SVM (linear kernel) and SVM (rbf kernel). As shown in Table 6.1, different machine learning-based models have varying levels of accuracy on both datasets. However, the SVM classifier (with rbf kernel) produces the best accuracies of 99.04% and 99.71% on GTI and Kaggle datasets respectively as compared to other classifiers.

Table 6.1: Accuracy attained before and after applying feature selection procedure by different machine learning models.

Classifier	GTI dataset		Kaggle dataset	
	Accuracy (Using original feature set)	**Accuracy (Using selected feature set)**	**Accuracy (Using original feature set)**	**Accuracy (Using selected feature set)**
Naive Bayes	90.01%	92.83%	90.63%	93.77%
Decision Tree	91.53%	92.49%	91.10%	93.10%
SVM (linear kernel)	93.54%	97.54%	94.90%	98.93%
SVM (rbf kernel)	**95.83%**	**99.04%**	**97.63%**	**99.71%**

6.4.2.2 Precision

By considering precision, we can estimate the number of correct predictions that were actually positive. As far as precision cases are concerned, FPs pose a greater challenge than FNs. Any e-commerce website, music or video recommendations, or anything else is dependent on precision. According to the definition of precision, precision means the ratio of positive samples classified correctly (TP) to positive samples classified either incorrectly or correctly (either correctly or incorrectly). As a percentage, precision is defined by the difference between true positives and predicted positives.

$$Precision = \frac{TP}{(TP+FP)} \tag{7}$$

Table 6.2 shows the precision scores attained before and after applying filter-based feature selection procedure on both the datasets by four different machine learning models such as Naïve Bayes, Decision Tree, SVM (linear kernel) and SVM (rbf kernel). As shown in Table 6.2, different machine learning based models have varying levels of precision scores on both the datasets. However, SVM classifier (with rbf kernel) produces the best precision scores of 99.03% and 99.72% on GTI and Kaggle datasets respectively as compared to other classifiers.

Table 6.2: Precision scores attained before and after applying feature selection procedure by different machine learning models.

Classifier	GTI dataset		Kaggle dataset	
	Precision (Before using feature selection)	Precision (After using feature selection)	Precision (Before using feature selection)	Precision (After using feature selection)
Naive Bayes	90.90%	92.71%	91.60%	94.77%
Decision Tree	91.49%	92.39%	92.81%	94.01%
SVM (linear kernel)	94.52%	97.54%	95.90%	98.92%
SVM (rbf kernel)	**95.81%**	**99.03%**	**96.64%**	**99.72%**

6.4.2.3 Recall

It describes how many positive cases our model predicted correctly out of the actual cases. Since FNs are of greater concern than FPs, so this metric is useful. There is a crucial difference between raising a false alarm and spreading the word about a positive case when it comes to medical cases. Positive samples are counted as such when they are correctly classified as such compared to the total number of positive samples. Detecting positive samples is measured by the recall.

$$Recall = \frac{TP}{(TP+FN)} \qquad (8)$$

Table 6.3 shows the recall scores attained before and after applying the filter-based feature selection procedure on both datasets by four different machine learning models such as Naïve Bayes, Decision Tree, SVM (linear kernel) and SVM (rbf kernel). As shown in Table 6.3, different machine learning-based models have varying levels of recall scores on both datasets. However, the SVM classifier (with rbf kernel) produces the best recall scores of 99.03% and 99.71% on GTI and Kaggle datasets respectively as compared to other classifiers.

Table 6.3: Recall attained before and after applying feature selection procedure by different machine learning models.

Classifier	GTI dataset		Kaggle dataset	
	Recall (Before using feature selection)	Recall (After using feature selection)	Recall (Before using feature selection)	Recall (After using feature selection)
Naive Bayes	90.04%	92.89%	91.62%	93.99%
Decision Tree	89.42%	92.47%	90.78%	94.89%
SVM (linear kernel)	94.52%	97.49%	95.89%	98.93%
SVM (rbf kernel)	**96.84%**	**99.03%**	**95.62%**	**99.71%**

6.4.2.4 F1 Score

Precision and recall metrics are combined in this chart. A measurement's precision is maximum when its recall equals its precision. The F1 Score is calculated by averaging Precision and Recall.

$$F1\ Score = 2 * \frac{(precision * Recall)}{(precision + Recall)} \tag{9}$$

Table 6.4 shows the F1 scores attained before and after applying the filter-based feature selection procedure on both datasets by four different machine learning models such as Naïve Bayes, Decision Tree, SVM (linear kernel) and SVM (rbf kernel). As shown in Table 6.4, different machine learning-based models have varying levels of F1 scores on both datasets. However, the SVM classifier (with rbf kernel) produces the best F1 scores of 99.03% and 99.74% on GTI and Kaggle datasets respectively as compared to other classifiers.

Table 6.4: F1 Score attained before and after applying feature selection procedure by different machine learning models.

Classifier	GTI dataset		Kaggle dataset	
	F1 Score (Before using feature selection)	F1 Score (After using feature selection)	F1 Score (Before using feature selection)	F1 Score (After using feature selection)
Naive Bayes	90.96%	92.78%	90.01%	93.77%
Decision Tree	89.45%	92.43%	91.61%	94.02%
SVM (linear kernel)	93.52%	97.52%	96.90%	98.93%
SVM (rbf kernel)	**95.83%**	**99.03%**	**95.64%**	**99.74%**

6.4.3 Analysis of results

In this section, we have shown the ROC curves produced by the proposed methodology on both GTI and Kaggle datasets which is illustrated in Figure 6.10. Here, FP rates are typically plotted on the X-axis of the ROC curve, while the true positive rate is displayed on the Y-axis. An FP rate of zero and a TP rate of one can be found in the top left corner of the plot. It indicates better performance when the curve reaches the top-left corner of the chart. For random classification, a diagonal distribution is expected (where FPR = TPR). It is less accurate for ROC graphs to have curves that approach the diagonal of the ROC space at a 45-degree angle.

If the model is to be accurate, it must be able to predict zero as zero and one as one. From 0 to 1, the true positive rate increases and is set to 1, resulting in high accuracy. High accuracy is the result of a high true positive rate.

The confusion matrices produced by the proposed filter-based feature selection framework for both datasets are shown in Figure 6.11. In a confusion matrix, the predicted category labels are compared to the true labels on a two-dimensional array. As a summary of what a classification model does, a confusion matrix is also called an error matrix. Based on count values, each class is broken down as to how many correct and incorrect predictions there are.

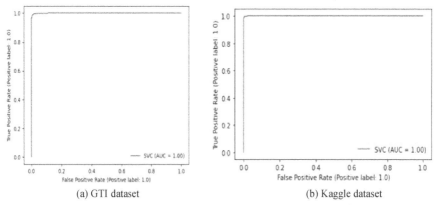

(a) GTI dataset   (b) Kaggle dataset

Figure 6.10: ROC curves produced by the proposed framework on the test data of: (a) GTI dataset and (b) Kaggle dataset.

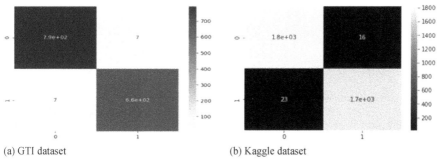

(a) GTI dataset   (b) Kaggle dataset

Figure 6.11: Confusion matrix produced by the best-performing model on both GTI and Kaggle datasets.

Confusion matrixes are tables that demonstrate how classification models perform. Colors are depicted as individual values in a matrix, which is a two-dimensional graphical representation of data. It can also help you determine the usefulness of the model by providing data that can be used to calculate measures. Columns represent true classes, while rows represent predicted classifications.

6.5 Conclusion and future scope

The purpose of this chapter is to study some standard vehicle detection methods that have been proposed in the literature to date. Until now, there have been no such methods tested using the filter ranking method for vehicle detection problems. Motivated by the above fact, in this work, we proposed a filter-based feature selection methodology for vehicle/non-vehicle classification problems. In this study, HOG feature descriptor has been applied to extract the features from the input image and then by applying a correlation matrix, some redundant features are removed from the original feature vector. Finally, we have tested our proposed filter-based feature selection framework on both GTI and Kaggle datasets using an SVM classifier (having rbf kernel) to attain overall classification accuracies of 99.04% and 99.71% respectively. It can also be concluded from the performance results that an increment of about 4–5% in the overall classification accuracy has been attained while utilizing only 50% of the original feature vector. This two-fold utility validates the need of applying a feature selection procedure before the classification phase.

A multi-class classification can be performed in the future using the present model to classify vehicles like cars, buses, trucks, scooters, bikes, etc. In addition, we can localize and highlight areas where vehicles appear in a scene image. In the future, some more benchmark datasets will be used, and other standard feature extraction techniques, as well as feature selection algorithms, will be developed. This will help to achieve much superior performance results.

References

Arora, N., and Kumar, Y. 2022. Automatic vehicle detection system in Day and Night Mode: Challenges, applications and panoramic review. Evolutionary Intelligence, 1–19.

Arróspide, J., Salgado, L., and Nieto, M. 2012. Video analysis-based vehicle detection and tracking using an MCMC sampling framework. EURASIP Journal on Advances in Signal Processing, 2012(1): 1–20.

Batavia, P. H., Pomerleau, D. A., and Thorpe, C. E. 1997. Overtaking vehicle detection using implicit optical flow. In Proceedings of the Conference on Intelligent Transportation Systems, Boston, MA, USA, 12 November 1997.

Bhagat, P. K., Choudhary, P., and Singh, K. M. 2019. A comparative study for brain tumor detection in MRI images using texture features. In Sensors for Health Monitoring (pp. 259–287). Academic Press.

Bhattacharya, D., Bhattacharyya, A., Agrebi, M., Roy, A. and Singh P. K. 2022. DFE-AVD: Deep feature ensemble for automatic vehicle detection. In Proceedings of International Conference on Intelligence Computing Systems and Applications (ICICSA 2022).

Blessie, E. C., and Karthikeyan, E. 2012. Sigmis: A feature selection algorithm using correlation based method. Journal of Algorithms & Computational Technology, 6(3): 385–394.

Dalal, N., and Triggs, B. 2005, June. Histograms of oriented gradients for human detection. In 2005 IEEE computer society conference on computer vision and pattern recognition (CVPR'05) (1: 886–893). IEEE.

Déniz, O., Bueno, G., Salido, J., and De la Torre, F. 2011. Face recognition using histograms of oriented gradients. Pattern Recognition Letters, 32(12): 1598–1603.

Ebrahimzadeh, R., and Jampour, M. 2014. Efficient handwritten digit recognition based on histogram of oriented gradients and SVM. International journal of computer Applications, 104(9).

Furey, T. S., Cristianini, N., Duffy, N., Bednarski, D. W., Schummer, M., and Haussler, D. 2000. Support vector machine classification and validation of cancer tissue samples using microarray expression data. Bioinformatics, 16(10): 906–914.

Girshick, R. 2015. Fast r-cnn. In Proceedings of the IEEE International Conference On Computer Vision (pp. 1440–1448).

Girshick, R., Donahue, J., Darrell, T., and Malik, J. 2015. Region-based convolutional networks for accurate object detection and segmentation. IEEE Transactions on Pattern Analysis and Machine Intelligence, 38(1): 142–158.

Gupta, V., Sachdeva, S., and Dohare, N. 2021. Deep similarity learning for disease prediction. Trends in Deep Learning Methodologies, 183–206.

Han, S., Han, Y., and Hahn, H. 2009. Vehicle detection method using Haar-like feature on real time system. World Academy of Science, Engineering and Technology, 59: 455–459.

Hira, Z. M., and Gillies, D. F. 2015. A review of feature selection and feature extraction methods applied on microarray data. Advances in Bioinformatics, 2015.

https://www.kaggle.com/datasets/brsdincer/vehicle-detection-image-set?resource=download   Accessed on 2022-10-21.

https://www.kaggle.com/datasets/iamprateek/vehicle-images-gti Accessed on 2022-10-21.

Hu, J., Sun, Y., and Xiong, S. 2021. Research on the cascade vehicle detection method based on CNN. Electronics, 10(4): 481.

Hu, X. G., and Liu, Z. Z. 2011. Improved vehicle detection algorithm based on Gaussian background model. Computer Engineering and Design, 32(12): 4111–4114.

Jain, S., and Salau, A. O. 2019. An image feature selection approach for dimensionality reduction based on kNN and SVM for AkT proteins. Cogent Engineering, 6(1): 1599537.

Kumar, K., Talluri, M. T., Krishna, B., and Karthikeyan, V. 2022, July. A novel approach for speed estimation along with vehicle detection counting. In 2022 IEEE Students Conference on Engineering and Systems (SCES) (pp. 1–5). IEEE.

Laopracha, N., Sunat, K., and Chiewchanwattana, S. 2019. A novel feature selection in vehicle detection through the selection of dominant patterns of histograms of oriented gradients (DPHOG). IEEE Access, 7: 20894–20919.

Li, L., Deng, Y., and Rao, X. 2015. Application of color feature Model in static vehicle detection. J. Wuhan Univ. Technol, 37: 73–78.

Lin, B. F., Chan, Y. M., Fu, L. C., Hsiao, P. Y., Chuang, L. A., Huang, S. S. et al. 2012. Integrating appearance and edge features for sedan vehicle detection in the blind-spot area. IEEE Transactions on Intelligent Transportation Systems, 13(2): 737–747.

Lin, C. J., Jeng, S. Y., and Lioa, H. W. 2021. A real-time vehicle counting, speed estimation, and classification system based on virtual detection zone and YOLO. Mathematical Problems in Engineering, 2021.

Liu, W., Anguelov, D., Erhan, D., Szegedy, C., Reed, S., Fu, C. Y. et al. 2016, October. Ssd: Single shot multibox detector. In European conference on computer vision (pp. 21–37). Springer, Cham.

Maity, S., Bhattacharyya, A., Singh, P. K., Kumar, M., and Sarkar, R. 2022. Last decade in vehicle detection and classification: A comprehensive survey. Archives of Computational Methods in Engineering, 1–38.

Murphy, K. P. 2006. Naive bayes classifiers. University of British Columbia, 18(60): 1–8.

Nidhyananthan Selva, Shebiah Newlin, Kumari, B. and Gopalakrishnan, K. 2022. Deep learning for accident avoidance in a hostile driving environment. Cognitive Systems and Signal Processing in Image Processing. Academic Press, pp. 337–357. 10.1016/B978-0-12-824410-4.00002-7.

Patil, S. P., and Patil, M. B. 2014. Moving vehicle detection: A review. International Journal of Computer Applications, 87(15).

Redmon, J., Divvala, S., Girshick, R., and Farhadi, A. 2016. You only look once: Unified, real-time object detection. In Proceedings of the IEEE Conference on Computer Vision and Pattern Recognition (pp. 779–788).

Safavian, S. R., and Landgrebe, D. 1991. A survey of decision tree classifier methodology. IEEE Transactions on Systems, Man, and Cybernetics, 21(3): 660–674.

Shi, L., Deng, X., Wang, J., and Chen, Q. 2017. Multi-target Tracking based on optical flow method and Kalman Filter. Computer Applications, 37: 131–136.

Singh, P. K., Mondal, A., Bhowmik, S., Sarkar, R., and Nasipuri, M. 2015. Word-level script identification from handwritten multi-script documents. *In*: Satapathy, S., Biswal, B., Udgata, S., and Mandal, J. (eds.). Proceedings of the 3rd International Conference on Frontiers of Intelligent Computing: Theory and Applications (FICTA) 2014. Advances in Intelligent Systems and Computing, vol 327. Springer, Cham. https://doi.org/10.1007/978-3-319-11933-5_62.

Singh, P. K., Sarkar, R., and Nasipuri, M. 2016. Significance of non-parametric statistical tests for comparison of classifiers over multiple datasets. International Journal of Computing Science and Mathematics, 7(5): 410–442.

Sonka, M., Hlavac, V., and Boyle, R. 1993. Image Processing, Analysis and Machine Vision. doi:10.1007/978-1-4899-3216-7.

Surasak, T., Takahiro, I., Cheng, C. H., Wang, C. E., and Sheng, P. Y. 2018, May. Histogram of oriented gradients for human detection in video. In 2018 5th International conference on business and industrial research (ICBIR) (pp. 172–176). IEEE.

Taherzadeh, G., Zhou, Y., Liew, A. W. C., and Yang, Y. 2016. Sequence-based prediction of protein–carbohydrate binding sites using support vector machines. Journal of Chemical Information and Modeling, 56(10): 2115–2122.

Tanveer, M., Khan, M. A., and Ho, S. S. 2016. Robust energy-based least squares twin support vector machines. Applied Intelligence, 45(1): 174–186.

Yang, H., and Qu, S. 2018. Real-time vehicle detection and counting in complex traffic scenes using background subtraction model with low-rank decomposition. IET Intelligent Transport Systems, 12(1): 75–85.

Zhang, Y. 2012, September. Support vector machine classification algorithm and its application. In International conference on information computing and applications (pp. 179–186). Springer, Berlin, Heidelberg.

7

Augmented Visual Inertial Wheel Odometry Through Slip Compensation

Niraj Reginald,[1] *Omar Al-Buraiki,*[1] *Baris Fidan*[2,]* and *Ehsan Hashemi*[3]

7.1 Introduction

Visual inertial navigation system (VINS) algorithms are considered state of the art for localization in cases where a global positioning system (GPS) is not available. The initialization procedure of VINS algorithms play a vital role in the overall accuracy and robustness of these algorithms. The estimation procedures used in VINS initialization can be classified as joint procedures vs the disjoint ones [Campos et al., 2020]. The joint estimation procedures build a closed form algebraic system of equations, which is typically solved using least squares based methodologies. On the other hand, the disjoint estimation procedures typically assume accurate measurement of up-to scale camera trajectory using monocular vision, which is used to estimate the inertial parameters. Regardless of these methods, there are certain degenerate motions which a wheeled mobile robot undergoes and fail to initialize, or initializes with very large errors, which affect the overall accuracy and robustness. In the recent past, considering these challenges, researchers have fused monocular visual, inertial, and wheel encoder measurements to estimate the robot states and initialize the state estimation, robustly to degenerate motions. However, the wheel encoder measurements can be faulty due to wheel slippages. Hence, when a VINS is augmented with wheel odometry (WO) one should take care of the errors arising due to wheel slippages and compensate for

---

[1] Department of Mechanical and Mechatronics Engineering University of Waterloo.

[2] 200 University Avenue West, Waterloo, Ontario, Canada, N2L 3G1.

[3] Department of Mechanical Engineering University of Alberta.

* Corresponding author: fidan@uwaterloo.ca

them. Considering the aforementioned challenges, this chapter introduces a method for augmenting VINS using slip compensated WO.

Because of the low cost of monocular vision and improvements in monocular VINS algorithms, these algorithms are widely utilized in mobile robotic applications. Also using monocular cameras has various advantages in building space constrained miniature robots. However, there exist some inherent issues with monocular vision based algorithms. The motivation to use WO pre-integration is to assist monocular VINS state estimation and initialization of such estimation, when the robot agent navigates through degenerate motion trajectories. Degeneracy [Yang et al., 2019] describes situations/trajectories which cause VINS state estimation challenging due to the additional unobservable directions.

In general, degenerate motions should be avoided as they diminish the system robustness. Furthermore, especially for monocular VINS algorithms, uniform linear and circular motion trajectories lead to loss of scale and orientation (pitch and roll) observability [Wu et al., 2017]. Hence, directly applying VINS algorithms can result in inaccurate state estimates. Considering these fall backs, researchers have utilized WO measurements to aid in robust initialization and improved performance. A tightly coupled visual inertial wheel odometry (VIWO) scheme is proposed in [Liu et al., 2019] where WO measurements are used for robust initialization. Another study provided a VIWO scheme with two degrees of freedom (DOF) bicycle model where the preintegrated WO measurements are used for accurate initialization [Kang et al., 2019]. Furthermore, in [Lee et al., 2020], online calibration of the wheel encoder intrinsic and extrinsic parameters in VIWO schemes is studied. The VIWO schemes utilizing such online calibration have shown improved accuracy compared to the schemes that assume there are no or negligible wheel slippages. Although VINS design augmented with WO measurements have been well studied in the recent past [Jung et al., 2022, Zhu et al., 2021], these studies assume ideal conditions without any wheel slippage. In certain cases, due to wheel slippages, the WO measurements can be faulty and therefore fusing of VINS with WO becomes a challenging task.

To improve the pre-integration accuracy of WO, this chapter introduces a wheel slip compensation method using Gaussian process regression to improve the localization accuracy of VINS when augmented with WO. The chapter's main contribution is integration of a wheel slip estimation and compensation scheme to improve the accuracy of WO measurements, and thereby to enhance the accuracy of the robot localization and state estimation by augmenting this slip compansation scheme with VINS.

The remaining sections of the chapter are structured as follows: Section 7.2 states the system description and defines the problem. Section 7.3 presents the overall structure of the studied VIWO scheme. Section 7.4 presents the proposed wheel slip estimator and compensator design. Section 7.5 focuses on state estimation via multi-state constrain Kalman filter (MSCKF) and augmentation of the wheel slip compensation to the state estimator. In Section 7.6, simulated experimental results are provided and discussed based on a real world dataset. Finally, in Section 7.7 the concluding remarks are provided along with future directions of this research.

7.2 Robot system, sensors, and measurements

In this section, we present the key components of our visual inertial wheel odometry (VIWO) system design. Figure 7.2 outlines these key system components of the proposed method. To describe the system, we first define the frame notations. The notations $^b(\cdot), ^w(\cdot), ^c(\cdot), ^o(\cdot)$ denote the body-fixed inertial frame $\{b\}$, world frame $\{w\}$, camera frame $\{c\}$, and wheel encoder frame $\{o\}$ respectively. The origin of frame $\{o\}$ is located in the mid-point of the axle linking the two wheels of the robot. The translation and orientation (using quaternions) in frame $\{w\}$ with reference to frame $\{o\}$ are denoted as $^w_o\mathbf{p}, ^w_o\mathbf{q}$ respectively. Furthermore, $\mathbf{R}$ represents a rotation matrix and $^{o_k}\mathbf{R}$ represents the rotation in $\{o\}$ frame when the kth image is taken. $\otimes$ is used to denote the multiplication operator between two quaternions.

7.2.1 Inertial state of the robot

The inertial state vector of the robot at each sampling time $t = t_k = k\Delta t$ (where $\Delta t = 0.01$ sec is the sampling time) is denoted by

$$\bar{\mathbf{x}}_{I_k} = \begin{bmatrix} \bar{\mathbf{x}}_k^T & ^w\bar{\mathbf{v}}_{b_k}^T & \mathbf{b}_g^T & \mathbf{b}_a^T \end{bmatrix}^T,$$

where $\bar{\mathbf{x}}_k = \begin{bmatrix} ^b_w\mathbf{q}^T(t_k) & ^w\mathbf{p}_b^T(t_k) \end{bmatrix}$ captures the robot orientation and position in frame $\{b\}$ at step k, $^b_w\bar{\mathbf{q}}$ is the quaternion corresponding to the rotation $^b_w\mathbf{R}$, and $^w\mathbf{v}_{b_k}$ is the velocity of the frame $\{b\}$ in reference frame $\{w\}$, and $\mathbf{b}_a, \mathbf{b}_g$ are the accelerometer and gyroscope biases of the inertial measurement unit (IMU), respectively.

7.2.2 Inertial measurements and dynamic model

The inertial state $\bar{\mathbf{x}}_{I_k}$ is measured using a 6-axis IMU continuously. The local angular velocity and linear acceleration measurements by the IMU at each step k are given by [Castro-Toscano et al., 2017]

$$\omega_{m,k} = \omega_k + \mathbf{b}_g + \mathbf{n}_g, \tag{7.1}$$

$$\mathbf{a}_{m,k} = \mathbf{a}_k + ^b_w\mathbf{R}\,^w\mathbf{g} + \mathbf{b}_a + \mathbf{n}_a, \tag{7.2}$$

where ω and $\mathbf{a}$, respectively, denote the actual angular velocity and acceleration. $\mathbf{n}_g$ and $\mathbf{n}_a$ denote the gyroscope and accelerometer measurement noises that are assumed to be zero-mean Gaussian random processes. $^w\mathbf{g} \approx \begin{bmatrix} 0 & 0 & 9.81 \end{bmatrix}^T$ is the global gravity vector. The camera measurements are obtained at a sampling time $\Delta\bar{t} = 0.1$ sec, which is 10 times the main (inertial) sampling time Δt. We denote this factor as $\tau = \dfrac{\Delta\bar{t}}{\Delta t} = 10$. Accordingly, the inertial state vector at the camera and odometry measurement sampling time $t = \bar{t}_{\bar{k}} = \bar{k}\Delta\bar{t}$ is defined as

$$\mathbf{x}_{I_{\bar{k}}} = \begin{bmatrix} \mathbf{x}_{\bar{k}}^T & ^w\mathbf{v}_{b_{\bar{k}}}^T & \mathbf{b}_g^T & \mathbf{b}_a^T \end{bmatrix}^T = \bar{\mathbf{x}}_{I_{10\bar{k}}} = \begin{bmatrix} \bar{\mathbf{x}}_{10\bar{k}}^T & ^w\bar{\mathbf{v}}_{b_{10\bar{k}}}^T & \mathbf{b}_g^T & \mathbf{b}_a^T \end{bmatrix}^T. \tag{7.3}$$

Below we define the pre-integrated IMU measurements between two camera frames $C_{\bar{k}}$ and $C_{\bar{k}+1}$. The pre-integrated velocity ${}^w\mathbf{v}_b$ of frame $\{b\}$ with respect to frame $\{w\}$ of the robot is obtained by integrating the acceleration $\mathbf{a}_m$ measured by the IMU given as

$$
{}^w\mathbf{v}_{b_{\bar{k}+1}} = {}^w\mathbf{v}_{b_{\bar{k}}} + \Delta\bar{t} \sum_{q=10\bar{k}}^{10\bar{k}+10} ({}^w\mathbf{R}\mathbf{a}_{m,q} - {}^w\mathbf{g}), \tag{7.4}
$$

where ${}^w\mathbf{R}$ is the orientation of the robot represented by the rotation matrix in world frame. Further integrating (7.4), the translation of the system between two inertial frames $b_{\bar{k}}$ and $b_{\bar{k}+1}$ with respect to the world frame is obtained as

$$
{}^w\mathbf{p}_{b_{\bar{k}+1}} = {}^w\mathbf{p}_{b_{\bar{k}}} + {}^w\mathbf{v}_{b_{\bar{k}}}\Delta\bar{t} + \Delta\bar{t}^2 \sum_{q=10\bar{k}}^{10\bar{k}+10} \sum_{p=10\bar{k}}^{q} ({}^w\mathbf{R}\mathbf{a}_{m,p} - {}^w\mathbf{g}). \tag{7.5}
$$

Similarly the IMU also measures the angular velocity ω of the robot. The rotation $\mathbf{q}$ of the robot between two frames is obtained by integrating the angular velocity given as

$$
{}^w\mathbf{q}_{b_{\bar{k}+1}} = {}^w\mathbf{q}_{b_{\bar{k}}} \otimes \Delta\bar{t} \sum_{q=10\bar{k}}^{10\bar{k}+10} \left(\frac{1}{2}\Omega(\omega m, q) {}^b\mathbf{q}_q\right). \tag{7.6}
$$

Using the pre-integrated measurements (7.4),(7.5),(7.6), the inertial dynamics is represented in terms of the state $\mathbf{x}_I$ given in (7.3) by the generic process model [Chatfield, 1997]

$$
\mathbf{x}_{I_{\bar{k}+1}} = f(\mathbf{x}_{I_{\bar{k}}}, \mathbf{a}_{\mathbf{m},\bar{k}}, \omega_{\mathbf{m},\bar{k}}, \mathbf{n}_{I,\bar{k}}), \tag{7.7}
$$

the IMU measurement noise is represented by the zero-mean Gausssian random process $\mathbf{n}_I = [\mathbf{n}_a^T, \mathbf{n}_g^T]^T$.

7.2.3 Camera measurements

The bearing measurement vector of feature i at each sampling time $t = \bar{t}_{\bar{k}} = \bar{k}\Delta\bar{t}$, by a camera with camera projection function $\pi([x, y, z]^T) = [\frac{x}{z}, \frac{y}{z}]^T$, is given by

$$
\mathbf{z}_{m(i),\bar{k}} = \pi({}^{C_{\bar{k}}}\mathbf{P}_{f(i)}) + \mathbf{n}_{i,\bar{k}}, \tag{7.8}
$$

$$
{}^{C_{\bar{k}}}\mathbf{P}_{f(i)} = {}^C_I\mathbf{R}{}^{I_{\bar{k}}}_w\mathbf{R}({}^w\mathbf{P}_{f(i)} - {}^w\mathbf{P}_{I_{\bar{k}}}) + {}^C\mathbf{P}_I, \tag{7.9}
$$

where ${}^w\mathbf{P}_{f(i)}$ is the 3D feature position, $\mathbf{n}_{i,\bar{k}} \sim \mathcal{N}(0, \mathbf{R}_{m,\bar{k}})$ is the measurement noise, ${}^C_I\mathbf{R}, {}^C\mathbf{P}_I$ are the extrinsic parameters between the camera and IMU. The filtered measurement estimates $\hat{\mathbf{z}}_{m(i),\bar{k}}$ and state estimates $\hat{\mathbf{x}}_{v_{\bar{k}}}$ are generated via Kalman filtering, as described later in Section 7.5, utilizing the residuals $\tilde{\mathbf{z}}_{m(i),\bar{k}} = \mathbf{z}_{m(i),\bar{k}} - \hat{\mathbf{z}}_{m(i),\bar{k}}$, $\tilde{\mathbf{x}}_{v_{\bar{k}}} = \mathbf{x}_{v_{\bar{k}}} - \hat{\mathbf{x}}_{v_{\bar{k}}}$, and the process model

$$
\tilde{\mathbf{z}}_{m(i),\bar{k}} = \mathbf{H}_{x_i}\tilde{\mathbf{x}}_{v_{\bar{k}}} + \mathbf{H}_{f_i}{}^w\tilde{\mathbf{P}}_{f(i)} + \mathbf{n}_{i,\bar{k}}, \tag{7.10}
$$

where

$$\mathbf{x}_{V_{\bar{k}}} = [\mathbf{x}_{I_{\bar{k}}}^T, \mathbf{x}_{C_{\bar{k}}}^T]^T, \tag{7.11}$$

$$\mathbf{x}_{C_{\bar{k}}} = \begin{bmatrix} \mathbf{x}_{\bar{k}-1}^T & \cdots & \mathbf{x}_{\bar{k}-n}^T \end{bmatrix}^T,$$

is the lumped vector of the prior n world to inertial frame transformations. $\mathbf{H}_{x_i}$ is the Jacobian matrix corresponding to the robot state, $\mathbf{H}_{f_i}$ is the Jacobian matrix corresponding to the feature position. Concatenating the measurement residuals $\tilde{\mathbf{z}}_{m(i),\bar{k}}$ for all feature points i and performing the nullspace marginalization operation based on (7.10), a feature-position-independent camera measurement process model is derived as

$$\tilde{\mathbf{z}}_{m(i),\bar{k}} = \check{\mathbf{H}}_{x_i} \tilde{\mathbf{x}}_{V_{\bar{k}}} + \mathbf{n}_{i,\bar{k}}, \tag{7.12}$$

and is directly used for robot state estimation via MSCKF as in [Lee et al., 2020]. The measurement function obtained in (7.12) provides higher computational efficiency compared to extended Kalman filter (EKF) approaches since this eliminates the necessity to store feature positions in the state vector.

7.2.4   *Wheel encoder measurements*

The wheel encoder (i.e., WO) measurements of the robot orientation and position are represented in frame {o} by $\mathbf{x}_{o_{\bar{k}}} = \begin{bmatrix} {}^o_w \mathbf{q}_{\bar{k}}^T & {}^w \mathbf{p}_{o_{\bar{k}}}^T \end{bmatrix}$, where ${}^o_w \mathbf{q}$ is the quaternion corresponding to the rotation ${}^o_w \mathbf{R}$. The corresponding ordinary differential equation for robot motion is expressed as

$$\begin{aligned} {}^w_o \dot{\mathbf{R}} &= {}^w_o \mathbf{R} \lfloor {}^o \omega \rfloor_\times, \\ {}^w_o \dot{\mathbf{p}} &= {}^w_o \mathbf{v} = {}^w_o \mathbf{R} \, {}^o \mathbf{v}, \end{aligned} \tag{7.13}$$

where ${}^o \omega$ is the angular velocity in frame {o} which is denoted as ${}^o \omega = \begin{bmatrix} 0 & 0 & \frac{v_r - v_l}{b} \end{bmatrix}^T$, ${}^o \mathbf{v} = \begin{bmatrix} \frac{v_l + v_r}{2} & 0 & 0 \end{bmatrix}^T$ is the linear velocity in frame {o}, v_l, v_r are the left and right wheel velocities, respectively. The wheel encoder provides measurements at a significantly higher frequency (100 Hz) as opposed to the camera (10 Hz). Therefore, it is computationally too costly to implement the MSCKF update at the rate of wheel encoder measurements. Hence, they are pre-integrated between two consecutive imaging time steps $\bar{k}$ and $\bar{k}+1$ [Zhang et al., 2021]. Considering this pre-integration, the WO measurement model is formed as

$$\mathbf{z}_{o_{\bar{k}+1}} = \begin{bmatrix} \int_{\tilde{t}_{\bar{k}}}^{\tilde{t}_{\bar{k}+1}} v_{\bar{k}} \cos\theta dt \\ \int_{\tilde{t}_{\bar{k}}}^{\tilde{t}_{\bar{k}+1}} v_{\bar{k}} \sin\theta dt \\ \int_{\tilde{t}_{\bar{k}}}^{\tilde{t}_{\bar{k}+1}} \omega_{\bar{k}} dt \end{bmatrix} + \mathbf{n}_{o_{\bar{k}}}, \tag{7.14}$$

where $\mathbf{n}_{o_{\bar{k}}}$ denotes the 3×1 zero-mean Gaussian measurement noise vector. Considering approximate planar motion (in $x - y$ plane) of the robot we augment the measurement model as

$$
\bar{\mathbf{z}}_{o_{k+1}} =
\begin{bmatrix}
\int_{\bar{t}_k}^{\bar{t}_{k+1}} v_{\bar{k}} \cos\theta \, dt \\
\int_{\bar{t}_k}^{\bar{t}_{k+1}} v_{\bar{k}} \sin\theta \, dt \\
0 \\
0 \\
0 \\
\int_{\bar{t}_k}^{\bar{t}_{k+1}} \omega_{\bar{k}} \, dt
\end{bmatrix}
+ \bar{\mathbf{n}}_{o_{\bar{k}}} = h(\mathbf{x}_{o_{\bar{k}}}, {}^o v_{\bar{k}}, {}^o \omega_{\bar{k}}) + \bar{\mathbf{n}}_{o_{\bar{k}}},
\tag{7.15}
$$

where $\bar{\mathbf{n}}_{o_{\bar{k}}}$ is the augmented 6×1 noise vector having $\mathbf{n}_{o_{\bar{k}}}$ entries in its first, second, and last entries, and having the other three entries equal to zero.

7.3 Proposed methodology

The robot considered in this chapter is equipped with wheel encoders which measure the left and right wheel linear velocities v_l, v_r, an accurate fiber optics gyro (FOG) which provides accurate heading velocity $\dot{\psi}$, an IMU and a stereo camera. The dynamic model used in our application is a differential drive robot (see Figure 7.1).

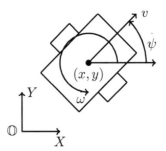

Figure 7.1: Robot model.

    The outline of our proposed VIWO scheme is shown in Figure 7.2. We take in three streams of data to our VIWO state estimation. The camera provides data which is used to obtain front-end visual odometry (VO). IMU data are pre-integrated to match with camera data. Finally, we utilize WO data which is compensated for slippage and other errors prior to pre-integration. Once the slippage is compensated. the WO data are pre-integrated to match with camera data. Then, the three data streams are fused together in an MSCKF framework to produce VIWO state estimates.

    The slip compensation methodology is described in Figure 7.3 and is explained in detail in Section 7.4.

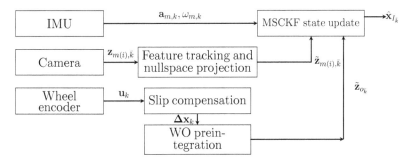

Figure 7.2: Outline of the proposed VIWO scheme.

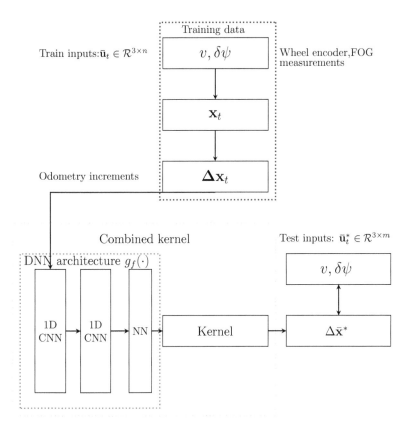

Figure 7.3: Slip compensation scheme.

7.4 Slip compensation via Gaussian process estimation

Our slip compensator design involves learning based estimation of the (error) residuals between the ground truth and the physical WO model considering a planar motion differential drive robot. In the process of training this learning based estimator design utilizing Gaussian process regression (GPR), the robot odometry dynamics is represented by the state vector

$$\xi_k = \begin{bmatrix} \xi_{1k} \\ \xi_{2k} \\ \xi_{3k} \end{bmatrix} = \begin{bmatrix} x_k & y_k & \psi_k \end{bmatrix}^T, \tag{7.16}$$

where (x_k, y_k) denotes the position of the robot and ψ_k denotes orientation of the robot at training sample k for the residual estimator design in the sequel. The inputs of the dynamic system are the velocity v_k and the heading angle increment $\delta\psi_k$ (measured by the FOG), represented in stacked vector form by

$$\mathbf{u}_k = \begin{bmatrix} v_k & \delta\psi_k \end{bmatrix}^T, \tag{7.17}$$

where $v = \dfrac{v_l + v_r}{2}$, v_l is the left wheel speed, and v_r is the right wheel speed. For representing the state increment $\Delta\xi_k$ with input $\mathbf{u}_k$, we use the discrete-time dynamic system model [Carlevaris-Bianco et al., 2016]

$$\Delta\xi_k = \xi_{k+1} - \xi_k = \bar{\mathbf{u}}_k + \mathbf{w}_k, \tag{7.18}$$

$$\bar{\mathbf{u}}_k = \begin{bmatrix} \bar{u}_{1k} \\ \bar{u}_{2k} \\ \bar{u}_{3k} \end{bmatrix} = \mathbf{f}_o(\mathbf{u}_k) = \begin{bmatrix} v_k \cos(\delta\psi_k)\delta_k \\ v_k \sin(\delta\psi_k)\delta_k \\ \delta\psi_k \end{bmatrix}, \quad \mathbf{w}_k = \begin{bmatrix} w_{1k} \\ w_{2k} \\ w_{3k} \end{bmatrix},$$

where $\mathbf{w}_k$ denotes the Gaussian process noise such that $w_{ik} \sim \mathcal{N}(0, \sigma_{w_{ik}}^2)$ and Δk denotes the sampling time. Next, a GPR is formulated for predictive correction of the odometry increments $\Delta\xi_k$ governed by (7.18). Consider a sequence of inputs (from training data sequences) collected in the individual input vector $\bar{\mathbf{U}}_i = [u_{i_k}, \dots, u_{i_{kn}}]^T \in \mathcal{R}^n$ and the corresponding sequence of state increments collected in the vector $\Delta\mathbf{X}_i = [\Delta\xi_{i_k}, \dots, \Delta\xi_{i_{kn}}]^T \in \mathcal{R}^n$. For predictions $\Delta\mathbf{X}_i^* = [\Delta\xi_{i_k}^*, \dots, \Delta\xi_{i_{km}}^*]^T$ on new data $\bar{\mathbf{U}}_i^* \in \mathcal{R}^m$ (test sequences), the predictive inference is given by

$$p(\Delta\mathbf{X}_i^* | \bar{\mathbf{U}}_i, \Delta\mathbf{X}_i, \bar{\mathbf{U}}_i^*) \sim \mathcal{N}(\Delta\bar{\mathbf{X}}_i^*, \mathbf{cov}(\Delta\mathbf{X}_i^*)), \tag{7.19}$$

where

$$\Delta\bar{\mathbf{X}}_i^* = \mathbf{K}(\bar{\mathbf{U}}_i^*, \bar{\mathbf{U}}_i)[\mathbf{K}(\bar{\mathbf{U}}_i, \bar{\mathbf{U}}_i) + \sigma_{w_i}^2 \mathbf{I}]^{-1} \Delta\mathbf{X}_i \tag{7.20}$$

is the mean prediction,

$$\mathbf{cov}(\Delta\bar{\mathbf{X}}_i^*) = \mathbf{K}(\bar{\mathbf{U}}^*, \bar{\mathbf{U}}^*) - \mathbf{K}(\bar{\mathbf{U}}^*, \bar{\mathbf{U}})[\mathbf{K}(\bar{\mathbf{U}}, \bar{\mathbf{U}}) + \sigma_{w_i}^2 \mathbf{I}]^{-1} \mathbf{K}(\bar{\mathbf{U}}, \bar{\mathbf{U}}^*) \tag{7.21}$$

is the prediction covariance, $\mathbf{K}(\bar{\mathbf{U}}^*, \bar{\mathbf{U}}^*) \in \mathcal{R}^{m \times m}$, $\mathbf{K}(\bar{\mathbf{U}}^*, \bar{\mathbf{U}}) \in \mathcal{R}^{m \times n}$, $\mathbf{K}(\bar{\mathbf{U}}, \bar{\mathbf{U}}^*) \in \mathcal{R}^{n \times m}$, and $\mathbf{K}(\bar{\mathbf{U}}, \bar{\mathbf{U}}) \in \mathcal{R}^{n \times n}$ are the kernel matrices where the element (i,j) of $\mathbf{k}_{ij} = \mathbf{k}(u_i, u_j)$. $\mathbf{k}(\cdot, \cdot)$ is the kernel function which consists of the base kernel $\bar{\mathbf{k}}$ (Matern kernel [Tronarp et al., 2018])) combined with the NN (neural network) architecture $g_f(\cdot)$ in the form [Brossard and Bonnabel, 2019]

$$\mathbf{k}(\cdot, \cdot) = \bar{\mathbf{k}}(\mathbf{g}_f(\cdot), \mathbf{g}_f(\cdot)). \tag{7.22}$$

In (7.22), $\bar{\mathbf{k}}(u_i, u_j) = \sigma_k^2 \left(1 + \dfrac{\sqrt{5}|u_i - u_j|}{l} + \dfrac{\sqrt{5}|u_i - u_j|^2}{3l^2} \right) \exp \left(-\dfrac{\sqrt{5}|u_i - u_j|}{l} \right)$, where σ_k is the magnitude parameter and $l > 0$ is the scale parameter. Using the optimized hyperparameters (σ_k, l), the kernel $\mathbf{k}(\cdot, \cdot)$, the corrected state vector increment $\Delta \xi_{i_q}$, for $i = 1, 2, 3$, and $q = 1, \ldots, m$ is obtained. Once the corrected set of odometry increments $\Delta \xi_q$ are obtained for a test sequence, similar to in (7.15) we obtain the augmented measurement

$$
\check{\mathbf{z}}_{o_{\bar{k}+1}} = \begin{bmatrix} \sum_{q=10\bar{k}}^{10\bar{k}+10} \Delta x_q \\ \sum_{q=10\bar{k}}^{10\bar{k}+10} \Delta y_q \\ 0 \\ 0 \\ 0 \\ \sum_{q=10\bar{k}}^{10\bar{k}+10} \Delta \psi_q \end{bmatrix}, \tag{7.23}
$$

which is used by the MSCKF state estimator.

7.5 State estimation

Based on the dynamic model developed in Section 7.2.2 and the methodology of [Mourikis and Roumeliotis, 2007], we develop an MSCKF as follows: The main state update rule is in the form of

$$
\hat{\mathbf{x}}_{I_{\bar{k}+1}} = f(\hat{\mathbf{x}}_{I_{\bar{k}}}, \mathbf{a}_{\mathbf{m}, \bar{k}}, \omega_{\mathbf{m}, \bar{k}}, \mathbf{0}) + \Delta_{I_{\bar{k}}}, \tag{7.24}
$$

where $\Delta_{I_{\bar{k}}}$ represents the correction term that is produced considering the camera measurement residual functions $\tilde{\mathbf{z}}_{m(i), \bar{k}}$, and the slip-compensated WO measurement residual $\tilde{\mathbf{z}}_{o_{\bar{k}}} = \check{\mathbf{z}}_{o_{\bar{k}}} - h(\hat{\mathbf{x}}_{o_{\bar{k}}}, {}^o v_{\bar{k}}, {}^o \omega_{\bar{k}})$, and the corresponding covariance matrices $\mathbf{P}_{\bar{k}}$ and $\mathbf{P}_{o_{\bar{k}}}$. Note that the MSCKF keeps track of a sliding window of n poses $\mathbf{x}_{C_{\bar{k}}} = \begin{bmatrix} \mathbf{x}_{\bar{k}-1}^T & \cdots & \mathbf{x}_{\bar{k}-n}^T \end{bmatrix}^T$ as described in (7.11), which leads to the augmented state estimate vector $\hat{\mathbf{x}}_{v_{\bar{k}}} = \begin{bmatrix} \hat{\mathbf{x}}_{I_{\bar{k}}}^T & \hat{\mathbf{x}}_{C_{\bar{k}}}^T \end{bmatrix}^T = \begin{bmatrix} \hat{\mathbf{x}}_{I_{\bar{k}}}^T & \hat{\mathbf{x}}_{\bar{k}-1}^T & \cdots & \hat{\mathbf{x}}_{\bar{k}-n}^T \end{bmatrix}^T$ with $\hat{\mathbf{x}}_{I_{\bar{k}}} \in \mathcal{R}^{15}, \hat{\mathbf{x}}_{C_{\bar{k}}} \in \mathcal{R}^{6n}$.

Note here that the robot state estimate is updated via two different types of measurements; camera and slip-compensated WO. Hence, we update the robot state estimate at each time step based on the most confident measurement using a gating test based on Mahalanobis distance γ [Li and Mourikis, 2013]. For visual measurement update step we denote this distance measure as $\gamma_{v_{\bar{k}}}$. Similarly we obtain $\gamma_{o_{\bar{k}}}$ for wheel encoder measurement update. Then, the measurement that produces the lowest Mahalanobis distance measure (γ) is used for updating the state estimate.

7.6   Real-time data simulations

In this section, we provide experimental results obtained through publicly available datasets. We demonstrate the approach using the KAIST [Jeong et al., 2019] data-set which is collected in an urban area. KAIST dataset is chosen since it also provides wheel encoder data which is missing in most of the available visual inertial datasets. Table 7.1 provides the KAIST dataset sensor specifications. The real world data simulations were carried out on an Intel core i7 laptop equipped with an NVIDIA Geforce GTX 1660 Ti GPU.

Table 7.1: Sensor specifications for the KAIST dataset.

Sensor	Manufacturer	Model	Description	freq.(Hz)	Accuracy
IMU	Xsens	MTi-300	Enhanced attitude and heading reference system	100	10^0/h
Camera	Pointgray	Flea3	1600×1200 RGB, 59 FPS	10	-
Wheel encoder	RLS	LM13	Magnetic rotary encoder	100	4096 (resolution)
VRS GPS	SOKKIA	GRX2	VRS-RTK GPS	1	H:10mm, V:15mm
FOG	KVH	DSP-1760	Fiber optics gyro	1000	0.05/h

7.6.1   *Dataset training*

We partition the data set into training, cross-validation, and testing sequence sets. In total, 17 sequences are used for training, 4 sequences for cross-validation, and 2 sequences for testing. Table 7.2 provides the parameters used for training the GP. The GP model was constructed using Pyro [Bingham et al., 2019] library for deep probabilistic programming and PyTorch. The training time to execute 100 epochs was 141.66 seconds. Furthermore, we show the training time for each epoch in Figure 7.4.

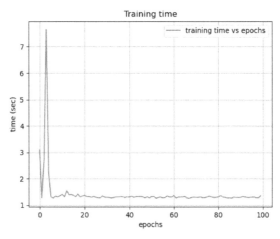

Figure 7.4: Training time for each epoch.

Table 7.2: Parameters for training GP.

Training parameter	value
Optimizer	Adam
Learning rate	0.01
No. of epochs	100
sample rate	100 Hz

7.6.2 *Results*

We ran two MSCKFs, one with and one without slip compensation, to demonstrate the properties of the proposed scheme. To demonstrate the improvements by the proposed scheme, we compare the mean absolute trajectory error (MATE) and mean absolute rotation error (MRTE) between the slip-compensated VIWO and VIWO obtained without slip compensation.

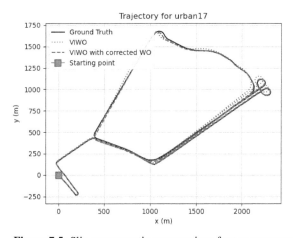

Figure 7.5: Slip compensation comparison for test sequence 1.

In Figures 7.5 and 7.6 the robot trajectories depict VIWO with corrected WO and VIWO without slip compensated WO. It is shown that the accuracy of the VIWO scheme with integrated slip compensation is closer to the ground truth of the test sequences. This is quantitatively displayed in Figures 7.7 and 7.8. The red color bar plot shows the MATE/MRTE for VIWO without slip compensation correction while the green color bar plot shows the MATE/MRTE for VIWO with slip compensation correction. When slip compensation is integrated into VIWO there is a significant reduction in MATE and MRTE.

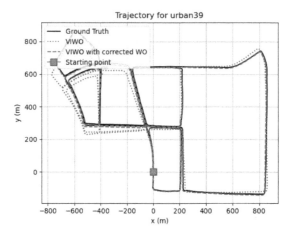

Figure 7.6: Slip compensation comparison for test sequence 2.

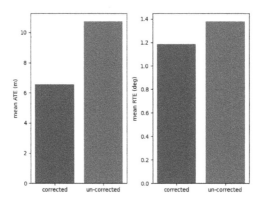

Figure 7.7: Trajectory error for test sequence 1.

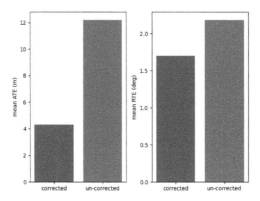

Figure 7.8: Trajectory error for test sequence 2.

7.7   Conclusion and future work

This chapter has presented a VIWO scheme that incorporates compensation of noisy measurements from wheel encoders mainly due to slippage. In this scheme, the error in WO between the physical model and ground truth is estimated by a learning and GP based estimator that is trained using a set of training data. Then the learned WO error estimate is used to correct the WO measurements. The corrected WO measurements are used to update an MSCKF based VIWO state estimation scheme.

As future directions of this work, it is planned to add online calibration of intrinsic and extrinsic parameters of the wheel encoders. This extension is essential especially when the robot is navigating in harsh environments where parameters such as wheel radius change with time, reducing the localization accuracy. In order to develop more generalized deep GP based methods the designs are aimed to be tested via further simulations with other relevant datasets as well as real-world experiments. Finally, since the proposed methodology requires supervised learning, further research is needed to explore unsupervised learning approaches to make the design more suitable for real-world applications.

Acknowledgment

This work is supported by Canadian Mitacs Accelerate Project IT16435 and Avidbots Corp, Kitchener, ON, Canada.

References

Bingham, E., Chen, J. P., Jankowiak, M., Obermeyer, F., Pradhan, N., Karaletsos, T. et al. 2019. Pyro: Deep universal probabilistic programming. The Journal of Machine Learning Research, 20(1): 973–978.

Brossard, M. and Bonnabel, S. 2019. Learning wheel odometry and imu errors for localization. In 2019 International Conference on Robotics and Automation (ICRA), pp. 291–297. IEEE.

Campos, C., Montiel, J. M., and Tardós, J. D. 2020. Inertial only optimization for visual-inertial initialization. In 2020 IEEE International Conference on Robotics and Automation (ICRA), pp. 51–57. IEEE.

Carlevaris-Bianco, N., Ushani, A. K., and Eustice, R. M. 2016. University of Michigan North Campus long-term vision and lidar dataset. The International Journal of Robotics Research, 35(9): 1023–1035.

Castro-Toscano, M. J., Rodríguez-Quiñonez, J. C., Hernández-Balbuena, D., Lindner, L., Sergiyenko, O., Rivas-Lopez, M. et al. 2017. A methodological use of inertial navigation systems for strapdown navigation task. In Proc. IEEE 26th Int. Symp. on Indust. Electronics, pp. 1589–1595.

Chatfield, A. B. 1997. Fundamentals of High Accuracy Inertial Navigation. American Institute of Aeronautics and Astronautics.

Jeong, J., Cho, Y., Shin, Y. -S., Roh, H., and Kim, A. 2019. Complex urban dataset with multi-level sensors from highly diverse urban environments. International Journal of Robotics Research, 38(6): 642–657.

Jung, J. H., Cha, J., Chung, J. Y., Kim, T. I., Seo, M. H., Park, S. Y. et al. 2022. Monocular visual-inertial-wheel odometry using low-grade IMU in urban areas. IEEE Transactions on Intelligent Transportation Systems, 23(2): 925–938.

Kang, R., Xiong, L., Xu, M., Zhao, J., and Zhang, P. 2019. Vins-vehicle: A tightly-coupled vehicle dynamics extension to visual-inertial state estimator. In 2019 IEEE Intelligent Transportation Systems Conference (ITSC), pp. 3593–3600.

Lee, W., Eckenhoff, K., Yang, Y., Geneva, P., and Huang, G. 2020. Visual-inertial-wheel odometry with online calibration. In 2020 IEEE/RSJ International Conference on Intelligent Robots and Systems (IROS), pp. 4559–4566.

Li, M. and Mourikis, A. I. 2013. High-precision, consistent EKF-based visual-inertial odometry. The International Journal of Robotics Research, 32(6): 690–711.

Liu, J., Gao, W., and Hu, Z. 2019. Visual-inertial odometry tightly coupled with wheel encoder adopting robust initialization and online extrinsic calibration. In 2019 IEEE/RSJ International Conference on Intelligent Robots and Systems (IROS), pp. 5391–5397.

Mourikis, A. I., and Roumeliotis, S. I. 2007. A multi-state constraint kalman filter for vision-aided inertial navigation. In Proceedings 2007 IEEE International Conference on Robotics and Automation, pp. 3565–3572.

Tronarp, F., Karvonen, T., and Särkkä, S. 2018. Mixture representation of the Matern class with applications in state space approximations and Bayesian quadrature. In 2018 IEEE 28th International Workshop on Machine Learning for Signal Processing (MLSP), pp. 1–6.

Wu, K. J., Guo, C. X., Georgiou, G., and Roumeliotis, S. I. 2017. Vins on wheels. In 2017 IEEE International Conference on Robotics and Automation (ICRA), pp. 5155–5162. IEEE.

Yang, Y., Geneva, P., Eckenhoff, K., and Huang, G. 2019. Degenerate motion analysis for aided INS with online spatial and temporal sensor calibration. IEEE Robotics and Automation Letters, 4(2): 2070–2077.

Zhang, M., Zuo, X., Chen, Y., Liu, Y., and Li, M. 2021. Pose estimation for ground robots: On manifold representation, integration, reparameterization, and optimization. IEEE Transactions on Robotics, 37(4): 1081–1099.

Zhu, J., Tang, Y., Shao, X., and Xie, Y. 2021. Multisensor fusion using fuzzy inference system for a visual-imu-wheel odometry. IEEE Transactions on Instrumentation and Measurement, 70: 1–16.

8

Methodology for Developing Models of Image Color of Terrain with Landmarks for Their Detection and Recognition by Autonomous Mobile Robots

*Oleksandr Poliarus** and *Yevhen Poliakov*

8.1 Introduction

Autonomous mobile robots (AMR) have been used recently in various fields of human activity, especially in areas related to security and military operations. Robots can perform multiple functions in the air, water, and earth, but this chapter mainly deals with ground robots that independently perform their assigned tasks to them. In many situations, the capabilities of the global positioning system are not effective [Nilwong et al. 2019] and may be suppressed by interference. Overlapping visibility, equipment failure and other reasons lead to a significant decrease in the effectiveness of GPS. Hence, there is a need to use AMR. A general approach to the construction of AMR and a review of the literature is presented in [Zghair and Al-Araji 2021]. To implement its plan, a robot must orient itself well in the territory and, in the absence of GPS, have one or more landmarks divided into different classes:

Kharkiv National Automobile and Highway University, Ukraine 61002, Ukraine, Kharkov, st. Yaroslava Mudrogo, 25.
Email: eug_p@ukr.net, https://orcid.org/0000-0002-3248-7461, https://orcid.org/0000-0002-8023-5189
* Corresponding author: poliarus.kharkov@ukr.net

synthetic and natural, permanent and temporary, radiating and non-radiating, used indoors and outdoors, etc. In the chapter, artificial and natural landmarks placed on arbitrary terrain outside the buildings are selected for analysis. Algorithms for processing information from different landmarks should be similar. AMR traverse unknown environment by detecting obstacles using various sensors to choose an obstacle-free path on the ground. Some separate obstacles can be used as landmarks. As a rule, space scanning is carried out by laser scanners that measure the distance to surrounding objects linked to a digital terrain map. The results of scan-matching navigation are similar to a digital image. Sometimes digital terrain maps may not be available or may not correspond to reality, for example, due to man-made disasters in the area or military operations that lead to the destruction of objects on the terrain. In such situations, many dangerous jobs can be given to robots. A robot without GPS and a digital map of the area must find a local landmark and calculate its coordinates from it. On the steppe terrain, landmarks concentrated in space are easily detected by laser scanners and other emitting devices (radar, sonar, etc.). If there are buildings, trees, etc., behind and near the landmark, its detection is a difficult problem. In this case, passive detection means are preferred, in particular, systems based on color features.

Many methods and technical means based on various physical principles are used to detect and recognize landmarks in the interests of AMR. This chapter considers only optical ways based on information registration using video cameras and subsequent processing of signals using the latest technologies, which can be combined with previous deep learning of neural networks and artificial intelligence. Traditional object detection algorithms can be divided into manual and automatic [Deng et al. 2020]. Manual methods are not considered here. Modern automated methods use a convolutional neural network (CNN) [Krizhevsky et al. 2012]. Another approach is proposed in this chapter. It does not require the mandatory presence of an artificial neural network as part of the information processing system. As a result, the robot becomes less dependent on the type of environment. The given signal processing method can be used in night conditions when the effectiveness of video cameras is very low and night vision systems replace them.

The authors of [Jin et al. 2021] solved the problem of eliminating significant positioning errors as well as increasing the speed and accuracy of object recognition by industrial robots in wireless telecommunication networks 5G using a convolutional neural network model and a deep learning algorithm. This chapter does not consider the problems of robot navigation in the presence of radiation sources specially installed on a terrain.

The requirements for image compression, storage, and video camera characteristics should be set to improve the quality of landmarks detection and recognition. A methodology for image preprocessing was developed by [Announcia and Godwin 2009]. The first method uses four video cameras. One of the cameras focuses on the front objects of the image, for example, on possible landmarks, and the other pair focuses on the back things, that is, on the background. The generated mismatch vector reduces the forecast error during information preprocessing.

A priori information for object recognition is contained in the database and can reach 10 million photos of the scene, labeled with semantic categories of the stage [Zhou et al. 2017]. The analysis begins with the classification of objects that need to be detected. Type and tags determine what is in the image and how reliable this information is. While classification recognizes only one class of objects, tagging can recognize several ones for a given image. This algorithm, along with the added tags, will try to return all the best classes that match the image. The most significant difference between training an image classification model and training an object detection model is the tagging of photos. While image classification requires one or more tags applied to the entire image, object detection requires that each mark consists of a tag and a region that defines a bounding box for each object in the picture. Bounding box segmentation identifies objects for each pixel in the image, resulting in a very accurate map. However, the segmentation accuracy depends on long-term training of the neural network. So, the quality of automatic recognition is largely determined by the type of neural network and its training technology. Hence, requirements for reducing such dependence by switching to information processing algorithms without neural networks follow.

Many reasons cause the problems of automatic landmark recognition. Firstly, it is necessary to detect the landmark in conditions of optical interference reliably, and secondly, to eliminate the possible consequences of image blurring, occlusion, illumination, a non-standard viewing angle of the object, etc. Difficulties in performing this task are increased due to temporal and spatial changes of these factors, and the background on which a landmark is located. As a result, all problems require a statistical evaluation and real-time computing. Landmark recognition algorithms are based either on neural networks with deep machine learning or models obtained directly from images. The aim of the chapter is to create new models of image color for landmarks with the background which make it possible to use these models in autonomous mobile robots navigation.

8.2 Background

The areas of AMR application are given in many scientific works. The primary operations of the robot, in addition to localization, are the detection and recognition of landmarks or other objects of interest to the customer. These objects, like the robot itself, can be mobile or stationary. Algorithms that detect and recognize moving objects are more complex [Ahmed et al. 2018]. Robots are provided with various sensors for a complete performance of basic operations at any time of the day: laser, infrared, sonar, inertial, etc. All sensors in conditions of use in an unfamiliar environment and different weather conditions always produce inaccurate measurement information and create false alarms when making decisions [Tawiah 2020]. The chapter does not consider semantic navigation [Astua et al. 2014]. The studies were conducted only using video cameras without information that can come from lidar, sonar, radar, etc. The analysis is not carried out for narrowly specialized tasks, such as, for example, detection of doors in corridors [Antonazzi et al. 2022], but for a wide range of functions.

Therefore, one or several video cameras are used as a sensor. Information from two video cameras is processed using stereo algorithms [Novak et al. 2004]. The recognition of landmarks and other objects is based on comparing the received image with a template, including fuzzy pattern matching [Fukuda et al. 1995]. In the absence of the ability to make a decision, in some robots, communication with a person is provided [Gopalakrishnan et al. 2005]. Intelligent recognition systems also use contextual information [Ruiz-Sarmiento et al. 2017]. Qualitative recognition is possible based on a priori information about the image, which is obtained either in advance if the area on which the AMR performs the task is well known or during its operation, for example, with the help of a qualitative panoramic description of scenes [Zhengt et al. 1991]. For navigation tasks, a generator of landmarks that creates templates can be used [Nasr and Bhanu 1988], and specially designed milestones are made to check recognition quality [Zhong et al. 2017]. For a rough estimation of the landmark's shape, it is sometimes appropriate to use color histograms of detected objects [Elmogy and Zhang 2009]. Most often, recognition algorithms use a geometric selection of known landmarks [Hayet et al. 2007]. In modern information processing systems, comparison with templates, assessment of similarity, and detection of local features of images are instead carried out in point clouds [Bore et al. 2017]. Processing algorithms for moving objects tend to work in real-time [Qazwan et al. 2021]. Algorithms for tracking moving targets or landmarks are essential here [Ahmed et al. 2018]. Object recognition in many systems is carried out in two stages [McGreavy et al. 2016]: first, a set of candidates for similarity with a real landmark is chosen, and then among this set, the best one according to the selected criterion is selected. The localization of the landmark can be complicated due to the repeatability of its shape in the territory [Ge et al. 2022]. This can be typical indoors, for example, in corridors or in the area when a tree is chosen as a landmark, and there are many such trees. This circumstance forces us to develop special algorithms. Assistive autonomous robots and collaborative algorithms can improve the quality of real-time recognition [Martinez-Martin and Pobil 2016]. The robot's hardware becomes more complicated to enhance the quality of navigation and recognition, leading to energy consumption problems. Therefore, there is a problem with optimizing the volume of equipment and the capacity of power sources [Alparslan and Çetin 2021]. Internal and external calibration of video cameras is also important [Elmogy and Zhang 2009] to obtain a detailed three-dimensional image of the environment around the robot. For robots performing complex movements, unconventional models are being developed, such as quantum process modeling [Peng et al. 2020].

Modern object recognition methods use artificial neural networks [Furlán et al. 2020], even in real-time [Asiain and Gomez-Allende 2001]. The most common is the convolutional neural network [Nilwong et al. 2019], and there is the possibility of combining algorithms with voice commands [Guilherme De Souza Silva et al. 2020, Czygier et al. 2020]. Other types of neural networks are also implemented in information processing algorithms, particularly back-propagation neural networks [Thin and Zaw 2019]. Deep machine learning on 3D point clouds [Zhou et al. 2022, Rauer et al. 2019] is appropriate for the flexible performance of recognition tasks. During training, various additional obstacles can be installed [Thin and Zaw 2019], lighting conditions can be artificially changed [Aoyagi et al. 2022], and other conditions are characteristic of robot navigation. Sometimes deep learning methods are combined with human-robot symbiotic learning [Cartucho et al. 2018] in systems containing two neural networks. An overview of neural networks with reinforcement learning for AMR is given by [Cheng and Chen 2021]. Reinforcement learning neural network is used for AMR obstacle avoidance [Huang et al. 2005]. A neural network model via supervising learning using the collected data for decision-making without global environment information with the existence of obstacles is represented in [Chen et al. 2022]. The authors of [Quan et al. 2020] introduce a novel navigation method based on deep reinforcement learning for path planning of agents. This method reduces the global path search time by 5–8%. For generating navigation policies, in [Xiao et al. 2022] an observation-action consistency model is introduced to ensure that the agent reaches the subgoals by means of collision penalty to reshape the reinforcement learning reward function. The paper [Samadi and Jond 2020] proposes a hybrid GPS—adaptive neuro-fuzzy inference system-based method for collision-free navigation of autonomous mobile robots.

Models have long been used for robot navigation [Akai et al. 2015]. In [Carballo et al. 2018] end-to-end and model-based navigation are considered for real outdoor environments: with pedestrians, bicycles, children, and possibly other robots, no matter the weather. The convolutional neural network supports end-to-end navigation: when there is an obstacle or the robot has deviated from its trajectory, the model-based system steers this robot which moves to the target direction. In [Wang et al. 2011] simulation is used for path planning and avoiding collision. An overview of path planning methods is presented in [Sánchez-Ibáñez et al. 2021]. In [Song et al. 2012] autonomous mobile robot uses a neural network for studying the navigation task and moving out of specific mazes in an unknown environment. The author of [Alhawary 2018] studied reinforcement learning of neural networks for evaluating a robot's optimal trajectory in an unknown environment and avoiding obstacles and overcoming the skidding effects. 3D laser scanning vision system and mobile robot navigation system with the neural network using Levenberg–Marquardt method are the base for obtaining a digitized map of the robot's surrounding by means of optical measurements [Básaca-Preciado et al. 2014]. Wavelet neural network with high learning speed and fast convergence is proposed in [Panigrahi and Sahoo 2014] for deducing a path for the robot to a given goal position. In [Pandey and Parhi 2016] a fuzzy model with a simulated annealing hybrid algorithm is used for obstacle avoidance in a cluttered environment. The models of robot navigation were built with help of the inductive method of self-organization of models [Andrakhanov 2013]. In [Miranda-Vega et al. 2022] defuzzification algorithms with artificial intelligence are used for robot localization and navigation tasks. The authors [Lucca Siqueira et al. 2022] proposed a framework to apply semantic information to AMR navigation.

There is a large number of scientific works devoted to the tasks of classification and pattern recognition using neural networks, but we do not know the results of their application for the detection and recognition of landmarks for AMR in unfamiliar terrain. Most existing methods using neural networks for navigating AMR consider path planning, collision avoidance, faster convergence, and generalization. To estimate the advantages of the proposed method compared to neural networks, let's use the general theory. Training neural networks is an important operation that requires a set of learning examples on the basis of which generalization will be ensured. The training becomes a problem when it is not known in which terrain the robot will be used. In emergency situations, it is difficult to predict the state of the area in advance. A neural network trained for a wide range of conditions has low generalization properties and is therefore ineffective in making decisions. The proposed method is based on current information about the terrain, which is obtained from active and passive sensors. The development of a landmark detection and recognition system based on current information is a complex task and goes beyond the scope of the chapter.

However, neural networks can learn based on real-world data from unknown environments. After natural and man-made catastrophes, and military operations, a reconnaissance robot can be sent to the affected territory. It will collect information about the state of the environment with the help of many different sensors. The proposed method is able to create environment models using this information. By changing the parameters of the model, you can get a wide range of examples for training neural networks in specialized robots that will perform certain types of work. In our opinion, there is a prospect of simultaneous use of neural networks and the proposed method in the detection and recognition of landmarks and other navigational tasks.

It follows from the conducted review that most existing detection, localization, and recognition methods are used for landmarks known by their shape, size, and color. For some robots, milestones are specially created; for example, patterns of concentric circular rings are applied to objects. As a rule, robots do not automatically classify objects as landmarks in challenging environmental conditions. Many robots are not autonomous and need information from the human environment or other robots in the same area. Complex systems provide detection and recognition of landmarks in real-time for processing data from various types of sensors. These systems have powerful computing resources, and they are also energy-consuming, which puts forward requirements for the simplification of the robot's hardware, as well as for the optimization of algorithms and resources under the influence of many factors. At this time, landmark color information needs to be used more, and color histograms are intended mainly for rough estimates of landmark characteristics.

In modern object recognition systems, neural networks of various types have become the most widely used. They have certain limitations; in particular, they need more flexibility. Training neural networks prepare the network to perform a narrowly specialized task, for example, recognizing a landmark of a certain type. Training is time-consuming and can only be carried out by qualified specialists. There is a need to develop algorithms for the automatic solution of important practical tasks by robots in complex environmental conditions. For this purpose, a system of differential equations was synthesized in [Poliarus and Poliakov 2021] for the optimal real-time determination of the color parameters of objects, which can then be used to recognize landmarks. The greatest efficiency of detection, localization, and recognition of objects is achieved when algorithms of processing systems are designed for landmarks of a specific shape. Thus, in [Poliarus et al. 2021], two optimized methods for processing information about the color of the environment are proposed for detecting targets elongated in the vertical plane, for example, pillars.

Thanks to the accumulation of signals describing color, it is possible to exceed the corresponding thresholds and detect the corresponding landmark. For detection tasks, a significant reduction in the influence of non-stationarity of processes occurs by decomposing the color parameters into Hilbert-Huang modes and using the first three modes, which contain information about color jumps due to the presence of landmarks in the field of the video camera view.

So, at this time, many scientific works are devoted to detecting, localization, and recognizing landmarks of predetermined shape, size, color, etc., which are in familiar environments. Only a few pieces have been dedicated to the execution of these tasks in unfamiliar environments, the characteristics of which change over time, and the determination of the type of landmark is entrusted to the robot itself. As a rule, they describe only some aspects of this problem. This chapter presents new approaches for solving such problems, and therefore, models of an object's color against the background of arbitrary terrain are proposed.

8.3 General requirements for models of environment color

As a rule, system models are built based on a priori data about the system and current measurement results. Robot navigation in unfamiliar terrain can generally occur with a limited amount of a priori data. The primary data source is current measurements of environment parameters necessary for navigation, particularly the color parameters of objects located in the robot's viewing area. Even for a known area, these parameters can randomly change over time, for example, due to changes in lighting, shadows falling on the object, precipitation, etc. With this approach, the number of models can be unlimited. However, for practice, it is advisable to have one or more general models that can be improved for specific navigation conditions. Therefore, the model of color should be simple, with no prior assumptions about the environment. It follows from this that no a priori data are entered into the computer memory of the information processing system that the robot receives during its navigation in an unfamiliar environment. That is why, below, only photographs of real terrain are considered, from which it is possible to draw conclusions about the possibility of finding acceptable landmarks for the robot in the area using the developed models. These models and algorithms of information processing for the task under consideration should reveal spatial structures and features of photographs for their interpretation during recognition and their possible assignment to the class of predefined landmarks. Since color parameters are random, their models must be statistical in nature. Finally, photographs are described by pixels of high-dimensional matrices. It follows from this that the model should contain mechanisms that make it possible to reduce the dimensionality of matrices and make decisions based on such matrices.

We will consider possible image models using well-studied modal decompositions in fluid mechanics to meet these requirements. The general thing is that the image of the terrain and the flow of liquid in the pipe represent a two-dimensional picture that changes over time. Previously, complicated Navier-Stokes differential equations were used to describe fluid flows. However, in recent decades, methods based on the analysis of "snapshots", such as pressure in pipe cross-sections, have begun to develop. The mathematical basis for such an analysis is matrix methods. It is logical to also describe the distribution of color in photographs using matrices. The main problems are the possible large dimensions of the matrices and the limitation of the methods to linear systems only. These problems can be overcome, and the field of application of matrices is expanded. Of course, image flow modeling has its characteristics compared to fluid flows in pipes. In addition, the purpose of image modeling is different and is aimed at building systems of detection and recognition of landmarks. All this is described in the chapter of the book.

8.4 Mathematical model of image color based on "snapshots"

To develop algorithms for detecting and recognizing landmarks, it is necessary to have a mathematical model of the environment color. It is clear that in each practical situation, the models may be different. However, the model's structure and the operations necessary for its construction should be the same for all cases. In the chapter, the specified requirements are implemented with the help of a matrix model of the environment color. The matrix approach is based on linear operations. A model of an arbitrary environment can often be nonlinear, which forces the chapter to look for methods to overcome the difficulties caused by nonlinearity. Let's describe the essence of the approach using specific examples.

Let's choose two different arbitrary photographs (Figure 8.1a,b), on which the image of a possible landmark will be installed later. There are different types of terrain relief, which are considered in the chapter in terms of landmark detection and recognition based on color features. The landmark model is a vertical pillar with a background around it. The absence of any objects near the landmark (for example, a steppe) or, conversely, the presence of a continuous object (for example, a dense continuous forest) means a "uniform background". If the surrounding objects are discontinuous (for example, trees alternate with artificial structures), then we call such a background heterogeneous, that is one which has inhomogeneities. For our chapter, both backgrounds are named "typical terrain backgrounds".

In the first stage, the photograph is converted into three matrices of pixels, each of which includes the distribution of pixels of one of the three colors (red, green, and blue) on the plane of the video camera matrix. This is implemented, for example, in the mathematical package MATLAB®. All or any of the three matrices can be used for analysis. This is not important for understanding the essence of the proposed method. From these two-dimensional color matrices, one can select the necessary fragments for analysis, for example, with the help of operators:

R=double(im1(351:550,1:200,1));

G=double(im1(351:550,1:200,2));

B=double(im1(351:550,1:200,3));

with 351:550 being the row range and 1:200 being the column range. The numbers 1, 2, and 3 denote matrices of red, green, and blue pixels, respectively.

The matrices R, G, and B can be used to extract dynamic information from the image color field directly based on a sequence of snapshots, as is done, for example, in [Schmid 2010] for fluid-dynamical and transport processes.

Figure 8.1: The examples of photographs for analysis: a—for the first background; b—for the second background.

After selecting a photograph of the area, a square transformation matrix is determined

$$\mathbf{A} \approx \vec{x}_{k+1} \cdot \vec{x}_k^{\dagger}, \tag{1}$$

which connects two adjacent columns of image pixels $\vec{x}_k$ and $\vec{x}_{k+1}$, where $\vec{x}_k^{\dagger}$ is the Moore-Penrose inversion, i.e., an analogue of the inverse matrix for non-square matrices. For example, in the MATLAB package for the matrix describing the red color we have:

$$A = R(:,2)*pinv(R(:,1)),$$

where pinv implements the inversion operator for a non-square matrix (column). The accuracy of approximation (1) is estimated in the form of the column vector of differences

$$\vec{\Delta} = \vec{x}_{k+1} - \mathbf{A}\vec{x}_k \tag{2}$$

For $k = 1$ all elements of this vector are close to zero. For $k = 2$ the result is significantly different (Figure 8.2).

The maximum absolute pixel color error can be equal to 255, and the minimum one – is 0. For adjacent columns with numbers 200 and 201, the graph of similar errors looks like this (Figure 8.3):

Errors were calculated using the program: d = A*R(:,200)-R(:,201).

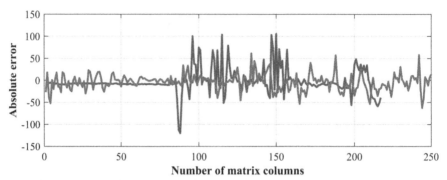

Figure 8.2: Dependence of absolute error of approximation (2) of the relationship between the color of adjacent columns (second and third) on the column number of the image matrix R: blue color—for the first background, red—for the second one.

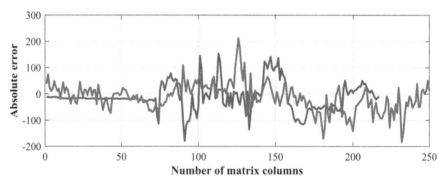

Figure 8.3: Dependence of absolute error of approximation (2) of the relationship between color of adjacent columns (with numbers 200 and 201) on the column number of the image matrix R: blue color— for the first background, red—for the second one.

Similar errors are observed for adjacent columns, except for the first and second ones. The main reason for such errors is the application of a linear transformation for conditions in which the relationship between adjacent columns has lost linearity. Matrix **A** was defined for the relationship between the first and second columns and then applied to adjacent relationships with other numbers. If the background were uniform, then matrix **A** would be almost the same for all adjacent columns. Otherwise, it is necessary to create such a transformation matrix, the elements of which would be functions of column numbers. We should expect a nonlinear dependence of the values of the matrix **A** determined for different numbers of adjacent columns; for each color R, G, B, and background, the type of nonlinear dependence will be different, which is a disadvantage of this method.

Now let's estimate not a vector, but a matrix of differences $\vec{\Delta} = \vec{x}_{k+1} - \mathbf{A}\vec{x}_k$, where $\vec{x}_k, \vec{x}_{k+1}$ are no longer columns, but two-dimensional matrices shifted by one column or more. The matrix for the first background color has 960 columns. Let's divide it into two parts. Consider the matrix $\vec{x}_k$, which includes columns with numbers from 1 to 480, and the matrix $\vec{x}_{k+1}$, which contains columns with numbers from 2 to 481. Then the matrix **A** is determined by the previously given formula using the program A = R(:,2:481)*pinv(R(:,1:480)). For error matrices (2), a more generalized approximation parameter is the Frobenius norm, which is calculated by the formula [Torokhti and Howlett 2007]

$$\left\| \vec{\Delta} \right\| = \sqrt{\sum_{j=1}^{n} \sum_{k=1}^{m} \Delta_{jk}^2} \ . \tag{3}$$

Since it depends on the number of pixels in the matrix, to ensure the same analysis conditions for different images, the Frobenius norm was divided by the total number of matrix elements. We will call such a reduced Frobenius norm. Figure 8.4, a, b shows the dependence of the reduced norm on the number of columns of the matrix $\vec{x}_k$.

Figures 8.4, a, and b shows that the largest approximation errors of relation (1) are observed with a small number of matrix columns $\vec{x}_k$. From physical considerations, it is obvious detecting landmarks concentrated in the vertical plane requires just a small number of columns of the image matrix. Eliminating approximation errors is possible if the matrix **A** is calculated according to (1) at each scanning step. This is an example of the irrational use of computing resources.

An object in the video camera's field of view to be detected changes the distribution of red, green, or, blue pixel colors. According to this character, it is possible to obtain the result of the mentioned operations, that is, to detect, recognize or classify the object. The laws of color distribution for the background and the background on which the object is located will differ. This provides a basis for carrying out the operations described above. For an AMR, a landmark can be an

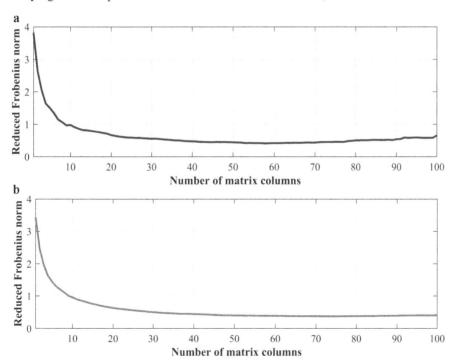

Figure 8.4: Dependence of the reduced Frobenius norm on the number of matrix $\vec{x}_k$ columns: a—for the first background, b—for the second one.

object concentrated in the vertical direction, for example, a pillar, a single tree, etc. In this case, it is advisable to choose a small number of columns of the matrix of color so that their total width is commensurate with the width of the landmark. However, as shown earlier, linear color transformations for an arbitrary background are not possible with a small number of selected columns. Suppose the values of individual elements of the approximation errors vector exceed some preselected threshold. In that case, this can be interpreted as a loss of linearity of the transformation of one column into the adjacent one for one, two, or three color R, G, B components. Choosing such a threshold is one of the research tasks.

It should be expected that the appearance of a landmark in the area will affect the local distribution of color. Figure 8.5 shows a photo with a pillar, which in some cases can be considered as a landmark.

The presence of the pillar leads to the loss of local homogeneity of the terrain image, and then the approximation errors at the location of the pillar are characterized by jump-like changes (Figure 8.6).

The presented jump-like change of approximation errors can be a sign for identifying a landmark and determining its position on the image matrix. Its color must be significantly different from the color of the environment at the landmark's location. There is a threshold exceeding, which indicates the presence of a landmark in the local area. In detail, the method of estimating the probability of detecting such landmarks with a preselected error threshold is described by [Poliarus et al. 2021].

Figure 8.5: The photograph of the first background with a possible landmark.

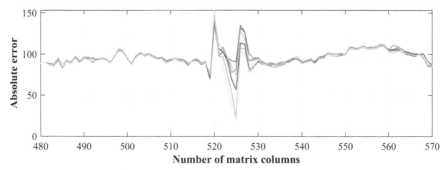

Figure 8.6: Absolute errors of approximation (2) at the location of the pillar.

No significant dependence of approximation errors on the shape of the landmark was found. Therefore, the proposed method can detect landmarks that are concentrated in space and have a color that is different from the background.

Therefore, the described operations are the basis for obtaining a linear transformation model of the components of various typical terrain backgrounds. Linear models are suitable for homogeneous backgrounds. For non-uniform backgrounds, nonlinear models based on the **A** matrix with elements that nonlinearly depend on the column numbers of the color matrix can be applied. A detailed analysis of possible nonlinear models is given below.

8.5 Analysis of possible nonlinear models of image color

As already mentioned, image formation can be represented as the registration of pixels color in the process of imaginary scanning of the vertical array of receiving optical sensors in the horizontal plane. As a result, virtual temporal color signals are formed for each array sensor, which in shape fully correspond to the distribution of color along the horizontal coordinate. Here we have a mapping of virtual temporal space into real spatial space. Previously, the relationship between adjacent image matrices was described by relation (1) regardless of the number of columns of these matrices. This process can be considered virtual filtering of a multi-channel time signal. The channel number corresponds to the sensor number in the vertical array. Matrix transformation (1) corresponds to signal filtering by a virtual system with an infinite bandwidth that does not distort the signals. As was shown, such transformations can be both linear and nonlinear. Nonlinear system transformation functions are easily calculated in MATLAB by polynomial approximation or nonlinear regression.

Actual signal reception and processing systems are inertial and have a finite bandwidth. If they are linear, then the signal transformation is described by the convolution equation. Nonlinear signal distortions by a system with infinite bandwidth can be close to signal distortions due to the limited bandwidth of a linear inertial system. In the general case, signals are distorted under the influence of both the inertia of the system and its nonlinear transformation function or under the influence of interference.

In [Poliarus et al. 2019], the method of identification of nonlinear inertial measuring systems is considered using the example of a pressure measuring channel. To obtain a mathematical model of the channel, it is necessary to measure the input and output signals and use the well-known Hammerstein model, which divides the channel into two virtual blocks. A polynomial of finite degree describes the transformation function of the first nonlinear non-inertial block, and the convolution integral describes the transforming properties of the second linear inertial block. This allows recording the channel's output signal in the form of a polynomial with unknown coefficients and a convolution integral with unknown parameters of the pulse response of the linear block. After transitioning to the functional space with a quadratic metric, the distance between the specified theoretical dependence and the output measured signal is minimized. The global random search method uses the minimization of this distance. As a result, the coefficients of the polynomial and the parameters of the inertial system's pulse response are determined, indicating the completion of the system identification problem solution.

In general, the universal model of a dynamic system is the Volterra model [Novak 2007]. It can be used to analyze a nonlinear inertial system, but due to its computational difficulties, it is not used in engineering studies. In systems with both nonlinear and inertial properties, the Wiener and Hammerstein models are used instead of the Volterra model, in which the functions of nonlinearity and inertia are artificially separated [Bai and Fu 2002]. In such nonlinear identification algorithms, the convergence problem is only sometimes well solved since the target function can have several local extrema. Least squares and singular value decomposition methods [Brouri et al. 2014] have good convergence, but the inverse matrices need to be more coherent. In general, the process of identification of nonlinear inertial systems is extremely cumbersome and time-consuming. This is why well-trained neural networks are used for the identification of nonlinear systems, as well as for recognition. The meaning of the method outlined in [Poliarus et al. 2019] is as follows.

Let's denote by $x(t)$ and $y(t)$ the realizations of random input and output signals, respectively. In the discrete version for images, the form of these realizations can be matrices $\bar{x}_k$ and $\bar{x}_{k+1}$. The intermediate signal between two virtual blocks of the Hammerstein model (nonlinear non-inertial and linear inertial ones) will be denoted as $z(t)$. The intermediate signal is described by a polynomial dependence

$$z(t) = a_0 + a_1 x(t) + a_2 x^2(t) + \ldots + a_{n-1} x^{n-1}(t),\qquad(4)$$

where a_i, $(i = 0,\ldots, n-1)$ are unknown dimensional coefficients that must be determined.

Output signal of the system

$$y(t) = \int_{-\infty}^{+\infty} z(t) h(t - \tau) d\tau,\qquad(5)$$

where $h(t)$ is the pulse response of the linear inertial block of the Hammerstein model. For the channel in [Poliarus et al. 2019], is represented by an exponential function

$$h(t) = \frac{A}{\tau_0} e^{-\frac{t}{\tau_0}},\qquad(6)$$

where τ_0 is the time constant of the linear channel, A is the amplitude coefficient. Applying this method to image description requires additional studies of the system's pulse response. A priori information about the dynamic system is contained in the coefficients a_0, a_1,... and A, τ_0.

To determine these coefficients, the output signal (2) is recorded using (1), for example

$$y(t) = a_0 \int_{-\infty}^{+\infty} h(t-\tau)d\tau + a_1 \int_{-\infty}^{+\infty} x(t)h(t-\tau)d\tau$$

$$+ a_2 \int_{-\infty}^{+\infty} x^2(t)h(t-\tau)d\tau + ... + \qquad (7)$$

$$+ a_{n-1} \int_{-\infty}^{+\infty} x^{n-1}(t)h(t-\tau)d\tau.$$

The theoretical signal (7) must coincide with the experimental one $y_{exp}(t)$, and then the functional characterizing the distance between the signals $y(t)$ and $y_{exp}(t)$ has the form

$$J(a_0, a_1, ..., a_{n-1}, A, \tau_0) = \int_{-\infty}^{\infty} [y(t) - y_{exp}(t)]^2 dt \qquad (8)$$

Its minimization by the random search of the global minimum allows obtaining a model of a nonlinear inertial system and estimating the degree of its nonlinearity and inertia. The presence of local minima of the functional can lead to incorrect parameters of the model and loss of convergence. To reduce the probability of obtaining similar results, a priori data should be used. The method does not require linearization because it uses a separate linear block for the inertial part of the virtual system. Other methods of modeling nonlinear systems involve linearization of the transformation function near the operating point; that is, they are not workable in a wide range of input signals. In recent decades, as mentioned in the introduction, methods have appeared that perform global linearization of dynamic systems. They are based on the methods of their orthogonal decomposition and are useful for terrain image processing.

8.6 The image color model is based on its own orthogonal decomposition

The most famous among the modal decomposition methods are the methods that create a set of orthogonal modes for the best restoration of a set of colors R, G, B. Such methods include, for example, the method of principal components analysis, Karhunen-Loev, etc. Let's build a model of terrain images using the modal decomposition method.

Formulation of the problem. Each sensor of the virtual system consisting of m optical sensors receives optical information R, G, B about the environment color in a very narrow angular sector and, in essence, is a pixel in practice. The pixels are placed along the vertical coordinate, and their number is equal to m. Let the array of m pixels scan the space along the horizontal coordinate and after a discrete time Δt the following values R, G, B are recorded. The scan ends when this array has taken N measurements for time $N\Delta t$. In essence, a virtual array of imaginary optical sensors has built a matrix of real images that has m rows and N columns. Here, the vertical coordinate represents space, and the horizontal coordinate represents time. In reality, it is clear that both coordinates are spatial ones. This approach makes it possible to present the spatiotemporal distribution of each of the components R, G, B in the form [Chatterjee 1999]

$$z(t,x) \approx \sum_{k=1}^{M} a_k(t) \cdot \phi_k(x), \qquad (9)$$

where $M \rightarrow \infty$. If the domain x is bounded by an interval X along the vertical coordinate, then the functions $\phi_k(x)$ are orthogonal basis functions, for example, harmonic ones or Legendre, Hermite polynomials, etc. Their scalar product is zero. The time functions are determined by the relation

$$a_k(t) = \int_X z(x,t) \cdot \phi_k(x) dx \qquad (10)$$

as projections of a function $z(x,t)$ onto orthogonal functions $\phi_k(x)$ in the function space. Qualitatively selected orthogonal functions make it possible to well approximate the spatial-temporal distribution R, G, B, i.e., $z(x,t)$. Expression (9) is called proper orthogonal decomposition. In image processing, discrete pixel color values are used, and therefore it is important to move from a continuous form of recording (1) to a discrete one based on matrix theory.

Let's build a matrix $\mathbf{Z}$ with dimension $N \times m$. Each element of this matrix Z_{ij} describes the values R, G, B at the j-th point ($j = 1...m$) at the i-th moment of time ($i = 1...N$). In essence, the matrix $\mathbf{Z}$ is one of the components R, G, B of the environment image, which is rotated relative to the usual one by 90°. A singular value decomposition of the matrix $\mathbf{Z}$

$$\mathbf{Z} = \mathbf{U\Sigma V}^T, \qquad (11)$$

where $\mathbf{U}$ is an orthogonal matrix with dimension $N \times N$, an orthogonal matrix $\mathbf{V}$ has dimension $m \times m$, and a matrix $\mathbf{O}$ with dimension $N \times m$ has all zero elements except diagonal ones. In the MATLAB, this operation is performed using the svd operator. The diagonal elements Σ_{ij} consist of $r = \min(N,m)$ non-negative numbers σ_i, which are always arranged in descending order $\sigma_1 \geq \sigma_2 \geq ... \geq \sigma_r \geq 0$ and are called singular for matrices $\mathbf{Z}$ and the transposed matrix $\mathbf{Z}^r$. The rank of the matrix $\mathbf{Z}$ is equal to the number of nonzero singular values σ_i. In the presence of noise, the number of singular values, as a rule, increases. The index k in the k-th singular value is the number of the singular value.

The matrix $\mathbf{Q} = \mathbf{U}\Sigma$, like the matrix $\mathbf{Z}$ itself, has dimension $N \times m$ and then $\mathbf{Z} = \mathbf{Q}\mathbf{V}^T$. Each element of this matrix

$$z_{ij} = q_{i1}v_{j1} + q_{i2}v_{j2} + \ldots + q_{im}v_{jm} = \sum_{k=1}^{m} q_{ik}v_{jk}. \tag{12}$$

Equation (12) is the discrete form of equation (9), where the continuous function $z(x,t)$ is an analogue of the matrix $\mathbf{Z}$ [Chatterjee 1999]. Continuous functions $a_k(t)$ and $\phi_k(x)$ are represented respectively by the row matrix (q_{ik}) and the column matrix (v_{jk}). The columns of the matrix $\mathbf{V}$ create an optimal orthogonal basis for the experimental data and are the eigen orthogonal modes for the selected image. The matrix $\mathbf{Z}$ with dimension $N \times m$ is a linear operator that maps vectors from m-dimensional space to N-dimensional space. The matrices $\mathbf{U}$ and $\mathbf{V}$ can be found by computing the SVD directly using MATLAB. The Table 8.1 presents the results of modeling the matrix $\mathbf{Q}$ which contains elements whose numerical values determine the time color distribution.

So, the model allows you to move from a spatial image to a time signal, the methods of processing of which are well developed. Similar studies have been done for orthogonal matrices $\mathbf{U}$ and $\mathbf{V}$.

The obtained results show that the peculiarities of the orthogonal matrices behavior and the matrix $\mathbf{Q}$ due to appearance of a landmark are completely invisible for the heterogeneous background and are partially visible for a homogeneous one. This consequence is not unexpected and is the result of integral approach to analysis. A similar effect is observed in analysis of the spectrum of harmonic signal with a very short amplitude jump. This jump is little noticeable in the spectrum. In our situation, a narrow pillar (landmark) is an analogue of a short jump in the sinusoidal signal. Detection of the landmark is possible, for example, using the method described in the second subsection.

The continuous representation of the color distribution (9) involves the multiplication of predefined orthogonal functions $\phi_k(x)$ by time coefficients $a_k(t)$, which for the problem under consideration, are coefficients related to the horizontal coordinate of the image. In the discrete form (12), the color of each pixel is determined by products of matrix elements $\mathbf{Q}$ by matrix elements $\mathbf{V}$. The latter creates an orthogonal basis for the selected image. For another image, they will change, unlike (1), where the orthogonal functions are fixed. The modeling of the calculated matrices $\mathbf{Q}$ and $\mathbf{V}$ shows that they change little for the images (Figure 8.1) and (Figure 8.5); that is, the presence of a landmark has almost no effect on these matrices. This is similar to how a short amplitude jump of a signal has almost no effect on its spectrum.

The use of the matrix $\mathbf{A}(k)$ is associated with nonlinear transformations, which, with large dimensions of this matrix, leads to significant time consumption during data processing. To simplify model (1) with a non-uniform background on the image, one can apply the dynamic mode decomposition (DMD) method, which includes the Arnoldi algorithm [Schmid et al. 2010]. This method for recognizing ground objects

Table 8.1: Plots of the orthogonal matrix Q for homogeneous and heterogeneous images.

The photo of a homogeneous image without a landmark	The photo of a homogeneous image with the landmark
The plot of matrix **Q** for a homogeneous image without a landmark	The plot of matrix **Q** for a homogeneous image with the landmark
The photo of a heterogeneous image without a landmark	The photo of a heterogeneous image with the landmark
The plot of matrix **Q** for a heterogeneous image without a landmark	The plot of matrix **Q** for a heterogeneous image with the landmark

with the help of a linear operator $\mathbf{A}$ maps a field of vectors $\vec{v}$ as analogues $\vec{x}_k$ to a sequence of fields $\mathbf{A}\vec{v}$ with a time interval Δt. It is a field due to the distribution of color along the vertical coordinate. Since this distribution is taken discretely with a time interval Δt, then as a result we have a space-time or flow field. Based on the sequence of vectors $\vec{v}$, an orthonormal basis $\mathbf{V}$ is created by the Gram-Schmidt orthogonalization method, in which the dynamics of the system are described by the Hessenberg matrix of reduced dimension [Chatterjee 1999]

$$\mathbf{H} = \mathbf{V}^H \mathbf{A} \mathbf{V}. \tag{13}$$

This matrix has eigenvalues ω close to $\mathbf{A}$.

According to Arnoldi's algorithm, the action of a matrix $\mathbf{A}$ on a set of column vectors $\mathbf{V}$ of an orthonormal basis is represented by the expression

$$\mathbf{H} = \mathbf{V}\mathbf{H} + \vec{r}\vec{e}_n^T, \tag{14}$$

where $\vec{r}$ is the residual vector and $\vec{e}_n$ is the unit vector with number n. Minimization of the residual vector is carried out after replacing the matrix $\mathbf{H}$ with a matrix optimized in the mean square sense

$$\mathbf{S} = \arg\min \left\| \mathbf{V}_2^n - \mathbf{V}_1^{n-1}\mathbf{S} \right\|. \tag{15}$$

The problem (15) can be solved using the QR-decomposition V_1^{n-1}, that is, the representation of the matrix in the form of the product of the unitary matrix $\mathbf{Q}$ and the right triangular matrix $\mathbf{R}$. In MATLAB, the operator qr is used for this. After determining the matrix $\mathbf{S}$, its eigenvalues and eigenvectors are calculated, which leads to obtaining dynamic modes of a sequence of images together with their temporal behavior. The eigenvectors of the matrix $\mathbf{S}$ contain the coefficients of the dynamic mode, which is expressed in snapshots of the basis V_1^{n-1}. The eigenvalues of the matrix $\mathbf{S}$ represent mappings between snapshot sequences. If the modules of the eigenvalues do not exceed one, the image transformation process is stable and perhaps this is characteristic of a monotonous background. The modulus of the eigenvalues of the matrix will exceed one if an object appears on the terrain, and it is significantly different in color and shape from the environment.

A given sequence of n snapshots over a time interval Δt forms two data matrices V_1^{n-1} and V_2^n, containing the first $n-1$ snapshots and exactly such a sequence, shifted to Δt respectively. The QR-decomposition of the first sequence is used to solve the first problem (15). The final step is to calculate the eigenvalues and eigenvectors of the matrix $\mathbf{S}$, transforming the eigenvalues from the time format to the more general format and reconstructing the dynamic modes from a weighted basis of snapshots of the eigenvectors of the matrix $\mathbf{S}$. Analyzing a sequence of data generated by a nonlinear dynamical system by linear mapping from one snapshot to another is related to Koopman analysis [Rowley et al. 2009].

8.7 Global linearization of image color models

Modeling dynamic systems obtained from high-dimensional data is a promising direction in processing video images. The method of transition to such a dynamic system based on its orthogonal decomposition is discussed above. A powerful approximation is the DMD method, which can be reduced to decomposing the images into spatial-temporal structures. In many cases, these structures can be used in processing information about images for AMR navigation. Rowley et al. [2009]

show that the DMD method can be suitable for nonlinear dynamic systems when the Koopman operator is applied. The mathematical and physical foundations of the Koopman operator are outlined in the book [Kutz et al. 2016].

The DMD method is based on data $\vec{x}_k$ collection, which are snapshots of processes. As shown above, matrix images were transformed into a spatial-temporal process formed by a virtual dynamic system at time instants t_k, where $k = 1,2,\ldots, m$. Adjacent images $\vec{x}_k$ and $\vec{x}_{k+1}$ are connected by the matrix relation (1), and the matrix **A** is chosen from the condition of minimization $\|\vec{x}_{k+1} - \mathbf{A}\vec{x}_k\|_2$ under the number of snapshots $k = 1,2,\ldots, m-1$. The method is convenient for image processing because it does not require any assumptions about the system.

The number of states $\vec{x}_k = \vec{x}(k\Delta t)$ is usually large. The map F of discrete-time flow is described as

$$\vec{x}_{k+1} = F(\vec{x}_k). \tag{16}$$

The effect of various optical interferences leads to the fact that instead of a pixel with color $\vec{x}_k$, a pixel with color $\vec{y}_k$ is obtained

$$\vec{y}_k = g(\vec{x}_k), \tag{17}$$

where g is some function, generally nonlinear one.

In this chapter, we believe that color registration takes place under ideal conditions and therefore $\vec{y}_k = \vec{x}_k$.

The DMD procedure locally approximates a linear dynamical system [Kutz et al. 2016]

$$\frac{d\vec{x}}{dt} = \mathcal{A}\vec{x}. \tag{18}$$

The initial conditions for the differential equation (18) are $\vec{x}(0)$, and its solution is well known [Boyce and DiPrima, 2008]:

$$\vec{x}(t) = \sum_{k=1}^{n} \phi_k \exp(\omega_k t) b_k = \Phi\exp(\Omega t)\mathbf{b}, \tag{19}$$

where ϕ_k and ω_k are the eigenvectors and eigenvalues of the matrix $\mathcal{A}$, which expresses the continuous dynamics from (18). The coefficients b_k are coordinates in the basis of eigenvectors.

For discrete time

$$\vec{x}_{k+1} = \mathbf{A}\vec{x}_k, \tag{20}$$

where

$$\mathbf{A} = \exp(\mathcal{A}\Delta t). \tag{21}$$

System solutions

$$\vec{x}_k = \sum_{j=1}^{r} \phi_j \lambda_j^k b_j = \mathbf{\Phi \Lambda^k b}. \tag{22}$$

Here ϕ_k are the eigenvectors, λ_k are the eigenvalues of the discrete-time mapping $\mathbf{A}$ and $\mathbf{b}$ are the coefficients of the initial conditions of the vector $\vec{x}_1$ in the basis of the eigenvectors, where $\vec{x}_1 = \mathbf{\Phi b}$.

The local linear approximation (20), as before, is written in terms of shifted image matrices

$$\mathbf{X'} = \mathbf{AX}, \tag{23}$$

and the best approximation of the matrix by the minimum of the Frobenius norm is determined by the relation

$$\mathbf{A} = \mathbf{X'X^\dagger}, \tag{24}$$

where the sign "†" is the Moore-Penrose inversion.

Since the matrix $\mathbf{A}$ has, as a rule, a large dimension, linear transformations are difficult to calculate. To reduce this problem, in [Kutz et al. 2016] an algorithm for transitioning it to a matrix $\tilde{\mathbf{A}}$ of reduced dimension is described to calculate leading nonzero eigenvalues and eigenvectors of a full-dimensional operator $\mathbf{A}$.

The DMD method is suitable for finite-dimensional linear systems. The Koopman operator κ allows the global linearization of a nonlinear system by moving it into an infinite-dimensional space. The modes of the infinite dimension Koopman linear operator are approximated based on the DMD method. Limiting the dimensionality of this operator in practice leads to approximation errors. The action of an operator κ on a nonlinear function g in the general case is described by a dependence [Kutz et al. 2016]

$$\kappa g(\vec{x}_k) = g(F(\vec{x}_k)) = g(\vec{x}_{k+1}). \tag{25}$$

The main points of the algorithm for transition from a matrix $\mathbf{A}$ to a matrix $\tilde{\mathbf{A}}$ of reduced dimension are as follows [Kutz et al. 2016]:

1. Singular value decomposition of the matrix $\mathbf{X}$

$$\mathbf{X} \approx \mathbf{U\Sigma V^*}, \tag{26}$$

where $*$ means complex conjugate transposition. The left $\mathbf{U} \in \mathbb{C}^{n \times r}$ and right $\mathbf{V} \in \mathbb{C}^{m \times r}$ singular vectors are described above. The diagonal matrix $\mathbf{\Sigma} \in \mathbb{C}^{r \times r}$ is square one with the rank r of reduced dimension.

2. Determination of the matrix $\mathbf{A}$ based on SVD and pseudoinversion $\mathbf{X}$:

$$\mathbf{A} = \mathbf{X'V\Sigma^{-1}U^*}, \tag{27}$$

Full matrix projection on proper orthogonal decomposition modes

$$\tilde{\mathbf{A}} = \mathbf{U}^*\mathbf{A}\mathbf{U} = \mathbf{U}^*\mathbf{X}'\mathbf{V}\mathbf{\Sigma}^{-1}, \tag{28}$$

where a low-dimensional linear model of the image conversion system is determined using a matrix $\tilde{\mathbf{A}}$:

$$\tilde{\vec{x}}_{k+1} = \tilde{\mathbf{A}}\tilde{\vec{x}}_k. \tag{29}$$

3. Calculation of the proper decomposition of the matrix $\tilde{\mathbf{A}}$:

$$\tilde{\mathbf{A}}\mathbf{W} = \mathbf{W}\mathbf{\Lambda}, \tag{30}$$

where the columns of the matrix $\mathbf{W}$ are the eigenvectors of the matrix $\tilde{\mathbf{A}}$, and $\mathbf{\Lambda}$ is a diagonal matrix with eigenvalues λ_k.

4. Determination of eigenvectors ϕ_k of a matrix $\mathbf{A}$ as columns of a non-square matrix $\mathbf{\Phi}$:

$$\mathbf{\Phi} = \mathbf{X}'\mathbf{V}\mathbf{\Sigma}^{-1}\mathbf{W}. \tag{31}$$

Approximate solution using the formula $\omega_k = \ln\dfrac{\lambda_k}{\Delta t}$

$$\vec{x}(t) \approx \sum_{k=1}^{r} \phi_k \exp(\omega_k t)b_k = \mathbf{\Phi}\exp(\mathbf{\Omega}t)\mathbf{b}, \tag{32}$$

where b_k is the initial amplitude of each mode, $\mathbf{\Omega} = \text{diag}(\omega)$ is a diagonal matrix with eigenvalues ω_k.

Formula (32) describes the best approximation of the selected images in the mean square sense, which is described by the relation (1). The initial values of the vector $\vec{b}$ are determined using pseudoinversion according to the formula

$$\vec{b} = \mathbf{\Phi}^{\dagger}\vec{x}_1. \tag{33}$$

According to [Kutz et al. 2016], the Koopman operator $\mathcal{K}_t$ can be determined for time-discrete dynamical systems described by the relation

$$\vec{x}_{k+1} = F_t(\vec{x}_k), \tag{34}$$

This operator forms a new dynamic system on the observed functions g:

$$\mathcal{K}_t g(\vec{x}_k) = g(F_t(\vec{x}_k)) = g(\vec{x}_{k+1}). \tag{35}$$

The solution (35) is obtained on the basis of the spectral decomposition of the Koopman operator with the determination of its eigenfunctions $\varphi_k(\vec{x})$ and eigenvalues λ_k:

$$\mathcal{K}\varphi_k = \lambda_k \varphi_k. \tag{36}$$

The vector of the observed functions g can be written in terms of the components of the Koopman eigenfunctions

$$g(\vec{x}) = \begin{bmatrix} g_1(\vec{x}) \\ g_2(\vec{x}) \\ ... \\ g_p(\vec{x}) \end{bmatrix} = \sum_{k=1}^{\infty} \varphi_k(\vec{x}) \vec{v}_k, \tag{37}$$

where $\vec{v}_k$ is the k-th mode associated with the k-th Koopman eigenfunction φ_k. All eigenfunctions are orthonormal and (37) can be written explicitly as

$$g(\vec{x}) = \sum_{k=1}^{\infty} \varphi_k(\vec{x}) \begin{bmatrix} \langle \varphi_k, g_1 \rangle \\ \langle \varphi_k, g_2 \rangle \\ ... \\ \langle \varphi_k, g_p \rangle \end{bmatrix} = \sum_{k=1}^{\infty} \varphi_k(\vec{x}) \vec{v}_k. \tag{38}$$

As a rule, the DMD method is used to approximate eigenvalues λ_k and modes $\vec{v}_k$.

The finite-dimensional nonlinear dynamic system determined in (34) and the linear infinite-dimensional system described by the operator $\mathcal{K}$ in (35) are two equivalent representations of the same image. Then [Kutz et al. 2016]

$$\mathcal{K} g(\vec{x}) = \mathcal{K} \sum_{k=1}^{\infty} \varphi_k(\vec{x}) \vec{v}_k = \sum_{k=1}^{\infty} \mathcal{K} \varphi_k(\vec{x}) \vec{v}_k = \sum_{k=1}^{\infty} \lambda_k \varphi_k(\vec{x}) \vec{v}_k. \tag{39}$$

Therefore, the nonlinear image transformation can be replaced by an infinite sum of products of eigenvalues, eigenfunctions, and Koopman modes, and the nonlinear dynamic system is transformed into a linear one. Eigenvalues and Koopman modes are determined directly from image matrices using the DMD algorithm.

The Koopman eigenvalues are the DMD eigenvalues of the matrix

$$\mathbf{A}_X = \mathbf{X}'\mathbf{X}^{\dagger}. \tag{40}$$

Let's denote the column vector of the observed functions as $\vec{g} = [g_1, g_2, ..., g_p]$. We build image data matrices $\mathbf{Y}$ and $\mathbf{Y}'$ from the condition $\vec{y}_k = g(\vec{x}_k)$. The columns $\mathbf{Y}'$ are given over time Δt and represent the output vector through the observables, $\vec{y}_k' = g(f(\vec{x}_k))$. The matrix $\mathbf{A}_Y = \mathbf{Y}'\mathbf{Y}^{\dagger}$ gives the necessary Koopman approximation of image sequences. Matrices $\mathbf{Y}$ and $\mathbf{Y}'$ compute DMD in the space of observables instead of computing modes in the space of states.

Koopman's eigenfunctions are defined as a linear combination of the observed functions [Kutz et al. 2016]

$$\varphi_k(\vec{x}) = w_1 g_1(\vec{x}) + w_2 g_2(\vec{x}) + ... + w_p g_p(\vec{x}) = \vec{w} \cdot \vec{g}, \tag{41}$$

where $\vec{w}$ is a left eigenvector $\mathbf{A}_Y$ with eigenvalue λ_k, so that $\tilde{\vec{w}}^* \mathbf{A}_Y = \lambda_k \tilde{\vec{w}}^*$.

The application of the Koopman operator is accompanied by limitations: (1) matrices $\mathbf{X}$ and $\mathbf{X}'$ characterize the color of the image, but the nonlinear dependence $f(\mathbb{C})$ is unknown, although, as shown before, it can be determined; (2) the calculation of an infinite sum is impossible, and therefore the sum (37) must be replaced by a finite one; and (3) there are strict requirements for the selection of the observed functions $g(\vec{x})$ to approximate the nonlinear dynamics $f(\mathbb{C})$ using the Koopman operator qualitatively. The finite dimensionality of the operator follows from the limitations in collecting color data. The method is effective with a well-chosen set of observable functions and expert knowledge of the color conversion system.

The Koopman operator application algorithm involves the following stages.

1. Obtaining the image matrices $\mathbf{X}$ and $\mathbf{X}'$, and from them further the matrices of the observed functions $\mathbf{Y}$ and $\mathbf{Y}'$, where each observed function g is related to the elements of the matrix $\mathbf{X}$ by the expression $\vec{y}_k = g(\vec{x}_k)$, where each column is given by the relations $\vec{y}_k = g(\vec{x}_k)$ or $\vec{y}'_k = g(\vec{x}'_k)$.

2. Calculation of the matrix $\mathbf{A}_Y$ based on the DMD algorithm

$$\mathbf{A}_Y = \mathbf{Y}'\mathbf{Y}^\dagger \tag{42}$$

and Koopman eigenvalues and modes, based on the selected set of observables.

3. Determination of the extended modes $\mathbf{\Phi}_Y$ based on DMD that can approximate Koopman modes

$$\mathbf{\Phi}_Y = \mathbf{Y}'\mathbf{V}\mathbf{\Sigma}^{-1}\mathbf{W}, \tag{43}$$

where $\mathbf{W}$ is determined from the eigenvalue problem $\tilde{\mathbf{A}}_Y \mathbf{W} = \mathbf{W}\mathbf{\Lambda}$ and $\mathbf{Y} = \mathbf{U}\mathbf{\Sigma}\mathbf{V}^*$.

4. Evaluation of the next state in the space of observable functions

$$\vec{y}(t) = \mathbf{\Phi}_Y \, diag(\exp(\omega t))\vec{b}, \tag{44}$$

where $\vec{b} = \mathbf{\Phi}_Y^\dagger \vec{y}_1$, and ω is the set of eigenvalues λ_k generated from the matrix $\mathbf{\Lambda}$, where $\omega_k = \dfrac{\ln(\lambda_k)}{\Delta t}$.

5. The inverse transition from observables back to state-time:

$$\vec{y}_k = g(\vec{x}_k), \; \rightarrow \; \vec{x}_k = g^{-1}(\vec{y}_k). \tag{45}$$

The DMD algorithm is close to the finite-dimensional Koopman operator algorithm. The selection of acceptable observables is important for this algorithm and provides a good approximation of the subsequent image.

8.8 Future research directions

The monograph results are expected to be based on a well-proven theory in hydrodynamics. The parameters of fluid flow in pipes and pixel color flows are close from a mathematical point of view. The limitations of the presented methods, which are related to the nonlinearity of the connection between neighboring images, are eliminated by applying the Koopman operator. However, this study needs an analysis of the observed functions for a wide range of terrain images. There is also no comparison of the proposed methods for different conditions of detecting landmarks and their recognition. No research has been conducted on the possibilities of robot recognition of possible landmarks of different shapes. An acceptable result would be obtaining image models for typical terrains with and without landmarks. All this should be carried out in future studies. Finally, the transition proposed in the study from image analysis in space to analysis in the time domain makes it possible to use the well-studied Markov theory of linear and nonlinear filtering for landmark detection.

8.9 Conclusions

This chapter describes the methodology of creating image models that can be used for training neural networks and, in the future, in video image processing systems for detecting and recognizing landmarks by an autonomous mobile robot. The method is based on transforming a sequence of images into a virtual dynamic system described by high-dimensional matrices, the elements of which are pixel color values. This transformation often loses its linearity. Therefore, modified models of Wiener and Hammerstein and methods based on their orthogonal decomposition and decomposition of dynamic modes are proposed for image processing. They make it possible to detect spatial-temporal structures of images. These structures can model images close to the selected area for training neural networks. Using Koopman modes creates conditions for the global linearization of the dynamic system and the reduction of the dimensionality of image matrices, which increases the efficiency of information processing in robot navigation. A feature for landmark detection can be exceeding the threshold of the Frobenius norm for the error matrix between the real image matrix and its model representation. The developed models can be used as a part of the improved general theory of detection and recognition of objects based on color; for expanding the scope of application of the global linearization method in nonlinear models, which are often encountered in the practice of detection, recognition and identification of objects; for improving the quality of autonomous mobile robot navigation.

References

Ahmed, S. A., Topalov, A. V., Shakev, N. G., and Popov, V. L. 2018. Model-free detection and following of moving objects by an omnidirectional mobile robot using 2D range data. IFAC-PapersOnLine, 51(22): 226–231.

Akai, N., Yamauchi, K., Inoue, K., Kakigi, Y., Abe, Y., and Ozaki, K. 2015. Development of mobile robot SARA that completed mission in real world robot challenge 2014. Journal of Robotics and Mechatronics, 27(4): 327–336.

Alhaway, M. 2018. Reinforcement-learning-based navigation for autonomous mobile robots in unknown environments. https://purl.utwente.nl/essays/76349/.

Alparslan, Ö., and Çetin, Ö. 2021. Comparison of Object Detection and Classification Methods for Mobile Robots. Year 2021, 25(3): 751–765, 30.06.2021, https://doi.org/10.16984/saufenbilder.828841.

Andrakhanov, A. 2013. Navigation of Autonomous Mobile Robot in Homogeneous and Heterogeneous Environments on Basis of GMDH Neural Networks. - International Conference in Inductive Modelling ICIM' 2013, pp. 134–138.

Anouncia, S. M. and Godwin, J. J. 2009. Approaches for automated object recognition and extraction from images – a study. Journal of Computing and Information Technology - CIT 17, 2009, 4: 359–370. doi:10.2498/cit.1001363.

Antonazzi, M., Luperto, M., Basilico, N., and Borghese, A. 2022. Enhancing Door Detection for Autonomous Mobile Robots with Environment-Specific Data Collection. https://doi.org/10.48550/arXiv.2203.03959.

Aoyagi, S., Ushiro, S., Fukuda, M., Takahashi, T., and Suzuki, M. 2022. Recognition and grasping of objects by active vision using indoor autonomous mobile robot. Transactions of the Institute of Systems, Control and Information Engineers, 35(2): 19–28.

Asiain, J. L., and Gomez-Allende, D. M. 2001. Landmark recognition for autonomous navigation using odometric information and a network of perceptrons. Conference: Bio-inspired Applications of Connectionism, 6th International Work-Conference on Artificial and Natural Neural Networks, IWANN 2001 Granada, Spain, June 13-15, 2001, Proceedings, Part II.

Astua, C., Barber, R., Crespo, J., and Jardon, A. 2014. Object detection techniques applied on mobile robot semantic navigation. Sensors (Basel). 2014 Apr; 14(4): 6734–6757.

Bai, E. W., and Fu, M. 2002. A blind approach to hammerstein model identification. IEEE Transactions on Signal Processing, 50(7): 291–304.

Básaca-Preciado, L. C., Sergiyenko, O. Yu., Rodríguez-Quinonez, J. C., García, X., Tyrsa, V. V., Rivas-Lopez, M. et al. 2014. Optical 3D laser measurement system for navigation of autonomous mobile robot. Optics and Lasers in Engineering, 54, March 2014, Pages 159–169.

Bing-Qiang Huang, Guang-Yi Cao, and Min Guo. 2005. Reinforcement learning neural network to the problem of autonomous mobile robot obstacle avoidance. International Conference on Machine Learning and Cybernetics, China, 2005, pp. 85–89. doi: 10.1109/ICMLC.2005.1526924.

Bore N., Ambrus, R., Jensfelt, P., and Folkesson, J. 2017. Efficient retrieval of arbitrary objects from long-term robot observations. Robotics and Autonomous Systems Journal, Volume 91, May 2017, Pages 139–150.

Boyce, W. E. and DiPrima, R. C. 2008. Elementary Differential Equations, 9th Ed. Wiley, 2008.

Brouri, A., Giri, F., Mkhida, A., Chaoui, F.Z., Elkarkri, A. and Chhibat, M.L. 2014. Identification of nonlinear systems structured by hammerstein-wiener model. International Journal of Electrical, Computer, Energetic, Electronic and Com-munication Engineering, 8(5): 738–742.

Carballo, A., Seiya, S., Lambert, J., Darweesh, H., Narksri, P., Morales, L. Y. et al. 2018. End-to-End autonomous mobile robot navigation with model-based system support. Journal of Robotics and Mechatronics. August 2018, 30(4): 563–583. DOI:10.20965/jrm.2018.p0563.

Cartucho, J., Ventura, R., and Veloso, M. 2018. Robust object recognition through symbiotic deep learning in mobile robots. Preprint submitted to 2018 IEEE/RSJ International Conference on Intelligent Robots and Systems. Received March 1, 2018.

Chatterjee A. 1999. An Introduction to the Proper Orthogonal Decomposition. Current Science, 15 p.

Chen, Y., Cheng, C., Zhang, Y., Li, X., and Sun, L. 2022. A neural network-based navigation approach for autonomous mobile robot systems. Appl. Sci., 12(15): 7796. https://doi.org/10.3390/app12157796.

Cheng, C., and Chen, Y. 2021. A neural network based mobile robot navigation approach using reinforcement learning parameter tuning mechanism. Proceedings of the IEEE. 2021 China Automation Congress (CAC), 22–24 October, 2021Beijing, China.

Czygier, J., Dąbrowski, P., Grabowy, R., Rećko, M., and Dzierżek, K. 2020. Autonomous searching robot with object recognition based on neural networks. Mechanical Engineering and Robotics Research, 2020, 9(9), September 2020.

Deng, J., Xuan, X., Wang, W., Li, Z., Yao, H., and Wang, Z. 2020. A review of research on object detection based on deep learning, AINIT 2020. Journal of Physics: Conference Series. IOP Publishing, 1684 (2020) 012028, doi:10.1088/1742-6596/1684/1/012028.

Elmogy, M., and Zhang, J. 2009. Robust real-time landmark recognition for humanoid robot navigation. Proceedings of the 2008 IEEE International Conference on Robotics and Biomimetics Bangkok, Thailand, February 21–26.

Fukuda, T., Ito, S., Arai, F., Yokoyama, Y., Abe, Y., Tanaka, K. et al. 1995. Navigation system based on ceiling landmark recognition for autonomous mobile robot-landmark detection based on fuzzy template matching (FTM). Proceedings 1995 IEEE/RSJ International Conference on Intelligent Robots and Systems. Human Robot Interaction and Cooperative Robots.

Furlán, F., Rubio, E., Sossa, H., and Ponce, V. 2020. CNN based detectors on planetary environments: A performance evaluation. Frontiers in Neurorobotics, pp. 63–70, Original research published: 30 October 2020 doi: 10.3389/fnbot.2020.590371.

Ge, G., Zhang, Y., Wang, W., Jiang, Q., Hu, L., and Wang, Y. 2022. Text-MCL: Autonomous mobile robot localization in similar environment using text-level semantic information. Machines, 10(3): 169; https://doi.org/10.3390/machines10030169.

Gopalakrishnan, A., Greene, S., and Sekmen, A. 2005. Vision-based mobile robot learning and navigation. 2005 IEEE International Workshop on Robots and Human Interactive Communication.

Guilherme De Souza Silva, C., Souza Padua, Y., and Cintra Felipussi, S. 2020. LoCAR – low-cost autonomous robot for object detection with voice command and mobile nets. Applied Artificial Intelligence. An International Journal, 34(11).

Hayet, J. B., Lerasle, F., and Devy, M. 2007. A visual landmark framework for mobile robot navigation. Image and Vision Computing, 25: 1341–1351.

Jin, Z., Liu, L., Gong, D., and Li, L. 2021. Target recognition of industrial robots using machine vision in 5G Environment. BRIEF RESEARCH REPORT article, Frontiers in Neurorobotics, 25 February 2021, https://doi.org/10.3389/fnbot.2021.624466.

Krizhevsky, A., Sutskever, I., Hinton, G. 2012. ImageNet classification with deep convolutional neural networks. Advances in Neural Information Processing Systems, 25: 1097–1105.

Kutz, J. Na., Brunton, S. L., Brunton, B. W., and Proctor, J. L. 2016. Dynamic mode decomposition. Data-Driven Modeling of Complex Systems. SIAM, 2016. 241 p.

Lucca Siqueira, F., Della Mea Plentz, P., and De Pieri, E. R. 2022. Semantic trajectory applied to the navigation of autonomous mobile robots. 2016 IEEE/ACS 13th International Conference of Computer Systems and Applications (AICCSA), Agadir, Morocco, 2016, pp. 1-8, doi: 10.1109/AICCSA.2016.7945766.

Martinez-Martin, E., and Pobil, A. P. 2016. Object Detection and Recognition for Assistive Robots. Robotics & Automation Magazine, Vol. X, No. X, September 2016.

McGreavy, C., Kunze, L., and Hawes, N. 2016. Next best view planning for object recognition in mobile robotics. Conference: PlanSIG 2016 Workshop.

Miranda-Vega, J. E., Díaz-Ramírez, A., Sergiyenko, O., García-González, W., Flores-Fuentes, W. and Rodríguez-Quiñonez, J. C. 2022. Improvements of an optical scanning system for indoor localization based on defuzzification methods. IEEE Sensors Journal, 22(11): 4808–4815, 15 March 15, 2022, doi: 10.1109/JSEN.2021.3068643.

Nasr, H., and Bhanu, B. 1988. Landmark recognition for autonomous mobile robots. Conference: Robotics and Automation, 1988. Proceedings, 1988 IEEE International Conference on Robotics and Automation.

Nilwong, S., Hossain, D., Kaneko, S., and Capi, G. 2019. Deep learning-based landmark detection for mobile robot outdoor localization. Machines, 7: 25.

Novak, A. 2007. Identification of Nonlinear Systems: Volterra Series Simplification. Acta Polytechnica, 47(45): 72–75.

Novak, G., Bais, A., and Mahlknecht, S. 2004. Simple stereo vision system for real-time object recognition for an autonomous mobile robot. Second IEEE International Conference on Computational Cybernetics, 2004. ICCC 2004, DOI: 10.1109/ICCCYB.2004.1437710.

Pandey, A. and Parhi, D. R. 2016. Autonomous mobile robot navigation in cluttered environment using hybrid Takagi-Sugeno fuzzy model and simulated annealing algorithm controller. World Journal of Engineering, 13(5): 431–440. https://doi.org/10.1108/WJE-08-2016-0055.

Panigrahi, P. K. and Sahoo, S. 2014. Navigation of autonomous mobile robot using different activation functions of wavelet neural network. International Conference for Convergence for Technology-2014, Pune, India, 2014, pp. 1–6, doi: 10.1109/I2CT.2014.7092044.

Peng, M., Gang, Y. D., Qian, K. J., Fu, Q. Z., and Yang, F. J. 2020. Quantum-based creative generation method for a dancing robot. Frontiers in Neurorobotics, pp. 71–93, Original research published: 01 December 2020 doi: 10.3389/fnbot.2020.559366.

Poliarus, O., Koval, O., Medvedovska, Ya., Poliakov, Ye., and Ianushkevych, S. 2019. Identification of a nonlinear inertial measuring pressure channel. Ukrainian Metrological Journal, №1, pp. 63–70.

Poliarus, O., Poliakov, Ye., and Lebedynskyi, A. 2021. Detection of landmarks by autonomous mobile robots using camera-based sensors in outdoor environments. IEEE Sensors Journal, 21(10.): 11443–11450, doi: 10.1109/JSEN.2020.3010883.

Poliarus, O. V., and Poliakov, Ye. O. 2021. Detection of landmarks by mobile autonomous robots based on estimating the color parameters of the surrounding area. pp. 224–257. *In*: Oleg Sergiyenko, Wendy Flores-Fuentes, Julio Cesar Rodríguez-Quiñonez (eds.). Examining Optoelectronics in Machine Vision and Applications in Industry 4.0. - IGI Global, 2021. DOI: 10.4018/978-1-7998-6522-3. ch008.

Qazwan, A., Nor, S. M. S., Mahathir, M., Muaammar, H. K. A., Nabil, F., Adeb, S. et al. 2021. Real-time autonomous robot for object tracking using vision system. Distributed, Parallel, and Cluster Computing (cs.DC); Robotics (cs.RO), arXiv:2105.00852.

Quan, H., Li, Y., and Zhang, Y. 2020. A novel mobile robot navigation method based on deep reinforcement learning. International Journal of Advanced Robotic Systems, 17(3). doi:10.1177/1729881420921672.

Rauer, J. N., Wöber, W., and Aburaia, M. 2019. An autonomous mobile handling robot using object recognition. Proceedings of the ARW and OAGM Workshop 2019, doi: 10.3217/978-3-85125-663-5-06, https://doi.org/10.5281/zenodo.3675257.

Rowley, C. W., Mezic, I., Bagheri, S., Schlatter, S., and Henningson, D. S. 2009. Spectral analysis of nonlinear flows. Journal of Fluid Mechanics, 641: 115–127.

Ruiz-Sarmiento, J. R., Günther, M., Galindo, C., González-Jiménez, J., and Hertzberg, J. 2017. Online context-based object recognition for mobile robots. 2017 IEEE International Conference on Autonomous Robot Systems and Competitions (ICARSC), DOI: 10.1109/ICARSC.2017.7964083.

Samadi, M., and Jond, H. 2020. Hybrid global positioning system-adaptive neuro-fuzzy inference system based autonomous mobile robot navigation. Robotics and Autonomous Systems. 134. 103669. 10.1016/j.robot.2020.103669.

Sánchez-Ibáñez, J. R., Pérez-del-Pulgar, C. J., and García-Cerezo, A. Path. 2021. Planning for autonomous mobile robots: A review. Sensors, 21: 7898. https://doi.org/10.3390/s21237898.

Schmid, P. J. 2010. Dynamic mode decomposition of numerical and experimental data. Journal of Fluid Mechanics, 656: 5–28.

Schmid, P. J., Li, L., Juniper, M. P., and Pust, O. 2010. Applications of the dynamic mode decomposition. Theory of Computing Fluid Dynamics, pp. 1–15.

Song, X., Fang, H., Jiao, X. and Wang, Y. 2012. Autonomous mobile robot navigation using machine learning, 2012 IEEE 6th International Conference on Information and Automation for Sustainability, Beijing, pp. 135–140, doi: 10.110 9/ICIAFS.2012.6419894.

Tawiah, T. A.-Q. 2020. A review of algorithms for image-based recognition and inference in mobile robotic systems. International Journal of Advanced Robotic Systems, 17(6), November 2020.

Thin, K. K., and Zaw, N. W. 2019. Object detection system of an autonomous mobile robot by using artificial neutral network. International Journal of Scientific and Research Publications, 9(3), March 2019.

Torokhti, A., and Howlett, P. 2007. Computational methods for modeling of nonlinear systems. Series: Mathematics in Science and Engineering. Elsevier, 212: 1–199. ISBN: 9780444530448.

Wang, Y., Yang, Y., Yuan, X., Zu, Y., Zhou, Y., Yin, F. et al. 2011. Autonomous mobile robot navigation system designed in dynamic environment based on transferable belief model. Measurement, 44(8): October 2011, pp. 1389–1405.

Xiao, W., Yuan, L., He, L., Ran, T., Zhang, J., and Cui, J. 2022. Multigoal visual navigation with collision avoidance via deep reinforcement learning. IEEE Trans. Instrum. Meas., 71: 1–9.

Zghair, N. A. K., and Al-Araji, A. S. 2021. A one decade survey of autonomous mobile robot systems. International Journal of Electrical and Computer Engineering (IJECE), December 2021, 11: 4891–4906. ISSN: 2088-8708, DOI: 10.11591/ijece.v11i6.

Zhengt, J. Y., Barth, M., and Tsuji, S. 1991. Autonomous landmark selection for route recognition by a mobile robot. Proceedings of the 1991 IEEE International Conference on Robotics and Automation Sacramento, California - April 1991.

Zhong, X., Zhou, Y., and Liu, H. 2017. Design and recognition of artificial landmarks for reliable indoor self-localization of mobile robots. International Journal of Advanced Robotic Systems.

Zhou, Z., Li, L., Fürsterling, A., Durocher, H. J., Mouridsen, J., and Zhang, X. 2022. Learning-based object detection and localization for a mobile robot manipulator in SME production. Robotics and Computer-Integrated Manufacturing, 73, February 2022, 102229.

Zhou, B., Lapedriza, A., Khosla, A., Oliva, A., and Torralba, A. 2017. Places: A 10 million image database for scene recognition. IEEE Transactions on Pattern Analysis and Machine Intelligence, doi 10.1109/tpami.2017.2723009.

9

Machine Vision
A Measurement Tool for Agricultural Automation

Duke M Bulanon,* Isaac Compher, Garrisen Cizmich, Joseph Ichiro Bulanon and *Brice Allen*

9.1 Introduction

Machine vision is defined as the application of existing technology, such as sensors, image processing, and artificial intelligence to provide a visual sense to machines. However, that visual sense is limited to some degree specifically by the nature of its applicability and its working environment. It is not the same kind of vision that is provided by the human visual system.

A general machine vision system model (Awcock and Thomas 1996) was defined which could be used and adapted to any type of environment. The necessary functions of the machine vision model are:

(1) application of environmental characteristics,

(2) capture of an image,

(3) analysis of the image,

(4) recognition of the desired objects,

(5) initiation of subsequent tasks to be taken.

From these functions, the elements of this model were defined. The model, which is illustrated in Figure 9.1, has four elements. These are (1) scene constraints, (2) image acquisition, (3) image processing and analysis, and (4) actuation.

Department of Engineering and Physics, Northwest Nazarene University.
* Corresponding author: dbulanon@nnu.edu

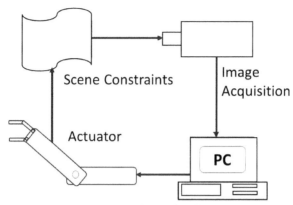

Figure 9.1: A generic machine vision system

(1) Scene constraint

The scene constraint refers to the location where the machine vision system will operate. This location includes the objects of interest and the background environment that will be captured by the image acquisition system. The physical and reflective properties of the objects and their background are critical parameters that need to be considered. Taking advantage of these properties helps differentiate the objects from the system's environment. Furthermore, it will simplify subsequent processes, especially image analysis for object recognition. Thus, it is the first critical design decision made in developing a machine vision system. To cite an example from a machine vision developed for robotic apple harvesting, the difference in the color and shape of the fruit (foreground) from the other parts of the tree (background) were used for recognizing and locating the target (Bulanon et al. 2002). On the other hand, a machine vision system for navigating in an orchard uses the configuration of the trees as features for operating the vehicle in the orchard (Durand-Petiteville et al. 2018). The main objective of the scene constraint setup is to enhance the distinctive characteristics of the desired objects and to facilitate the extraction of the desired information from the scene. This objective can be done by controlling the factors that affect image acquisition which include lighting (natural and artificial), type of camera, object position, and the proper installation of the machine vision equipment. Some factors of the scene may be controlled like object position. A machine vision system for inspecting products in sorting lines is an example where object position can be controlled (Nandi et al. 2016). However, a machine vision system for fruit harvesting will have no control over the fruit position (Bulanon and Kataoka 2010).

(2) Image acquisition

Image acquisition refers to the part of the machine vision system that uses photosensors to translate the falling reflected light of a scene into image data that will then be processed by a computer. A digitized image is typically a 512×512-pixel resolution. The image acquisition unit may be a black-and-white video camera that is relying on grayscale intensity, a colored video camera that uses the visible spectrum, or an infrared camera that uses the object's surface temperature. The type of acquisition equipment depends on the relevant parameters identified in the scene constraint step. The advancement of sensor technologies and graphic processing units have brought about cameras sensitive beyond the visible spectrum and resolutions in megapixels. Some researchers have investigated the spectral properties of objects using frequencies other than the visible frequencies. An example is a machine vision system that employed a hyperspectral imaging technique (multiple wavelengths) to identify fruits with different surface conditions (Bulanon et al. 2013). Hyperspectral and multispectral imaging have been utilized for the safety and quality inspection of agricultural products.

(3) Image processing and analysis

The acquired image data is then used as input to an image processor or a computer to discern the necessary information about the objects. The processing and analysis of image data using a computer is called digital image processing, which is a subsystem of the machine vision system (Gonzalez et al. 2009). This subsystem is divided into three areas to simplify its development: (1) low-level processing, (2) intermediate-level processing, and (3) high-level processing. As the name implies, low-level processing requires no intelligence on the part of the image processing and it is used to prepare the image data for subsequent processing. Examples of these are the capture and digitization of the image or the transformation of the image from one color model to another. Intermediate-level processing deals with the discrimination of the desired object from its background and the determination of the object's properties. Several steps are involved in this level of image processing, and selecting the steps depends on the goal of the project. As an example, considering an acquired apple image, the image would consist of fruits, leaves, branches, and a background. Image processing would locate the fruits and remove the other portions. Several steps are involved in the extraction of the data:

(a) Preprocessing

Preprocessing is the initial step of image processing with the goal of modifying and preparing the raw image to facilitate the subsequent image processing operations. Examples of image processing include contrast enhancement, low-pass filtering to remove the noise of the hardware, and correction for camera distortion (Ni et al. 2013).

(b) Segmentation

Segmentation is the process of dividing the digitized image into meaningful regions, such as foreground and background. The foreground includes the object that needs to be analyzed. For this reason, segmentation is considered the first critical step in image analysis because the decision to classify a pixel or group of pixels is made. The most common segmentation method to classify a pixel into a foreground or background is thresholding. Thresholding uses the statistical distribution of the pixel intensity such as a histogram. The Ohtsu method (Bulanon et al. 2002) is one of the popular thresholding techniques because it is very effective and easy to implement.

(c) Feature Extraction

Feature extraction is the process of describing the segmented objects using descriptors that facilitates classification. These descriptors are typically scalars that characterize the geometry of the objects, which include area, centroid, perimeter, major diameter, compactness, and thinness (Corke 2017). These descriptors are used simultaneously to have a good description of the object and are useful specifically if the machine vision system is used for measurement (Cetinkunt 2015).

(d) Classification

Classification is the process of sorting feature-extracted objects into predefined classes. Take for example a machine vision system for fruit counting, the objects in the image can be predefined as fruits, leaves, branch, ground, and sky. This process may be done by template matching, by a statistical method, or by training an AI (Artificial Intelligence) network (Femling et al. 2018). Template matching is a pattern recognition technique that compares unknown objects to a set of known templates to classify the object.

(4) Actuation

After the machine vision system has classified the object, the overall system decides on what action to take based on the classification. This task is known as the actuation process. This process closes the loop of the machine vision system shown in Figure 9.1. It is how the system interacts with the scene or the environment. Usually, machine vision is linked to a robotic system, and this is a basic component of automated operations (Zhou et al. 2022).

9.2 Visual feedback control

9.2.1 Control system definition

A control system can be defined as the assembly of systems and processes with the goal of obtaining a desired output with a desired response performance from a given specified input (Bolton 2021). Take for example the fruit harvesting robot (Figure 9.2). In this example, the robot uses a camera-in-hand sensor, and the robot centers the fruit in the image from this sensor. The distance needed to move the robot and position the fruit to the center of the image is the specified input. The desired output is the fruit located at the image center, and how the robot moves from its initial position to its final position is the desired response. The response of a system is composed of the transient response and the steady-state response (Katsuhiko 2007). These two parts of the system's response provide the measures of the performance of the control system.

The transient response describes the change in the output when the system receives an input. For the robotic system response, how fast the robot moves to the specified position describes the transient response. If the gain of the robot's motor is low, it will take a long time for the robot to center the fruit. However, if the gain

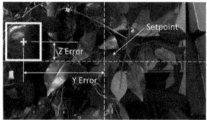

a) Initial Fruit Position on Image

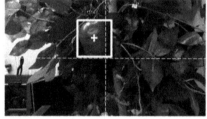

b) Fruit Position on Image after robot motion

Figure 9.2: Fruit centering.

of the motor is high, it will take a shorter time to reach the center. Too much of a gain might result in the robot overshooting the center position. One of the tasks of a controls engineer is to analyze the system and determine the optimal gain for a desired transient response. Only a stable system has the transient response decay to zero. Stability is another important criterion for a control system. If the system's transient response increases as time approaches infinity, then the system is unstable.

The other component of the system's response is the steady-state response. The steady-state response describes the status of the output once the transient part has reduced to zero. In the case of the fruit centering operation, the robot should stop close to or near the center of the image. The steady-state response describes how close the system's output is to the desired output. The steady-state error, which quantifies the steady-state responses, is usually set at 2% from the desired value.

There are two classifications of control systems: open loop and closed loop (Richard and Bishop 2007). For an open loop system (Figure 9.3), the input goes to the first subsystem, the controller. The controller processes the input variable and uses the output to drive the process, which is the next subsystem. If an open loop controller is developed for the robot to move a certain distance, the robot's motors would be powered on at a precalculated power level for a certain time and then turned off. The disadvantage of an open loop system, although it is easy to implement, is the inability to adapt to disturbance. If there is some resistance to the rotation of the motors, an open loop system has no way of knowing that the cart has not reached the desired position. If the robot overshoots the position because of too much gain or running the motor for too long, the cart has no method of correcting its position.

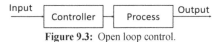

Figure 9.3: Open loop control.

9.2.2 Feedback control

Unlike an open-loop control system, a closed-loop control system has the ability to know the status of its output, in this case, the position of the robotic cart. A closed-loop control system (Figure 9.4) still has the controller and the process subsystems like the open-loop system, but the output of the process is fed back into a summing junction. The summing junction compares the input and the output, and the difference drives the controller. By feeding back the output and comparing it to the input, the closed loop system can adjust to disturbances to the system (Nise 2015). The disadvantage of the closed-loop system as compared to the open-loop system is the addition of a subsystem to feedback the output. The addition of this subsystem allows the system to provide a corrective action to the system output. Taking the harvesting for example, the additional subsystem could be a camera or an ultrasonic sensor to measure position. By feeding back the measured current position of the robot and comparing it with the desired position, the difference can then be used to drive the motors until there is no difference between the desired position and the current position.

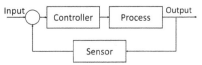

Figure 9.4: Closed loop control.

9.2.3 Visual feedback control

In a visual feedback control system, the sensor that feeds back the output is a camera. The status of the output is monitored by a camera, and image data is the signal being fed back. Visual feedback control is what humans use to perform everyday tasks such as driving or playing pickleball (Vitale and Liu 2020). When a person playing pickleball, as shown in Figure 9.5, is about to hit the ball, their eyes track the position of the ball (the image being fed back to the brain). Their brain then processes that information to adjust their arms and strike the ball.

To develop a closed loop control for a robotic motion using a visual feedback control system, the sensor is a vision system, such as a color camera, and the controlled process is the robot motion. The controller acts on the error and determines the speed and direction of the motor, which controls the robot's motion. The output of the robot's motion is monitored by the vision system. Because of the nature of the vision system, the status of the output will be dependent on the features found on the scene where the robot is located. For example, if the robot's motion is fruit harvesting, the scene will be composed of fruits on a tree. The position of the fruits on the tree can be used as features to determine the motion of the robot. The next sections will demonstrate the use of machine vision as a feedback sensor for closed-loop control.

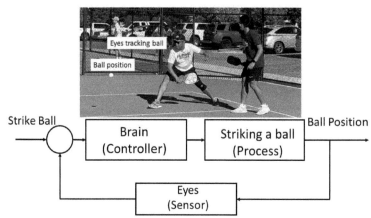

Figure 9.5: Closed loop control system for striking a ball.

9.3 Machine vision for navigation

9.3.1 Autonomous navigation in agriculture

The development of an effective navigation system is one of the main goals of autonomous guidance (Li et al. 2019). Although manually driving a car on the street seems to be a trivial task, driving a vehicle using autonomous navigation is not an easy undertaking. Autonomous navigation is a technology that will be very useful to production agriculture, especially with the current labor shortage. Researchers around the world have studied and developed different methods to apply autonomous navigation to farming. These methods include the use of global positioning systems, mechanical feelers, dead reckoning, radio frequency identification tags, laser radar, and machine vision (Reid et al. 2002).

In this section, a machine vision system is presented as one of the methods for autonomously guiding a vehicle in an orchard. To use machine vision for navigation, the control system measures the position of the vehicle with respect to an object or landmark and uses this relative position to estimate the vehicle's heading. Since the vehicle's relative position is measured using machine vision, the vision sensor is mounted on the vehicle. The position of the vehicle with respect to an object in front of it is estimated using the images captured by the vision sensor. The position of the objects in the images combined with the camera position and its intrinsic parameters is used to calculate the relative position of the vehicle. Since farming involves planting a row of crops or trees, these rows of crops can easily be used as a landmark for guidance similar to human drivers using lines on the road as a guide. Ma et al. (2021) developed a machine vision system and used the trunk position of wolfberries to guide a picking robot moving in the orchard. However, developing a machine vision for outdoor applications such as field orchards needs to deal with the varying ambient lighting condition. The color of the landmarks such as the row of crops is affected by the ambient lighting condition.

Similar to Ma et al. (2021) where the tree trunks were used as landmarks, current research in autonomous navigation using machine vision utilizes ground-based features for image processing. These features include planting patterns, leaf patterns, crop types, or other ground features that can be used as a guidance directrix. This technique of using ground features is very logical because these features are already embedded in the vehicle's path. So, taking advantage of these landmarks is a good strategy. However, applying this technique to orchards poses a certain challenge. The trees in an orchard are planted using a certain pattern and the tree positions do not change. However, the trees themselves change over the season. There will be blossoms during the spring season followed by the development of the leaves. The fruits appear during summer. After harvesting, leaves change color and fall off the tree, and the cycle begins again. When developing a machine vision, this variation should be taken into consideration. In addition to the physical changes during the year, the ambient lighting condition affects the spectral reflectance of the crops. A very good example is a machine vision system that was developed for citrus groves (Subramanian et al. 2006). The machine vision system used the tree canopies and the image processing employed an adaptive thresholding technique to deal with the ambient lighting condition. The variance in these environmental settings leads to challenges with navigation, especially if that navigation relies on physical characteristics as indicators as shown in Figure 9.6. Along with adapting to these constraints, researchers must develop algorithms that adapt to the season while remaining low-cost and simple for farmers to use.

This section describes a machine vision-based navigation system that does not use ground features, but instead focuses on looking up at the sky. The image processing uses the sky combined with the tree canopies. The rationale behind this method is that by looking up to the sky with some tree canopy, the variance coming from environmental factors is drastically minimized. Unlike the trees themselves, the skylines do not change much throughout the seasons and always remain one of

a) Raw Image b) Finding the tree trunks

c) Identifying Individual trunks c) Finding center between trunk rows

Figure 9.6: Using trunks as guide for navigation.

the most luminescent parts of the image, a key in pinpointing an object in image processing. By using the sky as a guidance system, this section provides a unique approach to autonomous navigation using machine vision.

9.3.2 Machine vision navigation system

The system diagram of the visual feedback system of an unmanned ground vehicle (UGV) seen in Figure 9.7 has three subsystems: the unmanned ground vehicle platform, the machine vision, and the controller. The input to the navigation system is the desired vehicle path and this input is compared with the current vehicle path. The difference between the desired path and the current path, which is the error, is used by the controller to calculate the response of the vehicle as it moves in between the tree rows.

The unmanned ground vehicle (Figure 9.8), that was used in this study, was a differentially steered vehicle. With differential steering, the difference between the angular velocity of the motors on the left side and the motors on the right side controls the direction of the vehicle. If there is no difference in angular velocity, the vehicle travels a straight path. For the machine vision subsystem, a color camera was used as the vision sensor and the camera was mounted on the front of the vehicle.

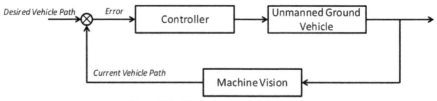

Figure 9.7: Block diagram for navigation.

Figure 9.8: Unmanned ground vehicle.

The camera was connected to a personal computer to capture and process the image data, and then the computer sends the navigation signals to the motor drivers, which are the magnitude and direction of the motors (Radcliffe et al. 2018).

The visual feedback control system was an image-based position servoing system (Corke 2017), where features of the image were used as control variables to estimate the vehicle's heading. The image processing of this visual feedback system did not rely on ground features but on sky features. This method is a sky-based approach, and the image processing is shown in Figure 9.9. After the image was acquired, it was cropped to remove the portion of the sky in the field of view that was closest to the camera. This was done to improve the sensitivity of the control system. It was found that slight changes in the direction of the vehicle were magnified when using the centroid of a point that was further away from the camera. Furthermore, cropping the image reduced the data to be processed later, resulting in faster processing time and a more rapid response from the ground vehicle platform. Since the green color plane provided the highest contrast between the sky and the tree canopy, the green plane was extracted to use for segmentation. A simple thresholding approach was employed to extract the path plane of the vehicle because of the high contrast between the canopy and the sky. The 'salt-and-pepper' noise was removed by filtering the

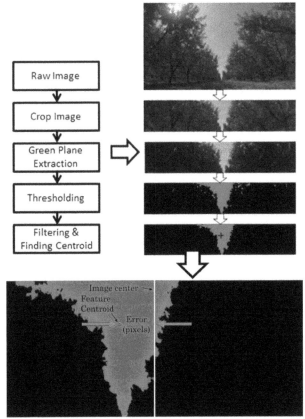

Figure 9.9: Image processing for the sky-based approach.

image after thresholding. Finally, the vehicle's heading was calculated by finding the centroid of the path plane.

9.3.3 Modeling the visual feedback control system

The transfer function of the ground vehicle platform with the visual feedback system was determined by applying a step input and characterizing its response. Even though the system may be higher in order, it was assumed that it can be approximated as a second-order system. The model used for the system is shown in Figure 9.10.

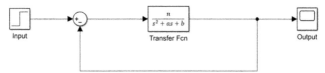

Figure 9.10: Control System model.

Here, the specified input is the desired angle we would like the robot to turn, the transfer function, G(s), is the open-loop transfer function of the robot, and the output is the actual angle that the robot turns. Since we would like the robot to rotate by the desired (input) angle, a unity feedback system was used to keep the comparison on a 1:1 scale.

We then note that the overall transfer function, T(s), is given by

$$T(s) = \frac{G(s)}{1 + G(s)}$$

Since we can find T(s) experimentally, we can solve for G(s), finding that

$$G(s) = \frac{T(s)}{T(s) - 1}$$

Finally, noting that the experimentally derived T(s) will be of the form

$$T(s) = \frac{n}{s^2 + as + b}$$

We know that the steady-state error for a step input will be equal to the limit of $sR(1 - T(s))$ as s approaches 0, which, for a step input of magnitude 1, evaluates to

$$e(\infty) = 1 - \frac{n}{b}$$

Experimentally, the error is found by subtracting the final angle from the desired (input) angle. With this information, we can perform lab tests on the robot to find a transfer function for simulation.

To test the robot, the following methodology was used:

(1) Using orange cones as the objects of interest, two cones were placed within the line of sight of the robot's webcam such that the centroid between the two cones was at a predetermined angle from the central axis of the robot, as shown in Figure 9.11.

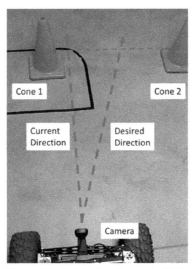

Figure 9.11: Lab testing of ground vehicle.

(2) The robot was set to run with no forward gain and a specified maximum angular power.

(3) Before performing the test, the robot was turned off and the program was started, allowing the camera time to adjust.

(4) After the camera auto-adjusted to its surroundings and detected the objects, a video recording of the robot was started, and the robot itself was switched on.

(5) When the robot finished moving, the angle between its initial position and its final position was measured.

(6) The video recording was then reviewed and analyzed to determine the peak time and settling time of the robot's response based on the timestamps embedded in the video data.

Two tests were conducted, each using a maximum angular power of 60 and an initial angle of 15 degrees. Table 9.1 below contains the results for peak time, settling time, and final angle for each of the two tests.

Table 9.1: Lab Test Results.

Test	Peak time (s)	Settling time (s)	Final angle (degrees)
1	0.60	1.54	11.2
2	0.60	1.54	11.6

The results of the two tests match remarkably well. We can now find the damping ratio, ζ, and the natural frequency, ω_n, using the equations

$$T_p = \frac{\pi}{\omega_n \sqrt{1 - \zeta^2}}$$

$$T_s = \frac{4}{\zeta \omega_n}$$

These equations form a nonlinear system which can be solved to find $\zeta = 0.444$ and $\omega_n = 5.84$ rad/s. Then, because the denominator of T(s) has the form, $s^2 + 2\zeta\omega_n s + \omega_n^2$ we get a denominator of $s^2 + 5.19s + 34.2$. Now, all we need is the numerator of T(s). Since the steady-state error was found to be approximately 15–11.4 degrees, or 3.6 degrees, on average, we have

$$\frac{3.6}{15} = 1 - \frac{n}{34.2}$$

giving n = 26.0. Thus, the overall transfer function for the robot, T(s), is

$$T(s) = \frac{26}{s^2 + 5.19s + 34.2}$$

we then find G(s) to be

$$G(s) = \frac{26}{s^2 + 5.19s + 8.2}$$

With this transfer function, we can use simulation software, such as MATLAB's Simulink, to simulate the system (Martyanov et al. 2015). For example, if we use a step input of magnitude 1, we get the time-domain response shown in Figure 9.12.

The response of the system is underdamped, as we would expect, and it shows the error in the output, as the steady-state value is under 0.8 of the input value. Of course, other simulations can be run on the transfer function to see approximately how the robot will respond to various stimuli in the real world.

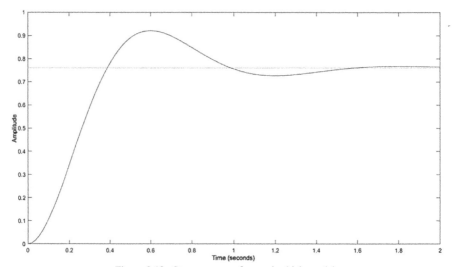

Figure 9.12: Step response of ground vehicle model.

9.3.4 Orchard test

The navigation system for the unmanned ground vehicle was tested in a commercial peach orchard in Caldwell, Idaho, USA. One of the tree rows was selected as the path to be tested for the machine vision navigation system. To evaluate the performance of the navigation system, the distance from the unmanned ground vehicle to one of the rows was measured. An ultrasonic sensor was used to measure the distance from the unmanned ground vehicle to the cardboard positioned along the tree rows. Cardboards were used to maintain constant tree row position, especially in the gaps where there were no trees. The distance covered for this ultrasonic measurement was 27 meters, and the remaining section of the row was evaluated using visual observation.

For the first 27 meters of travel and measured by the ultrasonic sensor, the unmanned ground vehicle had a maximum deviation of 3.5 cm. Although this was a short distance of quantifiable performance, this result demonstrated that the machine vision system worked in guiding the unmanned ground vehicle. As the unmanned ground vehicle traversed the rest of the row, it was observed that it had a larger deviation from the center of the row when approaching sections of missing trees. However, the unmanned ground vehicle was able to correct itself once another tree was captured in the image. The unmanned ground vehicle successfully completed the entire row.

As mentioned in the first section, taking advantage of the characteristics of the scene constraints will facilitate the development of an effective machine vision system. The scene in an orchard, which is an outdoor application, is affected by varying lighting conditions, shadows on the ground and canopies, and spectral reflectance inconsistencies. Focusing on the sky as the main background minimizes the issue of varying lighting conditions because the sky is the brightest part of the image regardless of the ambient lighting condition. This approach simplifies the segmentation process, which is the first step of object recognition. When developing a machine vision system, it is very important to note that all parameters of the environment should be taken into account even if it is as trivial as the sky.

9.4 Machine vision for Orchard roBot (OrBot)

9.4.1 The need for agricultural automation

It is projected that our current crop production will need to double to provide food for the world in 2050 (Rahman 2016). The problem of food sustainability was exposed during the pandemic when there were food security issues. The pandemic was a wake-up call for us to prioritize research into food sustainability.

The irony of increasing population and food sustainability is that fewer people are willing to work on the farms. A labor shortage is one of the problems that farmers are facing now, and it is true, especially for farm work that is labor intensive like harvesting. However, with the advancement of science and technology, we can find a solution to the labor shortage. Development in robotics technology, sensors, smart actuators, and artificial intelligence are the keys to creating a smart farm that could help improve food sustainability (King 2017).

Robotic technologies (Marinoudi et al. 2021) are being developed for agricultural tasks that are labor intensive, and fruit harvesting was identified as one of those areas. Robotic fruit harvesting has been studied since late 1970. One of the first researchers used a grayscale camera to find the fruit and then developed a Cartesian-based robot to pick the fruit (Parrish and Goksel 1977). This project showed the feasibility of robotic harvesting. Development has been made to improve fruit detection by using color cameras (Bulanon and Kataoka 2010), stereo cameras, ultrasonic sensors, thermal cameras, and multispectral cameras (Cubero et al. 2016). For manipulators used for harvesting, Cartesian robots, cylindrical robots, spherical robots, and articulated robots have been used (Li et al. 2011). One of the challenges in the development of robotic harvesting is finding and locating the fruits on the tree. Several image processing algorithms have been developed including grayscale thresholding, multi-color segmentation, pattern recognition approaches, artificial neural networks, and deep learning (Kapach et al. 2012). In addition to finding the fruits, properly picking the fruit from the tree is another challenging task. Different techniques have been employed to remove the fruit from the tree's branches such as a vacuum-based end effector, multi-fingered grippers, and a cutting end effector, to name a few (Davidson et al. 2020).

Although there have been several studies on agricultural robotics, there hasn't been a commercially available harvesting robot. There are multiple issues that need to be addressed including target detection, visual servoing, obstacle avoidance, and target handling. The main goal of this study is to develop a robotic platform to investigate these areas of concern. Specifically, the robotic platform will be tested on fruit harvesting to evaluate its performance.

9.4.2 Robotic prototype platform

The Robotics Vision Lab of Northwest Nazarene University has developed a robotic prototype platform called OrBot, Orchard robot. OrBot, which is shown in Figure 9.13, is composed of the following subsystems: a multiple-degree-of-freedom manipulator, a vision system, an end effector, a personal computer, a power supply, and a transportable platform (Bulanon et al. 2021).

OrBot uses a 3rd generation Kinova robotic manipulator. This manipulator has six degrees of freedom with a reach of up to 902 mm. The manipulator has a full-range payload of 2 kg, which is more than the weight of an average apple fruit. The Cartesian translation speed could reach up to 500 mm/s and it only consumes an average of 36 W. These characteristics of the manipulator are more than acceptable for developing a robotic way to mimic any agricultural tasks including fruit harvesting.

The vision system that comes with the manipulator combines a color sensor with a depth sensor. The pixel resolution of the color sensor (Omnivision OV5640) is 1920 × 1080 pixels and it has a field of view of 65 degrees. The depth sensor (Intel RealSense Depth Module D410) has a lower resolution of 480 × 270 pixels and the field of view is 72 degrees. The depth sensor employs stereo vision techniques and active IR sensing. The color sensor is used to recognize the target and its two-dimensional position while the depth sensor is used to estimate how far the target is from the end effector (Figure 9.14).

The end effector uses a single motor to control a standard two-finger gripper. The grip force ranges from 20 to 235 N and it could handle an object with a width

Figure 9.13: Orchard robot (OrBot).

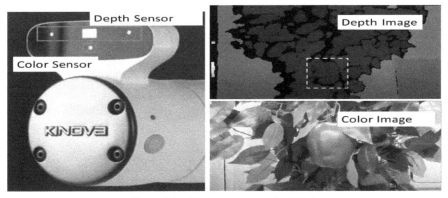

Figure 9.14: Dual vision system for OrBot.

of 85 mm. To properly handle the fruits, customized 3D-printed gripper fingers were designed and developed.

The overall harvesting task was controlled using a Lenovo Thinkpad laptop computer. The manipulator has its own manufacturer-provided control software called the Kinova Kortex. A customized program to perform the harvesting operation was developed using MATLAB®, the Digital Image Processing toolbox, the Image Acquisition toolbox, and the Kinova API tools (Bulanon et al. 2021).

As shown in Figure 9.13, the robotic manipulator with the gripper and the vision system is mounted on a transportable platform. The platform also carries the laptop computer and the power supply. The platform is a modified hand-pulled cart with extruded aluminium structure connected with 3D-printed parts. The aluminum structure also allows vertical adjustment of the manipulator height.

9.4.3 Machine vision system

A very important function of an agricultural robot is its ability to recognize the target. In addition to recognizing the target, it is equally important to direct the end effector towards the target: essentially, hand-eye coordination. To direct the end effector, a control system using machine vision was developed, which is called the visual control system. The visual servo control (Figure 9.15), which is based on a negative feedback system, has three subsystems. The controlled process is the Kinova robot's motion in handling the object. The machine vision subsystem finds and locates the target fruit. The goal of the visual servo control is to move the robot and make the end effector position equal to the target fruit position. Using the forward kinematics of the robot, the position of the end effector is known. The position of the target fruit is determined using the machine vision system. The difference between the end effector position and the target fruit position is the error. The error between the gripper and the target fruit position is used to control the manipulator motion.

The two configurations to implement a visual servo system are the eye-in-hand and the eye-to-hand configurations. In the eye-in-hand configuration, the camera is integrated with the hand, while the eye-to-hand configuration has the camera in a fixed position. The Kinova Robot comes with an eye-in-hand configuration. In addition to the camera positioning, visual servoing can be done using the position of the fruits in the image, image-based visual servoing (IBVS), or using the absolute position of the fruits derived from the image, position-based visual servoing (PBVS) (Corke 2017). PBVS calculates the absolute position of the fruit using the features extracted from the image combined with the camera's intrinsic parameters. On the

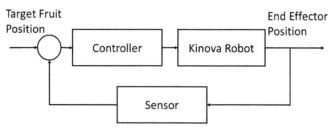

Figure 9.15. Block diagram for harvesting.

Figure 9.16: Fruit position with respect to robot position.

other hand, IBVS only uses the extracted features such as the object's centroid to implement visual servoing. IBVS was selected for the visual servoing of OrBot because it uses the eye-in-hand configuration. IBVS is suited for the eye-in-hand configuration because the camera is not in a fixed position.

Figure 9.16 shows the position vector relationship between the fruit and the camera and between the fruit and the origin. Using basic vector addition, visual servoing is simplified. In implementing IBVS, the first step is to move the robot so that the target fruit is in the center of the image, which will result in a straight path for the end effector. This fruit-centering process also simplifies the distance measurement as the depth sensor is combined with the color sensor. It is important to clarify that IBVS is effective if the target's features are properly determined.

9.4.4 Fruit harvesting task

As OrBot is designed for different agricultural tasks, we tested it for fruit harvesting. The target fruit is the Pink Lady apple grown in a commercial orchard in Idaho. The visual servo control is integrated into the harvesting process as defined by the following tasks:

1. The manipulator is moved to a predefined home position where the initial fruit search is initiated.

2. An image is acquired from the color sensor.

3. The captured image is then processed to segment the fruits from the background. The segmentation process to discriminate the fruit pixels used an artificial neural network that has the pixel's chromaticity r and g as inputs, and the neural network identifies the pixel as a fruit or a background.

4. The segmented fruit regions are filtered for size and the region's characteristic such as area and centroid are calculated using blob analysis.

5. The fruit region with the largest area is selected as the target.

6. The robot is moved to position the target fruit in the center of the image and the fruit distance is calculated.

7. The manipulator is then actuated to pick the fruit and then goes back to the predefined home position until no fruits are found.

9.4.5 Fruit harvesting evaluation

9.4.5.1 Visual servoing

Since OrBot uses IBVS and eye-in-hand configuration, the target object is brought to the center of the camera image using visual servoing. This prepares the robot for estimating the distance to the target and then approaching and handling the target object. Figure 9.17 shows a sample of the image processing that was used for visual servoing. The process starts with the original image and then segments the image to separate the target fruits from the background. The segmented image was then filtered, and features of the target object such as centroid were determined. The visual servo system moves the manipulator so the target object is in the center of the image (setpoint) based on the object's centroid. The visual servo control was evaluated by randomly placing the target fruits in different positions, and having the robot center the target fruit in the image. OrBot was able to center the target fruit in all fifteen attempts.

Figure 9.18 shows the system's response when centering the target object on the z-axis (Nise 2020). The visual servo system had an overdamped response, which is more favorable in avoiding oscillation. The Fast Speed has the shortest settling time with a steep transient response. The response of the system in the y-axis is very similar to the z-axis. Further investigation into tuning the controller parameters will be conducted to improve the response behavior of the system.

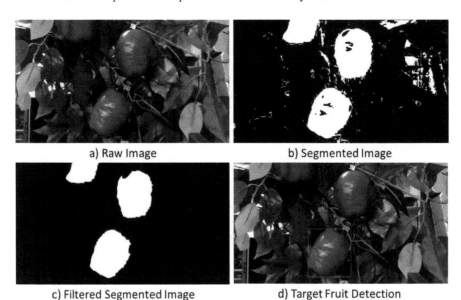

a) Raw Image   b) Segmented Image

c) Filtered Segmented Image   d) Target Fruit Detection

Figure 9.17: Image processing for locating fruit

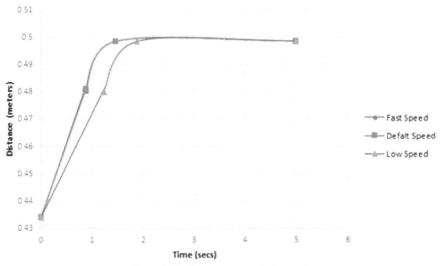

Figure 9.18: System response in the z-axis.

9.4.5.2 Fruit harvesting

OrBot was tested in a commercial orchard in Idaho. Table 9.2 shows the time for the different sections of the harvesting process. The average harvesting time is almost 10 seconds. Removal of the fruit, which includes approaching the fruit from the center position and picking the fruit, took most of the time. The location and centering of the fruit only took a little more than a second.

OrBot was tested in a commercial orchard in November 2022. Two hundred harvesting attempts were made and OrBot was able to harvest 87% of the fruits successfully. There were three main reasons for the missed attempts. The first was the target fruit was not recognized because the reflectance of the fruit was affected by direct sunlight. The second reason was when the target fruit was partially recognized because it was covered by a leaf or a branch. The last reason was the miscalculation of distance. The depth camera was really affected by the sunlight especially if it was directly facing it. The proper recognition of the target fruit directly affects the subsequent process of centering the fruit and measuring the distance and so is the key to successful harvesting.

Future developments for the robotic harvesting project using OrBot include improving the visual servoing control, harvesting at night, adding a fixed camera (eye-to-hand configuration), and developing of a soft adaptive fruit gripper.

Table 9.2: Robotic harvesting processing time.

Process	Time (Second)
Target recognition	0.12
Target centering	1.13
Depth estimation	0.01
Approach and pick	8.69
TOTAL	9.94

9.5 Machine vision for fruit yield estimation

9.5.1 Fruit yield estimation

Precision agriculture, which is a site-specific technique for farming, is a helpful tool for farmers today and in the future. One of its components is yield monitoring where farmers have the ability to determine the amount of crop produced by a certain field. Yield monitoring systems (Fulton et al. 2018) have been used by row crop growers over the years and have helped farmers identify parts of their fields which are not performing well. Most of the methods that have been developed for yield monitoring specifically for row crops involve measuring the weight of the crops after they have been harvested. This has been very successful for row crops such as corn and soybeans. However, this could be challenging when applied to speciality crops considering the geometric parameters of the fruits and vegetables. There have been yield monitors that have been studied for speciality crops (He et al. 2022), but the other issue with these current yield monitors is that they are used during harvesting to tell the farmers how much they have produced. However, fruit farmers would also like to know how much they could produce early in the season so that they can market their products competitively and can properly plan the logistics for the next harvesting and post-harvesting operations, specifically labor.

Currently, the practice is fruit growers count fruits during the early fruit drop and estimate their yield for that season. Since counting fruits from each tree is very laborious, they select a number of trees to count, calculate the average, and then obtain the estimated fruit yield. This process is time-consuming and inaccurate. To help farmers facilitate fruit counting, the Robotics Vision Lab of Northwest Nazaarene University (Braun et al. 2018) has developed an image processing and analysis method for counting blossoms and estimating fruit yield. It has been found that the photosynthetic activity of fruit trees increases during the blossom period (Fujii and Kennedy 1985). The photosynthetic activity directly correlates with the fruiting process. Figure 9.19 shows the relationship between the blossoms detected and the actual number of fruits on the tree. By deriving the correlation between blossoms and fruit number, we could easily estimate the number of fruits using the blossom count.

9.5.2 Fruit counting development

Images of 30 randomly selected blossoming apple trees were taken in the mid-morning of April 2018. The images were of Pink Lady apple trees in a commercial orchard located in Caldwell Idaho. The trees were in a row running north-south, with pictures taken of both the west and east sides of the trees. The images were taken using a point and shoot color camera on default settings in the landscape orientation resulting in 3000×4000-pixel images. The camera was held approximately five feet in the air at a horizontal distance of eight feet from the trunk of the apple tree.

An algorithm was developed in MATLAB (Paluszek and Thomas 2020) to detect and count the number of blossoms visible in each image. The blossoms were detected using a deep neural network object detector. The network was created by

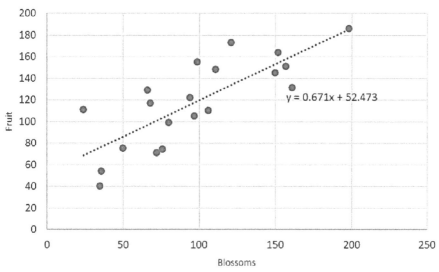

Figure 9.19: Blossom fruit correlation

starting with a pre-trained AlexNet which was modified by replacing the final three layers with a new untrained fully connected layer with 2 classes, a softmax layer, and a classification layer. The network was then trained to detect blossoms.

The training data was created by cropping 227 × 227-pixel images containing blossoms from the original images taken at the orchard. This size was chosen because AlexNet requires input images to be 227 × 227 pixels (Vadera 2022). The 227 × 227 images were then labeled using the image labeler in MATLAB by drawing bounding boxes by hand around the blossoms apparent in the image. The labeled images were then used to train the network for the detection of blossoms using the trainRCNNObjectDetector function in MATLAB. After the network had been

a) Original image of tree   b) Image subdivided into   c) Training of network
227 x 227

Figure 9.20: Deep learning training

trained, the 60 full-size images (an east side and a west side image of each of the 30 trees) were cropped to remove the trees on either side of the desired tree and the cropped images were then analyzed using the deep neural network object detector.

A count of the fully developed fruit on each of the 30 trees was taken before the apples were harvested in the fall of 2018. The apples were counted by placing a sticker on each apple found on a tree, and then counting how many stickers had been used. This method reduced the chances of apples being counted multiple times. The number of apples counted on each tree at the end of the season was then compared to the number of detected blossoms in the images for that tree taken at the beginning of the season.

a) Original image of tree   b) Detected Blossoms

Figure 9.21: Blossom detection and counting.

9.5.3 Fruit yield estimation

The resulting blossom count of each tree had a correlation of 0.79 to the number of fruits harvested at the end of the season. A linear equation was derived using the blossom versus fruit data from 20 trees, shown in Figure 9.19. The equation was then used to estimate the fruit yield of 10 new trees, with the plot of the actual fruit yield versus the estimated fruit yield shown below. It can be seen from the results that the deep learning approach to early fruit yield estimation has some potential. It should be noted that the deep learning network was trained with a limited set of image data and with the simplest deep learning network. With a correlation of almost 0.80, the deep learning approach can be improved by using a deeper network and training it with more image data.

Combined Estimated vs Actual Number of Apples

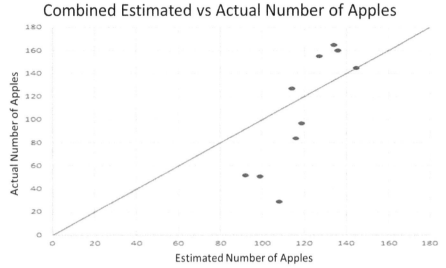

Figure 9.22: Estimated fruit count vs actual fruit count.

9.5.4 Mobile app for fruit yield estimation

Once a fruit yield estimation algorithm has been developed, the algorithm could then be ported to a mobile device through an app (Karkhile and Ghuge 2015). The app can then be provided to farmers to use for early fruit yield estimates in their orchards.

Figure 9.23: Picture of the mobile device taking a photo of an apple tree.

The platform selected to develop the Blossom Counting App was iOS. Then, the user interface was designed in the Swift programming language, as this is the iOS programming language for application development. The backend functionality was written in C++ and OpenCV, following the user interface. We then tested the application using the images acquired from the study site.

9.5.4.1 Planning and designing the front end of the mobile application

When developing a mobile device application, the designer must consider two aspects: the front end and the back end (Brambilla 2014). The front end of a mobile application is responsible for displaying the information to the user and serving the user experience with the application.

The development of the application was done using the iOS platform. The iOS language for designing a mobile application is Swift. When designing the user interface for the application, the intention was to keep it straightforward. The first portion of the front-end development was to establish what information needed to be displayed. The user interface components can be seen in Figure 9.24. Through the design process, the information chosen to be presented was:

1. The original image the user selected from either the camera or the photo library

2. The image processed through the back end

3. The value representing the number of blossoms detected

4. A button that allows the user to select a new image.

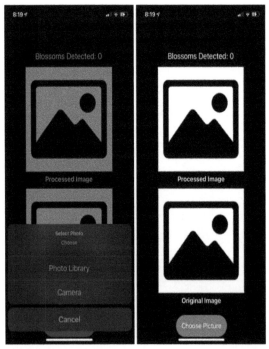

Figure 9.24: User interface of mobile app for early fruit estimation.

5.4.2 Development of the back end of the mobile device app

The back end of the mobile application is responsible for taking the data from the user and transforming it into the desired information. Development of the back-end function used the common programming language C++ and a library called OpenCV, which is known for its image processing tools. The architecture of the overall application can be described as a Model View Controller or MVC. Essentially this architecture is broken down into three pieces. First is the model, which is the data we pass into the application. Then, the view is provided by the frontend, which displays the information. The third is the Controller, which handles the data in the backend. Since the application uses C++, a language separate from Swift, a wrapper was required. The wrapper allows the application to call functions that are foreign to the primary language, Swift in this case.

The first step in creating the backend is to read the image from the user. Swift stores its image as a UIImage while OpenCV handles image processing through matrix transformation and uses the image processing that was developed in the previous section.

9.6 Conclusion

This chapter has shown the importance of machine vision in automation, specifically in agriculture. Three different applications were discussed, namely autonomous navigation, fruit harvesting, and early fruit yield estimation. In these applications, machine vision was used as a sensor for feedback. As a sensor, the machine vision system must make measurements that will be used for corrective actions. It has been shown that the key elements for the development of a machine vision system are analysis of the scene, selection of an appropriate image acquisition unit, development of an image processing algorithm, and development of a control algorithm using the image features. These image features are critical especially if the machine vision system is used as a tool for measurement.

Acknowledgements

The authors would like to acknowledge the support of the Idaho State Department of Agriculture through the Specialty Crop Block Grant, Idaho Space Grant Consortium, Symms Fruit Ranch, and Williamsons Orchard.

References

Awcock, G. J., and Thomas, R. 1995. Applied image processing. Macmillan International Higher Education.

Bolton, W. 2015. Instrumentation and Control Systems. (2nd Edition). Elsevier.

Brambilla, M., Mauri, A., and Umuhoza, E. 2014. Extending the interaction flow modeling language (IFML) for model driven development of mobile applications front end. In International Conference on Mobile Web sand Information Systems, 176–191.

Braun, B., Bulanon, D. M., Colwell, J., Stutz, A., Stutz, J., Nogales, C. et al. 2018. A fruit yield prediction method using blossom detection. In 2018 ASABE Annual International Meeting (p. 1). American Society of Agricultural and Biological Engineers.

Bulanon, D. M., Kataoka, T., Ota, Y., and Hiroma, T. 2002. A segmentation algorithm for the automatic recognition of Fuji apples at harvest. Biosystems Engineering, 83(4): 405–412.

Bulanon, D. M., and Kataoka, T. 2010. Fruit detection system and an end effector for robotic harvesting of Fuji apples. Agricultural Engineering International: CIGR Journal, 12(1).

Bulanon, D. M., Burks, T. F., Kim, D. G., and Ritenour, M. A. 2013. Citrus black spot detection using hyperspectral image analysis. Agricultural Engineering International: CIGR Journal, 15(3): 171–180.

Bulanon, D. M., Burr, C., DeVlieg, M., Braddock, T., and Allen, B. 2021. Development of a visual servo system for robotic fruit harvesting. AgriEngineering, 3(4): 840–852.

Cetinkunt, S. 2015. Mechatronics with Experiments. (2nd Edition). John Wiley & Sons.

Corke, P. 2017. Robotics, Vision and Control: F undamental Algorithms in MATLAB. (2nd Edition). Springer Tracts in Advanced Robotics.

Cubero, S., Lee, W. S., Aleixos, N., Albert, F., and Blasco, J. 2016. Automated systems based on machine vision for inspecting citrus fruits from the field to postharvest—A review. Food and Bioprocess Technology, 9(10): 1623–1639.

Davidson, J., Bhusal, S., Mo, C., Karkee, M., and Zhang, Q. 2020. Robotic manipulation for specialty crop harvesting: A review of manipulator and end-effector technologies. Global Journal of Agricultural and Allied Sciences, 2(1): 25–41.

Durand-Petiteville, A., Le Flecher, E., Cadenat, V., Sentenac, T., and Vougioukas, S. 2018. Tree detection with low-cost three-dimensional sensors for autonomous navigation in orchards. IEEE Robotics and Automation Letters, 3(4): 3876–3883.

Femling, F., Olsson, A., and Alonso-Fernandez, F. 2018. Fruit and vegetable identification using machine learning for retail applications. In 2018 14th International Conference on Signal-Image Technology & Internet-Based Systems (SITIS), 9-15 . IEEE.

Fujii, J. A., and Kennedy, R. A. 1985. Seasonal changes in the photosynthetic rate in apple trees: a comparison between fruiting and nonfruiting trees. Plant Physiology, 78(3): 519–524.

Fulton, J., Hawkins, E., Taylor, R., and Franzen, A. 2018. Yield monitoring and mapping. Precision Agriculture Basics, 63–77.

Gonzalez, R., Woods, R., and Eddins, S. 2009. Digital Image Processing Using MATLAB. (2nd Edition). Gatesmark Publishing.

He, L., Fang, W., Zhao, G., Wu, Z., Fu, L., Li, R., and Dhupia, J. 2022. Fruit yield prediction and estimation in orchards: A state-of-the-art comprehensive review for both direct and indirect methods. Computers and Electronics in Agriculture, 195: 106812.

Kapach, K., Barnea, E., Mairon, R., Edan, Y., and Ben-Shahar, O. 2012. Computer vision for fruit harvesting robots–state of the art and challenges ahead. International Journal of Computational Vision and Robotics, 3(1/2): 4–34.

Karkhile, S. G., and Ghuge, S. G. 2015. A modern farming techniques using android application. International Journal of Innovative Research in Science, Engineering and Technology, 4(10): 10499–10506.

Katsuhiko, O. 2007. MATLAB for Control Engineers. (1st Edition). Pearson.

King, A. 2017. Technology: The future of agriculture. Nature, 544(7651): S21–S23.

Li, P., Lee, S. H., and Hsu, H. Y. 2011. Review on fruit harvesting method for potential use of automatic fruit harvesting systems. Procedia Engineering, 23: 351–366.

Li, S., Xu, H., Ji, Y., Cao, R., Zhang, M., and Li, H. 2019. Development of a following agricultural machinery automatic navigation system. Computers and Electronics in Agriculture, 158: 335–344.

Ma, Y., Zhang, W., Qureshi, W. S., Gao, C., Zhang, C., and Li, W. 2021. Autonomous navigation for a wolfberry picking robot using visual cues and fuzzy control. Information Processing in Agriculture, 8(1): 15–26.

Marinoudi, V., Sørensen, C. G., Pearson, S., and Bochtis, D. 2019. Robotics and labour in agriculture. A context consideration. Biosystems Engineering, 184: 111–121.

Martyanov, A. S., Solomin, E. V., and Korobatov, D. V. 2015. Development of control algorithms in MATLAB/Simulink. Procedia Engineering, 129: 922–926.

Nandi, C. S., Tudu, B., and Koley, C. 2016. A machine vision technique for grading of harvested mangoes based on maturity and quality. IEEE Sensors Journal, 16(16): 6387–6396.

Ni, Z., Burks, T. F., and Lee, W. S. 2016. 3D reconstruction of plant/tree canopy using monocular and binocular vision. Journal of Imaging, 2(4): 28.

Nise, N. S. 2015. Control Systems Engineering. (7th Edition) John Wiley & Sons.

Paluszek, M., and Thomas, S. 2020. Practical MATLAB deep learning. A Project-Based Approach. (2nd Edition). Apress. Michael Paluszek and Stephanie Thomas.

Parrish, E. A. and Goksel, A. K. 1977. Pictorial pattern recognition applied to fruit harvesting. Transactions of the ASAE, 20(5): 822–0827.

Radcliffe, J., Cox, J., and Bulanon, D. M. 2018. Machine vision for orchard navigation. Computers in Industry, 98: 165–171.

Rahman, M. H. 2016. Exploring sustainability to feed the world in 2050. Journal of Food Microbiology, 1(01).

Reid, J. F., Zhang, Q., Noguchi, N., and Dickson, M. 2000. Agricultural automatic guidance research in North America. Computers and Electronics in Agriculture, 25(1-2): 155–167.

Richard, D., and Bishop, R. 2007. Modern Control Systems. (11th Edition). Pearson College Div.

Subramanian, V., Burks, T. F., and Arroyo, A. A. 2006. Development of machine vision and laser radar based autonomous vehicle guidance systems for citrus grove navigation. Computers and Electronics in Agriculture, 53(2): 130–143.

Vadera, S., and Ameen, S. 2022. Methods for pruning deep neural networks. IEEE Access, 10: 63280–63300.

Vitale, K., and Liu, S. 2020. Pickleball: review and clinical recommendations for this fast-growing sport. Current Sports Medicine Reports, 19(10): 406–413.

Zhou, H., Wang, X., Au, W., Kang, H., and Chen, C. 2022. Intelligent robots for fruit harvesting: Recent developments and future challenges. Precision Agriculture, 1–52.

10

Occlusion-Aware Disparity-based Direct Visual Servoing of Mobile Robots

Xiule Fan,[1] *Baris Fidan*[2,]* and *Soo Jeon*[1]

10.1 Introduction

Accurate positioning is an essential task in mobile robot control to ensure safe operation of the robots. Pose feedback is widely used in the control strategy to achieve accurate tracking performance. The most direct approach to obtaining pose information is through positioning systems, e.g., a global navigation satellite system (GNSS) [Huang et al., 2018]. Since this approach relies on the availability of satellite signals, it is not applicable in scenarios involving indoor or underground operations. Alternatively, the robot's pose can be estimated using different sensor systems and localization techniques [Brossard et al., 2018, Biswas and Veloso, 2010]. However, the accuracy of the estimated pose depends on the sensor models, the sensor setup, and the localization algorithms. Instead of using pose feedback, visual servoing [Chaumette and Hutchinson, 2006], especially image-based visual servoing (IBVS), offers another solution based on direct use of the images captured by a camera to calculate the control actions.

IBVS computes the robot's control inputs based on the differences between the current and desired visual features in the images. The early attempts in IBVS utilize various image processing approaches to extract these visual features and match them across different frames. Examples of these im-

---

[1] Department of Mechanical and Mechatronics Engineering University of Waterloo.
[2] 200 University Avenue West, Waterloo, Ontario, Canada, N2L 3G1.
* Corresponding author: fidan@uwaterloo.ca

age features include corner features [Hager et al., 1994], colors [Cai et al., 2013], the Scale-Invariant Feature Transform (SIFT) [Shademan and Janabi-Sharifi, 2004], the Speeded-Up Robust Features (SURF) [Djelal et al., 2012], image moments [Chaumette, 2004, Hoffmann et al., 2006]. These complex image processing algorithms may introduce errors, such as mismatched and unmatched features, into the controller. Therefore, feature extraction and matching are often the limiting factors in IBVS [Collewet and Marchand, 2011, Teulière and Marchand, 2014]. The recent development of direct IBVS algorithms address these limitations by utilizing features such as color intensities [Collewet and Marchand, 2011], depth [Teulière and Marchand, 2014], image histograms [Bateux and Marchand, 2017], and photometric moments [Bakthavatchalam et al., 2018] at constant pixel locations, which removes the need of error-prone feature extraction and matching steps.

Many of the above IBVS techniques require the depth information of the image features. In robotic applications, this depth information can be obtained by a stereo camera in the form of disparity maps. The stereo camera can capture a pair of stereo images and compute the disparity map from these images with a stereo-matching algorithm, such as a traditional stereo-matching method [Hirschmuller, 2008, Mei et al., 2011] or a more accurate data-driven method [Kendall et al., 2017, Chang and Chen, 2018, Khamis et al., 2018, Fan et al., 2022]. Although incorporating the stereo camera in IBVS approaches has been studied previously [Hager et al., 1994, Cai et al., 2013], these methods still need to be improved to address the errors introduced by feature extraction and matching. A more accurate direct visual servoing approach designed for a stereo camera still needs to be included.

This work proposes a disparity-based direct visual servoing controller for a mobile robot equipped with a stereo camera. The controller is derived according to the relationship between the camera's velocity and a disparity map computed from the stereo images. An occlusion mask is utilized to design an occlusion-aware controller to address the occlusion problem inherited from the stereo camera setup. A deep learning-based stereo-matching pipeline computes the disparity map and occlusion mask with confidence-guided raw disparity fusion (CRD-Fusion) [Fan et al., 2022]. Lastly, extensive simulations and experiments verify the proposed controller design.

The rest of this work is organized as follows: Section 10.2 provides a brief survey of the relevant literature, Section 10.3 outlines the overall architecture, Section 10.4 offers an overview of the self-supervised stereo-matching algorithm used in this work, Section 10.5 describes the proposed disparity-based direct visual servoing framework and Section 10.6 presents the integration of occlusion information in the controller design. Simulation and experimentation results of the proposed algorithm are presented in Section 10.7, and the concluding remarks are provided in Section 10.8.

10.2 Related work

10.2.1 Stereo matching

Stereo matching is a common technique to obtain depth information about an environment using images. To apply stereo matching in robotic applications, it is common to use a stereo camera to capture a pair of stereo images of the scene from two lenses simultaneously. If an object is visible by these two lenses, this object can be found in both images. The pixels corresponding to this object in the stereo images form a corresponding pair. Searching for the other corresponding pixel given a pixel in one of the images is the most important step in stereo matching. To simplify this search, the stereo images are typically rectified such that the search is limited to a one-dimensional (1D) horizontal scan line [Szeliski, 2022]. As shown in Figure 10.1, the distance between two corresponding pixels along the scan line is known as disparity, which is inversely proportional to the object's depth.

As [Scharstein et al., 2001] pointed out, stereo-matching algorithms generally consists of four steps: matching cost generation, matching cost aggregation, optimization to compute disparity, and optional disparity refinement. In the first step, pixels in one of the stereo views are compared against corresponding candidate pixels in the other to obtain the matching cost. The cost is then aggregated by considering the costs associated with the neighboring pixels. A disparity map is then regressed from the aggregated cost. Lastly, the disparity map may be further refined to improve its quality. Traditionally, model-based stereo-matching algorithms [Lee et al., 2013, Kolmogorov and Zabih, 2001, Hirschmuller, 2008, Mei et al., 2011] have been proposed and widely used by following these four steps. These methods rely on careful design choices at each step to obtain accurate results.

In recent years, data-driven stereo matching by utilizing deep neural networks (DNNs) have gained popularity. The early attempt in [Zbontar and LeCun, 2015] adopts a convolutional neural network (CNN) to extract image features to construct the matching cost for a model-based algorithm [Hirschmuller, 2008]. The first end-to-end design in [Kendall et al., 2017] mimics the four steps mentioned previously with different convolutional layers. Building upon this work, many end-to-end models [Chang and Chen, 2018, Khamis et al., 2018, Xu and Zhang, 2020, Cheng et al., 2020] have been proposed to predict accurate disparity. However, these

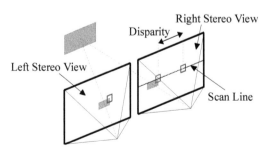

Figure 10.1: Illustration of disparity from two corresponding pixels along a scan line.

methods are designed for supervised training using a large dataset with ground truth disparity. Such a dataset is time-consuming and difficult to collect. To address this problem, researchers have exploited a supervisory signal based on the presence of corresponding pixels in both stereo views and designed several self-supervised stereo DNNs [Zhou et al., 2017, Li and Yuan, 2018, Wang et al., 2021, Wang et al., 2022, Fan et al., 2022], which do not require ground truth disparity for training. CRD-Fusion [Fan et al., 2022] predicts high-quality disparity maps and occlusion masks among these self-supervised methods. Occluded regions in stereo matching refer to pixels only visible in one of the stereo views. Since their correct corresponding pixels cannot be found, their predicted disparity may need to be revised. The occlusion masks can be used to identify these regions.

10.2.2   Visual servoing

Visual servoing algorithms utilize image data to generate the control actions of a robot. The algorithms are usually divided into position-based visual servoing (PBVS) and IBVS. An overview of visual servoing can be found in [Chaumette and Hutchinson, 2006] and [Hutchinson et al., 1996].

In PBVS, the camera images are used in pose estimation to perform pose control. An extended Kalman filter (EKF) is used to estimate the relative pose between a camera and an object from the image captured by the camera in [Wilson et al., 1996]. The estimated pose is then used as a feedback signal for the controller. Images are also used [Thuilot et al., 2002] to estimate the pose between the current camera frame and a reference frame for control. However, one major problem of PBVS algorithms is that their performance relies on accurate camera calibration and high-quality estimated pose [Cai et al., 2013, Chaumette, 1999].

IBVS algorithms generate control actions according to the difference in image features at the current and target frames. Different IBVS approaches have been designed with different types of image features. In the early work [Espiau et al., 1992], simple visual features, such as points, straight lines, and circles, are explored in visual servoing. In [Hager et al., 1994], a stereo camera captures the same corner feature in two lenses, and a control algorithm based on the epipolar constraint is proposed. The SIFT features [Lowe, 1999] are adopted for robust feature selection and matching in the control framework proposed in [Shademan and Janabi-Sharifi, 2004]. Chaumette [Chaumette, 2004] first performed segmentation on the images and then computed the image moments for the image segments as the image features in visual servoing. The uses of SIFT and image moments are combined by [Hoffmann et al., 2006]. The Speeded-Up Robust Features (SURF) [Bay et al., 2006] are also considered in visual servoing [Djelal et al., 2012]. [Cai et al., 2013] used color as the image features in their visual servoing approach designed for an uncalibrated stereo camera.

Since the feature extraction step generally serves as a bottleneck in the algorithm [Teulière and Marchand, 2014], removing this step in visual servoing has been a recent research direction that has led to the development of direct visual servoing. In these approaches, the differences of certain pixel-wise properties at all pixel locations are used to generate the control actions, resulting in control algorithms without the need for feature extraction. These properties include the color intensity of each pixel [Collewet and Marchand, 2011], image histograms [Bateux and Marchand, 2017], and photometric moments [Bakthavatchalam et al., 2018]. Note that depth from the camera to the image features is typically required in the above IBVS schemes. A previous work [Teulière and Marchand, 2014] has exploited the depth information generated by an RGB-D camera directly in their design. Since depth at each pixel location is used as an image feature, no other pixel-wise properties are considered in their design. In addition to RGB-D cameras, stereo matching is another popular choice to obtain depth perception in robotics. However, using disparity computed by a stereo-matching algorithm directly in visual servoing is yet to be studied.

All of the above visual servoing algorithms assume the robot is capable of 6-DOF motion. However, the motion of a mobile robot is constrained to a 2D plane. Some researchers have attempted to extend different IBVS algorithms to mobile robot control, such as visual servoing using SIFT features [Fu et al., 2013] and using depth maps [Xiong et al., 2017, Liu et al., 2019].

10.3   Overall architecture

The architecture of our system is shown in Figure 10.2. After obtaining a pair of stereo images from a stereo camera on a robot, an existing self-supervised stereo-matching pipeline [Fan et al., 2022] is used to compute a predicted disparity map and an occlusion mask for the scene. The predicted disparity map, occlusion mask, reference disparity map, and reference occlusion mask are sent into the proposed occlusion-aware visual servoing framework. The visual servoing algorithm computes the appropriate control signals to move the robot toward its goal, where the reference disparity map and occlusion mask are recorded.

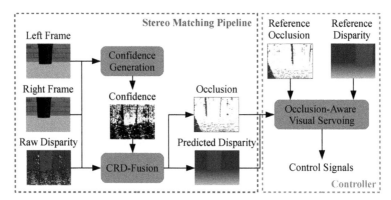

Figure 10.2: Overall architecture of the system with the stereo-matching pipeline and the proposed visual servoing controller.

10.4 Stereo-matching pipeline

The stereo-matching pipeline considered in this work has been described in details in [Fan et al., 2022] and a summary of this approach is provided here. This method consists of two main steps: a confidence generation step and a deep neural network named CRD-Fusion.

The confidence generation module receives a pair of stereo images and a (raw) disparity map as inputs. The raw disparity map is computed using a traditional model-based stereo-matching algorithm or a commercial stereo camera. The confidence generation module then computes a confidence map based on two simple measures: zero-mean sum of absolute difference [Haeusler et al., 2013] and mean disparity deviation [Park and Yoon, 2019]. The confidence map describes the accuracy of the raw disparity map at different regions in the image.

In the CRD-Fusion network, a feature extractor based on 2D convolutional layers and residual blocks [He et al., 2016] is first used to downsample and extract high-level image features from the input stereo pair. A cost volume for stereo matching is then constructed by comparing the difference between the left extracted features and the right extracted features spatially shifted according to all disparity candidates. Cost aggregation is performed on the matching cost by using a series of 3D convolutions. From the aggregated cost, a low-resolution preliminary disparity map is regressed. This preliminary disparity map is fused with the raw disparity map under guidance from the confidence map to obtain an initial disparity map. Lastly, a modular refinement module consisting of upsampling layers and 2D convolutions is utilized to upsample and refine the initial disparity map gradually and to predict an occlusion mask.

The proposed framework is trained in a self-supervised manner, allowing it to quickly adapt to different datasets and scenarios without collecting new data with expensive ground truth disparity. Additionally, this framework can extract useful information from the raw disparity to make high-quality predictions. Mobile robots these days are often equipped with commercial stereo cameras. These cameras often utilize their onboard hardware and algorithms to compute raw disparity maps, which can be exploited by this framework to improve the quality of depth perception. Furthermore, the predicted occlusion mask can effectively identify occluded regions where the predicted disparity values may not be as accurate as the ones in non-occluded regions.

10.5 The proposed visual servoing framework

10.5.1 Stereo vision modeling

A mobile robot equipped with a stereo camera oriented horizontally is assumed to move in a workspace. During its motion, the camera continuously records stereo images. These images are used in a stereo-matching algorithm to compute the disparity. A schematic of the stereo camera capturing a pair of rectified images is shown in Figure 10.3. At an arbitrary time instant t, consider an arbitrary 3D point, which is visible to both camera lenses, with coordinates $\mathbf{P} = (x_o, y_o, z_o) \in \mathbb{R}^3$ in a reference

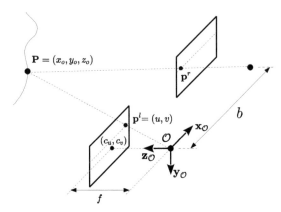

Figure 10.3: Schematic of a stereo camera capturing a pair of rectified images.

frame $\mathcal{O}$ attached to the camera's left optical center. The 3D point **P** is projected to the right and left image planes at $\mathbf{p}^r$ and $\mathbf{p}^l = (u,v)$ in the continuous image coordinates, respectively, by using a pinhole camera model. The coordinates of **P** and $\mathbf{p}^l$ are related by

$$\begin{cases} \bar{u} = \frac{u-c_u}{f} = \frac{x_o}{z_o} \\ \bar{v} = \frac{v-c_v}{f} = \frac{y_o}{z_o} \end{cases}, \qquad (10.1)$$

where $\bar{u}$ and $\bar{v}$ denote the adjusted image coordinates, f is the focal length in pixels, and (c_u, c_v) is the principal point.

At the same left image plane and time instant, the stereo-matching algorithm computes a disparity map $\mathcal{D} \in \mathbb{R}_{>0}^{W \times H}$ of width W and height H. The disparity information can be further expressed in a vector form as

$$\mathbf{D} = \begin{bmatrix} \mathbf{D}(1) \\ \mathbf{D}(2) \\ \vdots \\ \mathbf{D}(W(\bar{v}_j - 1) + \bar{u}_i) \\ \vdots \\ \mathbf{D}(N) \end{bmatrix} = \begin{bmatrix} \mathcal{D}(\bar{u}_1, \bar{v}_1) \\ \mathcal{D}(\bar{u}_2, \bar{v}_1) \\ \vdots \\ \mathcal{D}(\bar{u}_i, \bar{v}_j) \\ \vdots \\ \mathcal{D}(\bar{u}_W, \bar{v}_H) \end{bmatrix} \in \mathbb{R}_{>0}^N, \qquad (10.2)$$

where $N = WH$, $\bar{u}_i \in \{\bar{u}_1, \bar{u}_2, ..., \bar{u}_W\}$ and $\bar{v}_j \in \{\bar{v}_1, \bar{v}_2, ..., \bar{v}_H\}$ denote the discrete image coordiantes (pixel indices) corresponding to the continuous adjusted image coordinates $(\bar{u}, \bar{v})$.

10.5.2 *Disparity-based direct visual servoing*

Following the IBVS formulation introduced in [Chaumette and Hutchinson, 2006, Hutchinson et al., 1996, Teulière and Marchand, 2014], the instantaneous velocity $\mathbf{v} = \begin{bmatrix} v_{o,x} & v_{o,z} & \omega_{o,y} \end{bmatrix}^\top \in \mathbb{R}^3$ of the camera frame $\mathcal{O}$ and the temporal variation of

D is defined as

$$\frac{\partial \mathbf{D}}{\partial t} = \mathcal{L}_{\mathbf{D}} \mathbf{v}, \tag{10.3}$$

where $\mathcal{L}_{\mathbf{D}} \in \mathbb{R}^{N \times 3}$ is the full interaction matrix. The camera velocity $\mathbf{v}$ contains two translational components $v_{o,x}$ and $v_{o,z}$ in the $\mathbf{x}_\mathcal{O}$ and $\mathbf{z}_\mathcal{O}$ axis, respectively, as well as the rotational component $\omega_{o,y}$ about the $\mathbf{y}_\mathcal{O}$ axis. Consider the error vector

$$\Delta \mathbf{D} = \begin{bmatrix} \mathbf{D}(1) - \mathbf{D}^*(1) \\ \vdots \\ \mathbf{D}(W(\bar{v}_j - 1) + \bar{u}_i) - \mathbf{D}^*(W(\bar{v}_j - 1) + \bar{u}_i) \\ \vdots \\ \mathbf{D}(N) - \mathbf{D}^*(N) \end{bmatrix}, \tag{10.4}$$

where $\mathbf{D}^* \in \mathbb{R}^N_{>0}$ denotes the vector form of a reference disparity map captured at the robot's target pose. The proposed velocity control law is designed to minimize $e = \|\Delta \mathbf{D}\|^2 / 2$ along (10.3), by guaranteeing

$$\frac{\partial e}{\partial t} = (\Delta \mathbf{D})^\top \frac{\partial \mathbf{D}}{\partial t} = (\Delta \mathbf{D})^\top \mathcal{L}_{\mathbf{D}} \mathbf{v} < 0 \tag{10.5}$$

for nonzero $\mathcal{L}_{\mathbf{D}}^\top \Delta \mathbf{D}$. Hence, the corresponding control law is chosen as

$$\mathbf{v} = -\lambda \mathcal{L}_{\mathbf{D}}^+ \Delta \mathbf{D}, \tag{10.6}$$

where $\mathcal{L}_{\mathbf{D}}^+ = \left(\mathcal{L}_{\mathbf{D}}^\top \mathcal{L}_{\mathbf{D}} \right)^{-1} \mathcal{L}_{\mathbf{D}}^\top$ is the pseudoinverse of $\mathcal{L}_{\mathbf{D}}$ and $\lambda > 0$ is the controller gain. The local asymptotic stability of controller (10.6) is ensured within a neighborhood of $\mathbf{D} = \mathbf{D}^*$ when $\mathcal{L}_{\mathbf{D}}$ is of rank 3 [Chaumette and Hutchinson, 2006]. In the actual implementation, $\mathcal{L}_{\mathbf{D}}^+$ is computed by using singular value decomposition, which eliminates any potential problem for matrix inversion.

In order to derive the full interaction matrix $\mathcal{L}_D$, a procedure similar to that in [Teulière and Marchand, 2014] is followed. The depth z_o captured at time instant t is modeled as a surface $z_o(\bar{u}, \bar{v}, t)$. The disparity is also considered as a time varying surface $D(\bar{u}, \bar{v}, t)$. Note that the disparity image $\mathbf{D}$ is essentially a discrete representation of this surface. Taking the full time derivative of $D(\bar{u}, \bar{v}, t)$ yields

$$\frac{dD}{dt} = \frac{\partial D}{\partial \bar{u}} \dot{\bar{u}} + \frac{\partial D}{\partial \bar{v}} \dot{\bar{v}} + \frac{\partial D}{\partial t}, \tag{10.7}$$

which can be rearranged as

$$\frac{\partial D}{\partial t} = \frac{dD}{dt} - \frac{\partial D}{\partial \bar{u}} \dot{\bar{u}} - \frac{\partial D}{\partial \bar{v}} \dot{\bar{v}}. \tag{10.8}$$

By triangulation, the depth $z_o(\bar{u}, \bar{v}, t)$ is geometrically related to the disparity $D(\bar{u}, \bar{v}, t)$ given the camera's baseline b as

$$D(\bar{u}, \bar{v}, t) = \frac{bf}{z_o(\bar{u}, \bar{v}, t)}, \tag{10.9}$$

which implies that

$$\frac{dD}{dt} = -\frac{bf}{z_o^2}\dot{z}_o. \tag{10.10}$$

Time derivatives of the adjusted image coordinates are obtained by differentiating (10.1) as

$$\begin{cases} \dot{u} = \frac{\dot{x}_o z_o - x_o \dot{z}_o}{z_o^2} \\ \dot{v} = \frac{\dot{y}_o z_o - y_o \dot{z}_o}{z_o^2}. \end{cases} \tag{10.11}$$

Following the derivation steps in [Chaumette and Hutchinson, 2006] for the planar motion with $v_{o,y} = \omega_{o,x} = \omega_{o,z} = 0$, the relationships between the velocity components $(\dot{x}_o, \dot{y}_o, \dot{z}_o)$ of the 3D point **P** and the camera velocity **v** are found as

$$\begin{cases} \dot{x}_o = -v_{o,x} - \omega_{o,y} z_o \\ \dot{y}_o = 0 \\ \dot{z}_o = -v_{o,z} + \omega_{o,y} x_o \end{cases}. \tag{10.12}$$

Substituting (10.1), (10.9), and (10.12) into (10.10) and (10.11) yields

$$\frac{dD}{dt} = \frac{D^2}{bf} v_{o,z} - D\bar{u}\omega_{o,y}, \tag{10.13}$$

$$\begin{cases} \dot{u} = -\frac{D}{bf} v_{o,x} + \frac{D\bar{u}}{bf} v_{o,z} - \left(\bar{u}^2 + 1\right)\omega_{o,y} \\ \dot{v} = \frac{D\bar{v}}{bf} v_{o,z} - \bar{u}\bar{v}\omega_{o,y} \end{cases}. \tag{10.14}$$

Substituting (10.13) and (10.14) into (10.8) leads to

$$\frac{\partial D}{\partial t} = \begin{bmatrix} \frac{D}{bf}\frac{\partial D}{\partial \bar{u}} \\ \frac{D}{bf}\left(D - \bar{u}\frac{\partial D}{\partial \bar{u}} - \bar{v}\frac{\partial D}{\partial \bar{v}}\right) \\ -D\bar{u} + \left(\bar{u}^2 + 1\right)\frac{\partial D}{\partial \bar{u}} + \bar{u}\bar{v}\frac{\partial D}{\partial \bar{v}} \end{bmatrix}^{\top} \begin{bmatrix} v_{o,x} \\ v_{o,z} \\ \omega_{o,y} \end{bmatrix}. \tag{10.15}$$

From (10.15), an interaction manifold, which is also referred to as interaction matrix in previous works, is defined based on an arbitrary point on the disparity surface $D(\bar{u}, \bar{v}, t)$ as

$$\mathbf{L}_D = \begin{bmatrix} \frac{D}{bf}\frac{\partial D}{\partial \bar{u}} \\ \frac{D}{bf}\left(D - \bar{u}\frac{\partial D}{\partial \bar{u}} - \bar{v}\frac{\partial D}{\partial \bar{v}}\right) \\ -D\bar{u} + \left(\bar{u}^2 + 1\right)\frac{\partial D}{\partial \bar{u}} + \bar{u}\bar{v}\frac{\partial D}{\partial \bar{v}} \end{bmatrix}^{\top}. \tag{10.16}$$

The full interaction matrix $\mathcal{L}_\mathbf{D}$ is constructed as a stack of interaction manifolds $\mathbf{L}_D$ as

$$\mathcal{L}_\mathbf{D} = \begin{bmatrix} \mathbf{L}_D(\bar{u}_1, \bar{v}_1, t) \\ \vdots \\ \mathbf{L}_D(\bar{u}_i, \bar{v}_j, t) \\ \vdots \\ \mathbf{L}_D(\bar{u}_W, \bar{v}_H, t) \end{bmatrix}, \tag{10.17}$$

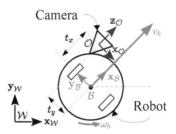

Figure 10.4: Model of a mobile robot with a camera.

where $\mathbf{L}_D(\bar{u}_i, \bar{v}_j, t)$ is the interaction manifold evaluated with the discrete pixel indices $(\bar{u}_i, \bar{v}_j)$ and $\mathbf{D}(W(\bar{v}_j - 1) + \bar{u}_i)$ recorded at time instant t. Additionally, when evaluating (10.16) in the actual implementation, the spatial gradients can be computed based on (10.1) as

$$
\begin{cases}
\frac{\partial D}{\partial \bar{u}} = \frac{\partial D}{\partial u}\frac{\partial u}{\partial \bar{u}} = f\frac{\partial D}{\partial u} \\
\frac{\partial D}{\partial \bar{v}} = \frac{\partial D}{\partial v}\frac{\partial v}{\partial \bar{v}} = f\frac{\partial D}{\partial v}
\end{cases}
, \qquad (10.18)
$$

where $\frac{\partial D}{\partial u}$ and $\frac{\partial D}{\partial v}$ are approximated by the Sobel filters.

In the above derivation of $\mathcal{L}_\mathbf{D} \in \mathbb{R}^{N \times 3}$, the camera motion is restricted to a 2D plane since it is attached to a mobile robot. The same procedures can be followed to derive a more generic $\mathcal{L}_\mathbf{D} \in \mathbb{R}^{N \times 6}$ for applications with robot manipulators by setting $v_{o,y} \neq 0$, $\omega_{o,x} \neq 0$, and $\omega_{o,z} \neq 0$ in (10.12).

After obtaining the full interaction matrix $\mathcal{L}_\mathbf{D}$, the camera velocity $\mathbf{v}$ can be computed by the control law (10.6). However, $\mathbf{v}$ is based on frame $\mathcal{O}$ attached to the camera. It needs to be transformed to the robot's base frame to properly move the robot. Given the model of a nonholonomic differential drive mobile robot shown in Figure 10.4, the velocity of the robot base $\mathbf{v}_b = \begin{bmatrix} v_b & \omega_b \end{bmatrix}^\top$ with respect to the robot's base frame $\mathcal{B}$ is related to the camera's velocity [Fu et al., 2013] by

$$
\mathbf{v} = \mathbf{T}\mathbf{v}_b = \begin{bmatrix} 0 & -t_x \\ 1 & -t_y \\ 0 & -1 \end{bmatrix} \mathbf{v}_b, \qquad (10.19)
$$

where t_x and t_y are the offsets of the camera from the robot base as shown in Figure 10.4. Hence, given the camera's velocity from (10.6), the control law in the form of the robot velocity is

$$
\mathbf{v}_b = \mathbf{T}^+\mathbf{v}, \qquad (10.20)
$$

where $\mathbf{T}^+$ is the pseudoinverse of the transformation $\mathbf{T}$. It is important to note that the controller in (10.20) does not consider the robot's nonholonomic motion constraints.

10.6 Occlusion-aware visual servoing and final design

Due to the setup of a stereo camera, some regions in one of the views may not be visible in the other. These regions are known as the occluded regions. Stereo algorithms often remove the occluded predictions or attempt to provide disparity estimates based on contextual information. Since these estimates rely on something other than the general principle of stereo matching, their accuracy is often lower than the estimates for non-occluded areas. Including them in the control law may affect the performance. Therefore, they should be removed from the visual servoing algorithm.

The stereo-matching method used in this work is [Fan et al., 2022]. One of the benefits of this approach is its ability to predict an occlusion mask for each predicted disparity map. For the vectorized disparity image $\mathbf{D}$, denote the corresponding occlusion mask in a vector form as $\mathbf{O}$, which has the same size as $\mathbf{D}$. For a pixel $(\bar{u}_i, \bar{v}_j)$, $\mathbf{O}(W(\bar{v}_j - 1) + \bar{u}_i) \in (0, 1)$ indicates how likely the pixel belongs to a non-occluded region according to the model's knowledge. This occlusion mask can effectively include non-occluded pixels and exclude the occluded ones in the computation of the control signals.

To incorporate the occlusion information at the time instant t and at the robot's target pose, consider $\mathbf{O}$ and the target occlusion mask in its vector form $\mathbf{O}^* \in \mathbb{R}^N$. A joint occlusion mask is obtained by

$$\bar{\mathbf{O}} = \mathbf{O} \otimes \mathbf{O}^* \in \mathbb{R}^N, \tag{10.21}$$

where $\otimes$ indicates element-wise multiplication between the two masks. The joint occlusion mask $\bar{\mathbf{O}}$ can be viewed as a weighting matrix based on the occlusion predictions of all pixels. In [Teulière and Marchand, 2014], a different weighting matrix is used in the control law to address the problem where the structure of the scene changes during the visual servoing process. By extending this technique, the controller in (10.6) is modified to include the joint occlusion mask as

$$\mathbf{v} = -\lambda \left(\bar{\mathbf{O}}^D \mathcal{L}_\mathbf{D} \right)^+ \left(\bar{\mathbf{O}}^D \Delta \mathbf{D} \right), \tag{10.22}$$

where the occlusion weight

$$\bar{\mathbf{O}}^D = \text{diag} \left(\bar{\mathbf{O}}(1), ..., \bar{\mathbf{O}}(N) \right) \in \mathbb{R}^{N \times N} \tag{10.23}$$

is a diagonalized matrix form of $\bar{\mathbf{O}}$. Equation (10.22) explicitly lowers the contribution of pixels that are identified as parts of the occluded regions to the calculated camera velocity.

In the final design of the control framework, the predicted disparity and occlusion from [Fan et al., 2022] are first used to compute the interaction matrix (10.17), the error vector (10.4), and the joint occlusion mask (10.21). Equation (10.22) utilizes all this information to compute the camera's commanded velocity. Lastly, the camera velocity is transformed to the robot's velocity command according to (10.20).

10.7 Simulation and experimental results

10.7.1 *System setup*

Using the Robot Operating System (ROS) [Quigley et al., 2009], the proposed visual servoing algorithm is verified in both a simulation environment and on a physical

(a)   (b)

Figure 10.5: Setup in the (a) simulation and (b) physical environments.

robot, as shown in Figure 10.5. In the simulation environment, a Turtlebot 3 with a simulated Intel RealSense D435 camera is used, while a Turtlebot 2 with a RealSense D415 camera is utilized in the physical experiments. The simulated camera captures stereo images at a resolution of 800×600 with focal length $f = 435$ px and baseline $b = 0.05$ m. The local block matching method from OpenCV [OpenCV, 2018] computes the raw disparity maps from these simulated stereo images. In the physical experiments, the camera outputs stereo images at a resolution of 640×480 with $f = 608.3$ px and $b = 0.055$ m. The raw disparity maps (converted from raw depth maps) are generated by the camera directly.

After obtaining the stereo images and raw disparity maps, the CRD-Fusion pipeline [Fan et al., 2022] computes the final predicted disparity maps and occlusion masks. To reduce the runtime of the entire framework, the images are cropped to $W = 320$ and $H = 240$ before sending them into CRD-Fusion. The controller utilizes the predicted disparity and occlusion with its gain set to $\lambda = 30$ in the simulations and $\lambda = 5$ in the experiments. The simulations are run on a desktop with an Intel i7-10700K CPU and an NVIDIA 3060 GPU, resulting in approximately 0.075 sec per iteration. A laptop with an Intel i5-7500HQ and an NVIDIA 1050 is used in the experiments, leading to a runtime of 0.095 sec per iteration. To evaluate the results from the experiments, the robot's ground truth poses are captured by an Optitrack camera tracking system.

To predict accurate disparity in the simulation and physical environments with CRD-Fusion, the pre-trained model from [Fan et al., 2022] is fine-tuned with images recorded in each setting using PyTorch [Paszke et al., 2019]. The dataset captured in the simulation consists of 5,056 frames, while the one recorded with the physical robot contains 12,814 frames. In both cases, 80% of the samples are used in training while the remaining ones are saved for validation. The pre-trained model is fine-tuned for 40 epochs using the simulated dataset or 30 epochs using the real dataset with an initial learning rate of 0.0001. The learning rate is reduced midway through training by factors of 0.5 and 0.1, respectively. Other training settings are consistent with the ones in [Fan et al., 2022] to obtain the pre-trained model. After fine-tuning, the model trained with simulated images achieves high accuracy in disparity prediction with an endpoint error of 0.3301 px and only 0.3852% pixels with an error larger

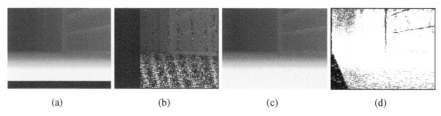

(a)	(b)	(c)	(d)

Figure 10.6: Sample qualitative results from the simulated dataset: (a) ground truth disparity; (b) raw disparity; (c) predicted disparity; (d) occlusion mask.

(a)	(b)	(c)

Figure 10.7: Sample qualitative results from the real dataset: (a) raw disparity; (b) predicted disparity; (c) occlusion mask.

than 3 px on the validation set. Sample qualitative outputs of the fine-tuned model in both cases are shown in Figures 10.6 and 10.7.

10.7.2 Simulation results

10.7.2.1 Verification of the proposed design

A positioning task is performed in simulation to verify the proposed disparity-based visual servoing scheme. Note that the motions considered here and in Section 10.7.3 consists mostly of forward movements with certain rotational movements. The feasible rotation range is limited by the camera's field of view (FOV) and the robot's nonholonomic motion constraints. The results are shown in Figure 10.8. The task error in Figure 10.8(a) quantifies the occlusion-aware difference between the robot's current disparity map and the desired one, and it is defined as

$$e_d = \frac{1}{N} \sum_{n=1}^{N} \bar{\mathbf{O}}(n) |\Delta \mathbf{D}(n)|. \tag{10.24}$$

The tracking error in Figure 10.8(b) includes the translational error Δ_x and Δ_y and the rotational error Δ_z, all based on the world coordinate frame $\mathcal{W}$, as shown in Figure 10.4. Figure 10.9 shows the disparity map and occlusion mask at the robot's desired, initial, and final pose.

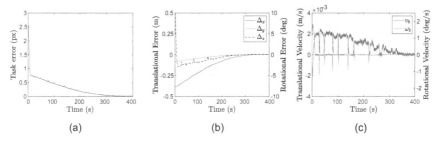

(a)   (b)   (c)

Figure 10.8: Results from the positioning task in simulation: (a) task error; (b) tracking error; (c) robot's velocity.

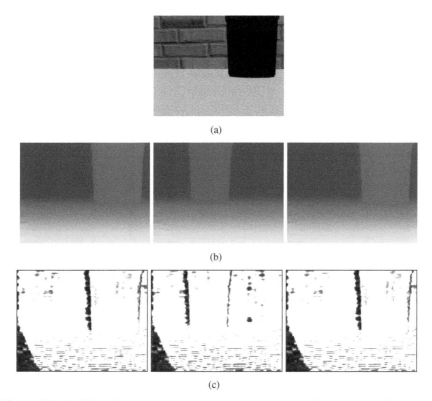

Figure 10.9: (b) Disparity maps and (c) occlusion masks captured in the (a) simulated scene for the positioning task. For (b) and (c), images from left to right are disparity (occlusion) recorded at the target, initial, and final pose.

According to Figure 10.8, the proposed controller in (10.22) can provide the appropriate control actions to move the robot toward its desired pose. After the robot reaches its steady-state pose, its translational and rotational errors are close to zero. Additionally, the task error also decreases as the simulation time increases. Hence, the proposed servoing scheme can continuously drive the robot's current disparity maps toward the desired one. This can be further observed in Figure 10.9, where the robot's final disparity map and final occlusion mask are visually similar to the reference ones.

10.7.2.2 Comparison with other approaches

The performance of our visual servoing controller is compared against two traditional approaches. Both of these baseline controllers are derived from the approach relying on image feature locations as outlined in [Chaumette and Hutchinson, 2006]. One of the baseline approaches extracts and matches SIFT features [Lowe, 1999] from the current and target stereo views, while the other utilizes the oriented FAST and rotated BRIEF (ORB) descriptors [Rublee et al., 2011]. The extraction and matching algorithms provided by open-source libraries [van der Walt et al., 2014, Bradski, 2000] are used directly.

Table 10.1 shows the final positioning error obtained by these controllers. The controller relying on SIFT features yields the highest positioning error, while the controller based on ORB descriptors leads to much more accurate results. Compared to the feature-based controllers, the proposed direct controller has the best performance. The final positioning errors based on the proposed controller in all three dimensions are significantly lower than the ones from feature-based controllers. The feature extraction and matching steps can be avoided with the direct controller. Any potential inaccuracies associated with these steps can also be removed.

Table 10.1: Initial and final positioning error for different visual servoing approaches.

	Δ_x (m)	Δ_y (m)	Δ_z (°)
Initial error	-0.375	-0.080	10.873
SIFT	-0.232	-0.040	1.337
ORB	0.013	-0.004	0.555
Proposed	**0.002**	**0.003**	**0.124**

10.7.2.3 Significance of occlusion masks

One feature of the proposed visual servoing scheme is the inclusion of the occlusion mask. It is observed that the occlusion mask plays a major role in the controller performance, especially when occlusion is significant in the disparity map. When the CRD-Fusion network predicts accurate disparity values at occluded regions, the contribution of the occlusion mask is negligible.

In order to verify the occlusion-aware design, a second positioning task is performed where the robot's target pose is in close proximity to an object. As shown in Figure 10.10, the robot's target disparity map in this case contains notably inaccurate disparity estimates at the occluded regions. Meanwhile, the occlusion mask can effectively detect these occluded areas.

The tracking results for this positioning task are given in Figure 10.11. Figure 10.11(a) shows the error obtained with the controller from (10.22), while Figure 10.11(b) is the error from the controller in (10.6). With the occlusion-aware controller, the robot can successfully track the desired pose. However, the robot does

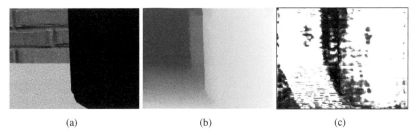

(a)   (b)   (c)

Figure 10.10: Images recorded at the robot's target pose for occlusion study: (a) left stereo view; (b) disparity map; (c) occlusion mask.

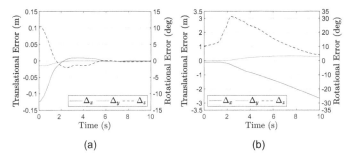

(a)   (b)

Figure 10.11: Tracking error for the robot (a) with and (b) without the proposed occlusion-aware control law.

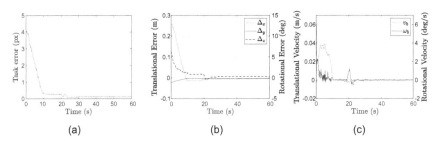

(a)   (b)   (c)

Figure 10.12: Results from the positioning task in the physical environment: (a) task error; (b) tracking error; (c) robot's velocity.

not converge to the target when using the controller without occlusion consideration. The incorrect disparity at the occluded region contaminates the calculated velocity, which leads to unsatisfactory performance.

10.7.3   *Experimental results*

Similar to the test case in the simulation environment, a positioning task is also performed on the physical system. Figure 10.12 shows the experimental results obtained from the disparity maps and occlusion masks shown in Figure 10.13. Shortly after

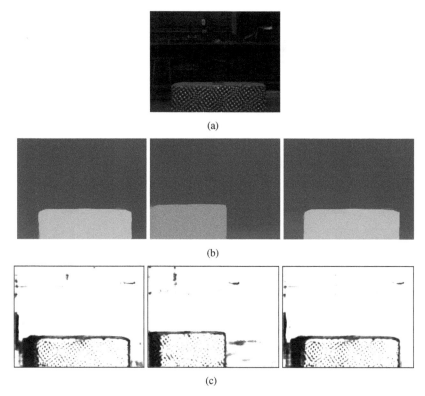

Figure 10.13: (b) Disparity maps and (c) occlusion masks captured in the (a) physical scene for the positioning task. For (b) and (c), images from left to right are disparity (occlusion) recorded at the target, initial, and final pose.

starting the experiment, the robot's tracking and task errors quickly approach zero. This is supported by Figure 10.13(b) and Figure 10.13(c), where the disparity map and occlusion mask captured at the robot's final pose are visually similar to those obtained at the target posture. The results verify that the proposed disparity-based controller also applies to a physical robot with specifications and sensor setup different from the simulated one. This indicates that the proposed pipeline is generic and can be applied to different mobile robotic systems.

In addition to the positioning task, a navigation experiment is also performed. After recording a sequence of disparity maps and occlusion masks, shown in Figure 10.14, the robot moves to the poses corresponding to the recorded images with the proposed controller. Initially, the robot uses the first disparity map and occlusion mask in the sequence as the reference images. The task error given in (10.24) is computed online based on the current disparity, occlusion, and the target ones. When the task error is less than 0.3 px, target disparity map and occlusion mask are switched to the next recorded pair.

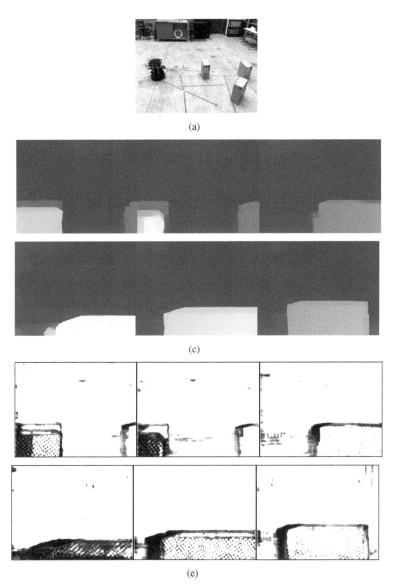

(a)

(c)

(e)

Figure 10.14: (b) Disparity and (c) occlusion sequences recorded in the (a) navigation experiment setup. The order for (b) and (c) is in the clockwise direction from the upper left image.

Figure 10.15 shows the results of this navigation experiment. It can be observed that the robot can successfully move toward the target poses and change the target when the robot is near the previous one. Besides successfully completing this navigation task, Figure 10.15 reveals that the robot has more difficulty correcting its lateral error than its longitudinal error. This shortcoming may be attributed to the nonholonomic motion constraints on the robot. To correct the robot's lat-

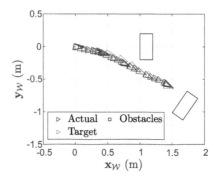

Figure 10.15: Actual robot poses and target poses from the navigation experiment. Obstacles' poses are approximate.

eral error under these constraints, the robot needs to move along its longitudinal direction and about its rotational axis. However, these constraints are not considered in the controller shown in (10.22). Incorporating them in the controller design [Cherubini et al., 2011, Huang and Su, 2019] may lead to better performance.

10.8   Concluding remarks

To relieve the dependence on feature extraction and matching in previous stereo-based visual servoing, a direct visual servoing algorithm has been proposed for a mobile robot equipped with a stereo camera by following (10.17) and (10.20)-(10.22). The basic principle of the proposed approach is to utilize the disparity maps and occlusion masks computed by a self-supervised stereo-matching deep neural network. Extensive simulations and experiments have shown satisfactory accuracy of the proposed approach. However, the proposed method is limited by two factors: lack of consideration of the robot's nonholonomic motion constraints in the controller design and unsatisfactory performance when the robot encounters planar scenes.

In the future, there are multiple possible directions to explore in order to improve the visual servoing performance. Further compressing the deep neural network is necessary to deploy the proposed method on edge devices and in production. A controller that considers the robot's dynamical modeling and nonholonomic constraints can be designed to achieve better performance. A more sophisticated control strategy other than proportional control can also be studied.

References

Bakthavatchalam, M., Tahri, O., and Chaumette, F. 2018. A direct dense visual servoing approach using photometric moments. IEEE Trans. Robot., 34(5): 1226–1239.

Bateux, Q. and Marchand, E. 2017. Histograms-based visual servoing. IEEE Robot. Autom. Lett., 2(1): 80–87.

Bay, H., Tuytelaars, T., and Van Gool, L. 2006. SURF: Speeded up robust features. In Proc. Eur. Conf. Comput. Vis., pp. 404–417.

Biswas, J., and Veloso, M. 2010. Wifi localization and navigation for autonomous indoor mobile robots. In Proc. IEEE Int. Conf. Robot. Autom., pp. 4379–4384.

Bradski, G. 2000. The OpenCV Library. Dr. Dobb's Journal of Software Tools, 25(11): 120–123.

Brossard, M., Bonnabel, S., and Barrau, A. 2018. Unscented kalman filter on lie groups for visual inertial odometry. In Proc. IEEE/RSJ Int. Conf. Intell. Robots Syst., pp. 649–655.

Cai, C., Dean-León, E., Mendoza, D., Somani, N., and Knoll, A. 2013. Uncalibrated 3d stereo image-based dynamic visual servoing for robot manipulators. In Proc. IEEE/RSJ Int. Conf. Intell. Robot. and Syst., pp. 63–70.

Chang, J. -R., and Chen, Y. -S. 2018. Pyramid stereo matching network. In Proc. IEEE/CVF Conf. Comput. Vis. Pattern Recog., pp. 5410–5418.

Chaumette, F. 1999. Potential problems of unstability and divergence in image-based and position-based visual servoing. In Proc. Eur. Control Conf., pp. 4549–4554.

Chaumette, F. 2004. Image moments: A general and useful set of features for visual servoing. IEEE Trans. Robot., 20(4): 713–723.

Chaumette, F. and Hutchinson, S. 2006. Visual servo control. I. Basic approaches. IEEE Robot. & Autom. Mag., 13(4): 82–90.

Cheng, X., Zhong, Y., Harandi, M., Dai, Y., Chang, X., Li, H. et al. 2020. Hierarchical neural architecture search for deep stereo matching. In Proc. Int. Conf. Neural Information Processing Systems, pp. 22158–22169.

Cherubini, A., Chaumette, F., and Oriolo, G. 2011. Visual servoing for path reaching with nonholonomic robots. Robotica, 29(7): 1037–1048.

Collewet, C., and Marchand, E. 2011. Photometric visual servoing. IEEE Trans. Robot., 27(4): 828–834.

Djelal, N., Saadia, N., and Ramdane-Cherif, A. 2012. Target tracking based on SURF and image based visual servoing. In Proc. Int. Conf. Commun. Comput. and Control Appl., pp. 1–5.

Espiau, B., Chaumette, F., and Rives, P. 1992. A new approach to visual servoing in robotics. IEEE Trans. Robot. Autom., 8(3): 313–326.

Fan, X., Jeon, S., and Fidan, B. 2022. Occlusion-aware self-supervised stereo matching with confidence guided raw disparity fusion. In Proc. Conf. Robot. Vis., pp. 132–139.

Fu, W., Hadj-Abdelkader, H., and Colle, E. 2013. Visual servoing based mobile robot navigation able to deal with complete target loss. In Proc. Int. Conf. on Methods and Models in Autom. Robot., pp. 502–507.

Haeusler, R., Nair, R., and Kondermann, D. 2013. Ensemble learning for confidence measures in stereo vision. In Proc. IEEE Conf. Comput. Vis. Pattern Recog., pp. 305–312.

Hager, G., Chang, W. -C., and Morse, A. 1994. Robot feedback control based on stereo vision: Towards calibration-free hand-eye coordination. In Proc. IEEE Int. Conf. Robot. Autom., 4: 2850–2856.

He, K., Zhang, X., Ren, S., and Sun, J. 2016. Deep residual learning for image recognition. In Proc. IEEE Conf. Comput. Vis. Pattern Recog., pp. 770–778.

Hirschmuller, H. 2008. Stereo processing by semiglobal matching and mutual information. IEEE Trans. Pattern Anal. Mach. Intell., 30(2): 328–341.

Hoffmann, F., Nierobisch, T., Seyffarth, T., and Rudolph, G. 2006. Visual servoing with moments of SIFT features. In Proc. IEEE Int. Conf. Syst., Man, Cybern., 5: 4262–4267.

Huang, P., Zhang, Z., Luo, X. J., and Huang, P. 2018. Path tracking control of a differential-drive tracked robot based on look-ahead distance. In Proc. IFAC Conf. Bio-Robotics, pp. 112–117.

Huang, Y., and Su, J. 2019. Visual servoing of non-holonomic mobile robots: A review and a novel perspective. IEEE Access, 7: 134968–134977.

Hutchinson, S., Hager, G., and Corke, P. 1996. A tutorial on visual servo control. IEEE Trans. Robot. Autom., 12(5): 651–670.

Kendall, A., Martirosyan, H., Dasgupta, S., Henry, P., Kennedy, R., Bachrach, A. et al. 2017. End-to-end learning of geometry and context for deep stereo regression. In Proc. IEEE Int. Conf. Comput. Vis., pp. 66–75.

Khamis, S., Fanello, S., Rhemann, C., Kowdle, A., Valentin, J., and Izadi, S. 2018. StereoNet: Guided hierarchical refinement for real-time edge-aware depth prediction. In Proc. Eur. Conf. Comput. Vis., pp. 573–590.

Kolmogorov, V., and Zabih, R. 2001. Computing visual correspondence with occlusions using graph cuts. In Proc. IEEE Int. Conf. Comput. Vis., 2: 508–515.

Lee, Z., Juang, J., and Nguyen, T. Q. 2013. Local disparity estimation with three-moded cross census and advanced support weight. IEEE Trans. Multimedia, 15(8): 1855–1864.

Li, A., and Yuan, Z. 2018. Occlusion aware stereo matching via cooperative unsupervised learning. In Proc. Asian Conf. Comput. Vis., pp. 197–213.

Liu, C. -Y., Chang, Z. -W., and Chen, C. -L. 2019. Visual servo tracking of a wheeled mobile robot utilizing both feature and depth information. In Proc. IEEE Conf. Ind. Electron. Appl., pp. 1045–1050.

Lowe, D. 1999. Object recognition from local scale-invariant features. In Proc. IEEE Int. Conf. Comput. Vis., 2: 1150–1157.

Mei, X., Sun, X., Zhou, M., Jiao, S., Wang, H., and Zhang, X. 2011. On building an accurate stereo matching system on graphics hardware. In Proc. IEEE Int. Conf. Comput. Vis. Workshops, pp. 467–474.

OpenCV (Nov. 17, 2018). cv::StereoBM class reference. Accessed on: Mar. 29, 2022. [Online]. Available: https://docs.opencv.org/3.4.4/d9/dba/classcv_1_1StereoBM.html.

Park, M. -G., and Yoon, K. -J. 2019. Learning and selecting confidence measures for robust stereo matching. IEEE Trans. Pattern Anal. Mach. Intell., 41(6): 1397–1411.

Paszke, A., Gross, S., Massa, F., Lerer, A., Bradbury, J., Chanan, G. et al. 2019. PyTorch: An imperative style, high performance deep learning library. In Proc. Int. Conf. Neural Information Processing Systems, pp. 8026–8037.

Quigley, M., Gerkey, B., Conley, K., Faust, J., Foote, T., Leibs, J. et al. 2009. ROS: An open-source robot operating system. In Proc. IEEE Int. Conf. Robot. Autom. Workshop on Open Source Robotics, pp. 1–6.

Rublee, E., Rabaud, V., Konolige, K., and Bradski, G. 2011. ORB: An efficient alternative to sift or surf. In Proc. Int. Conf. Comput. Vis., pp. 2564–2571.

Scharstein, D., Szeliski, R., and Zabih, R. 2001. A taxonomy and evaluation of dense two-frame stereo correspondence algorithms. In Proc. IEEE Workshop on Stereo and Multi-Baseline Vision, pp. 131–140.

Shademan, A., and Janabi-Sharifi, F. 2004. Using scale-invariant feature points in visual servoing. In Machine Vision and its Optomechatronic Applications, 5603: 63–70. SPIE.

Szeliski, R. 2022. Computer Vision: Algorithms and Applications. Springer.

Teulière, C., and Marchand, E. 2014. A dense and direct approach to visual servoing using depth maps. IEEE Trans. Robot., 30(5): 1242–1249.

Thuilot, B., Martinet, P., Cordesses, L., and Gallice, J. 2002. Position based visual servoing: Keeping the object in the field of vision. In Proc. IEEE Int. Conf. Robot. Autom., 2: 1624–1629.

van der Walt, S., Schönberger, J. L., Nunez-Iglesias, J., Boulogne, F., Warner, J. D., Yager, N. et al. 2014. Scikit-image: Image processing in Python. PeerJ, 2: e453.

Wang, H., Fan, R., Cai, P., and Liu, M. 2021. PVStereo: Pyramid voting module for end-to-end self-supervised stereo matching. IEEE Robot. Autom. Lett., 6(3): 4353–4360.

Wang, L., Guo, Y., Wang, Y., Liang, Z., Lin, Z., Yang, J. et al. 2022. Parallax attention for unsupervised stereo correspondence learning. IEEE Trans. Pattern Anal. Mach. Intell., 44(4): 2108–2125.

Wilson, W., Williams Hulls, C., and Bell, G. 1996. Relative end-effector control using cartesian position based visual servoing. IEEE Trans. Robot. Autom., 12(5): 684–696.

Xiong, Y., Zhang, X., Peng, J., and Yu, W. 2017. 3d depth map based optimal motion control for wheeled mobile robot. In Proc. IEEE Int. Conf. Syst., Man, Cybern., pp. 2045–2050.

Xu, H., and Zhang, J. 2020. AANet: Adaptive aggregation network for efficient stereo matching. In Proc. IEEE/CVF Conf. Comput. Vis. Pattern Recog., pp. 1956–1965.

Zbontar, J., and LeCun, Y. 2015. Computing the stereo matching cost with a convolutional neural network. In Proc. IEEE Conf. Comput. Vis. Pattern Recog., pp. 1592–1599.

Zhou, C., Zhang, H., Shen, X., and Jia, J. 2017. Unsupervised learning of stereo matching. In Proc. IEEE Int. Conf. Comput. Vis., pp. 1576–1584.

11

Development of a Software and Hardware Complex for the Visualization of Sedimentation Inside a Vortex Chamber

DO Semenov, SV Dvoinishnikov, VG Meledin, VV Rakhmanov, GV Bakakin, VA Pavlov and *IK Kabardin**

11.1 Introduction

An important part of an experiment or ongoing process is observation. In many fields of science and production, there is a great need for visual monitoring of the occurring process or its result [Irodov n.d.]. However, the inspection may be difficult or even unattainable due to the closed space in which the process under study takes place. One such example is vortex chambers, which serve to mix various gases and substances under pressure or at high temperatures. These are large chambers of a round or conical shape where everything that takes place inside is hidden from the direct view of the observer due to the need to seal the chamber itself. The operation principle of such chambers is based on the multiple circulations of a substance at high velocity in the cavity of the housing, where various substances can be supplied under pressure [Aronson et al. 2015].

At the moment, informative surveillance over objects with temperatures reaching 1200°C is impossible [Migal and Migal 2018]. The reason is that, when heated to such temperatures, solids begin to glow in the visible range. That create an illumination on the camera matrix, blocking the picture of what is happening in the experiment. Standard cameras do not allow a visual assessment of the geometry of heated objects; in addition, regular-acting devices are not intended for long-term operation at high temperatures and polluted environments, leading them to their failure.

Kutateladze Institute of thermophysics SB RAS. Lavrentyeva avenue 1, Novosibirsk, Russia, 630090.
* Corresponding author: ivankabardin@gmail.com

Modern vortex chambers are complex conical or cylindrical tanks expanding upwards and having several inlets (Figure 11.1) [Aronson et al. 2015]. They serve both for high-quality mixing of various mixtures of gas and liquid and for burning various types of fuel. Works on such setups come amid difficult conditions inside the measuring volume. High-temperature air overheat optical and electronic devices of diagnostic systems and intense thermal radiation from surfaces avoid the application of standard video surveillance systems [Lisienko 1988]. In addition, the residue of burned substances accumulates on the external elements and hampers the transmission of light. The task of creating an installation for observation inside vortex chambers, using the capabilities of a modern computer for the convenience of the experimenter, becomes urgent. The operation of such a system without software is impossible.

Kutateladze Institute of Thermophysics SB RAS is developing a system for visualizing deposits inside a vortex chamber, designed to work in conditions of severe surface contamination and temperatures reaching 1200°C. The design of this system should provide cooling of the housing, observation through a small-diameter hole, illumination of the inner cavity of the vortex chamber, as well as monitoring of the system overheating.

The purpose of this work is to create a complete software package for the operation of the sediment visualization system inside the vortex chamber. To achieve this goal, it is necessary to perform the following tasks:

- analyze the state of the art in observation of high-temperature experiments;
- formulate the requirements;
- choose a hardware platform;
- develop a subsystem for monitoring the device performance;
- develop a user application for a personal computer;
- realize the remote control via a PC;
- develop algorithms to improve the visual diagnostics of deposits;
- test the system under conditions similar to operating conditions.

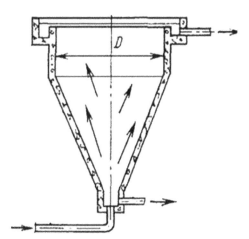

Figure 11.1: Schematic representation of a standard vortex chamber.

As a result of the work, it is expected to create a complete system of monitoring over sedimentation inside the vortex chamber, which will function in conditions of high pollution density and background radiation using active illumination. The control and demonstration of the image will be done in a fully remote mode, which will allow monitoring of the state of the system at a distance.

11.2 Overview of the subject area

11.2.1 Thermal radiation

To solve the above problems, below is a brief introduction to black body luminosity. Thermal radiation is electromagnetic radiation emitted by solids due to their internal energy. Solids with a temperature over 0 K emit in a continuous spectrum, and the location and intensity of their maximum depends on the solid temperature. When heated, this peak shifts to the short-wavelength part of the spectrum.

The distribution of energy over wavelengths in the blackbody radiation at a given temperature T is characterized by an emissivity $r(\lambda, T)$, equal to the radiation power from a unit of the body surface in a single wavelength interval. The product of the emissivity and the wavelength interval $(\Delta\lambda)$ is equal to the power of radiation emitted by a single surface area in all directions in the wavelength interval $\Delta\lambda$. An energy distribution over frequencies $r(v, T)$ may be introduced in a similar way. The function $r(\lambda, T)$ (or r (v, T)) is often called spectral luminosity, and the total flux $R(T)$ of radiation of all wavelengths, equal to

$$R(T) = \int_0^\infty r(\lambda, T)d\lambda = \int_0^\infty r(v, T)dv$$

According to the Stefan–Boltzmann law, introduced in 1884, the integral luminosity R(T) of a blackbody is proportional to the fourth power of the absolute temperature T:

$$M = \sigma T^4$$

where σ is the Stefan–Boltzmann constant and M is the radiation density. This formula represents the power radiated by a body depending on its temperature.

11.2.2 Overview of diagnostic methods

Later it was established that the wavelength λ_{max}, which accounts for the maximum energy of the blackbody radiation, is inversely proportional to the absolute temperature T (Wien's displacement law). At temperatures achievable in laboratory conditions, the maximum emissivity $r(\lambda, T)$ lies in the infrared region. As a consequence of the spectrum distribution, part of the radiation is in the visible region of the spectrum [Irodov n.d.].

The most common option for diagnosing closed combustion or heating chambers is complete disassembly and defect identification in all components of the system [Aronson et al. 2015]. This method is difficult to implement and it is resource-intensive.

Figure 11.2: Video-endoscope for automotive diagnostics.

It requires a complete shutdown of the process and cooling of the entire system, which takes a lot of time and forces the entire installation to be reheated. This leads to huge heat losses and equipment downtime, which entails financial losses. Breakdowns of parts of the system become noticeable only at the end of disassembly, although observation during the operation would allow to stop work earlier and to preserve valuable parts of the device [Aronson et al. 2015].

Technical video endoscopes help to solve the disassembly problem [Migal and Migal 2018, Lisienko 1988]. This is a group of special optical devices used to inspect hard-to-reach cavities of machinery and equipment during maintenance and performance assessment and they enable monitoring through a small diameter hole without interfering with the system design. There are both rigid and flexible endoscopes (Figure 11.2) that allow examining the area under study from all sides. A rigid endoscope is a rigid tube in which a lens system is used to transmit visual information. The basis of flexible endoscopes is a light fiber, which acts as an image transmission channel, covered with a durable shell.

Standard endoscopes are not designed to work at high temperatures, which leads to the destruction of the device body and the melting of the internal components. Therefore, only short-term observations are practicable, and visual surveillance over the experimental process remains unattainable [Migal and Migal 2018].

There exist high-temperature cameras, representing an endoscope inside a cooled case. Usually, these cameras operate in the infrared range and are designed to measure the temperature of observed objects, acting as a two-dimensional pyrometer or thermal imaging camera. There are also cameras operating in the full visible spectrum of wavelengths, but they only allow the assessment of the overall picture of the experiment, since thermal illumination by hot objects disguises their geometry [Lisienko 1988].

As can be seen in Figure 11.3, it is not possible to estimate the geometry of the manufactured material during the experiment due to the bright radiation in the visible spectrum of the heated material itself. Which can be solved by the application of the light filter. The light filter is an optical device that serves to suppress or isolate part of the electromagnetic radiation spectrum. A single-band or narrow-band filter is a colored glass or film that is transparent in one part of the radiation spectrum. The rest of the spectrum is absorbed or reflected due to the physical properties of the filter itself. This allows cutting off some areas of radiation or keeping only a narrow band

Figure 11.3: An example of visual observation of the cement and lime manufacturing process using a CESYCO HTO 70 high-temperature endoscope.

of the spectrum (10–15 nm). The latter is called monochromatic and it is used mainly in scientific photography and technical systems.

The electromagnetic radiation is absorbed by the light filter. In the case of open observation, the glass light filter will be able to withstand a short-term increase in temperature, but in a closed heated chamber without additional cooling, the glass of the light filter will begin to melt. This will lead to equipment failure, allowing radiation to access the camera, which can overheat it as well. In a closed area without thermal radiation there will be no light sources, so nothing will be visible without additional lighting.

Moreover, such a monitoring system is not protected from the effects of environmental pollution, which can be impossible when burning fuel or manufacturing volatile substances.

11.3 Goals and objectives

The purpose of this work is to create a complete software package for the operation of the sediment visualization system inside the vortex chamber.

Tasks that need to be solved to achieve the goal:

- Formulate the requirements;
- Choose the hardware platform;
- Develop a subsystem to monitor the device performance;
- Develop a user application;
- Implement a remote control via a PC;
- Develop algorithms to improve visual diagnostics;
- Test the system in real operating conditions;

11.3.1 Requirements for the monitoring module

The software package of the visualization system must meet the following requirements:

- Observation of objects with high temperatures. The system being created must discern the geometry of objects with temperatures reaching 1200°C.

- Visualization. The most important element of the system is to demonstrate the picture of what is happening inside a closed chamber to the researcher. To do this, the image from the video camera should show the settings on the monitor screen to the user.
- Remote control. The experimenter should be able to change the observation parameters while being away from the installation.
- User Interface. The user interface should be understandable to any researcher and be convenient to control the system.
    - Image enhancement. The original images from the camera may not be legible enough. The software should be able to select shooting parameters independently, as well as support image enhancement algorithms.

11.3.2 Analysis of requirements

To observe high-temperature objects in chamber 1, a narrow-band light filter 4 is installed on camera body 5 to remove a significant part of the background radiation (Figure 11.4).

Visualization of what is happening inside chamber 1 will be done using camera 5 installed inside the case. The image from it will be sent to the computer over the Ethernet network 6 and shown to the user in the main application window on PC 7.

Remote control over the entire installation will be carried out via the Ethernet network 6. Frame parameters will be transmitted to the camera using the built-in API. Communication with the microcontroller 3 will also be done remotely using an Ethernet-Shield expansion board. Microcontroller allows control by the light illuminator and can obtain additional data from temperature sensors to estimate the system state.

Access to all controls will be provided to the user on the main interface screen in the form of buttons with a clear indication.

Since the observation is supposed to be through a small-diameter hole, the camera optics are arranged in such a way that they have strong distortions of space in the form of spherical distortion. To correct this effect, it is necessary to use distortion correction algorithms.

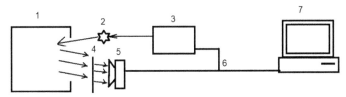

Figure 11.4: Scheme of the visualization system. 1 – closed chamber under study, 2 – light illuminator, 3 – controller, 4 –light filter, 5 – camera, 6 – Ethernet, 7 – Computer.

11.3.3 Correction of distortion

To correct the distortion, it is useful to determine the lens calibration coefficients [Voronov et al. 2012]. Camera calibration allows us to measure internal and external parameters via the received photos. Calibration of the camera allows for correcting the image's distortion. A [u,v] column-vector present the 2D coordinates of the camera plane point, and vector set the position of the 3D point world coordinates:

$$[u \ v \ 1] = A[R \ T] \ [x_w \ y_\omega \ z_w \ 1], \tag{1}$$

where A is the internal calibration matrix, which has 5 dominant variables. These variables have information about the focal length, the angle of inclination of the pixels and the intersection point of the image plane with the optical axis coinciding with the center of the photo. The matrix is presented as (2):

$$A = [\alpha_x \ \gamma \ u_0 \ 0 \ \alpha_y \ v_0 \ 0 \ 0 \ 1]. \tag{2}$$

where R is the 1×3 vector or the 3×3 rotation matrix, and T is the 3×1 transfer vector. These are external calibration parameters that determine the coordinate transformation or those that set the camera's position in the world coordinate system. These parameters are directly related to the scene being photographed, so each photo has its own set of such parameters. An algorithm developed by Zhengyou Zhang [Zhang et al. n.d.] uses a flat calibration object in the chessboard form [Zhang 2000].

11.3.4 Background subtraction

The quality of visualization deteriorates greatly in the presence of external noise or thermal illumination. The differential method of image registration for background subtraction by the software was applied to improve the visualization quality. The system registers two images: one without using an illuminator to capture external radiation, and the other using an illuminator to highlight the geometry of the object. The first image contains the intensity distribution without illumination I_b. The second image I_l contains the sum of the intensity of illumination scattered on the surface of the observed objects I_f and the background glow I_b. Then, in order to obtain the intensity distribution I_f, it is necessary to agree on the energy function of the photodetector and the intensity of the illuminator radiation, and pixel by pixel subtract the second frame from the first one:

$$I_f = I_l - I_b. \tag{3}$$

As a result, one will obtain an image that only registers the scattered radiation of the illuminator. This will significantly increase the informativeness of the received images when visualizing high-temperature processes.

11.4 Implementation of the software module

11.4.1 Installation structure

The device consists of a hollow cylindrical housing with double walls, which passes water between them removing heat from the inner casing. There are two holes in the lower part: the first one is a diaphragm with a diameter of 1 mm for observation using a photodetector through a spherical lens; the second one is intended for an illuminator. In the temperature range from 630 to 730°C, heat-resistant glasses begin to melt (soften), which is why the LED is covered from the outside with a transparent quartz glass that can withstand 1500°C with no change in structure. Inside, in front of the LED, there is a light filter, which absorbs thermal radiation to avoid heating the LED by ambient radiation. Since the illuminator window is quite large and a substantial amount of external light penetrates, the light filter can heat up significantly. Therefore, its water cooling is provided in the same circuit as the housing. A lens with a complex optical system with a spherical lens is mounted on the photodetector matrix (Figure 11.5a). This enables monitoring through a small-diameter hole. The use of a diaphragm is due to the fact that, on the one hand, thermal radiation does not allow applying larger-aperture optics, otherwise the internal components would get very hot, and, on the other hand, it is necessary to avoid contamination of optical surfaces. Such optics creates strong spherical distortions in the final image (Figure 11.5b), also called the "fish eye" effect. This impedes the correct assessment of the geometry of objects observed inside the study area. In this regard, it is necessary to develop algorithms for post-processing camera data to improve the quality of the observed image and to plug them into the computer software.

A narrow-band light filter with a 450 nm bandwidth is installed in front of the matrix and matched with the wavelength of the monochromatic illuminator. This allows for filtering out all the excess radiation on the camera and recording only the reflection from the light source. For less heating and greater productivity, pulsed illumination—short-term switching-on of the light source using a larger current—is applied. This imposes additional requirements on the synchronization of the camera and the illuminator. It should also be taken into account that the LED, powered by the power supply, has some delay in switching on. These delays must be taken into account before the start of the camera frame so that the entire frame is illuminated evenly, since the camera with a sliding shutter polls the reading matrix sequentially.

The DMM 25GP031-ML camera manufactured by the Imaging Source is used for shooting. Such cameras are designed specifically for the development of computer vision systems and are supplied with a set of original software in the form of a library for the C# programming language [https://www.theimagingsource. com/products/board-cameras/gige-monochrome/dmm25gp031ml/ 2021]. DS18b20 temperature sensors are installed inside the housing and fixed at critical points of the

Figure 11.5: a—Photo of a test lens with a spherical lens. b—Photo of a chessboard taken with this lens.

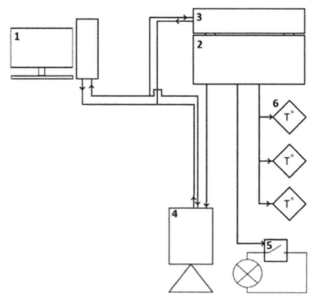

Figure 11.6: Functional diagram of the developed visualization system: 1 – computer, 2 – microcontroller, 3 – microcontroller expansion board, 4 – photodetector, 5 – illuminator with electronic power control relay, 6 – temperature sensors.

system: on the camera, the illuminator and the hottest point—at the bottom of the housing (Figure 11.6). The temperature measurement error does not exceed 0.5°C [https://datasheets.maximintegrated.com/en/ds/DS18B20.pdf 2021]. These sensors have their own connection interface and can be identified by serial number, which allows pre-configuring their position using only one interaction bus.

The gas (nitrogen) used inside the chamber is supplied to the housing under pressure. Using the usual atmospheric air is not an option due to the oxygen in its composition, since it may cause combustion at high temperatures inside the chamber. Due to this, excessive pressure is created inside the housing and prevents pollutants from penetrating through the diaphragm.

11.4.2 *Choosing a hardware platform*

The Iskra Neo programmable platform based on the ATmega32U4 8-bit microcontroller is used. This board is compatible with many extensions that allow configuring flexibly the system. The built-in microcontroller operates at a frequency of 16 MHz and has 32 Kb flash memory for storing firmware upgrades, which is sufficient to record all the necessary software. Additionally, 1Kb of built-in non-volatile memory is enough to store more than 100 integer parameters. The number of general-purpose I/O ports is 20, which enables simultaneous control over multiple external devices.

11.4.3 Microcontroller software

The microcontroller software has been written to work out system operation in various scenarios. Several hardware visualization system operation modes were implemented: video recording, standby mode and loading of new image frame parameters. With the help of a microcontroller, the camera shutter is controlled. This is implemented by a sync signal sent from the microcontroller [Bieker et al. 2006] to the camera. A microcontroller operated the LED power supply. It provides the frame full illumination, switching on and off the illuminator, and synchronizing the lighting and the camera, Figure 11.7.

In case of shooting the frame without synchronously switching on the illuminator, the user can observe a partially unilluminated frame (Figure 11.8a). Synchronization prevents this and guarantees a full view period (Figure 11.8b).

There is a small time delay between the arrival of the power-on signal to the power driver and the turn-on of the LED [Kalitov and Kornishev 2019, Petkovic et al. 2021], which also needs to be taken into account before opening the camera shutter (Figure 11.9).

To monitor the temperature of the system, the DS18b20 temperature sensors, being on the same line without additional power, are polled using the MODBUS protocol.

The control is realized remotely using a computer over the Ethernet network. For distant configuration of the device over a wired network, an Ethernet Shield expansion board is used (Figure 11.10) with a connection speed of up to 100 Mbit/sec. This serves to configure the device parameters while being away from it and without stopping the main operation process.

closed   1-st line   last line   closed

Figure 11.7: Synchronization of switching on the illuminator and reading data from the camera matrix.

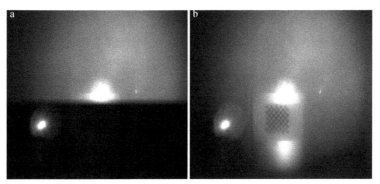

Figure 11.8: Synchronization of switching on the illuminator and reading data from the camera matrix.

A communication protocol is implemented over TCP-IP, which includes the code of the packet or response, the data and the checksum of the entire packet, which allows for verifying the packet integrity (Figure 11.11).

The microcontroller performs the function of a server, waiting for a request from a user's computer to execute a command or responding to a request for temperature or for recording new parameters.

A wired connection is selected because it is less susceptible to interference associated with nearby equipment and is capable of maintaining a stable connection [https://www.theimagingsource.com/products/board-cameras/gige-monochrome/ dmm25gp031ml/ 2021]. Shielded wires are used for better interaction in production conditions or other electrically loaded rooms [https://datasheets.maximintegrated. com/en/ds/DS18B20.pdf 2021].

Three main types of commands have been created: "start video recording", "load new parameters" of the frame, "stop video recording" and "request for temperature". "Start" and "stop" are responsible for enabling the sync signal mode for the camera and the illuminators, starting or completing the data transmission from the camera to the computer. The packet with the command "load new parameters" contains data about the time between frames and a flag encoding whether to use the illuminator or not.

The microcontroller polls temperature sensors regularly with a second interval, but this data is transmitted on external request. This reduces the load on the network and saves headroom for exchanging a greater video stream.

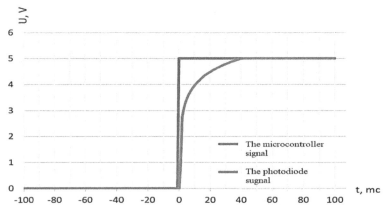

Figure 11.9: A delay of 20–40 ms for the activation of the LED power supply.

Figure 11.10: Photo of the installed expansion board.

```
typedef struct t_RIProtoRequest
{
    uint8_t version;
    uint8_t cmd;
    uint8_t data[RI_PROTO_DATA_LEN];
    uint8_t sign;
} RIProtoRequest_t;

typedef struct t_RIProtoResponse
{
    uint8_t version;
    uint8_t ok;
    uint8_t answer;
    uint8_t data[RI_PROTO_DATA_LEN];
    uint8_t sign;
} RIProtoResponse_t;
```

Figure 11.11: Listing of the code describing the structure of interaction and data exchange between a microcontroller and a computer over the Ethernet network.

To debug equipment or check errors in case of signal loss, the debugging mode with the output of information about the current state of the system has been added. Communication is carried out via COM-port'y via micro-USB input.

11.4.4 User application

A personal computer application has been developed to visualize the real-time camera image and to adjust the frame parameters by transmitting the parameters directly to the photodetector. The user interface provides access to the illuminator control. The current state of temperatures that the application receives from the microcontroller is demonstrated to the user. The program is the Windows application for controlling the visualization system and displaying images from it to the end user. The program is delivered as an executable file, several files and folders—application resources. Among them it is worth mentioning: a file for configuring the application; a file for configuring the camera during initialization; a folder in which all photos are stored while the application is running; and a folder in which log files of the application are recorded. Work with the camera is realized through a development tool supplied by the manufacturer. It allows wrapping all the work with camera drivers in a higher-level programming language.

Remote connection to the microcontroller is implemented using standard operating system libraries based on the use of the Windows Socket API, which determines how network software will access network services.

11.4.5 User interface

The user interface of the program consists of the main window frame, several menus, buttons for controlling video playback and image parameters, a window for demonstrating the internal temperature of the device and an image demonstration window (Figure 11.12).

The application can control the on-and-off switching of the image monitoring mode. The control over camera settings (Exposure, Contrast, Amplification—the

Figure 11.12: User interface of the program VUOR.exe.

coefficient of hardware signal amplification when reading data from the matrix, dB) is implemented. All parameters are stored in the PC memory in a separate file, so the user does not need to configure them again when the program is restarted. The camera settings are loaded automatically. The service of turning on and off the illuminator is implemented. There is also protection against unexpected light switching on when the device is examined by the user. Since a powerful light source with pulsed illumination is used, bright light can be harmful to vision. The control of the image is implemented: correction of distortion; approaching the central image; removal of background illumination; images can be deleted and uploaded; The diagnostics of probe temperatures are available.

The option of viewing visualization in real-time is implemented. In full-screen mode, the image is centered and has the maximum size. In the upper left corner, there is a frame counter that allows tracking of new images coming from the camera. When a new image is received, the counter increases by one and is briefly highlighted in red to attract attention.

11.4.6 Image enhancement algorithms

11.4.6.1 Distortion correction

To correct lens distortion, it is necessary to obtain the calibration coefficients. Since these are static characteristic of the lens, this can only be done once after assembling and adjusting the camera unit and lens. A separate camera calibration console application has been developed for this purpose.

To calibrate the lens, the "Camera calibration" function from the OpenCV image processing library is used to return a matrix of coefficients characterizing this camera and distortion coefficients. To use this function, it is necessary to specify points that in the real world are on one straight line, and are located on a curve in a distorted image [Alaniz-Plata 2022]. To do this, one should take a photo of a chessboard and find the corners of the chess squares on it [Zhang et al. n.d.].

The ways of searching for the corners of the chessboard are implemented: the automatic method (Figure 11.13) analyzes the original images of the chessboard (Figure 11.13a), using an image of one corner as a template for searching (Figure 11.13b) or an image of an ideal corner (a square divided into four equal parts with diagonally identical colors). The algorithm builds a cross-correlation function (Figure 11.13c) and finds the positions of the corners (Figure 11.13d) to the extremes of this function. The local maximum of this function is the maximum match with the template, and vice versa, the minimum is a complete discrepancy, that is, the inverted position of the colors on the chessboard.

The manual method of searching for corners is implemented to analyze images. The user manually applies the location of the corner (Figure 11.14b) on the original image (Figure 11.14a) in any graphic editor in the form of a red dot with a size of 1 pixel. The exact coordinates of these points are automatically determined inside the program.

Next, the array of all found corners must be sorted in the order of their location on the chessboard, that is, on a straight line in the real image, from top to bottom. For this purpose, the Graham algorithm for constructing a convex shell [Cormen et al. 2001] is used, since it is performed in the shortest time and evaluated by complexity as $O(n*\lg(n))$. The implementation implies selecting a point with a minimum or maximum coordinate by one of the coordinates and searching for the next one among those sorted by the polar angle. Points are removed from the shell until the last two points in the current shell form a non-right turn (Figure 11.15). Two lines are excluded from the resulting shell: the lower and the upper, to be stored as the desired lines of the chessboard. The procedure continues until all the lines are found.

Figure 11.13: Automatic search for corners of chess squares.

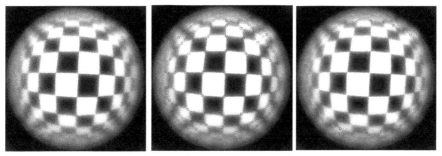

Figure 11.14: Manual search for the corners of chess squares.

The resulting vertically sorted lines of points are passed to the function to calculate the distortion coefficients [https://docs.opencv.org/master/d7/da8/tutorial_ table_of_content_ imgproc.html 2021].

The obtained lens and distortion coefficients can be used to transform the image obtained from the camera matrix to correct spherical distortion. We substitute them into the formula

$$u_{Corrected} = u(1 + k_1 \, r^2 + k_2 \, r^4 + k_3 \, r^6) \tag{4}$$

$$v_{Corrected} = v(1 + k_1 \, r^2 + k_2 \, r^4 + k_3 \, r^6) \tag{5}$$

where u,v are the coordinates of the points on the original image, k are the distortion coefficients, and r is the distance to the point u,v. After all the transformations, we get an image with corrected distortion (Figure 11.16).

These coefficients are recorded in the application configuration file and are used continuously in the distortion correction mode. After disassembling the device for maintenance or upgrade, if the lens is disassembled, the calibration procedure may be realized independently of the main software, providing the end user with only a new application configuration file.

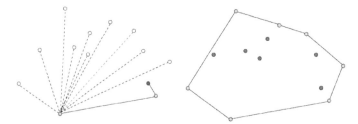

Figure 11.15: Steps of the convex shell construction algorithm.

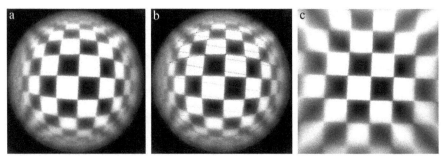

Figure 11.16: Correction of image distortion. A – the original image, b – the corners of the chess squares line by line, c – the image with corrected distortion.

11.4.6.2 Background subtraction

To improve the visual quality of the images recorded by the system, the background subtraction method is implemented [Cormen et al. 2001]. With this view in mind, a picture is taken with the illuminator turned off, in which only the thermal illumination of the observed scene is visible. After that, the illuminator is turned on and a second picture is taken. This is implemented by turning on and off the illuminator by a command of the microcontroller. Thus, the thermal illumination on the camera is separated, and only the areas of light and shadow are observed to improve the quality.

If there are illuminated areas in the frame, assessing the geometry of the objects under study becomes complicated. It is impossible to estimate the geometry of hot objects because they have a strong thermal glow, which impedes visual determination of the distance to one or another part of the object. To improve the quality of visualization, it is necessary to use an external light source, which will create areas of light and shadow. For the object's own glow to not interfere with observation, it is necessary to apply a differential method of image registration using background subtraction algorithms. To do this, a picture is taken with the illuminator turned off, in which only the thermal illumination of the observed scene is visible. After that, the illuminator is turned on and a second picture is taken. This is implemented by turning on and off the illuminator by a command of the microcontroller. The first image contains an intensity distribution without illumination—background radiation I_b.

The second image I_l contains the sum of the illumination intensities I_f and the background glow I_b. Then in order to obtain the intensity distribution I_f it is necessary to coordinate two frames and subtract the second frame from the first one pixel by pixel:

$$I_f = I_l - I_b \tag{6}$$

As a result, only the light scattered from the illuminator will be shown in the resulting image. This will significantly increase the informativeness of the studied images during visual inspection of surfaces in high-temperature processes. When this mode is enabled, the refresh rate of the image frames on the user interface is halved as a result of combining two frames.

11.4.7 Experimental studies

The stability of communication between the computer and the microcontroller was checked using a test application that sent packets via the exchange protocol and counted the ratio of the number of sent and received messages. For the experiment, packets were sent continuously in accordance with the protocol with a frequency of up to 10 pieces per second. In real working conditions, such a high frequency of the exchange is not expected, but it can be limited to two or three packets per second to update device parameters and request temperatures. Both correct requests according to the communication protocol and artificially damaged packets were sent. In response, it was expected to get packets with a confirmation code for the correct package received, or a response with an error flag of the received message. The one hundred per cent information acquisition has been achieved.

11.5 Results of practical application

This chapter provides examples of practical use of the created system on real problems and shows the obtained results of observing the geometry of high-temperature objects.

To test the operability of the assembled device, a test bench enabling the cooling and power supply of the entire device was assembled. An observation scene was constructed consisting of a dark canvas to create a background and a lighter object of study, a colored rectangle. As can be seen in Figure 11.17a, a rectangular object has strong distortions at standard observation through a camera lens. By enabling the distortion correction function, a straight angle is restored and the true geometry of the object is seen.

To test the algorithms for subtracting the background, an incandescent lamp was installed in front of the edge of the rectangle. It emits just in the visible region, close to infrared radiation. When the lamp is turned on, despite the installed light filter, there is a strong illumination. It becomes impossible to distinguish the edge of the object (Figure 11.18a). When the background subtraction mode is turned on, noises from the installed light source are noticeable, but the boundaries of the object behind the light source become discernible.

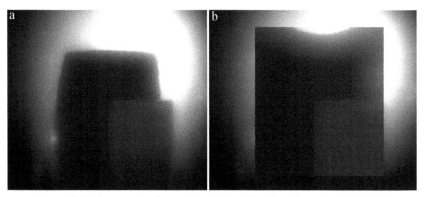

Figure 11.17: An example of correcting spherical distortion of a rectangular object.

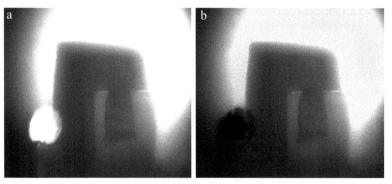

Figure 11.18: An example of correcting spherical distortion of a rectangular object.

In addition, temperature tests during which were carried out the device housing was heated with an open flame from the front side.

11.6 Conclusion

As a result of the work, a software and hardware system for visualizing sedimentation inside the vortex chamber has been developed. The microcontroller software of the hardware part of the software complex of the visualization system has been created to provide control of the entire system. A subsystem for monitoring the device's operability has been implemented. The software has been developed for a personal computer to provide remote monitoring of the image from a video camera and to control of the operating modes of the system. The communication protocol between the microcontroller and the computer is implemented. The microcontroller receives commands from the computer and accepts new operating parameters. The microcontroller also controls the camera shutter, switches on the illuminator according to algorithms that depend on commands coming from the computer, polls temperature sensors and, if critical values are exceeded, signals to the operator on the computer.

Algorithms for background subtraction and correction of distortion on the received images have been implemented. As a result of the developed algorithms, the quality of visualization of the technological process under limited lighting and difficult operating conditions has been enhanced.

The developed software and hardware system for diagnosing deposits inside the vortex chamber has successfully passed full-scale tests for visualizing sedimentation inside the vortex chamber with a temperature of more than 1000°C.

In the future, it is planned to develop software image processing and add correction of the brightness histogram and the mode of combining multiple frames.

Acknowledgments

The study of the flow was carried out within the framework of the IT SB RAS state assignment (project 121032200034-4), and the method development was carried out within the framework of the IT SB RAS state assignment (AAAA-531 A19-119052190039-8).

References

Alaniz-Plata, R., Sergiyenko, O., Flores-Fuentes, W., Tyrsa, V. V., Rodríguez-Quiñonez, J. C., Sepúlveda-Valdez, C. A. et al. 2022. ROS and stereovision collaborative system. In: Sergiyenko, O. (ed.). Optoelectronic Devices in Robotic Systems. Springer, Cham. https://doi.org/10.1007/978-3-031-09791-1_4.

Aronson, K. E., Blinkov, S. N., Brezgin, V. I., Brodov, Yu. M., Kuptsov, V. K., Larionov, I. D. et al. 2015. Heat exchangers of power plants, Educ. El. Publ. UrFU, Yekaterinburg.

Bieker, H. P., Slupphaug, O., and Johansen, T. A. 2006. Real time production optimization of offshore oil and gas production systems: a technology survey SPE 99446, SPE Intelligent Conference and Exhibition, Amsterdam, Netherlands, 11–13 April.

Cormen, Thomas H., Leiserson, Charles E., Rivest, Ronald L., and Stein, Clifford. 2001. Introduction to Algorithms (2nd ed.). MIT Press and McGraw-Hill. pp. 949–955.

[https://datasheets.maximintegrated.com/en/ds/DS18B20.pdf2021]URL: https://datasheets. maximintegrated.com/en/ds/DS18B20.pdf (дата обращения: 01.06.2021).

[https://docs.opencv.org/master/d7/da8/tutorial_table_of_content_ imgproc.html 2021]URL: https:// docs.opencv.org/master/d7/da8/tutorial_table_of_content_ imgproc.html (дата обращения: 01.06.2021).

[https://www.theimagingsource.com/products/board-cameras/gige-monochrome/dmm25gp031ml/ 2021]URL: https://www.theimagingsource.com/products/board-cameras/gige-monochrome/ dmm25gp031ml/ (дата обращения: 01.06.2021).

Irodov, I. E. 2010. Quantum physics. Basic laws: A textbook for university spec. physics. – 3rd ed. ster. – M.: BINOM. Laboratory of Knowledge.

Kalitov, M. A., and Kornishev, N. P. 2019. Computer Simulation of the Formation of Digital Spektrozanal Images Journal of Physics: Conference Series, 1352: 012025.

Lisienko, V. G. 1988. High-temperature heat-technological processes and installations. Minsk, 1988

Migal, V. D., and Migal, V. P. 2018. Methods of technical diagnostics of cars, Moscow, "Forum – infra-M" Publishers.

Petkovic, T., Pribanic, T., Đonlic, M., and D'Apuzzo, N. 2021. Software Synchronization of Projector and Camera for Structured Light 3D Body Scanning, Hometrica Consulting, Ascona, Switzerland.

Shakhrova, M. M. Color photography. Kyiv.

Voronov, A., Borisov, A., and Vatolin, D. 2012. System for automatic detection of distorted scenes in stereo video. Proc. of Sixth International Workshop on Video Processing and Quality Metrics for Consumer Electronics.

Zhang, C., Helferty, J. P., McLennan, G., and Higgins, W. E. 2000. Nonlinear Distortion Correction in Endoscopic Video Images, Penn State University, Department of Electrical Engineering, University Park, PA. - P. 16802.

Zhang, Z. 2000. A flexible new technique for camera calibration, IEEE Transactions on Pattern Analysis and Machine Intelligence, 22(11): 1330–1334.

12

Machine Vision for Astronomical Images using The Modern Image Processing Algorithms Implemented in the CoLiTec Software

Sergii Khlamov,* Vadym Savanevych, Iryna Tabakova,
Vladimir Kartashov, Tetiana Trunova and *Marina Kolendovska*

12.1 Introduction

In general, astronomical images are made by the charge-coupled device (CCD) [Smith 2010] or other cameras/sensors. Also, such astronomical images can be received from other different sources in raw or already processed forms: servers/clusters, historical archives, databases, catalogues, Virtual Observatories (VO) [Vavilova et al. 2016], predefined series of CCD images and even online video streams.

The machine vision (MV) goals related to the astronomical image processing are focused on the following tasks: understanding digital images, filtering [Gonzalez and Woods 2018], analyzing/processing/extraction of high-dimensional information to produce numerical and symbolic data in form as decisions [Burger and Burge 2009], object recognition [Khlamov et al. 2022b], object's image detection [Mykhailova et al. 2014], moving object detection [Khlamov et al. 2017], object's astrometry (estimation of the positional coordinates of object in the image that are converted into position in the sky) [Akhmetov et al. 2020], object's photometry (estimation of the brightness of object in the magnitude) [Kudzej et al. 2019],

Kharkiv National University of Radio Electronics, 14 Nauki Avenue, 61166 Kharkiv, Ukraine.
* Corresponding author: sergii.khlamov@gmail.com

determination of the different parameters of the image and apparent motion of object [Khlamov et al. 2016], reference objects cataloging and selection [Savanevych et al. 2020], visual data cross-matching [Akhmetov et al. 2019b], Wavelet coherence analysis [Baranova et al. 2019], and others.

Because of the huge number of astronomical images, it is very helpful to also use the big data analysis [Starck and Murtagh 2007] and data mining [Khlamov et al. 2022c] approaches before applying the MV techniques. So, information and communication technologies are very closely connected with data and knowledge engineering as well as MV [Steger 2018].

12.2 Big data in astronomy

The world's data and information in the astronomy direction becomes big data and increases very fast to Terascale or even Petascale volume. The reason for this is the development of different ground- and space-based telescopes. In this case, the following question is very important: how to automatically discover useful data from such a big volume of information using various MV techniques [Klette 2014]., and this is a big challenge for astronomers and scientists around the world. To solve such challenges there were a lot of different research was performed, as well as scientific programs/projects initiated. As a result of such research, the created virtual observatories, services, and databases solve the various research problems by usage of the Knowledge Discovery in Databases (KDD) approach [Zhang et al. 2002].

12.3 Knowledge discovery in databases

The Cross-industry standard process for data mining (CRISP-DM) implements a structure of the KDD process, which consists of the following six major stages: selection -> pre-processing -> transformation -> data mining -> interpretation -> evaluation [Grossman et al. 2013]. But from one research field to another research field such sequence of the KDD phases can be modified according to the appropriate purposes and goals of the research field.

The astronomical KDD process includes the following stages of the raw astronomical data transformation till human knowledge: receiving, selecting, storing, cleaning, preprocessing, transforming, data mining, and interpretation or useful data (knowledge) extraction according to the recognition patterns. A high-level schema of the main stages of the KDD process described above is illustrated in Figure 12.1.

As mentioned above the data mining phase is like an investigation step of the KDD process [Luo 2008]. So, in astronomy, it carries out useful data (knowledge) extraction from the input data sets for further use. The data mining uses different intelligent/mathematical methods for transforming the data into an obvious structure using the appropriate attributes and patterns.

The whole astronomical big data analysis flow using the KDD process with all intermediate steps/phases of the data transformation during the scientific analysis and data mining processes is presented in Figure 12.2 [Brescia and Longo 2012].

Astronomical data mining as a part of the KDD process is used in various directions, like statistics [Shvedun and Khlamov 2016], knowledge gathering,

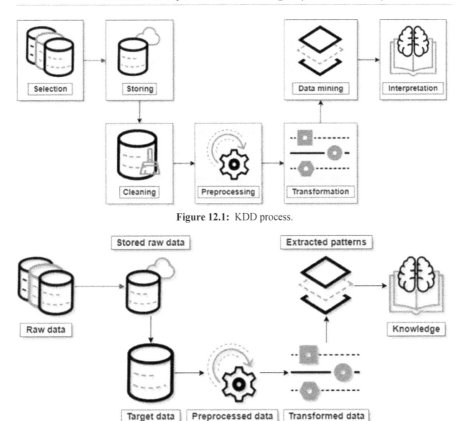

Figure 12.1: KDD process.

Figure 12.2: Astronomical big data analysis flow using the KDD process during the scientific analysis and data mining.

high-performance computing, morphology, machine learning, databases, data visualization, etc.

The data mining process itself can accidentally cause misunderstanding and astronomical data mixing when producing the obvious volume of processing results that can't be reproduced and used for further behavior prediction. In general, such processing results can be received by the verification of too many hypotheses and not properly testing statistical hypotheses [Lehmann et al. 2005].

So, a selection of the correct data only is a recommended or even required pre-processing step in analyzing high-dimensional data sets, videos, or streams before applying the data mining algorithms, and intelligent/mathematical methods to the formed useful data. Such a process of selecting the correct data (mining) is a very time-consuming and complex process. So, to optimize it different techniques are used for the data stream processing, which reduces the execution time and improves the accuracy.

The major intelligent/mathematical methods that are used during data mining in astronomy are described below.

12.3.1 Classification and Identification

The problems with the classification and identification of the astronomical data sets also depend on the data mining problems. Such problems can be resolved in different modes: semi-automatic or automatic.

The classification process is developed for the proper organization of the investigated scientific data, which will be used in the future. Also, it is used to clarify each predefined class of objects in more proper detail. This will help with the prediction of the properties and behaviors of such objects. The classification process is also used with the different astronomical images and spectrums for the separation and defining of the various galaxies by morphology. In general, the classification is performed using the appropriate properties of objects and applying to them the special recognition patterns that will be described in the next sections.

The identification process is developed to find the investigated objects in the different reference sources and catalogs by certain characteristics, like specific spectral class, position, brightness, etc. In all cases, such characteristics should almost be the same between investigated object and object from the reference sources or catalogues that meet the different requirements and have a long history of observations.

In the common case, the classification and identification processes also include cluster analysis and regression applied for different purposes.

Cluster Analysis. One more important process in astronomy is cluster analysis. It is a multidimensional procedure, the purpose of which is to put the investigated objects into the appropriate homogeneous groups. In such a group the investigated objects have a relationship with other relevant objects in the group.

The cluster analysis is only heuristic in its nature, so it is not related to the statistical theory. In this case, cluster analysis requires making the appropriate decisions by individuals and this way affects the whole results of such analysis. Also, it is widely used for more objective classification of the subsets of objects with their further identification with reference sources and catalogues.

Regression. The tags/labels/markers of the astronomical information are real and even continuous in the regression analysis. In astronomy, there were a lot of discoveries made using regression analysis, which was applied to the archives with historical astronomical data. The regression analysis in the common case is implemented on the basis, of Hubble's law and the Hertzsprung-Russell diagram.

12.3.2 Image processing

The different common intelligent/mathematical methods and algorithms are used to process astronomical CCD images [Adam et al. 2019]. But they can also be applied to the usual signal and image processing. Some of such intelligent/mathematical methods and algorithms for the processing of astronomical images and MV purposes are presented below:

- Fast Fourier transform—mathematical algorithm, which calculates the discrete Fourier transform of a sequence, or its inverse variant [Haynal and Haynal 2011].

- Low-pass filtering—data cleaning process for bypassing the different artifacts of the instrumental measurements. Such a filtering algorithm also attenuates signals with frequencies higher than the cutoff frequency and passes only the signals with a frequency lower than a selected cutoff frequency [Karki 2000].

- Deconvolution—the deblurring process of the object movements as well as the atmospheric blurring in astronomical CCD images to improve the processing quality [Campisi and Egiazarian 2017].

- Compression—process for the effective collecting and storing of historical astronomical data in archives/catalogues for the long-term period. This process includes different compressing techniques and algorithms, which are used even during the development of the CCD/detectors for ever-larger image sizes [Pata and Schindler 2015].

- Edge detection—identifying the process of the edges as curves of the investigated objects in the astronomical CCD images. For such identified edges or curves the brightness changes sharply or even has discontinuities [Park and Murphey 2008].

- Corner detection—identifying the process of the various corners of the investigated objects in the astronomical CCD images. Commonly, corner detectors are used within MV techniques to extract certain kinds of features and infer the contents of an astronomical CCD frame [Rosten and Drummond 2006].

- Blob or point detection—identifying process of the various regions of the investigated objects in the astronomical CCD images. Such regions have differences in color and brightness/gray shade, which are comparable with the adjacent regions. The blob is a kind of region with points or even pixels that have the same constant or approximately constant properties, so all such points or even pixels in the blob are the same [Lindeberg 2013].

- Ridge detection—localization process of the various ridges of the investigated objects in the astronomical CCD images. Such a process determines the curves that contain only points with the local maximums of the image function [Lindeberg 1998].

- Segmentation—the partitioning process of an astronomical CCD image of the investigated objects or even the whole CCD frame into the plural image areas/regions, like the various arrays of the image pixels related to such areas/regions [Haigh et al. 2021].

- Pattern recognition—process for the assignment of an image of the investigated astronomical object to a certain astronomical class using selecting the main similarity of properties, features, and parameters that can characterize this certain astronomical class of the investigated astronomical objects [Svensén and Bishop 2007].

- Hough transform—process for extraction of the special feature for discovering the deficient images of the investigated astronomical objects within a certain astronomical class of form using the process of voting [Massone et al. 2015]. Such a voting process works in the parameter space, from which a candidate of the investigated astronomical objects is obtained as a local maximum in the so-called accumulator space. This space is explicitly constructed by the computing method for the Hough transform. The classical Hough transform algorithm is focused on line detection in the series of CCD images. Also, it is very useful for the detection of the investigated moving astronomical objects that have their own image in each CCD image in the series.

12.4 Astronomical big data sources

Such a big volume of observational and historical astronomical information requires a lot of free storage space in hard disks, servers, clusters, etc. All these astronomical data can't be collected on one single server, which will be universal and public for the scientific society. So, the disturbed systems, online catalogues with public access, and cloud technologies should be used to resolve this complicated issue of storing astronomical information.

The Virtual Observatory (VO) concept becomes more and more popular and important in astronomy, as a platform for easy access to the astronomical information stored in the different digital catalogues, archives, and servers [Vavilova et al. 2020]. The International Virtual Observatory Alliance (IVOA) has provided the different VO standards and protocols for the realization and development of the VO. Also, IVOA has prepared special methods and algorithms for data interoperability. On a regular basis, the IVOA organizes the needed collaboration between the scientific society, information providers, and researchers.

There are a lot of astronomical scientific programs, communities, and data centers that create and maintain the different image archives, catalogues with common astronomical information for KDD processing and data mining.

For example, the SIMBAD database contains scientific data about more than 3 million astronomical objects [Kuhn et al. 2022]. It is based on the identifiers of 7.5 million astronomical objects. The SIMBAD database is continuously updated by the collaborative effort between all astronomical communities. The DAME (DAta Mining & Exploration) research contains a set of various web services that perform a scientific analysis of a big volume of astronomical information [Cavuoti et al. 2012].

The KDD, data mining, and MV tasks for data analysis, gathering and visualization [Akhmetov et al. 2019a] from the big astronomical catalogues become more and more difficult. Because such big catalogues contain billions of astronomical objects and are continuously updated with new scientific data from fresh massive data sets, such as WISE (Wide-field Infrared Survey Explorer) [Wright et al. 2010], 2MASS (Two Micron All Sky Survey) [Skrutskie et al. 2006], ESA Euclid space mission [Racca et al. 2016], ESA GAIA (Global Astrometric Interferometer for Astrophysics) space mission [Carry et al. 2021].

Collaboration of the new surveys projects and development of the new networks of the automated ground-based or space-based observational systems equipped with different large CCD cameras with a wide field of view (FOV) lead to a fast growth of the scientific information. Some of them are the Large Synoptic Survey Telescope (LSST) [Borne et al. 2008], Pan-STARRS (Panoramic Survey Telescope and Rapid Response System) [Kaiser et al. 2002], and Thirty Meter Telescope (TMT) [Nelson and Sanders 2008].

For example, the Pan-STARRS currently consists of two 1.8-m aperture telescopes (see Figure 1.3). Each such telescope has a FOV of 3 square angular degrees and is equipped with the largest in the world CCD camera, which produces ~ 1.400 million pixels per astronomical image., and each such image requires ~ 2 Gb of free disk storage and the exposure time of one shot can be up to one minute.

The time for saving such astronomical images to disk storage is about one minute or even more. Totally, more than 10 Tb of scientific information is obtained every observational night and such data are taken as an online stream on a continuous basis.

The LSST currently is under development. It is a reflecting telescope with an 8.4 meters primary mirror, which is part of a wide-field survey. The design of each telescope includes 3 mirrors. Both have a very wide FOV of 3.5 square angular degrees. The resolution of the equipped CCD camera is 3.2 Gpixel (see Figure 12.4).

In the future LSST plans to take astronomical images every few nights by observing the whole sky. In such case, according to the planned LSST productivity,

Figure 12.3: Pan-STARRS.

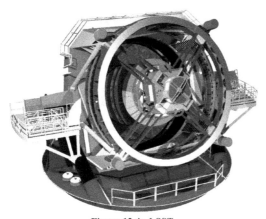

Figure 12.4: LSST.

there will be more than 200 thousand of uncompressed astronomical images per year, which will be more than 1.3 petabytes of scientific information.

It will be a big challenge for LSST to manage, the data mining, and processing of such big astronomical data in an effective way. The approximate requirements for servers and clusters for LSST are about 100 Tflops of power and about 15 Pb of disk storage.

The TMT currently is under development. It will be an extremely large telescope (ELT), which is equipped with the segmented Ritchey-Chrétien telescope with a 492-segment primary mirror with a diameter of 30 meters (see Figure 12.5).

The secondary mirror of TMT will be with a diameter of 3.1 meters. The design of such a telescope is adapted for the near-ultraviolet to mid-infrared (0.31 to 28 μm wavelengths) observations. Also, it will help in correcting image blur because of the adaptive optics.

The TMT will be at the highest altitude of all the proposed ELTs, and it is supported on the government level by several nations. In the future TMT plans to collect each night about 90 Tb of the scientific astronomical data.

There are a lot more such big telescopes, which produce a big volume of very huge astronomical images, like the Very Large Telescope (VLT) [Beuzit et al. 2019], the Canada-France-Hawaii Telescope (CFHT) in Hawaii, which is equipped with the MegaCam camera with a resolution of 16000 × 16000 (32 bits per pixel) [Ilbert et al. 2006].

The Sloan Digital Sky Survey (SDSS) is the most successful sky survey in astronomical history. The SDSS includes the most detailed Universe 3D maps with deep multi-color images of the third part of the whole sky, and spectra for more than 3 million astronomical objects [Eisenstein et al. 2011].

So, in multi-directional astronomy, the main goal is to collect and merge such big scientific data and astronomical information received from the big telescopes and surveys for further processing, which uses different technologies for data mining,

Figure 12.5: Thirty meter telescope.

MV, short time series analysis [Kirichenko et al. 2020], and even Wavelet coherence analysis [Dadkhah et al. 2019] with the possibility of the further forecasting [Dombrovska et al. 2018].

12.5 CoLiTec Software

The modern Collection Light Technology (CoLiTec) software was developed using the described above technologies and approaches for big data processing, data mining, and MV. In the astronomy direction, the CoLiTec software is designed to perform the following main stages of MV and image processing: pre-processing (astronomical data collection -> worst data rejection -> useful data extraction -> classification -> clustering -> background alignment -> brightness equalization), processing (recognition patterns applying -> machine vision -> object's image detection -> astrometry -> photometry -> tracks detection), knowledge extraction (astronomical objects to be discovered, tracks parameters for the investigation, light curves of the variable stars).

More features of the CoLiTec software are detailed described below:

- processing images with the very wide FOV (< 10 degrees^2);
- calibration and cosmetic correction in automated mode using the appropriate calibration master frames and their creation if necessary;
- brightness equalization and background alignment of the images in series using the mathematical inverse median filter;
- rejection of the bad and unclear observations and measurements of the investigated astronomical objects in automated mode;
- fully automatic robust algorithm of the astrometric and photometric reduction of the investigated astronomical objects;
- detection of the faint investigated astronomical moving objects in a series of CCD images with a signal-to-noise ratio (SNR) of more than 2.5 in automated mode;
- detection of the very fast investigated astronomical objects (< 40.0 pix./frame) in automated mode;
- detection of the astronomical objects with near-zero apparent motion (from 0.7 pix./frame) in automated mode;
- rejection of the investigated astronomical objects with bad and corrupted measurements in automated mode;
- viewer of the processing results with simple and understandable graphical user interface (GUI) by the LookSky software;
- confirmation of the most interesting astronomical objects at the night of their preliminary discovery;
- multi-threaded processing support;
- multi-cores systems support;
- support of managing the individual threads and processes;

- processing pipeline managed by the On-line Data Analysis System (OLDAS);
- deciding system of the processing results, which allows to adapt the end-user settings and inform the user about the processing results at each stage in the pipeline;
- subject mediator as a major part of the data control in the pipeline during processing.

In the next section, the technical implementation of the CoLiTec software is provided with some major and interesting details of such implementation with the appropriate screenshots.

12.6 Technical implementation

The CoLiTec software is a cross-platform software, which is a package of the appropriate tools for the near real-time processing of the series of images with the investigated astronomical objects for their discovery, identification, and tracking.

All such tools from the package are related to the various steps of astronomical machine vision and image processing and all of them were developed in scope of the CoLiTec research project [Khlamov and Savanevych 2020].

The CoLiTec software and the appropriate user guides for its components can be requested from the official website at https://colitec.space.

12.6.1 Minimum system requirements

The CoLiTec software has the following minimum system requirements for the installation:

- Windows system from 7 (32, 64-bit) version, UNIX system (32, 64-bit);
- CPU more than 1.5 GHz;
- RAM more than 2 GB;
- Free storage space more than 400 Mb;
- Installed Java Runtime Environment (JRE) more than 1.8.0.77 version;
- Minimum resolution more than 1360×600;
- Access to the Internet with no proxy use.

12.6.2 Supported formats of files

The CoLiTec software supports the astronomical files in Flexible Image Transport System (FITS) format using the following extensions: *.fit, *.fits, *.fts, *.FIT, *.FITS, *.FTS. Such FITS format is commonly used for the transformation, transfer, and archiving of astronomical data.

The FITS format was developed by the National Aeronautics and Space Administration (NASA) [Pence et al. 2010] and is accepted as an international astronomical standard and is used by many astronomical and scientific organizations, like International Astronomical Union (IAU) [Andersen et al. 2019], and other national and international organizations that deal with the astronomy or related scientific fields.

The FITS format is commonly used for storing the data without the image, like spectrums, photons list, data cubes or even structured data, such as databases with multiple tables. The FITS format includes many provisions to describe the photometric, astrometric, and spatial calibration, as well as image metadata.

The structure of the FITS file consists of a header with metadata and a binary image. The header, body, and structure of astronomical files should be filled according to the standards provided by NASA. The example of a header with metadata of the real astronomical FITS file is presented in Figure 12.6.

```
SIMPLE   =                    T
BITPIX   =                   16 /8 unsigned int, 16 & 32 int, -32 & -64 real
NAXIS    =                    2 /number of axes
NAXIS1   =                  512 /fastest changing axis
NAXIS2   =                  512 /next to fastest changing axis
BSCALE   =    1.0000000000000000 /physical = BZERO + BSCALE*array_value
BZERO    =   32768.000000000000 /physical = BZERO + BSCALE*array_value
DATE-OBS= '2017-03-30T21:39:16' /YYYY-MM-DDThh:mm:ss observation start, UT
EXPTIME  =   60.000000000000000 /Exposure time in seconds
EXPOSURE=   60.000000000000000 /Exposure time in seconds
SET-TEMP=  -40.000000000000000 /CCD temperature setpoint in C
CCD-TEMP=  -40.062500000000000 /CCD temperature at start of exposure in C
XPIXSZ   =   48.000000000000000 /Pixel Width in microns (after binning)
YPIXSZ   =   48.000000000000000 /Pixel Height in microns (after binning)
XBINNING=                    2 /Binning factor in width
YBINNING=                    2 /Binning factor in height
XORGSUBF=                    0 /Subframe X position in binned pixels
YORGSUBF=                    0 /Subframe Y position in binned pixels
READOUTM= '1 MPPS  ' /          Readout mode of image
FILTER  = 'V       ' /          Filter used when taking image
IMAGETYP= 'Light Frame' /       Type of image
OBJECT  = 'DO Dra  '
OBJCTRA = '11 43 38' /          Nominal Right Ascension of center of image
OBJCTDEC= '+71 41 20' /         Nominal Declination of center of image
OBJCTALT= ' 67.3413' /          Nominal altitude of center of image
OBJCTAZ = '  0.2784' /          Nominal azimuth of center of image
OBJCTHA = ' -0.0226' /          Nominal hour angle of center of image
SITELAT = '48 56 06' /          Latitude of the imaging location
SITELONG= '22 16 27' /          Longitude of the imaging location
JD      =    2457843.4022685187 /Julian Date at start of exposure
JD-HELIO=    2457843.4039910869 /Heliocentric Julian Date at exposure midpoint
AIRMASS =    1.0833536254388081 /Relative optical path length through atmosphere
FOCALLEN=    9000.0000000000000 /Focal length of telescope in mm
APTDIA  =    1000.0000000000000 /Aperture diameter of telescope in mm
APTAREA =    777544.20340061188 /Aperture area of telescope in mm^2
SWCREATE= 'MaxIm DL Version 5.12' /Name of software that created the image
SBSTDVER= 'SBFITSEXT Version 1.0' /Version of SBFITSEXT standard in effect
TELESCOP= 'VNT     ' /          telescope used to acquire this image
INSTRUME= 'FLI     ' /          instrument or camera used
OBSERVER= 'DPV     '
NOTES   = '       '
FLIPSTAT= '       '
SWOWNER = 'Amigo   ' /          Licensed owner of software
END
```

Figure 12.6: The example of a header with metadata of the real astronomical FITS file.

The header size is 2880 bytes and contains the list of human-readable metadata in fixed string form of 80 symbols. Each string is an ASCII [Elshoush et al. 2022] stroke, which contains the pair with key and value, and has the common form: "*KEYNAME = value/comment string*".

Each header block should be ended with the special key "*END*" with the empty value. The header of astronomical files should use the common mandatory and recommended keywords.

There is a minimum list of the required keywords to make the header and the whole FITS file valid. They are:

- "*SIMPLE*" (file conforms to FITS standard);
- "*BITPIX*" (bitrade of FITS file, bits per pixel);
- "*NAXIS*" (number of axes);
- "*NAXIS1*" (number of points along axe 1);
- "*NAXIS2*" (number of points along axe 2);
- "*END*".

For the correct processing of the astronomical files, the CoLiTec software implements the official NASA FITS input/output (I/O) library for the selected programming language for development.

12.6.3 *Main components*

The CoLiTec software contains a lot of processing components and mathematical modules on the various architecture layers: database, computation process, processing pipeline, user interaction, reporting, and visualization. Detailed information about these various architecture layers of the CoLiTec software is described in a book chapter [Khlamov and Savanevych 2020]. The main modules of the CoLiTec software are provided below.

CoLiTec Control Center. The CoLiTec Control Center (3C) is a main module with GUI for interaction with the end user and managing/controlling the computation processing of all available types of astronomical information. 3C allows the user to launch the various stages of the processing pipeline by using the appropriate sub-modules.

The user interface of main window of the 3C module of the CoLiTec software is presented in Figure 1.7, where 1 – Management buttons; 2 – Modes for processing; 3 – Area for processing; 4 – Button to open the window with log information during the processing; 5 – Settings.

Such sub-modules have different input and output data control on the various levels of architecture and can write the log information (debug, info, warning, error) during the processing of astronomical data in the pipeline. All such log information is available in the special pop-up window with processing messages, which are immediately updated. An example of the log information in the window of the 3C module is presented in Figure 12.8.

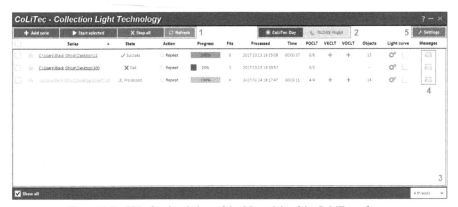

Figure 12.7: GUI of main window of the 3C module of the CoLiTec software.

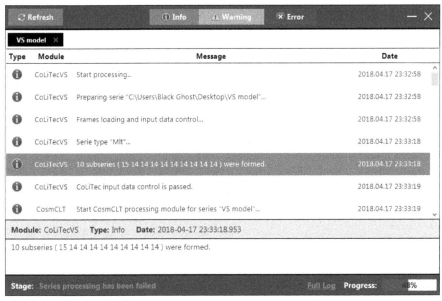

Figure 12.8: Log information in the window of the 3C module.

The CoLiTec Control Center was developed using the Java programming language. The IntelliJ IDEA was used as the cross-platform integrated development environment (IDE). The reason of selecting the Java programming language as a preferred language for the development is the ability for customization of the GUI and the operating system (OS) cross-platforming. So, the whole GUI of the 3C module has a modern Windows 10 style and is pretty simple. The JavaFX visualization library was used for the GUI creation.

ThresHolds. Each processing pipeline, which includes a lot of processing components and mathematical modules, should have a big volume of processing parameters to be set. Before the first processing of the astronomical data, it is required to perform the initial set-up of the processing parameters. These parameters can be set using a module called settings editor ThresHolds. It is available for launching right from the settings window of the 3C module.

The ThresHolds module was also developed using the Java programming language and the JavaFX library in the cross-platform IDE IntelliJ IDE. The next main parameters for the initial setup should be set:

- astronomical catalogues for photometry and astrometry;
- basic information about the observer, observatory, telescope, CCD camera, etc.;
- parameters for the background alignment, brightness equalization of images in series, and for their calibration (master frames);
- settings for the appropriate reports to be sent to the different astronomical services.

There are some examples of pages with processing parameters to be set using the settings editor ThresHolds presented in Figure 12.9.

ThresHolds has the option to show the amateur or professional set of parameters. The professional set of parameters includes the list of configurable variables that are used in the developed mathematical and computational methods and algorithms to tune the accuracy of processing.

LookSky. One more main module with GUI is the frames viewer LookSky. It is designed for a visualization of the raw and processed astronomical data for further analysis of them.

Below is a more detailed list of the LookSky features:

- visual analysis of the moving astronomical objects (satellites, asteroids, and comets) detected by the CoLiTec software in automation mode;
- deleting the falsely detected astronomical objects;
- re-analyzing of previously unknown objects, because it can be a new discovery;
- hand measuring of the astronomical objects (satellites, asteroids, and comets) that were not detected in automation mode;
- hand measuring of the investigated variable star;
- creating a special task file for the investigated variable star;
- selecting the comparison stars for the light curve creation of the investigated variable star;
- tuning visualization parameters (brightness, contrast, color palette, etc.);
- working with a list of the astronomical objects, which were found by the CoLiTec software based on the processed series;
- generating and sending a report for the entire list of series.

The user interface of the main window of the LookSky module of the CoLiTec software is presented in Figure 12.10.

The LookSky software was developed using the Delphi programming language. The Lazarus was used as the cross-platform IDE. Using such astronomical frames

Figure 12.9: ThresHolds settings editor module of the CoLiTec software.

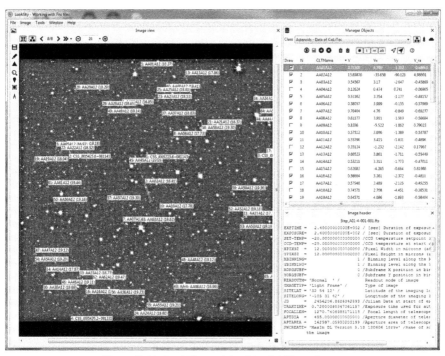

Figure 12.10: LookSky module of the CoLiTec software.

viewer, the results after processing by the CoLiTec software can be visualized, and analyzed right after their appearance.

12.7 Astronomical data mining

The list of astronomical big data sources significantly grows as well as the scientific information, which is produced by them. So, the ability to analyze such astronomical big data is lagging. In this case, interest in using KDD and data mining approaches is growing for collecting and analyzing such a big volume of astronomical information.

The CoLiTec software is specially developed with implementing such KDD and data mining approaches for MV and processing of astronomical images [Borne 2008]. It allows the processing of the input astronomical data in the near-real-time mode. The CoLiTec software is a very complex system for processing the various astronomical big data, which includes the various features for KDD, data mining, and MV that are based on the developed mathematical and computational methods.

Also, the CoLiTec software includes a very important part of data mining, called Online Data Analysis System (OLDAS). Using the OLDAS, the astronomical data sets and even data streams can be processed as soon as they are successfully saved right from the telescope to the storage or uploaded to the server/cluster. The OLDAS allows for speeding up the processing of astronomical information by preventing data blocking and collision.

Using the implemented OLDAS, the CoLiTec software provides an ability for the near real-time process of the astronomical big data, which includes the investigated variable stars, because the photometry process of them requires such near real-time processing. This is needed for the online creation and updating of the light curve for the appropriate variable star to analyze the value changes of their brightness. Also, the OLDAS provides immediate notification about emerging issues for the end user. The processing stages of the CoLiTec software with implementation of the KDD and data mining approaches are described below.

Pre-Processing. As a pre-processing stage, the CoLiTec software has the special OLDAS mode that allows the processing of the input astronomical big data received from the different archives/clusters/servers/sources in the various modes (offline, archives, online). The raw astronomical information is moderated and analyzed before starting the machine vision and computational process. The moderation step includes a rejection of the corrupted and unsupported astronomical frames. So, only useful scientific-related data is selected from the input astronomical big data for further machine vision and computational processes. In case, when the input astronomical data is encrypted, the CoLiTec software applies the appropriate decryption algorithm according to the security and data protection protocols [Buslov et al. 2018].

Clustering. The prepared useful scientific-related data from the input astronomical big data is separated into clusters using the special attributes in the astronomical frame's header, such as telescope name, equatorial coordinates of the FOV center, main parameters of the telescope, filter type, investigated object, etc. The prepared useful scientific-related data from the input astronomical information based on such special attributes are split into subsets with common identical information and stored at the various distributed servers/clusters/networks.

Classification. After the clustering process (dividing the processes of similar information into servers/networks), the created subsets of useful scientific-related data are classified by the application of a known pattern of the raw astronomical files, which is specified in the FITS standard described above. The main part of the FITS format is metadata, which includes various useful helpful scientific-related data. Then the digital files that were classified as astronomical FITS files, are sent to the processing pipeline for further machine vision and image processing.

Identification. The identification step follows next after the classification step in the processing pipeline. In this step, all previously classified astronomical FITS files will be processed. There are various forms of astronomical FITS files: raw light frames, raw service frames, and master service frames. The raw light frames are the images of investigated part of the sky made by the telescope with an astronomical object under study. The raw service frames are the images, which can be used for the frame's calibration with the following types: bias, dark, dark flat, flat. The master service frames are the images combined and created from the raw service frames in accordance with their types from a collection of them.

In this case, the appropriate master service frames are created from the existing raw service frames during the processing pipeline. Such created master service frames will be used for further frame's calibration as a precondition part of the astronomical machine vision and image processing. After that, the raw light frames will be sent to the computational process in the processing pipeline.

Processing. The OLDAS mode includes two main stages for the machine vision and image processing during the calculating process in the pipeline: intraframe and interframe processing. The detailed list of modules from the processing pipeline is presented in Figure 12.11.

The intraframe processing stage is designed for an estimation of the positional coordinates (astrometry) and photometry of all astronomical objects (asteroids/comets, stars, galaxies) in the CCD frame during their shooting. Also, the calibration, background alignment, brightness equalization, and pattern recognition processes are performed at the intraframe processing stage as a precondition before the astrometry.

The inter-frame processing stage is designed for the detection of moving astronomical objects and the estimation of their trajectories and their parameters. A core of the CoLiTec software implements the preliminary detection of astronomical objects by an accumulation of statistics by using the multi-valued transformation of the object's coordinates, which is corresponded to the Hough space-time transformation.

12.8 Astronomical machine vision

Each astronomical CCD image consists of coarse-grained and fine-grained image components, which are presented in Figure 12.12. Each of such components has a different nature of origin.

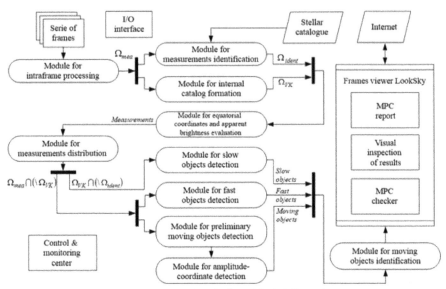

Figure 12.11: Processing pipeline of the CoLiTec software.

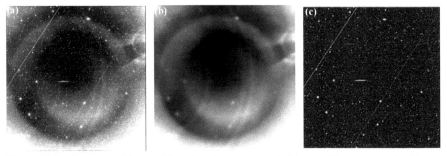

Figure 12.12: Astronomical image: (a) – original raw astronomical image; (b) – coarse-grained image component; (c) – fine-grained image component

In the common case, the coarse-grained image component is related to the backlight of the image during the astronomical observation at the full Moon, or at the moment of the sunset or sunrise. Such a backlight occupies a significant part of the CCD image.

The fine-grained image component is commonly related to the original images of astronomical objects (stars, galaxies, asteroids, comets). The size of the fine-grained image component is about 5–10 pixels and does not exceed 50–60 pixels.

However, there are a lot of different observational conditions that affect how the astronomical object will look in the CCD image. Some of them are telescope tracking mode, side wind, weather in general, mechanical failure of diurnal tracking, vignetting, telescope coma, and others.

So, under unfavorable observational conditions, images of individual astronomical objects or even the entire CCD image can be blurred [Khlamov et al. 2022d] or corrupted. There are some examples of corrupted astronomical images presented in Figure 12.13.

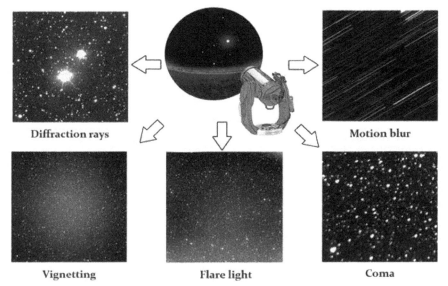

Figure 12.13: Different types of corrupted astronomical images.

This circumstance significantly reduces the quality indicators of detection of the astronomical objects under investigation as well as the accuracy of the computational processes.

There are different common intelligent/mathematical methods and algorithms used for the MV and image processing of astronomical CCD images. Below are described only those methods and algorithms, which are implemented in the CoLiTec software.

12.8.1 Brightness equalization

To fix the corruptions of astronomical images described above, astronomical image calibration, brightness equalization, matched filtration [Khlamov et al. 2023], and background alignment should be done to increase the quality of such CCD images before the machine vision.

The CoLiTec software performs the next operations for the astronomical image calibration, brightness equalization, and background alignment:

- alignment of the astronomical CCD image's background and reducing of the redundant noises by applying the inverse median filtration at the edges of the image;
- searching for the required raw service frames (bias, dark, dark flat, flat) for calibration if they are not predefined;
- creating the required master service-frames (master bias, master-dark, master flat) from the raw service frames (bias, dark, dark flat, flat);
- pixel subtraction of the master dark frame from the raw astronomical CCD image;
- pixel division of the received astronomical CCD image on the master flat frame;

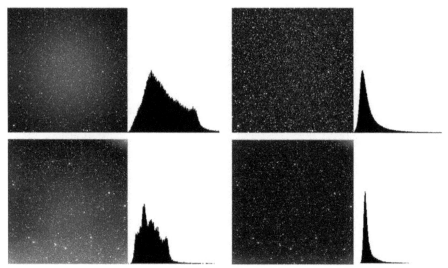

Figure 12.14: Examples of the corrupted astronomical CCD images with their histograms before (left) and after (right) brightness equalization by the CoLiTec software.

- dividing the received astronomical CCD image into the image fragments to save the processor and memory resources during image processing and to speed up it;
- applying the inverse median filtration to each image fragment;
- bonding of the received astronomical CCD image fragments into one image.

Some examples of the corrupted astronomical CCD images with their histograms before (left) and after (right) performing the brightness equalization by the CoLiTec software are presented below in Figure 12.14.

12.8.2 *Pattern recognition*

Pattern recognition techniques are the base of the machine vision prospects in astronomical image processing. Such techniques are used for an assignment of the initial input astronomical information to a certain class or group by selecting the important and major features, which characterize this certain class or group [Howard 2007]. So, the pattern recognition techniques help with the image classification of all investigated astronomical objects in the entire CCD image.

In general, the astronomical CCD images are monochrome and have a simpler graphical structure compared to the color images. So, they can easily be used for MV and pattern recognition prospects [Kirichenko et al. 2021].

The following different recognition patterns can be applied to the various object types in the astronomical CCD images, which are received as the real series of CCD images/videos or the online data streams [Khlamov et al. 2022a].

Point Object. The astronomical point object in the CCD image is the object, which has a round shape on its edges. The such astronomical object has only one brightness peak in their center. The spatial domain of the CCD image with the astronomical point objects (left) and its frequency domain (right) are presented in Figure 1.15.

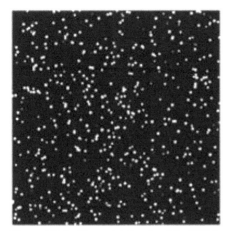

Figure 12.15: The spatial domain of the CCD image with the astronomical point objects (left) and its frequency domain (right).

Extended (Long) Object. The astronomical extended (long) object in the CCD image is the object, which has a round shape at the end of its form and has at least a 1:4 and more semi-axes ratio. The such astronomical object has several brightness peaks that can lie along a line in the direction of the object. Almost always brightness peaks are located very close to each other.

The spatial domain of the CCD image with the astronomical long objects (left) and its frequency domain (right) are presented in Figure 1.16.

Blurred Object. The astronomical blurred object in the CCD image is the object, which has a round shape at the end of its form and has up to 1:4 semi-axes ratio. The such astronomical object has similar properties to extended (long) object but has different origin and nature. The reasons for the formation of such astronomical images with blurred objects are some chromatic, monochromatic aberrations of the

Figure 12.16: The spatial domain of the CCD image with the astronomical long objects (left) and its frequency domain (right).

telescope system, telescope coma, different fails in the diurnal tracking, and others [Schroeder 1999].

The blurred astronomical object as well as the long object has several brightness peaks that can lie along a line in the direction of the object. The main difference is that such brightness peaks are equidistant at the same distance from each other.

The spatial domain of the CCD image with the astronomical blurred objects (left) and its frequency domain (right) are presented in Figure 12.17.

Object With Flare or Intersection with Another Object. This type of recognition pattern for astronomical objects is not so general but can be presented as a conjunction of other recognition patterns of the astronomical objects, e.g., point, extended (long) or blurred objects. The major singularity of it is the crossing with other astronomical objects in the CCD image where the brightness of the neighbor object is more than the brightness of the investigated astronomical object.

Another case of the appearance of such superfluous flare is the very long exposure time. Because the root of such appearance is that more and more photons hit the same pixel in the CCD matrix and overfull the pixel's brightness value in the buffer. This case is very complicated for machine vision and pattern recognition in the automated mode because the brightness peaks of several objects that have an intersection with each other are unspecified and mixed.

The spatial domain of the CCD image with the astronomical objects with flare and intersection with another object (left) and its frequency domain (right) are presented in Figure 1.18.

Applying the appropriate correct recognition pattern to the detected image of the investigated astronomical object in the CCD image simplifies the further process of machine vision, image recognition, and image processing.

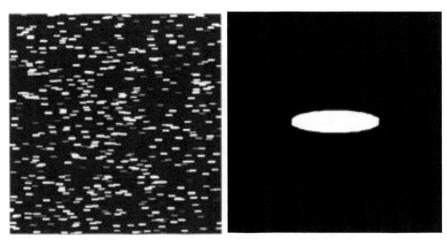

Figure 12.17: The spatial domain of the astronomical CCD image with the blurred objects (left) and its frequency domain (right).

Figure 12.18: The spatial domain of CCD image with the astronomical objects with flare and intersection with another object (left) and its frequency domain (right).

12.8.3 Astrometry

The recognition patterns can be applied both to one astronomical object and even to the whole astronomical CCD image if it does not have instabilities and corruption in any parts of it. But before applying the appropriate correct recognition pattern to the investigated astronomical object in the CCD frame, the image of a such an astronomical object should be detected.

It means, that the image signals of the investigated astronomical object should be analyzed against the noise flat substrate in the CCD frame plane [Savanevych et al. 2022b]. An example of the asteroid's signal in the image is presented in Figure 12.19.

As described above, an analysis of the image signals should be performed in accordance with the appropriate magnitude or brightness peak of the investigated astronomical object. That is why the extraction of the noise flat substrate, which is performed during the brightness equalization, is also a very important step in the MV of astronomical objects.

The main goal of an astrometry process is to determine the positional coordinates of the investigated astronomical object in the CCD frame and recalculate these coordinates from the image plane into the stellar positional coordinates in the sky.

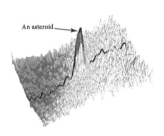
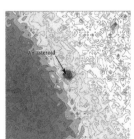
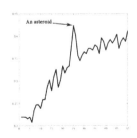

Figure 12.19: Image signal of the astronomical object (asteroid) on the noise flat substrate.

Regarding MV purposes, astrometry means the ability to find the positional coordinates of an image of the investigated astronomical object in the CCD frame and observe/track this object in other CCD frames in a series.

Implementation. To perform the astrometry of all investigated astronomical objects in the CCD frame the CoLiTec software implements the specially developed iteration method for the coordinates estimate. Such a method was developed with using the subpixel Gaussian model of the discrete image of an astronomical object as a basis [Savanevych et al. 2015a].

The developed method uses the continuous parameters (astronomical object coordinates) in the discrete observational space (set of the pixel's potential/ amplitude) in the astronomical CCD frame. In this developed model, a type of positional coordinates distribution of the photons hitting a pixel in the CCD frame is known a priori, while the associated parameters are determined from the real image of the investigated astronomical object in CCD frame.

The developed method based on the subpixel Gaussian model is more flexible in adapting to the different forms of an image of the astronomical object or to its recognition pattern (see above). Such implementation in the CoLiTec software has a higher accuracy of determined measurements along with a low determining complexity due to the maximum likelihood method. The last one was used for obtaining best fit instead of the ordinary least-squares (OLS) method and the Levenberg-Marquardt algorithm for the minimization of the quadratic form.

Based on the developed methods, the CoLiTec software provides a high efficiency of the astronomical information processing as well as a high measuring accuracy of the investigated astronomical object's position.

Comparison. In this subsection, a comparison of the functional features and statistical characteristics of the positional measurements is provided between the CoLiTec and Astrometrica [Raab 2012] software using the same test set of astronomical data [Savanevych et al. 2015b].

The comparison of the functional features of the CoLiTec and Astrometrica software is presented in Table 12.1, where 1 – CoLiTec, 2 – Astrometrica. Table 12.1 shows that the CoLiTec software has much more advantages compared with Astrometrica software.

To perform a comparison of the statistical characteristics of the positional measurements between the CoLiTec (v.1.8) and Astrometrica (v.4.11) software, the set of 2002 positional measurements was selected from the same series of astronomical CCD frames. The positional measurements include the determined stellar position for two coordinates: right accession (RA) and declination (DE). The root mean square (RMS) deviation was selected as a statistical characteristic for comparison.

The comparison of the distribution of the deviations of positional measurements of the numbered astronomical objects by SNR ranges performed by the CoLiTec and Astrometrica software is presented in Table 12.2.

A comparison from the Table 12.2 demonstrates that the limits of more realistic positional measurements for the CoLiTec software are wider than those for Astrometrica one for the measurements with the extremely low SNR.

Table 12.1: Comparison table with functional features of the CoLiTec and Astrometrica software.

Functional features	1	2
The ability for quick selection of the user's set of parameters	+	+
Calibration of the astronomical CCD frames	+	+
Image transformation tool and settings editor	+	+
Astrometric reduction of wide FOV (> 2°)	+	–
Supporting of local astrometric and photometric catalogs	+	+
List of supported local astrometric and photometric catalogs	Tycho-2 USNO A2.0 USNO B1.0 XPM UCAC3 UCAC4	USNO A2.0 USNO B1.0 UCAC3 UCAC4 CMC-14 CMC-15 PPMXL
Supporting of online astrometric and photometric catalogs	+	+
List of supported online astrometric and photometric catalogs	USNO B1.0 NOMAD UCAC4 UCAC5 SDSS DR9 APASS DR9 Tycho-2 GAIA-DR2	USNO B1.0 NOMAD UCAC3 UCAC4 CMC-14 CMC-15 PPMXL GAIA-DR2
The possibility to split astrometric and photometric catalogs for further using	+	–
Inserting the coordinates information (WCS) into the header of CCD frame	+	+
Astrometric reduction of the extended (long) objects	+	–
Track & Stack technique	+	+
Easy way to measure the astronomical object in CCD frame	+	+
Magnifying loupe for zooming	+	+
Search of moving astronomical objects in automated mode	+	+
Search of moving faint astronomical objects (SNR > 2.5) in automated mode	+	–
Automatic processing pipeline	+	+
Visual analysis of the detected moving astronomical objects in automated mode	+	+
Creating of the processed data with astrometric measurements in the Minor Planet Center (MPC) format	+	+
The possibility to send the received measurements to MPC from the GUI	+	+
The possibility to save the processing results (detected real astronomical objects and rejected false objects)	+	–
Identification of the detected moving astronomical objects with a local database MPCORB	–	+

Table 12.1 contd. ...

...*Table 12.1 contd.*

Identification of the detected moving astronomical objects with an online database MPCORB (MPC)	+	–
Identification of the stationary astronomical objects with a database of the variable stars (VSX)	+	–
Identification of the stationary astronomical objects with a database of the galaxies (HyperLeda)	+	–
The possibility to view the known real astronomical objects from catalogs as well as detected objects	+	+
Multicomponent architecture (ability to include the individual modules inside the processing pipeline)	+	–
Open source availability	–	–

Table 12.2: Comparison table with distribution of deviations of positional measurements of numbered asteroids by SNR ranges by the CoLiTec and Astrometrica software.

SNR		Number of measurements	Astrometrica		CoLiTec	
min	max		RMS RA	RMS DE	RMS RA	RMS DE
1.8	3.5	119	0.97	1.02	0.78	0.68
3.5	6.8	804	1.10	0.95	0.62	0.49
6.8	10.1	397	0.39	0.27	0.46	0.32
10.1	13.4	215	0.26	0.18	0.26	0.20
13.4	16.7	130	0.23	0.16	0.21	0.18
16.7	20.0	69	0.28	0.16	0.24	0.16
20.0	23.3	65	0.16	0.13	0.15	0.13
23.3	26.6	49	0.16	0.10	0.15	0.11
26.6	29.9	36	0.14	0.09	0.26	0.14
29.9	33.2	26	0.12	0.08	0.11	0.10
33.2	36.5	13	0.10	0.06	0.10	0.09
36.5	274.8	79	0.22	0.17	0.22	0.11
Total/Average		2002	0.77	0.67	0.50	0.39

12.8.4 *Photometry*

After detecting the image signals of the investigated astronomical object against the noise flat substrate in the CCD frame plane and determining its positional coordinates, the determining of the object's apparent brightness (magnitude) should be done. Regarding the MV purposes, photometry means the ability to determine the magnitude of an image of the investigated astronomical object in the CCD frame and maintain the magnitude determination of this object in other CCD frames in a series.

In astronomy, photometry is one of the important research directions. The scientific information about the photometric variability of the different types of stars/variable stars and other transient objects is necessary for understanding the structures and evolution of our galaxy as well as the processes occurring in them. The most interesting transient objects are microlensed stars, supernovas, optical flashes associated with gamma-ray bursts and variable stars of different origins, extrasolar planets (exoplanets), etc. Also, with the help of photometric variability, the distances to distant objects such as globular clusters and close galaxies, as well as their luminosity, can be determined.

The photometry process in the scope of machine vision means the analyzing of time series of astronomical observations with determining the apparent brightness (magnitude) of the investigated astronomical objects and their visualization using the plots called light curves. Using such plots, the variations in magnitude can be easily measured. But the light curve creation process is a time-consuming task even for the one investigated astronomical object., and massive photometry as the simultaneous creation of the light curves for several or even all investigated astronomical objects presented in each CCD frame in series requires much more processing time and resources.

So, accurate machine vision (image detection, classification, and estimation of the investigated astronomical objects) requires as high accuracy as possible for the photometry process. To perform accurate photometry it is required to prepare the astronomical CCD frames before their direct use. Such preparation contains the following tasks: flat-field division, considering the read noise (bias), dark-field subtraction, and the calibration of these brightness variations to the reference object or even a group of reference objects.

An accurate understanding of the brightness variability provides the possibility to generate the key parameters and processes of the investigated astronomical objects. In general, the estimation of an apparent brightness of the astronomical object is performed after the estimation of its signal amplitude. The brief workflow of the apparent brightness estimation is presented in Figure 12.20.

The photometry process (also called the brightness calibration of the astronomical object) is always finished by the light curve creation. For example, the light curve of the GZAnd variable star created from the 107 photometric measurements using the data from the C11 telescope and filter "I" is presented in Figure 12.21.

Such a photometry process in common cases requires verification of images in time series for at least one reference source, but more will be even better (Akhmetov et al. 2019a). All such reference sources should have certain characteristics, like the specific brightness and spectral class with similar values of such characteristics compared to the original investigated astronomical object.

Also, the reference sources can be selected as standards from the reference photometric catalogue and should have a long history of observations and meet the appropriate requirements. The photometry accuracy can be significantly improved if more than one reference source or catalogue is available and used during calibration. But during the manual processing mode, using several reference sources will take more effort and time.

The calibration process should be repeated for each astronomical image in a series with considering the corrections. Such results of correction can include the different predictable adjustments caused by an estimation of the atmospheric extinction (absorption) because of changes in the air mass. Also, the different unpredictable adjustments caused by the bright nearby objects, light from the Moon, or various types of diffused light encountered during observations should be made.

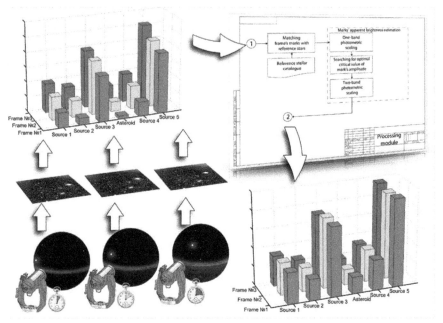

Figure 12.20: Brief workflow of the apparent brightness estimation.

And, of course, such adjustments complicate the processing of astronomical information and reduce the accuracy of the light curve determination. So, all such corrections are needed to create a harmonious (internally consistent) and homogeneous light curve.

Implementation. To perform accurate photometry, the CoLiTec software implements the specially developed algorithm [Savanevych et al. 2022a]. Below are described the stages for determining the photometric measurements of the appropriate variable star using the series of astronomical frames.

1. Best photometry aperture radius selection:
   - Determining the average SNR of the investigated variable star and each candidate for comparison stars in all frames in the series;
   - Selection of two control candidates for comparison stars with the smallest differences between their average SNR and the average SNR of the investigated variable star;
   - Determining the instrumental brightness for each control candidate for comparison stars;
   - Determining the RMS dependence of the instrumental brightness for two control candidates for comparison stars in all frames;
   - Selection of a radius with the minimal RMS of difference of the instrumental brightness of two control candidates for comparison stars in all frames as the best photometry aperture radius.

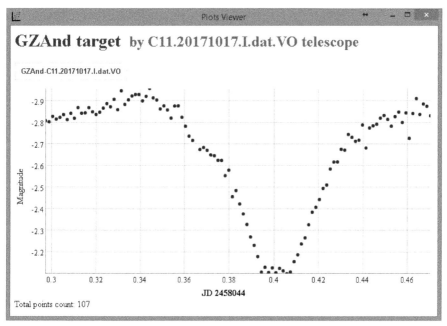

Figure 12.21: Light curve of the GZAnd variable star using the data from the C11 telescope.

2. Exclusion of the anomalous errors in all photometric measurements of the investigated variable star.

3. Final comparison stars selection from the control candidates.

4. Preparation of the most suitable combinations of the comparison stars that will be used for the photometry calibration.

The more detailed steps and flows of this algorithm as well as the accurate estimation of the aperture photometry are presented in the paper mentioned above.

Comparison. In the next subsection, we provide the main functional and photometry features of the CoLiTec software and the comparison with the same features of some other popular astronomical software, like Muniwin as the implementation of C-Munipack with GUI (v. 2.1) [Motl 2009], APPHi (release from Jul 2, 2018) [Sánchez 2019], MaxIm DL (latest version) [Walker 2004], Tangra 3 (v. 3.6.17) [Pavlov 2020], and Astropy (v. 5.2) [Astropy et al. 2018] as a new generation of IRAF and PyRAF packages [Luan 2001].

The comparison of the functional features of the described above popular astronomical photometric software is presented in Table 12.3, where 1 – MaxIm DL, 2 – Muniwin, 3 – Astropy, 4 – APPHi, 5 – Tangra 3, 6 – CoLiTec.

The Table 12.3 shows that the CoLiTec software (column 6) has much more advantages in the functional features in comparison with other popular astronomical photometric software described above.

Table 12.3: Comparison table with functional features of the popular astronomical software.

Functional features	1	2	3	4	5	6
Possibility to individual parameters for telescope	+	–	–	–	–	+
Possibility to select the required astro-, photometry catalogs	+	+	–	–	–	+
Parameters setting of the telescope aperture	+	+	+	+	+	+
Calibration of raw CCD frames using calibration frames in manual mode	+	+	+	+	+	+
Calibration of raw CCD frames using calibration frames in automated mode	–	–	–	–	–	+
Using of the mathematical inverse median filter for the brightness equalization	–	–	–	–	–	+
Support of the localization for GUI	+	–	–	–	–	+
Support of the multi-threaded processing	–	–	–	–	–	+
Support of the multi-cores systems with the ability to manage individual thread	–	–	–	–	–	+
Detection of the faint moving objects (SNR > 2.5) in automated mode	–	–	–	–	–	+
Detection of the very fast objects (up to 40.0 pix./frame) in automated mode	–	–	–	–	–	+
Detection of the objects with near-zero apparent motion (from 0.7 pix./frame) in automated mode	–	–	–	–	–	+
Rejection of objects with bad and unclear measurements in automated mode	–	–	–	–	–	+

Table 12.3 contd. ...

...Table 12.3 contd.

Functional features	1	2	3	4	5	6
Support of the processing a very wide FOV (< 20 degrees²)	–	–	–	–	–	+
Data validation during processing	+	+	+	+	+	+
Full robust algorithm in the pipeline	–	–	–	–	–	+
Simple, user-friendly, and understandable GUI	+	+	–	–	+	+
Modern GUI (Windows 10 style)	+	–	–	–	–	+
Console interface	–	+	+	+	–	–
Simple installation	+	–	–	–	–	+
Free open source	–	+	+	+	+	–
Cross-platform	+	+	+	+	+	+
Compilation required	–	–	+	+	+	–

The main advantages in the functional features of the CoLiTec software are the following: fully automated robust algorithm in the pipeline; support of the processing using multi-threaded and multi-cores systems; user-friendly, modern, simple, and understandable GUI.

The comparison of the photometry functions of the described above popular astronomical photometric software is presented in Table 12.4, where 1 – MaxIm DL, 2 – Muniwin, 3 – Astropy, 4 – APPHi, 5 – Tangra 3, 6 – CoLiTec.

Table 12.4 shows that the CoLiTec software (column 6) has much more advantages in the photometry functions in comparison with other popular astronomical photometric software described above.

The main advantages in the photometry functions of the CoLiTec software are the following: massive photometry; automated plotting of the light curve of the investigated variable star and its online changing during the calibration process; automated selection of the aperture size; automated selection of the comparison stars.

Also, Table 1.4 shows that the CoLiTec software (column 6) performs all actions without any human interactions in the automated mode in one processing pipeline. Such approach simplifies the processing of a series of astronomical frames and the creation of a light curve of the investigated variable stars.

12.8.5 Tracks detection

Also, the CoLiTec software allows detecting the moving objects in a series of CCD frames. This process is always performed after the astrometry when the positional coordinates of the investigated astronomical object are finally defined in each CCD frame of a series. Such a process is also called track detection, when not only the fact

Table 12.4: Comparison table with photometry functions of the popular astronomical software.

Photometry functions	1	2	3	4	5	6
Creation of the light curve in manual mode	+	+	+	+	+	+
Creation of the light curve in automated mode	−	−	−	−	−	+
Online analysis during the light curve changes	−	−	−	−	−	+
Analysis of the light curve in the viewer tool	+	+	−	−	+	+
Comparison stars selection in manual mode	+	+	−	−	−	+
Comparison stars selection in automated mode	−	−	−	−	−	+
Comparison stars selection optimization	−	−	−	−	−	+
Massive photometry	−	−	−	+	−	+
Photometry of the moving astronomical objects	−	−	−	−	−	+
Aperture size determination in autonomous mode	−	−	−	−	−	+
Task-file creation for the investigated stars	+	+	+	−	+	+
Using of the ensemble-photometry	+	+	+	+	+	+
File with instrumental brightness saving in automated mode	+	+	+	+	+	+
AAVSO report saving in automated mode	−	+	−	−	−	+
AAVSO report sending in automated mode	−	−	−	−	−	+

of the object's movement is detected, but the parameters of the track/trajectory of such investigated astronomical object is estimated and finally determined.

Commonly, the track detection fully depends on the verification of the following hypothesis and alternative hypothesis: hypothesis H_0, which is related to the zero/null apparent motion of the investigated astronomical object (fixed object), and the alternative hypothesis H_1, which is related to the non-zero apparent motion of the investigated astronomical object (moving object). In the common case, all moving astronomical objects are related to the Solar System objects (SSOs), and the fixed astronomical objects—to the stars. Also, the moving objects can be belonged to robots [Ivanov et al. 2019, Yeromina et al. 2021], drones [Tantsiura et al. 2019], satellites [Akhmetov et al. 2019c], and even rockets.

The main principle for the moving objects and their tracks detection is based on using the following specific quality indicators: conditional probabilities of the false detection (CPFD) and the conditional probability of the true detection (CPTD).

The different approaches implemented in the CoLiTec software for moving objects and their tracks detection are described below.

Maximum Likelihood Criterion. In general, hypothesis H_0 and alternative H_1 are verified by the maximum likelihood criterion or another criterion from the statistical checking group called Bayesian [Ando 2010]. In this case, the likelihood ratio will be like the final value of statistics for the appropriate criteria. Such value in the common case assimilates with the predefined critical values (calculated or even from the table) [Myung 2003].

A likelihood function for the moving objects and their tracks detection is determined as the common density distribution of positional measurements of the astronomical object in a set. The ordinary least square (OLS) evaluation of the parameters of the apparent motion of the astronomical objects as well as the estimation of the positional variance of the astronomical objects in a set should be determined. Based on these parameters, the maximum allowable (critical) value of the likelihood ratio can be obtained to estimate the moving objects and their tracks detection using the substitutional methods.

There are several various situations for the maximum likelihood ratio. Almost all of them depend on the knowledge of the position variance of the astronomical object. So, in general, the following variations of the substitutional methods for maximum likelihood detection can be used:

- the position variance of the astronomical object is known;
- the position variance of the astronomical object is unknown and only the estimation of such variance can be used;
- external variance estimation of the astronomical object's position can be used based on the previous calculations according to the accuracy of previous measurements sets (for example, the already known instrumental error during observation);

In some cases, the position variance of the astronomical object can be known, otherwise, the external estimation of the position variance of the astronomical object is used for this purpose. Such external estimation in the common case is calculated from the estimation accuracy from the previous array of positional measurements.

Fisher F-Criterion. The insufficient justification of applying the substitutional computational methods based on maximum likelihood criteria when some parameters of the likelihood ratio are unknown is one of the main disadvantages. The second disadvantage is a requirement to select the value of boundary decisive statistics.

Models of the independent apparent motion of the astronomical object along each coordinate are the classical models of linear regression with two parameters (velocity along each coordinate and start position). Thus, the alternative hypothesis H_1, which is related to the astronomical object belonged the SSO, is identical to the hypothesis about the statistical significance of the apparent motion. So, the checking of the statistical significance of the entire velocity for the moving objects and their tracks detection is equivalent to checking hypothesis H_1.

In cases where it is not possible and realistic to use the known variance of the position of the astronomical object, authors suggested using the developed detection algorithm implemented on the Fisher f-criterion [Savanevych et al. 2018]. Using such Fisher f-criterion, the statistical significance of the object's velocity along two axes (coordinates x and y) can be easily checked. In such a case, a statistic of the f-distribution has any dependencies on the distribution of errors of the object's position.

Also, the Fisher distribution statistics have already predefined statistical values from the table [Mélard 2014].

According to the known count of measurements of the investigated astronomical object from each image in series, the degrees of freedom for the f-distribution can be easily determined [Yazici and Cavus 2021]. Also, the predefined significance level helps to select the appropriate threshold of the f-distribution from the table.

Hough Transform. Also, for the movement objects and their tracks detection, the CoLiTec software encapsulates the specially developed method for image accumulation along a trajectory with locally unchanged parameters of visible apparent motion. The brief workflow for an algorithm for the moving astronomical objects detection is presented in Figure 12.22.

Such a method is the basis of the developed two-stage computational method for astronomical data processing for moving object detection. It is a modification of the common well-known Hough transform method [Massone et al. 2015].

The developed method ensures the accumulation of data along the trajectory of an astronomical object with unknown motion parameters by using the proposed multivalued transformation of coordinates of the investigated object. Due to this, the method provides potentially possible indicators of the quality of detection of moving astronomical objects, which are identical to the values of the quality indicators of detection of stationary/fixed astronomical objects.

The computational costs of the developed method are stabilized at an acceptable level due to the two-stage implementation of the data accumulation along possible trajectories and the linear dependence of the computational costs on the number of processed astronomical measurements, in contrast to the exponential dependence when using strobe methods.

The developed method provided the possibility for significantly reducing the thresholds in devices and tools for primary processing, which made it possible to detect moving objects and their tracks with a reduced contrast of their images.

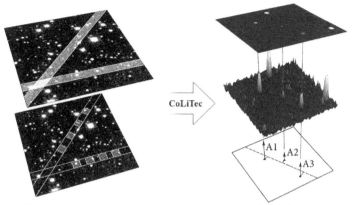

Figure 12.22: Algorithm for the moving astronomical objects detection.

Also, to speed up the processing algorithm, the astronomical objects, which are stationary/fixed in a series of CCD images are removed from the investigated collection before detecting the moving objects.

12.8.6 Astronomical test data

Testing of the CoLiTec software was performed during the regression after the development of each new algorithm/method/component/module/package as well as deployment of the new build or release.

For such testing, we especially selected the different astronomical images for machine vision purposes with the various resolutions (4008×2672, 3056×3056, 768×512, 512×512 pixels). Also, the different observational conditions of the investigated astronomical objects were selected from the different observatories equipped with various telescopes.

The appropriate astronomical test data for astronomical MV were selected in the scope of the current research from the following real observatories: ISON-NM/ISON-Kislovodsk [Molotov et al. 2009], ISON-Uzhgorod [Kudak et al. 2010], Vihorlat Observatory in Humenne [Parimucha et al. 2019] and Mayaki observing station of "Astronomical Observatory" Research Institute of I. I. Mechnikov Odessa National University [Kwiatkowski et al. 2021] with unique observatory codes "H15", "D00", "K99", "Humenne" and "583" accordingly.

The observatory codes are unique and approved by the Minor Planet Center (MPC) from the International Astronomical Union (IAU) [MPC Codes].

Detailed information about the observatories described above including MPC code and telescope information is provided in Table 12.5.

The astronomical test examples for MV are consisting of the different series of astronomical CCD frames that were collected during the regular observations by the various CCD cameras. The information about the CCD cameras that are installed on the telescopes from the observatories listed above is presented in Table 12.6. This table contains the following information about the CCD camera: model and its parameters, like resolution, pixel size, and exposure time.

Table 12.5: Information about observatories.

Observatory	Code	Telescope
ISON-Kislovodsk	D00	VT-78 as the GENON wide-field telescope with main mirror of 19.2 cm
ISON-NM	H15	0.4 m SANTEL-400AN telescope
ISON-Uzhgorod	K99	0.4 m ChV-400 telescope
ISON-Uzhgorod	K99	25 cm BRC-250 M telescope
Vihorlat Observatory	Humenne	Vihorlat National Telescope (VNT) as the Kassegren telescope with main mirror of 1 m and a focal length of 8925 mm
Vihorlat Observatory	Humenne	Celestron C11 telescope as the Schmidt-Cassegrain telescope with main mirror of 28 cm and a focal length of 3060 mm
Astronomical Observatory	583	0.48 m AZT-3 reflector telescope (focal length of 2025 mm)

Table 12.6: Information about CCD cameras.

Code	CCD camera	Resolution	Pixel size	Exposure time
D00	FLI ML09000-65	4008 × 2672 pixels	9 microns	180 seconds
H15	FLI ML09000-65	3056 × 3056 pixels	12 microns	150 seconds
K99	FLI PL09000	3056 × 3056 pixels	12 microns	150 seconds
K99	Apogee Alta U9	3072 × 2048 pixels	9 microns	180 seconds
Humenne	FLI PL1001E	512 × 512 pixels	12 microns	150 seconds
Humenne	G2-1600	768 × 512 pixels	9 microns	180 seconds
583	Sony ICX429ALL	795 × 596 pixels	12 microns	150 seconds

12.8.7 Processing results

As mentioned above the CoLiTec software performs a lot of different MV steps in the pipeline during processing, so the common result for a series of astronomical CCD frames is shown in Figure 12.23.

A final stage of the CoLiTec processing is the detection and identification of astronomical objects as is shown in Figure 12.24. Such objects can have different sizes and apparent motions in a series of images. So, it is very important that the CoLiTec software can detect such different astronomical objects in images at the same time.

During a long time of exploitation and testing of the CoLiTec software, a lot of very important observations and discoveries of the Solar System objects (SSOs) were made. The number of them is presented in Table 12.7.

There are a lot of official observational circulates from the Minor Planet Center (MPC) [MPC] that were created in accordance with the observations and discoveries performed by the CoLiTec software.

Figure 12.23: Processing results of the CoLiTec software.

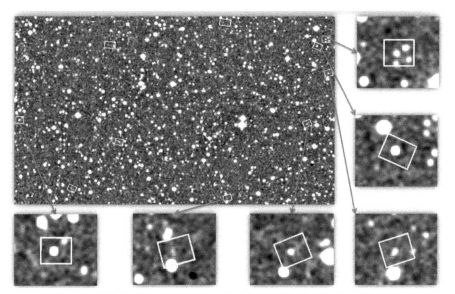

Figure 12.24: Different astronomical objects detected by the CoLiTec software.

Table 12.7: Processing results of the CoLiTec software.

Processing results	Number
Astronomical observations	> 700 000
Discoveries of the Solar System objects (SSOs)	> 1600
Discoveries of the Comets	5
Discoveries of the Near-Earth objects (NEOs)	5
Discoveries of the Trojan asteroids of Jupiter	21
Discoveries of the Centaurs	1

12.9 Conclusions

The chapter describes the different modern machine vision and image processing algorithms with their implementation in the CoLiTec software. Also, a comparison with other astronomical software packages and tools is provided to show the pros and cons of the suggested algorithms and software.

The modern CoLiTec software was developed using data mining, knowledge discovery in databases, machine vision, and image processing technologies and approaches. In the astronomy direction the CoLiTec software was designed to perform the following main stages: pre-processing (astronomical data collection -> worst data rejection -> useful data extraction -> classification -> clustering -> background alignment -> brightness equalization), processing (recognition patterns applying -> objects detection -> astrometry -> photometry -> tracks detection), knowledge extraction (astronomical objects to be discovered, tracks parameters for the investigation, light curves of the variable stars).

The trial version of the CoLiTec software and user guides for its components can be requested from the official website at https://colitec.space.

Using the CoLiTec software, more than 1600 small Solar system objects (SSOs) were discovered, including asteroids, five near-Earth objects (NEOs), 21 Trojan asteroids of Jupiter, and one Centaur. It was used in more than 700 000 observations, and five comets were also discovered.

Also, the CoLiTec software was approved by the coordinator of the Gaia-FUN-SSO network Mr. W. Thuillot [Thuillot et al. 2015] as a well-adapted software to the Gaia-FUN-SSO conditions of observation (https://gaiafunsso.imcce.fr).

References

Adam, G., Kontaxis, P., Doulos, L., Madias, E. -N., Bouroussis, C. and Topalis, F. 2019. Embedded microcontroller with a CCD camera as a digital lighting control system. Electronics, 8(1): 33. doi: 10.3390/electronics8010033.

Ando, T. 2010. Bayesian model selection and statistical modeling, CRC Press.

Akhmetov, V., Khlamov, S., Tabakova, I., Hernandez, W., Hipolito, J., and Fedorov, P. 2019a. New approach for pixelization of big astronomical data for machine vision purpose. In Proceedings of the IEEE International Symposium on Industrial Electronics, pp. 1706–1710. doi: 10.1109/ISIE.2019.8781270.

Akhmetov, V., Khlamov, S., and Dmytrenko, A. 2019b. Fast coordinate cross-match tool for large astronomical catalogue. Advances in Intelligent Systems and Computing, 871: 3–16. doi: 10.1007/978-3-030-01069-0_1.

Akhmetov, V., Khlamov, S., Savanevych, V., and Dikov, E. 2019c. Cloud computing analysis of Indian ASAT test on March 27, 2019. In Proceedings of the 2019 IEEE International Scientific-Practical Conference: Problems of Infocommunications Science and Technology, pp. 315–318. doi: 10.1109/PICST47496.2019.9061243.

Akhmetov, V., Khlamov, S., Khramtsov, V., and Dmytrenko, A. 2020. Astrometric reduction of the wide-field images. Advances in Intelligent Systems and Computing, 1080: 896–909. doi: 10.1007/978-3-030-33695-0_58.

Andersen, J., Baneke, D., and Madsen, C. 2019. The International Astronomical Union: Uniting the Community for 100 Years, Springer.

The Astropy Collaboration, Price-Whelan, A., Sipőcz, B., Günther, H., Lim, P. and Crawford, S. 2018. The astropy project: building an open-science project and status of the v2.0 Core Package. The Astronomical Journal, 156(3): 123. doi: 10.3847/1538-3881/aabc4f.

Baranova, V., Zeleni, O., Deineko, Zh., Bielcheva, G. and Lyashenko, V. 2019. Wavelet coherence as a tool for studying of economic dynamics in infocommunication systems. In Proceedings of the IEEE International Scientific-Practical Conference Problems of Infocommunications, Science and Technology, pp. 336–340. doi: 10.1109/PICST47496.2019.9061301.

Beuzit, J. -L., Vigan, A., Mouillet, D., Dohlen, K., Gratton, R., Boccaletti, A. et al. 2019. SPHERE: the exoplanet imager for the Very Large Telescope. Astronomy & Astrophysics, 631, A155. doi: 10.1051/0004-6361/201935251.

Borne, K., Becla, J., Davidson, I., Szalay, A. and Tyson, J. 2008. The LSST data mining research agenda. AIP Conference Proceedings, 1082(1): 347–351, American Institute of Physics. doi: 10.1063/1.3059074.

Borne, K. 2008. Scientific data mining in astronomy. Chapman and Hall/CRC Data Mining and Knowledge Discovery Series, pp. 115–138. doi: 10.1201/9781420085877.CH5.

Burger, W., and Burge, M. 2009. Principles of digital image processing: fundamental techniques. New York, NY: Springer.

Buslov, P., Shvedun, V., and Streltsov, V. 2018. Modern Tendencies of Data Protection in the Corporate Systems of Information Consolidation. In Proceedings of the IEEE International Scientific-Practical Conference on Problems of Infocommunications Science and Technology, pp. 285–288. doi: 10.1109/INFOCOMMST.2018.8632089.

Brescia, M., and Longo, G. 2012. Astroinformatics, data mining and the future of astronomical research. Nuclear Instruments and Methods in Physics Research Section A: Accelerators, Spectrometers, Detectors and Associated Equipment, 720: 92–94. doi: 10.1016/j.nima.2012.12.027.

Campisi, P., and Egiazarian, K. 2017. Blind image deconvolution: theory and applications. CRC press.

Carry, B., Thuillot, W., Spoto, F. et al. 2021. Potential asteroid discoveries by the ESA Gaia mission: Results from follow-up observations. Astronomy and Astrophysics, 648, A96. doi: 10.1051/0004-6361/202039579.

Cavuoti, S., Brescia, M., and Longo, G. 2012. Data mining and knowledge discovery resources for astronomy in the Web 2.0 age. SPIE Astronomical Telescopes and Instrumentation, Software and Cyberinfrastructure for Astronomy II, 8451. doi: 10.1117/12.925321.

Dadkhah, M., Lyashenko, V., Deineko, Zh., Band, Sh. and Jazi, M. 2019. Methodology of wavelet analysis in research of dynamics of phishing attacks. International Journal of Advanced Intelligence Paradigms, 12(3-4): 220–238. doi: 10.1504/IJAIP.2019.098561.

Dombrovska, S., Shvedun, V., Streltsov, V., and Husarov, K. 2018. The prospects of integration of the advertising market of Ukraine into the global advertising business. Problems and Perspectives in Management, 16(2): 321–330. doi: 10.21511/ppm.16(2).2018.29.

Eisenstein, D. et al. 2011. SDSS-III: Massive spectroscopic surveys of the distant universe, the Milky Way, and extra-solar planetary systems. The Astronomical Journal, 142(3): 72. doi: 10.1088/0004-6256/142/3/72.

Elshoush, H., Mahmoud, M., and Abdelrahman, A. 2022. A new high capacity and secure image realization steganography based on ASCII code matching. Multimedia Tools and Applications, 81(4): 5191–5237. doi: 10.1007/s11042-021-11741-y.

Gonzalez, R., and Woods, R. 2018. Digital image processing. 4th edition, NY: Pearson.

Grossman, R., Kamath, Ch., Kegelmeyer, Ph., Kumar, V. and Namburu, R. 2013. Data Mining for Scientific and Engineering Applications, Vol. 2, Springer Science & Business Media.

Haigh, C., Chamba, N., Venhola, A., Peletier, R., Doorenbos, L., Watkins, M. et al. 2021. Optimising and comparing source-extraction tools using objective segmentation quality criteria. Astronomy & Astrophysics, 645: A107. doi: 10.1051/0004-6361/201936561.

Haynal, S., and Haynal, H. 2011. Generating and searching families of FFT algorithms. Journal on Satisfiability, Boolean Modeling and Computation, 7(4): 145–187. doi: 10.48550/arXiv.1103.5740.

Howard, W. 2007. Pattern recognition and machine learning, Kybernetes.

Ilbert, O., Arnouts, S., McCracken, H., Bolzonella, M., Bertin, E., Le Fèvre, O. et al. 2006. Accurate photometric redshifts for the CFHT legacy survey calibrated using the VIMOS VLT deep survey. Astronomy & Astrophysics, 457(3): 841–856. doi: 10.1051/0004-6361:20065138.

Ivanov, M., Sergiyenko, O., Mercorelli, P., Perdomo, W., Tyrsa, V., Hernandez-Balbuena, D. et al. 2019. Effective informational entropy reduction in multi-robot systems based on real-time TVS. In

Proceedings of the IEEE International Symposium on Industrial Electronics, pp. 1162–1167. doi: 10.1109/ISIE.2019.8781209.

Kaiser, N., Aussel, H., Burke, B., Boesgaard, H., Chambers, K., Chun, M. et al. 2002. Pan-STARRS: A large synoptic survey telescope array. In Proceedings of the Conference on Survey and Other Telescope Technologies and Discoveries, 4836: 154-164, International Society for Optics and Photonics. doi: 10.1117/12.457365.

Karki, J. 2000. Active low-pass filter design. Texas Instruments application report.

Khlamov, S., Savanevych, V., Briukhovetskyi, O., and Oryshych, S. 2016. Development of computational method for detection of the object 's near-zero apparent motion on the series of CCD–frames. Eastern-European Journal of Enterprise Technologies, 2: 9(80): 41–48. doi: 10.15587/1729-4061.2016.65999.

Khlamov, S., Savanevych, V., Briukhovetskyi, O., and Pohorelov, A. 2017. CoLiTec software – detection of the near-zero apparent motion. In Proceedings of the International Astronomical Union: Cambridge University Press, 12 (S325): 349–352. doi: 10.1017/S1743921316012539.

Khlamov, S., and Savanevych, V. 2020. Big astronomical datasets and discovery of new celestial bodies in the Solar System in automated mode by the CoLiTec software. Knowledge Discovery in Big Data from Astronomy and Earth Observation, Astrogeoinformatics: Elsevier, pp. 331–345. doi: 10.1016/B978-0-12-819154-5.00030-8.

Khlamov, S., Tabakova, I., and Trunova, T. 2022a. Recognition of the astronomical images using the Sobel filter. In Proceedings of the International Conference on Systems, Signals, and Image Processing, 4 p. doi: 10.1109/IWSSIP55020.2022.9854425.

Khlamov, S., Savanevych, V., Tabakova, I., and Trunova, T. 2022b. The astronomical object recognition and its near-zero motion detection in series of images by in situ modeling. In Proceedings of the International Conference on Systems, Signals, and Image Processing, 4 p. doi: 10.1109/IWSSIP55020.2022.9854475.

Khlamov, S., Savanevych, V., Briukhovetskyi, O., Tabakova, I., and Trunova, T. 2022c. Data Mining of the Astronomical Images by the CoLiTec Software. CEUR Workshop Proceedings, 3171: 1043–1055.

Khlamov, S., Vlasenko, V., Savanevych, V., Briukhovetskyi, O., Trunova, T., Chelombitko, V. et al. 2022d. Development of computational method for matched filtration with analytic profile of the blurred digital image. Eastern-European Journal of Enterprise Technologies, 5, 4(119): 24–32. doi: 10.15587/1729-4061.2022.265309.

Khlamov, S., Savanevych, V., Vlasenko, V., Briukhovetskyi, O., Trunova, T., Levykin, I. et al. 2023. Development of the matched filtration of a blurred digital image using its typical form. Eastern-European Journal of Enterprise Technologies, 1, 9(121): In Print. doi: 10.15587/1729-4061.2023.273674.

Kirichenko, L., Alghawli, A.S.A., and Radivilova, T. 2020. Generalized approach to analysis of multifractal properties from short time series. International Journal of Advanced Computer Science and Applications, 11(5): 183–198. doi: 10.14569/IJACSA.2020.0110527.

Kirichenko, L., Zinchenko, P., and Radivilova, T. 2021. Classification of time realizations using machine learning recognition of recurrence plots. Advances in Intelligent Systems and Computing, 1246 AISC: 687–696. doi: 10.1007/978-3-030-54215-3_44.

Klette, R. 2014. Concise computer vision. Springer, London.

Kudak, V., Klimik, V., and Epishev, V. 2010. Evaluation of disturbances from solar radiation in orbital elements of geosynchronous satellites based on harmonics. Astrophysical Bulletin, 65(3): 300–310. doi: 10.1134/S1990341310030120.

Kudzej, I., Savanevych, V., Briukhovetskyi, O., Khlamov, S., Pohorelov, A., Vlasenko, V. et al. 2019. CoLiTecVS – A new tool for the automated reduction of photometric observations. Astronomische Nachrichten, 340(1–3): 68-70. doi: 10.1002/asna.201913562.

Kuhn, L., Shubat, M., and Barmby, P. 2022. Comparing NED and SIMBAD classifications across the contents of nearby galaxies. Monthly Notices of the Royal Astronomical Society, 515 (1): 807-816. doi: 10.1093/mnras/stac1801.

Kwiatkowski, T., Koleńczuk, P., Kryszczyńska, A., Oszkiewicz, D., Kamiński, K., Kamińska, M. et al. 2021. Photometry and model of near-Earth asteroid 2021 DW1 from one apparition. Astronomy and Astrophysics, 656: A126. doi: 10.1051/0004-6361/202142013.

Lehmann, E., Romano, J., and Casella, G. 2005. Testing statistical hypotheses, vol. 3, NY: Springer.

Lindeberg, T. 1998. Edge detection and ridge detection with automatic scale-selection. International Journal of Computer Vision, 30(2): 117–156. doi: doi.org/10.1023/A:1008097225773.

Lindeberg, T. 2013. Scale selection properties of generalized scale-space interest point detectors. Journal of Mathematical Imaging and Vision, 46(2): 177–210. doi: 10.1007/s10851-012-0378-3.

List of Observatory Codes: IAU Minor Planet Center. https://minorplanetcenter.net/iau/lists/ObsCodesF. html.

Luan, J. 2001. Book review: Practical algorithms for image analysis: Description, examples, and code. Discrete Dynamics in Nature and Society, 6(3): 219–220. doi: 10.1155/s1026022601000243.

Luo, Q. 2008. Advancing knowledge discovery and data mining. In Proceedings of the First International Workshop on Knowledge Discovery and Data Mining, pp. 3–5. doi: 10.1109/WKDD.2008.153.

Massone, A., Perasso, A., Campi, C., and Beltrametti, M. 2015. Profile detection in medical and astronomical images by means of the Hough transform of special classes of curves. Journal of Mathematical Imaging and Vision, 51(2): 296–310. doi: 10.1007/s10851-014-0521-4.

Mélard, G. 2014. On the accuracy of statistical procedures in Microsoft Excel 2010. Computational statistics, 29(5): 1095–1128, 2014. doi: 10.1007/s00180-014-0482-5.

Molotov, I., Agapov, V., Kouprianov, V., Titenko, V., Rumyantsev, V., Biryukov, V. et al. 2009. ISON worldwide scientific optical network. In Proceedings of the Fifth European Conference on Space Debris, ESA SP-672, 7.

Motl, D. 2009. C-munipack. http://c-munipack.sourceforge.net.

Mykhailova, L., Savanevych, V., Sokovikova, N., Bezkrovniy, M., Khlamov, S., and Pogorelov, A. 2014. Method of maximum likelihood estimation of compact group objects location on CCD-frame. Eastern-European Journal of Enterprise Technologies, 5(4): 16–22. doi:10.15587/1729-4061.2014.28028.

Myung, I. 2003. Tutorial on maximum likelihood estimation. Journal of mathematical Psychology, 47(1): 90–100. doi: 10.1016/S0022-2496(02)00028-7.

Nelson, J., and Sanders, G. 2008. The status of the Thirty Meter Telescope project. Ground-based and Airborne Telescopes II, 7012: 70121A, 18, International Society for Optics and Photonics. doi: 10.1117/12.788238.

Parimucha, Š., Savanevych, V., Briukhovetskyi, O., Khlamov, S., Pohorelov, A., Vlasenko, V. et al. 2019. CoLiTecVS – A new tool for an automated reduction of photometric observations. Contributions of the Astronomical Observatory Skalnate Pleso, 49(2): 151–153.

Park, J., and Murphey, Y. 2008. Edge detection in grayscale, color, and range images. Wiley Encyclopedia of Computer Science and Engineering, pp. 1–16, John Wiley & Sons, Inc. doi: 10.1002/9780470050118.ecse603.

Pata, P., and Schindler, J. 2015. Astronomical context coder for image compression. Experimental Astronomy, 39(3): 495–512. doi: 10.1007/s10686-015-9460-3.

Pavlov, H. 2020. Tangra: Software for video photometry and astrometry. Astrophys. Source Code Libr., record ascl:2004.002.

Pence, W., Chiappetti, L., Page, C. Shaw, R., and Stobie, E. 2010. Definition of the flexible image transport system (fits), version 3.0. Astronomy & Astrophysics, 524: A42. doi: 10.1051/0004-6361/201015362.

Raab, H. 2012. Astrometrica: Astrometric data reduction of CCD images. Astrophysics Source Code Library, record ascl:1203.012.

Racca, G., Laureijs, R., Stagnaro, L., Salvignol, J. -Ch., Alvarez, J., Criado, G. et al. 2016. The Euclid mission design. Space Telescopes and Instrumentation 2016: Optical, Infrared, and Millimeter Wave. In Proceedings of the SPIE, 9904: 235–257. doi: 10.1117/12.2230762.

Rosten, E., and Drummond, T. 2006. Machine learning for high-speed corner detection. Lecture Notes in Computer Science, 3951: 430–443. doi: 10.1007/11744023_34.

Sánchez, E. et al. 2019. APPHI: An automated photometry pipeline for high cadence, large volume data. Astron. Comput, 26: 1–13. doi: 10.1016/j.ascom.2018.09.009.

Savanevych, V., Briukhovetskyi, O., Sokovikova, N., Bezkrovny, M., Vavilova, I., Ivashchenko, Yu. et al. 2015a. A new method based on the subpixel Gaussian model for accurate estimation of asteroid coordinates. Monthly Notices of the Royal Astronomical Society, 451(3): 3287–3298. doi: 10.1093/mnras/stv1124.

Savanevych, V., Briukhovetskyi, A., Ivashchenko, Yu. et al. 2015b. Comparative analysis of the positional accuracy of CCD measurements of small bodies in the solar system software CoLiTec and Astrometrica. Kinematics and Physics of Celestial Bodies, 31(6): 302–313. doi: 10.3103/S0884591315060045.

Savanevych, V., Khlamov, S., Vavilova, I., Briukhovetskyi, A., Pohorelov, A., Mkrtichian, D. et al. 2018. A method of immediate detection of objects with a near-zero apparent motion in series of CCD-frames. Astronomy & Astrophysics, 609, A54: 11. doi: 10.1051/0004-6361/201630323.

Savanevych, V., Akhmetov, V., Khlamov, S., Dikov, E., Briukhovetskyi, A., Vlasenko, V. et al. 2020. Selection of the reference stars for astrometric reduction of CCD-frames. Advances in Intelligent Systems and Computing, 1080: 881–895. doi: 10.1007/978-3-030-33695-0_57.

Savanevych, V., Khlamov, S., Akhmetov, V., Briukhovetskyi, A., Vlasenko, V., Dikov, E. et al. 2022a. CoLiTecVS software for the automated reduction of photometric observations in CCD-frames. Astronomy and Computing, 40(100605): 15. doi: 10.1016/j.ascom.2022.100605.

Savanevych, V., Khlamov, S., Vlasenko, V., Deineko, Zh., Briukhovetskyi, O., Tabakova, I. et al. 2022b. Formation of a typical form of an object image in a series of digital frames. Eastern-European Journal of Enterprise Technologies, 6(2-120): 51–59. doi: 10.15587/1729-4061.2022.266988.

Schroeder, D. J. 1999. Astronomical optics, Elsevier.

Skrutskie, M., Cutri, R., Stiening, R., Weinberg, M., Schneider, S., Carpenter, J. et al. 2006. The two micron all sky survey (2MASS). The Astronomical Journal, 131(2): 1163. doi: 10.1086/498708.

Shvedun, V., and Khlamov, S. 2016. Statistical modelling for determination of perspective number of advertising legislation violations. Actual Problems of Economics, 184(10): 389–396.

Smith, G. 2010. Nobel Lecture: The invention and early history of the CCD. Review of Modern Physics, 82(3): 2307–2312. doi: 10.1103/RevModPhys.82.2307.

Starck, J.-L., and Murtagh, F. 2007. Astronomical image and data analysis. Astronomy and Astrophysics Library, 2nd edition, Springer.

Steger, C., Ulrich, M., and Wiedemann, C. 2018. Machine vision algorithms and applications. John Wiley & Sons.

Svensén, M., and Bishop, C. 2007. Pattern recognition and machine learning. Springer.

Tantsiura, A., Kolomiets, D., Tabakova, I., Hannoshyna, I., Serdiuk, N., Yelieazarov, O. et al. 2019. Evaluation of the potential accuracy of correlation extreme navigation systems of low-altitude mobile robots. International Journal of Advanced Trends in Computer Science and Engineering, 8(5): 2161–2166. doi: 10.30534/ijatcse/2019/47852019.

The Minor Planet Center (MPC) of the International Astronomical Union. https://minorplanetcenter.net.

Thuillot, W., Bancelin, D., Ivantsov, A., Desmars, J., Assafin, M., Eggl, S. et al. 2015. The astrometric Gaia-FUN-SSO observation campaign of 99942 Apophis. Astronomy and Astrophysics, 583: A59. doi: 10.1051/0004-6361/201425603.

Vavilova, I., Yatskiv, Y., Pakuliak, L. et al. 2016. UkrVO astroinformatics software and web-services. In Proceedings of the International Astronomical Union, 12, S325: 361–366. doi: 10.1017/S1743921317001661.

Vavilova, I. et al. 2020. Surveys, catalogues, databases, and archives of astronomical data. Knowledge Discovery in Big Data from Astronomy and Earth Observation. Astrogeoinformatics: Elsevier, pp. 57–102. doi: 10.1016/B978-0-12-819154-5.00015-1.

Walker, S. 2004. MaxIm DL/CCD 4.01. Sky Telesc. 108, 91W.

Wright, E., Eisenhardt, P., Mainzer, A., Ressler, M., Cutri, R., Jarrett, Th. et al. 2010. The Wide-field Infrared Survey Explorer (WISE): Mission Description and Initial On-orbit Performance. AJ, 140: 1868–1881. doi: 10.1088/0004-6256/140/6/1868.

Yeromina, N., Tarshyn, V., Petrov, S., Samoylenko, V., Tabakova, I., Dmitriiev, O. et al. 2021. Method of reference image selection to provide high-speed aircraft navigation under conditions of rapid change of flight trajectory. International Journal of Advanced Technology and Engineering Exploration, 8(85): 1621–1638. doi: 10.19101/IJATEE.2021.874814.

Yazici, B., and Cavus, M. 2021. A comparative study of computation approaches of the generalized F-test. Journal of Applied Statistics, 48(13–15): 2906–2919. doi: 10.1080/02664763.2021.1939660.

Zhang, Y., Zhao, Y., and Cui, C. 2002. Data mining and knowledge discovery in database of astronomy. Progress in Astronomy, 20(4): 312–323.

13

Gallium Oxide UV Sensing in Contemporary Applications

Naif H Al-Hardan,[1,*] *Muhammad Azmi Abdul Hamid,*[1] *Chaker Tlili,*[2] *Azman Jalar,*[1] *Mohd Firdaus Raih*[1,3] and *Naser M Ahmed*[4]

13.1 Introduction

Since the discovery of the polychromatic nature of light by Isaac Newton, new laws have been discussed to understand the nature of light and, later, electromagnetic waves; at the beginning of the eighteenth century, Johann Ritter discovered ultraviolet light. As part of his experiments, he split sunlight with a prism and measured how silver chloride (a chemical used in photographic paper) darkened with wavelength. The region beyond the optical violet light produced the most darkening, known as ultraviolet or ultraviolet radiation [Berg 2008, Diffey 1980]. After almost a century, Niels Finsen's work laid the foundation for modern ultraviolet photobiology. He proved that contrary to what the name would imply, sunburn is caused by ultraviolet radiation from the sun's spectrum [Diffey 1980].

In electromagnetic radiation, ultraviolet radiation (UV) has wavelengths varying from 100 nm to 400 nm. The UV broad spectrum was later divided into four regions

[1] Department of Applied Physics, Faculty of Science and Technology, Universiti Kebangsaan Malaysia, 43600 Bangi, Selangor, Malaysia.

[2] Chongqing Key Laboratory of Multi-scale Manufacturing Technology, Institute of Green and Intelligent Technology, Chinese Academy of Sciences, Chongqing, People's Republic of China.

[3] Institute of Systems Biology, Universiti Kebangsaan Malaysia, 43600 UKM Bangi, Selangor, Malaysia.

[4] School of Physics, Universiti Sains Malaysia, 11800 USM, Penang, Malaysia.

* Corresponding author: naifalhardan@ukm.edu.my, Orcid/0000-0001-7309- 9660

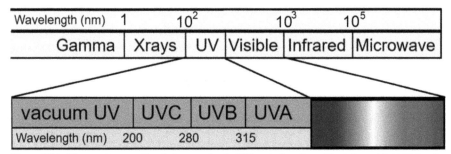

Figure 13.1: The spectrum portion that covers the far UV up to the edge of the infra-red light [Schwalm 2007].

based on their wavelength range [Chen et al. 2015, Huffman 1992, Shama 2014], as shown in Figure 13.1.

- UV-A, which includes wavelengths within 320 and 400 nm.
- UV-B, which includes wavelengths within 280 and 320 nm.
- UV-C, which includes wavelengths within 200 and 280 nm.
- V-UV, which includes wavelengths within 100 and 200 nm.

The ozone layer absorbs some UV-B and nearly all UV-C radiation from the sun in the stratosphere. Solar radiation with wavelengths longer than 280 nm (UV-A and UV-B), on the other hand, can reach the earth by diffusing through the atmosphere [Hatsusaka et al. 2021]. Exposure to moderate UV light from natural or artificial sources has been found to affect human health significantly, including integrating Vitamin D and handling or avoiding rickets [Chen et al. 2015, Michael F. Holick 2006]. However, extreme exposure to UV light causes premature ageing and skin cancers, cataracts, pterygium, severe cell membrane, proteins, and DNA damage [Brand 2018, Hatsusaka et al. 2021, Michael F. Holick 2004, Kanellis 2019, Ombra et al. 2017, Shahraki et al. 2021]. The stratospheric ozone layer begins to deteriorate as a result of the widespread use of several chemicals, which raises the total of UV light reaching the earth and consequently worsens the health effects on living species, in addition to severe crop yield damage and decreased building longevity [Barnes et al. 2019, Chen et al. 2015, Ozel et al. 2021]. Over the past century, measures have been taken to ensure the stratospheric ozone layer recovery [Barnes et al. 2019]. Nevertheless, UV light has found several practical applications that benefited the livelihood of humankind, such as healthcare and medical treatments [Ahad et al. 2022, Baltadourou et al. 2021, Buonanno et al. 2020, Wu et al. 2022], various industrial fields [Delorme et al. 2020, Hinds et al. 2019], UV communication systems [Arya and Chung 2021, Vavoulas et al. 2019], research and developments [Cruse and Goodpaster 2021], UV astrophysics and satellite surveillance [Jebar et al. 2017, Fujinawa et al. 2019, Jia et al. 2020, Kuzin et al. 2018], fire/flame and arc detectors [Muñoz et al. 2000], detecting toxic airborne gases [Khan et al. 2021], and aircraft landing assistance [Lavigne et al. 2006]. In light of the UV source's significance with $\lambda < 280$ nm for several applications and the fact that the stratosphere layer blocks this range of UV radiation, efforts have been made to artificially produce them through low-pressure mercury lamps, excimer (Xe) and deuterium lamps, and recently through UV light emitted diodes (LEDs) and lasers. In light of these and other factors, sensing UV light has become challenging and expanded globally.

Several articles in chapters and review papers deal with UV photodetectors, covering the materials used as the media of reaction, platforms, and performance. In this chapter, we will explore some advanced applications of UV-C photodetectors.

13.2 Semiconductor based UV photodetectors

There are two types of UV photodetectors: vacuum and solid-state devices. Photomultiplier tubes are an example of vacuum devices. These devices are well-known and have been in use for quite some time. However, due to its high-power consumption, low efficiency, fragility, need for cooling, and high operating voltage, it was deemed unsuitable for several applications [Kingston 2003, Wu et al. 2020]. The solid-state UV photodetectors, however, are primarily made of semiconductor materials. Since they consume low power, are small, have a wide bandwidth, are fast to detect, and have a high signal-to-noise ratio, they have received much consideration due to their applicability to various applications [Chen et al. 2022, Zhou et al. 2022a, Zou et al. 2018].

Semiconductors can be composed of two or more elements or be a single element, such as silicon (Si). Since silicon photodetectors are relatively mature production technologies, they are also commercially available as UV photodetectors [Decoster and Harari 2013, Jia et al. 2020, Li et al. 2020]. However, due to its narrow bandgap, interference will occur between the visible and even infrared signals with the UV signals. Therefore, it cannot be used directly in the ultraviolet field. To overcome this limitation, the main feature of Si photodetectors is the presence of filters that block infrared and visible light. Furthermore, the lifetime of silicon UV photodetectors is reduced because of exposure to such radiation with much higher energy than the Si energy bandgap [Monroy et al. 2003, Xie et al. 2019b]. In addition, Si photodetectors exhibit serious thermal instability due to the narrow bandgap, which suppresses their deployment in high-temperature applications [Hou et al. 2022]. In the short term, however, it is challenging to replace Si UV photodetectors with other types of wide bandgap semiconductor-based UV photodetectors due to their poor reproducibility and reliability [Jia et al. 2020].

To develop UV photodetectors, semiconductors with wide band gaps are used, such as gallium oxide, zinc oxide, tin oxide, and gallium nitride. These semiconductors are sensitive, selective, and inexpensive. Wide-bandgap semiconductor UV photodetectors have drawn significant interest in industrial manufacturing, biological detection, and environmental surveillance. Due to the high energy of UV radiation, semiconductors with wide-bang gap energy of ($E_g > 3$ eV approximately

400 nm) are the most suitable [Tsai et al. 2018, Jia et al. 2020, Sang et al. 2013]. Furthermore, if a UV photodetector only detects UV-C and VUV radiation with a wavelength shorter than 280 nm, it is called "solar-blind". A UV photodetector that detects UV-A, UV-B, UV-C, and far UV radiation and blocks a wavelength of more than 400 nm is known as "visible-blind" [Sang et al. 2013]. Numerous wide bandgap semiconductors have been widely studied, covering different UV regions. Furthermore, the tuning process of the energy bandgap by alloying or doping process proves to be an essential step to tune the semiconductors to function at specific UV regions. III-nitride (AlGaN and InGaN) [Cai et al. 2021, Lv et al. 2021] and II-VI semiconductors such as $Mg_xZn_{1-x}O$ [Shiau et al. 2020, Hongbin Wang et al. 2022, Xie et al. 2019b] are few examples on how alloying or doping process can modify the energy bandgap of these semiconductors making them attractive for solar-blind sensing applications.

13.2.1 Evaluating UV photodetectors' performance

Several parameters have been established to evaluate and understand the performance of these UV photodetectors. Here we present the most common parameters utilized by the research community.

Photocurrent (I_{ph})

The photocurrent of a photodetector is the initial parameter to be measured once the light is irradiated to the sensitive layer of the device. Electron–hole pairs are photogenerated by photons whose energies are near or more significant than the energy bandgap of the sensitive layer. Light intensity and bias voltage affect the amount of photocurrent [Nguyen et al. 2022, Xu et al. 2019].

Dark Current (I_{dark})

Whenever no photon passes through the photodetectors, a tiny current is still generated on the device. The random generation of carriers causes the dark current in the sensitive layer of devices due to specific defects in the sensitive layer [Xu et al. 2019].

Photosensitivity

Another characteristic of a photodetector is its photosensitivity, which determines how well it can reject noise based on the ratio between the photocurrent and the dark current [Li et al. 2022] and can be expressed as [Naif H. Al-Hardan et al. 2017, Pan and Zhu 2015].

$$S = \frac{I_{ph} - I_{dark}}{I_{dark}}$$

Photoresponsivity (R$_\lambda$)

This factor is the most studied, which reflects the ratio of photocurrent obtained by a photodetector per unit area to the incident light flux at a specific wavelength and can be calculated as follows [Al-Hardan et al. 2014, Jia et al. 2020, Li et al. 2022]

$$R_\lambda = \frac{I_{ph}}{I_{P_{in}} \times A}$$

where I_{ph} is the photocurrent, P_{in} is the input optical power in Watt/cm^2, and A is the active area of the photodetector. The photoresponsivity of photosensitive materials is also affected by carrier mobility and carrier lifetime [Jia et al. 2020]. A further method of determining the detector's spectral response is plotting the responsivity with wavelength [Alaie et al. 2015].

External Quantum efficiency (EQE)

EQE is a measure of how well a photodetector converts light into charge carriers based on how many incident photons it collects [Dechao Guo et al. 2021]. The spectral response can be quantified as the EQE of a photodetector

$$EQE = \frac{Rhc}{q\lambda}$$

where *c* is the speed of light, *R* is the observed responsivity, *h* is Planck's constant, *q* is the elementary electron charge, and λ is the wavelength of the incident light.

Response Time (τ)

Another important factor in testing UV photodetectors is the response time. Response time is the time required for a photodetector to respond to an optical input. It is typically measured in terms of how long it took for the photocurrent to increase from 10% to 90% of its maximum value (rise time) after applying light pulses or the time needed for the photocurrent to fall from 90% to 10% of its maximum (fall time). The importance of this parameter is evident in applications such as transmitting and receiving data in which the photodetectors should be faster to collect the signals [Jia et al. 2020].

Photoconductive gain (G)

Electrons collected per unit of time versus photons absorbed (P$_{photons}$) can be defined as this factor, which can be calculated as

$$G = \frac{N_{electrons}}{N_{photons}} = \left(\frac{I_{ph} - I_{dark}}{q} \right) \left(\frac{h\nu}{P} \right) \frac{1}{\eta}$$

where I_{ph} is the photocurrent, I_{dark} is the dark current, q is the electron charge, hv is the photon energy of the incident light, P is the power of incident light, and η is the quantum efficiency, defined as the current responsivity multiplied by the photon energy of the incident radiation [Alaie et al. 2015].

Specific detectivity (D*)

Detectivity is crucial in comparing photodetectors made of different materials and shapes. It denotes the ability of the photodetector to differentiate the most negligible light intensity from noise. Detectivity is calculated by [Alaie et al. 2015, Lan et al. 2022];

$$D^* = \frac{\sqrt{AB}}{NEP} \quad (cm\,(Hz)^{1/2}\,W^{-1}\,(Jones))$$

where A is the photodetector area (cm^2), B is the bandwidth of the measuring system (Hz), and NEP presents the equivalent noise power, defined as the minimum optical power necessary for generating a photocurrent with an S/N equal to 1.

13.2.2 Solar-blind photodetector

Earlier, we mentioned that the ozone in the atmosphere layer absorbed almost all the UV in the range of UV-C (also known as deep-UV (DUV) [Sharma and Demir 2022] and V-UV. As a result, hard work was put into developing UV light sources that cover this range of UV radiation and can be used in several applications that could be applied in modern industrial applications, including manufacturing, advanced communication, astronomy, and other areas discussed in this chapter. We focus on the UV-C radiation because the interference with the neutral source of UV at these ranges is almost null, and they will not produce any noticeable signal if exposed to standard outdoor lighting, which results in the reduction of the noise source, and the signal to noise ratio will be maximized. These detectors are based on semiconductors with ultra-energy bandgaps close to or lower than the cut-off wavelength of $\lambda = 280$ nm (Eg > 4.4 eV). Some semiconductors with wide bandgaps (Eg < 4.4 eV) can be modified and tuned by doping or alloying with other elements [Xuanhu Chen et al. 2020, Park et al. 2022].

Currently, ultra-wide bandgap semiconductors (Eg > 4.4 eV) like $Al_xGa_{1-x}N$, $Mg_xZn_{1-x}O$, diamond, and gallium oxide are leading the research in solar-blind UV photodetectors. $Al_xGa_{1-x}N$ and $Mg_xZn_{1-x}O$ with high Mg and Al contents demonstrate deterioration in quality and phase separation. The fixed bandgap of diamond limits its detection range to less than 225 nm. As a result, there are still difficulties in applying these materials to solar-blind photodetectors [Chen et al. 2018, Guo et al. 2019, Elías Muñoz 2007, Pandit et al. 2020, Xie et al. 2019b]. On the other hand, gallium oxide Ga_2O_3 (with its energy bandgap of 4.4–4.8 eV [Wu et al. 2022]) has drawn the attention of many research groups globally due to its easy preparation methods as compared to its competitors, such as $Al_xGa_{1-x}N$, and $Mg_xZn_{1-x}O$. Furthermore, due to its energy bandgap being within the UV-C range, Ga_2O_3 can be used directly without bandgap modulation via doping or alloying [Hou et al. 2022]. Several studies have been conducted on Ga_2O_3, focusing on its performance in UV-C detection. The effect of different preparation conditions and parameters of Ga_2O_3 with different forms (such as bulk, thin films, and different micro/nanostructure) is well documented in several comprehensive review articles

[Xuanhu Chen et al. 2020, Chen et al. 2019, Guo et al. 2019, Hou et al. 2020, Kaur and Kumar 2021, Qin et al. 2019, J. Xu et al. 2019].

13.3 Classification of solid-state UV photodetectors and applications

UV photodetectors operate on the base where light interacts with photoresponsive material. During photoelectric absorption, electron-hole pairs are generated when photons with energy close to or greater than the semiconductor material's bandgap are absorbed. A current signal proportional to the flux of the incident photon is generated by either an internal or external voltage [Kingston 2003] and can be monitored by an external unit [Kingston 2003, Monroy et al. 2003, Huan Wang et al. 2022]. According to their operating mechanism, semiconductor UV photodetectors fall into two main categories: a semiconductor photo detects the photoconductive effect, which is a consequence of the semiconductor photoconductor effect, while a second type uses the photovoltaic effect of heterojunction (Schottky or p-n) junction to separate charges [Su et al. 2017].

A photoconductive-based UV detector is the most straightforward type of photodetector. As a result, this type of photodetector relies on the absorption of UV light with energy larger than or close to the semiconductor's energy bandgap. Therefore, the absorbed UV light will induce photocarriers (electron-hole pairs) which will then be separated by the influence of the external bias. Consequently, changing the conductivity of the semiconductor. The generated carriers contribute to the current, which can be electrically measured via the external circuit [Nguyen et al. 2022, Yang 2020]. It is, therefore, possible to achieve high gains with these types of photodetectors. Metal ohmic contacts are usually coated at both ends of semiconductors to manufacture these photoconductors.

Photoconductive-based UV-C photodetectors have been employed for several applications due to their high internal gain [Reverchon et al. 2004] and responsivity compared to photovoltaic-based photodetectors [Chen et al. 2019, Jia et al. 2020, Liu et al. 2022].

Ga_2O_3 is deemed potential for solar-blind photodetectors as it is chemically and thermal stability, has high radiation resistance with an energy bandgap of 4.4 to 4.9 eV and a significant absorption coefficient [Kumar et al. 2014, Lin et al. 2019, Oh et al. 2015]. Ga_2O_3 has five different polymorphs, which are [Pearton et al. 2018] the cubic (δ), monoclinic (β-Ga_2O_3), rhombohedral (α), orthorhombic (ε), or defective spinel (γ) structures. The monoclinic (β-Ga_2O_3) has been widely used as the most consistent form under normal conditions. Various processes were employed to grow Ga_2O_3 for UV-C detection, such as atomic layer deposition (ALD), hydrothermal, pulsed laser deposition (PLD), and radio frequency (RF) magnetron sputtering [Atilgan et al. 2020, Gu et al. 2022, Pintor-Monroy et al. 2020, Yang et al. 2022]. Furthermore, Ga_2O_3 has been prepared in different forms, such as nanostructures (nanowires and nanorods) [Chen et al. 2022, Kumar et al. 2014], thin films [Pintor-Monroy et al. 2020], and bulk single crystals [Galazka et al. 2021].

To ensure that the device is functioning in photoconductor mode, the metallization of the electrode should be ohmic. Using titanium/gold (Ti/Au) thin films as contacts in Ga_2O_3-based photodetectors is common. There have also been studies on several other metals, with Ti/Au thin films remaining the best choice for Ga_2O_3 to act as an ohmic contact [Ahmadi and Oshima 2019]. Various substrates were used to grow Ga_2O_3 for optoelectronic applications, including sapphire [Pintor-Monroy et al. 2020], Si/SiO_2 [R. Lin et al. 2019], and MgO [Xinrong Chen et al. 2020]. There are several review articles [Chen et al. 2019, Hou et al. 2020, Kaur and Kumar 2021, Qin et al. 2019] that deal with the structure, optical, and preparation methods for Ga_2O_3. Thus, for this reason, we will focus on the application of Ga_2O_3 in the field of C-UV photodetectors.

The primary research on Ga_2O_3 focused on the optoelectronic properties of the device, i.e., their output response once illuminated by light in the UV-C range, to ensure that the devices will work properly under specific applications. Features such as response time and gain became crucial in applications such as flame detectors, image detectors, communication receivers, and others. The UV-C blind sensors must detect UV-C light rather than visible light or infrared, especially from the sun, to reduce the chance of false detection [Razeghi 2002]. In recent years, Ga_2O_3 has drawn the attention of various research groups due to its potential application in UV-C image sensing. In this direction, Lin [Lin et al. 2019] prepared Ga_2O_3 thin film over Si/SiO_2 substrates. The thin film was annealed under an oxygen atmosphere to ensure crystalline growth with standard stoichiometry β-phase Ga_2O_3. The device was prepared as an array of (16 × 16) by an etching process. A low background noise was measured, which is helpful for weak signal detection. The authors reported that the detector attains a responsivity of 1.75 A/W and an external quantum efficiency EQE of 854.3% with a detectivity value of 2.3×10^{11} Jones at a bias voltage of 10 V. Additionally, the linear-arrayed detector, which consists of 20 pixels, was only able to generate a photocurrent when exposed to a specific light source. Each pixel's photocurrent can be used to estimate the diameter of a light spot by using linear-arrayed detectors. The UV-C image of linear array detectors with Ga_2O_3 is shown in Figure 13.2.

Xie and co-workers introduced another attempt to use Ga_2O_3 as a photodetector array for optical imaging applications [Xie et al. 2021]. Two steps were involved in the construction of the device. Initially, a thin metal film of Ga with a thickness of 22 nm was deposited over a SiO_2/Si substrate by evaporating metallic Ga in a periodic square array (8 × 8 device units). The substrate was oxidized at 1100°C with a constant flow of O_2 gas. The device was tested under UV-C irradiance at a 265 nm wavelength. A low dark photocurrent was recorded at a bias voltage of 20 V. The photodetector array demonstrates excellent UV-C photoresponse property: the ratio of I_{ph}/I_{dark} is more than 10^4, with a response of ~ 0.72 A/W, and a specific detectivity of ~ 4.18×10^{11} Jones, respectively.

The device also showed an outstanding solar-blind spectral selectivity for UV/visible rejection with ~ 1.45×10^3 and ~ 5.86×10^2 at wavelengths (nm) 250/400

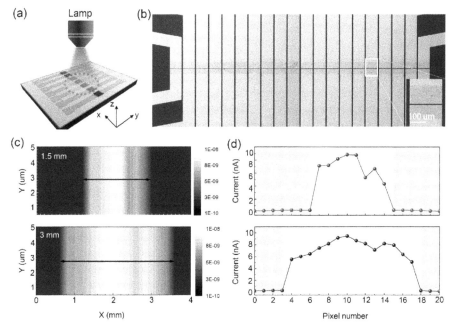

Figure 13.2: UV-C imaging of the linear-arrayed detector (a). The Diagram of the linear arrayed detector, A quartz lens is used to focus the UV-C light, producing a circular light spot (b). Optical image of the 20-pixel linear array detector with a 5 μm gap (c). Photocurrent image with 1.5 mm (upper) and 3 mm (lower) circular light spots illumination on it. Bright stripes indicate the size of the light spots (d). Photocurrent in the linear-arrayed detector as a function of pixels, corresponding to part c [Lin et al. 2019].

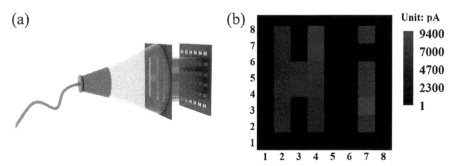

Figure 13.3: Presents the schematic of the linear-arrayed detector with the 265 nm filtered light (a). An optical photograph of 20 pixels UV-C image detector with a 5 μm gap (b) [Xie et al. 2021].

and 250/300, respectively. An array of Ga_2O_3 thin film photodetectors can work as a UV-C image sensor. Figure 13.3 reveals the pattern of the "Hi" character recorded after the UV-C illuminated the photodetectors array. The remaining array remained dark, shaded with the hollow mask.

Zhou and co-authors [Zhou et al. 2022b] studied the effect of three transparent conductive oxides, namely aluminium zinc oxide (AZO), indium tin oxide (ITO), and indium gallium zinc oxide (IGZO) films as electrodes. In their work, the authors prepared another phase of Ga_2O_3 known as ε-Ga_2O_3 with a hexagonal phase structure [Guo et al. 2019]). Each of the three photodetectors has extremely high responsivity, remarkable detectivity, excellent stability, and a fast photoresponse time. The results of the tested devices differed, likely due to their different resistivities and concentrations of carriers. The prepared devices with high-uniformity 5×4 arrays were tested as an ultraviolet imager. The arrays have high-fidelity characteristics that can be useful in imaging and machine vision applications. Chen and co-authors [Chen et al. 2022] proposed an alternative co-planer electrode over a flexible substrate. After coating an array of 7×7 Al metal, a layer of alumina oxide was deposited over the Al metal arrays, where the thin Ga_2O_3 film was then deposited. A thin layer of graphene nanosheet was assembled to complete the circuit. The Al metal will serve as a conductor and a reflector for the 260 nm UV-C light. In this structure $Al/Al_2O_3/Ga_2O_3$, the incident light will be reflected to the Ga_2O_3 thin film, which will increase the flux of the light to react with the Ga_2O_3. The device was tested for its imageability in UV-C for ultra-weak light detection and provided a path to high-performance solar-blind photodetectors.

Not only crystalline structures of Ga_2O_3 have been used as a media for the UV-C region, amorphas (a-Ga_2O_3) found their way as an image photodetector. Qin and co-authors [Qin et al. 2021] developed a 32×32 a-Ga_2O_3 image sensor array. The device exhibits superhigh sensitivity of 733 A/W and a high response time of 18 ms, a high gain bandwidth of 10^4 at 5 V and a high specific detectivity of 3.9×10^{16} Jones. A clear image of a target object with high contrast was attained due to the high sensitivity and uniformity of the a-Ga_2O_3 array.

Robust UV-C photodetectors that withstand potential extreme conditions like elevated temperatures are necessary for applications including space exploration, flame detection, and combustion monitoring [Ding et al. 2022, Kalra et al. 2022, Nguyen and Bark 2022, Toda et al. 2003, Zhou et al. 2020]. Furthermore, flexible UV-C photodetector for wearable electronics applications is also highly demanded. Ding and co-authors [Ding et al. 2022] prepared ultrathin Ga_2O_3 (15 nm thickness) through inkjet printing over SiO_2/Si wafer and flexible mica substrate with both devices operated at 250°C. Acceptable results of responsivity and detectivity are calculated with 0.14 A/W and 6.6×10^{11} Jones, and fast decay speed of 26 ms. The photocurrent of the devices increased under the illumination of UV-C light with a wavelength of 254 nm ranging from 72 to 540 $\mu W\ cm^{-2}$. The consistent results in the study performed by Ding and co-authors confirmed the potential of UV-C photodetection application in harsh-environment. The flexible printed Ga_2O_3 photodetector was tested in practical deep UV imaging applications with a prepared array of 4×4 photodetectors. A UV light with a wavelength of 254 nm passed through the steel mask with different letters, which the photodetector array can then detect. The sharp imaging capability of the flexible Ga_2O_3 deep UV photodetector array confirms the ability of the Ga_2O_3 photodetector for image applications. Another study on the effect of a high-temperature environment on the imaging performance of Ga_2O_3 thin film array was performed by Hou and co-authors [Hou et al. 2022]. In this study, the array was heated to 280 °C to investigate the performance of harsh conditions of the photodetector. The results reveal the high stability of the array and its capability of producing sharp imaging at elevated temperatures up to 280 °C. In addition, the results manifest the thermal stability of Ga_2O_3 thin film for harsh-environment applications.

The reproducibility and repeatability of the photodetector array published so far indicate the ability of Ga_2O_3 as a potential compound in applications such as imaging and machine vision. Table 13.1 compares the important parameters of Ga_2O_3 solar-blind PDs for imaging applications.

Since the 1960s, UV communications have been studied primarily for outdoor naval communications [Xu and Sadler 2008]. The optimal suppression of background radiation in a communication system requires solar-blind UV detectors under solar radiation [Brien 2011]. In short-range military communications, solar-blind deep ultraviolet (SDUC) has become a popular solution. Unlike other optical-based communication systems, the UV-C region of electromagnetic radiation has a low background noise that will not need an optical filter to reduce the stray background noise [Brien 2011, Lin et al. 2019]. Zhou and co-authors [Zhou et al. 2022a] introduced UV-C photodetectors based on β-G_2O_3 for SDUC. The device has a high responsivity of 1.93 A/W, exceptional detectivity of 6.53×10^{13} Jones, and a photo-to-dark current ratio of 3.58×10^5, with an ultrafast response, which is crucial for a communication system. The prepared device was integrated into the SDUC system as a signal receiver. Their results showed a significant accuracy in receiving transmittance code up to a data rate of 10 kbps. On the other hand, Zhou and co-authors [Zhou et al. 2022b] extended their work with an attempt to utilize ε-Ga_2O_3 with fully transparent electrodes (ITO, AZO, and IGZO) as a receiver for a communication system. Data was transmitted using a homemade solar-blind ultraviolet transmission system (photodetector). Figure 13.4 (a) illustrates the principle of ultraviolet communication using a solar-blind photodetector as an optical receiver. Figure 13.4 (b) illustrates how a faster photodetector would increase the transmission rate of a solar-blind deep-ultraviolet communication system. In this case, the photodetector using ITO shows the best and most reliable performance due to its faster response time.

Flame detectors based on UV-C photodetector play a significant role in building safety. Avila-Avendano [Avila-Avendano et al. 2021] prepared a Ga_2O_3 thin film via a sputtering process over Si/SiO_2 substrate as a part of a CMOS amplifier device. The maximum response of 51 A/W at 232 nm was achieved with a high gain of 210. Moreover, the Ga_2O_3 thin film rejected approximately 100 UV-C rays because of its blind UV-C characteristic. When exposed to deep UV light generated by the flame, the prepared sensor produced voltage pulses with amplitudes up to 2 V. As a result of the Ga_2O_3 sensor's intrinsic low sensitivity to visible light, no optical filter was required to detect the flame's signal despite visible background illumination. Another attempt by Oshima and co-authors [Oshima et al. 2009] proposed a flame detector using a Ga_2O_3 Schottky junction. The device was initially

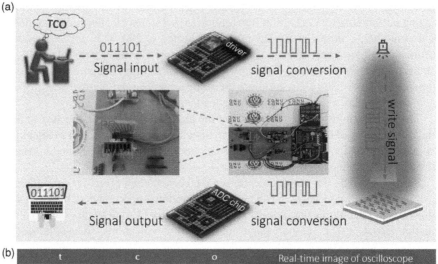

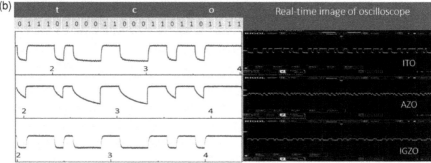

Figure 13.4: The proposed solar-blind ultraviolet communication principle is depicted in a sketch diagram (a). Waveform and real-time image of an optical signal-receiving photodetector [Zhou et al. 2022b].

tested for long wavelengths (greater than 300 nm) and a large rejection ratio of 1.5×10^4 for the 250/300 nm, showing that the Ga_2O_3 Schottky junction detector was solar blind. Furthermore, the photoresponsivity at 250 nm was 37 mA/W with a rise and fall time of approximately 9 ms. The results demonstrated that the proposed Ga_2O_3 Schottky junction could be used for furnace control and gas flame safety.

Solar-blind photodetectors were utilized as position-sensitive detectors. Li and co-anthers [Li et al. 2020] prepared β-Ga_2O_3 for position detectors with the preparation of four quadrant position-sensitive detectors. All photodetector components have high uniformity and fast rise/fall times of 22 ms/2.8 ms. The demonstration manifested the potential application of the UV-C photodetectors in optical tracking, positioning, and communication. Amorphous Ga_2O_3 films grown on polyethylene terephthalate (PET) substrates created a 3D solar-blind photodetector array [Chen et al. 2019]. The photodetector cells have a dark current of 0.17 nA and a peak responsivity of approximately 8.9 A/W at 250 nm. The detectivity of the photodetector was 3.3×10^{13} Jones at 15 V bias. Figure 13.5 reveals the schematic

Table 13.1: Comparison of arrayed photoconductive Ga_2O_3 solar-blind PDs.

Materials	Array dimension	electrode material	R A/W	D^* Jones	τ_{raise} /τ_{fall} ms	References
a-Ga_2O_3 (amorphous)	8×3	Au	8.9 (12 V)	3.3×10^{13}	0.015/0.308	[Chen et al. 2019]
a-Ga_2O_3 (amorphous)	32×32	Ti/Au	733 (5V)	3.9×10^{16}	1/18	[Qin et al. 2021]
ε-Ga_2O_3	5×4	ITO	286 (10V)	4.73×10^{14}	5.6/7.2	[Zhou et al. 2022b]
ε-Ga_2O_3	5×4	AZO	262 (10V)	2.16×10^{14}	70/200	[Zhou et al. 2022b]
ε-Ga_2O_3	5×4	IGZO	284 (10V)	5.06×10^{15}	6.9/9.5	[Zhou et al. 2022b]
β-Ga_2O_3	4×4	Au	1.2 (10V)	1.9×10^{12}	---	[Chen et al. 2019]
β-Ga_2O_3	4×4	Ti/Au	1.3 (15V)	1.46×10^{14}	313/26	[Ding et al. 2022]
β-Ga_2O_3	16×16	Ti/Au	1.75 (10V)	2.3×10^{11}		[Lin et al. 2019]
β-Ga_2O_3	8×8	Au	0.72 (20V)	4.18×10^{11}	1100/30	[Xie et al. 2021]
β-Ga_2O_3	7×7	graphene film	295 (10V)	1.7×10^{15}	1.7×10^{-3}/ 79.7×10^{-3}	[Chen et al. 2022]
β-Ga_2O_3	4×4	Ti/Au	634 (10V)	5.93×10^{11}	---	[Liu et al. 2022]
Ga_2O_3 nanowires	Single	Au	233 (10V)	8.16×10^{12}	480/40	[Xie et al. 2019a]
Sn-doped Ga_2O_3 nanowires	1×10	Ti/Au	211 (5V) 2,409 (40V)	---	7.9/1180	[Lu et al. 2022]

of the proposed 3D Ga_2O_3 photodetector array with the rise/fall time of the response process was 308 μs/1.7 ms, respectively. However, the 3D Ga_2O_3 photodetector array preparation over PET flexible substrate and the bending of the device showed an insignificant effect on its uniformity performance. Multipoint light distribution detection is possible with 3D photodetector arrays compared to 2D arrays [Chen et al. 2019, Li et al. 2020].

In previous applications, the photodetectors were based on the photoconductive detection mechanism. The main advantage of photoconductor-based UV-C sensors is their high gain and fast response, which is crucial to prevent the problem of weak UV-C signals [Mahmoud 2016]. The gain and the time response of photoconductors material are typically a magnitude or higher than that of photovoltaic detectors for the specific material. However, other operational characteristics, such as the bandwidth and UV/visible ratio, are typically lower than those of photovoltaic photodetectors,

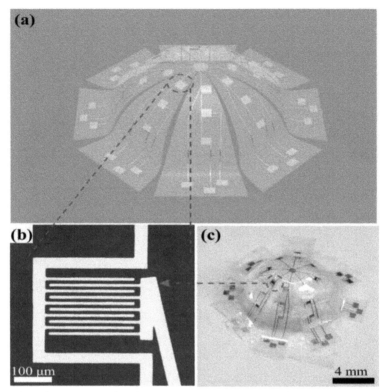

Figure 13.5: The 3D Ga$_2$O$_3$ photodetector array schematic (a). A microscope image of a single photodetector cell (b), and a visual photograph of a 3D Ga$_2$O$_3$ photodetector array (c) [Chen et al. 2019].

which often limits the scope of its potential applications [Decoster and Harari 2013]. Traditionally, UV photodetectors require external power. However, batteries are not the best option for today's energy-saving and environmentally friendly practices, primarily due to their hazardous nature. Schottky barrier, heterojunction, and p-n junction photodetectors operate without an external voltage source due to the induced electric fields within the junction that the separate electron-hole pairs. Since this separation occurs under the influence of the electric field, it can be used for an extended period in remote areas and outer space [Wang et al. 2020]. In the coming paragraphs, we will explore cutting-edge applications for UV-C sensors based on photovoltaic mechanisms.

The main limitation of emerging Ga$_2$O$_3$ technology might be the problem of preparing p-type Ga$_2$O$_3$ and the lack of an intrinsic conductivity because of its wide band energy gap [Chikoidze et al. 2017, Wu et al. 2022]. Nevertheless, there are several attempts to prepare p-type Ga$_2$O$_3$ [Chikoidze et al. 2017, Jiang et al. 2020, Yan et al. 2021]. Due to the lack and early manufacturing stages of p-type Ga$_2$O$_3$, several alternative substrates with high stability performance are employed in the fabrication of p-n junction devices, such as p-Si [Pedapudi and Dhar 2022], SiC [Yu

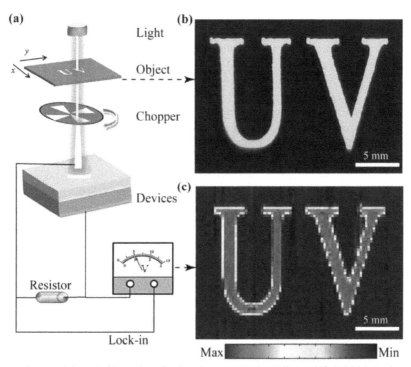

Figure 13.6: (a) Schematic illustration of an imaging system using a diamond/ β-Ga2O3 heterojunction photodetector as a sensing pixel with a bias of 0 V. (b) An image of the object with the letters "UV" written on black paper. (c) Image captured by the imaging system [Chen et al. 2018].

et al. 2020], diamond [Kim et al. 2020], GaN [Chen et al. 2022], NiO [Wang et al. 2020], and conductive polymers [Wu et al. 2022].

Next, we will focus on the applications of Ga_2O_3 that work under the photovoltaic concept, as several published review articles dealing with the manufacturing, detection mechanism, and performance of the Ga_2O_3 junctions. Compared to metal-semiconductor-metal (MSM) ohmic photodetectors, heterojunctions operate at zero voltage, which is a significant advantage for flexible devices such as biosensors and space applications that require zero voltage operation. As a result, many studies focus on Ga_2O_3 junctions for UV-C photodetectors [Chen et al. 2019, Jamwal and Kiani 2022, Xu et al. 2019]. The self-powered diamond/β-Ga_2O_3 photodetectors for UV-C imaging demonstrated good repeatability and consistency without any additional power supply with a responsivity of 0.2 mA/W at a wavelength of 244 nm and a detectivity of 6.9×10^9 jones [Chen et al. 2018]. An imaging system with a photodetector as a sensing pixel was built to investigate the self-powered photodetector's imaging capability. The device shows a sharp image of the mask as shown in Figure 13.6.

The Song team introduced an alternative design for UV-C image sensing [Liu et al. 2022]. The self-powered device was composed of G_2O_3 grown over p-type NiO/SiC and a photo-responsivity of approximately 0.51 mA/W at 266 nm (at V = 0V) with a fast response time of 0.59 μs. It also has a large voltage on/off ratio (V_{Iph}/V_{dark} > 100). The proposed structure of Ga_2O_3/NiO/SiC heterojunction using a 266 nm nanosecond laser system for its image detection highly exhibited position sensitivity of 750.86 mV/mm. Even at a low laser power of 130 mW (to micro W), the device records a position sensitivity of 6.51 mV/mm. Further testing of the self-operated device was conducted under additional circumstances, which included varying laser power, varying background illumination, and a broad range of ambient temperatures, ranging from –75°C to 200°C. Due to its excellent thermal stability, this device is suitable for astronomical and military applications. Another Ga_2O_3-based self-powered photodetector [Wu et al. 2022] heterojunction was prepared by attaching Ga_2O_3 with small-molecule hole transport materials (SMHTMs) such as triphenylamine. Four different types of triphenylamine were tested as SMHTMs with a high on/off ratio of up to 10^5 times and detectivity in the range of 8.3×10^{12} to 1.02×10^{13} Jones at 0 V. The device shows a fast response speed with rising and decay times of 190 – 270 and 50 – 130 ms, respectively. Further, the device has been tested as a receiver in the solar-blind optical communication system. The Ga_2O_3/SMHTM device received and displayed the accepted code in the current-time graph by decoding the transmitter UV-C light using Morse code. The optical communication setup with its received code is depicted in Figure 13.7.

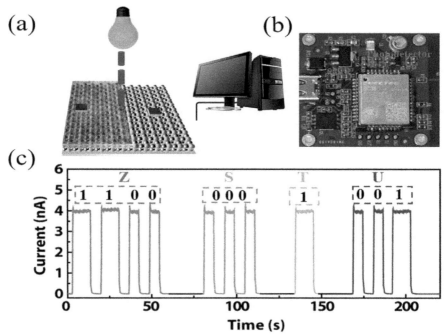

Figure 13.7: Solar-blind optical communication system schematic diagram (a). A solar-blind communication system proof-of-concept (b). The Morse code-based photodetector decoding process used in optical communication (c) [Wu et al. 2022].

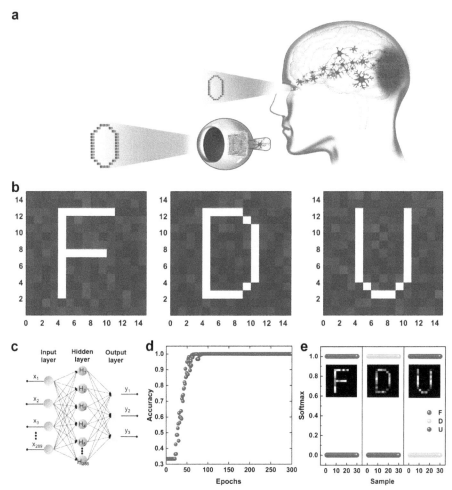

Figure 13.8: The fabricated β-Ga$_2$O$_3$ phototransistor was used to simulate an artificial neural network (ANN). (a) diagram of the human nerve visual system. (b) Illustration of the corresponding UV detector arrays. (c) An illustration of an artificial visual-neural network (d) Image recognition rate of UV detector arrays. (e) Using the letters in the image database, a trained artificial neural network calculates [Li et al. 2022].

Another exciting application of a robust UV-C phototransistor based on Ta-doped β-Ga$_2$O$_3$. The prepared device reveals outstanding optoelectrical properties with a high responsivity of 1.32×10^6 A/W, a high detectivity of 5.68×10^{14} Jones with a fast response time of ~ 3.50 ms [Li et al. 2022]. Moreover, the team studied the possibility of applying phototransistors to artificial intelligence and robotics. In Figure 13.8, an artificial neural network (ANN) simulates the human visual system where the UV detector perceives the image. Images representing the letters F, D, and U (Figure 13.8 (b)) served as a database for the artificial neural visual system. As a result of the large I_{ph} produced by the phototransistor, the image of letters formed was in sharp contrast, making it easier for robots to recognize them.

ANN algorithms are used in traditional machine vision systems to train and recognize images through a three-layer artificial neural network (Figure 13.8 (c)). Input (128 neurons), hidden (225 neurons), and output (3 neurons) make up the three-layer ANN. Phototransistor arrays reach 99% image recognition after 64 training epochs, indicating high image recognition efficiency (Figure 13.8 (d)). For further validation of the trained ANN's high image recognition rate, 90 examples of "F" images, "D" images, and "U" images were selected and fed into the ANN. The probabilities were computed and plotted based on the three possible outcomes (Figure 13.8 (e)). The results demonstrate that the trained ANN has excellent recognition ability and the β-Ga$_2$O$_3$ UV phototransistors array's ability to perform high imaging processes for different cutting-edge applications.

13.4 Summary

In this article, we outlined the ability of gallium oxide (Ga$_2$O$_3$) for modern optoelectronics applications in the field related to machine vision. Ga$_2$O$_3$ is a potential compound for UV detection in the blind solar UV region of electromagnetic radiation (UV-C, which covers wavelengths between 200 and 280 nm). Ga$_2$O$_3$ is a promising ultrawide energy bandgap material that attracted the attention of several groups globally for its cost-effective preparation methods, energy bandgap that covers the UV-C range without doping or alloying process, hence making it superior in their mechanical, thermal, and electrical stability performance as compared with the other competitive compound such as Al$_x$Ga$_{1-x}$N.

The result also reveals the potential application of Ga$_2$O$_3$ in UV vision applications that have many promising applications in industry, out space, machine vision and other applications.

Despite the early stages of research and the development of Ga2O3-based devices, it has proven its concepts at the laboratory scale. However, more research is required to fully understand and control its manufacturing process for real-life applications.

Acknowledgments

The authors acknowledge the financial support from the Universiti Kebangsaan Malaysia (UKM).

Conflict of interest

The authors declare that they have no known competing financial interests or personal relationships that could have appeared to influence the work reported in this paper.

References

Ahad, Tashmeeta, Wang, Elle Yueqiao, Liu, Yi A., Lee, Tim K., Lui, Harvey, Crawford, Richard I. et al. 2022. Incidence of skin cancers in patients with eczema treated with ultraviolet phototherapy. Journal of the American Academy of Dermatology, 87(2): 387–389. doi:https://doi.org/10.1016/j.jaad.2021.11.048

Ahmadi, Elaheh, and Oshima, Yuichi. 2019. Materials issues and devices of α- and β-Ga_2O_3. Journal of Applied Physics, 126(16): 160901. doi:https://doi.org/10.1063/1.5123213.

Al-Hardan, N. H., Jalar, Azman, Abdul Hamid, M. A., Keng, Lim Kar, Ahmed, N. M., and Shamsudin, R. 2014. A wide-band UV photodiode based on n-ZnO/p-Si heterojunctions. Sensors and Actuators A: Physical, 207: 61–66. doi:https://doi.org/10.1016/j.sna.2013.12.024.

Alaie, Z., Mohammad Nejad, S., and Yousefi, M. H. 2015. Recent advances in ultraviolet photodetectors. Materials Science in Semiconductor Processing, 29: 16–55. doi:https://doi.org/10.1016/j.mssp.2014.02.054.

Arya, S., and Chung, Y. H. 2021. Novel Indoor Ultraviolet Wireless Communication: Design Implementation, Channel Modeling, and Challenges. IEEE Systems Journal, 15(2): 2349–2360. doi:https://doi.org/10.1109/JSYST.2020.2995919.

Atilgan, A., Yildiz, A., Harmanci, U., Gulluoglu, M. T., and Salimi, K. 2020. β-Ga_2O_3 nanoflakes/p-Si heterojunction self-powered photodiodes. Materials Today Communications, 24: 101105. doi:https://doi.org/10.1016/j.mtcomm.2020.101105.

Avila-Avendano, Carlos, Pintor-Monroy, Maria I., Ortiz-Conde, Adelmo, Caraveo-Frescas, Jesus A., and Quevedo-Lopez, Manuel A. 2021. Deep UV Sensors Enabling Solar-Blind Flame Detectors for Large-Area Applications. IEEE Sensors Journal, 21(13): 14815–14821. doi:https://doi.org/10.1109/jsen.2021.3071980.

Baltadourou, M. S., Delibasis, K. K., Tsigaridas, G. N., Sandalidis, H. G., and Karagiannidis, G. K. 2021. LaUV: A physics-based UV light simulator for disinfection and communication applications. IEEE Access, 9, 137543–137559. doi:https://doi.org/10.1109/ACCESS.2021.3118302.

Barnes, Paul W., Williamson, Craig E., Lucas, Robyn M., Robinson, Sharon A., Madronich, Sasha, Paul, Nigel D. et al. 2019. Ozone depletion, ultraviolet radiation, climate change and prospects for a sustainable future. Nature Sustainability, 2(7): 569–579. doi:https://doi.org/10.1038/s41893-019-0314-2.

Berg, Hermann. 2008. Johann Wilhelm Ritter - The Founder of Scientific Electrochemistry. Review of Polarography, 54(2): 99–103. doi:https://doi.org/10.5189/revpolarography.54.99.

Brand, R. M., Wipf, P., Durham, A., Epperly, M. W., Greenberger, J. S. and Falo, L. D. Jr. 2018. Targeting Mitochondrial Oxidative Stress to Mitigate UV-Induced Skin Damage. Front. Pharmacol., 9: 920. doi:https://doi.org/10.3389/fphar.2018.00920

Brien, D. C. O'. 2011. Visible Light Communications: Challenges and potential. Paper presented at the IEEE Photonic Society 24th Annual Meeting.

Buonanno, Manuela, Welch, David, Shuryak, Igor, and Brenner, David J. 2020. Far-UVC light (222 nm) efficiently and safely inactivates airborne human coronaviruses. Scientific reports, 10(1): 10285. doi:https://doi.org/10.1038/s41598-020-67211-2.

Cai, Qing, You, Haifan, Guo, Hui, Wang, Jin, Liu, Bin, Xie, Zili et al. 2021. Progress on AlGaN-based solar-blind ultraviolet photodetectors and focal plane arrays. Light: Science & Applications, 10(1): 94. doi:https://doi.org/10.1038/s41377-021-00527-4.

Chen, Hao, Ma, Xinzhou, Zhang, Jingtao, Li, Qiuguo, Liu, Huiqiang, Chen, Zuxin et al. 2018. Avalanche solar blind photodetectors with high responsivity based on MgO/MgZnO heterostructures. Optical Materials Express, 8(4): 785–793. doi:https://doi.org/10.1364/OME.8.000785.

Chen, Hongyu, Liu, Kewei, Hu, Linfeng, Al-Ghamdi, Ahmed A., and Fang, Xiaosheng. 2015. New concept ultraviolet photodetectors. Materials Today, 18(9): 493–502. doi:https://doi.org/10.1016/j.mattod.2015.06.001.

Chen, Rongrong, Wang, Di, Liu, Jie, Feng, Bo, Zhu, Hongyan, Han, Xinyu et al. 2022. Ta-Doped Ga$_2$O$_3$ Epitaxial Films on Porous p-GaN Substrates: Structure and Self-Powered Solar-Blind Photodetectors. Crystal Growth & Design, 22(9): 5285–5292. doi:https://doi.org/10.1021/acs.cgd.2c00401.

Chen, Wei-Han, Ma, Chun-Hao, Hsieh, Shang-Hsien, Lai, Yu-Hong, Kuo, Yen-Chien, Chen, Chia-Hao et al. 2022. High stability flexible deep-UV detector based on all-oxide heteroepitaxial junction. ACS Applied Electronic Materials, 4(6): 3099–3106. doi:https://doi.org/10.1021/acsaelm.2c00470.

Chen, Xinrong, Mi, Wei, Wu, Jianwen, Yang, Zhengchun, Zhang, Kailiang, Zhao, Jinshi et al. 2020. A solar-blind photodetector based on β-Ga$_2$O$_3$ film deposited on MgO (100) substrates by RF magnetron sputtering. Vacuum, 180, 109632. doi:https://doi.org/10.1016/j.vacuum.2020.109632

Chen, Xuanhu, Ren, Fang-Fang, Ye, Jiandong, and Gu, Shulin. 2020. Gallium oxide-based solar-blind ultraviolet photodetectors. Semiconductor Science and Technology, 35(2): 023001. doi:http://dx.doi.org/10.1088/1361-6641/ab6102.

Chen, Xuanhu, Ren, Fangfang, Gu, Shulin, and Ye, Jiandong. 2019. Review of gallium-oxide-based solar-blind ultraviolet photodetectors. Photonics Research, 7(4): 381–415. doi:https://doi.org/10.1364/PRJ.7.000381.

Chen, Yan-Cheng, Lu, Ying-Jie, Lin, Chao-Nan, Tian, Yong-Zhi, Gao, Chao-Jun, Dong, Lin, and Shan, Chong-Xin. 2018. Self-powered diamond/β-Ga$_2$O$_3$ photodetectors for solar-blind imaging. Journal of Materials Chemistry C, 6(21): 5727–5732. doi:http://dx.doi.org/10.1039/C8TC01122B.

Chen, Yan-Cheng, Lu, Ying-Jie, Liu, Qian, Lin, Chao-Nan, Guo, Juan, Zang, Jin-Hao et al. 2019. Ga$_2$O$_3$ photodetector arrays for solar-blind imaging. Journal of Materials Chemistry C, 7(9): 2557–2562. doi:http://dx.doi.org/10.1039/C8TC05251D.

Chen, Yancheng, Lu, Yingjie, Liao, Meiyong, Tian, Yongzhi, Liu, Qian, Gao, Chaojun et al. 2019. 3D Solar-Blind Ga$_2$O$_3$ Photodetector Array Realized Via Origami Method. Advanced Functional Materials, 29(50): 1906040. doi:https://doi.org/10.1002/adfm.201906040.

Chen, Yancheng, Yang, Xun, Zhang, Yuan, Chen, Xuexia, Sun, Junlu, Xu, Zhiyang et al. 2022. Ultra-sensitive flexible Ga$_2$O$_3$ solar-blind photodetector array realized via ultra-thin absorbing medium. Nano Research, 15(4): 3711–3719. doi:https://doi.org/10.1007/s12274-021-3942-6.

Chikoidze, Ekaterine, Fellous, Adel, Perez-Tomas, Amador, Sauthier, Guillaume, Tchelidze, Tamar, Ton-That, Cuong et al. 2017. P-type β-gallium oxide: A new perspective for power and optoelectronic devices. Materials Today Physics, 3: 118–126. doi:https://doi.org/10.1016/j.mtphys.2017.10.002.

Cruse, Courtney A., and Goodpaster, John V. 2021. Optimization of gas chromatography/vacuum ultraviolet (GC/VUV) spectroscopy for explosive compounds and application to post-blast debris. Forensic Chemistry, 26: 100362. doi:https://doi.org/10.1016/j.forc.2021.100362.

Decoster, Didier, and Harari, Joseph (eds.). 2013. Optoelectronic sensors]: John Wiley & Sons.

Delorme, Mariana M., Guimarães, Jonas T., Coutinho, Nathália M., Balthazar, Celso F., Rocha, Ramon S., Silva, Ramon et al. 2020. Ultraviolet radiation: An interesting technology to preserve quality and safety of milk and dairy foods. Trends in Food Science & Technology, 102: 146–154. doi:https://doi.org/10.1016/j.tifs.2020.06.001.

Diffey, B. L. 1980. Ultraviolet radiation physics and the skin. Physics in Medicine and Biology, 25(3): 405–426. doi:http://dx.doi.org/10.1088/0031-9155/25/3/001.

Ding, Mengfan, Liang, Kun, Yu, Shunjie, Zhao, Xiaolong, Ren, Huihui, Zhu, Bowen et al. 2022. Aqueous-Printed Ga$_2$O$_3$ Films for high-performance flexible and heat-resistant deep ultraviolet photodetector and array. Advanced Optical Materials, 10(16): 2200512. doi:https://doi.org/10.1002/adom.202200512.

Fujinawa, Tamaki, Noguchi, Katsuyuki, Kuze, Akihiko, Richter, Andreas, Burrows, John P., Meier, Andreas C. et al. 2019. Concept of small satellite UV/visible imaging spectrometer optimized for tropospheric NO$_2$ measurements in air quality monitoring. Acta Astronautica, 160: 421–432. doi:https://doi.org/10.1016/j.actaastro.2019.03.081.

Galazka, Zbigniew, Ganschow, Steffen, Irmscher, Klaus, Klimm, Detlef, Albrecht, Martin, Schewski, Robert et al. 2021. Bulk single crystals of β-Ga$_2$O$_3$ and Ga-based spinels as ultra-wide bandgap transparent semiconducting oxides. Progress in Crystal Growth and Characterization of Materials, 67(1): 100511. doi:https://doi.org/10.1016/j.pcrysgrow.2020.100511.

Gu, Keyun, Zhang, Zilong, Tang, Ke, Huang, Jian, Liao, Meiyong, and Wang, Linjun. 2022. Effects of sputtering pressure and oxygen partial pressure on amorphous Ga_2O_3 film-based solar-blind ultraviolet photodetectors. Applied Surface Science, 154606. doi:https://doi.org/10.1016/j.apsusc.2022.154606.

Guo, D., Guo, Q., Chen, Z., Wu, Z., Li, P., and Tang, W. 2019. Review of Ga_2O_3-based optoelectronic devices. Materials Today Physics, 11: 100157. doi:https://doi.org/10.1016/j.mtphys.2019.100157.

Guo, Dechao, Yang, Liqing, Zhao, Jingcheng, Li, Ji, He, Guo, Yang, Dezhi et al. 2021. Visible-blind ultraviolet narrowband photomultiplication-type organic photodetector with an ultrahigh external quantum efficiency of over Materials Horizons, 8(8): 2293–2302. doi:http://dx.doi.org/10.1039/D1MH00776A.

Hatsusaka, Natsuko, Yamamoto, Naoki, Miyashita, Hisanori, Shibuya, Eri, Mita, Norihiro, Yamazaki, Mai et al. 2021. Association among pterygium, cataracts, and cumulative ocular ultraviolet exposure: A cross-sectional study in Han people in China and Taiwan. PLOS ONE, 16(6): e0253093. doi:https://doi.org/10.1371/journal.pone.0253093.

Hinds, Laura M., O'Donnell, Colm P., Akhter, Mahbub, and Tiwari, Brijesh K. 2019. Principles and mechanisms of ultraviolet light emitting diode technology for food industry applications. Innovative Food Science & Emerging Technologies, 56: 102153. doi:https://doi.org/10.1016/j.ifset.2019.04.006.

Holick, Michael F. 2004. Vitamin D: importance in the prevention of cancers, type 1 diabetes, heart disease, and osteoporosis. The American Journal of Clinical Nutrition, 79(3): 362–371. doi:https://doi.org/10.1093/ajcn/79.3.362.

Holick, Michael F. 2006. Resurrection of vitamin D deficiency and rickets. The Journal of Clinical Investigation, 116(8): 2062–2072. doi:https://doi.org/10.1172/JCI29449.

Hou, Xiaohu, Zhao, Xiaolong, Zhang, Ying, Zhang, Zhongfang, Liu, Yan, Qin, Yuan et al. 2022. High-Performance Harsh-Environment-Resistant GaO_x Solar-Blind Photodetectors via Defect and Doping Engineering. Advanced Materials, 34(1): 2106923. doi:https://doi.org/10.1002/adma.202106923.

Hou, Xiaohu, Zou, Yanni, Ding, Mengfan, Qin, Yuan, Zhang, Zhongfang, Ma, Xiaolan et al. 2020. Review of polymorphous Ga_2O_3 materials and their solar-blind photodetector applications. Journal of Physics D: Applied Physics, 54(4): 043001. doi:http://dx.doi.org/10.1088/1361-6463/abbb45.

Huffman, Robert E. 1992. Atmospheric ultraviolet remote sensing (Vol. 52): Academic Press.

Jamwal, Nishant Singh, and Kiani, Amirkianoosh. 2022. Gallium Oxide Nanostructures: A Review of Synthesis, Properties and Applications. Nanomaterials, 12(12): 2061. doi:https://doi.org/10.3390/nano12122061.

Jebar, A., Mustapha, A., Parisi, Alfio V., Downs, Nathan J., and Turner, Joanna F. 2017. Validation of Ozone monitoring instrument UV satellite data using spectral and broadband surface based measurements at a queensland site. Photochemistry and Photobiology, 93(5): 1289–1293. doi:https://doi.org/10.1111/php.12784.

Jia, Lemin, Zheng, Wei, and Huang, Feng. 2020. Vacuum-ultraviolet photodetectors. PhotoniX, 1(1), 22. doi:https://doi.org/10.1186/s43074-020-00022-w.

Jiang, Z. X., Wu, Z. Y., Ma, C. C., Deng, J. N., Zhang, H., Xu, Y. et al. 2020. P-type β-Ga_2O_3 metal-semiconductor-metal solar-blind photodetectors with extremely high responsivity and gain-bandwidth product. Materials Today Physics, 14: 100226. doi:https://doi.org/10.1016/j.mtphys.2020.100226.

Kalra, Anisha, Muazzam, Usman Ul, Muralidharan, R., Raghavan, Srinivasan, and Nath, Digbijoy N. 2022. The road ahead for ultrawide bandgap solar-blind UV photodetectors. Journal of Applied Physics, 131(15): 150901. doi:https://doi.org/10.1063/5.0082348.

Kanellis, Vangelis, George. 2019. Ultraviolet radiation sensors: a review. Biophysical Reviews, 11(6): 895–899. doi:https://doi.org/10.1007/s12551-019-00556-9.

Kaur, Damanpreet, and Kumar, Mukesh. 2021. A strategic review on gallium oxide based deep-ultraviolet photodetectors: Recent progress and future prospects. Advanced Optical Materials, 9(9): 2002160. doi:https://doi.org/10.1002/adom.202002160.

Khan, Sulaiman, Newport, David, and Le Calvé, Stéphane. 2021. A sensitive and portable deep-UV absorbance detector with a microliter gas cell compatible with micro GC. Chemosensors, 9(4): 63. doi:http://dx.doi.org/10.3390/chemosensors9040063.

Kim, Hyun, Tarelkin, Sergey, Polyakov, Alexander, Troschiev, Sergey, Nosukhin, Sergey, Kuznetsov, Mikhail et al. 2020. Ultrawide-Bandgap p-n Heterojunction of Diamond/β-Ga$_2$O$_3$ for a Solar-Blind Photodiode. ECS Journal of Solid State Science and Technology, 9(4): 045004. doi:http://dx.doi.org/10.1149/2162-8777/ab89b8.

Kingston, Robert H. 2003. Optical Detectors. *In*: Robert, A. Meyers (ed.). Encyclopedia of Physical Science and Technology (Third Edition) (pp. 237–253). New York: Academic Press.

Kumar, Sudheer, Tessarek, C., Christiansen, S., and Singh, R. 2014. A comparative study of β-Ga$_2$O$_3$ nanowires grown on different substrates using CVD technique. Journal of Alloys and Compounds, 587: 812–818. doi:https://doi.org/10.1016/j.jallcom.2013.10.165.

Kuzin, S. V., Pertsov, A. A., Kirichenko, A. S., Sachkov, M. E., Savanov, I. S., and Shugarov, A. S. 2018. Space Instrumentation of the WSO-UV Mission for Astrophysics Research. Journal of Surface Investigation: X-ray, Synchrotron and Neutron Techniques, 12(4): 678–681. doi:https://doi.org/10.1134/S1027451018040122.

Lan, Zhaojue, Lee, Min-Hsuan, and Zhu, Furong. 2022. Recent Advances in Solution-Processable Organic Photodetectors and Applications in Flexible Electronics. Advanced Intelligent Systems, 4(3): 2100167. doi:https://doi.org/10.1002/aisy.202100167.

Lavigne, Claire, Durand, Gérard, and Roblin, Antoine. 2006. Ultraviolet light propagation under low visibility atmospheric conditions and its application to aircraft landing aid. Applied Optics, 45(36): 9140–9150. doi:https://doi.org/10.1364/AO.45.009140.

Li, Kaiyong, Yang, Xun, Tian, Yongzhi, Chen, Yancheng, Lin, Chaonan, Zhang, Zhenfeng et al. 2020. Ga$_2$O$_3$ solar-blind position-sensitive detectors. Science China Physics, Mechanics & Astronomy, 63(11): 117312. doi:https://doi.org/10.1007/s11433-020-1581-4.

Li, Xiao-Xi, Zeng, Guang, Li, Yu-Chun, Zhang, Hao, Ji, Zhi-Gang, Yang, Ying-Guo et al. 2022. High responsivity and flexible deep-UV phototransistor based on Ta-doped β-Ga2O3. npj Flexible Electronics, 6(1): 47. doi:https://doi.org/10.1038/s41528-022-00179-3.

Li, Yuqiang, Zheng, Wei, and Huang, Feng. 2020. All-silicon photovoltaic detectors with deep ultraviolet selectivity. PhotoniX, 1(1): 15. doi:https://doi.org/10.1186/s43074-020-00014-w.

Lin, ChaoNan, Lu, YingJie, Tian, YongZhi, Gao, ChaoJun, Fan, MingMing, Yang, Xun et al. 2019. Diamond based photodetectors for solar-blind communication. Optics Express, 27(21): 29962–29971. doi:https://doi.org/10.1364/OE.27.029962.

Lin, Richeng, Zheng, Wei, Zhang, Dan, Li, Yuqiang, and Huang, Feng. 2019. Brushed crystallized ultrathin oxides: Recrystallization and deep-ultraviolet imaging application. ACS Applied Electronic Materials, 1(10): 2166–2173. doi:https://doi.org/10.1021/acsaelm.9b00536.

Liu, Mengting, Zhu, Senyin, Zhang, Hanxu, Wang, Xianjie, and Song, Bo. 2022. Triple layer heterojunction Ga$_2$O$_3$/NiO/SiC for ultrafast, high-response ultraviolet image sensing. Applied Physics Letters, 121(11): 112104. doi:https://doi.org/10.1063/5.0105350.

Liu, N., Zhang, T., Chen, L., Zhang, J., Hu, S., Guo, W. et al. 2022. Fast-response amorphous Ga2O3 solar-blind ultraviolet photodetectors tuned by a polar AlN template. IEEE Electron Device Letters, 43(1): 68–71. doi:https://doi.org/10.1109/LED.2021.3132497.

Liu, Zeng, Zhi, Yu-Song, Zhang, Mao-Lin, Yang, Li-Li, Li, Shan, Yan, Zu-Yong et al. 2022. A 4×4 metal-semiconductor-metal rectangular deep-ultraviolet detector array of Ga$_2$O$_3$ photoconductor with high photo response. Chinese Physics B, 31(8): 088503. doi:http://dx.doi.org/10.1088/1674-1056/ac597d.

Lu, Ya-Cong, Zhang, Zhen-Feng, Yang, Xun, He, Gao-Hang, Lin, Chao-Nan, Chen, Xue-Xia et al. 2022. High-performance solar-blind photodetector arrays constructed from Sn-doped Ga$_2$O$_3$ microwires via patterned electrodes. Nano Research, 15(8): 7631–7638. doi:https://doi.org/10.1007/s12274-022-4341-3.

Lv, Zhisheng, Liu, Lei, Zhangyang, Xingyue, Sun, Yan, Lu, Feifei, and Tian, Jian. 2021. Designs of photoabsorption-enhanced variable Al component GaN nanostructure for UV photodetectors. Physica E: Low-dimensional Systems and Nanostructures, 126: 114496. doi:https://doi.org/10.1016/j.physe.2020.114496.

Mahmoud, Waleed E. 2016. Solar blind avalanche photodetector based on the cation exchange growth of β-Ga_2O_3/SnO_2 bilayer heterostructure thin film. Solar Energy Materials and Solar Cells, 152: 65–72. doi:https://doi.org/10.1016/j.solmat.2016.03.015.

Monroy, E., Omn s, F., and Calle, F. 2003. Wide-bandgap semiconductor ultraviolet photodetectors. Semiconductor Science and Technology, 18(4): R33–R51. doi:http://dx.doi.org/10.1088/0268-1242/18/4/201.

Muñoz, E., Monroy, E., Pau, J.L., Calle, F., Calleja, E., Omnes, F., and Gibart, P. 2000. (Al,Ga)N Ultraviolet Photodetectors and Applications. physica status solidi (a), 180(1): 293–300. doi:https://doi.org/10.1002/1521-396X(200007)180:1<293::AID-PSSA293>3.0.CO;2-J.

Muñoz, Elías. 2007. (Al,In,Ga)N-based photodetectors. Some materials issues. physica status solidi (b), 244(8): 2859–2877. doi:https://doi.org/10.1002/pssb.200675618.

Nguyen, Thi My Huyen, and Bark, Chung Wung. 2022. Self-Powered UVC Photodetector Based on Europium Metal–Organic Framework for Facile Monitoring Invisible Fire. ACS Applied Materials & Interfaces. doi:https://doi.org/10.1021/acsami.2c13231.

Nguyen, Thi My Huyen, Shin, Seong Gwan, Choi, Hyung Wook, and Bark, Chung Wung. 2022. Recent advances in self-powered and flexible UVC photodetectors. Exploration, 2(5): 20210078. doi:https://doi.org/10.1002/exp.20210078.

Oh, Sooyeoun, Jung, Younghun, Mastro, Michael A., Hite, Jennifer K., Eddy, Charles R., and Kim, Jihyun. 2015. Development of solar-blind photodetectors based on Si-implanted B-Ga_2O_3. Optics Express, 23(22): 28300–28305. doi:https://doi.org/10.1364/OE.23.028300.

Ombra, Maria N., Paliogiannis, Panagiotis, Doneddu, Valentina, Sini, Maria C., Colombino, Maria, Rozzo, Carla et al. 2017. Vitamin D status and risk for malignant cutaneous melanoma: recent advances. European Journal of Cancer Prevention, 26(6): 532–541. doi:https://doi.org/10.1097/CEJ.0000000000000334.

Oshima, Takayoshi, Okuno, Takeya, Arai, Naoki, Suzuki, Norihito, Hino, Harumichi, and Fujita, Shizuo. 2009. Flame Detection by a β-Ga_2O_3 Based Sensor. Japanese Journal of Applied Physics, 48(1): 011605. doi:http://dx.doi.org/10.1143/JJAP.48.011605.

Ozel, Halil Baris, Abo Aisha, Adel Easa Saad, Cetin, Mehmet, Sevik, Hakan, and Zeren Cetin, Ilknur. 2021. The effects of increased exposure time to UV-B radiation on germination and seedling development of Anatolian black pine seeds. Environmental Monitoring and Assessment, 193(7): 1–11. doi:https://doi.org/10.1007/s10661-021-09178-9

Pan, A., and Zhu, X. 2015. Optoelectronic properties of semiconductor nanowires. pp. 327–363. *In*: Jordi Arbiol and Qihua Xiong (eds.). Semiconductor Nanowires: Woodhead Publishing.

Pandit, Bhishma, Schubert, E. Fred, and Cho, Jaehee. 2020. Dual-functional ultraviolet photodetector with graphene electrodes on AlGaN/GaN heterostructure. Scientific reports, 10(1): 22059. doi:https://doi.org/10.1038/s41598-020-79135-y.

Park, Sangbin, Park, Taejun, Park, Joon Hui, Min, Ji Young, Jung, Yusup, Kyoung, Sinsu et al. 2022. Ag_2O/β-Ga_2O_3 Heterojunction-based self-powered solar blind photodetector with high responsivity and stability. ACS Applied Materials & Interfaces, 14(22): 25648–25658. doi:https://doi.org/10.1021/acsami.2c03193.

Pearton, S. J., Yang, Jiancheng, CaryIV, Patrick H., Ren, F., Kim, Jihyun, Tadjer, Marko J. et al. 2018. A review of Ga_2O_3 materials, processing, and devices. Applied Physics Reviews, 5(1): 011301. doi:https://doi.org/10.1063/1.5006941.

Pedapudi, Michael Cholines, and Dhar, Jay Chandra. 2022. Ultrasensitive p-n junction UV-C photodetector based on p-Si/β-Ga_2O_3 nanowire arrays. Sensors and Actuators A: Physical, 344: 113673. doi:https://doi.org/10.1016/j.sna.2022.113673.

Pintor-Monroy, Maria Isabel, Murillo-Borjas, Bayron L., and Quevedo-Lopez, Manuel A. 2020. Nanocrystalline and Polycrystalline β-Ga$_2$O$_3$ Thin Films for Deep Ultraviolet Detectors. ACS Applied Electronic Materials, 2(10): 3358–3365. doi:https://doi.org/10.1021/acsaelm.0c00643.

Qin, Yuan, Long, Shibing, Dong, Hang, He, Qiming, Jian, Guangzhong, Zhang, Ying et al. 2019. Review of deep ultraviolet photodetector based on gallium oxide. Chinese Physics B, 28(1): 018501. doi:http://dx.doi.org/10.1088/1674-1056/28/1/018501.

Qin, Yuan, Li, Li-Heng, Yu, Zhaoan, Wu, Feihong, Dong, Danian, Guo, Wei et al. 2021. Ultra-High Performance Amorphous Ga$_2$O$_3$ Photodetector Arrays for Solar-Blind Imaging. Advanced Science, 8(20): 2101106. doi:https://doi.org/10.1002/advs.202101106.

Razeghi, M. 2002. Short-wavelength solar-blind detectors-status, prospects, and markets. Proceedings of the IEEE, 90(6): 1006–1014. doi:https://doi.org/10.1109/JPROC.2002.1021565.

Reverchon, J.-L., Mosca, M., Grandjean, N., Omnes, F., Semond, F., Duboz, J.-Y., and Hirsch, L. 2004. UV Metal Semiconductor Metal Detectors, Dordrecht.

Sang, Liwen, Liao, Meiyong, and Sumiya, Masatomo. 2013. A comprehensive review of semiconductor ultraviolet photodetectors: from thin film to one-dimensional nanostructures. Sensors, 13(8): 10482–10518. doi:http://dx.doi.org/10.3390/s130810482.

Schwalm, Reinhold. 2007. Introduction to coatings technology. pp. 1–18. *In*: Reinhold Schwalm (ed.). UV Coatings. Amsterdam: Elsevier.

Shahraki, Toktam, Arabi, Amir, and Feizi, Sepehr. 2021. Pterygium: an update on pathophysiology, clinical features, and management. Therapeutic Advances in Ophthalmology, 13, 1–21. doi:https://doi.org/10.1177/25158414211020152.

Shama, G. 2014. Ultraviolet light. pp. 665–671. *In*: Carl A. Batt and Mary Lou Tortorello (eds.), Encyclopedia of Food Microbiology (Second Edition). Oxford: Academic Press.

Sharma, Vijay Kumar, and Demir, Hilmi Volkan. 2022. Bright Future of Deep-Ultraviolet Photonics: Emerging UVC Chip-Scale Light-Source Technology Platforms, Benchmarking, Challenges, and Outlook for UV Disinfection. ACS Photonics, 9(5): 1513–1521. doi:https://doi.org/10.1021/acsphotonics.2c00041.

Shiau, Jr-Shiang, Brahma, Sanjaya, Huang, Jow-Lay, and Liu, Chuan-Pu. 2020. Fabrication of flexible UV-B photodetectors made of Mg$_x$Zn$_{1-x}$O films on PI substrate for enhanced sensitivity by piezophototronic effect. Applied Materials Today, 20: 100705. doi:https://doi.org/10.1016/j.apmt.2020.100705.

Su, Longxing, Yang, Wei, Cai, Jian, Chen, Hongyu, and Fang, Xiaosheng. 2017. Self-Powered Ultraviolet Photodetectors Driven by Built-In Electric Field. Small, 13(45): 1701687. doi:https://doi.org/10.1002/smll.201701687.

Toda, Tadao, Hata, Masayuki, Nomura, Yasuhiko, Ueda, Yasuhiro, Sawada, Minoru, and Shono, Masayuki. 2003. Operation at 700°C of 6H-SiC UV Sensor Fabricated Using N$^+$Implantation. Japanese Journal of Applied Physics, 43(1A/B), L27-L29. doi:http://dx.doi.org/10.1143/JJAP.43.L27.

Tsai, Si-Han, Basu, Sarbani, Huang, Chiung-Yi, Hsu, Liang-Ching, Lin, Yan-Gu, and Horng, Ray-Hua. 2018. Deep-Ultraviolet Photodetectors Based on Epitaxial ZnGa$_2$O$_4$ Thin Films. Scientific reports, 8(1): 14056. doi:https://doi.org/10.1038/s41598-018-32412-3.

Ultraviolet Sensors Based on Two-Dimensional Zinc Oxide Structures 251–267 (InTech 2017).

Vavoulas, A., Sandalidis, H. G., Chatzidiamantis, N. D., Xu, Z., and Karagiannidis, G. K. 2019. A survey on ultraviolet C-Band (UV-C) Communications. IEEE Communications Surveys & Tutorials, 21(3): 2111–2133. doi:https://doi.org/10.1109/COMST.2019.2898946.

Wang, Hongbin, Tang, He, Liu, Quansheng, and Li, Rui. 2022. Laser Thermal Treatment-Induced MgxZn$_{1-x}$O Gradient Film and Photodetector with Solar-Blind UV Response. physica status solidi (a), 219(14): 2200210. doi:https://doi.org/10.1002/pssa.202200210.

Wang, Huan, Qin, Pei, Feng, Yun-Hui, Sun, Hui-Liang, Wu, Hui-Xiang, Liao, Bo-Kai et al. 2022. Polypyrrole Film Deposited-TiO$_2$ Nanorod Arrays for High Performance Ultraviolet Photodetectors. Chemosensors, 10(7): 277. doi:http://dx.doi.org/10.3390/chemosensors10070277.

Wang, Yachao, Wu, Chao, Guo, Daoyou, Li, Peigang, Wang, Shunli, Liu, Aiping et al. 2020. All-oxide NiO/Ga$_2$O$_3$ p–n junction for self-powered UV photodetector. ACS Applied Electronic Materials, 2(7): 2032–2038. doi:https://doi.org/10.1021/acsaelm.0c00301.

Wu, C., Wu, F., Ma, C., Li, S., Liu, A., Yang, X. et al. 2022. A general strategy to ultrasensitive Ga$_2$O$_3$ based self-powered solar-blind photodetectors. Materials Today Physics, 23: 100643. doi:https://doi.org/10.1016/j.mtphys.2022.100643.

Wu, Junkang, Li, Zihao, Zhang, Ruijun, Fu, Zhao, Han, Shan, Chen, Jiadong et al. 2020. Mg$_x$Zn$_{1-x}$O Prepared by the Sol–Gel Method and Its Application for Ultraviolet Photodetectors. Journal of Electronic Materials, 49(8): 4518–4523. doi:https://doi.org/10.1007/s11664-020-08010-3.

Wu, Y.-H., Chou, C.-L., and Chang, H.-C. 2022. Risk of skin cancer after ultraviolet phototherapy in patients with vitiligo: a systematic review and meta-analysis. Clinical and Experimental Dermatology, 47(4): 692–699. doi:https://doi.org/10.1111/ced.15010.

Xie, Chao, Lu, Xing-Tong, Tong, Xiao-Wei, Zhang, Zhi-Xiang, Liang, Feng-Xia, Liang, Lin et al. 2019a. Recent progress in solar-blind deep-ultraviolet photodetectors based on inorganic ultrawide bandgap semiconductors. Advanced Functional Materials, 29(9): 1806006. doi:https://doi.org/10.1002/adfm.201806006.

Xie, Chao, Lu, Xing-Tong, Ma, Meng-Ru, Tong, Xiao-Wei, Zhang, Zhi-Xiang, Wang, Li et al. 2019b. Catalyst-Free Vapor–Solid Deposition Growth of β-Ga$_2$O$_3$ Nanowires for DUV Photodetector and Image Sensor Application. Advanced Optical Materials, 7(24): 1901257. doi:https://doi.org/10.1002/adom.201901257.

Xie, Chao, Lu, Xingtong, Liang, Yi, Chen, Huahan, Wang, Li, Wu, Chunyan et al. 2021. Patterned growth of β-Ga$_2$O$_3$ thin films for solar-blind deep-ultraviolet photodetectors array and optical imaging application. Journal of Materials Science & Technology, 72: 189–196. doi:https://doi.org/10.1016/j.jmst.2020.09.015.

Xu, Jingjing, Zheng, Wei, and Huang, Feng. 2019. Gallium oxide solar-blind ultraviolet photodetectors: a review. Journal of Materials Chemistry C, 7(29): 8753–8770. doi:http://dx.doi.org/10.1039/C9TC02055A.

Xu, Z., and Sadler, B. M. 2008. Ultraviolet Communications: Potential and State-Of-The-Art. IEEE Communications Magazine, 46(5): 67–73. doi:https://doi.org/10.1109/MCOM.2008.4511651.

Yan, Chongyong, Su, Jie, Wang, Yifei, Lin, Zhenhua, Zhang, Jincheng, Chang, Jingjing, and Hao, Yue. 2021. Reducing the acceptor levels of p-type β-Ga$_2$O$_3$ by (metal, N) co-doping approach. Journal of Alloys and Compounds, 854: 157247. doi:https://doi.org/10.1016/j.jallcom.2020.157247.

Yang, He. 2020. An introduction to ultraviolet detectors based on III group-nitride semiconductor. Paper presented at the 6th International Conference on Materials, Mechanical Engineering and Automation Technology, China.

Yang, Yue, Zhang, Xiao-Ying, Wang, Chen, Ren, Fang-Bin, Zhu, Run-Feng, Hsu, Chia-Hsun et al. 2022. Compact Ga$_2$O$_3$ thin films deposited by plasma enhanced atomic layer deposition at low temperature. Nanomaterials, 12(9), 1510. doi:https://doi.org/10.3390/nano12091510.

Yu, Jiangang, Dong, Linpeng, Peng, Bo, Yuan, Lei, Huang, Yu, Zhang, Lichun et al. 2020. Self-powered photodetectors based on β-Ga$_2$O$_3$/4H–SiC heterojunction with ultrahigh current on/off ratio and fast response. Journal of Alloys and Compounds, 821: 153532. doi:https://doi.org/10.1016/j.jallcom.2019.153532.

Zhou, Hai-tao, Cong, Lu-jia, Ma, Jian-gang, Chen, Ming-zhu, Song, Dong-yu, Wang, Hong-bin et al. 2020. High-performance high-temperature solar-blind photodetector based on polycrystalline Ga$_2$O$_3$ film. Journal of Alloys and Compounds, 847: 156536. doi:https://doi.org/10.1016/j.jallcom.2020.156536.

Zhou, Shuren, Peng, Xuan, Liu, Haowen, Zhang, Zhengfeng, Ye, Lijuan, Li, Honglin et al. 2022aHigh-performance β-Ga$_2$O$_3$-based solar-blind photodetector with ultralow dark current and fast photoresponse for deep-ultraviolet communication. Optical Materials Express, 12(1): 327–337. doi:http://dx.doi.org/10.1364/OME.449496.

Zhou, Shuren, Zhang, Hong, Peng, Xuan, Liu, Haowen, Li, Honglin, Xiong, Yuanqiang et al. 2022b. Fully Transparent and High-Performance ε-Ga$_2$O$_3$ Photodetector Arrays for Solar-Blind Imaging and Deep-Ultraviolet Communication. Advanced Photonics Research, n/a(n/a), 2200192. doi:https://doi.org/10.1002/adpr.202200192.

Zou, Yanan, Zhang, Yue, Hu, Yongming, and Gu, Haoshuang. 2018. Ultraviolet Detectors Based on Wide Bandgap Semiconductor Nanowire: A Review. Sensors, 18(7): 2072. doi:http://dx.doi.org/10.3390/s18072072.

14

Technical Vision System for Alive Human Detection in an Optically Opaque Environment

Oleg Sytnik[1],* and *Vladimir Kartashov*[2]

14.1 Introduction

The modern systems of technical vision are widely used in various robotic complexes for industrial, household, and military purposes. The capabilities of technical vision systems are much wider than those of human vision. They are capable of operating not only in the optical range but also in the infrared, ultraviolet, and X-ray wavelength ranges [Nguyen et al. 2019]. The unique capabilities of vision systems in the microwave and radio ranges make it possible not only to detect and identify objects in an optically opaque environment but also to "see" objects behind obstacles in the form of brick and concrete walls, snow screes, sand, etc.

The problem of creating effective vision systems is acute when developing devices for remote detection and identification of people affected by man-made or natural disasters [Sytnik 2015, Ivashov et al. 1999]. A person could be behind the rubble of brick or concrete walls, hidden in a smoky or dusty atmosphere, and the system must highlight the target against the background of many foreign objects. Within the boundaries of this task, the main problem is to create a system that could not only detect given objects against the background of stationary interference and in conditions of signal-absorbing dispersive media but also provide a constant level of false alarms.

[1] O.Ya. Usikov Institute for Radio Physics and Electronics, National Academy of Sciences of Ukraine, 12 Academician Proskura St., Kharkov 61085, Ukraine.
[2] Kharkov National University of Radio Electronics, 14 Nauky Ave., Kharkov 61085, Ukraine.
Email: volodymyr.kartashov@nure.ua
* Corresponding author: ssvp127@gmail.com

The classical way of fixing the constant level of the false alarm is using the suggestion of Gaussian approximation of the disturbing statistics [Scolnik 1990, Woodward 1953]. For most technical and robotic vision systems based on optical or radar technologies the Gaussian approximation is true and gives appropriate results. But a system that must see and identify alive people under optically opaque barriers ought to extract information about targets from very low-frequency signals [Sytnik 2021, Zhang et al. 2020]. The only sign that distinguishes a living person from stationary objects and from the obstacle itself is the movement of the chest during breathing and heartbeat, which generate a Doppler shift in the frequency of the signal reflected from the target. The frequency spectrum of informative signals is in a band of approximately 0.1...1.2 Hz [Sytnik 2022]. For example, in a calm state human breathing process causes a frequency response of 0.2...0.25 Hz and a heartbeat of 0.9...1.05 Hz respectively. The disturbing statistics in the low band are non-Gaussian [Ierley and Kostinski 2020]. In this range of signals, flicker noises predominate, and at the duration of the observation intervals, they are not stationary.

Classes of non-parametric methods [Hollander et al. 2013] of signal detection and identification in the technical vision systems are intensively developed because they can ensure the constancy of the false alarm probability for a wide class of distribution functions of statistics. To the automatic technical vision system is important three following characteristics of non-parametric methods of informative signal detection:

1. Robustness of a nonparametric detector at a fixed level of false alarm probability with concern to various types of perturbing statistics.
2. Fixed detection quality with non-Gaussian noise and a finite observation interval.
3. Complicated technical implementation in real-time.

The chapter focuses on the technical problems of creating a highly sensitive vision system for detecting and identifying living people behind optically opaque obstacles. It considers a non-parametric approach to the synthesis of the structure of a signal detector using sign criteria, analyzes the asymptotic characteristics of the detection, and discusses the advantages and disadvantages of possible options for the hardware implementation of the system.

14.2 Alive human being detection problem by technical vision system

The traditional way to get constant false alarm probability in a technical vision system, which is working under conditions of continually changing levels of the disturbing statistic, is the adjustment of sensitivity and detection threshold level depending on the statistics of the observed sample [Taylor 2012]. This approach was usually based on the assumption that the noises are Gaussian and that the task of implementing an information signal detection system is a strategy for estimating the statistical characteristics of the noise (for example, moments) that were used in the decision rules [Levanon and Mozeson 2004]. As was said above, for technical vision systems the main purpose of which is the detection and identification of alive human beings under optically opaque barriers, the Gaussian assumption about disturbing statistics cannot be approved. In addition, it is usually impossible to find a

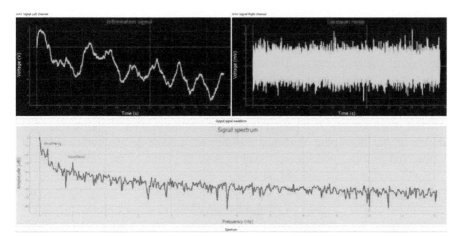

Figure 14.1: The interface of the technical vision system for detecting alive people under optically opaque barriers.

suitable noise probability density function that could be used to synthesize a decision rule regarding the presence or absence of an information signal of the target in the observed fluctuation process. Thus, it is necessary to synthesize such an information signal detection procedure that would not depend on the actual distribution function of interfering statistics. Such a procedure can be based on the theory of testing nonparametric statistical hypotheses [Hollander et al. 2013] and adapted to the problem of detecting living people behind optically opaque obstacles. Figure 14.1 shows the interface of the technical vision system for detecting alive people under optically opaque barriers.

At the top left corner is an oscillogram of informative signals in an additive mix with flicker-noise and Gaussian noise. In the upper right corner, there is a fragment of the implementation of the noise process in the absence of an information signal.

14.2.1 Non-parametric detection based on rank criterion

Non-parametric testing of the hypothesis about the presence of information signals from the target in the frequency range of (0.1...1.1) Hz (see the bottom graph in Figure 14.1) is performed by comparing a certain function $u(x)$ built on the spectral signal samples $x_1^s, x_2^s, x_3^s, \ldots x_M^s$ in this frequency range with a function built on reference noise samples. Noise reference samples should be taken in the frequency band of the spectrum near the band of possible signal occurrence, but at a distance that ensures that they are not affected by the signal from the target. In addition, the frequency interval between samples in the sample should ensure their un-correlation.

Unlike vision systems operating in the optical range, which use light scattered by an object to detect and recognize objects, a vision system for detecting living people behind optically opaque obstacles is based on radar technologies. This approach involves the use of a special type of probing signal, which, reflected from the target, carries information about both the object and the interference. To obtain high resolution both in range and frequency simultaneously the technical vision system uses a continuous phase-shift keyed signal with a periodic pseudo-random sequence (PPRS) [Smirnov et al. 2022], which has an ambiguity function close to the peak function. For example, the Mersenne code signals. So, in particular, the main advantage of signals based on Mersenne codes is that the period of the sequence can be very large which provides high frequency resolution and at the same time, the duration of the elementary pulse can be very short determines the high range resolution.

Thus, when sending each period of the PPRS of the probing signal, N reference samples of the disturbing statistics are formed. Let designate the samples of the observed process, which correspond to the j-th period of the PPRS signal as $x_{j1}^n, x_{j2}^n, x_{j3}^n, \dots x_{jN}^n$ and calculate the statistic

$$z_j = \sum_{k=1}^{N} u\left(x_j^s - x_{jk}^n\right), \tag{1}$$

where $u(x)$ - is the unit step function.

Then the nonparametric decision rule on the validity of hypotheses about the presence or absence of a target will be the inequality

$$T_G = \sum_{j=1}^{M} z_j \begin{matrix} \geq h_0 \\ < h_0 \end{matrix}, \text{ if } T_G \geq h_0 \text{ - target is detected; if } T_G < h_0 \text{ - target is not detected,} \tag{2}$$

where h_0 - is a threshold, which is chosen to satisfy the required level of false alarm probability.

In order for such a decision rule to be nonparametric, the following conditions must be met [Hansen and Olsen, 1971]: in the presence of only noise, the probability density of all samples of the observed process, which are calculated from one period of the signal PPRS, must belong to the same class; all statistics $z_1, z_2, z_3, \dots z_M$ must be independent. At the same time, it is not required that the spectral samples of the signal obtained from the ensemble of periods of the PPRS signal be independent.

The generalized structure of the rank detector is shown in Figure 14.2.

In practice, in order to provide a sufficiently large dynamic range, a logarithmic compressor (not shown in Figure 14.2) can be switched on after the correlator. At the same time, the theoretical estimates of the characteristics of the rank detector remain unchanged. In the generalized scheme shown in Figure 14.2, it is assumed that the statistics according to (2) are calculated for neighboring range gates and that for each new period of the signal PPRS, the data is updated similarly to the "moving average" algorithm [Carbone 2009]. It is interesting to note that for $N = 1$, the rank criterion (2) coincides with the well-known two-sample signed test, and for $N \geq 2$ it can be considered as a generalization of the sign criterion or as a special case of a two-sample problem for randomized Mann-Whitney (MW) statistics [Mann and Whitney 1947]. Considering that the Mann-Whitney criterion is usually regarded as the most efficient for the two-sample [Feustal and Davisson 1967] it will be interesting to compare it with the result of processing according to the rule (2). The Mann-Whitney statistic in the notation adopted in (1) can be written as

$$T_{MW} = \sum_{j=1}^{M} \sum_{i=1}^{M} \sum_{k=1}^{N} u\left(x_j^s - x_{ik}^n\right). \tag{3}$$

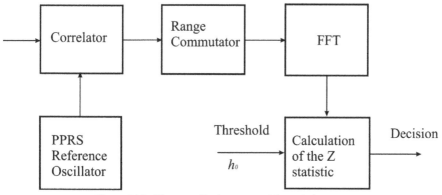

Figure 14.2: The generalized structure of the rank detector.

It is easy to see that criterion (3) is much more difficult to implement than rule (2). For comparison, it is convenient to take simple theoretical probability distribution functions, assuming that the result will be valid for arbitrary functions as well. If the output power of the observed fluctuation process is normalized to unity, then the probability density function of the signal entering the detector can be represented as

$$W_0(x) = \begin{cases} x\exp\left(-0.5x^2\right), & x \geq 0 \\ 0 & otherwise \end{cases}. \tag{4}$$

For a non-fluctuating signal, the joint probability density of the signal and noise can be written as follows

$$W_1(x) = \begin{cases} x\exp\left(-0.5x^2\right)\exp(-S)I_0\left(x\sqrt{2S}\right), & x \geq 0 \\ 0 & otherwise \end{cases}, \tag{5}$$

where $S = E\{E_s\}/N_0$ - is the average signal energy E_s normalized to the noise spectral density, $E\{\cdot\}$ - is the expectation operator, $I_0\{\cdot\}$ - is Bessel function [Korn and Korn 1968].

If take into account the fluctuations of the signal from one PPRS period to another, then (5) can be written as

$$W_1(x) = \begin{cases} x(1+S)^{-1}\exp\left(-0.5x^2(1+S)^{-1}\right), & x \geq 0 \\ 0 & otherwise \end{cases}. \tag{6}$$

So, in the following consideration, the function of probability density (4) will be taken into account as reference noise statistics of samples $\{x^n\}$, and functions (5), and (6) will be used for the statistical description of additive mix signal and noise $\{x^s\}$.

14.2.2 Rank detector efficiency

Asymptotic detection characteristics are convenient for performing a comparison of detectors when the number of observations M is large. The relative asymptotic efficiency of the considered detector G concerning the known MW detector can be defined as

$$E_{G,MW} = \lim_{SNR \to 0} \frac{n_{MW}(P_d, P_f, SNR)}{n_G(P_d, P_f, SNR)},$$

(7)

where $n(P_d, P_f, SNR)$ - is the number of observation samples at which the detector will meet the requirements of a given probability of correct detection P_d, false alarm probability P_f for a given signal-to-noise ratio SNR.

In the engineering practice of comparing systems, the indicator of the magnitude of the losses of the detector G in relation to the detector MW is more common for a fixed sample size n.

$$L = \lim_{n \to \infty} \frac{SNR_G(P_d, P_f, n)}{SNR_{MW}(P_d, P_f, n)}.$$

(8)

The generalized rank detector (2) and the MW - detector (3) were compared with the parametric detector, which is optimal when receiving signals against the background of white Gaussian noise. For small signal-to-noise ratios, the optimal detector uses the statistics

$$T_{opt} = \sum_{i=1}^{M} (x_i^s)^2,$$

(9)

which is equally suitable for both fluctuating and non-fluctuating signals. Using probability density functions (5) and (6) it is easy to show that $E_{opt} = 1$ for both models.

For the MW - detector, which uses statistics (3), the variance can be calculated by the formula

$$\sigma_0^2(T_{MW}) = \frac{M^2 N}{12}(M + N \cdot M + 1),$$

(10)

and expectation by

$$E\{T_{MW} / SNR\} = \sum_{k=1}^{M}\sum_{j=1}^{M}\sum_{i=1}^{M} E\{u(x_k^s - x_{ji}^n)\} = M^2 N \cdot E\{u(x^s - x^n)\} = M^2 N \Pr\{x^s > x^n\},$$

(11)

where

$$\Pr\{x^s > x^n\} = \int_{-\infty}^{\infty} p(x^s)\left\{\int_{-\infty}^{x^s} p(x^n)dx^n\right\}dx^s.$$

(12)

If probability density functions are given by expressions (5) and (6), then the detector performance estimate can be calculated as

$$\frac{\partial}{\partial(SNR)} E\{T_{MW} / SNR\} = \left(M^2 N / 4\right)\exp\left[-SNR/2\right].$$ (13)

then

$$E_{MW} = \lim_{M \to \infty} \left(\frac{MN/4}{\sigma_0^2\left(T_{MW}\right)}\right) = \frac{3}{4}\frac{1}{1+N^{-1}}.$$ (14)

From where the value of the relative asymptotic efficiency can be calculated as follows

$$E_{MW,opt} = \frac{E_{MW}}{E_{opt}} = \frac{3}{4}\frac{1}{1+N^{-1}}.$$ (15)

The same result is obtained if in (12) we substitute the model of the fluctuating signal probability density function (6). For a generalized rank detector, one can obtain the following estimates

$$\sigma_0^2\left(T_G\right) = M \cdot N \frac{N+2}{12}.$$ (16)

Next, by analogy with (11), it can be found

$$E\{T_G / SNR\} = N \cdot M \Pr\{x^s > x^n\},$$ (17)

and therefore efficiency

$$E_G = \lim_{M \to \infty} \frac{1}{M}\frac{\left(M \cdot N/4\right)}{\sigma_0^2\left(T_G\right)} = \frac{3}{4}\frac{1}{1+2N^{-1}}.$$ (18)

Whence the asymptotic relative efficiency turns out to be equal to

$$E_{G,opt} = \frac{E_G}{E_{opt}} = \frac{3}{4}\frac{1}{1+2N^{-1}}.$$ (19)

It is easy to show that in the case of incoherent signal processing with noise and probability densities given by expressions (5) and (6), the asymptotic losses will be

$$L_\infty = E^{-1/2}.$$ (20)

Calculations performed in accordance with (20) taking into account (15) and (19) show that at $N \to \infty$ both detectors have the same efficiency. At small $N = 1...10$ the generalized rank detector has a gain in losses within $(0.5...1.5)$ dB. But, as mentioned above, its implementation is simpler than that of the *MW* detector.

14.2.3 Rank detector characteristics

The characteristics of the generalized rank detector for a finite number of observations were determined analytically. Two cases were considered - a fluctuating and non-fluctuating signal. First, the distribution of statistics z_j (1) was determined for two cases: there is a signal and noise at the receiver input, and the only noise is present at the receiver input and all noise samples were independent.

From expression (1) the statistics for $M = 1$ is equal to

$$z = \sum_{k=1}^{N} u\left(x^s - x_k^n\right),$$

(21)

where, without loss of generality, the index j is omitted.

The statistic z can take all integer values from 0 to N. Let denote the probability density of x^s by $W_1(x^s)$, and the probability density for x^n by $W_0(x^n)$, then the probability that $z = l$ is equal to

$$P(z = l) = \binom{N}{l} \int_{-\infty}^{\infty} W_1(x^s) \left[\int_{-\infty}^{\infty} W_0(x^n) dx^n\right]^l \left[\int_{-\infty}^{\infty} W_0(x^n) dx^n\right]^{N-l} dx^s.$$

(22)

The distribution for x^n can be written as

$$F_0^c(x^n) = \int_{x^n}^{\infty} W_0(u) du.$$

(23)

After expanding the function $[1 - F_0^c(x^s)]^l$ into a series and substituting (23) into (22), we can obtain the following expression for the probability $P(z = l)$

$$P(z = l) = \binom{N}{l} \sum_{i=0}^{l} (-1)^i \binom{l}{i} \int_{-\infty}^{\infty} W_1(x^s) \left[F_0^c(x^s)\right]^{N-l+i} dx^s.$$

(24)

Now it is necessary to calculate the probability $P(z = l)$ at $W_0(x^n)$ from (4) and $W_1(x^s)$ from (5) or (6). For a non-fluctuating signal, the integral included in (24) is equal to

$$\int_{-\infty}^{\infty} W_1(x^s) \left[F_0^c(x^s)\right]^{N-l+i} dx^s =$$

$$= \exp(-SNR) \binom{N}{l} \int_{0}^{\infty} x^s \exp\left[-0.5\left(x^s\right)^2 (N - l + i + 1)\right] I_0\left(x^s \sqrt{2SNR}\right) dx^s =$$

(25)

$$= \frac{\exp(-SNR)}{N - l + i + 1} \exp\left[\frac{SNR}{N - l + i + 1}\right].$$

Then expression (24) for the probability $P(z = l)$ will take the form

$$
P(z = l) = \exp(-SNR) \binom{N}{l} \sum_{i=0}^{l} (-1)^i \binom{l}{i} \frac{1}{N-l+i+1} \times
$$
$$
\times \exp\left[\frac{SNR}{N-l+i+1}\right], l = 0,1,...,N. \tag{26}
$$

In the case when only noise is present in the observed process, expression (26) is simplified

$$
P(z = l) = \binom{N}{l} \sum_{i=0}^{l} (-1)^i \binom{l}{i} \frac{1}{N-l+i+1} = \frac{1}{N+1}, \quad l = 0,1,2,...,N. \tag{27}
$$

For a fluctuating signal, substituting function (6) into (24) gives the following formula for calculating the probability

$$
P(z = l) = \binom{N}{l} \sum_{i=0}^{l} (-1)^i \binom{l}{i} \frac{1}{(1+SNR)(N-l+i)+1}. \tag{28}
$$

Obviously, for $SNR = 0$ (28) is reduced in (27).

Figure 14.3 shows the loss in the signal-to-noise ratio of a non-parametric rank detector of an engineering vision system in comparison with the optimal parametric detector at a probability of correct detection $P_d = 0.5$ and false alarm probability $P_f = 10^{-6}$. The losses were calculated as a function of the number M of PPRS signal periods and the number N of reference noise samples per one signal sample mixed with noise.

As noted above, the Mann-Whitney criterion is known as the most efficient criterion in the two-sample problem. Therefore, it is interesting to compare the detection performance of the generalized rank detector with the Mann-Whitney detector and the optimal parametric detector. Figure 14.4 shows the characteristics of the detection of the generalized rank criterion in comparison with the characteristics of the optimal parametric detector and the detector based on the Mann-Whitney criterion.

The detection characteristics were calculated according to the probability distribution density (4). The set of observations x and x was used to calculate the expression (3). The values of x_j^s and x_{jk}^n found in this way were compared with the threshold, and a decision was made about the presence or absence of a signal. After 10,000 trials, the probability of correct detection was estimated as the number of detections divided by the total number of trials. A comparison of the detection characteristics is shown in Figure 14.4 presents that non-parametric detectors in the case of Gaussian statistics are inferior to the optimal parametric detector. However,

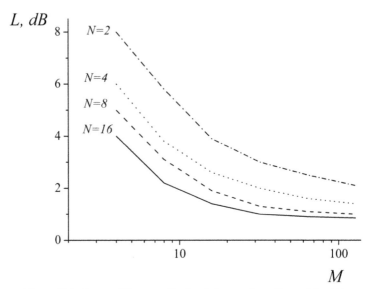

Figure 14.3: Losses of the generalized rank detector depending on M and N.

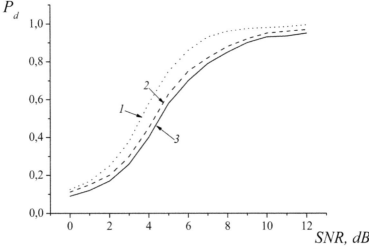

Figure 14.4: Detection characteristics of the generalized rank detector (curve 3), the optimal parametric detector (curve 1) and the Mann-Whitney detector (curve 2) at $M = 16$, $N = 8$ and $P_d = 10^{-6}$.

for a vision system designed to detect and identify living people behind optically opaque obstacles, the optimal parametric detector cannot be used due to the non-Gaussian nature of information and fluctuation processes. The detector based on the non-parametric Mann-Whitney test, as expected, gives somewhat better results, especially for small M, but it is much more difficult in relation to the generalized rank detector in technical implementation.

14.3 Identification of living people in the technical vision system

As noted above, the task of the vision system is not only to detect the desired object among the multitude of fluctuation and deterministic interference but also to identify the detected object as a living person. The only information feature that distinguishes a living person hidden behind an optically opaque obstacle from non-living objects (for example, fragments of walls, reinforced concrete floors, etc.) is the Doppler phase modulation of the reflected signal in the frequency range from 0.1 to 1.2 Hz. The spectrogram (Figure 14.1) shows the responses of the information signal corresponding to respiration and heartbeat. Moreover, it is important to note that the level of the signal characterizing the heartbeat is approximately 20 dB lower than the level of the spectral components corresponding to human breathing. It is obvious that for confident identification of a living person, it is necessary to detect and evaluate both signals—respiration and heartbeat. This is due to the fact that the breath signal, despite the higher level in relation to the heartbeat signal, is very difficult to distinguish from the fluctuation component of the interference due to the very low frequencies of both. This is especially the case for short, in comparison with the period of the information signal of respiration, and observation intervals. This is clearly seen on the oscillogram (upper left Figure 14.1). Consequently, the signal acquisition interval must be more than ten seconds for getting an acceptable spectral resolution. A portable technical vision system set operates in and hands of the rescuer. So it can't be motionless. The chaotic motion of the device generates Doppler modulation that reduces the probability of target detection. The new methods of spectra super-resolution [Marpl 1990] couldn't be used to solve this problem so it needs a carefully calculated data model and they do not operate properly under low signal-to-noise ratio. Therefore, for reliable identification of a living person behind an optically opaque obstacle, it is necessary to modify the spectral resolution algorithms, which would take these features into account.

14.3.1 Mathematical problem definition

Identification of real objects begins with the construction of a statistical model. In this case, the mathematical problem can be formulated as follows. On a certain observation interval T, a model of the correlation function of the process is built. In the technique of digital signal processing, instead of a continuous interval T, a discrete set of samples m, $(k = 1,2,..., m)$ taken through Δt, is used, where Δt is the interval between adjacent samples in accordance with the Nyquist theorem. The object can be represented as some functional transducer with an unknown static characteristic. Based on the knowledge of the samples of the observed process and the corresponding samples calculated from the observation model, it is necessary to minimize the error variance between the observation and the model. There are a number of methods for solving this problem, such as the least squares and maximum likelihood methods, as well as regression and correlation analysis algorithms and stochastic approximation procedures. When using these methods, the form of the approximating function must be chosen in advance up to a vector of unknown parameters. Since the form of the correlation function is initially unknown, the latter is represented by a finite series [Hamming 1962].

Let it is done the sequence of estimators of the correlation function B_k in the discrete set m $(k = 1,2,..., m)$

$$B_k = \sum_{j=1}^{r} \rho_j \cdot \exp(i \cdot \omega_j \cdot k), r \le m, \tag{29}$$

where i – is the imaginary unit; ρ_j, ω_j – is amplitude and phase of spectral components respectively.

The correlation function calculated by the ensemble of receiving signal plus noise realizations can be written in the following way,

$$R_k = A \cdot \sum_{j=1}^{r} \rho_j \cdot \exp(i \cdot \omega_j \cdot k) + n_k, \tag{30}$$

where A – unknown factor; n_k – noise discrete set (particularly, that may be a normal Gaussian noise set having average distribution equal to null and dispersion equal σ^2.

The problem is finding some spectral decomposition $F(\omega)$ associated with correlation function R as,

$$R_k = (2\pi)^{-0,5} \int_{-\pi}^{\pi} \exp(i \cdot \omega \cdot k) \cdot dF(\omega), \tag{31}$$

that the vectors $\vec{B} = (B_1, B_2,..., B_m)$ and $\vec{N} = (n_1, n_2,..., n_m)$ are orthogonal.

14.3.2 Orthogonal Decomposition

Let's examine the same, in generically, non-orthogonal and non-normed function system $\{\vec{\xi}_1, \vec{\xi}_2,..., \vec{\xi}_m\} = \{\vec{\xi}\}$ and then vector $\vec{B}$ expands by basic set $\{\vec{\xi}\}$

$$\vec{B} = B_1 \cdot \vec{\xi}_1 + B_2 \cdot \vec{\xi}_2 + \cdots + B_m \cdot \vec{\xi}_m. \tag{32}$$

As it follows from the problem definition, the vector $\vec{N}$ must satisfy the orthogonality condition of all vectors: $\vec{\xi}_1, \vec{\xi}_2,..., \vec{\xi}_m$, i.e., $(\vec{N}, \vec{\xi}) = 0$, where $(\cdot, \cdot)$ is the symbol of the scalar product. Then, in view of (32), it can be written the system of equations

$$
\begin{aligned}
(\vec{N}, \vec{\xi}_1) &= (\vec{R} - A \cdot \vec{B}, \vec{\xi}_1) \\
(\vec{N}, \vec{\xi}_2) &= (\vec{R} - A \cdot \vec{B}, \vec{\xi}_2) \\
\vdots \quad &\vdots \quad \vdots \\
(\vec{N}, \vec{\xi}_m) &= (\vec{R} - A \cdot \vec{B}, \vec{\xi}_m)
\end{aligned}
\tag{33}
$$

The determinant of system equations (33) can be written in following way

$$
\det = \begin{vmatrix}
\left(\vec{\xi}_1,\vec{\xi}_1\right) & \left(\vec{\xi}_2,\vec{\xi}_1\right) & \cdots & \left(\vec{\xi}_m,\vec{\xi}_1\right) \\
\left(\vec{\xi}_1,\vec{\xi}_2\right) & \left(\vec{\xi}_2,\vec{\xi}_2\right) & \cdots & \left(\vec{\xi}_m,\vec{\xi}_2\right) \\
\vdots & \vdots & \vdots & \vdots \\
\left(\vec{\xi}_1,\vec{\xi}_m\right) & \left(\vec{\xi}_2,\vec{\xi}_m\right) & \cdots & \left(\vec{\xi}_m,\vec{\xi}_m\right)
\end{vmatrix}.
\tag{34}
$$

The scalar product, under definition [Pugh 2015], is symmetrical, positively defined bilinear form. So the determinant (34) is nonzero. To find factor set B_j, where $j = 0,..., m$, let's solve system equations (33)

$$
B_j = \frac{1}{\det} \cdot \begin{vmatrix}
\left(\vec{\xi}_1,\vec{\xi}_1\right) & \cdots & \left(\vec{\xi}_{j-1},\vec{\xi}_1\right) & \left(\vec{R},\vec{\xi}_1\right) & \left(\vec{\xi}_{j+1},\vec{\xi}_1\right) & \cdots & \left(\vec{\xi}_{m-1},\vec{\xi}_1\right) & \left(\vec{\xi}_m,\vec{\xi}_1\right) \\
\left(\vec{\xi}_1,\vec{\xi}_2\right) & \cdots & \left(\vec{\xi}_{j-1},\vec{\xi}_2\right) & \left(\vec{R},\vec{\xi}_2\right) & \left(\vec{\xi}_{j+1},\vec{\xi}_2\right) & \cdots & \left(\vec{\xi}_{m-1},\vec{\xi}_2\right) & \left(\vec{\xi}_m,\vec{\xi}_2\right) \\
\vdots & \vdots & \vdots & \vdots & \vdots & \vdots & \vdots & \vdots \\
\left(\vec{\xi}_1,\vec{\xi}_m\right) & \cdots & \left(\vec{\xi}_{j-1},\vec{\xi}_m\right) & \left(\vec{R},\vec{\xi}_m\right) & \left(\vec{\xi}_{j+1},\vec{\xi}_m\right) & \cdots & \left(\vec{\xi}_{m-1},\vec{\xi}_k\right) & \left(\vec{\xi}_m,\vec{\xi}_m\right)
\end{vmatrix}
\tag{35}
$$

14.3.3 Spectral estimate

To calculate the estimate of spectral function $F(\omega)$ using estimates B_k, that had been calculated by the equation (35), it will be needed to follow the Pisarenko method [Pisarenko 1973] and keep in mind the model validity (29). The model (29) in terms of Caratheodory's theorem [Danninger-Uchida 2008] can be written as follow

$$
B_k = \rho_0 \cdot \delta_k + \sum_{j=1}^{r} \rho_j \cdot \exp\left(i \cdot \omega_j \cdot k\right),
\tag{36}
$$

where $\delta_0 = 1$, $\delta_k = 0$ when $k \neq 0$ and denotes Kroneker's delta.

The unknown factors r, ρ_j, ω_j in equation (36) can be calculated by the following way.

At first, it will be needed to form the correlation matrix

$$
\vec{B} = \begin{bmatrix}
B_0 & B_1 & \cdots & B_m \\
B_{-1} & B_0 & \cdots & B_{m-1} \\
\vdots & \vdots & \vdots & \vdots \\
B_{-m} & B_{-m+1} & \cdots & B_0
\end{bmatrix}.
\tag{37}
$$

In the next step it will be found the minimal eigenvalue μ_0 of the matrix (37) is equal to the amplitude factor $\rho_0 = \mu_0$. The order of eigenvalue μ_0 denotes as v. The difference in m and v defines parameter r

$$
r = m-v.
\tag{38}
$$

In the second step, it will be needed to build the matrix $\vec{Z} = \vec{B} - \mu_0 \cdot \vec{I}$, where $\vec{I}$ is an identity matrix and calculates the eigenvector $\vec{P} = (p_0, p_1, ..., p_r)$ that corresponds to an eigenvalue equal to zero. Roots of polynomial

$$p_0 + p_1 \cdot \alpha + ... + p_r \alpha^r = 0 \tag{39}$$

defines the frequencies of spectral function $F(\omega)$

$$\alpha_j = \exp\left(i \cdot \omega_j\right). \tag{40}$$

The system equations $\sum_{j=1}^{r} \rho_j \cdot \sin\left(\omega_j \cdot k\right) = \operatorname{Im}\{B_k\}$, that in matrix mode can be written as

$$\begin{bmatrix} \sin\left(\omega_1\right) & \sin\left(\omega_2\right) & \cdots & \sin\left(\omega_r\right) \\ \sin\left(2 \cdot \omega_1\right) & \sin\left(2 \cdot \omega_2\right) & \cdots & \sin\left(2 \cdot \omega_r\right) \\ \vdots & \vdots & \vdots & \vdots \\ \sin\left(r \cdot \omega_1\right) & \sin\left(r \cdot \omega_2\right) & \cdots & \sin\left(r \cdot \omega_r\right) \end{bmatrix} \begin{bmatrix} \rho_1 \\ \rho_2 \\ \vdots \\ \rho_r \end{bmatrix} = \begin{bmatrix} \operatorname{Im}\{B_1\} \\ \operatorname{Im}\{B_2\} \\ \vdots \\ \operatorname{Im}\{B_r\} \end{bmatrix}, \tag{41}$$

and the model's parameters can be calculated: $r, \vec{\rho} = (\rho_1, ..., \rho_r), \vec{\omega} = (\omega_1, ..., \omega_r)$ and then restore the function .

14.3.4 Numerical experimental data

The considered algorithm of signal processing used for detection and identification of some signal sources. There were four narrowband Gaussian with average of distribution equal to zero and carrier frequencies: $f_1 = 1.27$ Hz, $f_2 = 1.5$ Hz, $f_3 = 2.7$ Hz, $f_4 = 3.4$ Hz respectively. Observation interval was 10 s. As a noise factor was a wideband white noise with average distribution equal to zero and dispersion from 0.1 to 1.0. On Figure 14.5 has shown the spectral function under noise dispersion equal to 0.1.

The traditional Fourier analyses of those signals shown at Figure 14.6

As you can see in Figure 14.6 the first and second ($f_1 = 1.27$ Hz, $f_2 = 1.5$ Hz) signals, so as third and fourth ($f_3 = 2.7$ Hz, $f_4 = 3.4$ Hz), instead of the situation as shown in Figure 14.5, signals are irresoluble. Here and below, the arrows show the true position of the spectral components of the analyzed signal. In practice, the advantage of the considered method can manifest itself only when, in the absence of a priori information about the information process, it is possible to obtain an adequate partition of the correlation function embedded in the model. At the same time, at relatively short observation intervals, when the Fourier transform does not allow the resolution of individual spectral components, the proposed method has a significant advantage. High-frequency resolution is achieved here by requiring a significant signal-to-noise ratio. If this requirement is not met, then the errors of estimated signal amplitude and frequencies increase when the signal-to-noise ratio decreases (see Figure 14.6). So, the suggested signal processing algorithm hadn't efficient under a low signal-to-noise ratio.

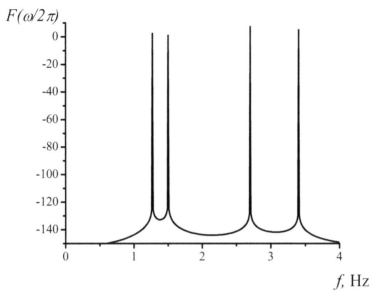

Figure 14.5: The spectral function under signal to noise ratio equal 40 dB.

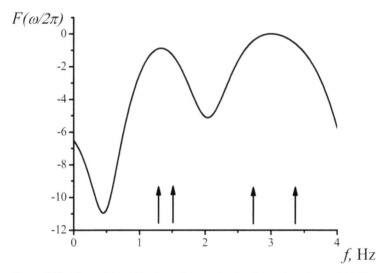

Figure 14.6: The traditional Fourier analyses under signal-to-noise ratio equal 40 dB.

The errors of frequency estimates can appear in signal processing algorithms as a result of a non-adequate choice of quantity discrete set base function or if a number of signal sources is more than the quantity discrete set of the correlation function in the model.

14.3.5 Objective experimental results

In Figure 14.7 it is shown the signal spectral function that had been reconstructed from the discrete-time series obtained from the output of the C-band ($f_0 = 0.9$–1.8 GHz) technical vision system which used the Doppler principle of identification targets. The system's sounding signal frequency carrier has been modulated by PPRS having a length 2^{16}. The duration of the elementary pulse of the PPRS signal was 10 ns. Therefore, the duration of the period of PPRS signal was 65 μs. The target (human being) has been covered under a breaks wall of 30 centimeter thickness. The antenna of the technical vision system has been placed from the back of that wall at a distance of 3 m.

It is obvious, as is seen in Figure 14.7, the target can't be detected and identified by this spectral density. In Figure 14.8, it is shown the signal spectral function calculated by the proposed algorithm.

As is seen from Figure 14.9, the spectral components of the information signal produced by breathing ($f_1 \approx 0.6$ Hz) and heart beating ($f_1 \approx 1.12$ Hz) are well resolved. Consequently, the simple comparison of Figure 14.7 and Figure 14.8 allow asserts that the target identification algorithm of the technical vision system is preferable to FFT signal processing under the condition that the model of correlation function (36) is correct.

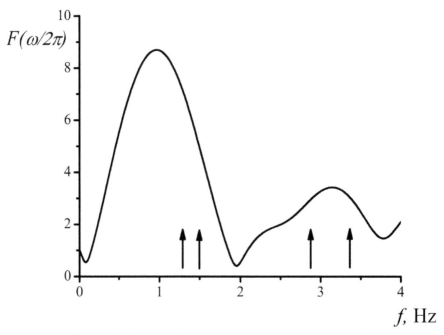

Figure 14.7: The spectral function under the signal-to-noise ratio equal 3.

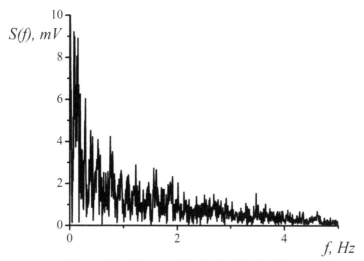

Figure 14.8: The spectral function by FFT algorithm.

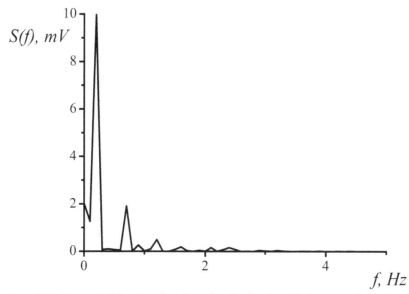

Figure 14.9: The spectral density of the information signal produced by the proposed algorithm.

14.4 Structure and hardware composition technical vision system for alive human detection in an opaque optical environment

14.4.1 Two channels coherent system

As it was mentioned above, the main advantage of PPRS signals is that the period of sequence can be very long but the width of the main pick of its correlation function is too narrow. That signal guarantees a high distance and velocity resolution. The technical problems of PPRS signals forming are solved by shift registers schematic. So, the PPRS signals are preferable to use them for technical vision systems for rescuer operations to search for living people behind optically opaque obstacles. The distinctive feature of the technical vision system with the PPRS sounding signal is the need to form coherent modulating functions for the transmit-and-receive channels. Therefore a general high stability master oscillator with a relative instability of signal frequency $\Delta f/f_0 = 10^{-5}...10^{-6}$ (where Δf–is the effective spectrum bandwidth of PPRS and f_0–is the carrier frequency of the probing signal) at a carrier frequency of 2 GHz is the basic element of the system. From a signal of the master, oscillators are formed: carrying the signal of the transmitter; a basic signal heterodyne oscillator to the receiver; a basic signal for the modulator; clock signals for the block of processing. The frequencies of all signals are generated either by division or multiplication of the master oscillator frequency. The automatic frequency control is not employed.

A block diagram of an analog part of the portable technical vision system for rescue operations, that has been used for collecting statistical data and which data was processed in experiments, is shown in Figure 14.10.

The analog part of the technical vision system is operated as follows. The output signal of master oscillator **1** simultaneously is fed to amplitude modulator **2** and two frequency dividers **3** and **4** with the division factors $n = 20$ and $m = 10$ respectively. At the other input of amplitude modulator 2, the 100 MHz oscillations are set up from divider 3. Narrow-band filters **8**, **9** are connected to the output of modulator 2 serve to sort out oscillations of the upper sideband (filter **8**) and lower sideband (filter **9**). Separations of coherent oscillations at the outputs of filters 8 and 9 is 200 MHz. The upper sideband oscillations are used in the system's transmitter to generate the sounding signal, and the lower sideband oscillations are used to generate the receivers heterodyne. A sounding signals in balanced modulator **7** are increased by amplifier **6** to the value of minus 10 dBW and radiated by transmitting antenna **5** in space. The pseudorandom modulating function generated in block **10** has affected the other input of balanced modulator 7. The clock rate of the reference oscillator is generated from 1 by dividing the frequency in block 3. The pseudorandom function is generated in block 10 by a numerical procedure. The subcarrier frequency is 1,3 kHz. The subcarrier oscillation period is made equal to two periods of pseudorandom signal. Upon multiplying the required delays of the pseudorandom signal are formed in block **11** for range target selection. The receiver heterodyne signal appears at the balanced modulator **12** output. The coherent transmitter signal and pseudorandom signal are fed to the inputs of block **12** from filter **9** and block **10**. The signals from the output of antenna **14** and amplified by amplifier **15**, with a noise factor of 2 dB and amplifying factor of 10 to 15 dB are fed to the first input of balanced mixer **16** while the heterodyne signal from block **13** is fed to the second input of block **16** (correlator). Bandpass filter **17** is connected to the output of mixer **16.** From the output of block **17** the signal at the intermediate frequency of 200 MHz is fed to two quadrature channels **18**, **19**. The information signal is transferred to a subcarrier frequency of 1,3 kHz in balanced mixers **20** of each channel. The quadrature signals are separated in each channel by means of phase shifter **27**. These signals are filtered in bandpass filters **21** and amplified

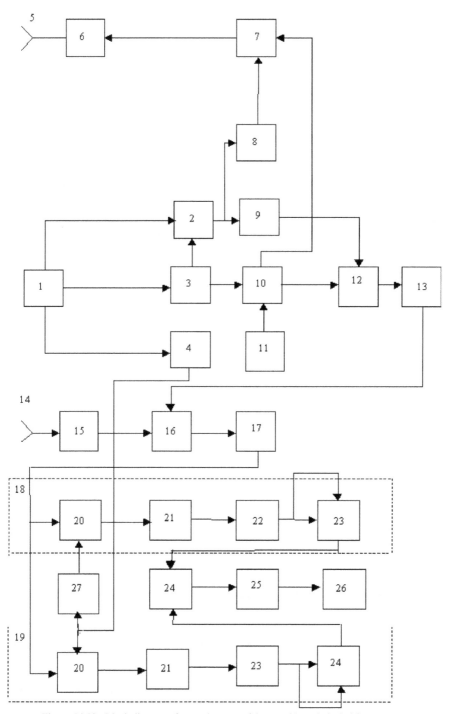

Figure 14.10: Block diagram of an analog part of the portable technical vision system.

in narrow-band low-frequency amplifiers **22.** These signals are then squared in blocks **23** and added in block **24.** The decision-making concerning the presence or absence of a target is accomplished by block **26.** Receive-transmit antennas (**14** and **5** respectively) are incorporated into a single design. All system's blocks are placed in separate screened cells in the common design. The power supply batteries are placed in a separate shockproof bag. The power supply unit is coupled to the radar through a separate cable. The main engineering characteristics of the technical vision system for live people detection is in Table 14.1.

The advantages of the considered structural diagram of the system for detecting living people behind optically opaque obstacles are high sensitivity, selectivity in spatial coordinates, and the ability to detect targets by phase modulation of echo signals, which is a fraction of the probing oscillation period. This option of constructing the analog part of the structural diagram of the system can be recommended for the tasks of detecting living people under the rubble of buildings when searching for targets behind brick and concrete walls. In practice, this system has shown satisfactory performance and sufficiently high sensitivity to weak signals from a person behind an obstacle with significant suppression of interfering reflections from stationary local objects. However, with its relatively simple structural scheme, the technical implementation of individual blocks causes certain difficulties.

Table 14.1: The main engineering characteristics of the technical vision system for live people detection.

№	Parameter name	Value	Commentary
1	Frequency band	1,5…3 GHz	
2	Transmitter average power	> 50,0 mWt	It can be controlled subject to a level of local interferences.
3	Receiver sensitivity	– 170 dBW	The receiver's bandwidth < 5Hz.
4	Modulation	Pseudonoise phase modulation of sounding signals	
5	Azimuth and elevation antenna beam width	15^0–25^0	Low then 15^0
6	Range resolution	1…2 m.	
7	Range of action to the first barrier	5…15 m.	
8	The responsibility zone range back from the first barrier	1,5…7 m.	The first digit corresponds to concrete box units and the second digit corresponds to dry sands.
9	Doppler's filter bandwidth	0,1…5 Hz.	
10	Side lobe level of ambiguity function	Less than minus 96 dB.	Modulation code length $N = 2^{15} - 1$ or $N = 2^{17} - 1$
11	Volume of radar's unit	8-10 dm^3	
12	Radar's mass with accumulators	3…5 kg.	

The requirements for the equipment are becoming more stringent when striving to obtain ideal signals during modulation, radiation, propagation over a complex path, reflection, reception, and signal processing. The efficiency of the correlator is influenced not only by its own characteristics, which can be obtained technically without much difficulty, but most importantly, by the degree of the ideality of the useful signals fed to it. The level of interference, other things being equal, is affected by the place and method of their occurrence for a given block diagram of the locator. For example, the disadvantage of this system according to the block diagram in Figure 14.9 is the criticality to the value of the mutual decoupling of the transmitting and receiving antennas, since when converting signals, the transmitter signal with all its parasitic components freely passes through all amplification paths, which can cause their overload. It is extremely difficult to obtain satisfactory isolation of antennas (at least 70 dB) at frequencies below 1.5 GHz, but as the author's experience has shown, when the frequency is increased to 2–3 GHz, this is possible, and in a wide frequency band. The signal reflected from the operator or nearby objects, even at a low level of the side lobes of the autocorrelation function, is a significant interference. Since, as a rule, it is not possible to suppress the spurious carrier in the spectrum of the PPRS signal, which gives uncontrolled reception from local objects in the area near the antennas, at the output of the modulator by more than 40–50 dB, and narrow-band rejection leads to inevitable losses in the spectrum of the PPRS signal, it is necessary to apply various methods of suppressing signals and interference received on the carrier, in particular, to increase the minimum operating range, to provide remote control of the system, etc.

14.4.2 One channel system

It is possible to build a system devoid of this shortcoming. As an example, consider the circuit of a single-channel of the technical visual system. Figure 14.10 shows a possible variant of the structural diagram of the system, which is insensitive to the leakage of the carrier wave of the transmitter into the receiving path.

In this scheme, one antenna can be used with simultaneous operation for receiving and transmitting, or two identical antennas, which do not have such stringent requirements for mutual isolation as in the scheme in Figure 14.9. Figure 14.10 shows a variant of the system with two antennas. The analysis of this scheme does not limit the generality of the presentation. The system works as follows. The microwave signal of the transmitter is formed in generator 8 and fed to modulator 5, the other input of which receives the digitally generated PPRS signal from generator 6. The signal received at the output of modulator 5 is radiated towards the target by antenna 2. The signals reflected from the target, obstacles, and local objects with some delay enter the receiving antenna 1 and then to the input of the multiplier 3. The reference signal for multiplier 3 is the branched part of the transmitter signal emitted at the current moment of time and which is used as a local oscillator. At the same time, since the signal reflected from the target and the transmitter signal is modulated by PPRS and differ from each other in amplitude and delay, the result of multiplying such oscillations in block 3 will be a new PPRS, the bandwidth of which will be about 200 MHz. Moreover, for each element of resolution

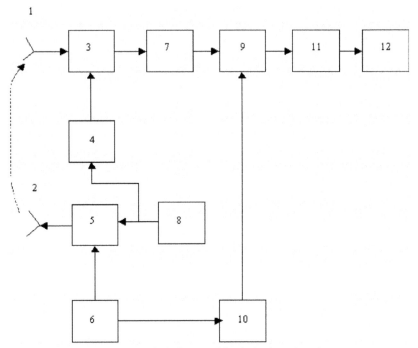

Figure 14.11: Block diagram of the single-channel receiver.

in range, the form of this newly formed PPRS will be different. This follows directly from the properties of signals based on the Mersenne code. It is important to point out that signals modulated by the Mersenne code have a unique property for Doppler radars. Changing the length of the code sequence allows to determine the frequency resolution of the rescuer radar, and changing the duration of the code elementary pulse gives the range resolution parameter. Carrier signal remnants that enter the receiving path due to sounding signal reflections from nearby obstacles and direct leakage due to low isolation between the transmitting and receiving antennas can be attenuated to an acceptable level in multiplier 3 by controlling the phase shift of the reference microwave signal, which installed in the phase shifter 4. In addition, in order to avoid overloading the first stages of the receiver with signals reflected from the operator, a fixed obstacle (for example, a wall), the surface of the earth, and other objects located within the first correlation zone in such a circuit, it is undesirable to use a low-noise amplifier at the input of the receiver. Unfortunately, this reduces the sensitivity limit of the single-channel circuit of the Figure 14.11 system compared to the two-channel circuit of Figure 14.9. A strong signal reflected from stationary objects, and signals from moving targets located in the zero-correlation zone, are attenuated after the multiplier by rejecting low-frequency signals. It is possible due to the fact that the multiplier 3 and the bandwidth-limited video amplifier 7 act as a correlator for these signals. The PPRS signal generated at the output of the multiplier is amplified by the video amplifier and fed to the input of the multiplier 9, the other input of which receives the PPRS signal converted by delay to a certain range element from the digital converter 10. At the output of block 11 (Figure 14.10), as in the circuit in Figure 14.9, there will be a constant voltage at the output of the integrator, corresponding to the response from a fixed obstacle, and a low-frequency oscillation due to phase modulation of echo signals reflected from a moving target. In decision device 12, statistics are accumulated in accordance with (1), low-frequency oscillations are selected, and a decision is made on the presence or absence of a target in accordance with the decision rule (2) for the selected range element. The advantage of a vision system built according to a single-channel scheme (Figure 14.10) is a low sensitivity to the leakage of the transmitter signal to the receiver input and to reflections from objects located near the antenna. However, in the task of detecting a person under the rubble of buildings, when the response from the target is on the verge of receiver sensitivity, the absence of a low-noise amplifier in front of multiplier 3 may be a fundamental limitation on the use of such a scheme.

The main advantages of this version of the system scheme are the simplicity of design and the ability to work on one antenna. Therefore, it is advisable to use a single-channel version of the technical vision system during rescue operations to detect people in snow avalanches, sand landslides and in free space (for example, in smoke or fog), when the target is at distances that exclude the reception of signals from the nearest local objects through the side lobes autocorrelation function (this is approximately over 15–25 m). Of course, it should be taken into account that in this case the weight and size parameters of the antenna and the power of the system transmitter can be increased. The main disadvantage of a single-channel version of the vision system is the inability to effectively use an additional quadrature channel (when working on one receiving antenna). Obviously, with a single-channel scheme and coherent signal processing, due to wave interference, there is a probability that the target is at a distance at which the microwave signal level at the mixer input is close to zero. A quadrature channel could increase the probability of detecting a signal with small Doppler shifts, which are usually observed when a reflective surface (for example, a chest when a person breathes) moves small and slowly. Technically, such a quadrature channel can only be realized using a similar receiver with an antenna shifted in space by about a quarter of the wavelength of the microwave signal along its axis. However, this solution is structurally inconvenient. In addition, due to the lack of pre-amplification in front of the first mixer and the low gain in the broadband video amplifier, the sensitivity of the system receiver according to a single-channel scheme is obviously lower than the sensitivity of the system built according to the scheme shown in Figure 14.10. Additionally, it is difficult to concentrate the main amplification of the information signal in a broadband amplifier 7 of a single-channel circuit, since the bandwidth of the amplifier must be matched to the spectrum of the PPRS signal, which is approximately 100–300 MHz. In this case, a wideband video amplifier must have a large dynamic range (up to 70–80 dB) and high linearity of the amplitude response, otherwise, the correlation functions will have large side lobes, and the advantages of suppressing near-field signals will be lost. The use of signal modulation of the reference PPRS can reduce the gain requirements of the video amplifier since the main gain and filtering are easier to provide after the correlator. Another advantage of the system design with a quadrature receiver (Figure 14.10) in relation to the single-channel circuit (Figure 14.11) is that the information signal can be amplified at an intermediate frequency in the band determined by the Doppler frequencies of the signal reflected from the target. As mentioned earlier, this range is very narrow and amounts to approximately 0.1...1.2 Hz. It is obvious that obtaining the necessary gain in such a band is quite simple. It should also be noted that the requirements for the shapers of PRRS signals in both schemes are the same.

14.5 Conclusion

Thus, in order to see and identify a living person behind an optically opaque obstacle, a vision system is needed, built on the principle of active target illumination. Obviously, the frequency range of the probing signals must be chosen so that the illumination signal penetrates the obstacle with minimal losses and, at the same time, with the help of this signal, it would be possible to obtain a sufficient resolution to detect a person. The frequency range from 0.9 to 2.4 GHz just satisfies these requirements. A distinctive information feature by which the vision system can distinguish a living person from foreign objects, wall fragments, etc., obstacles is the presence of Doppler phase modulation in the signal reflected from the person. The frequency range of information signals is extremely low. In particular, the breathing process generates an information signal with frequencies of the order of 0.1–0.25 Hz, and the heartbeat process gives a response at frequencies of 0.9–1.1 Hz. In this frequency band, the main electromagnetic interference is the flicker noise. This factor predetermines the use of nonparametric methods for detecting and identifying targets due to their robustness to a priori distributions of fluctuation noise. In particular, the nonparametric generalized criterion (2) in comparison with the well-known Mann-Whitney criterion (3) has sufficient simplicity with sufficiently high probabilities of correct detection at given levels of false alarms. A comparison of the detection characteristics shows that non-parametric detectors in the case of Gaussian statistics are inferior to the optimal parametric detector. However, for a vision system designed to detect and identify living people behind optically opaque obstacles, the optimal parametric detector cannot be used due to the non-Gaussian nature of information and fluctuation processes. The detector based on the non-parametric Mann-Whitney test, as expected, gives somewhat better results, especially for small M, but it is much more difficult in relation to the proposed generalized rank detector in technical implementation.

It is obvious that for confident identification of a living person, it is necessary to detect and evaluate both signals—respiration and heartbeat. This is due to the fact that the breath signal, despite the higher level in relation to the heartbeat signal, is very difficult to distinguish from the fluctuation component of the interference due to the low frequencies of both. This is especially the case for short, in comparison with the period of the information signal of respiration, observation intervals. Therefore, when identifying a living person behind optically opaque obstacles, signal processing algorithms must be expanded by spectral super resolution methods, which, based on relatively short realizations of the observed signal, allow one to single out the spectral components of information processes. The proposed method of representing the correlation function model in the form of its orthogonal expansion in terms of basic harmonic functions has shown in practice an advantage over known methods when, in the absence of a priori information about the information process, it is possible to obtain an adequate partition of the correlation function embedded in the model. This advantage is manifested at relatively short observation intervals when the Fourier transform does not allow resolution of individual spectral components. High-frequency resolution is achieved here due to a significant signal-to-noise ratio. If this requirement is not met, then the errors in estimating the amplitude and frequency of the signal increase as the signal-to-noise ratio decreases.

The hardware implementation of the vision system can be implemented as a coherent two-channel structure and as a simplified single-channel system. Each of the options has its own advantages and disadvantages. In particular, the coherent two-channel system has high sensitivity, high Doppler selection, and resistance to microwave signal interference due to the presence of two quadrature signal receiving channels. At the same time, the main disadvantage of this design is the requirement for high isolation between the transmitting and receiving antennas. Obviously, the increased complexity of the system design can also be attributed to its disadvantages. The main advantage of a vision system built according to a single-channel scheme is a low sensitivity to the leakage of the transmitter signal to the receiver input and to signal reflections from objects located near the antenna. Another important advantage of this scheme is the simplicity of design, which is especially important for portable rescue systems. The ability to work on one antenna is its advantage too. The main disadvantage of the single-channel version of the vision system is the inability to effectively use the additional quadrature channel. This is due to the fact that with a single-channel scheme and coherent signal processing, due to wave interference, there is a possibility that the target is at a distance at which the microwave signal level at the mixer input is close to zero.

The main recommendations for the use of the considered options for vision systems for rescue operations in places of the collapse of buildings, in mines, and in the event of avalanches, fires and other disasters are as follows. It is advisable to use a single-channel version of the vision system when carrying out rescue operations to detect people in conditions of snow avalanches, sand landslides and in free space (for example, in smoke or fog), when the target is at a distance, to exclude the reception of signals from the nearest local objects through the autocorrelation function of the side lobes (this is about 15–25 m). A two-channel coherent system must be used when searching for people under the rubble of buildings, in snow and sand screes, in mines, etc. at distances between 1–10 m.

References

Carbone, A. 2009. Detrending Moving Average Algorithm. In Science and Technology for Humanity (TIC-STH), IEEE International Conference, Toronto. DOI: 10.1109/TIC-STH.2009.5444412.

Danninger-Uchida, G. 2008. Carathéodory Theorem. Springer, Boston, MA. https://doi.org/10.1007/978-0-387-74759-0

Feustal, E., and Davisson, L. 1967. The asymthotic relative efficiency of mixed statistic tests. IEEE Trans., IT-13, Apr., pages 247–255.

Hansen, V., and Olsen, B. 1971. Nonparametric radar extraction using a generalized sign test. IEEE Trans, AES-7, no. 5, pages 942–950.

Hamming, R. 1962. Numerical Methods for Scientists and Engineers. – N.Y.: MC Gaw-Hill Book Company.

Hollander, M., Douglas, A., and Wolfe, E. 2013. Nonparametric Statistical Methods, 3rd Edition, New York: Willey.

Ierley, G., and Kostinski, A. 2020. Detection of Unknown Signals in Arbitrary Noise, Physical Review, E 102. (032221).

Ivashov, S. I., Sablin, V. N., and Vasilyev, I. A. 1999. Wide-span systems of mine detection. IEEE Aerospace & Electron. Systems Magazine, 14(5): 6–8.

Korn, G., and Korn, T. 1968. Mathematical Handbook for Scientists and Engineers, New York: McGraw-Hill.

Levanon, N., and Mozeson, E. 2004. Radar Signal, Hoboken, NJ: John Willey & Sons, Inc.

Mann, H., and Whitney, D. 1947. On a Test of Whether one of Two Random Variables is Stochastically Larger than the Other, Annals of Mathematical Statistics, 18(1): 50–60.

Marpl, S. 1990. Digital Spectral Analysis with applications, New Jersey: Prentice-Hall, Inc.,Englewood Cliffs.

Nguyen, T. V., Liqiong, T., Veysel, D., Syed, F. H., Nguyen, D. M., and Subhas, M. 2019. Review-microwave radar sensing systems for search and rescue purposes. Sensors (Radar Radiomet. Sensors Sensing), 19(13): 28–79.

Pisarenko, V. 1973. The Retrieval of Harmonics from a Covariance Function. Geophys. J. R. astr. Soc., 33: 347–366.

Pugh, C. 2015. Real Mathematical Analysis. Textbook, Springer Nature Switzerland AG.

Scolnik, I. (ed). 1990. Radar Handbook, New York: McGraw-Hill.

Smirnov, A., Bondar, V., Rozhenko, O., Mirzoyan, M. and Darjania, A. 2022. Mersenne numbers in the bases of systems of residual classes when transmitting data in serial communication channels. Journal of Mathematical Sciences, 260: 241–248.

Sytnik, O. V. 2015. Adaptive radar techniques for human breathing detection. J. Mechatron., 3(4): 1–6.

Sytnik, O. V. 2021. Problems and solutions of alive human detection behind the opaque obstacles. Telecommunication Radio Eng., 80(9): 1–13.

Sytnik, O. V. 2022. Adaptive technique to phase estimation in pseudo-noise informative signal of doppler radar for rescuers. Telecommunication Radio Eng., 81(2): 61–67.

Taylor, J. D. 2012. Ultra wideband Radar. Applications and Design. Review-Microwave Radar Sensing Systems for Search and Rescue Purposes, Sensors (Radar Radiomet. Sensors Sensing), Boca Raton, FL: CRC Press, 19(13): 28–79.

Woodward, P. M. 1953. Probability and Information Theory with Applications to Radar, Pergamon Press, N.Y.

Zhang, J., Du, Y., and Yan, He. 2020. Code Design for Moving Target-Detecting Radar in Nonhomogeneous Signal-Dependent Clutter, Mathematical Problems in Engineering, Article ID 7609547.

15

The Best Linear Solution for a Camera and an Inertial Measurement Unit Calibration

Miti Ruchanurucks,[1,*] *Ratchakorn Srihera*[2] and
Surangrak Sutiworwan[3]

15.1 Introduction

This chapter deals with linear least-squares error approximation. Readers will finally see that this document warns specifically about suboptimal solutions regarding the least-squares problem. If the suboptimal solutions are adopted, applications of x in (1), in any field, would also be suboptimal when specific noise is presented in the system. For example, in multi-sensor fusion and integration fields, geometrical calibrations between sensors' position and orientation are often required. Many geometrical calibrations rely on linear least-squares solvers. Thus, if any solver yields a suboptimal result (x), even the geometrical calibration can be complete, it would be suboptimal. Further uses of the sensor set would be affected by some certain sensory noise. In this paper, we use an example of the camera and the IMU calibration. Specifically, we will show that when image noise occurs, one must be very careful which his/her choice of the least-square solvers. The goals of this paper are not limited only to finding the best solver for the camera+IMU set of sensors; however, the finding would be beneficial to other types of problems as well.

[1] Electrical Engineering Department, Kasetsart University, Thailand, +66-27970999 Ext. 1505.
[2] Ryowa Co., Ltd., 10-5 Torigoe-Cho, Kanda-Machi, Miyako-Gun, Fukuoka, Japan, Japan.
   Email: ratchakorn.sr@ku.th
[3] Office of Information and Communications Technology, United Nations, Thailand.
   Email: surangrak.sutiworwan@un.org
* Corresponding author: miti.r@ku.th

We shall start from

$$Ax = B \tag{1}$$

or $(Ax - B)^2 = 0$, if B does not lie in the same range space of A, there is no exact solution (see the second and third scenarios below), or $(Ax - B)^2$ is not zero. The general solutions for this least-squares error approximation are among (2)–(4).

1. If A is square and non-singular, the exact solution is

$$x = A^{-1}B \tag{2}$$

2. If A has row > column (over specified), the least-squares solution is

$$x = (A^{T}A)^{-1}A^{T}B \tag{3}$$

3. If A has row < column (under specified), the least norm solution is

$$x = A^{T}(AA^{T})^{-1}B \tag{4}$$

This chapter experiments extensively when A is squared and non-singular*. We specifically test and prove that even if A is non-singular, there is a better linear solution than (2); this is strongly contradictory to the widely held belief above. It is an extension of a rotational calibration part in [Ruchanurucks et al. 2018]. In contrast to our previous paper, we will show in the present paper that in contrast to the widely known notion in the above paragraph, (2) is sometimes inferior to an iterative version of (3), as shown in (5), at least for a Lie group SO(3) or so-called rotational matrix, when there are one or more sources of noise in the system; the sources of noise could be, for example, from a rotational matrix generated from some certain pose estimation algorithm that does not guarantee Lie group SO(3) output.

$$x = \sum_i (A_i^T A_i)^{-1} \sum_i A_i^T B_i \tag{5}$$

Furthermore, the two solutions (averaging (2) or (3) or (4) versus (5)) would be different if and only if:

1. There are multiple sets of A and B; solutions of (2) are generally averaged to one x whereas (5) produces one x from the multiple sets.

2. One or more source of noise is present in B. Notably, noise here implies that it does not lie in the range space of a Lie group SO(3).

On the contrary, if only A is noisy, we find that averaging (2), or (3), or (4) versus (5) produces the same solution. These two facts are not widely known in the sensor-fusion field, hence, there might be some works (both academic and industrial) that produced their output sub-optimally.

---

* In the scope of this paper, (2), (3), and (4) produce the same solution. Notably, the finding as concluded in the final chapter could be extended to the over-specified case as well; A in this special case could be either non-singular or singular.

Before going into the benefits, it should be noted that from (3) and (4), an iterative form is only available with the left pseudo inverse and not the right pseudo inverse. Thus while we can extend (3) to (5), there is no such iterative form for (4) as $\sum_i A_i^T \sum_i (A_i A_i^T)^{-1} \sum_i B_i$ does not yield correct output, nor do $\sum_i A_i^T \sum_i (A_i A_i^T)^{-1} B_i$; $\sum_i A_i^T (A_i A_i^T)^{-1} \sum_i B_i$ is not tested for non-singular A.

This discovery and the experiments in this paper would be beneficial to many researchers dealing with the geometrical transformation between two matrices, such as the geometrical calibration between a camera and an orientation sensor on the same platform. The camera in this paper refers to a common RGB camera whereas the IMU refers to general inertial measurement unit, with any precision. The platform could be a multisensory fusion and integration for smart devices, such as an automatic driving vehicle, including but not limited to aerial vehicles. The calibration would enable the camera to be orientation-sensitive, without having to use any image feature, having application in an automatic landing assist system [Ruchanurucks et al. 2018] or planar area calculation [Sutiworwan et al. 2012]. In these specific applications, the rotational matrix of a camera concerning the world (chessboard calibration object) derived from certain perspective-n-point (PnP) algorithms would not belong to SO(3).

Furthermore, in our future work, we aim to adapt the findings in this paper to compare the iterative overdetermined solution (hereafter, iterative least-squares solution or ILS) versus a non-linear solution as we have optimized the homogeneous transformation, both linearly and non-linearly, in [Tulsuk et al. 2014] There might be other benefits in fields other than geometry; however, this is beyond the expertise of the authors.

In any case, for other applications, we provide some hints based on our experiments. The hints would be in the final section, discussion and conclusion. These hints would be benefit for readers to see as a precaution before writing an algorithm to find the solution x when the noise is presented in their systems' B.

15.2 Literature review

Methods related to those mentioned in the introduction can be found in computer engineering books, such as [Björck 1990], which presents least squares methods in the book's final pages. Numerical methods for linear least squares problems can be found in Health 1965.

Iterative methods for least-squares systems are shown in [Martin and Tee 1961], which considers a symmetric positive definite matrix. The paper deals with stationary methods as well as gradient methods. On the contrary [Fong and Saunders 2011], consider square unsymmetric systems. There are bidiagonalization methods for unsymmetric systems. The methods relate to the starting point of dense singular value decomposition (SVD); SVD is also utilized in our experiment. One such method is the Golab-Kahan process [Golub and Kahan 1965]. To find the solution x, the bidiagonalization is usually followed by QR decomposition. More recent general methods can be found in Saad and Van Der Vorst 2000.

For large matrices, there are methods that consider calculation complexity. [Khabaza 1963] deals with a wide variety of matrices and is not restricted to real, symmetric, or definite matrices. Numerical methods for such matrices have been documented. Recent methods for large matrices are in Meng et al. 2014.

For some specific applications [Romero and Mason 2011], consider many direct as well as iterative algorithms for overdetermined systems of the time of arrival problem; concerning several initialization methods.

On the other hand, for underdetermined systems, special considerations can be found in Shokri and Shokri 2012.

Our paper deals with both square and linear systems. We do not consider computation complexity/large matrices/underdetermined systems. Ultimately, we aim to solve both symmetric and unsymmetric systems, both singular and non-singular, as discussed in the conclusion. Readers will see that this paper considers specifically a new solution to the system when B does not lie in the same range space as A, which belongs to a Lie group SO(3). This is novel and different from the previously mentioned papers, where many consider mainly A or consider the whole system non-linear. To the best of our knowledge, there is no paper that documents or recommends the use of the iterative overdetermined solution over the basic solution for this particular problem.

15.3 Method

To enhance intuitiveness toward the application of rotational offset finding, without loss of general sense of the least-squares problems, in consecutive chapters we will also use these subsequent equations, which directly link with the notion of the needed offset between two rotational matrices, in place of (1).

$$R_l = R_{offset} R_r \tag{6}$$

where subscript l represents left and subscript r represents right. This implies we are considering a solution in the middle rotational matrix, or so-called offset (o), which relates to the leftmost and the rightmost matrices.

$$
\begin{bmatrix} l_{11} & l_{12} & l_{13} \\ l_{21} & l_{22} & l_{23} \\ l_{31} & l_{32} & l_{33} \end{bmatrix} =
\begin{bmatrix} o_{11} & o_{12} & o_{13} \\ o_{21} & o_{22} & o_{23} \\ o_{31} & o_{32} & o_{33} \end{bmatrix}
\begin{bmatrix} r_{11} & r_{12} & r_{13} \\ r_{21} & r_{22} & r_{23} \\ r_{31} & r_{32} & r_{33} \end{bmatrix} \tag{7}
$$

For calculation onward, we use both $R_{offset} = R_l R_r^{-1}$ that is related to (7) as well as (8) that can be further denoted by $x' = A'^{-1} B'$ due to the fact that x', A' and B' are internally arranged differently from the Lie group SO(3). Readers can see that we set (7) so that if we perform vector (*vec*) operator to (6)'s R_{offset} and R_r resulting in (8), then (8)'s matrix order conforms to $A'x'=B'$.

$$
\begin{bmatrix}
r_{11} & r_{21} & r_{31} & 0 & 0 & 0 & 0 & 0 & 0 \\
r_{12} & r_{22} & r_{32} & 0 & 0 & 0 & 0 & 0 & 0 \\
r_{13} & r_{23} & r_{33} & 0 & 0 & 0 & 0 & 0 & 0 \\
0 & 0 & 0 & r_{11} & r_{21} & r_{31} & 0 & 0 & 0 \\
0 & 0 & 0 & r_{12} & r_{22} & r_{32} & 0 & 0 & 0 \\
0 & 0 & 0 & r_{13} & r_{23} & r_{33} & 0 & 0 & 0 \\
0 & 0 & 0 & 0 & 0 & 0 & r_{11} & r_{21} & r_{31} \\
0 & 0 & 0 & 0 & 0 & 0 & r_{12} & r_{22} & r_{32} \\
0 & 0 & 0 & 0 & 0 & 0 & r_{13} & r_{23} & r_{33}
\end{bmatrix}
\times
\begin{bmatrix}
o_{11} \\ o_{12} \\ o_{13} \\ o_{21} \\ o_{22} \\ o_{23} \\ o_{31} \\ o_{32} \\ o_{33}
\end{bmatrix}
=
\begin{bmatrix}
l_{11} \\ l_{12} \\ l_{13} \\ l_{21} \\ l_{22} \\ l_{23} \\ l_{31} \\ l_{32} \\ l_{33}
\end{bmatrix}
\quad (8)
$$

Then, (8) is used exclusively for the herewith-so-called *vec* iterative overdetermined calculation $(x' = \sum_i (A'^T_i A'_i)^{-1} \sum_i A'^T_i B'_i)$, whereas (7) is straightforwardly used exclusively for the basic calculation $(R_{offset} = R_l R_r^{-1})$, as well as the *all-square* iterative overdetermined calculation $(x = \sum_i (A^T_i A_i)^{-1} \sum_i A^T_i B_i)$ for thorough consideration. It should be noted from (2) that A is R_l^{-1} whereas B is R_r^{-1}, which strongly contradicts those in A' and B' of (8). Ultimately, in the conclusion, we discuss exclusively B (that can be rearranged to A') that violates SO(3)'s definition.

15.4 Data generation and evaluation criteria

In this section, we explain how to prepare the experiment, namely how the sensors are installed. In addition, criteria for evaluating the validity of R_{offset} are explained.

To test multiple configurations or installations between the two sensors, we test not only the real hardware but also simulate the existing hardware configuration to show how to install them in many relative orientations to make the analysis reliable with no bias to one relative orientation between them. The camera is firmly glued to the base whereas the IMU is attached by screws and nuts. There are other ways (relative orientations) that the two sensors can be installed on the same platform. For those other relative orientations, instead of having to reattach the sensors, we shall use a simulation to test them. The testing aims to find the best least-square solver for the resulting relative orientation for each simulation setup.

In other words, we can call the configuration or installation in Figure 15.1 'relative orientation 1'.

$$
R_{l1} = R_{z,\alpha l1} \, R_{y,\beta l1} \, R_{x,\gamma l1} \tag{9}
$$

$$
R_{r1} = R_{z,\alpha r1} \, R_{y,\beta r1} \, R_{x,\gamma r1} \tag{10}
$$

$$
R_{offset1} = R_{l1} \, R_{r1}^{-1} \tag{11}
$$

Figure 15.1: Original configuration and installation between a camera and an IMU.

In this sense, we can also generate or simulate data for other relative orientations ($R_{offseti}$) so that the sensors do not need to be reinstalled.

$$R_{li} = R_{z,\alpha li}\, R_{y,\beta li}\, R_{x,\gamma li} \qquad (12)$$

$$R_{ri} = R_{z,\alpha ri}\, R_{y,\beta ri}\, R_{x,\gamma ri} \qquad (13)$$

$$R_{offseti} = R_{li}\, R_{ri}^{-1} \qquad (14)$$

Then, within each simulated installation (8 installations are tested), we simulate capture using the two sensors for 20 times per each installation. This attenuates any effect of error regardless of its source (imaging error or IMU internal error). It should be noted that the former error is the reason that some PnP solutions do not comply with the Lie group SO(3).

First, some noise is added to one or more of the nine components in one rotational matrix—either R_l or R_r. Noise added to both R_l and R_r will be portrayed in the last case. Noise sources are, for example, the camera's image noise.

The evaluation criteria consisted of both the determinant (of calculated R_{offset}, not the ground truth R_{offset} above, which always equals one) as well as the relative distance between the calculated R_{offset} and the ground truth R_{offset}. The determinant should be close to one* and the distance should be zero or as small as possible.

15.5 Experimental Result

We will show the resulting analysis of R_{offset} after adding:

(a) Random noise to one random component of R_l versus R_r.

(b) Random noise to all components of R_l versus R_r.

(c) Random noise to one random component versus all components of both R_l and R_r.

---

* We tested and found that the determinant is not a good indicator of a better R_{offset}.

The important question considered in this paper is does positioning the noisy rotational matrix, by putting it in R_l versus putting it in R_r, affect the calculations?

In this regard, we calculate R_{offset} in two different ways from 20 simulated captured data. First, we use the basic solution, and then we use the *all-square* iterative overdetermined solution as well as the *vec* iterative overdetermined solution, as mentioned in the method section. We tested and found that the *all-square* iterative overdetermined solution is the same with that as the basic solution.

So, in the below tables, we will show only the basic solution and the *vec* iterative overdetermined solution, which is widely known as Iterative Least Squares (ILS). 8 simulated installations (relative orientations between R_l and R_r) are tested and each is shown in each line of the sub table.

It should be noted that to calculate the distance between the calculated R_{offset} and its ground truth R_{offset} complying with the rotational matrix difference calculation definition, first, singular value decomposition (SVD) is used to force any noisy R_{offset} to be SO(3). Then, we use both the quaternion-based method and the axis-angle-representation-based method, and the resulting distances are the same*. Only the distance based on one method is presented consistently in the tables below.

For noise characteristics, we tested the noise ranges of [–0.1, 0.1], [–0.5, 0.5], and [–1, 1], etc. Due to limited space, below, we will show only the extreme noise range of [–1, 1]. Kindly observe the middle and final columns of each and every table. The middle column shows how far an output R_{offset} is from the ground truth value. The final column summarizes if the basic and the ILS solvers produce the same result or not; if the result is not the same, which solver produces a better R_{offset}.

Kindly be noted that computation complexity is low as both basic and ILS are linear equation solvers. Also, we do not consider large matrices as such the calibration is known to be complete with few input data from both rotational matrices. For some certain multi-sensor fusion and integration, non-linear methods could be further adopted to enhance the calibration result; non-linear solvers, instead, should be compared in the sense of computational complexity. In any case, non-linear solvers are beyond the scope of this work.

Reader can see from the third columns that, there are certain cases that ILS produces better solutions of the rotational matrix than the basic methods.

If we increase the number of iteration (number of times we move the sensor set, concerning world/chessboard, per each installation), the distance error is as followed. Due to limited space, we will show only one installation case: Roll, pitch, yaw between the camera and the IMU is 90, 90, and 90 degrees, respectively. We will not show the graph for the case that the basic solution and the *vec* iterative overdetermined solution produce the same result.

Readers might have already seen the superiority of the iterative overdetermined solution or the iterative least-squares (ILS) from the final column of the tables and the figures (kindly observe rigid lines, which are from ILS). We shall further discuss and conclude in the next chapter.

---

* Notably, the two distance calculating methods produce different results if we do not force inputs to be SO(3); however, such a non-SO(3) matrix does not comply with the rotational matrix difference calculation methods anyway. Hence, it is safe to say that, after forcing all inputs to be SO(3), the two distance calculating methods yield the same result.

Table 15.1: Simulation result.
(Real hardware calibration result is in [Ruchanuracks et al. 2018, Sutiworwan et al. 2012])
Case a Random noise to one random component of R_l versus R_r

Subcase (average using 20 captures)	Distance from calculated to ground truth (deg)		Note
One noise to a component of R_l (*Rcam*)	Basic	ILS	Basic and ILS produce exactly the same R_{offset}; on average, the distance is 2.07439672
	2.92828967	2.92828967	
	2.05000157	2.05000157	
	1.35810554	1.35810554	
	1.54432871	1.54432871	
	3.43535729	3.43535729	
	2.13932167	2.13932167	
	1.35026502	1.35026502	
	1.78950429	1.78950429	
One noise to a component of R_r (*Rimu*)	Basic	ILS	On average, the distance is 1.822558485 for basic solution and 1.788507224 for ILS solution
	0.40825169	0.42917575	
	1.874068234	1.87711706	
	1.699440708	1.70206722	
	2.007285658	1.93409815	
	1.872014987	1.67700284	
	2.403651473	2.34691547	
	1.724268114	1.70287503	
	2.591487019	2.63880627	

Case b Random noise to all components of versus

Subcase (average using 20 captures)	Distance from calculated to ground truth (deg)		Note
Multiple noises to all components of R_l (*Rcam*)	Basic	ILS	Basic and ILS produce exactly the same R_{offset}; on average, the distance is 10.96747867
	2.77633447	2.77633447	
	8.42294366	8.42294366	
	18.3306689	18.3306689	
	11.7293432	11.7293432	
	12.9196698	12.9196698	
	12.2954157	12.2954157	
	18.1095412	18.1095412	
	3.15591246	3.15591246	

Table 15.1 contd. ...

...Table 15.1 contd.

Multiple noises to all components of R_r (*Rimu*)	Basic	ILS	On average, the distance is 75.42229624 for basic solution and 8.450330375 for ILS solution
	17.7265519	10.3675169	
	32.0115288	10.1681197	
	12.843052	9.72823855	
	171.502977	3.32229429	
	168.236884	16.2266346	
	31.1193763	6.42568325	
	5.60075294	8.76353529	
	164.337247	2.60062042	

Case c Random noise to one random component versus all components of both

Subcase (average using 20 captures)	Distance from calculated to ground truth (deg)		Note
One noise to a component of each and every R_l and R_r	Basic	ILS	On average, the distance is 2.360445158 for basic solution and 2.676911936 for ILS solution
	2.32655727	2.4375994	
	2.314470807	2.29100428	
	2.088210558	3.16328491	
	0.681596766	1.59580751	
	2.97612313	3.00171998	
	1.028282656	1.09203984	
	5.503766171	5.46354418	
	1.964553905	2.37029539	
Multiple noises to all components of each and every R_l and R_r	Basic	ILS	On average, the distance is 124.2646654 for a basic solution and 19.11548969 for ILS solution
	160.71273	8.32939471	
	156.027599	22.9900911	
	146.967468	38.3968726	
	141.154487	10.9330196	
	151.971551	17.8469669	
	55.9629257	11.5975559	
	13.3508966	19.3150675	
	167.969666	23.5149492	

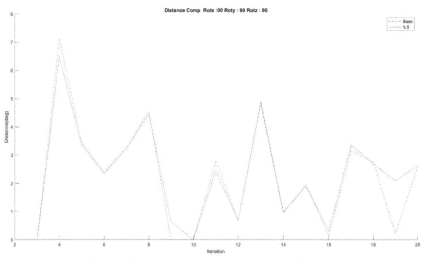

Figure 15.2: Case a: One noise to a component of $R_r(Rimu)$.

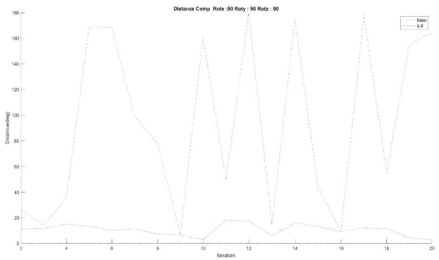

Figure 15.3: Case b: Multiple noises to all components of $R_r(Rimu)$.

15.6 Discussion and conclusion

In contrast to the widely known notion of "an exact solution when A is non-singular", there is one specific situation for minimizing $(Ax - B)^2$ when it would be better to use the iterative overdetermined solution over averaging multiple basic solutions. Namely, when B (R_r, in this paper) is noisy and does not lie in the range space of A and there are multiple* sets of A (R_l, in this paper) and B, regardless of how noisy A is, or even without any noise. This can be seen in Table 15.1. From the last row of

---

* If there is only one set of A and B, all linear solvers would produce the exact solution.

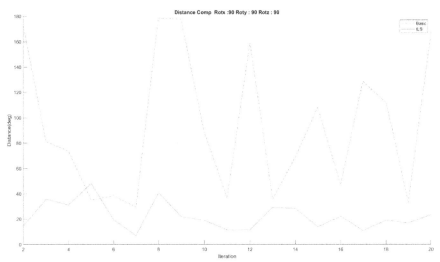

Figure 15.4: Case c: Multiple noises to all components of each and every R_l and R_r.

Case a/Case b/Case c: When B is noisy in the sense that it is not a proper rotational matrix (violates the Lie group SO(3) definition), there are discrepancies between the two solutions' result. Kindly be noted that the last row of **Case a**/the middle row of **Case C** shows that when noise is small, the discrepancy is also small. On the other hand, the middle row of **Case a/Case b** shows that, when A is noisy whereas B is not, there is no such discrepancy; all solutions yield the same result.

To comply with many prior arts, B must be rearranged as A'; shown in (8): Once the *vec* operator is performed appropriately as shown from (7) to (8), the problem could also be considered as minimizing $(A' x' - B)^2$. Thus, the matrix we must be careful about in the previous paragraph (B) is now A' as many literatures.

The benefit of this paper is we stress to users that, in such above case of noise in A', if one uses the basic method, the solution will tend to be suboptimal. Hence, the iterative overdetermined solution should be chosen.

The reason that the iterative overdetermined solution outperforms is that the purpose of the overdetermined solution is to minimize the least-squares error. If there are two solutions, as mentioned in the former paragraph, in most cases, the iterative overdetermined solution will produce less error than the basic solution. It should be noted that it is not possible to claim this will be so with all cases since the best result of the geometrical application mentioned is still based on the rotational differences and the best solution might not be the one that is the most optimized in the least-squares sense.

For the application of a relative rotational matrix, (R_{offset}) between a camera, where its rotational matrix from a PnP solver could violate the definition of SO(3), and an IMU, where its rotational matrix is generated from multiplying $R_z R_y R_x$ and thus belongs to SO(3), we recommend that from $R_l = R_{offset} R_r$:

1. Put R_{camera} as R_l and put R_{IMU} as R_r, and any linear solution can be used as all of them would produce the same output.

2. Put R_{IMU} as R_l and put R_{camera} as R_r, and generally, the iterative overdetermined solution can be used to solve for R_{offset}.

Furthermore, regarding the camera calibration object, here, a chessboard (IMU's calibration object is the earth itself), there are two schemes to put it on the ground correctly, assuming the ground is leveled.

1. If your application does not require the use of yaw (earth magnetic field pointing), you can arbitrarily put the chessboard on any leveled ground. After the offset calibration, the camera can correctly tell roll and pitch, as verified by [Sutiworwan et al. 2012].

2. If your application requires the use of yaw as well, you should use a compass to align any line of the chessboard with the earth's magnetic field pointing. After the offset calibration, the camera can then tell roll, pitch, and yaw.

The experiment in this paper actually could be extended for other noisy geometrical applications other than SO(3). For example, to linearly find a homogeneous transformation (4 × 4) between a camera and LiDAR installed on the same rigid platform, the previous paragraph should be able to be adapted to put any noisy matrix. In any case, non-linearity in a homogeneous matrix could be stronger than that of a noisy rotational matrix. Hence, we believe that non-linear methods, like Levenberg-Marquardt, could yield a better solution than those presented in this paper. However, this needs to be verified in our future work.

Due to the nature of the mathematics presented and experiments performed, for other applications that relate to minimizing $(Ax - B)^2$, regardless of whether A is non-singular or even for an over-specified case (row > column, thus, $x = (A^{\mathrm{T}}A)^{-1}A^{\mathrm{T}}B$ is conventionally used; A can be singular as well), we believe this paper can provide useful information as the iterative overdetermined solution could be better than averaging any basic solutions when one or more source of noise is present in B so that it does not lie within some ordinary range space and there are multiple sets of A and B, that produce one desired x.

References

Björck, Å. 1990. Least squares methods. pp. 465–652. *In*: Ciarlet, P. G., and Lions, J. L. (eds.). Handbook of Numerical Analysis, Vol 1. Finite Difference Methods (Part 1), Solutions of Equations in Rn (Part 1). Amsterdam, New York: Elsevier/North-Holland.

Fong, D. C.-L., and Saunders, M. A. 2011. LSMR: An iterative algorithm for least-squares problems. SIAM J. Sci. Comput., 33(5): 2950–2971. http://stanford.edu/group/SOL/software.

Golub, G. H., and Kahan, W. 1965. Calculating the singular values and pseudoinverse of a matrix. SIAM J. Numer. Anal., 2: 205–224.

Health, M. T. 1965. Numerical methods for large sparse linear least squares problems. SIAM J. Sci. and Stat. Comput., 5: 497–513.

Khabaza, I. M. 1963. An iterative least-square method suitable for solving large sparse matrices. The Computer Journal., 6: 202–206.

Martin, D. W., and Tee, G. J. 1961. Iterative methods for linear equations with symmetric positive definite matrix. The Computer Journal., 4: 242–254.

Meng, X., Saunders, M. A., and Mahoney, M. W. 2014. LSRN: A parallel iterative solver for strongly over- or underdetermined systems. SIAM J. Sci. Comput., 36(2): C95–C118.

Romero, L. A., and Mason, J. 2011. Evaluation of direct and iterative methods for overdetermined systems of TOA geolocation equations. IEEE Transactions on Aerospace and Electronic Systems, 47(2): 1213–1229.

Ruchanurucks, M., Rakprayoon, P., and Kongkaew, S. 2018. Automatic landing assist system using IMU+PnP for robust positioning of fixed-wing UAVs. Journal of Intelligent and Robotic Systems: Theory and Applications, 90(1-2): 189–199.

Saad, Y., and Van Der Vorst, H. A. 2000. Iterative solution of linear systems in the 20th century. Journal of Computational and Applied Mathematics, 123(1-2): 1–33.

Shokri, A., and Shokri, A. A. 2012. New iterative method for solving of underdetermined linear equations system. Acta Universitatis Apulensis, 30: 189–196.

Sutiworwan, S., Ruchanurucks, M., Apiroop, P., Siddhichai, S., Chanwimaluang, T., and Sato, M. 2012. Planar surface area calculation using camera and orientation sensor, pp. 377–381. In 2012 IEEE International Conference on Cyber Technology in Automation, Control, and Intelligent Systems.

Tulsuk, P., Srestasathiern, P., Ruchanurucks, M., Phatrapornnant, T., and Nagahashi, H. 2014. A novel method for extrinsic parameters estimation between a single-line scan lidar and a camera, pp. 781–786. In 2014 IEEE Intelligent Vehicles Symposium Proceedings.

16

Methods of Forming and Selecting a Reference Image to Provide High-Speed Navigation for Maneuvering Aircraft

Sotnikov Oleksandr,[1] Tymochko Oleksandr,[2] Tiurina Valeriia,[1] Trystan Andrii,[3] Dmitriev Oleg,[2] Olizarenko Serhii,[2] Afanasiev Volodymyr,[1] Fustii Vadym[1] and Stepanenko Dmytro[2],*

16.1 Introduction

The mass application of mobile robots (MR) in many branches of industry, medicine, and the military characterizes the modern period of engineering and technology development [Siciliano et al. 2016, Basset et al. 2014, Taha et al. 2018]. Mobile robots achieve the required quality of solving applied tasks while achieving a given navigation accuracy. Thus, when using the field of terrain elevations, the work of an autonomous navigation system of MR, equipped with a correlation-extreme navigation system (CENS), consists of the following. Onboard the aircraft (mobile robot) indirectly compares the measured terrain elevation at a specific trajectory point with its reference value. The result of the comparison in the onboard calculator is the value of the target function. It shows the correlation between the measured and the reference values. Naturally, the extremum is the desired solution to the navigation

[1] Kharkiv National Air Force University named after Ivan Kozhedub, Kharkiv, Ukraine.
  Emails: alexsot@ukr.net; valery.kharkiv@gmail.com; afvv74@ukr.net; vadimfustie1995@gmail.com
[2] Flight Academy of National Aviation University, Kropyvnytzkyy, Ukraine.
  Emails: timochko.alex@gmail.com; Dmitronik70@i.ua; solizarenko71@gmail.com
[3] State Scientific Research Institute of Armament and Military Equipment Testing and Certification, Cherkasy, Ukraine.
  Email: andr.tristan@gmail.com
* Corresponding author: stepanenko.dima.aspirant@gmail.com

problem, which will be shown in further studies. However, there are certain limitations concerning the implementation of CENS [Lindner et al. 2016, Lindner et al. 2017, Hornung et al. 2013, Kostyashkin et al. 2013, Loginov et al. 2015].

Firstly, it is the area in which mobile robots use and the tasks they perform. Secondly, it is the purpose and nature of information retrieval system construction. Thirdly, the procedures of preparation and extraction of reference information for the successful functioning of CENS. Fourth, the possible permanent or randomly performed effects of external interfering factors. Maneuvering aircraft (MA) navigation characterize by the need to change the flight trajectory in real-time and, accordingly, to introduce time and geographical (coordinate) constraints. They will concern rules of construction of reference images (RI) of reference areas and the selection of unambiguous landmarks on the sighting surface (SS) associated with these areas [Loginov et al. 2015, Yeromina et al. 2015, Tymochko et al. 2020a, Sotnikov et al. 2020, Yeromina et al. 2020]. Such unambiguous landmarks we will further call georeferencing objects. And the marked rules must work accurately and clearly in real-time, with steep trajectory changes, often under intentional and unintentional external influences.

It is necessary to allocate and consider the relevant information attributes to achieve a given navigation system accuracy. In such a formulation, the speed and accuracy of problem-solving can be affected by the degradation of the CENS secondary processing system. This system implements one of the algorithms (heuristic, searchless, search, combined, Bayesian) for the comparison of measured and reference signals. In practice, the combined systems make it possible to achieve an acceptable quality of solving such tasks [Tymochko et al. 2020b, Yeromina et al. 2021, Tymochko et al. 2022, Faessler et al. 2016, Starovoytov and Golub 2014].

So, a flight task preparation for MR over areas of interest (positioning) under the influence of the factors noted above becomes more complicated [Yeromina et al. 2021]. Therefore, these factors must consider when creating appropriate databases and implementing the specifics of MR flight. Such a database application in the conditions of imposed restrictions will make it possible to rapidly prepare RI, preserving the accuracy and reliability of the navigation system.

Many factors significantly affect the accuracy of a navigation system. These include the instability of shooting conditions, the type and number of objects on the SS, the completeness and stability of their description by informative features, and the scale of the influence of external factors. The sighting surface database modification for high-speed navigation of the maneuvering MR allows considering interference of these factors in the CENS [Tymochko et al. 2022, Faessler et al. 2016, Starovoytov and Golub 2014, Sotnikov et al. 2013, Keller et al. 2017].

The use and processing of Earth surface images will make it possible to form a database on the object composition of SS. The purpose of processing is to select informative features of SS objects necessary for the functioning of information retrieval systems [Loginov et al. 2015, Yeromina et al. 2015a, Tymochko et al. 2020a]. The obtained initial information is a set of informative parameters measured by remote sensing sensors of different physical natures (SDPN) [Yeromina et al. 2020, Tymochko et al. 2020b, Yeromina et al. 2021, Tymochko et al. 2022, Faessler et al. 2016].

Remote sensing makes it possible to determine brightness, contrast, and structural (geometrical) informative parameters. The corresponding informative fields represent the distribution of these parameters within the SS [Li and Savkin 2020, Somov et al. 2017, Sotnikov et al. 2013]. After generating sighting surface images, these information fields compare with the information from the database. The database fills with reliable information. Random nature information does not get into the database. Accounts for the information aging. The rules governing how the database fill and the information interpretation received from CENS are central to the database created by the sighting surface [Starovoytov and Golub 2014].

To classify SS objects efficiently, information is pre-processed, which consists of the following steps [Sotnikov and Tarshin 2012]:

- noise filtering to remove irrelevant elements in the image;
- scaling (thinning and interpolation);
- improving visual quality by sharpening;
- improving visual quality by highlighting the contours of image objects;
- complexing and combining images of different spectra.

Certain initial image acquisition conditions and the object composition of the SS can override some image pre-processing steps. For example, noise filtering and visual enhancement based on sharpening or highlighting the contours may not perform when there are increased contrast and a small number of objects in the image. These processing steps should be mandatory if the considered backgrounds have high object saturation and small and blurred contrast of individual SS objects. A preliminary analysis of the quality of the available images is the basis for the decision.

The elective images create after the pre-processing of images. Next, the informative features selected as invariants were extracted, and the database was filled.

The analysis of CC information as a sequence of interrelated procedures for obtaining, processing data, and filling the database is regarded as a single task. This approach enables the establishment of unified rules for the preparation of various data for imagery processing, analysis of informative fields, describing remote sensing results, and information processing about the current state and changes of the Earth's surface [Li and Savkin 2020, Somov et al. 2017, Sotnikov et al. 2013].

However, the implementation of these procedures does not consider the possible limitations caused by the specific functioning and tasks of the information extraction system when the flight tasks of mobile robots equipped with the CENS change.

16.2 General approach to generating selective reference images

16.2.1 Basic requirements for database information filling

The database for MR navigation under conditions of rapidly changing flight tasks shall meet the requirements corresponding to the general principles of database construction [Sotnikov et al. 2018, Vorobiov et al. 2018, Sotnikov et al. 2015]:

- the maximum volume of stored data;
- data independence—possibility to use individual elements;

– closed access to data;
– protection against unauthorized access to the information contained in the database;
– support of transactions with the guarantee of the corresponding properties;
– the guaranteed absence of failures;
– a system of user authorization.

These requirements do not consider the specific tasks assigned to the navigation system. Further, it is needed to develop the database information-filling concept.

The basic principles of database information filling for navigation systems in rapidly changing flight tasks must base on the existing developments in the development and modernization fields of CENS. Therefore, when developing and information filling the database, the following must consider [Yeromina et al. 2021]:

– existing effective approaches of SS description taking into account the type of measured parameters by sensors or a set of CENS-sensors;
– criteria and methods of forming RI in stochastic conditions of obtaining information;
– methods of formation of a decisive function as a command to correct the MR trajectory.

16.2.2 *Analysis of the influence of the object scene filling on the selective image*

It is proposing ways of forming selective RI that retain correlation with the original image based on experimental verification using the original sighting surface image [Tymochko et al. 2022, Faessler et al. 2016, Starovoytov and Golub 2014, Sotnikov et al. 2013]. It is suggested the image correlation analysis using the "sliding window" (SW) method.

In digital image processing, a window selects—a finite two-dimensional square area. During the recognition, this window shifts ("slides") across the image, consistently analyzing all picture pixels. A few words about a "sliding window". All the image-contained elements match according to the classical correlation algorithm for each fixed position of the window. Calculate pixel brightness values in the centre of the window and enter them into the corresponding matrix element. The process repeats after moving the window by one pixel. The algorithm runs cyclically until the window has visited all the pixels in the image.

Let it be necessary to make an element-by-element comparison of two images of the same object in brightness. The image's mutual binding (alignment) performs for comparison and relative spatial shifts, and geometric and brightness distortions are corrected. The result of this binding of a pair function is the value measuring their maxima positions and the correlation of the function. Let the fragments of the input image of size $M_w \times N_w$ (M_w, N_w sliding window size in pixels) in rotation shall be the "sliding window" in the correlation analysis. Every subsequent image fragment ("window") is shifted relative to the previous one by one pixel horizontally (vertically). A set of values of cross-correlated functions (CCFs) of image fragments and the whole source code is the result of the general analysis. Selective ("reduced") RI is formed in data array processing. It has image fragments that retain the correlation between the original and generated RI.

Such an approach to generating selective images allows for forming a set of initial data for the filling database, considering the sighting geometry and the peculiarities of the object composition of the scene itself. However, the influence of the SS object composition on the RI quality has not been covered in the literature adequately. The necessary relationship between the contents of the database to form a RI set for MR navigation is not shown.

The dependence of image quality on the scene object content was analyzed to determine the feasibility of the proposed approach for generating selective reference images.

The cross-correlation function of the source image (SI) and the generated binary selective image is used as a criterion for assessing the quality of the reference information:

$$K_{CCF}(i,j)_{mn} = \sum_{i=0}^{M-1} \sum_{j=0}^{N-1} [S_{OI}(i,j) S_W(i+m, j+n)], \tag{1.1}$$

where $K_{CCF}(i,j)_{mn}$ is a discrete two-dimensional CCF;

M, N – SI dimensions in pixels;

$m = [0, \ldots, M - M_W], n = [0, \ldots, N - N_W]$—offset (shift) of SW relative to SI;

$S_{OI}(i,j)$, $S_W(i,j)$, is the brightness (grey intensity) of SI and SW at the point with coordinates (i,j).

The resulting matrix $|\mathbf{K}|$ with the size $(M_1 - N_1) \times (M_2 - N_2)$ of elements that characterizes the distribution of the maximum CCF value in the plane of the analyzed image is the correlation analysis field (CAF). If the dimensions of the original image and the sliding window do not change during the informativity estimation process, the maximum CCF value used as an element of the CAF uniquely characterizes the sharpness of the CCF peak in the maxima area.

The luminance estimation of the FCA is the base of the luminance correlation analysis field (LCAF), and the SS images with saturated object content are the base of the simulation. This corresponds to typical conditions of urban infrastructure and heterogeneous landscape images. The correlation degree choosing between SI and selective RI at the level of 0.5...0.7 determine the influence of random factors on image formation. The source images are given in Figures 16.1, 16.4, 16.7, 16.10, 16.13; binary RIs derived from these SIs are in Figures 16.2, 16.5, 16.8, 16.11, 16.14, and their CCF are in Figures 16.3, 16.6, 16.9, 16.12, 16.15.

The input database data must consider not only the features of the SS itself but also the different angles at which solving the problem of locating MR using CENS. The formation of selective images of the objects of two highly saturated areas from two angles (Figures 16.1, 16.4) is investigated. For this purpose, selective images were formed for two values of LCAF cross sections: 0.6 and 0.7 (Figures 16.2, 16.5 respectively).

Figure 16.1: Source image of a densely populated area.

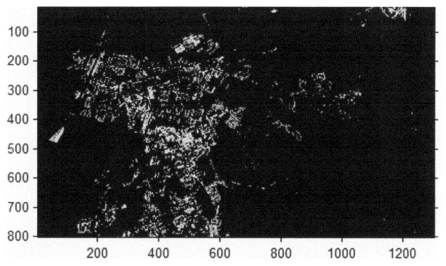

Figure 16.2: Binary selective image at correlation analysis field, sectional level 0.7 to Figure 16.1.

Figures 16.3 and 16.6 demonstrate the results of the CCF for the cases in question. If the correlation relationship value is between 0.6...0.7, there is a unimodal CCF between the source images and their selective images as their comparison result. To quickly generate RI when sighting angles change, it is sufficient to store rather than not the original SS images but their selective ones in the database. The values scatter in the correlation between the selective images equal 0.6...1 allows to avoid anomalous MR location errors with CENS. Similar CCF estimations using differently structured source images (Figures 16.7, 16.10, 16.13) let us generalize these results and extend them to other types of SSs. A correlation between 0.5 and 0.6 was used to form selective images.

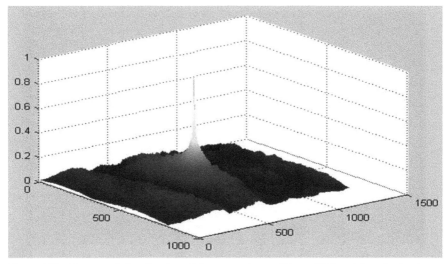

Figure 16.3: Cross-correlation function of the source image (Figure 16.1) and its selective image (Figure 16.2).

Figure 16.4: Source image at a 30-degree viewing angle.

The increase in CCF lateral outliers is due to a decrease in the degree of correlation between the images under study and the use of weakly saturated SS types by object composition. At the same time, maintaining the unimodality of the CCF emphasizes the possibility of using informative parameters derived from selective rather than source images to fill the database. The analysis of the numerical simulation results (Figures 16.1–16.15) shows the possibility of using invariants based on a set of binary selective images for the database information filling. The navigation system decisive function (DF) generation will significantly reduce the database size, ensure high MR navigation accuracy, and reduce the number of computational operations.

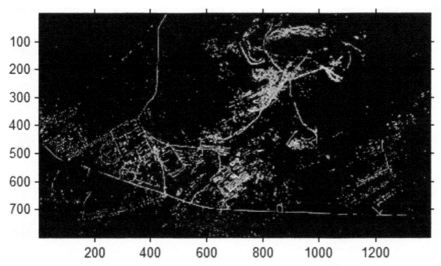

Figure 16.5: Binary selective image at correlation analysis field, sectional level 0.6 to Figure 16.4.

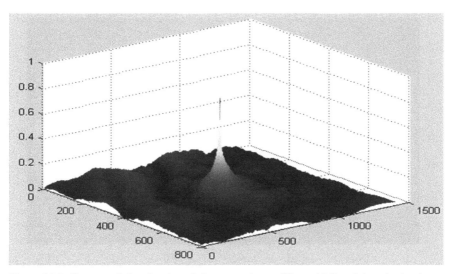

Figure 16.6: Cross-correlation function of the source image (Figure 16.4) and its selective image (Figure 16.5).

16.3 Generating reference images using image correlation analysis fields

16.3.1 Generation of reference images using luminance correlation analysis field

The purpose of brightness correlation analysis of the source image is to distinguish objects and areas with a predominant brightness on it [Tymochko et al. 2020a, Sotnikov et al. 2020, Yeromina et al. 2020, Tymochko et al. 2020b, Yeromina et al.

Figure 16.7: Source landscape image with large homogeneous areas.

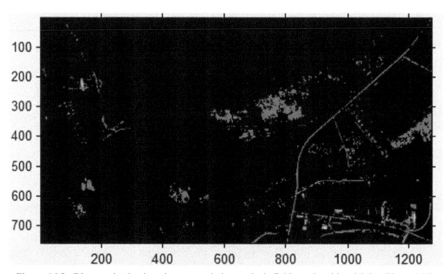

Figure 16.8: Binary selective imaging at correlation analysis field, sectional level 0.5 to Figure 16.7.

2021, Tymochko et al. 2022, Faessler et al. 2016]. Such objects, for example, can be roofs of buildings, a dirt road on a field background, etc. The result of applying the "sliding window" method when analyzing image elements is the brightness (color intensity) of the SI pixel in the center of the window.

All pixels processed in a "sliding window" by brightness become fragments of the input image. The obtained set of partial autocorrelation function (ACF) values of image fragments; and the weight of each one in the total image ACF forms a selective RI.

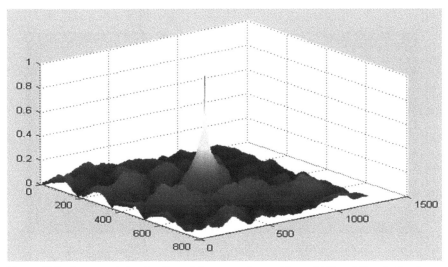

Figure 16.9: Cross-correlation function of the source image (Figure 16.7) and its selective image (Figure 16.8).

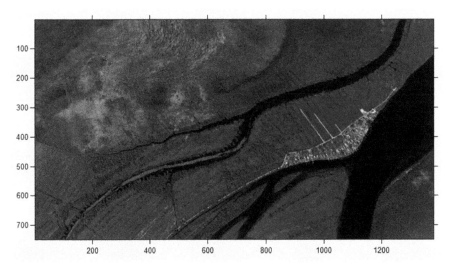

Figure 16.10: Source image of a typical landscape.

Figure 16.16 shows the acquiring SW image process and "sliding" it over the SI to calculate $K_{CCF}(i,j)_{mn}$. The luminance matrices replaced the images in the example.

Absolute brightness values affect forming brightness correlation analysis field based on the obtained $K_{CCF}(i,j)_{mn}$ functions. To exclude this influence, let us implement field normalization [Tymochko et al. 2022, Faessler et al. 2016]:

$$M_{FCAB} = \frac{M'_{FCAB}}{max[M'_{FCAB}]}. \tag{2.1}$$

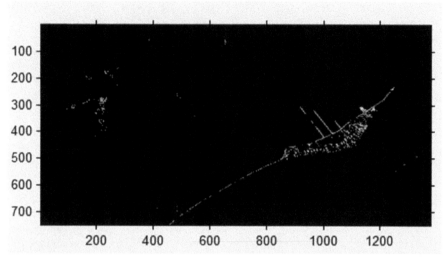

Figure 16.11: Binary selective imaging at correlation analysis field, sectional level 0.6 to Figure 16.10.

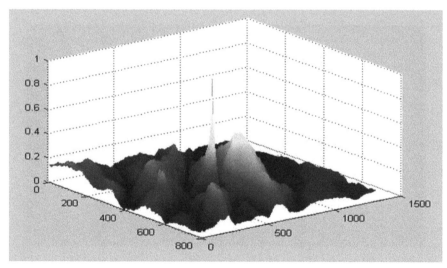

Figure 16.12: Cross-correlation function of the source image (Figure 16.10) and its selective image (Figure 16.11).

For a compressed color original image (OI) of size $M \times N$, the intensity of each color component $S_R(i, j)$, $S_G(i, j)$, $S_B(i, j)$ (i, j)-th pixel ($i \in 0...M - 1$, $j \in 0...N - 1$) is converted into the image pixel brightness in grayscale $S_{OI}(i, j)^*$ according to the expression [Starovoytov and Golub 2014]:

$$S_{OI}(i, j)^* = 0{,}2989 \cdot S_R(i, j) + 0.5870 \cdot S_G(i, j) + 0.1140 \cdot S_B(i, j).$$

In the grayscale test image, the results of calculating the LCAF for it with the size of SW 2×2 pixels, and the analysis of the transformations are in Figure 16.17.

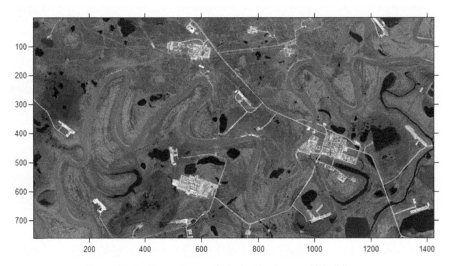

Figure 16.13: Source image of a typical landscape with buildings.

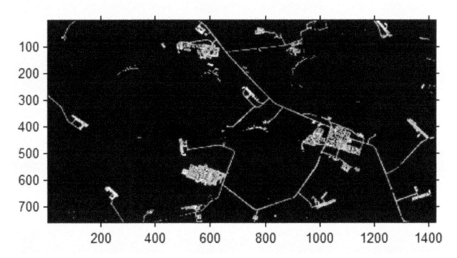

Figure 16.14: Binary selective imaging at correlation analysis field, sectional level 0.6 to Figure 16.13.

The results of the LCAF calculation showed that the brightness correlation analysis allows "highlighting" the image's bright areas. A fragment's image brightness increase increases its "highlighting" intensity.

Let us select the "highlighted" areas and calculate the original image ACF and the segmented image CCF. Autocorrelation and cross-correlation functions comparing show the contribution of the segmented area to the image ACF. Fragments with a normalized ACF level above a certain threshold, remaining on the original image, form a selective image. An example of the selective image with selected shapes of the highest brightness OI shows in Figure 16.18.

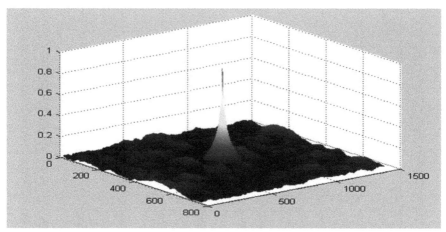

Figure 16.15: Cross-correlation function of the source image (Figure 16.13) and its selective image (Figure 16.14).

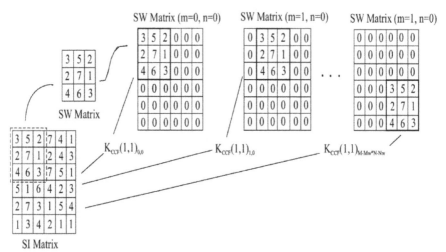

SI Matrix

Figure 16.16: Example illustration of the procedure for determining the $K_{CCF}(i,j)_{mn}$ using the SI matrix and sliding window.

A comparison of the ACF and CCF of the test and LCAF-selective images (Figure 16.19) shows their closeness. The difference consists of a certain narrowing of the main lobe and a noticeable decrease in the level of the side lobes in the CCF. The systemic nature of these changes may indicate a preference for using the selective images on board the aircraft as reference images due to the better characteristics of the decisive function.

A similar experiment in the visible electromagnetic range of the spectrum was conducted on a section of the Earth's surface. The image was reduced to grayscale in advance. The LCAF section level of 0.5 was applied to obtain a selective image. The results obtained (Figure 16.20) do not contradict those shown in Figure 16.19.

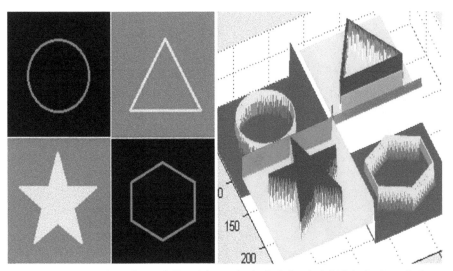

Figure 16.17: Grayscale test image (left) and the result of calculating the LCAF for it, shown in three-dimensional projection (right).

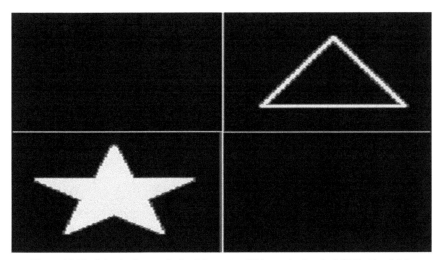

Figure 16.18: Selective image obtained from a test RI by sectioning the LCAF at level 0.5.

The CCF and ACF are almost identical. An increase in the distance between the input and selective images causes the acceleration of the "destruction" of the correlation relation between them, and is reflected on the plots as a slight narrowing of the main lobe of the ACF.

Figure 16.21 shows the selective image and the resulting CCF for the same image for the LCAF section level equal to 0.7, which are different from the previous case. The selection of a rational level of the LCAF section to reveal the necessary number of significant features in the selective image allows us to preserve the correlation between it and the original image.

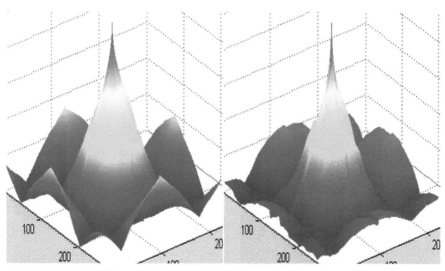

Figure 16.19: The test image ACF (left) and the test and selective images CCF (right).

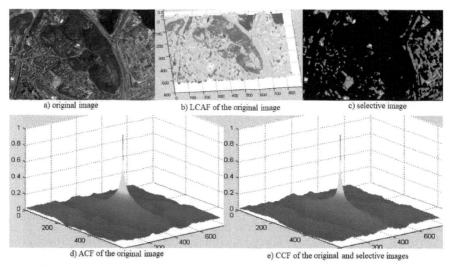

a) original image   b) LCAF of the original image   c) selective image

d) ACF of the original image   e) CCF of the original and selective images

Figure 16.20: Selective image based on satellite land sighting and its correlation function.

To compare the ACF (CCF) shown in the graphs (i.e., the quality of the generated selective image), we introduce a quantitative index equal to the ratio of the level of the main lobe to the average level of the correlation function. Physically, the index means the degree of dominance of the brightest areas of the image over the level of the "background" function. The selective image with the best value of such an indicator is the reference image. For all marked examples, the index has taken different values:

– for the ACF of the test image (see Figure 16.19) – 7;

– for CCF of the test image and the obtained selective image – 9;

- for ACF of the real image (see Figure 16.20) – 26;
- for the CCF of the real image with the LCAF section level of 0.5 – 27;
- for CCF of the real image with the LCAF section level of 0.7 – 48.

The introduced index of "quality" of correlation functions L_Q is sensitive to the slightest changes in the level of the LCAF section, which is displayed visually on the plotted dependencies.

Let the original image (in grayscale) compressed by a lossless archiver program is 450 kB. Then the SI volume is reduced from 70 kB to 20 kB when the LCAF section level grows from 0.5 to 0.7.

Thus, if the current image retains the brightest portions of the image used to form the reference image, the image-matching task in the CENS will solve correctly. This reduces the memory requirements of the MR board computer to store selective images and the bandwidth of communication channels to transmit such RIs between remote locations. If the CENS uses multiple correction points (multiple RIs), the benefits of using selective RIs become even more significant. In addition, a more "impoverished" selective image (see Figure 16.20c and Figure 16.21a) makes it possible to obtain a more "high-quality" CCF, characterized by a relatively low "background" level and a sharper main lobe.

The experiment was conducted to test the effectiveness of the developed method. The model experiment involved a simulation model of the CENS, which allows for obtaining statistics of misses (hits) of MR in the marked point. Images of the same terrain, taken at various times of the year by diverse sources, were used in the model. The starting value of the error of MR guidance by the inertial system for each iteration of the model experiment was determined randomly and was within 600 m. The number of correction points of the MR flight is equal to five. In this case, the correction began to conduct from an altitude of 6,000 m.

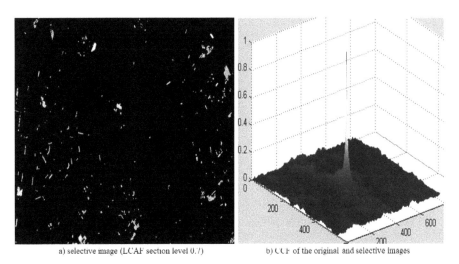

a) selective image (LCAF section level 0.7)　　　b) CCF of the original and selective images

Figure 16.21: Selective image for the LCAF section level 0.7 and results of the calculation of the CCF of this selective and original image.

The number of iterations in the simulation was 1,100, which can be considered a representative statistical sample. As a result, the resulting value of the MR circular probability deviation from the target point was 0.6 m with only two misses observed (which is less than 0.002% of the total number of iterations). This result is fully compliant with modern requirements for most MR navigation tasks.

Thus, selective RI for CENS with an application of a "sliding window" is formed by rather productive computers on the information coming in a wide spectral range. The computer power determines the time of preparation of reference images, which can be counted in hours. That is why it is recommended to use the method when there is enough time to solve the problem.

16.3.2 Generating reference images using a contrast correlation analysis field

The original image is not always characterized by brightness-dominant areas, especially under unfavorable conditions of the imagery. Images' informative features, except objects (areas) with dominant brightness, also include objects' contrast boundaries. Contrast boundaries of fragments on the image are more stable than brightness because brightness depends more significant brightness depends more significantly, for example, on the exposure interval of the image during shooting or weather clarity (illumination of objects), etc.

Correlation-based image processing can also be applied to distinguish contrasting object boundaries. This approach is like the previous one but with the correlation function normalization by amplitude [Sotnikov et al. 2018e]. Then the discrete two-dimensional correlation function was calculated as follows [Vorobiov et al. 2018, Sotnikov et al. 2018, Sotnikov et al. 2015, Sotnikov et al. 2017]:

$$K'_{CCF}(i,j)_{mn} = \sum_{i=0}^{M-1}\sum_{j=0}^{N-1} [S_{OI}(i,j) - \bar{S}_{OI}] \cdot [S_W(i+m,j+n) - \bar{S}_W], \qquad (2.2)$$

where $\bar{S}_W = \dfrac{1}{M_W N_W} \sum_{i=0}^{M-1}\sum_{j=0}^{N-1} S_W(i+m,j+n)$.

Based on the obtained values of $K'_{CCF}(i,j)_{mn}$ functions, a contrast correlation analysis field (CCAF) is formed. It is a matrix M'_{CCAF} of size $(M - M_W, N - N_W)$, the elements of which are values $M'_{CCAF}(i,j) = max[K'_{CCAF}(i,j)_{mn}]$. Similarly, to the formation of the correlation analysis field matrix by brightness, the normalization of the CCAF is conducted:

$$M_{CCAF} = \frac{M'_{CCAF}}{max[M'_{CCAF}]}.$$

Figure 16.22 shows the test image and the calculating CCAF for it using the "sliding window" which "highlights" only the boundaries of the objects. In other words, using the CCAF, as in the previous method of RI formation, allows obtaining from the OI selective image which represents the contours of contrasting objects.

As in the previous case, to check the "contribution" of the contours of contrast objects to the image autocorrelation function, consider a segmented image corresponding to a section of the CCAF at a given level (Figure 16.23). Then calculate the CCF of the segmented image and compare it with the previously obtained ACF of the test image (see Figure 16.18 (left)).

The ACF of the test image, and the CCF of the test and the selective image based on CCAF are shown in Figure 16.24 CCF has a narrower main lobe and a significantly lower level of the side lobes compared to the ACF.

The degree of dominance of the maximum of the main lobe of the correlation function over the average level of its "background" L_Q, in this case, is: for CCF $L_Q = 17$ (for ACF of the test image (see Figure 16.19) – $L_Q = 7$). The analysis of obtained ACF and CCF showed as follows. Using such a selective image to correct the MR flight, a slight shift of the current image relative to the RI will lead to a significant drop in the correlation decisive function level. In other words, MR using RIs based on the selected boundaries of contrasting objects on the original image can potentially navigate more selectively.

Figure 16.25 reflects the results of a similar experiment for an existing section of the earth's surface shown in Figure 16.20a. The CCAF section level of 0.25 was applied to obtain the selective image. As for the test image (see Figure 16.25), the CCF of the input and selective images has a narrower main lobe. The value for the CCF is $L_Q = 36$ (for the ACF of the input image $L_Q = 26$). Consequently, CENS can base on the sliding window method for iterative RI synthesis using contrast-correlation analysis of images. However, high computational complexity and tight timing requirements also limit the use of this approach for preparing reference images.

Figure 16.22: The grayscale test image (left) and the CCAF calculation result for it (right).

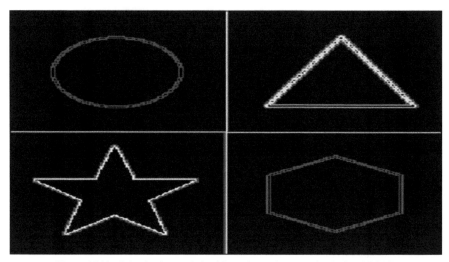

Figure 16.23: Selective image derived from the test image and calculated CCAF.

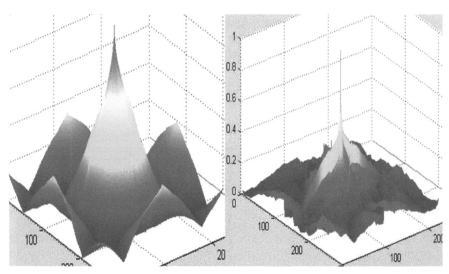

Figure 16.24: ACF of the test image (left) and CCF of the test and selective images (right).

16.3.3 A method for generating reference images using a fractal image analysis field

The proposed RI generation methods are based on image transformations and have a clear physical interpretation. The content of these methods approximates the approaches used to determine the CENS decisive function on board an MR [Sotnikov et al. 2015, Sotnikov et al. 2018, Sotnikov et al. 2019]. However, these approaches are time-consuming for RIs generation. Thus, it is necessary to find a method for fast RI generation [Sotnikov et al. 2019, Smelyakov et al. 2005, Hernandez and Mendez 2018, Shen and Song 2018].

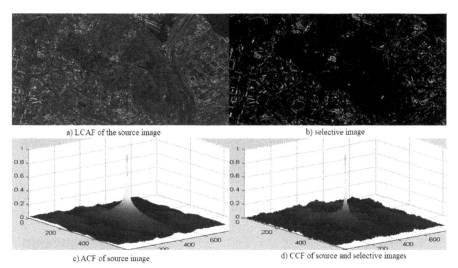

a) LCAF of the source image   b) selective image

c) ACF of source image   d) CCF of source and selective images

Figure 16.25: Results of selective image acquisition based on SI and correlation function calculations.

Recently, fractal methods have been widely used to solve image segmentation problems. At the fractal analysis in the given field the fractal characteristics of the image, and its separate objects or fragments are calculated. The fractal dimension (K'FS) as the main fractal characteristic in the sequential viewing of image fragments depends on the size of the "sliding window" (SW). The general approach to the formation of RI requires the calculation of K'FS for each image fragment «covered» by the "sliding window" [Sotnikov et al. 2015]:

$$K'_{FS}(i,j) = \frac{ln\big(S_{W\Sigma}(i,j)\big) - ln(max[S_W]/N_W)}{ln(N_W)}, \qquad (2.3)$$

where $S_{W\Sigma}(i,j) = \sum_{i=0}^{M_{W}-1} \sum_{j=0}^{N_{W}-1} S_W(i,j)$.

As a result, a field of fractal dimensionality (FFD) matrix M_{FFS} of size $(M - M_W, N - N_W)$ with $S_{W\Sigma}(i,j)$ elements are formed for SI. Fractal dimension values take fractional values in the range from 2 to 3.

From the analysis of the results of calculating the FFD for the test image with 2×2 pixel SW (Figure 16.26), it follows that the FFD distinguishes the monochrome parts of the image well, responding little to the intensity of gray color, except for black. The intermediate value of borders dimensionality between image parts of different brightness allows us to distinguish them by selecting a range of fragment dimensionality.

When the range of dimensionality is limited, the FFD behaves differently. When the FFD dimension is from 2 to 2.9, it is possible to highlight the borders of contrasting objects, and from 2.9 to 3 – image areas are "filled" with colors of the same brightness (except for black) (Figure 16.27). Often areas of an image with dominant brightness are characterized by high "filling" with bright color.

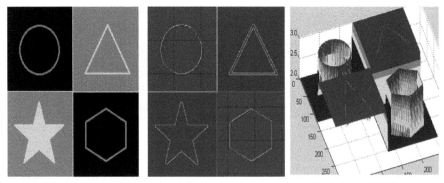

Figure 16.26: Test image in grayscale (left), result of calculation FFD for it in 2D (middle) and 3D projection (right).

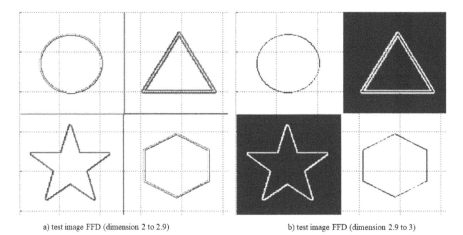

a) test image FFD (dimension 2 to 2.9)   b) test image FFD (dimension 2.9 to 3)

Figure 16.27: Results of the FFD calculation for the test image.

The analysis of FFD calculation data (Figure 16.28a) for a real area of the Earth's surface (see Figure 16.20a) and a selective image obtained on the basis of FFD with separation of parts of SI with fractal dimension from 2 to 2.75 (Figure 16.20b) confirm the closeness of segmentation results and selective image based on CCAF calculation. If the fractal dimension of the selective image is in the range from 2.96 to 3 (Figure 16.28c), then it, in turn, is similar to the LCAF-based image.

Cross-correlation functions (Figure 16.28d,e) of source and selective (Figure 16.28b,c) images can be used to distinguish objects of increased brightness and boundaries of contrasting objects on the images.

Thus, the method of image analysis is universal. The choice of the range of fractal dimensionality makes it possible to distinguish areas with dominant brightness and boundaries of contrast areas on the images. Even a superficial analysis of the computational complexity of LCAF, CCAF, and FFD calculations shows the advantages of using FFD to obtain RI. A modern computer calculates an FFD image of 1024 × 1024 pixels (2 × 2 pixels CO) in less than a minute.

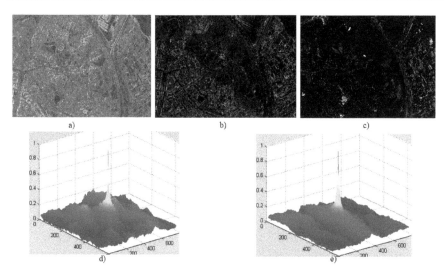

Figure 16.28: Results of calculations based on the original satellite image:
a) FFD of the original image;
b) selective image of fractal dimensionality from 2 to 2.75;
c) selective image of fractal dimensionality from 2.96 to 3;
d) CCF of the original image and the selective image (Figure 16.28b);
e) CCF of the original image and the selective image (Figure 16.28c).

It is found that fill color at uniform filling of image areas actually does not influence fractal dimensionality. Thus, fragments of the test image (range FFD is from 2,984 to 2,994), which differ greatly in color (brightness of contour is higher than the brightness of star's background on 134 gradations from 256), differ only by 0,01 in fractal dimensionality (Figure 16.24, Figure 16.29).

The mentioned facts complicate the search of the required dimension range for selecting the desired informative regions on the selective images. Therefore, the use of correlation methods is more effective than FFD, which confirms the quality level of L_Q for real images: not less than 25–30 for correlation analysis methods and 17–20 for obtained FFD.

So, the method of iterative formation of reference images using a "sliding window" based on fractal analysis allows the selection of bright informative areas and boundaries of contrasting objects on images [Sotnikov et al. 2015]. Despite the versatility and high speed of obtaining selective images by the fractal method, the quality of the solution to the problem of RI formation is inferior to correlation methods, at least in a simple procedure of fractal dimension ranges selection. However, this method can also be used in CENS systems of high-speed maneuvering mobile robots.

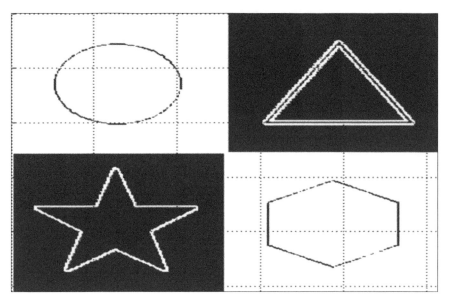

Figure 16.29: FFD of test image with fractal dimension from 2.984 to 2.994.

16.4 Method of reference image selection for mobile robot navigation under rapidly changing flight paths

16.4.1 Statement of problem on development of method and algorithm of reference image selection in secondary information processing system in correlation-extreme navigation system

The following assumptions were introduced to determine in space the position of an aircraft with an optoelectronic CENS that maneuvers and moves at high speed:

1. A wide range of variations of the MR flight altitude and the sighting angle of the reference area.

2. Absence of three-dimensional objects on the sighting surface, giving shadows in neighboring areas.

3. Constant brightness and/or coordinates of the illumination source, which determines the minimum difference in brightness of the corresponding image pixels $S_{CI}(m,n)$.

4. Absence of distortion of SS images in the CENS.

5. Description of the image by a special brightness distribution function $S(r(t),t)$, where $r(t) = (x(t), y(t))$ is the displacement vector in the coordinate system of the image plane.

6. The synthesis of frames with corresponding images in time $\psi_1 = \psi(r(t), t_0)$, $\psi_{2p} = \psi(r(t), t_p)$ where $t_p = t_0 + \Delta t_p$ by the correlation-extreme system.

The type of the problem determines the number of images, which, in turn, generates a different number of DFs.

Description of the set of RIs.

Let the MR move in the horizontal plane of the x, y, and z coordinate system associated with the SS (Figure 16.30).

The position of each partial antenna directional diagram (ADD) is characterized by the angles α and β. The opening angles of the ADD at the half-power level are equal θ_x – in the plane along the angle of location and θ_y – in the azimuthal plane. The intersection of the ADD with the xy plane is an ellipse for the Gaussian approximation. The width of the ADD at the half-power level is determined by the wavelength λ of the receiving path and the diameter of the antenna's opening d_a: $2\theta_{0.5} = \dfrac{\lambda}{da}$.

While performing the flight the MR constantly changes the altitude $h_i \in [h_{min}, h_{max}]$, sighting angles $\alpha_j \in [\alpha_{min}, \alpha_{max}]$, $\beta_l \in [\beta_{min}, \beta_{max}]$, directions of surface imaging, determined by the vector v, and carried out at different times t_p. For such conditions of flight, it is necessary to form a set of RIs:

$$S_{RI} (2\theta_{0,5}, h_i, \alpha_j, \beta_k, v_1, \varphi_s, t_m), i = \overline{1,I}, j = \overline{1,J}, k = \overline{1,K}, l = \overline{1,L}, p = \overline{1,P}, s = \overline{1,S}.$$

Each individual RI of size M,N corresponds to its own matrix of brightness values:

$$S_{RI} = |S_{RI} (m,n)|, m = \overline{1,M}, n = \overline{1,N}.$$

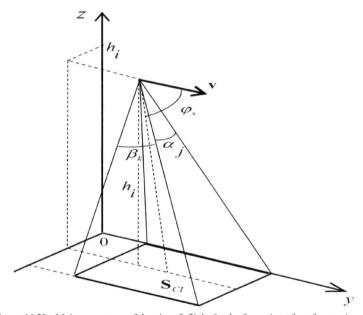

Figure 16.30: Main parameters of the aircraft flight for the formation of a reference image.

Each RI in the set is an 8-bit halftone image. To obtain the DF $R(r,t)$ using the operator F_{SP}, let's compare the current (CI) and reference images:

$$R(r,t) = F_{SP} (S_{CI} (r,t), S_{RI} (2\theta_{0,5}, h_j, \alpha_j, \beta_k, v_1, \varphi_s, t_p)), \tag{3.1}$$

Problem Statement. Using the considered models of current and reference images, select a single image from the existing set of RIs S_{RI} and form a DF on its basis without a complete search of all possible image comparison variants.

16.4.2 Method of RI selection for high-speed maneuvering MR navigation

The set of RIs $\{S_{RI} (2\theta_{0,5}, h_j, \alpha_j, \beta_k, v_1, \varphi_s, t_m)\}$ is a multidimensional matrix. A complex and not yet fully developed multidimensional matrix approach must be applied to analyze its data. Let us assume that any comparison operations are performed in an equal time interval. Then the criterion for choosing a single RI S_{RI} from the available totality $\{\bullet\}$ is the solution that provides the greatest matching of the compared images in the minimum time [Yeromina et al. 2021]. That is, according to (3.1), the parameters in the set $\{S_{RI}\}$ are found as close to the parameters (r, t) to be as possible. The problem has once again returned to combinatorics, namely, the enumeration of RI over the whole totality, which requires fixing some components from the totality [Yeromina et al. 2021].

The displacement vector in the coordinate system of the image plane $r(t) = (x(t), y(t))$ describes the ground surface fixation conditions. The elements $h_j, \alpha_j, \beta_k, v_1, \varphi_s$ of RI formation should correspond to this vector as much as possible. To determine these parameters, a typical image of SS with a natural landscape is analyzed (Figure 16.31). This and other images (Figures 16.33, 16.35, 16.37, 16.39, 16.41) are taken from the Google Earth collection.

Only achieving correlation values of 0.5 to 0.7 between the fragments of the RI will ensure the navigation accuracy of a high-speed mobile robot [Keller et al. 2017]. This is confirmed by the results of modeling the behavior of MR (Figure 16.32).

To ensure correlation, the brightness distribution graphs of objects for sighting angles of $-80°$ and $-70°$ on identical images under the same shooting conditions are compared (Figures 16.33–16.35).

Consider the coordinate x. The plots for angles of location $-90°$, $-80°$, and $-70°$ (Figures 16.32, 16.34, and 16.36, respectively) show brightness dips (image mismatches). Images for other angles (in the range from $-0°$ to $-60°$) are characterized by similar properties.

Set the reference (Figure 16.31) and the current (frame $\Psi1$) images (Figure 16.35). Then the deviation (offset) between frames $\Psi1$ and RI is approximately equal to $123-111 = 12$ pixels. Comparison of frame $\Psi2$ of the current image (Figure 16.33) with RI (Figure 16.31), gives a deviation of 5 pixels. The procedure will end at the g-step when the components of the offset vector $r(m, n)$ take values smaller than the threshold ($\sigma_{rmin} > 0$). This means that the current and the reference images $S_{RI} \subset \{S_{RI} (2\theta_{0,5}, h_j, \alpha_j, \beta k, v_1, \varphi_s, t_m)\}$ are coincide ($r_g = \underset{m,n}{min}\, r(m,n)$). The procedure is repeated g times for the number of RIs used out of the total number of RIs.

Figure 16.31: A nadir image of a standard surface area from an altitude of 500 m ($\varphi_s = -90°$).

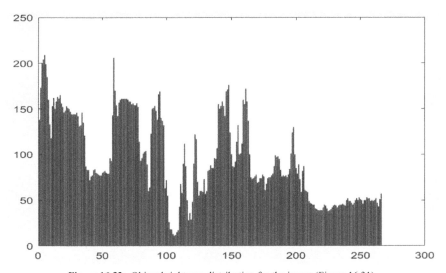

Figure 16.32: Object brightness distribution for the image (Figure 16.31).

Then the same operations are repeated for coordinate y. If the altitude of the aircraft flight is constant, the degree of mismatch of compared images will be determined by enumerating several image variants.

Let the MR fly the route with a change of profile (altitude) over the same area of SS, where the minimum values of object brightness are recorded. The choice of this section of the SS is due to the convenience of observing changes in brightness distribution when fixing it from different angles for a certain altitude, for example, 250 m (Figures 16.37–16.42). Let's determine the influence of changes in the altitude of the MR flight on the degree of discrepancy of the compared images.

Figure 16.33: Image of a typical landscape from a location angle $\varphi_s = -80°$.

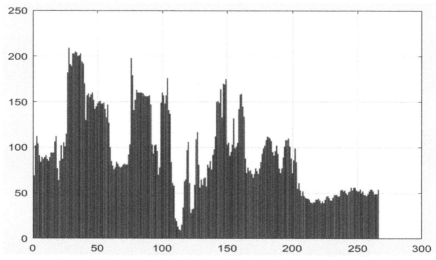

Figure 16.34: Brightness distribution of objects for the image (Figure 16.33).

The pairwise comparison of the graphs reflects the unevenness of the brightness distribution resulting from taking pictures from different altitudes but from the same angles. As sighting height increases, the viewing area increases, but the detail of the reference image decreases.

Analysis of the simulation results (Figures 16.32, 16.35, 16.36, 16.38, 16.40, 16.42) shows that the choice of the RI fragment is primarily influenced by the altitude parameter h_i. Most of the MRs can independently determine the altitude, which justifies the option of roughly selecting the image fragment by the flight altitude.

Figure 16.35: Image of a typical landscape from a location angle $\varphi_s = -70°$.

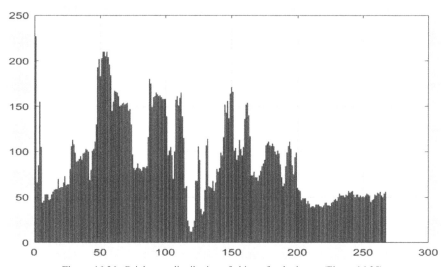

Figure 16.36: Brightness distribution of objects for the image (Figure 16.35).

Let the navigation system of the aircraft form CI at an unknown altitude. This unknown altitude is closest to the true altitude at which the RI was performed if the current and reference surface images have the highest degree of coincidence. To determine the real aircraft flight altitude, it is necessary to organize an iterative process of searching for exactly matching fragments. Let RI fragments, which differ by altitude parameter, be represented by columns in a multidimensional matrix, and a normal is chosen as a reference. Finding the desired RI is organized by one of the columns. The type of trajectory and the orientation of the CENS sensor influence the column choice. In the second step, the angular coordinates at which the RI fragment

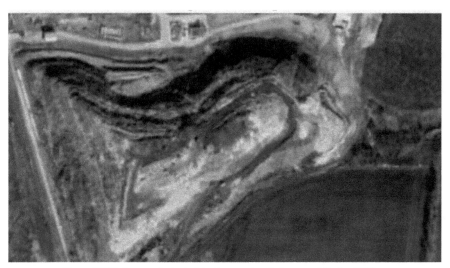

Figure 16.37: Image of a typical landscape at nadir from an altitude of 250 m.

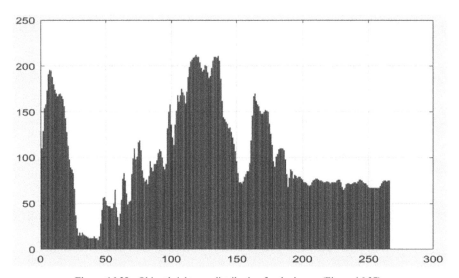

Figure 16.38: Object brightness distribution for the image (Figure 16.37).

will have the smallest deviation from CI are specified for the previously found value of the MR altitude. The procedure is also iterative but conducted on the rows of the matrix.

Consequently, the proposed iterative procedure makes it possible to find the sought RI fragment that most closely matches CI without conducting a complete search. The degree of coincidence (mismatch) of compared images characterizes the navigational accuracy of the aircraft.

The algorithm for the selection of CI is shown in Figure 16.43.

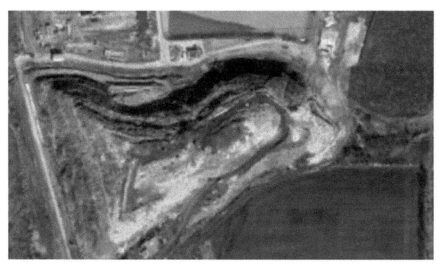

Figure 16.39: Image of a typical landscape from a location angle $\varphi_s = -80°$.

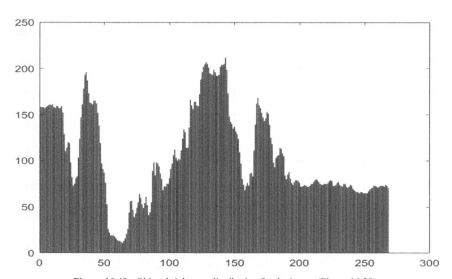

Figure 16.40: Object brightness distribution for the image (Figure 16.39).

16.4.3 Assessment of RI selection method for high-speed maneuvering MR navigation

Consider three images obtained for sighting angles of –90°, –80°, and –60°. Using the decisive rule, determine the measure of similarity of the images by comparing the first image with the second and the first with the third image. To determine the degree of similarity of the images obtained from different angles, shall build a CCF, and for nadir images, shall build an (ACF for heights of 500 m (Figure 16.44) and 250 m (Figure 16.45).

Figure 16.41: Image of a typical landscape from a location angle $\varphi_s = -70°$.

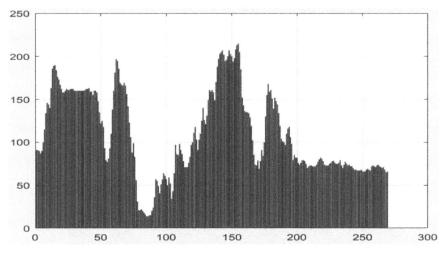

Figure 16.42: Object brightness distribution for the image (Figure 16.41).

Even intuitively, the closer the line of sight stands from the normal, the greater the similarity of the compared images. The graphs ACF and CCF (Figures 16.44, 16.45) confirm it, reflecting the result of the search for the greatest closeness of the RI fragment from the aggregate with the obtained CI. Objectively there is a directly proportional relationship between the degree of misalignment of compared images and the deviation of sighting angles from the normal. It does not depend on the altitude of the aircraft flight. Thus, if the MR is flying at an altitude of 500 m, a decrease in the sighting angle from –60° to –80° leads to a decrease in the RI deviation from CI from 0.91 to 0.75. Similar is the behavior of this dependence for an altitude of 250 m: at the same values of angles, the deviation is 0.92 and 0.83,

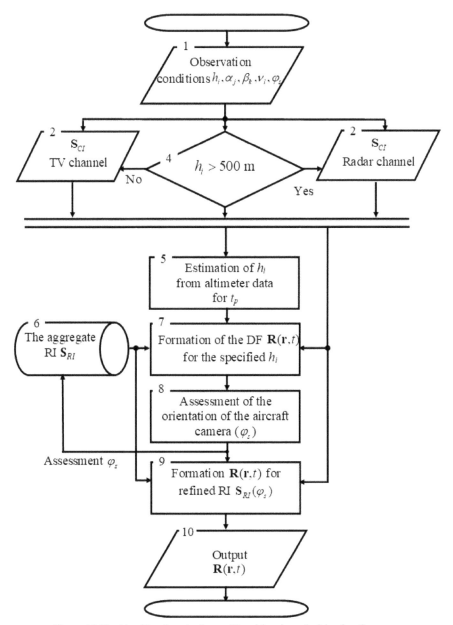

Figure 16.43: Algorithm for selecting an RI and forming a decisive function.

respectively. The previously obtained dependences of brightness distribution for the considered altitudes for the same MR flight conditions complement well the picture of image proximity determination.

To evaluate the effectiveness of the proposed method, first, take as a criterion the complexity of computational procedures for comparing images in set W. Secondly,

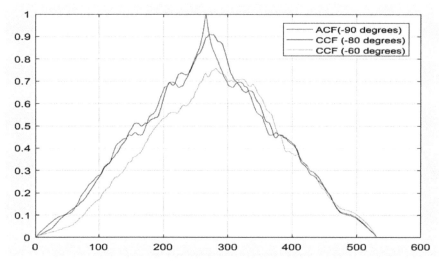

Figure 16.44: Results of ACF for sighting angle (–90°) and CCF for sighting angles –80° and –60° for altitude 500 m.

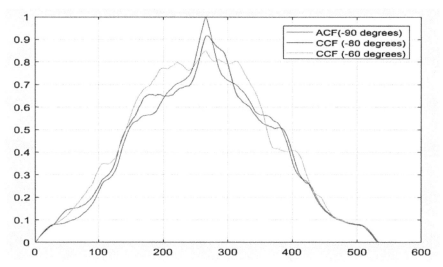

Figure 16.45: Results of ACF for sighting angle (–90°) and CCF for sighting angles –80° and –60° for altitude 250 m.

the relative reduction in computational complexity is taken as an indicator. Physically, it means how much the number of comparison operations will decrease when going from the complete enumeration of all fragments from the general population to the consideration of the RI fragment that the most exact matches CI.

Since the images are fixed from different altitudes, the complete set of RI fragments is a three-dimensional matrix. The two-dimensional image formed by the CI sensor (see Figure 16.30) based on the current image taken under certain conditions at a given flight altitude is a matrix element.

Consider how the application of the proposed iterative search procedure has changed the computational complexity of image comparison.

In the general case, the matrix describing the totality of RI has the dimension $B \cdot V \cdot C = W$. If for certainty, the dimensionality of the such matrix is $10 \times 10 \times 10$, and each individual element of the RI fragment is $4 \times 4 \times 4$, then during the search for the closest images, several fragments – 4 in height and 8 in the corners – are used in the refinement on each instance. In this case, the total number of iterations in the full enumeration of pairwise compared images is 4,000.

The proposed two-step procedure within the method allows setting a limited number of pairwise compared images at each of the stages: seven in the first step and twelve in the second step. Therefore, the total computational complexity of image comparison was reduced by about 210 times, preserving the required accuracy of mobile robot navigation using CENS.

The following demonstrates the objectivity, reliability, accuracy, adequacy, and unbiasedness of the obtained results. The Google Earth library was used as a repository, the images from which were randomly selected. The flights made by unmanned aircraft using TV cameras are, as a rule, conducted in the altitude range of 200–1000 m. Therefore, the images taken from altitudes of 500 m and 250 m were deliberately chosen for the research. There was no special binding of CENS to a particular type of image. The choice of a discreteness step of sighting angles of $10°$ when creating a set of images and constructing the corresponding CCFs for the class of tasks under consideration seems quite rational and can be explained by the following. On the one hand, it is necessary to constantly fix the reference object in the camera lens. On the other hand, the integrity of picture perception is not violated, and simultaneously the library of images is not clogged with unnecessary uninformative details. The use of sensors of different physical natures and the convenience of calculations, the CCF, led to the choice of an image dimension of 8 bits.

The decreasing computational complexity in the choice of RI did not affect the values of the main characteristics of CCF, in particular the side and main lobe, the width of which depends on the navigation accuracy. To compare the CI and RI, a simulation of the CENS solver function formation process was performed. For the current images obtained from a height of 500 m at different angles of sight (Figures 16.31, 16.33, 16.35), the corresponding CCFs are calculated (Figures 16.46–16.48). The highest correspondence of CI to the chosen RI (RI_{bvc}) is found for the image taken at the nadir (Figure 16.46). As the sighting angle increases with the unchanged altitude of the aircraft, mutual correlation decreases, and, accordingly, the discrepancy between current and reference images grows (Figures 16.47, 16.48). At the same time, navigation accuracy decreases, caused by the "spreading" of CCF main maxima peak and growth of the number and level of lateral residuals.

Thus, the developed approach to decrease the computational complexity of procedure formation procedures and rational choice of reference images (Figure 16.46) provides exact high-speed navigation of maneuvering dynamic MR performed in real-time.

Thus, summarizing the above considerations, the structure of the method is shown in Figure 16.49.

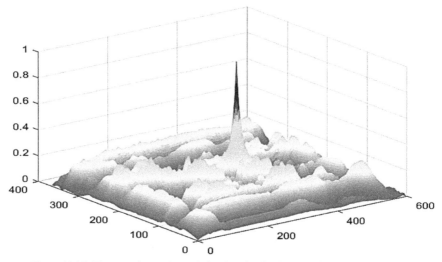

Figure 16.46: The mutual (cross-) correlation function for the RI to Figure 16.31 ($\varphi_s = -90°$).

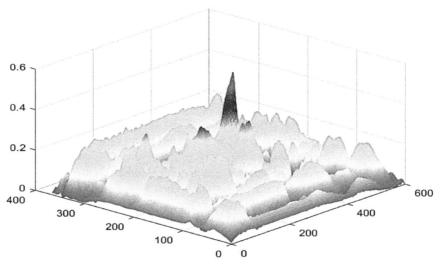

Figure 16.47: The mutual (cross-) correlation function for the RI to Figure 16.33 ($\varphi_s = -80°$).

The method and algorithm for selecting RIs from the general totality proposed to increase the speed of secondary data processing in CENS to allow for real-time re-planning of the route and trajectory of the MR flight. The sighting surface images are formed based on different-type data from sensors that implement different physical principles and are differentiated by accuracy parameters. This necessitates the selection of the RI dimensions according to the conditions of convergence of the iteration procedure.

The sensitivity and resolution of the sensors, which are the cornerstone elements of the primary information processing system, mainly affect the formation of the

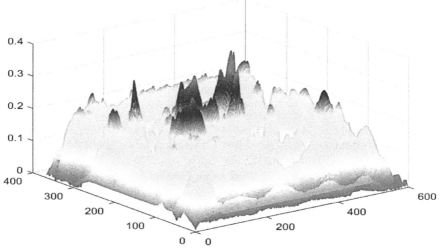

Figure 16.48: The mutual (cross-) correlation function for the RI to Figure 16.35 ($\varphi_x = -70°$).

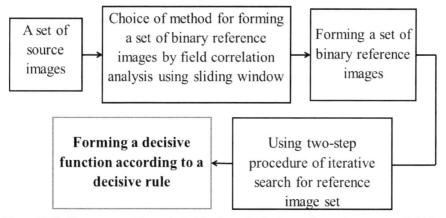

Figure 16.49: The structure of the method of forming and selecting a reference image to provide high-speed navigation for maneuvering aircraft.

threshold for the selection of the RI from the available totality in the combined type CENS and its comparison with the CI.

This method eliminates the ambiguity of selecting RI from a single database that stores reference images obtained from sources with different spatial resolutions. Comparison of image fragments by a cross-correlated function is reasonable when using the brightness (and/or reflectance) of objects as an informative parameter. However, this study has limitations.

Firstly, it is necessary to investigate additionally the influence of shadow binding, closing angles and restricted visibility zones, different illumination conditions (including artificial) in different weather and time of day, in different seasons, etc. on the object.

Secondly, a more detailed study of the peculiarities of diverse types of sighting surfaces requires special attention. Thus, the sighting area may contain objects with structural similarity, similar brightness distribution, infrastructure degradation, or high object saturation due to man-made or natural disasters, warfare, etc.

Thirdly, due to the diverse types and quality of information coming from sensors of different physical natures, the aircraft positioning will be formed CI with different parameters, which will inevitably affect the quality of the proposed algorithm.

The current stage in the development of robotics in general, and its navigational component, is characterized by an expansion in the field of application of these remarkable machines. Unfortunately, the latest news reports tell us about the meaningful results achieved by developers not only in industry, communications, and agriculture but on the battlefield. And in most cases, the specific methods and models underlying the development of new applications are hidden from us. This is particularly true in the military sector. And it is there that the products whose characteristics considered in the proposed work—highly maneuverable high-speed unmanned aerial vehicles performing tasks under the simultaneous influence of a group of factors complicating the functioning of mobile robots—are used [Ham et al. 2018, Tymochko and Podorozhnyak 2007, Sergiyenko et al. 2009, Yu. Sergiyenko 2010, Garcia-Cruz et al. 2014, Básaca-Preciado et al. 2014, Cañas et al. 2014, Straßberger et al. 2015, Sergiyenko et al. 2016, Ravankar et al. 2021].

It seems possible, that taking into account low-informative attributes, which the authors referred to as additional and not considered within the framework of this study, and their further formalization will allow finding effective application of the proposed basic solutions on high-speed navigation of MR in many new areas in different physical environments: not only in the air but also on land, including outside the Earth, in space, on water, and underwater. A lot of work is to be done to develop methods of navigation for mobile robots in conditions of low-informative terrain—over deserts, steppes, forests, and large areas of water surface. The authors consider it necessary to start developing decision support systems and training mobile robots to act intelligently in a rapidly changing environment when reference points are degraded due to the impact of technological or natural processes. In this case, the method developed and the perspectives voiced may complement known systems for modeling the behavior of mobile robots and pioneer the emergence of new ones [Rodríguez-Quiñonez et al. 2017, Sergiyenko et al. 2018, Sergiyenko et al. 2017, Oleg Sergiyenko and Julio Rodriguez-Quiñonez 2016, Ivanov et al. 2018, Sergiyenko et al. 2009, Rivas et al. 2008, Básaca et al. 2010, Yu Ishihara and Masaki Takahashi 2022, Zeinalova and Jafarov 2022, Gao and Huang 2022, Daza et al. 2021, Neggers et al. 2022, Zhu and Zhang 2021].

16.5 Conclusion

1. An improved model is characterized by a description of the process of formation of the CENS decisive functions of mobile robots, for the accurate navigation of which, considering their high speed and maneuvering characteristics, a rational selection of the right one from the array of reference images stored in the CENS

database is required. This model was the basis for the development of the method and algorithm of the same name.

2. To achieve accurate positioning of MR with autonomous CENS on board, which has a wide database of reference images, a two-step procedure for selecting a fragment of RI from this database was developed.

The main idea in the realization of the method was a fundamental reduction in the number of computational procedures while providing accurate navigational characteristics of the aircraft with autonomous CENS. Numerous experiments and simulation results showed that this goal was achieved. Namely, under conditions corresponding to real flight tasks, the number of performed image comparison operations is reduced by more than two orders of magnitude – 210 times.

3. The proposed approach to the formation and selection of reference images for the navigation of mobile robots using correlation-extreme systems significantly improves the process of their location. This method, with minor adjustments realized by considering additional factors, can be used in many new applications for land and surface (underwater) mobile robots and platforms and is adapted to known robot modeling systems.

References

Antyufeev, V. I., Bykov, V. N., Grichanyuk, A. M., Ivanchenko, D. D., Kolchigin, N. N., Krayushkin, V. A. et al. 2014. Matrichnyye radiometricheskiye korrelyatsionno-ekstremal'nyye sistemy navigatsii letatel'nykh apparatov: Monography: Khar'kov: Shchedraya usad'ba plyus 372 p. ISBN: 978-617-7188-XX-X. [In Russian].

Básaca, L. C., Rodríguez, J. C., Sergiyenko, O., Tyrsa, V. V., Hernández, W., Nieto, J. I. 2010. Starostenko. resolution improvement of dynamic triangulation method for 3D vision system in robot navigation task, Proceedings of IEEE-36th Annual Conference of IEEE Industrial Electronics (IECON-2010), Glendale-Phoenix, Arizona, USA, 7-10 November 2010, pp. 2880–2885.

Básaca-Preciado, L. C., Yu. Sergiyenko, O., Rodríguez-Quinonez, J. C., García, X., Tyrsa, V., Rivas-Lopez, M. et al. 2014. Optical 3D laser measurement system for navigation of autonomous mobile robot. In Optics and Lasers in Engineering, Elsevier, 54: 159–169.

Basset, P. M., Tremolet, A., and Lefebvre, T. 2014. Rotary Wing UAV pre-sizing: Past and Present Methodological Approaches at Onera. AerospaceLab, pp. 1–12.

Cañas, N., Hernandez, W., González, G., and Sergiyenko, O. 2014. Controladores multivariables para un vehiculo autonomo terrestre: Comparación basada en la fiabilidad de software. In RIAI-Revista Iberoamericana de Automática e Informática Industrial, Elsevier Doyma, 11(2) April–July 2014, pp. 179–190. [In Spanish]

Daza, M., Barrios-Aranibar, D., Diaz-Amado, J., Cardinale, Y., and Vilasboas, J. 2021. An approach of social navigation based on proxemics for crowded environments of humans and robots. Micromachines 2021, 12: 193. https://doi.org/10.3390/mi12020193.

Dunbabin, M., and Marques, L. 2012. Robots for environmental monitoring: significant advancements and applications. In IEEE Robotics & Automation Magazine, 19(1): 24–39, March 2012.

Faessler, M., Fontana, F., Forster, C., Mueggler, E., Pizzoli, M., and Scaramuzza. 2016. Autonomous, vision-based flight and live dense 3D mapping with a quadrotor micro aerial vehicle. In Journal of Field Robotics by Wiley, 33(4), Special Issue: Safety, Security, and Rescue Robotics (SSRR), Part 2, pp. 431–450, June 2016.

Gao, Y., and C.-M. Huang. 2022. Evaluation of Socially-Aware Robot Navigation. Front. Robot. AI 8:721317. doi: 10.3389/frobt.2021.721317.

Garcia-Cruz, X. M., Yu. Sergiyenko, O., Vera Tyrsa, Rivas-Lopez, M., Hernandez-Balbuena, D., Rodriguez-Quiñonez, J. C. et al. 2014. Optimization of 3D laser scanning speed by use of combined variable step. In Optics and Lasers in Engineering, Elsevier, 54: 141–151.

Ham, M. Cho, and Ponce, J. 2018. Robust guided image filtering using nonconvex potentials. In IEEE Transactions on Pattern Analysis and Machine Intelligence, 40(1): 192–207, 1 Jan. 2018.

Hernandez, W., and Mendez, A. 2018. Application of principal component analysis to image compression. In Statistics-Growing Data Sets and Growing Demand for Statistics. IntechOpen.

Hornung, K. M., Wurm, M., Bennewitz, C., Stachniss, W., and Burgard. 2013. OctoMap: an efficient probabilistic 3D mapping framework based on octrees. In Autonomous Robots, by Springer, 34(3): 189–206, April 2013.

Ivanov, M., Lindner, L., Sergiyenko, O., Rodríguez-Quiñonez, J. C., Flores-Fuentes, W. and Rivas-López, M. 2019. Mobile robot path planning using continuous laser scanning. Optoelectronics in Machine Vision-Based Theories and Applications. IGI Global, 2019. pp. 338–372. Web. 7 Dec. 2018. doi:10.4018/978-1-5225-5751-7.ch012.

Keller, J., Thakur, D., Likhachev, M., Gallier, J., and Kumar, V. 2017. Coordinated path planning for fixed-wing UAS conducting persistent surveillance missions. In IEEE Transactions on Automation Science and Engineering, 14(1): 17–24, Jan. 2017.

Kostyashkin, L. N., Loginov, A. A., and Nikiforov, M. B. 2013. Problem aspects of the combined vision system of flying vehicles // Izvestiya SFU. № 5. C. 61–65.

Li, H., and Savkin, A. V. 2018. Wireless sensor network based navigation of micro flying robots in the industrial internet of things. In IEEE Transactions on Industrial Informatics, 14(8): 3524–3533, Aug. 2018.

Lindner, L., Sergiyenko, O., Rodríguez-Quiñonez, J., Rivas-López, M., Hernández-Balbuena, D., Flores-Fuentes, W. et al. 2016. Mobile robot vision system using continuous laser scanning for industrial application. In Industrial Robot by Emerald, 43(4): 360–369.

Lindner, L., Sergiyenko, O., Rivas-Lopez, M., Hernandez-Balbuena, D., Flores-Fuentes, W., Rodríguez-Quiñonez, J. et al. 2017. Exact laser beam positioning for measurement of vegetation vitality. In Industrial Robot: An International Journal, by Emerald, 44(4): 532–541.

Loginov, A. A., Muratov, E. R., Nikiforov, M. B., and Novikov, A. I. 2015. Reducing the computational complexity of image matching in aviation vision systems // Dynamics of Complex Systems. T. 9, № 1. C. 33–40.

Neggers, M. M. E., Cuijpers, R. H., Ruijten, P. A. M. and Ijsselsteijn, W. A. 2022. Determining Shape and Size of Personal Space of a Human when Passed by a Robot. Int J of Soc Robotics 14: 561–572, 2022. https://doi.org/10.1007/s12369-021-00805-6.

Oleg Sergiyenko, and Julio C. Rodriguez-Quiñonez. 2016. Developing and Applying Optoelectronics in Machine Vision. Editorial: IGI Global, Hershey, Pennsylvania, USA. August, 2016, 341 Pages.

Oleg Sergiyenko, Wendy Flores-Fuentes, and Vera Tyrsa. 2017. Methods to Improve resolution of 3D Laser Scanning. Editorial: LAP LAMBERT Academic Publishing, 31/ 07/ 2017. - 132 p.

Ravankar, A., Ravankar, A.A., Rawankar, A., and Hoshino, Y. 2021. Autonomous and safe navigation of mobile robots in vineyard with smooth collision avoidance. Agriculture 2021, 11, 954. https://doi.org/10.3390/agriculture11100954.

Rivas, M., Sergiyenko, O., Aguirre, M., Devia, L., Tyrsa, V., and Rendón, I. 2008. Spatial data acquisition by laser scanning for robot or SHM task. IEEE-IES Proceedings. International Symposium on Industrial Electronics (ISIE-2008), Cambridge, United Kingdom, 30 of June–2 of July, 2008, pp. 1458–1463.

Rodríguez-Quiñonez, J. C., Sergiyenko, O., Flores-Fuentes, W., Rivas-lopez, M., Hernandez-Balbuena, D., Rascón, R. et al. 2017. Improve a 3D distance measurement accuracy in stereo vision systems using optimization methods' approach. Opto-Electronics Review by Elsevier, 25(1) May 2017, Pages 24–32.

Sergiyenko, O., Hernandez, W., Tyrsa, V., Devia Cruz, L., Starostenko, O., and Pena-Cabrera, M. 2009a. Remote sensor for spatial measurements by using optical scanning. MDPI, Sensors, 9(7): Basel, Switzerland, pp. 5477–5492.

Sergiyenko, O. Y., Tyrsa, V. V., Devia, L. F., Hernandez, W., Starostenko, O., and Rivas Lopez, M. 2009b. Dynamic Laser Scanning method for Mobile Robot Navigation. Proceedings of ICCAS-SICE

2009, ICROS-SICE International Joint Conference, Fukuoka, Japan, August 18–21, 2009, pp. 4884–4889.

Sergiyenko, O., Tyrsa, V., Flores-Fuentes, W., Rodriguez-Quiñonez, J., and Mercorelli, P. 2018. Machine vision sensors. In Journal of Sensors, Hindawi, Volume 2018 - Special Issue on "Machine Vision Sensors. Editorial article, Article ID 3202761, 2 pages.

Shen, Z., and Song, E. 2018. Dynamic Filtering of Sparse Signals via L1 Minimization with Variant Parameters. 2018 37th Chinese Control Conference (CCC), Wuhan, pp. 4409–4414.

Siciliano, B. and Khatib, O. (ed.). 2016. Springer handbook of robotics. 2nd Revised edition. Springer Verlag: Berlin. ISBN 978-3-319-32550-7; e-ISBN 978-3-319-32552-1. LXXVI, 2227 pp. https://dx.doi.org/10.1007/978-3-319-32552-1.

Smelyakov, K. S., Ruban, I. V., Smelyakov, S. V., and Tymochko, O. I. 2005. Segmentation of small-sized irregular images. In Proceeding of IEEE East-West Design & Test Workshop (EWDTW'05), Odessa, 2005, pp. 235–241.

Somov, Y., Butyrin, S., Somov, S., and Somova, T. 2017. In-flight calibration, alignment and verification of an astroinertial attitude determination system for free-flying robots and land-survey satellites. 2017 IEEE International Workshop on Metrology for AeroSpace (MetroAeroSpace), Padua, 2017, pp. 474–478.

Sotnikov, O. M., and Tarshin, V. A. 2012. Obosnovaniye printsipov postroyeniya i razvitiya modeli korrelyatsionno-ekstremal'noy sistemy navedeniya kombinirovannogo tipa. Sistema upravleniya navigatsiyey ta zvozdku. - K., № 4(24): 7–11. [In Russian]

Sotnikov, O. M., Tarshin, V. A., and Otkryto, P. V. 2013. Problemy i pryamoye razvitiye yadro-spetsificheskikh ekstremal'nykh sistem, nalozhennykh kerovanami apparatury. Sovremennyye informatsionnyye tekhnologii v sfere oborony bez oborony. № 3(18): 93–96. 2013. [In Russian]

Sotnikov, O. M., Antyufeyev, V. I., Bykov, V. N., Grichanyuk, A. M. et al. 2014. Matrichnyye radiometricheskiye korrelyatsionno-ekstremal'nyye sistemy navigatsii letatel'nykh apparatov" Book: Ministerstvo obrazovaniya i nauki Ukrainy. KHNU imeni V.N. Karazina - 2014. - 372 p. [In Russian]

Sotnikov, O., Tarshyn, V., Yeromina, N., Petrov, S., and Antonenko, N. 2017. A method for localizing a reference object in a current image with several bright objects. In Eastern-European Journal of Enterprise Technologies. 3. № 9(87): 68–74.

Sotnikov, O. M., Tantsiura, A. B., and Yu. Lavrov, O. 2018. Calculating method of error calculations of the object coordinating platform free inertial navigation systems of unmanned aerial vehicle. In Advanced Information Systems, 2(1): 32–41.

Sotníkov, O. M., Vorobey, O. M., and Tantsyura, O. B. 2018. Modelí potochnikh zobrazhen', shcho formuyut'sya kanalami kombínovanoï korelyatsíyno-yekstremal'noï sistemi navígatsíï bezpílotnogo lítal'nogo aparatu. Suchasní ínformatsíyní tekhnologíï u sferí bezpeki ta oboroni, №2(32): 29–38. [In Ukrainian]

Sotnikov, O., Kartashov, V., Tymochko, O., Sergiyenko, O., Tyrsa, V. Mercorelli, P. et al. 2020. Methods for ensuring the accuracy of radiometric and optoelectronic navigation systems of flying robots in a developed infrastructure (eds.). Machine Vision and Navigation. Springer, Cham. https://doi.org/10.1007/978-3-030-22587-2_16.

Starovoytov, V. V. 2014. Tsifrovyye izobrazheniya ot polucheniya do obrabotki / V. V. Starovoytov, YU. I. Golub – Minsk: OIPI NAN Belarusi, . – 202 s. ISBN 978-985-6744-80-1.

Straßberger, P. Mercorelli, and Sergiyenko, O. 2015. A decoupled MPC for motion control in robotino using a geometric approach. IOP Publishing, Journal of Physics: Conference Series, 659: 1–10.

Taha, H., Kiani, M., and Navarro, J. 2018. Experimental demonstration of the vibrational stabilization phenomenon in bio-inspired flying robots. In IEEE Robotics and Automation Letters, 3(2): 643–647.

Tymochko, O. I., and Podorozhnyak, A. O. 2007. Lokalizatsiya ob'ektu poshuku na potochnomu zobrazhenni navigatsinoy systemy z raiometrychnymy datchykamy. In Zbirnyk naukovykh prats Kharkivskoho universytetu Povitryanykh Syl. № 1(13): 47–50. [In Ukrainian]

Tymochko, O. I., Ttystan, A., Ushan, V., Yeromina, N., Dmitriiev, O., Mazharov, V. et al. 2020a. The synthesis of the reference image and algorithms for vehicle navigation systems, IJETER, 8(3): 853–858. doi:10.30534/ijeter/2020/40832020.

Tymochko, O., Trystan, A., Berezhnyi, A., Sotnikov, O., Matiushchenko, O., and Kryzhanivskyi, I. 2020b. Vehicles while monitoring behavior of dynamic objects in a forest-steppe area. IJETER, 8(7): 3208–3215. doi.org/10.30534/ijeter/2020/54872020.

Tymochko, O., Trystan, A., Matiushchenko, O., Shpak, N., and Dvulit, Z. 2022. Method of controlling a group of unmanned aircraft for searching and destruction of objects using artificial intelligence elements. MMC, 9(3): 694–710.

Vorobiov, O. M., Sotníkov, O. M. and Tantsyura, O. B. 2018. Modelí potochnikh zobrazhen', shcho formuyut'sya kanalami kombínovanoĭ korelyatsíyno-yekstremal'noĭ sistemi navígatsíĭ bezpílotnogo lítal'nogo aparatu. Suchasní ínformatsíyní tekhnologíĭ u sferí bezpeki ta oboroni, (32): 29–38. [In Ukrainian].

Yeromina, N., Petrov, S., Tantsiura, A., Iasechko, M., and Larin, V. 2018. Formation of reference images and decision function in radiometric correlation-extremal navigation systems, Eastern-European Journal of Enterprise Technologies, 4, No. 9 (94): 27–35. DOI: 10.15587/1729-4061.2018.139723.

Yeromina, N., Petrov, S., Samsonov, Y., Pisarevskiy, S., Kaplun, S., and Vlasenko, I. 2020. The simulation and performance evaluation of adaptive algorithm of image comparison in correlation-extreme navigation systems. IJETER, 8(8): 4146–4151, doi:10.30534/ijeter/2020/19882020.

Yeromina, N., Tarshyn, V., Petrov, S., Samoylenko, V., Tabakova, I., Dmitriiev, O. et al. 2021. Method of reference image selection to provide high-speed aircraft navigation under conditions of rapid change of flight trajectory. International Journal of Advanced Technology and Engineering Exploration, Vol. 8(85) ISSN (Print): 2394–5443 ISSN (Online): 2394-7454. http://dx.doi.org/10.19101/IJATEE.2021.874814.

Yu Ishihara, and Masaki Takahashi. 2022. Empirical study of future image prediction for image-based mobile robot navigation. Robotics and Autonomous Systems. - 2022, pp. 104018. DOI: 10.1016/j.robot.2021.104018.

Yu, O., and Sergiyenko. 2010. Optoelectronic system for mobile robot navigation. Springer/Allerton Press, Inc., Optoelectronics, Instrumentation and Data Processing, 46(5), October, 2010, pp. 414–428.

Yu. Sergiyenko, O., Ivanov, M. V., Tyrsa, V. V., Kartashov, V. M., Rivas-López, M., Hernández-Balbuena, D. et al. 2016. Data transferring model determination in robotic group", in Robotics and Autonomous Systems, Elsevier, vol. 83, September 2016, pp. 251–260.

Zeinalova, L. M., and Jafarov, B. O. 2022. Mobile robot navigation with preference-based fuzzy behaviors. - 11th International Conference on Theory and Application of Soft Computing, Computing with Words and Perceptions and Artificial Intelligence - ICSCCW-2021 - Lecture Notes in Networks and Systems. - 10.1007/978-3-030-92127-9_102 2022 .-pp. 774–782.

Zhu, K. and Zhang, T. 2021. Deep reinforcement learning based mobile robot navigation: A review. Tsinghua Science and Technology, 26(5): 674–691. https://doi.org/10.26599/TST.2021.9010012.

17

Application of Fibre Bragg Grating Arrays for Medical Diagnosis and Rehabilitation Purposes

Manish Mishra and *Prasant Kumar Sahu**

17.1 Introduction

Human health is an incessant query, which to date and in the future will remain an issue of paramount importance for the sustenance and survival of the Homo Sapiens race. To understand the issue at hand, i.e., health and well-being, it needs to be defined and the World Health Organisation does so by stating that "it is (health) not merely the absence of malady, but a condition of completeness of physical, social, and mental wellbeing" [World Health Organisation 1948]. This chapter, however, deals with a single entity, which is physical well-being. To further prove the merit of the study, it becomes essential to present some practical data associated with human physiological disorders and diseases. As per the study conducted, heart disease is most common among all age groups of humans, and leads to a single death every 34 seconds. Coronary artery disease is the most frequent type of heart condition and around 20 million people in their twenties suffer from it [Centre for Disease Control and Prevention 2020b]. Heart attack, another phenomenon, is witnessed by 0.8 million people every year and 1 out of 5 heart attacks are silent. Hypertension, a medical condition in which blood pressure accounts for values higher than nominal, is very prevalent among human beings. More than 0.6 million deaths occurred had

School of Electrical Sciences, Indian Institute of Technology, Bhubaneswar, Argul - Jatni Road, Kansapada, Odisha – 752050, India.
Emails: mm29@iitbbs.ac.in, Orcid Id: 0000-0001-9671-8209.
* Corresponding author: pks@iitbbs.ac.in

hypertension as a primary or contributing cause. Surprisingly, nearly half of the fully-grown struggle from hypertension and only 1 out of 4 have it under control. Not only is it dangerous in terms of health, but such ailments also prove themselves to be a costly endeavor too. As per the study, heart disease can cost $229 billion every year comprising of health services, medicines, and lost work productivity. Hypertension also costs around $131 billion every year comprising medical and health care services. Acquiring, analyzing, and evaluating various physiological parameters plays a significant part in understanding and maintaining a balanced state of health in human beings [Centre for Disease Control and Prevention 2020a]. Gauging deep inside the matter and understanding the gravity of the situation, it becomes essential to monitor health-related parameters for continuous analysis and assessment. Various physiological parameters such as Heart Rate (HR) or Pulse Rate (PR), Respiratory Rate (RR), Blood Pressure (BP) consisting of Systolic Blood Pressure (SBP) and Diastolic Blood Pressure (DBP), Oxygen Saturation Percentage (SpO2), etc., can be evaluated and supervised regularly for ahead of time detection of abnormalities or presence of life-threatening diseases. The above-mentioned parameters are acquired from a pulse (an impulse felt over an artery resulting from continuous contraction and expansion of the arterial walls of the heart) and can be acquired from different regions appearing from head to toe. Generally, there are nine pulsation points, which are Temporal (over the temple), Carotid (at the side of the neck), Apical (over the intercostal space), Brachial (on the crook of the arm), Radial (in the wrist below the thumb), Femoral (in the groin), Popliteal (behind the knee), Posterior Tibial (at the side of the ankle), and Dorsalis Pedis (on the front of the foot). By analyzing the pulse pattern obtained from these pulsation points, an evaluation of physiological parameters and efficient diagnosis can be performed.

Acquisition of any signal depends highly upon the sensor's design, operating methodology, and sensitivity towards the physiological variable under assessment. In the present era, optical technology has gained quite a stardom due to various advantages offered by them. Optical sensors offer various advantages such as being small in size and having accessibility to difficult places, solid state reliability, resistance to Electromagnetic Interference (EMI) and ionizing radiation, light spectrum variations for analyzing physical parameters, sensitivity towards external physical parameters for instance temperature, strain, and humidity, high accuracy as the wavelength is an absolute parameter, often don't require physical contact, non-electrical hence explosion proof, remote sensing and interfacing through communication systems with enhanced security is permissible, operation in harsh environments, and enhanced multiplexing capabilities [Kashyap 2010]. Optical sensors can be classified into many types based on their fiber type, geometry, sensing purpose (biological and chemical), scattering mechanisms, and topology. The current study is based on Fibre Bragg Grating Arrays (FBGA), which are the combination of two or more Fibre Bragg Gratings (FBG) placed at a distance apart from each other. FBGs are sensors based on back-reflecting spectra generated due to a combination of multiple small reflections occurring at the edges of grating planes. The reflected spectrum then can be analyzed to study the parameter under observation. The application of FBGs in medicine and healthcare has witnessed a lot of popularity in the past decade. Applications may vary from cardiorespiratory analysis, dental and bone health, temperature ablation, and thermography to strain mapping of the foot, curvature or bending analysis to gait and motion analysis. Myriad applications are reported previously and a variety of literature can be consulted for further analysis [Korposh et al. 2017, Lo Presti et al. 2020, Sirkis et al. 2017]. As the following study only deals with the analysis of pulse waves, further discussion of medical applications will be beyond the scope of the literature.

Various previous studies show the possibility of acquiring the pulse patterns utilizing FBGs and evaluation of physiological parameters say blood pressure, heart rate or pulse rate, and breathing rate. In the reported studies, FBGs have been utilized as sensing elements for acquiring the pulse pattern and then, further analysis and signal processing methods have been employed for the calculation of physiological parameters [Haseda et al. 2019, Koyama and Ishizawa 2019]. The acquired pulse wave and their derivatives (either first or second) were studied in detail and comparative analysis was reported based on information provided by each type of waveform. Although the FBG sensor is small, easily installable, and quite sensitive to minute pressure variation generated due to the pulses, still the values obtained can be affected by several factors such as sensor position or orientation. In previous studies, such effects were not taken into account and have been left as an entity that still needs to be expedited. To compensate for the location effects, sensor positioning or spatial orientation, Fibre Bragg Grating Arrays (FBGA) are employed for efficient and precise analysis. FBGA ensures proper coverage of the region of interest keeping in mind the effects of spatial orientation which can be either orthogonal or parallel to the artery region under analysis. FBGA being a composition of laterally placed FBGs at a certain distance not only ensures the coverage but, also provides multiple readings from the region of interest, hence compensating for the local referencing effects and proceeding for multiple numbers of trials, which is cumbersome. Furthermore, by acquiring the data from the common site, such signals can be averaged and a single signal can be obtained which can be treated as a reference for evaluating the physiological parameters. Averaging of the signals obtained can lead to reduced effects of local referencing and hence lead to the low noise signal (Lo Presti et al. 2021). In the presented study, fiber Bragg grating arrays (FBGA) are utilized for acquiring the pedal pulses from the Posterior Tibial and Dorsalis Pedis regions, and results based on the acquired data have been presented. The chapter contains the following sections, which are first, the Introduction, explaining the aim of the study; second, the theoretical background, explaining the schematics and theory of operation of FBGA; third, the Experimental Procedure, outlining the process outflow and necessary details for experimenting; Fourthly, Results and Discussions, containing the detailed analysis of the data acquired and stating various limitations of the study; and Fifth, Conclusion, concluding the results, discussion and future scope for the conducted study.

17.2 Fibre bragg gratings

Fibre Bragg Gratings, i.e., FBGs are periodic perturbations generated in the core of the optical fiber due to exposure of a focalized optical radiation (of particular frequency and wavelength). The relative variation in the refractive index is dependent upon the material properties of fiber, Ultra Violet (UV) exposure duration, and photosensitivity. While radiation traveling through the optical fiber is reflected through interacting with the grating planes; a condition known as Bragg condition is observed which is the result of constructive additions of all such minute reflections; hence creating a reflective vertex of a certain wavelength called Bragg Wavelength (λB). Bragg wavelength varies in direct proportion with the effective refractive index of core and cladding (nnff), and periodicity of the grating planes (Λ) as shown in equation (1),

$$\lambda_B = 2n_{eff}\Lambda \tag{1}$$

Efficient analysis of the characteristics of the FBGs can be done theoretically by utilizing Coupled Mode Theory (CMT) and various forms of grating patterns can be produced. As explained previously, FBGs are sensitive to physical parameters such as temperature and strain; equation (2) describes the relation of Bragg wavelength shift ($\Delta\lambda_B$) with strain (ε) and change in temperature (ΔT),

$$\frac{\Delta\lambda_B}{\lambda_B} = (\alpha + \eta)\Delta T + (1 - \rho_e)\varepsilon_z \tag{2}$$

where, α, η, ρ_e, and ε_z are thermal expansion, thermos-optic, elasto-optic, and temperature change coefficients respectively. Elasto optic coefficient is dependent on the core refractive index (n), Poisson ratio (υ), and strain optic coefficients (p_{11}, p_{12}) and can be described by equation (3),

$$\rho_e = \frac{(n^2)}{2} \{p_{12} - v(p_{11} + p_{12})\} \tag{3}$$

From the above equations, it is clear that the shift in the wavelength is dependent on the strain applied by external agents (Mishra and Sahu 2022). The values of strain are affected by the electro-optic coefficients and their dependence on strain optic coefficients, Poisson ratio, and refractive index. The lower value of the elasto-optic coefficient is preferred for higher deflection in wavelength shifts and vice versa. An interesting feature to note about the functioning of the FBGs is that it includes two opposite behaviors affecting the Bragg wavelength shift. When the optical fiber is stretched, then it produces a positive effect and the optical medium expands due to a decrease in the medium's density, the refractive index decreases, which leads to a negative effect. Typical values for a Ge-doped silica-based optical fiber are $\rho_e = 0.22$, $\alpha = 0.55 \times 10^{-6}/°C$ and $\eta = 8.6 \times 10^{-6}/°C$ which provide typical wavelength shift sensitivities of 14.18 pm/°C and 1.2 pm/$\mu\varepsilon$. The dependence of FBGs on strain and temperature simultaneously raises concerns over the matter of cross-sensitivity. Either providing temperature compensations for the acquired data or ensuring a constant room temperature can nullify the effects of temperature under a considerable range. FBGs are also available in different packaging materials, which makes them handy and versatile for their efficient utilization. For instance, to retrieve data FBGs can be glued using polymer adhesives directly to the location of interest. Such applications are found in bone health monitoring. Polymer-integrated FBGs are also being used for gait analysis as the FBGs are embedded inside the sheath of a polymer material such as resin to provide further robustness and flexural strength. Mesh-integrated FBGs, i.e., FBGs in elastic fabrics are used during the fabrication process and usually found in application in respiratory or cardiovascular monitoring. Smart Fibre Reinforced Polymer (SFRP) in which the FBGs are enclosed between the reinforcing layers of the composite material during manufacturing. Arrangements of such sorts are found in amputees or protection devices for fibers. Metal encapsulation is also a very well-known encapsulation methodology. FBGs are placed inside a metal container specifically designed to provide mechanical strength and protection to the sensors. Such arrangements are found in oil and refineries, pipelines or large structures such as bridges where structural health monitoring is of utter importance and sensing methods must be explosion-proof. Polymer encapsulation, is popular in acquiring physiological data from human beings, which protects the FBG and enhances flexural strength. Most such sheaths are biocompatible and possess no harm to the subjects.

Fibre Bragg Grating Arrays (FBGA) are another form of packaged FBGs in which two or more FBGs are placed side by side at some fixed distance apart. Such packaged FBGs act as quasi-distributed sensors facilitating the sensing of multiple physical factors (same or different) at different locations of the target region. In this setup, FBGs can be designed with varying features such as length, apodization profile or sensing parameter, etc., for industrial, research and development purposes. As different FBGs possess different Bragg wavelengths, the possibility of interference is reduced. It is up to the manufacturer or user to provide the necessary FBG profile or Bragg wavelengths to ensure zero overlaps. FBGs have narrow bandwidth, which can ensure the packaging of the maximum number of FBGs for coverage of the large region of interest or target area. Utilizing a single sensor for extracting data is not always ideal, as it does not account for location effects or spatial orientation effects in their implementation. In monitoring physiological parameters, as shown in Figure 17.1, the data obtained may likely vary from place to place in a single region of interest. For instance, obtaining heart rates from different regions of the chest may vary and differences can be observed. Ensuring well-defined and properly analyzed regions of interest can ensure a possible error band so that further analysis could be carried out for improving data acquisition and accuracy.

Revisiting the FBGA implementation, as explained above, can compensate for the location effects and can provide local referencing features. The spatial orientation of the sensor can also ensure a better way of acquiring the signal through the FBG sensor. Proper exposure to the area of interest, in this case, the pulsation point, enables each sensor to accommodate itself for maximum exposure and hence the degree of similarity of data obtained from all the sensors. Proper exposure to the regions of interest not only ensures a higher degree of similarity of the signal, but also solves the problem of the number of trials required for conducting the study and signal refining. Since two or more sensors are placed in the region of interest, multiple amounts of data can be acquired simultaneously and hence, provide a certain degree of relief in conducting repeated trials for a precise and efficient analysis. In terms of making the signal efficient and more accurate, the data acquired from the sensors can be averaged over the whole time interval for which data is acquired. The data acquired after averaging the whole data is far more refined and smoother as compared to the

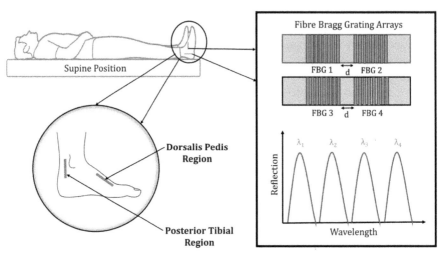

Figure 17.1: Physiological parameter monitoring with FBGA.

data acquired individually. The averaged data possesses a higher degree of similarity with both signals obtained individually. Averaging is a very basic operation that can be easily performed and no need for extra-complicated operations is required.

Although using FBGA is very advantageous and can offer many features as compared to single FBGs, knowing about the limitations of the applications is also necessary. To work in tandem with each other, the connection between the FBGs must be robust. Splicing separately the FBGs may result in fragile and non-homogeneous uniformity of the linkage point so it is a dire need that all the FBGs must be fabricated simultaneously. In addition, during fabrication, smooth and robust techniques like "the phase mask technique" must be used for fabricating the FBGA. Requiring an array of different types of FBGs can increase the cost of fabrication and complexity. Arrays of greater length can also be disadvantageous for small signal detection such as in the domain of medicine and healthcare. In such applications, brute force or sudden extensive movement can lead to breakage of the FBGA, so proper packaging of the sensor arrays with steadfast material without affecting signal detection efficiency is required. Utilizing FBGA in large-scale applications such as oil, mining, and pipelines, separate FBG can be connected with connectors and as each FBG is metallically encased, proper protection is provided beforehand. In the medical field, the usage of polymer-encapsulated FBGs has seen a lot of popularity in recent years and hence could be a viable solution for providing robustness and enhanced flexing capabilities [Lo Presti et al. 2019, Presti et al. 2019]. For the arrays to work properly, the distance must be as close as possible, for instance, 10 mm. A closer distance between FBGs ensures that there is no significant difference in the area of exposure to which the FBGs are subjected. If it so happens that the distance becomes larger than the specified measurement, a lot of dissimilarities obtained in the waveform could lead to absurd results. In the overall scenario, utilizing FBGA is quite an essential step toward opening new dimensions of sense. Enhanced with multiplexing qualities and capabilities such a sensor network could be applied to gather information from different areas of the region and such information could be assessed collectively.

Application of FBGA is quite suitable in medicine, as arrays can be implemented to study target areas and mapping of physical factors "such as strain and temperature" could be performed. For instance, in the tumor, the target area possesses a higher degree of temperature ranges as compared to the other body region in close vicinity. Therefore, depending on the thermal map generated from the sensors' location of the tumor, it could be exactly pinpointed and further diagnosis can be performed [Ambastha et al. 2020]. In strain mapping, a similar idea can be applied to the foot area. In the foot of a diabetic patient, an ulcer is witnessed quite often due to prolonged inactivity of the feet. Utilizing the arrays and targeting the specific areas, the formation of ulcers can be regulated. In gait and motion analysis, it has been found that different strain maps on the foot are formed for each person. By studying and analyzing the foot patterns and strain mapping, a classification can be done between the strain maps and the chances of security breach can be curtailed [Domingues et al. 2019, Suresh et al. 2015]. Placing the arrays in the regions of pulsation points can deliver physiological parameters say blood pressure, heart rate or pulse rate, heart rate variability, respiratory rate, etc., for critically analyzing the acquired data. There is a possibility that combining this data with strain mapping can enable the identification of the movement of a person or the activity being performed. Previous works regarding plantar pressure mapping have shown the possibility of obtaining the distribution data from the feet [Domingues et al. 2017]. It also shows the possibility of combining the FBGA instead of using a single FBG connected and placed at different locations. The accuracy of data obtained and the depth of strain data can be enhanced using the FBGA. In addition, integrating the FBGA to extract and evaluate the physiological parameters can ensure its application in gait and motion analysis. Expediting such features can prove to be a prudent step toward developing FBGA technologies. Utilizing the FBGA requires superior interrogation techniques and hence, it is necessary to have a piece of basic information about the interrogators, which is described below.

Shifting the focus from a theoretical description of FBGs design, schematics, and working methodology to interrogation techniques, a commercially available Bragg interrogator is used for data collection. An FBG interrogator comprises a light source, detector, and sensor. After connecting the gratings suitably with the interrogator, data can be acquired for longer time intervals. Firstly, the radiation is passed through the circulator to the sensor and the reflected spectrum is collected through another port of the circulator. The output from the port is then passed through a Mach – Zender interferometer for wavelength shift detection purposes. The subsequent output is then forwarded to the photodetectors assembly where the optical signals are converted to electrical signals. The electrical signals are then sent to the FPGA modules for further processing and data processing. The data can be acquired through available communication protocols (LAN) and with the help of the customized application, software data can be visualized and acquired. The capabilities of interrogators can vary from the different manufacturers in terms of operation methodologies, size and shapes, handheld or table setups, type of detectors and connectors, available sensor connections, multiplexing capabilities, and communication capabilities. The data can be acquired at different sampling rates varying from 50–1000 Hz. The number of sensors that can be connected to the interrogator can be in multiple hundreds but the sampling rates decrease gradually. The operating range for the interrogators usually lies between 1500–1600 nm. The operating temperature range lies between 0 to 50°C. Various communication protocols such as Ethernet (RJ45) and SCPI over TCP/IP are commonly available for accessing data.

17.3 Pulse wave signals

In human anatomy, the cardiovascular system is one of the most vital systems and it is responsible for supplying oxygenated blood throughout the entire system. The blood is supplied from the heart through a dense channel of vessels (arteries); for this function of carrying blood in both ways, the cardiovascular system is also known as the human pulse. A pressure wave is generated due to the blood impact on the walls of the heart, and henceforth this pressure wave is measured as the pulse in the human body. Sensing the pulse requires a region where it can sense clearly and is easily accessible. In human anatomy, as shown in Figure 17.2, nine such locations are identified which are Temporal (over the temple), Carotid (at the side of the neck), Apical (over the intercostal space), Brachial (on the antecubital fossa (crook) of the arm), Radial (in the wrist below the thumb), Femoral (in the groin), Popliteal (behind the knee), Posterior Tibial (at the side of the ankle), and Dorsalis Pedis (on the front of the foot).

Detection of the pulse wave and their subsequent analysis becomes necessary as they contain a lot of information regarding several physiological parameters such as heart rate or pulse rate, heart rate variability, respiration rate, and blood pressure. Electro Cardio Graph (ECG) and Photo Plethysmo Graph (PPG) are commonly and popularly available for pulse wave analysis. ECG provides sensitive information by recording electrical signals from the heart to observe different heart conditions. In ECG, the information is stored in the form of a P-QRS-T wave, which explains the complete cardiac cycle of the heart. The P wave symbolizes the depolarisation of the atria; the QRS complex denotes the depolarization of the ventricles, and T explains the repolarisation of the ventricles. Analyzing ECG for its temporal features can provide sensitive information for better diagnosis. The method is quite a standard to date but suffers from limitations like big-sized setup, the number of leads utilized, dependence on electrical signals, and contained artefacts [Vandenberk et al. 2017]. However, PPG offers a better alternative against ECG and the pulse obtained. PPG is an optical sensing-based device, which is based on reflectance spectra. Transmission spectra-based devices are dependent on the measurement site as their output varies according to the path length [Fujita et al. 2019]. PPG can be useful in terms of calculating other additional parameters such as blood vessel pulsations, cardiac output, oxygen saturation levels, and many more. PPG and ECG have a high degree of similarity as they both signify the cardiac rhythm (mechanical activity coupled with electrical activity) [Selvaraj et al. 2008]. Despite being small, cost-effective, and efficient, PPG has some limitations too. PPG waveforms suffer from poor undulation and baseline variations during physiological parameter calculations. Such signals are prone to noise and interference incorporated attitude as it utilizes the reflected

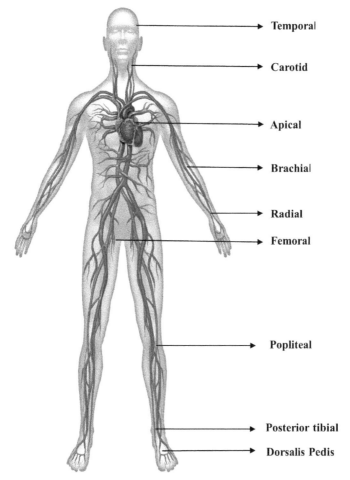

Figure 17.2: Pulsation points in the body.

spectra. Skin color and sweat can also affect the PPG waveform, hence alternating the data. Non-clarity of peaks in the PPG waveform also accounts for errors during analysis. To successfully reduce the effects of waveform defects, derivative forms can be utilized for the evaluation of physiological parameters. There are two derivative waveforms, i.e., first and second for the pulse wave obtained which are named velocity plethysmograph (VPG) and accelerated plethysmograph (APG). Velocity plethysmography possesses non-acceptable variations and is not generally used (Shriram et al. 2017). The main characteristics are peak-to-peak time difference (ΔT) which signifies the time taken for the pressure wave to travel from the heart to the periphery and back; and Crest Time (CT) which denotes the time difference from the foot to the peak of the waveform. To remove further noise from the signal, the velocity plethysmograph is again differentiated to obtain Accelerated Plethysmograph (APG). An APG consists of five parts and amplitudes of five distinct peaks (a to e), as shown in Figure 17.3a, which are utilized for the characterization of physiological parameters [Kim et al. 2019, Liang et al. 2018]. Proceeding in chronological order, a-wave (former systolic positive wave) to b-wave (former systolic negative wave) are systolic anterior components that denote pressure caused by blood ejection; c-wave (belated systolic re-increasing wave) to d-wave (belated systolic re decreasing wave) are systolic posterior components which denote reflection pressure wave (pressure wave propagated in the periphery that is reflected) and lastly; wave-e (former diastolic positive wave) which denotes diastolic component due to peripheral blood flow after the aortic valve closure.

The a-wave is foremost most suitable for heart rate evaluations as it is steep and has high amplitude. The relative heights of the waves (b/a, c/a, d/a, e/a, and (b-c-d-e)/a) are associated to age, blood pressure and artery stiffness. For instance, ratio b/a is an indicator for increased arterial stiffness, and vessel extensibility which increases with age, ratio c/a, d/a, and e/a reflect reduced arterial stiffness which decreases with age, and ratio (b-c-d-e)/a, also known as an aging index, describes the cardiovascular age which increases with age. The aging index is used for vascular aging and monitoring of arteriosclerotic disease. The a-wave tends to rise while the b-wave and e-wave tend to decrease with increased systolic blood pressure and vice versa for diastolic blood pressure. In addition, a-wave tends to increase and b-wave and e-wave tend to decrease with diminishing elastic modulus of the arteriolar valve. Patterns obtained with APG tend to change with age or if a person is suffering from cardiovascular disease. Medicinal effects or exercise routines can also result in changing patterns; in return, the effects of exercising routines or certain medications can be evaluated using APG (Atomi et al. 2017).

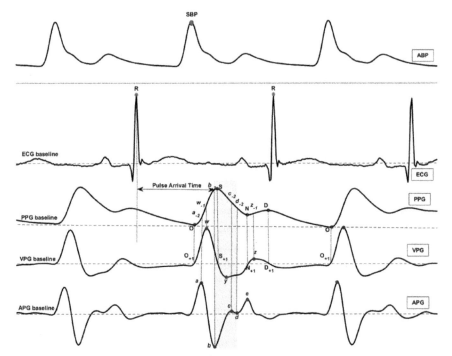

Figure 17.3a: Characteristics of different pulse wave signals (Liang et al. 2018).

17.4 Experimental methodology and data analysis

17.4.1 Experimental setup

In the following study, the aim was to investigate the pulse pattern from the foot region (Posterior Tibial and Dorsalis Pedis) to enquire about the feasibility of the data, and to check the suitability for evaluating the physiological parameters. To perform such analysis, firstly two FBGA (SAMYON TECH) inscribed in SMF-28 with FC/APC connectors and an FBG interrogator FS22DI with data acquisition package installed in a desktop were utilized. The data can be acquired on a real-time basis with a sampling rate fixed at 1 kHz. The wavelength characteristics of each FBGA were 1559.899 nm and 1564.149 nm, 1548.807 nm, and 1552.877 nm respectively. The length of each FBG in the FBGA was 10 mm, with a 10 mm space between each FBG and having reflectivity of around 93% each. All the experiments were performed in a controlled environment with constant thermal conditions (minor deflection was neglected). The FBGA were attached to the dorsalis pedis region and posterior tibia region firmly with a medical adhesive tape. For the simplicity of expression, the dorsalis pedis region can be referred to as "upper" (as in the upper visible region of the foot) and the posterior tibia "corner" (as it is lying beside the ankle). All the experiments were performed for a fixed duration of 300 seconds, i.e., 5 minutes and the subjects were in the supine position. A supine position was chosen for the experiment as in this position sudden movements do not occur and subjects are very relaxed without any tediousness as shown in Figure 17.3b. To experiment, 10 healthy subjects were chosen with no prior medical history. All the subjects were male and adults. The mean age, height, and weight were 27.9 years, 172.506 cm, and 76.3 Kg. The experiments were not conducted instantaneously, but each subject was prescribed to relax for 5 to 10 minutes before the experimentation. The experiment was conducted for 5 minutes and each minute physiological data such as oxygenation percentage (SpO2), pulse rate (per minute), systolic and diastolic blood pressure (mm/Hg), and body temperature (°F) were recorded every minute. The physiological data were acquired from a standard digital blood pressure meter, pulse oximeter, and non-contact IR thermometer. The data for each subject were acquired, averaged and based on those calculations were conducted.

17.4.2 Signal acquisition and analysis

As per the arrangement, the FBGA in the upper and corner region was firmly fixed by using medical tape. From a theoretical point of view, the pulsation happening in the arteries due to the continuous beating of the heart should generate enough strength for the sensors to detect it. The pulse due to blood flow will make the vessel expand, which in return will apply strain on the FBGA. The applied strain on the FBGA will make a change in the wavelength shift of the FBGA and the interrogator will record the resultant shift from the base value (Bragg wavelengths of individual arrays). The data acquired will be then analyzed for further processing.

The data acquired, ideally, is not reliable nor exactly accurate for computational analysis and carrying out physiological studies. There are several types of artifacts

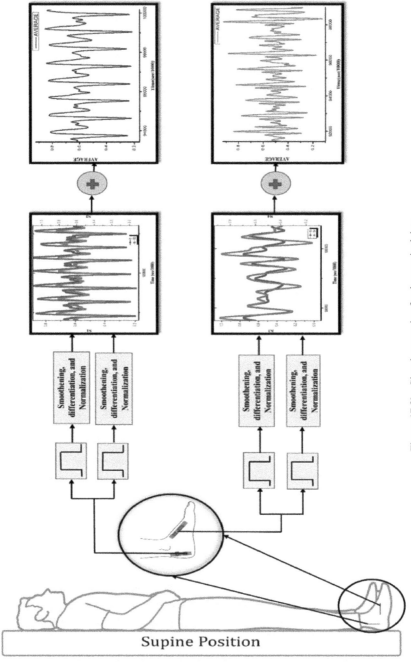

Figure 17.3b: Signal processing for the acquired data.

and noises that remain an inherent part of the signal. Therefore, firstly the data acquired is passed through a bandpass filter to remove excess deviations and noises from the signals. Since the data acquired is from low-intensity pulsation regions, it is required that the user should be careful of excessive filtering as it will remove the sensitive information from the signal and can provide a signal with lost information. After filtering the signal, it is passed through an FFT filter for smoothening so that the data can be refined and a uniform pattern could be acquired. During the process, the specifications of the filter are left to the user as the depth of smoothening is dependent on the kind of signal being monitored and how much smoothening is required. The smoothened data is then differentiated to acquire the Accelerated plethysmograph (APG) and then normalized to acquire the signal lying between the limits of 0 to 1. Normalization of a signal provides a uniform signal with well-defined boundaries and without any baseline deviations. The data then obtained represents a second-order differentiated pulse wave, as shown in Figure 17.3b, which is accurate and precise for data analysis purposes.

In the study, the data acquired from individual FBGs of the arrays are averaged to get a waveform, which is highly efficient and possesses a higher degree of similarity with both signals. Analyzing the whole signal for similarity seems quite an impossible task with the naked eye (as the number of data points will be 300 seconds × 1000 samples/seconds = 300000 samples). To mathematically analyze the similarity between the signals, a similarity tool called Coherence is utilized. Coherence is a measure that describes the linear dependency of two signals. The measure tests for similar frequency components without taking the phase information of the signals into account. The measure utilizes cross-spectrum for analysis of the two signals and provides a degree of similarity on a scale of zero to one. A signal, which is exactly similar and dissimilar, will be ranked with one and zero respectively. A signal with a degree of similarity lying between 0.8 to 1 is considered almost similar (Braun 2001).

17.5 Results and discussions

17.5.1 Sample set and physiological data

In the following study, the number of subjects who participated was 10 and their physiological characteristics varied from each other as explained in Figure 17.5. From the subjects who provided their data for the physiological analysis, the following features such as Age (years), Height (cm), Weight (Kgs), SpO2 (%), SBP (mm/Hg), DBP (mm/Hg), Pulse Rate (bpm), and Body Temperature (°F) were recorded as described in Table 17.1. The subject's height showed above average height, i.e., 172.05 cm, and the minimum height was close to 165.1 cm. The age of all the adults was in the range of 25–31 years. The weight of the subjects was in the range of 61–96 kg and showed a higher degree of variance. All the subjects were male and adults. The mean age, height, and weight were 27.9 years, 172.506 cm, and 76.3 Kg. After analyzing the physiological data, values of SBP, DBP, PR, SpO2 (%), and Body Temperature (°F) were monitored continuously during the experimentation. As the data changed regularly during the experiment procedure, for the ease of

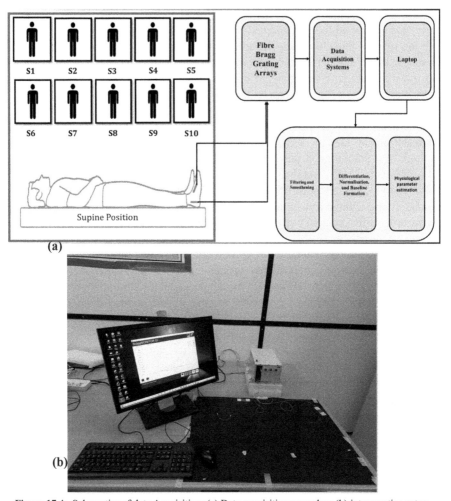

Figure 17.4: Schematics of data Acquisition: (a) Data acquisition procedure (b) interrogation setup

analysis of the data, average values (for subjects and average of the values obtained during five minutes of observations) of the data acquired for the above-mentioned parameters were calculated. The mean value of SpO2 levels was 97.83 which shows that the oxygenation levels in the subjects were good and as reported, no discomfort was observed during the experimentation. The mean values for SBP and DBP were 117.915 and 76.665 mm/Hg respectively. The variability of the range of SBP and DBP was 24.4 and 19.4, which is quite deep. A similar trend of variability was reported by the values of heart rate (bpm) which were 38.2 with a mean value of 76.65. The mean value for body temperatures was 97.7145°F with the least variability of 0.66 which again suggests that the temperature of the surroundings was well controlled and variations related to the temperature can be neglected.

In the proposed study, the sample set of the subject was a sum of 10. To perform such physiological studies, usually a higher number of subjects is suggested which

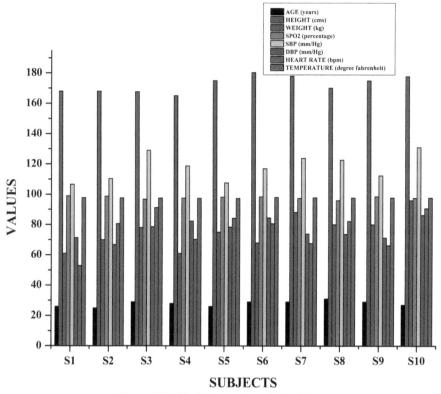

SUBJECTS

Figure 17.5: Physical parameters of the subjects.

Table 17.1: Physical parameters of the subjects.

Parameters	Age (years)	Height (cms)	Weight (Kgs)	SpO2 (%)	Pulse rate (bpm)	SBP (mm/Hg)	DBP (mm/Hg)	Temperature (°F)
SUM	279	1725.06	763	978.3	766.5	117.95	766.65	977.145
MEAN	27.9	172.506	76.3	97.83	76.65	117.915	76.665	97.7145
MEDIAN	28.5	172.59	76.5	97.9	80.6	117.875	76.1	97.72
RANGE	6	15.24	35	3	38.2	24.4	19.4	0.66
MINIMUM	25	165.1	61	96	53	106.6	66.8	97.42
MAXIMUM	31	180.34	96	99	91.2	131	86.2	98.08
QUARTILES (Q1, Q2, Q3)	26, 28.5, 29	168, 172.59, 177.8	68, 76.5, 80	97.4, 97.9, 98.6	67.6, 80.6, 84.2	110.4, 117.875, 123.8	71.4, 76.1, 82.25	97.58, 97.72, 97.86
Interquartile Range (IQR)	3	9.8	12	1.2	16.6	13.4	10.85	0.28

is quite well noted. Due to various limitations such as non-accessibility to varied age groups, regular presence for repeated trials, connectivity to access devices, transportation of analysis and data acquisition setups, etc., imposed, an issue of standardization which can be pointed out. Nonetheless, the study was conducted to show the possibility and mark the initiation of usage of FBGA in physiological parameters.

17.5.2 Signal similarities

As the data acquired from the sample set was complete, the waveforms signifying the pulse change acquired from the interrogator were recorded and analyzed. The period of analysis was five minutes (300 seconds) and the position in which data was recorded as chances of sudden movements are minimal; no complaints regarding discomfort were notified. As explained previously, the shift from the base Bragg wavelength happens due to the strain applied from the continuous throbbing of the pulsation points. The wavelength shift varies in direct proportion to the values of applied strain. So far, changes occurring due to the thermal variations were neglected as explained previously. The acquired signal was analyzed using custom-packaged software (Origins Pro 8.5) and processes of signal processing were performed. In the previous sections, the process of pre-processing the signals was explained which included four major parts, which are Filtering (removing noises and artifacts), Smoothening (smoothening the data freeing it from unnecessary irregularities), Differentiation (calculation of the second derivative of the smoothened waveform), and Normalisation (to limit the signal with a range of zero to one). Normalization of data enables the formation of a uniform pulse free from irregularities to facilitate easy computation and baseline formation to detect potential crossovers. The data was then checked for overall similarity, which was performed by evaluating the coherence values provided on a scale of zero to one.

The values of coherence were calculated for all 10 subjects from signals acquired through FBGA placed at upper and corner positions simultaneously as shown in Figure 17.6. The data observed between signals acquired from the two positions was quite surprising. The data acquired from the upper positions of all the subjects had a higher degree of coherence between the signals obtained from FBGA as compared to the FBGA placed in the corner position. Taking the upper position under attention, the minimum and maximum values of the coherence were 0.608 and 0.958. The average and median values of coherence were 0.8111 and 0.8405 which signify that data obtained from the upper position FBGA was in permissible ranges of similarity (0.8–1.0) as shown in Table 17.2. The range of variance was quite high at 0.35. On the other hand, the values of coherence for data acquired from the corner FBGA were not so appreciable. Taking the corner position under attention, the minimum and maximum values of the coherence were 0.001 and 0.712. The average and median values of coherence were 0.1209 and 0.001 which signify that data obtained from the upper position FBGA was not in permissible ranges of similarity (0.8–1.0). The range of variance was quite high at 0.711.

From the above-reported statistics of the degree, similarity following conclusions can be concluded. The degree of coherence of data from the upper position was

Table 17.2: Coherence value statistics for the acquired signals.

Parameters	Sum	Mean	Median	Range	Minimum	Maximum	Quartiles (Q1, Q2, Q3)	Inter Quartile Range (IQR)
UPPER COHERENCE VALUE	8.111	0.8111	0.8405	0.35	0.608	0.958	0.764, 0.8405, 0.885	0.121
LOWER COHERENCE VALUES	1.209	0.1209	0.001	0.711	0.001	0.712	0.001, 0.001, 0.027	0.026

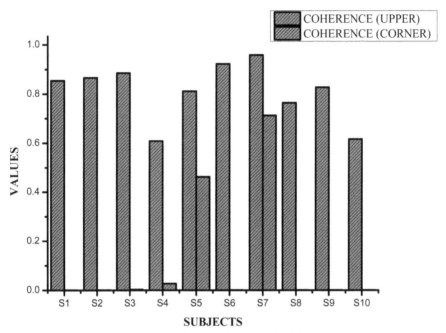

Figure 17.6: Coherence for the acquired signals.

much superior as compared to the corner position. The difference in their measure of similarity was by far very large and the difference between their average and median values was 0.6902 and 0.8395. It is to be pointed out that the measure of range for the corner position, i.e., 0.711, and the upper position was 0.35 which do not lie in a very close range. From the above data, the following inferences can be made. Firstly, the evaluation of data from the upper region which is dorsalis pedis, is far better as compared to the corner position. The upper region is far more exposed as compared to the posterior tibia region which is at the corner position. The placement of the sensor is far clearer and easy installation is possible. The irregularities in the foot region can also affect the data acquired from the sensors resulting from improper contact thus, incurring noise and artifacts in the acquired data. The sudden changes occurring in the regular coherence values, i.e., 0.001 for the corner position can be attributed to the types of feet and exposure to the pulsation point. If the pulsation points are better exposed, then acquiring the data becomes easy without having many dissimilarities. From all the above discussion, it can be inferred that data obtained from the upper region is far more reliable as compared to the corner position and sudden irregularities can be neglected.

Considering only the data from the upper region then becomes logical and further analysis was performed. Firstly, as per previous discussions, the data obtained from the upper region was similar within permissible limits so, they were suitable for further analysis. Secondly, the data obtained from the arrays were averaged and a single waveform for analysis was obtained. To compute the similarity of the averaged data as compared to the individual data obtained from FBGA, a coherence measure was obtained. The analysis shows that the average data possess a higher degree of coherence with two individual signals obtained from the arrays (FBG1 and FBG2 as S1 and S2), and the values reported concerning S1 and S2 were 0.99 and 0.988. In addition, it is to be noticed that the similarity measure of the average signal with the individual signals and between two signals, the former possessed a higher value. The values for average signal similarity and individual signal similarity were 0.99 and 0.958 respectively as shown in Figure 17.7.

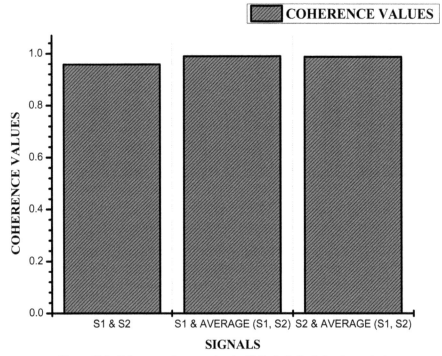

Figure 17.7: Coherence of average signal with the individual signals acquired.

17.5.3 Heart rate estimations

After the signal accuracy was determined, an estimation of the physiological parameter was performed. In the following study, heart rate was estimated by utilizing the averaged waveform obtained from the FBGA. The method of calculating the heart rate depended upon the identification of peaks of a wave. In the following study, it is to be pointed out that, the average of the five readings taken in five minutes of monitoring was taken into account. Secondly, the estimation done from the averaged wave can show some degree of error as the comparison is not for the exact value of heart rate of the defined time interval of observation but for the average value. Observing the statistical values of the heart rates observed for different participants as shown in Figure 17.8, a large variation was observed. Readings of HR observed can be as high as 90 bpm and around 50 bpm for its lowest possible values in the supine position. In heart rate, values (observed) such as the mean, median, and range were 76.665, 80.6, and 38 respectively. The range of variation for the heart rate was around 40, which was quite high.

After the estimation of heart rate, an analysis of data was performed over the errors in the estimation as shown in Table 17.3. The average error (%) was around

Table 17.3: Heart rate error statistics for the subjects.

Parameters	Sum	Mean	Median	Range	Maximum	Minimum	Quartiles (Q1, Q2, Q3)	Inter Quartile Range (IQR)
HEART RATE ERROR (%)	28.28	28.28	2.11	7.45	8.04	0.59	1.19, 2.11, 3.87	2.68

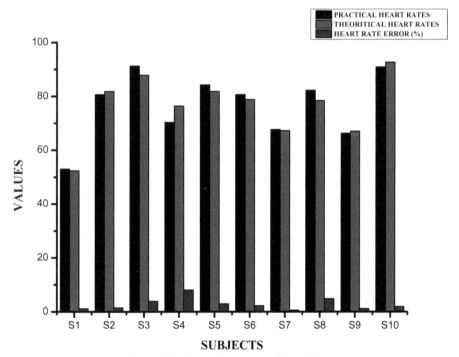

SUBJECTS

Figure 17.8: Physical parameters of the subjects.

2.82% with maximum and minimum values of 8.04 and 0.59 respectively. The range of error percentage was 7.45 for the dataset. From the above-reported values, the following conclusions can be inferred. Firstly, the average error was to be 2.28%, which can be considered an appreciable range. It also shows that it is possible and feasible to calculate the heart rate by analyzing pedal pulses. Secondly, a relatively high error percentage of around 8 was observed for subject 4. Following previous discussions, the value of coherence for the upper position of subject 4 was also around 0.6 which was below the permissible limits (0.8–1). Correlating the aspects, it can be concluded that, for lower coherence of signals or deviation from the permissible limits, evaluations contain a large degree of errors. Relating to the calculation of errors, the physiological parameter evaluation also depends upon the accuracy of the algorithm and parameter evaluation techniques. Several techniques based on different methods such as moving average after squaring the data, PLS regression, calibration curve analysis, etc., can lead to finer results.

17.6 Conclusion and future scope

In the previous sections of the following study, various matters related to human health, the need for measurement of physiological parameters for instance heart rate or pulse rate, respiratory rate, heart rate variability, and systolic and diastolic blood pressures, various popular methodologies like ECG and PPG with their advantages and disadvantages, and possibilities of integrating optical sensor technology with physiological parameter estimation and evaluation were discussed. Methods like ECG require large setups for physiological evaluation, the signals acquired are electrical and there is a high probability of signals being affected by artifacts. On the other hand, techniques like Pulse Plethysmo Graph (PPG) are dependent upon reflected spectra of light, free from complexities of size and the electrical nature of the signal. Although, even PPG waveforms are not free from errors; they suffer from poor undulation and baseline variations during physiological parameter calculations. Being prone to noise and interference due to utilization of the reflected spectra is a usual problem. PPG waveform can also get affected by skin color and sweat, hence alternating the data. The uncertainty of the peaks in the PPG waveform also accounts for numerous complications during analysis. Understanding all limitations, an effort was made to integrate FBGA as sensing units for analyzing and procuring the pulse waveforms to check their feasibility and report the details related to their applications. FBGA were employed in the dorsalis pedis (upper) and posterior tibia (corner) regions of the foot and the pulse patterns were acquired. Following conclusions can be drawn out from conducted study:

❖ FBGA can be more useful as they offer quasi-distributed sensing or multipoint sensing with enhanced multiplexing capabilities. FBGA can provide multiple data from a region of interest simultaneously, hence minimizing the effects of sensor location and facilitating locational referencing capabilities.

❖ Since multiple data are available at the same time, all the readings can be averaged and reference data can be obtained for analysis and evaluation purposes. Averaging the data allows the reduction of noise, and generates a dataset possessing a higher degree of similarity. Using the averaging technique also relieves the issue of employing complicated algorithms for analysis purposes.

❖ The study was conducted with 10 healthy young adults (all male) and data was procured simultaneously from both regions. The data obtained showed contrasting differences between the waveforms obtained. Data obtained from the upper region showed a higher degree of similarity between individual data obtained from FBGA as compared to the corner region. The reported average and median values for upper and corner regions were "0.8111 and 0.8405", and "0.1209 and 0.001" respectively.

❖ Furthermore, selecting and analyzing the data from the upper region seems to be the logical choice for evaluating physiological parameters. The similarity index for the averaged data with the individual data of FBGA was higher than the similarity index of individual data and values of 0.99 and 0.958 were reported.

❖ HR was computed using tracking of the instance of a-wave peaks and then, estimations were performed. The estimations performed were in a well-considered range of error and provided an average accuracy of 2.82%.

❖ There could be several reasons for errors out of which important ones were identified and reported. Firstly, the value of data for physiological estimation was the average of the collective data recorder for the defined time interval (300 seconds). So deviations can be expected, which can be reduced by increasing the sample set. Secondly, the identification of a-wave peaks is the essence, and if somehow, minute deviations occurring in the waveform interfered with rhythmic activity, that could result in erroneous outcomes. Thirdly, the basis of physiological parameter evaluations depends on the algorithm being used. Improving peak identification efficiency or using other possible methods can relatively increase the accuracy.

❖ It has also been observed from the data acquired that signals with low coherence values can lead to erroneous results. If the degree of similarity is relatively low, then the average of the signal will not possess the characteristics of both the signals acquired. In addition, the defined permissible limits (0.8–1) should be strictly followed; otherwise, physiological parameter estimation can lead to results with increased error percentages.

Although the above discussions show the feasibility of the FBGA for physiological parameter evaluation and analysis, the following study "for its limitations" also paves new pathways for future scope and improvement. Firstly, the following study sample set is small and limited by gender and age gap. Taking different age groups and conducting trials with large samples "say in hundreds" can provide further improved data. Secondly, the study can take into account different types of feet in terms of shapes, sizes, and exposure area of the pulsation point. By incorporating these factors, further analysis can be performed and the extent of feasibility for efficient application can be performed. Thirdly, for procuring the data, FBGA was directly placed on the target locations using medical adhesive tape. Issues of flexural strength and resistance towards forced bending and sudden stresses can be provided by polymer encapsulations; which ensure no sudden breakages and smooth operations for a long time. Fourthly, previous studies show a possibility of evaluating strain mapping for feet. The ability to acquire data from the foot and enable capabilities to evaluate multiple physiological parameters can be integrated with previously reported work for enhancing performance. In addition, such technology can be extended for activity recognition and gait analysis. At last, if features regarding blood pressure estimation and proper temperature compensation can be incorporated, the possibility of versatile application can be ensured. After scanning through the above discussions, it can be concluded that FBGA can offer premier solutions to the unusual problems of daily life. Ensuring accuracy, preciseness, and packaging variety can further solidify their claim for versatile applications.

Acknowledgements

The following study was conducted in the DST-FIST-sponsored MOE-Lab of the Indian Institute of Technology, Bhubaneswar, Odisha, India.

Conflict of interest

The authors declare no conflict of interest.

References

Ambastha, S., Pant, S., Umesh, S., Vazhayil, V., and Asokan, S. 2020. Feasibility study on thermography of embedded tumor using fiber bragg grating thermal sensor. IEEE Sensors Journal, 20(5): 2452–2459. https://doi.org/10.1109/JSEN.2019.2950973.

Atomi, K., Kawanaka, H., Bhuiyan, M. S., and Oguri, K. 2017. Cuffless blood pressure estimation based on data-oriented continuous health monitoring system. Computational and Mathematical Methods in Medicine, 2017. https://doi.org/10.1155/2017/1803485.

Braun, S. 2001. Identification, Fourier-Based Methods. Encyclopedia of Vibration, 665–672. https://doi.org/10.1006/rwvb.2001.0120.

Centre for Disease Control and Prevention. 2020a. CDC-HYP. https://www.cdc.gov/bloodpressure/facts.htm

Centre for Disease Control and Prevention. 2020b. CDC. https://www.cdc.gov/heartdisease/facts.htm#:~:text=Heart disease is the leading,groups in the United States.&text=One person dies every 34,United States from cardiovascular disease.&text=About 697%2C000 people in the,1 in every 5 deaths.

Domingues, M. F., Alberto, N., Leitao, C. S. J., Tavares, C., De Lima, E. R., Radwan, A. et al. 2019. Insole Optical fiber sensor architecture for remote gait analysis - an e-health solution. IEEE Internet of Things Journal, 6(1): 207–214. https://doi.org/10.1109/JIOT.2017.2723263.

Domingues, M. F., Tavares, C., Leitão, C., Frizera-Neto, A., Alberto, N., Marques, C. et al. 2017. Insole optical fiber Bragg grating sensors network for dynamic vertical force monitoring. Journal of Biomedical Optics, 22(9): 091507. https://doi.org/10.1117/1.jbo.22.9.091507.

Fujita, D., Suzuki, A., and Ryu, K. 2019. PPG-based systolic blood pressure estimation method using PLS and level-crossing feature. Applied Sciences (Switzerland), 9(2). https://doi.org/10.3390/app9020304.

Haseda, Y., Bonefacino, J., Tam, H. Y., Chino, S., Koyama, S., and Ishizawa, H. 2019. Measurement of pulse wave signals and blood pressure by a plastic optical fiber FBG sensor. Sensors (Switzerland), 19(23). https://doi.org/10.3390/s19235088.

Kashyap, R. 2010. Fiber bragg gratings. Fiber Bragg Gratings, 168–185. https://doi.org/10.1016/C2009-0-16830-7.

Kim, J., Campbell, A. S., de Ávila, B. E. F. and Wang, J. 2019. Wearable biosensors for healthcare monitoring. Nature Biotechnology, 37(4): 389–406. https://doi.org/10.1038/s41587-019-0045-y.

Korposh, S., Lee, S.-W., James, S., Tatam, R., and Morgan, S. P. 2017. Biomedical application of optical fibre sensors. Quantum Sensing and Nano Electronics and Photonics XIV, 10111, 101112Y. https://doi.org/10.1117/12.2243640.

Koyama, S., and Ishizawa, H. 2019. Vital Sign Measurement Using FBG Sensor for New Wearable Sensor Development. Fiber Optic Sensing - Principle, Measurement and Applications. https://doi.org/10.5772/intechopen.84186.

Liang, Y., Chen, Z., Ward, R., and Elgendi, M. 2018. Hypertension assessment via ECG and PPG signals: An evaluation using MIMIC database. Diagnostics, 8(3): 65. https://doi.org/10.3390/diagnostics8030065.

Lo Presti, D., Massaroni, C., D'Abbraccio, J., Massari, L., Caponero, M., Longo, U. G. et al. 2019. Wearable system based on flexible FBG for respiratory and cardiac monitoring. IEEE Sensors Journal, 19(17): 7391–7398. https://doi.org/10.1109/JSEN.2019.2916320.

Lo Presti, D., Massaroni, C., Jorge Leitao, C. S., De Fatima Domingues, M., Sypabekova, M., Barrera, D. et al. 2020. Fiber bragg gratings for medical applications and future challenges: A review. IEEE Access, 8: 156863–156888. https://doi.org/10.1109/ACCESS.2020.3019138.

Lo Presti, D., Santucci, F., Massaroni, C., Formica, D., Setola, R., and Schena, E. 2021. A multi-point heart rate monitoring using a soft wearable system based on fiber optic technology. Scientific Reports, 11(1): 1–10. https://doi.org/10.1038/s41598-021-00574-2.

Mishra, M., and Sahu, P. K. 2022. Fiber bragg gratings in healthcare applications: A review. IETE Technical Review (Institution of Electronics and Telecommunication Engineers, India), May. https://doi.org/10.1080/02564602.2022.2069608.

Presti, D. Lo, Massaroni, C., Di Tocco, J., Schena, E., Carnevale, A., Longo, U. G. et al. 2019. Single-plane neck movements and respiratory frequency monitoring: A smart system for computer workers. 2019 IEEE International Workshop on Metrology for Industry 4.0 and IoT, MetroInd 4.0 and IoT 2019 - Proceedings, 2018, 167–170. https://doi.org/10.1109/METROI4.2019.8792870.

Selvaraj, N., Jaryal, A., Santhosh, J., Deepak, K. K., and Anand, S. 2008. Assessment of heart rate variability derived from finger-tip photoplethysmography as compared to electrocardiography. Journal of Medical Engineering and Technology, 32(6): 479–484. https://doi.org/10.1080/03091900701781317.

Shriram, R., Martin, B., Sundhararajan, M., and Daimiwal, N. 2017. Comparison of acceleration plethysmogram acquired using optical signal and pressure signal. International Journal of Signal Processing, Image Processing and Pattern Recognition, 10(9): 57–68. https://doi.org/10.14257/ijsip.2017.10.9.06.

Sirkis, T., Beiderman, Y., Agdarov, S., Beiderman, Y., and Zalevsky, Z. 2017. Fiber sensor for non-contact estimation of vital bio-signs. Optics Communications, 391(January): 63–67. https://doi.org/10.1016/j.optcom.2017.01.013.

Suresh, R., Bhalla, S., Hao, J., and Singh, C. 2015. Development of a high resolution plantar pressure monitoring pad based on fiber Bragg grating (FBG) sensors. Technology and Health Care, 23(6): 785–794. https://doi.org/10.3233/THC-151038.

Vandenberk, T., Stans, J., Mortelmans, C., Van Haelst, R., Van Schelvergem, G., Pelckmans, C. et al. 2017. Clinical validation of heart rate apps: Mixed-methods evaluation study. JMIR MHealth and UHealth, 5(8): 1–15. https://doi.org/10.2196/mhealth.7254.

World Health Organisation. 1948. WHO. https://www.who.int/data/gho/data/major-themes/health-and-well-being.

Index

9 781032 381619